ULTRAMONTANISM AND TRADITION

OS JUSTI STUDIES IN CATHOLIC TRADITION

General Editor: Peter A. Kwasniewski

Ultramontanism *and* Tradition

❧ ❧

THE ROLE OF PAPAL AUTHORITY IN THE CATHOLIC FAITH

Edited by
PETER A. KWASNIEWSKI

OS JUSTI PRESS
LINCOLN, NEBRASKA

Os Justi Press
P.O. Box 21814
Lincoln, NE 68542
www.osjustipress.com

Send inquiries to
info@osjustipress.com

ISBN 978-1-960711-59-5 (paperback)
ISBN 978-1-960711-60-1 (hardcover)
ISBN 978-1-960711-61-8 (ebook)

Typesetting by Michael Schrauzer
Cover design by Julian Kwasniewski
Memorial monument to Pope Pius VI by Antonio Canova,
represented in a print by Pietro Fontana
after a drawing by Giovanni Tognolli
Rijksmuseum RP-P-OB-39.048, public domain

In honor of
St Paul († c. 64/65)
St Hilary of Poitiers (c. 310-c. 367)
St Leo II (c. 611-683)
St Bruno of Segni (c. 1045-1123)
Robert Grosseteste (c. 1168-1253)
St Bridget of Sweden (1303-1373)
St Catherine of Siena (1347-1380)
Ven. Bruno Lanteri (1759-1830)
St John Henry Newman (1801-1890)
St Padre Pio (1887-1968)

and all holy men and women
who, with Christian parrhesia, have
confronted, criticized, or circumvented
a wayward pope

I, *I* am the Tradition! I, *I* am the Church!

— Pope Pius IX (1870)

The Pope is the guardian of dogma and of morals; he is the custodian of the principles that make families sound, nations great, souls holy; he is the counsellor of princes and of peoples; he is the head under whom no one feels tyrannized because he represents God Himself; he is the supreme father who unites in himself all that may exist that is loving, tender, divine . . . . When one loves a person, one tries to adhere in everything to his thoughts, to fulfill his will, to perform his wishes . . . . Therefore, when we love the Pope, there are no discussions regarding what he orders or demands, or up to what point obedience must go, and in what things he is to be obeyed; when we love the Pope, we do not say that he has not spoken clearly enough, almost as if he were forced to repeat to the ear of each one the will clearly expressed so many times not only in person, but with letters and other public documents; we do not place his orders in doubt, adding the facile pretext of those unwilling to obey — that it is not the Pope who commands, but those who surround him; we do not limit the field in which he might and must exercise his authority; we do not set above the authority of the Pope that of other persons, however learned, who dissent from the Pope; for, however great their learning, they must be lacking in holiness, for there can be no holiness in dissension from the Pope.

— Pope Pius X (1912)

You know, we have stuck out for our position all our lives . . . unity, authority, etc., Peter the Rock and so on. I have, too, and believe it. I am always preaching that sort of thing, and yet is it now getting to a *reductio ad absurdum?* Centralisation grows and goes madder every century. Even at Trent they hardly foresaw this kind of thing. Does it really mean that one cannot be a member of the Church of Christ without being, as we are, absolutely at the mercy of an Italian lunatic [viz., Pius X]? . . . We must pull through even this beastliness somehow. After all, it is still the Church of the Fathers that we stand by and spend our lives defending. However, bad as things are, nothing else is possible. I think that when I look at Rome, I see powerful arguments against us, but when I look at the Church of England . . . I see still more powerful arguments for us. But of course, saving a total collapse, things are as bad as they can be. Give us back the tenth-century Johns and Stephens, or a Borgia! They were less disastrous than this deplorable person.

— Fr Adrian Fortescue (1910)

The infallibility of the pope does not mean in any way that he enjoys unlimited and arbitrary power in matters of government and teaching. The dogma of infallibility, while it defines a supreme privilege, is fixed in precise boundaries, allowing for infidelity, error, and betrayal. Otherwise in the prayers for the Supreme Pontiff there would be no need to pray *"non tradat eum in animam inimicorum eius"* [that he may not be delivered into the hands of his enemies]. If it were impossible for the pope to cross to the enemy camp, it would not be necessary to pray for it not to happen. The betrayal of Peter is the example of possible infidelity that has loomed over all of the popes through the course of history, and will be so until the end of time. The pope, even if he is the supreme authority on earth, is suspended between the summit of heroic fidelity to his mandate and the abyss of apostasy that is always present.

— Roberto de Mattei

❦ CONTENTS ❧

⟨ PREFACE ⟩

I T IS NOT POSSIBLE TO UNDERSTAND THE CRISIS IN THE Catholic Church today, much less begin to see how it might be overcome, without a careful study of the origins of the ecclesial current known as ultramontanism. While this current originated in the fierce anti-Liberalism of nineteenth-century conservatives, it tended, over the next century and a half, toward an unrestrained hyperpapalism that weakened subsidiarity, overrode local custom, and dismantled immemorial tradition, until with Pope Francis it has morphed into a veritable engine of progressivism.

What are the historical, theological, and cultural causes of this complex phenomenon—at once a quasi-doctrine, an attitude, and a political regime—and of its successive developments or deviations? Is an ultramontanist papacy the source of our ills, or their only possible remedy, or perhaps something of both (*corruptio optimi pessima*)? Did Vatican I comprehensively define the pope's role and prerogatives, or did it leave many questions undetermined and debatable? Might there be a "spirit of Vatican I" as harmful, in its own way, as the later and rightly denigrated "spirit of Vatican II"? Can popes be heretics, and what, if anything, can be done about a heretical pope? What is the relationship between papacy and episcopacy; between moral authority and coercive power; between legal positivism, blind obedience, and clerical abuse (sexual and otherwise)? In the face of pontifical monarchy, do churches *sui iuris*, organized communities, subordinate rulers, baptized faithful, venerable traditions, or time-honored liturgies enjoy their own inviolable rights?

These and related questions occupy the attention of the twenty-six scholars who have contributed to this anthology, which they offer as a service to their fellow Catholics and to the Church in a period of institutional upheaval. The nearly fifty essays do not represent or advocate for a single "correct view"—there is plenty of respectful disagreement among the authors as they respond and counter-respond to each another's work—but rather, aim to equip readers with the best of contemporary conservative and traditional writing on these controversial topics.

As this book is hefty, as its authors are well-known, and as the titles of the parts and chapters speak for themselves, no lengthy preface is needed. This anthology came together because of the intellectual friendship of the editor with the rest of the authors, and of these authors among themselves. The traditional Catholic world is well-connected and interacts frequently about matters of importance. We keep track of essays, books, and lectures, and try to pursue the truth as a common endeavor, for indeed truth is among the loftiest of common goods and counted as one of the Names of God. Our times make this common pursuit both easier and harder—easier in that Catholic writing usually becomes instantly and globally available; harder in that the sheer volume of analysis can be overwhelming, and the factions are more numerous and louder than ever before, so that one feels as if one is fighting a battle on ten fronts instead of one or two. Be that as it may, I find that the best writing tends to stand out, to soar above the maelstrom. Even after several years of journalistic inundation, one finds oneself remembering this or that special piece and going back to it or recommending it to a friend. In compiling this anthology, I strove to gather the "solid gold," no lead, no dross.

Although most of the chapters in this book were initially published elsewhere (the location and date is given in the first note of each chapter), four appear in this volume for the first time: the major study "What May Be Done about a Heretical Pope?" by a Friar of the Order of Preachers (chapter 9); the short but thought-provoking essay "The Tower, and the City, of Babel: A Warning against Ultramontanism" by Robert W. Keim (chapter 26); the masterful synthesis "Centripetal Governance and the Loss of Coherence" by Stuart Chessman (chapter 37); and a translation of a German interview on the papacy featuring Martin Mosebach and Thomas Sternberg (chapter 50). Moreover, three chapters are reworked and expanded versions of earlier publications: Phillip Campbell's study of Pope St Gregory VII (chapter 2), Thomas Pink's "Papal Authority and the Limits of Official Theology" (chapter 3), and John Lamont's "The Catholic Church and the Rule of Law" (chapter 7).

The chapters in Parts I and III follow principally a logical order, irrespective of their date of origin, whereas the chapters in Part II mainly follow the chronological order of publication since so many of them were written precisely as responses to earlier pieces (e.g., the courteous exchanges among Messrs. Chessman, Ureta, de Mattei, and Flanders). A few of the chapters are written as responses to authors whose work is not included in this volume; whenever that is the case, a footnote indicates where the reader may find that work.

Given that I myself have devoted much attention to the problem of hyperpapalism, the reader may wonder why I have contributed no chapters to this anthology. The reason is simple: my own recent work on these themes was sufficiently substantive to publish it as a separate volume that appeared last month under the title *Bound by Truth: Authority, Obedience, Tradition, and the Common Good* (Brooklyn, NY: Angelico Press, 2023). That book will surely appeal to the same readers to whom this one does.[1] It is also worth mentioning two new books that appeared after this manuscript was completed and that take up in greater detail the origins and consequences of Jorge Mario Bergoglio's theology: Serafino M. Lanzetta's *"Super Hanc Petram": The Pope and the Church at a Dramatic Moment in History* (Lincoln, NE: Os Justi Press, 2023) and Jean-Pierre Moreau's *The Synodal Pope: The True Story of the Theology and Politics of Pope Francis*, translated by Jeanne Smits (Gastonia, NC: TAN Books, 2023).

---

1 *Bound by Truth* joins several thematically related books that I have written or edited since 2021, namely, *The Road from Hyperpapalism to Catholicism* (Waterloo, ON: Arouca Press, 2022), *True Obedience in the Church* (Manchester, NH: Crisis Publications, 2022), and *From Benedict's Peace to Francis's War* (Brooklyn, NY: Angelico Press, 2021).

A word about the juxtaposition of the epigraphs. My quoting of Fr Fortescue's private outburst about Pius X, from a letter dated November 5, 1910, does not mean that I find (or, for that matter, that Fr Fortescue found) nothing admirable in the devout pontiff. Quite the contrary. The primary objection is to the ever-increasing centralization of Church governance around the pope, and the virtual equation of the pope's every thought and whim with the will of God, with all divine qualities, with the essence of holiness — that is the point of the accompanying over-the-top quotation from Pius X's allocution of November 18, 1912 (*Acta Apostolicae Sedis*, 1912, p. 695), which expresses a view of the papacy *far* beyond anything the Church has ever taught with a high degree of authority. And this, in turn, harks back to another and even more unfortunate outburst, that of Pius IX in a private meeting at the time of the First Vatican Council. Many Catholics today can relate to Fortescue's feelings of frustration, scribbled well over a hundred years ago. As Roberto de Mattei soberly says, the dogma of infallibility does not cancel out the possibility of infidelity, error, and betrayal — be they obvious cases, like *Amoris Laetitia* and Pachamama, or more subtle but still consequential ones, like the radical revision of the Roman Breviary in 1911 that paved the way for increasingly audacious papal actions against liturgical tradition in the ensuing decades.

I would like to express my thanks to *OnePeterFive*, *Crisis Magazine*, *Rorate Caeli*, *LifeSiteNews*, *The Lamp*, *Catholic World Report*, *Catholic Family News*, *The European Conservative*, *Herder Korrespondenz*, the Society of St Hugh of Cluny, and The American Society for the Defense of Tradition, Family, and Property for permission to republish.

Footnotes are by the author of each chapter unless otherwise noted; internal cross-references have, however, been added without further ado, and a measure of consistency has been imposed on citations, in spite of the diversity of countries from which the contributors hail. Over the centuries Gratian's *Decretum* has been cited in varying manners and we have decided to allow the authors here to cite it in the method they prefer. Please bear in mind that, because this book is equipped with a complete bibliography of works cited, short citations are the norm. Unsightly hyperlinks are not supplied for most online citations, except where the source might be difficult to find with a simple search.

Lastly, those who wish to view in color the Figures printed here in black and white (pp. 207–20) will find many of them in the online version of Stuart Chessman's essay "Ultramontanism: Its Life and Death" — either the original four posts at the blog of the Society of St Hugh of Cluny on December 20, 23, 27, and 31, 2021, or the single post that brought them all together at *Rorate Caeli* on January 7, 2022.

Peter A. Kwasniewski
December 11, 2023
Pope St Damasus I

⟨ ABBREVIATIONS ⟩

CIC *Codex Iuris Canonici*
(Code of Canon Law)

DH Denzinger-Hünermann

DTC *Dictionnaire de théologie catholique*

ED *Ecclesia Dei*

MD *Mediator Dei*

MGH EKA *Monumenta Germaniae Historica:*
Epistolarum Karolini Aevi

PL *Patrologia Latina*

ST *Summa theologiae*

TC *Traditionis Custodes*

❴ PART I ❵
Authority and Power
in the Church

The *Plenitudo Potestatis* of the Roman Pontiff in Service of the Unity of the Church[1]

RAYMOND LEO CARDINAL BURKE

INTRODUCTION

In one of the open discussions during the session of the Synod of Bishops held in October of 2014, the Synod Fathers were debating about the possibility of the Church permitting those living in irregular matrimonial unions to receive the sacraments of penance and the Holy Eucharist. At a certain point, one of the cardinals, thought to be an expert in canon law, intervened with what he judged to be a definitive solution to the difficulty. Making reference to the dissolution of marriages in favor of the faith, he strongly asserted that we have not at all begun to comprehend the extent of the *plenitudo potestatis* of the Roman Pontiff.

The implication was that the fullness of power which is, by divine law, inherent to the Petrine Office could permit the Holy Father to act in contradiction to the words of Our Lord Himself in chapter nineteen of the Gospel according to St Matthew and the Church's constant teaching in fidelity to the same words: "And I say to you: whoever divorces his wife, except for unchastity, and marries another, commits adultery; and he who marries a divorced woman, commits adultery" (Mt 19:9). The cardinal's quite shocking affirmation made me think again about something which the Holy Father himself had said, at the beginning of the 2014 session of the Synod, to all of the Synod Fathers.

He told the Synod Fathers: "It is necessary to say with *parrhesia* all that one feels."[2] He then concluded: "And do so with great tranquility and peace, so that the Synod may always unfold *cum Petro et sub Petro*, and the presence of the pope is a guarantee for all and a safeguard of the faith."[3] The juxtaposition of the classic words which describe the power of the pope, such that all things in the Church must be with Peter and under Peter, and the presence of the body of the pope

---

1 A paper delivered at the conference "Catholic Church: Where are you heading?," held in Rome, April 7, 2018. Translated by Diane Montagna and published at *LifeSiteNews* on April 13, 2018. The first few paragraphs, a personal tribute to Cardinal Meisner, have been omitted.

2 "Saluto del Santo Padre Francesco ai Padri Sinodali, 6 ottobre 2014," *La famiglia è il futuro. Tutti i documenti del Sinodo straordinario 2014*, ed. Antonio Spadaro (Milan: Àncora Editrice, 2014), 118. English translation: "Pope Francis's invitation to the Synod Fathers at the opening of the General Congregation: With honesty and humility," *L'Osservatore Romano*, October 10, 2014, p. 6.

3 *La famiglia è il futuro*, 118; *L'Osservatore Romano*, October 10, 2014, p. 6.

in a meeting risks a misunderstanding of the authority of the pope which is not magical but derives from his obedience to Our Lord.

Such magical thinking is also reflected in the docile response of some of the faithful to whatever the Roman Pontiff may say, claiming that, if the Holy Father says something, then we must accept it as papal teaching. In any case, it seems good to reflect a bit on the notion of the power inherent to the Petrine Office and, in particular, on the notion of the fullness of power (*plenitudo potestatis*) of the Roman Pontiff.

THE FULLNESS OF POWER IN THE TRADITION

The history of the terminology, *plenitudo potestatis*, to express the nature of the jurisdiction of the Roman Pontiff is succinctly described in a contribution of Prof. John A. Watt of the University of Hull to the Second International Congress of Medieval Canon Law, held at Boston College from August 12–16, 1963.[4] The term is first used by Pope St Leo the Great in 446. In his Letter 14, he writes about the authority of the bishop with these words: "Thus we have confided to your charity our duties, such that you are called unto a share of solicitude, not unto the fullness of power."[5] In his customary crystalline Latin, Pope St Leo the Great expresses the relationship of the Roman Pontiff with the bishops. While both the Roman Pontiff and the bishops share the solicitude for the good of the universal Church, the Roman Pontiff alone exercises the fullness of power, in order that the unity of the universal Church be effectively safeguarded and promoted.

The term, fullness of power, is found extensively in treatises on papal authority, especially in the canonical literature. Gratian includes the dictum of Pope St Leo the Great along with two others canons among his decrees. These decrees emphasized "papal primacy as expressed in the supreme appellate jurisdiction and the reservation of all major issues."[6] St Bernard of Clairvaux contributed greatly to the reception of the term, so that "by the time of Huguccio it had reached a high level of development."[7]

Pope Innocent III, grounding the term theologically in the reality of the papal office as the Vicar of Christ on earth (*Vicarius Christi*), emphasized the position of the Roman Pontiff "*supra ius*" and "as *iudex ordinarius omnium.*"[8] Regarding the term, *supra ius*, "over the law," it was clear that the Roman Pontiff could dispense from the law or interpret the law only for the purpose of serving the proper end of the law, not to subvert the law. The description of the exercise of the fullness

---

4   Cf. J. A. Watt, "The Use of the Term 'Plenitudo Potestatis' by Hostiensis," in Stephen Ryan and Joseph Kuttner, ed., *Proceedings of the Second International Congress of Medieval Canon Law*, Boston College, August 12–16, 1963 (Città del Vaticano: S. Congregatio de Seminariis et Studiorum Universitatibus, 1965), 161–87.

5   "Vices nostras ita tuae credidimus charitati, ut in partem sis vocatus sollicitudinis, non in plenitudinem potestatis" [*Ep.* 14, *PL* 54:671], quoted in Watt, 161.

6   Watt, 164.

7   Ibid.

8   Watt, 165.

of power as the action of Christ Himself, through His Vicar on earth, was made with "the qualification that the pope must avoid decreeing anything that was sinful or might lead to sin or subversion of the faith."[9]

Cardinal Henry of Susa, called Hostiensis, an illustrious canonist of the thirteenth century, treated amply the notion of the fullness of power of the Roman Pontiff, using the term in seventy-one individual contexts in his writings: the *Summa*, the *Apparatus* or *Lectura* on the *Gregoriana*, and the *Apparatus* on the *Extravagantes* of Innocent III. In Appendix A of his article, Prof. Watt provides a representative list of legislative texts of Pope Innocent III in which he uses the term, fullness of power, while in Appendix B of his article, he provides a list of all seventy-one usages of the term, fullness of power, by Hostiensis.[10]

Hostiensis introduced a distinction of two uses of the fullness of power: the pope's "ordinary power" (*potestas ordinaria* or *ordinata*) when by virtue of his "fullness of office" (*plenitudo officii*) he "acted according to the law already established," and "his absolute power" (*potestas absoluta*) when by virtue of his "fullness of power" (*plenitudo potestatis*) he "passed over or transcended existing law."[11] The adjective "absolute" must be understood in the context of Roman Law and its service to the development of canonical discipline, not according to the secular understanding of Machiavelli or of totalitarian dictators.

In Roman Law, it signified a dispensation from a law and supply of a defect in a law. In the words of Prof. Watt:

> Dispensation was a use of the absolute power to set aside existing law; *suppletio* was an act of absolute power to remedy defects that had arisen either through the non-observance of existing law or because existing law was inadequate to meet the particular circumstances. In both cases the absolute power, the *plenitudo potestatis*, stands revealed as a discretionary power over the established legal order, a prerogative power to act for the common welfare outside that order, if, in the pope's judgment, circumstances made this necessary.[12]

In other words, the fullness of power was understood not as an authority over the very constitution of the Church or her Magisterium but as a necessity for the governance of the Church in accord with her constitution and Magisterium. Hostiensis describes it as a necessary tool so that "curia business could be expedited, delays shortened, litigation curtailed,"[13] while, at the same time, "he considered that it was a power to be used with great caution, as a power in the Pauline phrase 'unto edification and not for destruction,' a discretionary power to maintain the constitution of the Church, not to undermine it."[14]

---

9   Watt, 166.
10 Watt, 175–87.
11 Watt, 167.
12 Watt, 167–68.
13 Watt, 168.
14 Watt, 168. Cf. 2 Cor 13:10.

It is clear that the fullness of power is given by Christ Himself and not by some human authority or popular constitution, and that, therefore, it can be rightly exercised only in obedience to Christ. Prof. Watt observes:

> It was axiomatic that any power which had been given by Christ to His Church was for the purpose of fulfilling the end of the society which He had founded, not to thwart it. Therefore the prerogative power could only be exercised within these terms. Therefore "absolutism" (*solutus a legibus*) was not licence for arbitrary government. If it was true that the will of the prince made the law, in the sense that there was no other authority which could make it; it was also true as a corollary that, where this will threatened the foundations of the society whose good the will existed to promote, it was no law. The Church was a society to save souls. Heresy and sin impeded salvation. Any act of the pope *in quantum homo* which was heretical or sinful in itself or might foster heresy or sin threatened the foundations of society and was therefore void.[15]

In other words, the notion of fullness of power was carefully qualified.

It was understood that it did not permit the Roman Pontiff to do certain things. For example, he could not act against the Apostolic Faith. Also, for the sake of the good order of the Church, it was a power to be used sparingly and with the greatest prudence. Watt observes:

> It was unfitting to depart from the *ius commune* too frequently or to do so *sine causa*. The pope could do so, but he should not, for the exercise of the *plenitudo potestatis* was to further the *utilitas ecclesie et salus animarum* and not the self-interest of individuals. The setting aside of the *ius commune* must therefore always be an exceptional act impelled by grave reasons. If the pope did so act *sine causa* or arbitrarily, he put his salvation in danger.[16]

Since the notion of fullness of powers contains the just-described limitations, how is the violation of the limitations judged and corrected? What is to be done if the Roman Pontiff so acts? Hostiensis is clear that the pope is not subject to human judgment. "He should be warned of the error of his ways and even publicly admonished, but he could not be put on trial if he persisted in his line of conduct."[17] For Hostiensis, the College of Cardinals, even though they do not share in the fullness of power, "should act as a *de facto* check against papal error."[18]

Hostiensis recognized the need for the exercise of the fullness of power at certain times, in order to "rectify the imperfections of the established order or thwart

---

15   Watt, 173.
16   Watt, 168. *Ecclesie* is a spelling found in medieval texts.
17   Watt, 169.
18   Ibid.

those who were manipulating it for private ends,"[19] but he also "thought as a general rule the pope should be slow to depart from the common law and he also thought that he should take the fraternal advice of his appointed advisers before doing so."[20] Apart from public admonition and prayer for divine intervention, he does not offer a remedy for the abuse of the fullness of power. If a member of the faithful believes in conscience that a particular exercise of the fullness of power is sinful and cannot bring his conscience to peace in the matter, "the pope must, as a duty, be disobeyed, and the consequences of disobedience be suffered in Christian patience."[21]

Time has not permitted me to examine the question of the correction of the pope who abuses the fullness of power inherent to the primacy of the See of Peter. As many will know, there is an abundant literature on the question. Certainly the treatise *De Romano Pontifice* of St Robert Bellarmine and other classical canonical studies must be examined. Suffice it to say that, as history shows, it is possible that the Roman Pontiff, exercising the fullness of power, can fall either into heresy or into the dereliction of his primary duty to safeguard and promote the unity of faith, worship, and practice. Since he is not subject to a judicial process, according to the first canon on the competent forum in the Code of Canon Law ("Prima Sedes a nemine iudicatur"),[22] how is the matter to be addressed?

A brief preliminary response, based upon the natural law, the Gospels, and canonical tradition, would indicate a twofold process: first, the correction of a supposed error or dereliction made directly to the Roman Pontiff himself; and, then, if he fails to respond, a public declaration. According to natural law, right reason demands that subjects be governed according to the rule of law and, in the contrary case, provides that they have recourse against actions in violation of the rule of law. Christ Himself teaches the way of fraternal correction which applies to all members of His Mystical Body.[23] We see His teaching embodied in the fraternal correction of St Peter by St Paul, when St Peter dissembled regarding the freedom of Christians from certain ritual laws of the Jewish faith.[24] Finally, the canonical tradition is summarized in the norm of can. 212 of the 1983 Code of Canon Law. While the first section of the canon in question makes clear that "the Christian faithful are bound to follow with Christian obedience those things which the sacred pastors, inasmuch as they represent Christ, declare as teachers of the faith or establish as rulers of the Church,"[25] the third section declares the

---

19　Watt, 174.
20　Ibid.
21　Watt, 173.
22　Cf. can. 1404.
23　Cf. Mt 18:15-17.
24　Cf. Gal 2:11-21.
25　"Quae sacri Pastores, utpote Christum repraesentantes, tamquam fidei magistri declarant aut tamquam Ecclesiae rectores statuunt, christifideles, . . . christiana oboedientia prosequi tenentur." Can. 212, §1 (English translation by the Canon Law Society of America).

right and duty of the faithful "to manifest to the sacred pastors their opinion
on matters which pertain to the good of the Church and to make their opinion
known to the rest of the Christian faithful, without prejudice to the integrity of
faith and morals, with reverence toward their pastors, and attentive to common
advantage and the dignity of persons."[26]

To conclude this too brief examination of the development of the notion of
the fullness of power from the time of Pope St Leo the Great, it must be observed
that the contribution of the medieval canonists constitutes a deepening of the
understanding of the Church's faith regarding Petrine primacy. It, in no way,
pretended to offer doctrinal novelty. Prof. Watt summarizes the matter thus:

> That the concept of ecclesiastical sovereignty expressed by this partic-
> ular term had been formulated before Hostiensis wrote, is clear from
> Innocent III's decretals and the early commentary thereon. Exam-
> ination of the decretist background to early decretalist work makes
> it clear that no novelty of doctrinal essence was here involved. The
> decretals register a crystallization of terminology; sure mark of the
> maturity of the canonist understanding of the notion in question. The
> *Professio Fidei* known to the Second Council of Lyons was but a more
> solemn acceptance of a position held generally much earlier, not least
> among canonists, expressed now with the help of a term which the
> canonists had made a technical one. In the form adopted at Lyons,
> *plenitudo potestatis* represented two things, both of which corresponded
> exactly to its canonistic history: the principle of jurisdictional primacy
> as such, in all its judicial, legislative, administrative and magisterial
> aspects, and more narrowly, the principle that prelates derived their
> jurisdiction from the pope.

There was, however, a third level of interpretation of the term: the plenitude of
power in its purest juristic form. This was the level at which the canonists were
most deeply engaged, in that it concerned the practical applications of supreme
authority and considered its relationship to law already in being and an *ordo iuris*
already established. In short, a problem of developed legal theory, the concept of
the power of the sovereign over law and the juridical order.

Progress was made with some simple distinctions about the nature of this
power. The pope's jurisdiction was said to be exercised in a twofold way. There
was an exercise which had a recognized and regular place, established by existing
law and translated into practice by existing procedures: his ordinary power. There
was further his extraordinary power, inhering in him personally and alone, by
which — manifestation *par excellence* of sovereign authority — existing law and
established procedures might be suspended, abrogated, clarified, or supplemented.

---

26   "...sententiam suam de his quae ad bonum Ecclesiae pertinent sacris Pastoribus manifestent
eamque, salva fidei morumque integritate ac reverentia erga Pastores, attentisque communi utilitate
et personarum dignitate, ceteris christifidelibus notam faciant." Can. 212, §3.

This was the prerogative power of the pope *supra ius* — the plenitude of power seen in its most characteristic juristic form as the right to regulate established legal machinery. *Solutus a legibus*, the absolute ruler might redispose any of the mechanisms of law. In the doing thereof, the plenitude of power was deployed in its most practical form.

Once the *plenitudo officii* had been distinguished from the *plenitudo potestatis* and the *potestas ordinaria* from the *potestas absoluta* (and with these distinctions Hostiensis seems to have made his most individual contribution to the common stock of canonist ideas on papal power), it followed logically that the circumstances in which this power was used *extra ordinarium cursum* should be examined.[27]

In fact, the ever-deepening understanding of the fullness of power of the Roman Pontiff during the medieval period has led to the ongoing study of the primacy of Peter and of the power connected with it. Any discussion of the matter would be incomplete without taking into account the essential work accomplished by canonists during the Middle Ages.

PLENITUDO POTESTATIS IN THE MAGISTERIUM

The term, fullness of power, was used in the definition of papal primacy at the First Vatican Council. Chapter 4 of the Dogmatic Constitution *Pastor Aeternus*, on the Church of Christ, promulgated on July 18, 1870, reads:

> Furthermore, with the approval of the Second Council of Lyon, the Greeks professed that "the holy Roman Church possesses the supreme and full primacy and authority over the universal Catholic Church, which she recognizes in truth and humility to have received with fullness of power from the Lord himself in blessed Peter, the prince or head of the apostles, of whom the Roman pontiff is the successor. And, as she is bound above all to defend the truth of the faith, so too, if any questions should arise regarding the faith, they must be decided by her judgment."[28]

The dogmatic definition makes it clear that the fullness of power of the Roman Pontiff is necessary if the Apostolic Faith is to be safeguarded and promoted in the universal Church. Later on in the same chapter of *Pastor Aeternus*, the Council Fathers declare:

27　Watt, 172–73.

28　"Approbante vero Lugdunensi Concilio secondo Graeci professi sunt: 'Sanctam Romanam Ecclesiam summum et plenum primatum et principatum super universam Ecclesiam catholicam obtinere, quem se ab ipso Domino in beato Petro Apostolorum principe sive vertice, cuius Romanus Pontifex est successor, cum potestatis plenitudine recepisse veraciter et humiliter recognoscit; et sicut prae ceteris tenetur fidei veritatem defendere, sic et, si quae de fide subortae fuerint quaestiones, suo debent iudicio definiri.'" Heinrich Denzinger, *Compendium of Creeds, Definitions, and Declarations on Matters of Faith and Morals*, ed. Peter Hünermann with Helmut Hoping, ed. Robert Fastiggi and Anne Englund Nash, 43rd ed. [hereafter *DH* followed by paragraph number] (San Francisco: Ignatius Press, 2012), no. 3067.

For the Holy Spirit was not promised to the successors of Peter that they might disclose a new doctrine by his revelation, but rather that, with his assistance, they might reverently guard and faithfully explain the revelation or deposit of faith that was handed down through the apostles. Indeed, it was this apostolic doctrine that all the Fathers held and the holy orthodox Doctors reverenced and followed, fully realizing that this See of St Peter always remains untainted by any error, according to the divine promise of our Lord and Savior made to the prince of his disciples: "But I have prayed for you that your faith may not fail; and when you have turned again, strengthen your brethren" [Lk 22:32].

Now this charism of truth and of never-failing faith was conferred upon Peter and his successors in this chair in order that they might perform their supreme office for the salvation of all; that by them the whole flock of Christ might be kept away from the poisonous bait of error and be nourished by the food of heavenly doctrine; that, the occasion of schism being removed, the whole Church might be preserved as one and, resting on her foundation, might stand firm against the gates of hell.[29]

Following the constant understanding of the Church down the centuries, the Council Fathers taught that Petrine primacy and the corollary fullness of power of the Roman Pontiff, instituted by Christ in His constitution of the Church as His Mystical Body, are directed exclusively to the salvation of souls by the safeguarding and promoting of the solid doctrine and sound discipline, handed down in an unbroken line by means of Apostolic Tradition.

Section 22 of the Dogmatic Constitution *Lumen Gentium* of the Second Vatican Ecumenical Council likewise used the expression "fullness of power." Describing the relationship of the College of Bishops to the Roman Pontiff, the Council Fathers declare:

But the college or body of bishops has no authority unless it is understood together with the Roman pontiff, the successor of Peter as its head. The pope's power of primacy over all, both pastors and faithful, remains whole and intact. In virtue of his office, that is, as vicar of Christ and pastor of the whole Church, the Roman pontiff has full, supreme, and universal power over the Church. And he is always free to exercise this power. The order of bishops, which succeeds to the college of apostles and gives this apostolic body continued existence, is also the subject of supreme and full power over the universal Church, provided we understand this body together with its head, the Roman pontiff, and never without this head. This power can be exercised only with the consent of the Roman pontiff. For Our Lord placed Simon alone as the rock and the bearer of the keys of the Church [cf. Mt 16:18-19] and made him shepherd of the whole flock; it is evident, however, that the power of binding and loosing, which was

---

29   *DH* 3070-71.

given to Peter [Mt 16:19], was granted also to the college of apostles, joined with its head [cf. Mt 18:18; 28:16–20].[30]

The distinct office of the Roman Pontiff with respect to the College of Bishops and indeed to the universal Church is described in section 23 of *Lumen Gentium* with these words: "The Roman pontiff, as the successor of Peter, is the perpetual and visible principle and foundation for the unity of the multiplicity of both the bishops and the faithful."[31]

In an earlier part of the same Dogmatic Constitution, the Council Fathers explain:

> This sacred synod, following in the steps of the First Vatican Council, teaches and declares with it that Jesus Christ, the eternal pastor, set up the holy Church by entrusting the apostles with their mission as he himself had been sent by the Father (cf. Jn 20:21). He willed that their successors, the bishops namely, should be the shepherds in his Church until the end of the world. In order that the episcopate itself, however, might be one and undivided he put Peter at the head of the other apostles, and in him he set up a lasting and visible source and foundation of the unity both of faith and of communion.[32]

After the symposium entitled "The Primacy of the Successor of Peter," organized by the Congregation for the Doctrine of the Faith from December 2–4, 1996, the Congregation published certain considerations regarding the subject of the Petrine Office and the power conferred upon it.

Regarding the relationship of the Petrine Office to the office of bishop, the document declared:

> All bishops are subjects of the care of all the Churches (*sollicitudo omnium Ecclesiarum*) inasmuch as they are members of the episcopal college which succeeds to the college of the Apostles, of which the extraordinary figure of St Paul was a member. This universal dimension of their *episkopè* (oversight) is inseparable from the particular dimension

---

30   "Collegium autem seu corpus Episcoporum auctoritatem non habet, nisi simul cum Pontifice Romano, successore Petri, ut capite eius intellegatur, huiusque integer manente potestate Primatus in omnes sive Pastores sive fideles. Romanus enim Pontifex habet in Ecclesiam, vi muneris sui, Vicarii scilicet Christi et totius Ecclesiae Pastoris, plenam, supremam et universalem potestatem, quam semper libere exercere valet. Ordo autem Episcoporm, qui collegio Apostolorum in magisterio et regimine pastorali succedit, immo in quo corpus apostolicum continuo perseverat, una cum Capite suo Romano Pontifice, et numquam sine hoc Capite subiecutm quoque supremae ac plenae potestatis in universam Ecclesiam exsistit, quae quidem potestas nonnisi consentiente Roman Pontifice exerceri potest. Dominus unum Simonem ut petram et cavigerum Ecclesiae posuit [cf. Mt 16:18–19], eumque Pastorem totius sui gregis constituit [cf. Io 21: 15–19]; illud autem ligandi ac solvendi munus, quod Petro datum est [Mt 16:19], collegio quoque Apostolorum, suo Capiti coniuncto, tributum esse constat [Mt 18:18; 28:16–20]." Second Vatican Council, Dogmatic Constitution on the Church *Lumen Gentium* (November 21, 1964), §22.

31   "Romanus Pontifex, ac successor Petri, est unitatis, tum Episcoporum tum fidelium multitudinis, perpetuum ac visibile principium et fundamentum." *Lumen Gentium* 23.

32   *Lumen Gentium* 18.

relative to the offices entrusted to them. In the case of the bishop of Rome — Vicar of Christ in the proper manner of Peter as Head of the College of Bishops —, the care of all the Churches acquires a particular force because it is accompanied by full and supreme power in the Church: a truly episcopal power, not only supreme, full, and universal, but also immediate, over all, both pastors and other faithful. The ministry of the Successor of Peter, therefore, is not a service which reaches each particular Church from outside, but is inscribed in the heart of every particular Church, in which "the Church of Christ is truly present and acts," and by this carries in itself the opening to the ministry of unity. This interiority of the ministry of the bishop of Rome to each particular Church is also an expression of the mutual interiority between the universal Church and the particular Church.[33]

The Petrine office is therefore in its proper essence and in its exercise different from offices of civil government.

The document of the Congregation goes on to explain how the Roman Pontiff carries out his office as a service, that is, in obedience to Christ:

The Roman Pontiff is — as are all the faithful — subject to the Word of God, to the Catholic faith, and is the guarantee of the obedience of the Church and, in this sense, is the servant of the servants (*servus servorum*). He does not decide according to his own will, but gives voice to the will of the Lord who speaks to man in the Scriptures lived and interpreted by the Tradition; in other terms, the *episkopè* of the Primate has the limits which flow from divine law and the inviolable divine constitution of the Church contained in Revelation. The Successor of Peter is the rock who, contrary to arbitrariness and conformism, guarantees a rigorous fidelity to the Word of God: the martyrological character of his primacy follows from this.[34]

The fullness of power of the Roman Pontiff cannot be properly understood and exercised except as obedience to the grace of Christ the Head and Shepherd of the flock in every time and place.

CANONICAL LEGISLATION

The fullness of the power of the Roman Pontiff is expressed in can. 218 of the 1917 Code of Canon Law, which reads:

§1. The Roman Pontiff, who is the successor of St Peter in the primacy, possesses not only a primacy of honor, but supreme and full power of jurisdiction in the entire Church in matters which belong to faith

---

33   "Il Primato del Successore di Pietro nel Mistero della Chiesa," in Congregation for the Doctrine of the Faith, *Documenti (1966-2013)* (Città del Vaticano: Libreria Editrice Vaticana, 2017), pp. 480-81, no. 6; *Communicationes* 30 (1998): 210-11, no. 6.

34   "Il Primato," p. 481, no. 7; *Communicationes* 30 (1998): 212, no. 7.

and morals as well as in those which pertain to discipline and the government of the Church throughout the world.

§2. This power is truly episcopal, ordinary and immediate over all and each of the churches and over all and each of the pastors and the faithful, and is independent of every human authority.[35]

What is important to note initially is that the fullness of power is required by the primacy of the Roman Pontiff, which is not merely honorary but substantial, that is, it is required for the fulfillment of the supreme, ordinary, full and universal responsibility of safeguarding the rule of faith (*regula fidei*) and the rule of law (*regula iuris*).

Can. 331 of the 1983 Code of Canon Law contains substantially the same legislation. It reads:

> The bishop of the Roman Church, in whom continues the office given by the Lord uniquely to Peter, the first of the Apostles, and to be transmitted to his successors, is the head of the college of bishops, the Vicar of Christ, and the pastor of the universal Church on earth. By virtue of his office he possesses supreme, full, immediate, and universal ordinary power in the Church, which he is always able to exercise freely.[36]

The power of the Roman Pontiff is understood from the adjectives which modify it.

It is *ordinary* because it is stably connected to the office of primacy by Christ Himself. It is part of the *ius divinum*. It is a divine disposition.[37] It is *supreme*, that is, the highest authority within the hierarchy and not subordinated to any other human power, while it remains always subordinate to Christ alive in the Church through the Tradition guarded and transmitted by the rule of faith and the rule of law. It is *full* in that it is equipped with all the faculties contained in the sacred power to teach, to sanctify, and to govern. It is thus connected with the exercise of the infallible magisterium and with the authentic non-infallible magisterium (cann. 749 §1 and 752), with legislative and judicial power, and with the moderation of the liturgical life and divine worship of the universal Church. It is *immediate*, that is, it may be exercised over the faithful and their

---

35 "Can. 218. §1. Romanus Pontifex, Beati Petri in primate Successor, habet non solum primatum honoris, sed supremam et plenam potestatem iurisdictionis in universam Ecclesiam tum in rebus quae ad fidem et mores, tum in iis quae ad disciplinam et regimen Ecclesiae per totum orbem diffusae pertinent. § 2. Haec potestas est vere episcopalis, ordinaria et immediate tum in omnes et singulas ecclesias, tum in omnes et singulos pastores et fidelis a quavis humana auctoritate independens." English translation: John A. Abbo and Jerome D. Hannan, *The Sacred Canons: A Concise Presentation of the Current Disciplinary Norms of the Church* (St Louis, MO: B. Herder Book Co., 1952), vol. 1, p. 281.

36 "Can. 331. Ecclesiae Romanae Episcopus, in quo permanet munus a Domino singulariter Petro, primo Apostolorum, concessum et successoribus eius transmittendum, Collegii Episcoporum est caput, Vicarius Christi atque universae Ecclesiae his in terris Pastor; qui ideo vi muneris sui suprema, plena, immediata et universali in Ecclesia gaudet ordinaria potestate, quam semper libere exercere valet." English translation: Canon Law Society of America, *Code of Canon Law: Latin-English Translation* (Washington, DC: Canon Law Society of America, 1998).

37 Cf. cann. 131 §1, and 145 §1; and "Nota Explicativa Praevia" of *Lumen Gentium*.

pastors wherever and without condition, and it is *universal*, that is, it extends to the entire ecclesial community, to all the faithful, to the particular Churches and their congregations, and to all of the matters which are subject to the jurisdiction and responsibility of the Church.

What is evident in the canonical legislation is that "the pope does not exercise the power connected to his office when he acts as a private person or simple member of the faithful."[38] Evidently, too, given the supreme character of the fullness of power entrusted to the Roman Pontiff, he does not have an absolute power in the contemporary political sense and, therefore, is held to listen to Christ and to His Mystical Body the Church. In the words of the considerations offered by the Congregation for the Doctrine of the Faith in 1998:

> To listen to the voice of the Churches is, in fact, a proper characteristic of the ministry of unity, also a consequence of the unity of the episcopal body and of the *sensus fidei* of the entire People of God; and this bond appears substantially endowed with greater force and certainty than juridical instances—a moreover inadmissible hypothesis because of lack of foundation—to which the Roman Pontiff would have to respond. The final and binding responsibility of the Roman Pontiff finds its best guarantee, on the one hand, in its insertion in the Tradition and in fraternal communion and, on the other hand, in the assistance of the Holy Spirit Who governs the Church.[39]

As one canonist comments on the fullness of the power of the pope:

> Without doubt, the end and the mission of the Church indicate well-articulated limits which are not of easy juridical formulation. But if we would wish juridical formulations, we could say that these limits are those that the divine law, natural and positive, establishes.
>
> Above all, the pope has to exercise his power in communion with the whole Church (c. 333, §2). Wherefore, these limits stand in relationship with the communion in the faith, in the sacraments, and in ecclesiastical governance (can. 205). The pope has to respect the deposit of faith—he holds the authority to express the Credo in a more adequate manner but he cannot act contrary to the faith; he has to respect all and each of the sacraments—he cannot suppress nor add anything that goes against the substance of the sacraments; and, finally, he has to respect the ecclesial rule of divine institution—he cannot prescind from the episcopate and has to share with the College of Bishops the exercise of the full and supreme power.[40]

---

38   ". . . el Papa no ejercita esta potestad aneja a su oficio cuando actúa come persona privada o como simple fiel." Eduardo Molano, "Potestad del Romano Pontifice," *Diccionario General de Derecho Canónico*, vol. VI (Cizur Menor [Navarra]: Editorial Aranzadi, SA, 2012), 304. English translation by author.

39   "Il Primato," p. 483, no. 10; *Communicationes*, 213.

40   Molano, "Potestad del Romano Pontifice," 306.

CONCLUSION

It is my hope that these reflections which are initial in character and require much further elaboration will help you to understand the necessity and the subtlety of the fullness of the power of the Roman Pontiff for the safeguarding and promoting of the good of the universal Church. According to Sacred Scripture and Sacred Tradition, the Successor to St Peter has power which is universal, ordinary, and immediate over all the faithful. He is the supreme judge of the faithful, over whom there is no higher human authority, not even an ecumenical council. To the pope belongs the power and authority to define doctrines and to condemn errors, to make and repeal laws, to act as judge in all matters of faith and morals, to decree and inflict punishment, to appoint and, if need be, to remove pastors. Because this power is from God Himself, it is limited as such by natural and divine law, which are expressions of the eternal and unchangeable truth and goodness that come from God, are fully revealed in Christ, and have been handed on in the Church throughout time. Therefore, any expression of doctrine or law or practice that is not in conformity with Divine Revelation, as contained in Sacred Scripture and the Church's Tradition, cannot be an authentic exercise of the Apostolic or Petrine ministry and must be rejected by the faithful. As St Paul declared: "There are some who trouble you and want to pervert the gospel of Christ. But if we, or an angel from heaven, should preach to you a gospel contrary to that which we preached to you, let him be anathema" (Gal 1:8).

As devout Catholics and servants of the Church's discipline, we must in all things teach and defend the fullness of the power with which Christ has endowed His Vicar on earth. At the same time, we must teach and defend that power within the teaching and defense of the Church as the Mystical Body of Christ, as an organic body of divine origin and divine life. I conclude with the words of Gratian:

> Let no mortal being have the audacity to reprimand a pope on account of his faults, for he whose duty it is to judge all other men cannot be judged by anybody, unless he should be called to task for having deviated from the faith.[41]

---

41   "Huius culpas istic redarguere presumit mortalium nullus, quia cunctos ipse iudicaturis a nemine est iudicandus, nisi deprehendatur devius; pro cuius perpetuo statu uniuersitas fidelium tanto instantius orat, quanto suam salutem post Deum ex illius incolumitate animaduertunt propensius pendere." *Decretum Magistri Gratiani. Concordia Discordantium Canonum,* 1a, dist. 40, c. 6, Si papa; Item ex gestis Bonifacii martyris. Gratian, *Decretals,* 1a, dist. 40, c. 6, *Si papa;* ex gestis Bonifacii martyris.

2

The Hyperpapalist Claims of Pope St Gregory VII[1]

PHILLIP CAMPBELL

IN LIGHT OF THE UNPRECEDENTED CENTRALIZATION of authority under the Francis pontificate, discussions on the extent of papal power take on a fresh urgency. What is in question is not so much the pope's doctrinal authority as the breadth of his disciplinary power. The novelties of the Francis pontificate have seemingly placed every Catholic discipline on the table. Could the pope, for example, dispense the entire Church from the Lenten fast? Could he add a clause to the Our Father? Or change the liturgical colors of the seasons? Questions of these sorts used to be academic thought exercises for manualists, hypotheticals discussed by scholastic specialists; now they are frighteningly relevant scenarios as the entire Church huddles in trepidation, waiting to see what our pope feels the God of Surprises wants to foist upon the Church from day to day.

There have been some excellent traditional responses to the dilemma of "hyperpapalism." I would like especially to cite Peter Kwasniewski's two-volume set *The Road from Hyperpapalism to Catholicism*, as well as the lecture "The Pope's Boundedness to Tradition as a Legislative Limit" by the same author. Mention also must be made of Dr John Joy's excellent book *Disputed Questions on Papal Infallibility*. These and other works of this nature are of great utility in understanding the theoretical limits of papal authority.

THE PAPACY AND HISTORICAL PRECEDENT

In the realm of history, however, the problem has always been more muddled. Of course, the institution of the papacy came with no written constitution of clearly enumerated powers; Christ gave no dogmatic handbook when He handed St Peter the keys of the kingdom. How, then, did the papacy delineate the scope of its actions?

Historically, papal power grew from implied authority, concretized in particular historical circumstances that established precedents. The popes preferred precedent to theory when defining the contours of their authority. That is to say, when the popes wanted to justify their authority at various junctures, their preferred approach was not an appeal to arguments dogmatic or theological (beyond the common Scriptural citations), but rather to examples historical, essentially saying, "I can

---

1   First published at *OnePeterFive* on August 29, 2022; revised and expanded for this book.

do such-and-such because here's some concrete examples of my predecessors doing the same thing." When King Henry VIII made the theological objection that the pope could not dispense a man to marry his brother's widow, one of the weightiest rebuttals of Queen Catherine's defenders, such as St John Fisher, was simply to point out historical examples where prior popes had done just that.[2] When papal prerogatives were challenged, we could say that precedent took precedence.

But precedent also allowed room for development. Popes have traditionally pushed the boundaries, using one inherited precedent to build upon another in the expansion of authority. An excellent example is the case of the pallium, the woolen garment bestowed by the pope upon a metropolitan archbishop. The pallium was originally a sign of honor given by a pope to a newly consecrated archbishop. But over time it came to represent the archepiscopal office itself, and then finally to *confer* the archepiscopal office, such that an archbishop was not considered installed until he received the pallium from the pope. This fascinating development is well documented in Steven Schoenig's *Bonds of Wool: The Pallium and Papal Power in the Middle Ages.*[3]

The primacy of precedent in the development of papal authority simply means that *the strongest argument that the popes can do something is the fact they have done something.*

Thus, like the old Roman god Janus, the papacy looks backward and forward in wielding power: it looks backward to precedent to find stable footing for its current actions, and it looks forward by pushing its inherited precedential boundaries, thus expanding the scope of action for future popes.

Here it is critical to note an important caveat: the growth in papal power, *contra* the claims of the Greek schismatics, was in large part to *counter* the ecclesiastical assertions of the eastern and (later) western Roman emperors promoting heresy or caesaropapist ambitions by making the bishops into government bureaucrats. Each individual precedent must be evaluated separately according to its historical circumstances. As a result, Catholic history smiles upon the courage of Pope St Gregory VII and Innocent III in growing papal power, even as it frowns upon the unjust excommunications decreed by Martin IV and Boniface VIII. But even this summarization is much too simplistic, as we'll see presently.

Does history offer nothing but bad news for traditionalists seeking to push back against the brute force of papal absolutism? Where does it leave us in the face of a pope determined to wield his authority to impose every manner of crude novelty on the Church?

Precedent is a two-sided coin. On the one hand, the tremendous danger is obvious. If the Church meekly accepts the expansion of authority accomplished under Francis, then this will create a precedent for future popes to claim these powers as

---

2   See J. J. Scarisbrick, *Henry VIII* (Los Angeles: University of California Press, 1970), 177–78. Popes Martin V, Alexander VI, Leo X, and even Clement VII himself had done the same on other occasions.

3   Washington, DC: Catholic University of America Press, 2016.

part of the legislative patrimony of the Petrine office. It leaves the door open for future pontificates to reorder every facet of Catholic life according to whatever fads are popular at the time. In short, as awful as it is that Pope Francis should presume to outlaw the traditional Roman Rite, subvert religious orders' autonomy, or sack bishops as if they are corporate middle managers, the long-term threat is that such deeds enter the stream of papal precedent—that a kind of historical consensus sprouts up that these are actions proper to papal governance itself.

But now, the other side of the coin: though papal power has grown by appeal to precedent, there have been occasions where papal overreach has failed to become precedent due to stiff resistance. Let us consider one of the examples from above to demonstrate the complexity of the historical precedents.

THE CASE OF POPE ST GREGORY VII

Pope St Gregory VII (1073–1085) is appropriately lauded for his courage against the Holy Roman Emperor. We rightly praise the Gregorian Reform as the Church's pushback against the abuse of lay investiture and the tyranny of the Holy Roman Emperors over the papacy. What we often forget, however, is that the reforms of Gregory VII were not simply meant to free the Church from lay tyranny; Gregory's philosophy envisioned an inversion of the entire relationship between the spiritual (clerical) and temporal (lay) powers within Christendom, substituting imperial dominance of the Church with clerical dominance over the empire.[4]

In pursuit of this, Gregory promoted ideas that even the most ardent hyperpapalists today would shrink from. We need only look at the Gregorian document *Dictatus Papae* (1075) which claimed, among other things, that the pope was *de facto* a saint by the grace of the Petrine office, that he had the right to use the imperial insignia, that he possessed unilateral authority to depose any bishop and to divide or combine dioceses at will.[5] While the authorship of *Dictatus Papae* is uncertain, all historians agree that it is a Roman document dating from the Gregorian period, and thus represents ideas circulating among the Gregorian reformers, even if it is not the literal writing of Pope Gregory VII.

A follow-up to *Dictatus Papae* was *Propriae auctoritates apostolicae sedis*.[6] Issued sometime prior to 1085, this document argued that even if the pope apostatized and renounced the Christian faith entirely, he would not be liable to any judgment.[7]

---

4   See Jacques Le Goff, *Medieval Civilization*, trans. Julia Barrow (Oxford: Blackwell Publishers, 1999), 96–97; 271: "This is an essential aspect of the Gregorian Reform—it proclaimed itself to be the head of the lay as well as of the religious hierarchy."

5   The holiness of the pope by virtue of the Petrine office is also reaffirmed in Gregory VII's Letter to Hermann of Metz, *Registrum*, Bk. 8, Letter 21, as found in *The Correspondence of Pope Gregory VII*, translated with an introduction by Ephraim Emerton (New York: W. W. Norton & Company, 1969), 166–75.

6   For a synopsis of *Propriae auctoritates apostolicae sedis*, see my essay of the same name at *Unam Sanctam Catholicam*, April 15, 2012, http://unamsanctamcatholicam.blogspot.com/2021/04/propriae-auctoritates-apostolicae-sedis.html.

7   Gregory VII, *Propriae auctoritates apostolicae sedis*, no. 7. The text may be found in a German-language work by Hubert Mordek, "Proprie auctoritates apostolice sedis. Ein zweiter Dictatus Papae Gregors VII?," *Deutsches Archiv für Erforschung des Mittelalters* 28 (1972): 105–32, trans. by T. Reuter.

Did Pope Gregory really believe that the papal office made him a saint? The assertion is found in *Dictatus Papae* article 23, a strange clause where the document argues that a canonically elected pope "is undoubtedly made a saint by the merits of St Peter."[8] But should this be taken literally? Could it not be simply another way of suggesting that the pope's authority comes by virtue of being successor of St Peter?

The Latin reads "meritis beati Petri indubitanter efficitur sanctus." Fortunately we are not left to wonder, for Gregory develops a similar idea elsewhere. In a letter to Hermann of Metz, Gregory expands upon the concept of *efficitur sanctus*. Commenting on the superiority of popes over kings, he says:

> If, then, men who fear God come under compulsion with fear and trembling to the Apostolic See where those who are properly ordained become stronger through the merits of the blessed Apostle Peter, with what awe and hesitation should men ascend to the throne of a king where even good and humble men like Saul and David become worse! What we have said above is thus stated in the decrees of the blessed pope Symmachus—though we have learned it through experience: "He, that is, St Peter, transmitted to his successors an unfailing endowment of merit together with an inheritance of innocence"; and again: "For who can doubt that he is holy who is raised to the height of such an office, in which if he is lacking in virtue acquired by his own merits, that which is handed down from his predecessor is sufficient. For either he [Peter] raises men of distinction to bear this burden or he glorifies them after they are raised up.[9]

We know Gregory is speaking of the same concept here as in *Dictatus Papae* article 23 because both his letter to Hermann and article 23 reference Pope Symmachus. This passage strongly suggests Gregory does indeed take *efficitur sanctus* to mean personal holiness. This is evident in several ways.

First, consider the contrast: Gregory contrasts kings who are "made worse" by their office with popes who "become stronger" through the merits of Peter. The references to Saul and David becoming "worse" are clearly references to their personal sins. Ergo, for the contrast to make sense, Gregory must be contrasting personal vices with personal virtues. Kingly office makes one "become worse" by temptation to personal vice; the occupant of the Apostolic See will "become stronger" by being supplied with personal virtue through the merits of Peter.

Second, notice that Gregory is speaking of the popes' *personal* merit. Each successor of Peter receives "an unfailing endowment of merit," but also "an inheritance of innocence." The phrase "inheritance of innocence" is awkward, but it seems clear that he is referring to a pontiff's personal innocence, with which he is provided by virtue of holding the Apostolic See. This is made explicit with his final clause, a striking passage that merits close attention:

---

8 All quotes from *Dictatus Papae* are taken from the English translation by Ernest F. Henderson, *Select Historical Documents of the Middle Ages* (London: George Bell and Sons, 1910), 366–67.

9 Gregory VII, Letter to Hermann of Metz, in *The Correspondence of Pope Gregory VII*, 174.

> For who can doubt that he is holy who is raised to the height of such an office, in which if he is lacking in virtue acquired by his own merits, that which is handed down from his predecessor is sufficient. For either he [Peter] raises men of distinction to bear this burden or he glorifies them after they are raised up.[10]

Again, Gregory says that "he is holy" by virtue of being raised to the Apostolic See: even if a pope lacks personal virtue, it is provided through the office—it comes to him as a Petrine "inheritance" that "glorifies" the pope after his canonical election.

This all suggests that Gregory believed that one who ascends to the papacy is possessed of a kind of "supplied holiness" by the merits of St Peter. This sanctity is described with the words "holy," "endowment of merit," "inheritance of innocence," "virtue," and "glorifies," all of which are used in a personal sense. The letter to Hermann of Metz thus provides the context for *Dictatus Papae* article 23. This is admittedly a hypothesis, but a strong one justified by the relevant texts.

Let it be granted that it is an obscure text and concept; but if it is so, it is precisely because it was *not* reaffirmed by successive popes, which leads us to our next consideration.

PUSHBACK TO GREGORY'S PROGRAM

Pope Gregory's ideas about papal authority were not universally embraced; some were resisted vigorously, not only by the Holy Roman Emperor, but by a broad coalition of bishops—especially those of northern Europe—who pushed back against the novelties they saw Gregory was imposing upon the Church.[11] Among such, he had the reputation of being a radical ideologue, pushing impracticable ideals that were guaranteed to sow confusion and chaos.[12] The eminent Bishop Ivo of Chartres protested that the pre-Gregorian social arrangement had broad support from clergy and laity alike, and was not contrary to canon law. Custom, he argued, ought to prevail over the radical agenda of the pope. If the pope and his supporters wanted reform, Ivo argued they should be content with incremental changes over time. Rome, irked by his moderate but persistent criticism, told him to keep silent. Today, Ivo is venerated as a saint; his feast day is on May 23.[13]

Another powerful opponent of the pope was the prominent Cluniac, Hugh of Fleury. Hugh wrote a treatise against the pope's pretensions to temporal authority, arguing that the pope was injuriously disrupting the right ordering of society.[14]

---

10   Ibid.

11   See Norman F. Cantor, *Medieval History*, 2nd ed. (Toronto: MacMillan Co., 1971), 286.

12   Medievalist Norman Cantor suggests that Gregory VII knew his teachings would be received as radical and was fully cognizant of their revolutionary nature: "*Dictatus Papae* was a sensational and extremely radical document, and it is inconceivable to think that Hildebrand [Gregory VII] was so naïve as to not realize that it would make that impression" (ibid.).

13   Cantor, 292.

14   Robert L. Benson, *The Gelasian Doctrine: Uses and Transformations* (Paris: Presses Universitaires de France, 1982), 34–35.

Cluny was at the time the most prestigious monastery in Christendom; the opposition of a man of the caliber of Hugh held considerable weight.

Of course, most German bishops opposed Gregory as well, usually from fidelity to the Holy Roman Emperor, but in some cases from genuine theological opposition to the pope's claims. [15] But it was not only the Germans who opposed the pope: the episcopate of Lombardy resisted the pope *en masse*, incurring excommunication for their obstinacy. In faraway England, Gerard, archbishop of York and chancellor of England, published a tract bitterly contesting Gregory's claims to temporal supremacy. [16] Gerard's tract was so polemical he published it anonymously so his name would not be associated with it.

These examples are not cited to argue that the positions of the pope's opponents were correct. Many of them had their own problems (like Gerard's assertion that kings were not lay people), and their hostility to Pope Gregory was seldom motivated by pure doctrinal considerations, often being mixed up with political considerations. And not a few of them ended up on the wrong side of the argument on the question of the Church's independence from lay control. This is all irrelevant; the point is simply that there was significant, sustained opposition from the European episcopate. This is irrefutable.

In the end, Gregory's pontificate was a mixed bag. He was thankfully successful in getting the emperors to renounce the right to invest bishops with ring and staff; he also undertook a very salutary reform of the sacrament of penance and may have died *in odium fidei*. [17] The Church rightly venerates him as a saintly pope.

But many of his more radical initiatives were abandoned by future pontiffs. His successors Clement III, Urban II, and Paschal II prudently stepped back from Gregory's more outlandish propositions, having little desire to perpetuate the chaos of Gregory's pontificate. We can see this, for example, in Alexander III's prudently diplomatic approach to the dispute between St Thomas Becket and Henry II of England, in which he preferred negotiated settlements rather than risk an open breach with the powerful Angevin king. As for the teachings of Gregory's pontificate, neither *Dictatus Papae* nor *Propriae auctoritates* passed into papal precedent. The documents do not appear in Denzinger, nor are they cited as dogmatic or canonical sources in Vatican I's teaching on papal infallibility. [18] The Church simply abandoned the documents and the ideology they represented.

---

15 Such as Bishop Wido of Osnabrück, who wrote a treatise against Gregory's assertions (Le Goff, *Medieval Civilization*, 268).

16 Norman F. Cantor, *Church, Kingship, and Lay Investiture in England, 1089–1135* (Princeton, NJ: Princeton University Press, 1958), 191. Another prominent English opponent of the pope was Herbert, Bishop of Norwich.

17 See Phillip Campbell, "Gregory the Great and the Reform of Penance," *Unam Sanctam Catholicam*, November 21, 2021, www.unamsanctamcatholicam.com/gregory-the-great-and-the-reform-of-penance.

18 *Pastor Aeternus* cites four popes, but Gregory VII is not among them. It also cites eight councils, ecumenical and regional, but none date from the period of the Gregorian Reform. Certainly, the fathers of Vatican I were familiar with the Gregorian documents but preferred not to use them in support of so weighty a doctrine. I conjecture their reticence was prompted by the Gregorian

THE CRITICAL JUNCTURE

My apologies if this historical detour seems tedious, but it is highly relevant. This essay is not a polemic against contemporary hyperpapalism. It is a historical observation about the ebb and flow of papal power in previous ages and how that may apply to current discussions about papal authority. That being said, it certainly has a bearing on our current situation. While theologians continue to delineate the theoretical limits of papal power—and I think Dr Kwasniewski's argument on the legislative limit posed by tradition is the correct answer—it is of utmost importance to make our opposition known to these actions *now*, before they enter the historical record as unresisted precedents. But more importantly, it is urgent that theologians and bishops in particular voice their protest. If the global episcopate, for example, does not protest the pope's arbitrary firing of Bishop Daniel Fernández Torres of Puerto Rico, it will become precedent that this, too, is within the scope of papal power.[19]

In the eleventh century, the popes who followed Gregory VII backed down from his platform because the late pontiff's measures had stirred up too much opposition from bishops, theologians, and emperors, causing chaos throughout the Church. Our current pope has stated that he welcomes disorder. "*¡Hagan lío!*" he proclaimed in 2013: "Make a mess!" If we don't want these novelties to become precedent, the best thing we can do at this point is stir up our own *lío*—respectfully, reasonably, charitably—but vigorously.

---

documents' claims about the *temporal* authority of the papacy. As *Pastor Aeternus* concerns only the teaching authority of the pope, appeals to Gregorian documents could have obfuscated the teaching of Vatican I about the role of the papacy—particularly at a time of such political upheaval as the late nineteenth century.

19   See Inés San Martin, "Pope removes Puerto Rican bishop from office after he refused to resign," *Crux*, March 9, 2022. [Indeed, the episcopate did not protest, and subsequently Francis did the same thing to Bishop Joseph Strickland of Tyler, Texas—who, in failing to resist his unjust deposition, further strengthened the injurious precedent. The "new *Dictatus Papae*" seems to be enjoying smooth sailing. See Peter Kwasniewski, *Bound by Truth: Authority, Obedience, Tradition, and the Common Good* (Brooklyn, NY: Angelico Press, 2023), 178–99.—*Ed.*]

3

Papal Authority and the Limits of Official Theology[1]

THOMAS PINK

H OW FAR ARE CATHOLICS MORALLY OBLIGED TO obey the pope? Some centuries ago this question arose politically. Suppose the pope commanded you, for the good of religion, to abandon allegiance to your political ruler; would you be morally bound to do so? Since the Second Vatican Council the question has arisen once again with regard to the liturgy. In 1969 Paul VI commanded the abandonment of the long-established Latin rite for a new rite that was a radical revision. The older rite was restricted, for many effectively forbidden. But then later popes began to remove these restrictions, and Benedict XVI even encouraged its celebration, claiming that it could never be right to suppress it. Now in *Traditionis Custodes* Francis has reimposed restrictions, limiting the discretion of bishops to permit the liturgy, as a path to the older rite's complete suppression. Papal decree reverses earlier papal decree, with spiritual burdens all along the way for many priests and for their people. Again we face the question: are we bound to obey the pope?

Some Catholics are in no doubt. On social media supporters of *Traditionis Custodes* gleefully cited *Pastor Aeternus*, the decree of the First Vatican Council that defined a papal primacy not only of teaching but also of jurisdiction. This decree seems to dictate unconditional obedience to papal legislation:

> Therefore in relation to this juridical authority [of the pope] clergy and faithful, of whatever rite and dignity, both singly and collectively, are bound by a duty of hierarchical subordination and true obedience, and this not only in matters concerning faith and morals, but also in those which regard the discipline and government of the Church throughout the world.[2]

One internet ultramontane posted this very passage, underlined in green ink, and claimed that even public criticism of *Traditionis Custodes* was "Protestant" and forbidden. *Pastor Aeternus* again:

---

1 An expanded and revised version of an article that originally appeared in *The Lamp* in the issue for the season of Christ the King of 2022. My thanks to the editor Matthew Walther for his invaluable assistance and advice in its original preparation, and for his kind permission to republish, and to John Joy for helpful discussion.

2 First Vatican Council, *Pastor Aeternus* (July 18, 1870), *Pastor Aeternus*, ch. 3.

The sentence of the Apostolic See (than which there is no higher authority) is not subject to revision by anyone, nor may anyone lawfully pass
judgment thereupon. [3]

Opponents of *Traditionis Custodes* struck back. They too appealed to the papalist
tradition in Catholic theology, this time not to the teaching of *Pastor Aeternus*, but to
the theology of the Counter-Reformation. Long before Vatican I many theologians
already defended a papal primacy of teaching and jurisdiction, opposing appeals
against papal decrees to any other authority within the Church and especially
opposing appeals to a general council. These theologians included Francisco Suárez
and St Robert Bellarmine, who in their turn cited eminent papalists preceding
Trent, such as Juan de Torquemada and Cajetan. These theologians all defended
something like the understanding of papal primacy taught in *Pastor Aeternus*; but
they still entertained the possibility not only of a pope who fell into heresy, but
also of a pope who misused his legislative authority to attack the Church, and
who, if he did so, would morally have to be opposed. Bellarmine insisted:

As it is lawful to resist a pope if he attacks the body, so it is lawful to resist
him if he attacks the soul or afflicts the state, and much more if he were
to seek to destroy the Church. It is permitted, I say, to resist him by not
doing what he commands and by preventing the execution of his will. [4]

For Bellarmine there was no unconditional duty of obedience to the pope.

Following Cajetan and Torquemada, Suárez insisted that a pope could even fall
into schism, detaching himself from the Church by legislating in a way hostile
to her unity and mission. One way he could do this would be through a radical
assault on the liturgy. A pope would fall into schism "if he wanted to abolish all
ecclesiastical ceremonies that are based on apostolic tradition." [5] Some opponents
of *Traditionis Custodes* imply that the motu proprio and the Pauline liturgical
reform that it enforces could amount to schismatic acts. But can we really use
the papalist theological tradition to win the liturgy wars, either for *Traditionis
Custodes* or against it? Not in the way that either of the opposing sides intends.

We must first make a distinction between magisterial teaching, which *Pastor
Aeternus* plainly is, and what one might call "official theology." [6] Magisterial teaching
is given by an officeholder within the Church, a pope or bishops, with magisterial
authority—with the authority, that is, to impose canonical obligations on belief.
These obligations are to an assent of faith in respect of what is taught infallibly
or to a religious submission of intellect and will to what is taught fallibly. [7] And

---

3   Ibid.

4   Robert Bellarmine, *De Romano Pontifice*, Bk. 2, ch. 29 (Ingolstadt, 1599), 311.

5   Francisco Suárez, *De Caritate*, disp. 12, sec. I, in *Opera*, ed. Charles Berton, vol. 12 (Paris:
Vivès, 1858), 734.

6   For the original use and discussion of the notion of official theology, see my "Vatican II and
Crisis in the Theology of Baptism," in *Integralism and the Common Good*, ed. P. Edmund Waldstein,
OCist, vol. 2 (New York: Angelico Press, 2022), 290–334.

7   See the 1983 *CIC*, cann. 750–54, which are footnoted with a reference to *Lumen Gentium* 25.

since not all utterances even of popes or bishops count as magisterial teaching, the teaching must signal an intention to impose some such obligation. Official theology, as the term suggests, is likewise produced by officeholders within the Church. It is, simply put, what such officeholders are expected to say. But it may still fail to count as magisterial teaching. It may be given by someone with magisterial authority, but without clear signal that he intends to place an obligation on the minds of the faithful. It may be a currently received view, but be given by a pope or bishop in his capacity as a private doctor. It may even be given in a forum which expressly disavows any exercise in its pronouncements of magisterial authority — such as a statement of the International Theological Commission. Or it may be given by officeholders who, though their role is central to the faith as it is communicated on a workaday basis, lack magisterial authority in their own right. It could be the content of a parish homily.

Official theology may represent and interpret what is magisterial teaching, and it may do so faithfully. But it does so without imposing any further claim of its own, independent of that which is already attached to the magisterial teaching referred to. Much of what passes for the communication of Church teaching, the stuff of parish homilies and catechesis, is not itself magisterial teaching, but at most refers to such teaching as a report or interpretation of its content. Suárez and Bellarmine were very eminent. Suárez was a theologian some of whose work was papally commissioned. Bellarmine was a cardinal and bishop and a member of the Congregation of the Roman Inquisition. Their writings, however, generally amounted at most to official theology of a highly prestigious and influential kind. Their accounts of magisterial teaching might in many cases be accurate. But like similar reports and interpretations today they remain perfectly open to debate.

Official theology is fundamental to the life of the Church. It is the main medium through which the Church's teaching is represented and understood by her members. For that reason, it is often difficult for many of them to distinguish the official theology of the age from magisterial teaching proper. That official theology, to the extent that they grasp it, commonly provides their understanding of the teaching. More than providing a common understanding of magisterial teaching, official theology can even help shape the content of that teaching. The assumptions on which the magisterial teaching of a general council is based generally come as official theology. At Trent, as we shall see, received assumptions about the moral force of canonical legislation were crucial to the formulation and approval of dogmatic canons.

Unlike much (not all) magisterial teaching, including the magisterial teaching that it helps form, official theology is not itself protected from error. Far from being so protected, official theology can be various and inconsistent, taking local forms that contradict official theologies within the Church of other times and places. Official theology in Rome in 1600 was broadly papalist in its view of ecclesial authority; that was not the official theology of then more Gallican Paris. In both places the official theology of limbo and the destiny of infants who die unbaptized of 1600 was not that of 1500, nor is it that of either Catholic Rome or Paris in 2022. As it mutates and changes, official theology may repeat magisterial teaching, or it may go beyond it; it may pass over some magisterial teaching in silence, or even begin to contradict it.

If Suárez and Bellarmine were purveyors of official theology, does that alone show that the opponents of *Traditionis Custodes* are wrong to invoke them? Certainly not. Official theology is indispensable to our understanding of the faith. But it is only as good as its interpretations of magisterial teachings and the arguments on which those interpretations rely. On the specific points cited these two theologians were surely right. The immunity of papal legislation to "judgment" which *Pastor Aeternus* teaches is clearly an immunity to any "higher" *juridical* sentence. There can be no juridical appeal against it in any earthly forum. That does not mean, however, that all public criticism of it is forbidden morally, or even that it cannot be so morally faulty as to fail to impose a moral obligation to obey. The duty of obedience that *Pastor Aeternus* teaches is juridical. The Church is a *potestas* — a sovereign legislator with jurisdiction over a community which her authority serves. The Church shares this character of *potestas* with states, as Leo XIII taught. A state is sovereign in civil matters over a political community for which it issues civil law. The Church is the one sovereign authority for religion on this earth, with jurisdiction over the Christian faithful for whom she issues canon law: the discipline of the Church of which *Pastor Aeternus* treats. *Pastor Aeternus* teaches that the faithful are canonically subject to papal authority, with a legal obligation to obedience without any legal forum for appeal. But, as Bellarmine and Suárez well knew, it does not follow that the faithful need be bound morally. As Bellarmine took some trouble to explain in *De Romano Pontifice*, just as a valid legal directive of the state may fail to bind its citizens morally because of some defect in it, so too the faithful may fail to be bound morally by a valid but defective legal directive of the Church. The legal directive could be immoral and unjust; or it could simply be too damaging to the community to be morally binding on them. A legal obligation is not necessarily a moral obligation.

Pastor Aeternus teaches that the pope has a primacy in respect of two distinct kinds of authority: an authority to teach and an authority to direct and legislate. It further defines conditions under which the pope will teach infallibly, without possibility of falsehood. But note well: there is no parallel definition of conditions under which the pope will legislate "infallibly," that is without possibility of legislative fault, let alone a fault substantial enough to remove a moral obligation to obey. Had *Pastor Aeternus* meant to teach about our moral obligation to obey the pope, it would have had to specify such conditions, which it did not.

Newman was very aware of this distinction between infallibility in teaching and in legislation. In his *Letter to the Duke of Norfolk* just after the Vatican Council he discussed the force of *Pastor Aeternus*, which asserted the infallibility of the pope as teacher; but not an infallibility of the pope as a legislator:

> In doing this, I shall, with him, put aside for the present and at first the pope's prerogative of infallibility in general enunciations, whether of faith or morals, and confine myself to the consideration of his authority (in respect of which he is not infallible) in matters of conduct, and our duty of obedience to him. . . . But a pope is not infallible in his laws, nor in his commands, nor in his acts of state, nor in his administration, nor in his public policy.[8]

Others have ignored Newman's distinction – not only the internet ultramontanes of today, but the arch-ultramontane Manning at the time, who flatly claimed in a letter to his clergy:

> In a word, the whole magisterium or doctrinal authority of the Pontiff as the supreme Doctor of all Christians, is included in this definition of his infallibility. And also all legislative or judicial acts, so far as they are inseparably connected with his doctrinal authority; as, for instance, all judgments, sentences, and decisions, which contain the motives of such acts as derived from faith and morals. Under this will come laws of discipline, canonisations of Saints, approbation of religious Orders, of devotions, and the like; all of which intrinsically contain the truths and principles of faith, morals, and piety.[9]

Cardinal Manning certainly did not exclude papal legislation from infallibility. Nor did another eminent author of the early twentieth century, Cardinal Billot, who in his *De Ecclesia Christi* expressly extended infallibility to include legislation as well as teaching:

> Infallibility always attaches to the exercise of the supreme legislative authority [within the Church] in so far as the Church has divine assistance and can never establish discipline opposed to the rules of faith and of evangelical holiness.[10]

The real problem with using Suárez and Bellarmine to oppose *Traditionis Custodes* is that their theology was far closer to Manning and Billot than the brief passages cited on the internet, torn from context, might suggest. Of course Suárez and Bellarmine admitted at least some bare possibility of moral error in papal legislation, and they were right to do so. But they did this hypothetically. In fact, their considered view accorded immense force to bind or obligate morally both to papal legislation and to ecclesial legislation in general. And this force to obligate morally was explained, in turn, by a claim that not only the teaching but the settled law of the popes and of the Church could not conflict with faith and morals.

Thus Suárez raised the issue of whether the canonical punishment of the baptized for heresy was morally objectionable. It could not be, he reasoned, because the Church had long provided for this in her canon law:

---

8   John Henry Newman, *Letter Addressed to the Duke of Norfolk* (London: Longmans, 1900), 223; 256.
9   Henry Edward Manning, *The Vatican Council and Its Definitions* (London: Longmans, 1870), 89.
10   Louis Billot, *De Ecclesia Christi* (Prato: Giachetti, 1909), 466.

> Secondly I prove the claim from the custom of the Church: for the
> whole Church makes use of an authority to do this, an authority that
> has been so employed since ancient times. But the whole Church cannot
> err in moral questions and in matters pertaining to religion and justice.
> It is in itself quite unbelievable that the Church usurped this authority
> tyrannically and without legitimate title.[11]

For Suárez the settled canon law of the Church simply could not be in moral error. Nor was Suárez's view eccentric for his time. Dogmatic canons of Trent anathematizing Protestant claims could be argued for on canonical grounds by the council fathers and by the theologians advising them. What the heretics were proposing could be anathematized because it conflicted with established canon law. The punishment of heresy in the baptized by means other than mere exclusion from the sacraments was an example. Objection to such punishment was anathematized in canon XIV of session VII on baptism, and the anathema was argued for at Trent by appeal to law. Theologians formulating the canon appealed to the decree of a provincial council in Visigothic Spain calling for such punishment, a decree that by the time of Trent remained in general canonical force within the Church as part of Gratian's *Decretum*.[12] An important part of Counter-Reformation official theology, the assured morality of settled canon law, fed into the delivery of magisterial teaching at a general council.

Suárez and Bellarmine thought that just as canon law was generally morally impeccable, so was the legislation of the pope as canonically supreme. A bare possibility that a papal decree might be morally objectionable was conceded. But the hypothetical cases were of isolated and particular decrees, not law for the Church as a whole. Why was the concession made? Because papal authority was plainly answerable to a higher authority that was not human: moral law as known by reason alone (natural law) and as revealed (the divine law of the New Covenant). The authority of the popes, like all legal authority, served the good of a community, in this case that of the Church and of her mission. This left open the possibility of some misfunction in papally imposed law—for some conflict with moral law, or for some harm to the Church and her mission, even to the point of a particular pope putting himself in schism. Thus Suárez and Bellarmine could not dismiss out of hand a hypothetical papal decree that failed to bind morally.

There were further reasons for discussing such cases. Conciliarists argued that because some defective papal legislation was possible on any view, provision for remedy was required: some forum of legal appeal against the pope, such as to a general council. The answerability of papal law to moral law and to the mission of the Church was common ground, yet threatened to lend support to

---

11   Francisco Suárez, *De Fide*, disp. 20, sec. 3, in *Opera*, ed. Charles Berton, vol. 12 (Paris: Vivès, 1858), 513.

12   For further discussion and references to the Council *Acta*, see my "John Finnis's Alternative History of Trent," www.academia.edu/37861294/John_Finniss_Alternative_History_of_Trent.

the conciliarists. So the papalists insisted that their theology too could provide for remedy: not appeal to a juridically higher authority, for there was none, but the possibility of morally legitimate disobedience on a scale sufficient to disable an errant pope and block the execution of his decrees. As Bellarmine insisted:

> It is permitted, I say, to resist [the pope] by not doing what he com-
> mands and by preventing the execution of his will. But it is not lawful
> to judge him, or to punish him, or to depose him, which alone is the
> business of a superior. [13]

It is clear that Suárez and Bellarmine did not seriously intend such concessions to provide a practical theology of resistance to papal authority. They were instead thought experiments meant to clarify their own understanding of the authority in question; they conceded its non-arbitrary nature and its service to the Church, but in a way designed to stave off conciliarist inferences. These thought experiments ask us to suppose that a pope did X, where X is so fantastic and so absurdly damaging to the good of the Church that of course a pope doing *that* should not be obeyed, nor would he be; but equally (it is also hard not to suppose) Providence would surely not let such a thing happen. They really amount to "Suppose, *per impossibile*, a pope did X . . ."

Suárez discusses, as we have seen, the case of a pope who put himself in schism from the Church by "abolishing apostolic liturgies." Now Suárez does not further specify what such an act might involve. But since it amounts to the pope detaching himself from the rest of the Church completely, it must come to something rather more radical than the Pauline liturgical reform. One suspects that Suárez had notionally in mind some wholesale papal attack on anything even recognizable as an ordered Church liturgy. Suárez cites in his support an earlier discussion by Torquemada of just such a hypothetical schismatic attack by a pope on the liturgy. Torquemada's discussion gives more detail and what he envisages is indeed drastic. It extends to a pope's refusal of all sacred vestments and even of the sign of the cross. [14] Furthermore Suárez parallels a pope's attack on the liturgy with another case which is very evidently fantastic: a pope, he suggests, might also put himself in schism by excommunicating absolutely everyone else in the Church. Did Suárez really think that God would ever let this happen? This is obviously a formal thought experiment meant to drive home the point that punishment legitimately imposed by a pope cannot be arbitrary; since papal authority serves the Church's unity, its legitimate exercise cannot directly attempt that unity's destruction.

Bellarmine's considered view still leaves papal legislative authority infallible to a very significant degree. When the pope legislates for the whole Church, his decrees cannot directly conflict with moral law, natural or revealed. And even when papal decrees given for the whole Church misfunction in other ways, still

---

13   Bellarmine, *De Romano Pontifice*, Bk. 2, ch. 29, p. 311.
14   Juan de Torquemada, *Summa de Ecclesia*, Bk. 4, pt. 1, ch. 11 (Salamanca, 1560), 552.

we are morally obligated to obey. Not only that, as subordinates we are forbidden even to criticize:

> The supreme pontiff not only cannot err in doctrines of faith but neither can he err in moral directives which are given for the whole Church, and which are concerned with matters necessary to salvation or with what is per se good or bad . . . So the pontiff cannot direct to what is vicious, such as usury . . . or direct to what is now contrary to salvation, the practice of circumcision . . . or forbid what is necessary to salvation, the practice of baptism. . . . But it is not absurd to say he could direct what is neither good nor bad in itself, nor in itself contrary to salvation but merely useless or harmful (inutile) . . . . But it is not for subjects to debate this issue, but only to obey.[15]

"Uselessness" in papal law is possible for Bellarmine, provided the law is not directly contrary to morals or the needs of salvation. But such "uselessness" could still be extremely damaging. Could there not be a "useless" law which, though in itself strictly consistent with morals and salvation, still, because of attendant circumstances, threatened immense damage to the Church and her mission? Imagine a liturgical reform that provided for valid celebration of the sacraments, with texts and rubrics that under some conditions might be harmless. This liturgical reform would still be "useless" if in existing circumstances it would be dangerously corrosive of existing belief and devotional practice. For example, in existing circumstances the reform might involve radical omissions of previous text and custom, omission dangerously apt to suggest some change in doctrine. Bellarmine's theory leaves room for that sort of "uselessness" in law, which would surely warrant public criticism lest the damage to the Church's mission be too great. It might even warrant disobedience. But Bellarmine will not entertain that possibility: "It is not for subjects to debate this issue, but only to obey."

Why suppose that canonical decrees issued for the Church as a whole cannot be directly contrary to moral law? The official theology of the Counter-Reformation generally did suppose this. An inference was frequently made from the infallibility of the pope or the Church as a teacher, an infallibility as teacher that extended to the content of moral law both natural and revealed, to a comparable infallibility as legislator. We find the inference being made very explicitly by Melchior Cano in his greatly respected and highly influential work of 1563, De Locis Theologicis. As with Bellarmine, for Cano the infallibility of the Church as legislator involved an impossibility of her issuing canon law that directly contravened moral law. And that was because the Church teaches infallibly what the moral law contains, natural and revealed:

> Then the Church cannot define something to be a vice that is morally good, or to be virtuous what is morally bad. Therefore in the law which

---

15   Bellarmine, De Romano Pontifice, Bk. 4, ch. 5, pp. 489–90.

she makes the Church cannot approve something that is contrary to the gospel or to reason . . . For which reason just as a council cannot put forward falsehoods to people as what they are to believe, so it cannot put forward evil as to be done.[16]

But why cannot the Church be protected from error in her teaching, including her teaching about what is good or bad, without *ipso facto* being protected from legally directing the doing of what is bad?

There is one basis for inferring infallibility in legislation from infallibility in teaching. This is the educational function of law. A *potestas* makes law; but it also teaches through its legislation. This applies to every *potestas*, state as well as Church. When a state forbids theft and punishes it heavily as a crime, it conveys the message — teaches — that theft is morally wrong. Correspondingly, when the state puts us under a legal obligation to do X, it conveys the message that insofar as doing X is required by law, it must be good morally, or at least not bad. States of course are not infallible as teachers about morals; but the Church is. If the Church as *potestas* legally directed us to do what is morally bad, she would then be teaching error about morals, which is impossible.

There is a fatal difficulty for this line of thought, however. In directing that X be done, the Church would certainly be teaching in the sense of conveying or implying a belief. She would be conveying the belief that doing X would at least not be bad. But as our discussion of official theology has emphasized, the Church's officeholders, including those with magisterial authority, convey lots of beliefs, without teaching magisterially and without any guarantee that these beliefs are true. Teaching is only ever protected from error (and even then not always) when it takes magisterial form — when it is proposed as imposing a canonical obligation on the mind. But canonical direction to do X, whilst it may convey that what it directs is at least moral, does not itself impose any canonical obligation to believe this. It imposes merely an obligation to do X, to act as canonically directed.

Let us return to Bellarmine's deferential view even of harmful papal decrees, which (he thought) we are morally obliged not only to obey but to avoid criticizing. His view gives rise to the question of whether compliance with such laws might still, in some cases, be immensely damaging to the mission of the Church. In such cases, why should disobedience, still less open criticism, be morally excluded?

There is one doctrine of the Church which might justify Bellarmine's insouciance. This is not the infallibility of the magisterium as a teacher, but the Church's more general indefectibility. The doctrine of indefectibility — the Church cannot fail — may resolve the tension within Counter-Reformation official theology: its concession of the possibility of defective legislation, but its effective refusal to allow for legitimate disobedience. Because canon law is in service to an end, the

---

16 Melchior Cano, *De Locis Theologicis*, in *Opera*, ed. Hyacinthe Serry (Padua, 1734), 169. Cano was a Dominican and personally hostile to the Jesuit order; this official theology of legislative infallibility was not peculiar to Jesuits such as Suárez and Bellarmine.

Church's good, and subject to a higher moral authority, ecclesial and papal legislation must in principle be capable of going wrong. But Providence's protection of the Church's good is bound to limit how far ecclesial legislation really can go wrong, and thereby limit too the harm that can ever come from complying with it when it does. Given this protection, the balancing good of respect for authority and ecclesial order dictates not only obedience but complete docility. We should not even dare to criticize, because in the end Providence has assured that it is non-criticism and compliance that turn out for the best.

This is a very familiar line of thought in Catholic circles. But does the doctrine of indefectibility really preclude legitimate disobedience? How far really is the Church protected from failure? She may not be permitted to fail completely. But otherwise her guaranteed protection is hardly total. Loss of communion with the East, the Reformation, the collapse not only in Mass attendance but in vocations and the decline of catechesis in Europe and the Americas since Vatican II — all these have been allowed to happen, partly through the sins and mistakes of officeholders in the Church, popes very much included. If serious damage to the Church's mission can occur through other means by which popes fail, why not through their legislative errors? The extent to which her own legislation can do serious damage to the Church's mission, especially when complied with, is surely for the historical record to establish, not for appeals to indefectibility to prejudge.

There is a deeper problem with the appeal to indefectibility. What if the Church is sometimes to be preserved by God from failure precisely through open criticism by the faithful of her laws, and even by noncompliance? God might sometimes protect the Church from failure not by preventing very bad, even flatly immoral, papal legislation in the first place, but through raising up internal opposition to it when it does occur. In the absence of some magisterial teaching otherwise, it is obsequious clericalism to assume that it is only hierarchical authority that God uses to preserve the Church from failure, and not, at least on occasion, Christian noncompliance with hierarchical authority. Sometimes, perhaps, noncompliance may not be merely permitted by God as an evil but, where the papal laws are sufficiently bad, may even be His will. At any rate, appeals to indefectibility alone do not prove otherwise.

The official theology of the Counter-Reformation sought to block this line of thought. The drafting of canonical legislation was directly assisted by God, and so directly willed by him, and hence was not a potential source of damage to the Church's mission. Disobedience could not be justified. In *De Locis Theologicis*, Melchior Cano appealed to the authority of a great fourth-century pope: "But the canons of the Church are issued on the prompting of the Holy Spirit, as Damasus says."[17] Cano refers to teaching from a doctrinal passage in Gratian's *Decretum*. This is a letter from Pope Damasus I in the fourth century to Aurelius, bishop of Carthage:

---

17   Cano, *De Locis Theologicis*, 247.

> Those who voluntarily breach the canons are harshly judged by the
> holy fathers and condemned by the Holy Spirit at whose prompting
> they are issued, since someone who shamelessly does or speaks some-
> thing against the same canons when not compelled by necessity to
> do so but acting freely, or who freely consents to others willingly so
> doing is rightly seen to be blaspheming against the Holy Spirit. Such
> presumption is clearly of one kind with blasphemy against the Holy
> Spirit since as we have already said they are acting against him at whose
> prompting and by whose grace the holy canons are issued.[18]

But, unfortunately for the official theology that appealed to it, the papal
teaching which Cano cited was imaginary. The alleged letter from Damasus to
Aurelius was a forgery, from the false decretals of Pseudo-Isidore. This was a
fabricated collection of ecclesiastical decrees and teachings formed, probably, in
ninth-century northern France (it is a matter of continuing scholarly discussion),
possibly in part to support the cause of a bishop deposed — irregularly, in the
view of his clerical supporters — by a Carolingian ruler.[19] One purpose of the
collection, very possibly assembled by these very supporters, seems to have been
to establish, in part through manufactured papal teaching, a highly convenient
official theology of the moral authority of canon law. Canon law was supposed
to carry an absolute morally binding force for Christians generally, and so for
Carolingian rulers too. Hence Damasus's supposed letter, inserted prominently
at the collection's beginning, with its eloquent and forceful assurance of the
assistance guaranteed the Church, as legislator, by the Holy Spirit. The letter
convinced Gratian and through him passed into the *Decretum* as a genuine teaching.
The spurious nature of the Pseudo-Isidorean collection was already evident to
humanist and Protestant critics by Cano's time. But its importance to the official
theology of the Counter-Reformation, shown by Cano's reliance, delayed acceptance of its origins for Catholic theologians, who resisted the growing weight of
criticism until the seventeenth century.

Appeals to Pope Damasus were eventually discredited. But even in the nineteenth and twentieth centuries, theologians continued to base the moral duty
of the faithful to obey the pope and the Church on a supposed infallibility of
canonical legislation — and to link this supposed legislative infallibility, in turn,
to divine assistance. And they still appealed to magisterial teaching, though
this time from a text that did exist. This was *Auctorem Fidei*, the bull of Pius
VI that condemned, with varying degrees of force, a numbered collection of
propositions associated with the Synod of Pistoia in 1787. This synod had met
to reform the church in Tuscany on Italian Jansenist lines with the approval
of the Grand Duke, Joseph II's brother Leopold.

---

18   Emil Friedberg, ed., *Corpus Iuris Canonici*, vol. 1 (Leipzig: Tauchnitz, 1879), 1008.
19   See Eric Knibbs, "Ebo of Reims, Pseudo-Isidore and the Date of the False Decretals," *Speculum* (2017): 144–83.

We have already noted Cardinal Billot's exalted view of papal legislation. Why was the infallibility of the pope as legislator so clear to him as it certainly was not to Cardinal Newman? Billot appealed to Pius VI's condemnation in *Auctorem Fidei* of a Jansenist proposition.[20] As cited by Pius VI, this proposition claimed:

> That which pertains to faith and to the essence of religion must be distinguished from that which is proper to discipline... In this [discipline] itself there is to be distinguished what is necessary or useful to retain the faithful in spirit, from that which is useless or too burdensome for the liberty of the sons of the New Covenant to endure, but more so, from that which is dangerous or harmful, namely leading to superstition and materialism.

Pius VI then issued his condemnation:

> In so far as by the generality of the words it [the proposition] includes and submits to a prescribed examination even the discipline established and approved by the Church, as if the Church which is ruled by the Spirit of God could have established discipline which is not only useless and burdensome for Christian liberty to endure, but which is also dangerous, harmful, leading to superstition and materialism: false, rash, scandalous, destructive, offensive to pious ears, injurious to the Church and to the Spirit of God by whom she is guided, at least erroneous.[21]

As Shaun Blanchard has written, *Auctorem Fidei* was a central magisterial text for nineteenth-century Catholic theology.[22] It was treated as of great importance at Vatican I. But as Newman's case shows, not quite everyone seems to have understood it in Billot's terms.

The problem with Billot's use of Pius VI is clear. Billot is not convincing about what specifically is being condemned and precisely what, correspondingly, is being magisterially taught instead. For *Auctorem Fidei* to extend infallibility to ecclesial legislation, Pius VI must have meant formally to teach that the legislative authority of the Church has from the beginning been guaranteed the direct assistance of the Holy Spirit. The Jansenist error specifically condemned would then be the denial of this guarantee. But the condemnation seems not to focus on any such error. There is no specific mention of any guarantee of assistance. The condemnation seems merely to presuppose instead a fact—that of the Spirit's actual assistance—and then insist that, given this assistance, the Church's discipline could never have gone wrong.

Note that the error is condemned as one injurious "to the Spirit of God by whom [the Church] is guided." And that suggests that the particular error condemned is not likely to be that of denying any guarantee of divine assistance to

---

20   See Billot, *De Ecclesia Christi*, 469.

21   Denzinger-Schönmetzer, *Enchiridion*, 2678 (Freiburg: Herder, 1965).

22   Shaun Blanchard, *The Synod of Pistoia and Vatican II: Jansenism and the Struggle for Catholic Reform* (Oxford: Oxford University Press, 2020).

the Church's legislation. Suppose someone does disbelieve in such a guarantee. Even if erroneous, how would such disbelief be erroneous in a way that was especially "injurious to God"? After all, it is entirely down to God's will how far he chooses to assist his Church, a will that if it extends both to guaranteeing her legislation and to binding us to believe in such a guarantee, must on that point have been revealed to us. But then the error would be an heretical denial of that revelation. It would not, however, involve any particular injury to God. Whereas of course there would be injury specifically to the Spirit if anyone supposed that legislation could go wrong *even when assisted by God*. For then one would be denigrating God's nature. God's goodness and omnipotence definitely exclude him from assisting error. But they do not exclude him, if that is his will, from failing to guarantee assistance in the first place, merely permitting the error instead.

The preamble to *Auctorem Fidei* insists that the errors it condemns go beyond propositions expressly stated by the Synod, but also include further propositions that might be conveyed or "introduced through ambiguity" (*per ambiguitatem insinuatas*) through its teachings. Pius VI was concerned not just with the explicit claims of the Synod, or what its members and leaders did or did not themselves believe, but with the errors that could result within the wider Church, including the effect on "those of simple faith who come to know some part or other of the Synod published for all in the vernacular." Now it was very much the official theology of Pius VI's Rome, and believed within the wider Church, that the Holy Spirit did assist the Church in her legislation. Assuming that generally accepted theology, the Synod's critical attitude to that legislation would then insinuate or imply the inefficacy of that assistance. And that was the error condemned: that even when assisted in her legislation by the Spirit the Church could impose discipline that was harmful. This second reading leaves the assistance guaranteed the Church by God entirely outside the condemnation rather than its focus. No doubt (unlike the Synod) the pope had a generous view of the guarantee available. But that generous view was not itself defined.

On the first reading we would have a definition concerning revelation – how far the Church has from the outset been guaranteed the legislative assistance of the Holy Spirit. On the second reading we have, on the assumption of actual assistance, condemnation of an erroneous and impious disregard of its implications. The second reading seems better to fit the text. Hence the pope's accusation not of heresy about revelation (an accusation made in *Auctorem Fidei* of other condemned propositions) but of impiety and injury to the Spirit.

This proposition (number LXXVIII) was cited by subsequent popes, Gregory XVI and Leo XIII.[23] Leo XIII in *Testem Benevolentiae* was the most specific – but again he only disparaged as injurious to the Holy Spirit too critical an attitude to the Church's law. There was no explicit teaching of a guarantee of the Spirit's

---

23 Gregory XVI, *Quo Graviora* (1833) and Leo XIII, *Testem Benevolentiae* (1899).

assistance and of conditions under which, based on that guarantee, the Church's legislation would always be preserved from fault. And despite its concern with defining a legislative primacy for the pope, we have noted that Vatican I entirely bypassed the issue.

It is worth examining the *Dictionnaire de théologie catholique*, that major work of theological reference produced in the Francophone church between 1899 and 1950. The entries for "Église" and "Infaillibilité du pape" are another indication of the state of official theology in the twentieth century before Vatican II. Their author, Edmond Dublanchy, a very eminent Marist theologian, contributed many important entries to the *Dictionnaire* before his death in 1938.[24] He is extremely confident. The infallibility of the Church, he assures us, must certainly extend to doctrinal or moral teaching that is "included practically" or "indirectly" in "what is commanded, approved or authorized by the general discipline of the Church, whether the discipline comes from the positive law of the whole Church, or whether it be a custom adopted or approved by the universal Church."[25] Why are we to believe Dublanchy on this matter? The author's argument is revealing, both in what it claims and in what it avoids claiming.

First, Dublanchy claims that his view is a strict consequence both of New Testament teaching that Christ will be with the Church until the end of time (Mt 28:20) and the further consideration that teaching "necessarily included indirectly" in laws has the same effect as what the Church directly claims in explicit teaching.[26] Now of course that may be true, in the sense of conveying beliefs to those addressed by the Church. But as we have already seen, the mere fact that the Church conveys a belief to us as true does not guarantee its truth. After all, it is generally agreed that even magisterial teaching, when not given definitively, can be fallible.

And this brings us to a further difficulty that afflicts this entire official theology of the Church's supposed infallibility in legislation. This theology claims that the Church's universal legislation is preserved from implying error, at least in relation to faith and morals. But as Dublanchy himself admits, along with most theologians, magisterial teaching on faith and morals can take forms that are fallible as well as infallible.[27] Fallible teaching binds us, in his view, to belief or assent—but an assent based on a moral certainty rather than the certainty of faith demanded by infallible teaching. As we have already noted, in the 1983 Code of Canon Law the Church binds us canonically to an *obsequium intellectus et voluntatis* to teaching that is not given definitively—a submission of intellect and will. Now this is a canonical obligation that very clearly implies the truth of what is taught. For it involves, as Dublanchy and *Lumen Gentium* both claim, an obligation to assent to

---

24   "Église" dates from 1911; "Infaillibilité du pape" from 1923.
25   "Église," col. 2197; see also "Infaillibilité du pape," col. 1706.
26   "Église," col. 2197.
27   "Église," col. 2199 and "Infaillibilité du pape," col. 1709-14.

the teaching as true.[28] Were the Church ever to doubt that fallible teaching's truth, she would certainly withdraw the canonical obligation to *obsequium*. So even in teaching fallibly the Church is legislating universally in a way that presupposes the truth of what she teaches, binding canonically to belief that what is taught is true. But then that teaching's falsehood would amount to exactly what the official theology of infallibility in legislation supposes to be impossible — a case of universal legislation implying error about faith and morals. Were the Church really infallible in her legislation then fallible magisterial teaching on faith or morals would be impossible. But such fallible magisterial teaching is possible.[29]

In support of the infallibility of the Church as legislator, Dublanchy further claims that appeal has often been made by popes and general councils to the Church's canon law and discipline in establishing magisterial teaching.[30] Indeed we saw this from the case of Trent. However, Dublanchy also admits, as is conventional, that the theologies and arguments on which magisterial teachings are based do not themselves count *ipso facto* as magisterially taught, and so are not themselves guaranteed to be true.[31] But that would include any general theory of the Church's canon law as infallible. Finally, Dublanchy appeals to past theological consensus for his official theology — a consensus he dates from the sixteenth century.[32] But we were looking for good arguments for that theology — not further cases of belief in it. In particular, Dublanchy fails to support his view with actual magisterial teaching. Unlike Billot, he avoids appeal even to Pius VI's *Auctorem Fidei*, though in his *Dictionnaire* article on papal infallibility he claims that *Auctorem Fidei* was an exercise of the pope's infallible magisterium.[33] We have by the 1920s an official theology supported increasingly only by appeal to its own authority and nothing more.

In the contemporary Church we find the issue addressed by the Congregation for the Doctrine of the Faith in *Donum Veritatis*. The Congregation now clearly disavows a legislative "infallibility" for the Church, but it still gestures, without being specific, at some level of divine assistance and at some related duty to obey. Because all acts of the magisterium have their source in Christ, "magisterial decisions in matters of discipline, even if they are not guaranteed by the charism of infallibility, are not without divine assistance and call for the adherence of the

---

28 *Lumen Gentium* 25: "The faithful are bound to agree (*concurrere*) with the judgment of their bishop on matters of faith and morals when this is given in the name of Christ and adhere to it with a religious submission of the mind (*religioso animi obsequio*). This submission of will and intellect (*hoc religiosum voluntatis et intellectus obsequium*) should be given with especial reason to the authentic magisterium of the Roman pontiff even when he does not speak *ex cathedra*."

29 Were it to become clear that some fallible magisterial teaching is in fact false, any canonical obligation to believe it would be deprived of moral force. The law would prove to have been defective, and there would be no moral obligation to comply.

30 "Église," col. 2197–98.

31 "Infaillibilité du pape," col. 1713.

32 "Église," col. 2198.

33 "Infaillibilité du pape," col. 1704.

faithful."[34] This passage denies legislative "infallibility" but fudges what follows from this denial. Of course, since ecclesial authority is divinely instituted, its acts must in this respect, as the Congregation insists, have their source in Christ. But if legislative infallibility is excluded, then some ecclesial legislation could still be faulty. As faulty, how would that legislation be divinely assisted? Surely the faultiness would at most be divinely permitted as an evil. And again if faulty, how far then, depending on the fault, could legitimate criticism and even disobedience be morally excluded?

Donum Veritatis seems clear on one point at least. Whatever the official theology of the past, neither pope nor Church is magisterially taught to be divinely preserved from error in legislation. How far then can canonical legislation go wrong? Very far wrong, judging from history. Consider a body of canon law that was once settled, papally approved, and that applied throughout the Church. I mean the law of the Church that once bound the faithful canonically in their conduct towards the Jews.

This was the Church's law for *centuries*. Through the compliance of the faithful, the law aimed to ring-fence the existing Christian community of the baptized from Judaism. Christians were to limit their social contact with Jews; for example, they were forbidden to work as servants in Jewish households. Christian rulers were required by the Church to enforce identifying dress upon the Jews; they were forbidden to tolerate the building of new synagogues; and they were commanded to confine Jews to their houses on the holiest Christian days. Jews who had received baptism were restricted from contact with those who still practiced Judaism (the parents and siblings of those baptized included), and so families were to be split. These unlovely regulations were to be found as settled canon law, applying throughout the Church, in the *Corpus Iuris Canonici* — for example, as parts of Gratian's *Decretum* and of the decretals of Gregory IX.[35]

What was the effect of all this legislation, and its moral status? Such laws, by their very character, clearly prioritized protecting the existing Christian community from Judaism over a sharing of Christian fellowship and thereby of the Gospel, at least in ways likely to be inviting, with the Jewish people for whose salvation too Christ surely came. Laws such as these, to the degree that they were complied with, would not have conveyed love but contempt and fear, and harmed, rather than advanced, the Christian mission. The memory of them certainly discredits the Church now. In relation to the Jewish people in particular, these laws also breached a basic moral requirement — that of charity. Here, then, are two faults in settled canon law that Bellarmine clearly thought impossible: real and discrediting damage to the Church herself and her mission, and direct offence against morality. It is hard to see how these detestable laws were ever binding morally on anyone.

---

34   Congregation for the Doctrine of the Faith, *Donum Veritatis* (May 4, 1990), 17.
35   See *Corpus Iuris Canonici*, ed. Friedberg, 1:1087–89, and 2:771–78. For the continuing canonical force of these laws at the Counter-Reformation, see Suárez, *De Fide*, disp. 18, secs. 5–6, in *Opera* 12:452–60.

There is unfortunately more. We have noted law that forcibly detached the Jewish people from interaction with Christians — law that prioritized ring-fencing over conversion. It is not surprising that where the Church's mission to convert the Jewish people did come into focus, that mission was distorted in a similarly coercive reverse direction: Jews, having been forcibly removed from the society of Christendom, were, for the purposes of their conversion and for short and carefully regimented periods, to be equally coercively returned to it. This was not a coercion of Jews into the faith, which was forbidden, but a no less morally objectionable coercion of them into at least hearing the faith. By the 1580s, having confined the Jews of Rome in a newly established ghetto, the popes would regularly extract them from it by compulsion, on the afternoons of the Jewish sabbath, to hear preached to them a Christian interpretation of the Old Testament and of Jewish history. These were the famous conversionary sermons that persisted in Rome under papal rule until their final abolition by Pius IX in 1847, and that were satirized in Browning's poem "Holy Cross Day."[36] Gregory XIII, who had instituted these sermons in Rome itself, made their arrangement a legal obligation for the universal Church. In 1584 he issued the bull *Sancta Mater Ecclesia* binding bishops throughout the Church to arrange them wherever there was a Jewish community large enough to support a synagogue. All Christians were bound to exclude Jews who failed to attend these sermons from their business dealings, and bishops were invited to employ their authority to devise further methods of enforcement. All Catholic rulers, from the emperor downwards, were to give these sermons support through their civil law. Any Catholic who impeded the execution of the bull was subject to excommunication.[37] Happily, outside Italy at least, this law was generally disobeyed.[38]

These sermons seem to have functioned more as a public display against unbelief than as a serious source of conversions, which their compulsory nature was not very apt to encourage. Consider John Evelyn's description of one such sermon which he witnessed visiting Rome on January 7, 1645:

> A sermon was preach'd to the Jewes at Ponte Sisto, who are constrained to sit till the houre is don: but it is with so much malice in their countenances, spitting, humming, coughing and motion that it is almost impossible they should heare a word from the preacher. A conversion is very rare.[39]

---

36   For the history of these conversionary sermons in the sixteenth century, see Emily Michelson, "Conversionary Preaching and the Jews in Early Modern Rome," *Past and Present* 235 (2017): 68–104. She gives a more general history in *Catholic Spectacle and Rome's Jews: Early Modern Conversion and Resistance* (Princeton, NJ: Princeton University Press, 2022).

37   See *Bullarum Sanctorum Romanorum Pontificum a Gregorio XIII ad Sixtum V* (Turin, 1868), 487–89. As we might expect, Suárez sought to establish the morality of compelling unbelievers to at least hear the faith by appealing to the existence of (guaranteed-to-be-moral) papal legislation for this and, in particular, *Sancta Mater Ecclesia*. See Suárez, *De Fide*, disp. 17, sec. 2, in *Opera* 12:442–43.

38   For belated application of *Sancta Mater Ecclesia* in Modena in 1635, and some immediate Jewish success in negotiating moderation of its provisions, see Katherine Aron-Beller, *Jews on Trial: The Papal Inquisition in Modena 1598-1638* (Manchester, UK: Manchester University Press, 2011), 24.

39   For discussion of the adverse Jewish reaction to the conversionary sermons, see Michelson, "Conversionary Preaching" and *Catholic Spectacle and Rome's Jews.*

It is a great irony of our subject that Manning, defender of the infallibility of papal legislation, also came to be a committed and active defender of the civil rights of the Jewish people. In 1890 backing a public appeal for the civil rights of Russian Jews, Manning observed that the Russian state was violating a "universal common law" which "when this is anywhere broken, or wounded, it is not sympathy but civilisation that has the privilege of respectful remonstrance."[40] Unlike Newman, Manning's strength did not lie in the area of church history. We have here a not uncommon phenomenon within modern Catholicism — an exaggerated view of papal and ecclesial authority that depends on amnesia even about the fairly recent past.

History shows, then, just how very far ecclesial law can degrade from its proper function. The pious view according to which ecclesiastical legislation issues directly from the Holy Spirit may be no more sound than another, which associates the Holy Spirit with the selection of individual popes. The career of Paul IV Carafa refutes both pieties. Paul IV was the pope who first forced Rome's Jewish population into a ghetto. He was as unloved and as unlovely morally as many of the canons he was so zealous in applying. In August 1559 at the news of his death the population of Rome erupted in celebration. Order collapsed. A mob attacked the statue of the pope that stood on the Capitol. They broke off its head and kicked it through the streets into the Tiber, having first covered the head with the identifying yellow hat which Paul IV had imposed on Rome's Jews.[41]

Just as history fails to guarantee the quality, even the basic morality, of canonical legislation, no more does *Pastor Aeternus*. But *Pastor Aeternus* does unquestionably guarantee something else, namely, that no law, no matter how horrible, which issues from papal authority admits of juridical appeal. The discomfort felt by the conciliarists now returns. If papal legislation can go so very wrong, how can the constitution of the Church fail to provide for remedy?

The notional remedy of the Counter-Reformation papalist theologians was disobedience, a remedy which, however, in practice they withdrew. Now disobedience does look to be rather more morally justifiable than past official theology ever supposed. But there is an obvious difficulty. Without juridical protection — which *Pastor Aeternus* rules out — even morally justified disobedience may achieve little. Unless the disobedience spreads among the bishops, or is at least tolerated by them (which its moral justification certainly does not guarantee), it may simply be extinguished.

Perhaps there is a less bleak and more important lesson to be drawn. The absence of a juridical remedy against the pope has one central and perhaps providential consequence. It is that Catholics cannot simply exploit procedure to

---

40   See James Pereiro, "'Am I my brother's keeper?' Cardinal Manning and the Jewish People," *Bulletin of the John Rylands Library* 97 (2021): 195–208.

41   See Miles Pattenden, *Pius IV and the Fall of the Carafa* (Oxford: Oxford University Press, 2013), 29, and Mary Hollingsworth, *Conclave 1559: Ippolito d'Este and the Papal Election of 1559* (London: Head of Zeus, 2021), 41.

block papal legislation, no matter how noxious such papal legislation might be. To reverse legislation that is defective and damaging one must ultimately appeal to truth, not to a constitution. And in a Church founded on truth, it must be truth that matters.

Papal and ecclesial legislation generally reflects a current official theology. If the legislation is defective, that is often because the official theology upon which it is based is bad. This might be a fearful, contempt-ridden theology of Judaism, or it might be a recently invented and pastorally damaging liturgical theology. The only sure route to reversing the legislation is public and effective criticism of the underlying theology: establishing not only its erroneous nature but also the clear distinction between the official theology and genuine magisterial teaching, especially magisterial teaching that really is infallible. The critique must be effective enough to convince, if not a reigning pope (who may well be beyond convincing), then at least his eventual successors. That means convincing, over time, the clergy from whom those successors will be drawn.

Of course past canonical legislation governing conduct towards the Jews was morally quite different from the modern papal legislation reforming liturgies and forbidding traditional forms. Just in its content the former legislation was in immediate conflict with morality as the liturgical legislation plausibly is not. But if the Church really can gravely damage her own mission by legislating in ways that violate morality directly—the impossibility of this, remember, was supposed to be especially obvious—we can hardly exclude serious damage to her mission from legislation that is defective in other ways.

The legislative primacy of the pope serves unity—but a Christian unity that rests, ultimately, on truth. Truth will win the sooner if within the Church there is a culture that tolerates, even encourages, legitimate criticism of the exercise of papal primacy and especially of the theology on which that exercise relies. Without such a culture of open criticism, as history shows, the damage from bad Church law can be immense and last for centuries.[42]

---

42   The escape from bad laws imposed by popes and from the bad theologies on which these laws rest must be by open criticism and discussion, even disobedience—but certainly not by formal appeals to councils. Not only has conciliarism been doctrinally condemned, but appeals to councils against popes would not necessarily help against bad official theologies in any case, which when especially damaging are often shared by popes and councils alike. It was in 1434 that the conciliarist council of Basel first imposed conversionary sermons on the Jews; Gregory XIII's papal law of 1584 was strikingly like that of Basel. Popes and councils alike are equally capable of basing important decisions on official theologies that are quite false, and of doing great harm thereby. It is unclear that any New Pentecost of the Spirit has recently occurred to leave either modern popes or modern general councils suddenly immune to this.

4

Hyperpapalism and the Body Politic[1]

CHARLES A. COULOMBE

W E ARE AT A VERY CURIOUS TIME IN ECCLESIASTICAL history. On the one hand, the shaky ecclesiology of the Orthodox Churches, already shaken further when Constantinople and Moscow excommunicated each other over the status of Ukrainian Orthodoxy, has received another blow when the section of the latter body that had given its allegiance to Moscow broke it when Putin launched his invasion. The Orthodox seemed reduced to the *reductio ad absurdum* of their organizational principles. But on the other hand, the current Successor of St Peter appears to have achieved a similar reduction by living up to their grimmest charges of the papacy as a tyranny whose wielder believes he can alter Apostolic Tradition on his own whim. Certainly the time has come for believing Catholics to look carefully at that office which has so long defined them.

INTEGRATION OF POPE AND PRINCE

When Christ established the Mass and the priesthood at the Last Supper, He also united His Davidic kingship with the *Communio* of the Church. From that time until the conversion of Armenia in 303, the Catholic Church and her leaders, the successors of the Apostles—with the spiritual heirs of St Peter at their head—negotiated their way through persecutions at the hands of various pagan, secular regimes. But as successively Armenia, Georgia, Ethiopia, and at last the Roman Empire itself (thanks to Theodosius the Great's Edict of Thessalonica in 380) adopted the faith as their official religion, Christian Sovereigns—and especially the Roman Emperors—came to see themselves as cooperators with the popes and the episcopate in the administration of the Catholic body.

This reality was most fully expressed in the role played by successive emperors in convoking various ecumenical councils, from Constantine and Nicaea to Charles V and Trent. It was expressed by Pope Gelasius I in a letter, *Famuli Vestrae Pietatis* written in 494 to Byzantine Emperor Anastasius I Dicorus and enshrined in the opening words of Emperor Justinian's famed legal code: "We desire that all peoples subject to Our benign Empire shall live under the same religion that the Divine Peter, the Apostle, gave to the Romans, and which the said religion declares was

---

1   First published at *OnePeterFive* on July 20, 2022.

introduced by himself . . ." What Viscount Bryce wrote of the Holy Roman Empire was also true of the Byzantine Empire — both being continuing manifestations of the Christian Imperial idea: "Thus the Holy Roman Church and the Holy Roman Empire are one and the same thing seen from different sides; and Catholicism, the principle of the universal Christian society, is also Romanism . . ."[2]

The various Christian kingdoms, though functionally independent, held the same relationship between themselves and the Church. Despite the 1054 excommunications between Rome and Constantinople, the same theoretical relationship between Church and State continued on both sides. Church and State in East and West were the two halves of the *Res publica Christiana*. Wars between Christian princes were considered civil wars, which the Church tried to mitigate through the Truce of God (forbidding warfare at certain times) and the Peace of God (forbidding it around certain places). Such struggles as the various Crusades were seen as wars on behalf of the whole Christian body.

This reality was expressed in innumerable ways. Liturgically, the rites for coronations and the prayers for the various kings and for the emperor expressed their roles, as did the specific place the Holy Roman Emperor and the kings of France and Spain occupied in papal ritual. They and the king of England were canons of certain basilicas in Rome. The pope was a sovereign in his own right over the Papal States, could and did take kingdoms as fiefs, and called the Western Roman Empire back into being — and reserved the right to crown the emperors. But by the same token, the major Catholic monarchs had the right to veto one candidate each at the conclave. Emperors and kings maintained particular national institutions in Rome and the Holy Land (and many of their successor governments still do). The discovery of the East and West Indies led sixteenth-century popes to extend the right of Patronage (whereby princes or nobles who endowed abbeys or parishes maintained certain rights over them) to the kings of Spain and Portugal in their American, Asian, and African dominions.

This same deep relationship between Church and State continued down to the lowest level of governance: if the local nobles and gentry exercised patronage over the ecclesiastical foundations, bishops and abbots often had *ex officio* noble titles attached to their specific positions, and were members of the Provincial or National Estates. In addition to the cathedral, every city and town had a civic church where the mayor and corporation attended Mass; so too did the guilds. Throughout Europe, the parish was the lowest level of both ecclesiastical and temporal governance, with the same council both overseeing church repairs and the expenses of the liturgy on the one hand, and dealing with the poor, militia, and policing matters on the other.

This system — which had gradually developed as the inherited pagan institutions became ever more Christian — worked very well in many places and times.

---

2   On this theme, see Alan Fimister, *The Iron Sceptre of the Son of Man: Romanitas as a Note of the Church* (Lincoln, NE: Os Justi Press, 2023).

But like any human arrangement, it gave rise to tensions between the various players from time to time—not over basic principles, but in particular cases. A prince-bishop might owe allegiance to the pope in his episcopal role, and to the emperor in his noble one. Usually, this would not pose too much of a problem; but if his two masters were in conflict, he and his flock would suffer. As the thirteenth and fourteenth centuries passed, successive popes came into conflict with various emperors and kings. In Germany and Italy, this led to the rise of the pro-Imperial Ghibellines and the pro-papal Guelphs, whose fighting reduced Italy to chaos, and affected Dante heavily. Then the Great Schism broke out, giving Christendom the chaos of two and then three rival claimants to the papacy. The Emperor Sigismund was seen as the only authority capable of ending the strife—even as his predecessor Otto I had ended the "pornocracy" of the tenth century.[3] He convoked the Council of Constance, which settled the matter with one pope in 1415. A little over a century later two major events occurred: the election of Charles V as emperor, who would be the last thus far to try to realize concretely the idea of the *Res publica Christiana*, and the Protestant revolt, which would end it for the foreseeable future. But if the Guelph idea had triumphed in the West (only to lose the victory thanks to Luther, Calvin, and company), it was the opposite impulse that triumphed in the East. There—both in Constantinople, and in Orthodoxy's later center at Moscow—it was the Church's autonomy that was sunk by the Imperial supremacy, despite the efforts of such men as Emperor Constantine XI and Alexius of Moscow.

Rooted in the horrors of the Western religious wars of the seventeenth century, the indifferentist Enlightenment arose in the eighteenth century; its ideas were given horrible life by the French and following revolutions. The nineteenth and early twentieth centuries saw the successive destruction of the remaining Catholic monarchies; peacefully or otherwise, Liberalism triumphed in country after country. Seeking to separate Catholicism or whatever dominant religious body from any effective role in public life was what united Liberalism, Communism, National Socialism, and Fascism.

From the age of revolution forward, successive popes and their clergy acted as the leaders of the resistance to these manifestations, as royals and nobles were defeated or coopted in country after country. This role was augmented by the fact that pope after pope was in this era much holier and wiser than the average layman, to say nothing of their opponents. A perfect specimen of the breed was Bl. Pope Pius IX, who called valiant young men from all over the Catholic world to defend the Papal States. At the same time, a generation

---

3   On the use of the term "pornocracy" to refer to ages in which the leadership of the Church is especially compromised by the worldliness that displays itself in a *porneia* at once physical and spiritual, and on the identification of three pornocracies—the first, from 882 to 964; the second, from 1471 to 1563; the third, from 1965 to the present—see Timothy S. Flanders, "The Third Pornocracy: What We Are Living Through," *OnePeterFive*, December 16, 2021; idem, "Pornocracy and the Coming Reign of Antichrist," *OnePeterFive*, December 23, 2021.

of Catholic lay politicians arose, who carried on the fight wherever the Church was threatened, be it on the battlefield or in parliaments. Far more deferential to the clergy than their royal and noble predecessors, they relied upon them for strategic direction. These were called the ultramontanes;[4] they formed the great Catholic political parties of the era. It was against this backdrop that Vatican I dogmatically defined papal infallibility.

AFTER VATICAN I

If anything, the loss of the Papal States increased the spiritual prestige of the popes. World War I saw the ruin of most of the last bit of the Catholic temporal order in Europe, although Bl. Charles I of Austria-Hungary briefly shot across the sky like a comet from the days of chivalry. Unfortunately, his betrayal – not merely by politicians, but by Vienna's Cardinal Piffl – was a presage of worse things to come, and not just in Central Europe. In the interwar years Pius XI and XII were the unquestioned leaders of the Catholic people; as with Leo XIII, they issued many fine social and political statements designed for the new liberal republican era, and the Catholic politicians – often clerics themselves – tried dutifully to carry them out. Meanwhile, the theological Modernism that St Pius X had attempted to squelch (unsuccessfully, as it turned out) slowly grew in nooks and crannies. World War II saw Catholic politicians given the choice of either collaborating with the Germans in hopes of saving something and perhaps eventually achieving their goals – and so being destroyed with them in 1945, or else joining Liberals, Socialists, and Communists in the Resistance. Those who took the latter option would be the fathers of postwar Christian Democracy.

POSTWAR PAPALISM

The 1950s were perhaps the apogee of papal prestige. Enough of the old ceremonial remained to give the papal court a patina of antique charm unequalled anywhere save perhaps the Court of St James. Pius XII's personal holiness and air of ethereality seemed to give him a kind of personal infallibility. He saw there were troubles brewing ahead. He wrote against them, if unconsciously abetting their fomenters: to deal with dogmatic issues, he wrote *Humani Generis* – but allowed Karl Rahner to edit Denzinger; he gave us *Mediator Dei*, a fine exposé of liturgical malfeasance – and allowed Annibale Bugnini to begin his ritual redesign. As he had been a staunch ally of the United States against the Nazis, so too did he work with them against the Communists. Whatever it was, if it came from Rome, most Catholics believed it to be infallible and Pius XII did indeed define the dogma of the Assumption of the Blessed Virgin Mary.

His death brought John XXIII to the throne of St Peter; while maintaining the formality of his predecessor in most respects, he did so with a twinkle in

---

4   Although often capitalized in older sources, in this book "ultramontane" and "ultramontanist" will normally be in lowercase. – *Ed.*

his eye, and won the hearts of millions. John's deep piety made him encourage devotion to the Precious Blood, and ordered the use of Latin in seminaries in no uncertain terms. But these were overshadowed and then forgotten due to his calling of Vatican II, at the beginning which he died.

Without wanting to go too much into the Council, in its wake every aspect of Catholic life was shaken up. The immense prestige of the papacy was brought to bear to enforce such changes. Paul VI's attempts to "modernize" the papal court primarily consisted of removing most of its remaining lay positions, and dulling down those that remained. But when Paul VI would attempt to actually defend Catholic teaching—as with *Humanae Vitae*—entire national conferences of Catholic bishops happily ignored him, and encouraged dissent. This, and the same bodies' refusal to support Catholic politicians keen on fighting both birth control and abortion, had the effect of reducing the Christian Democratic parties of Western Europe and Latin America into the mere groups of hunters for government jobs they have been ever since (those in Central Europe tend to be rather different, thanks to their experiences under Communism).

After the sad last decade of Paul VI and the brief reign of his immediate successor, John Paul II roared into town. Young and vibrant at the beginning of his pontificate, he became a travelling pope like none other. Attracting crowds across the planet with the consummate media savvy of a born actor, his phenomenologically-inflected language might have been hard to understand, but there was no mistaking his devotion and personal piety. Young people loved him, and he successfully threw his prestige into the ultimately victorious struggle against Communism. He also restored Eucharistic adoration, and began slowly and against much opposition to return liturgical and theological tradition to the mainstream of the Church. As the years went by, and he became sick, old, and feeble, this pope was obviously walking the Way of the Cross; his greatest regret—a lack of attention to the appointment of bishops—he not only drew attention to, but attempted to rectify in the last few years of his life.

His successor, Benedict XVI, increased the prestige of the papacy even further than had John Paul II—at least if we measure this in terms of pilgrims to Rome. Learned in both the Church Fathers and the Scholastics, as well as a participant at Vatican II, he struggled manfully to bring about a reconciliation of the machinery of the Church with its own soul. Piece by piece he restored papal symbols abandoned by his immediate predecessors—realizing, in his humility, that the world and the Church needed not *his* personality, but renewed papal symbolism. So it went, until he left us.

He was succeeded by Francis, who seems to believe that as pope he has the right to do anything he pleases, and alter the faith at will. When Paul VI attempted something similar, the vast majority obeyed, because of the huge prestige the office had come to have—and because of a sort of "creeping infallibilism" (in the late Chuck Wilson's pithy phrase) which (because of the historical occurrences we have looked at) had come to be attached to all the popes since Vatican I. But that prestige had been largely dissipated by the time of John Paul II and Benedict. They were both wise men in their very different ways—much aware that the Church was not their personal property. In Francis's pontificate, that awareness appears entirely absent.

LESSONS FROM HISTORY

So what lessons may we draw from this toboggan ride through Church history? Very often, the solution to one crisis in the Church's life leads to the next crisis—Arianism's defeat led to Nestorianism, which in turn spawned Monophysitism in response, as Islam sparked Iconoclasm. The decentralization brought about by the Great Schism fed into the Protestant Revolt, which was quelled by the centralizing of Trent, which was reinforced by the collapse of Catholic lay authorities; this in turn led to ultramontanism, a necessary thing, indeed, for fighting Liberalism and Modernism—but deadly if the latter should ever gain control over the Holy See.

Of course, a great deal depends upon the next few pontificates. But sooner or later, when Catholicity is again dominant at the Holy See—something as much dependent upon generational demographics as anything else, including the wishes of the current tenants—the work of Vatican I, interrupted by the Italian seizure of Rome in 1870, shall have to be returned to. The truth of the great gift of infallibility, which has kept the Church from ever fully and finally embracing heresy at her highest levels, is not the question. What is needed is a clearer definition of the *limits* of the papacy. It has been implied by many things in ages past; but as with any other time a doctrine has been defined, it must be made explicit. So too with the limits and even the definition of the "ordinary Magisterium," in whose name at different times and places in the past century the most solemn teachings have been concealed.

It may well be that a future Council would benefit from the presence of the Orthodox Patriarchs, who were invited as full participants to Vatican I by Bl. Pius IX—partly to end the Schism, but perhaps to get their counsel regarding the papal office in the first millennium. In their pride, they refused; it may be that their current travails are a punishment for this. But certainly the current position of the Holy See embodies all their worst fears of Roman domination. What makes the current situation so difficult is that in this pontificate those fears have come to be shared by so many loyal Catholics. Eastern Catholics, on the other hand, have a great deal to teach us at the moment.

❦ 5 ❧
Refuting the Hyperpapalist Approach to the Death Penalty Debate[1]

EDWARD FESER

I N 2018, POPE FRANCIS REVISED THE SECTION OF THE *Catechism of the Catholic Church* dealing with the topic of capital punishment, so that it now states that "the death penalty is inadmissible because it is an attack on the inviolability and dignity of the person." Flatly to assert that capital punishment is "an attack on the inviolability and dignity of the person" might be read as implying that the death penalty is *intrinsically* evil, or immoral *of its very nature* and not just under the wrong circumstances. Such a claim would contradict Scripture and two millennia of consistent magisterial teaching. For this reason, the revision has been criticized as at least badly formulated, even by some Catholic thinkers who support the abolition of capital punishment. For example, after the revision was announced, an appeal was made by forty-five prominent Catholic academics and clergy to the cardinals of the Catholic Church to call upon the pope clearly to reaffirm traditional teaching on the subject.[2]

In a four-part series of articles entitled "Capital Punishment and Magisterial Authority,"[3] theologian Robert Fastiggi criticizes those who have criticized the revision. He cites the appeal, specifically, as among the criticisms that he objects to. In this chapter, I respond to Fastiggi's arguments. I apologize for the length, but Fastiggi's series is itself quite long and addresses a variety of complex issues. In this first part, I address what Fastiggi has to say about the obligations of theologians and Catholics in general vis-à-vis the teaching of the Magisterium. In the second part, I address what he says about Scripture and the teaching of previous popes.

I want to say at the outset that while I think Fastiggi makes serious errors of judgment, I have nothing but respect for him as a scholar, a gentleman, and a loyal Catholic. In my experience, too many defenders of the revision refuse to

---

1   First published in two parts at Edward Feser's blog (https://edwardfeser.blogspot.com/) on August 26 and 30, 2023. Unless otherwise noted, articles by Feser referenced in the notes to this chapter are published on his blog.

2   For the text of the appeal, see *Defending the Faith Against Present Heresies: Letters and Statements Addressed to Pope Francis, the Cardinals, and the Bishops with a Collection of Related Articles and Interviews*, ed. John R. T. Lamont and Claudio Pierantoni (Waterloo, ON: Arouca Press, n.d.), 161–65.

3   Published August 14–17, 2023, at the website *Where Peter Is*.

address or even to bother reading what I and other critics have written on the topic, but prefer to attack straw men and attribute bad motives. Fastiggi is not guilty of that. Too many defenders of the revision are also woefully ignorant of the history of the Church's teaching on capital punishment and of the relevant theological literature. Fastiggi, by contrast, knows it well, even if I disagree with his interpretations of the relevant evidence. I also admire Fastiggi's loyalty to the pope, even though I think it blinds him to grave deficiencies in some of Pope Francis's words and actions. For I think this loyalty is clearly motivated by love of the Church and the papacy. I do not see in it any of the self-righteousness and lack of charity and basic fairness that is evident in the work of too many of Pope Francis's other defenders. Finally, Fastiggi is a good sport. He and I have tangled over this issue many times, and occasionally our exchanges have been somewhat heated. But he has always shown an admirable even temper.

On to Fastiggi's series, then. In part 1, he writes: "Who has the authority to resolve the dispute? The answer, of course, is the Magisterium, which consists of the Catholic bishops in communion with the successor of Peter." And again: "Who has the authority to determine the context, meaning, and ongoing applicability of Scripture? It is the Magisterium of the Church, not a group of scholars and clerics."

So far so good. I know of no participant in the debate over the change to the Catechism who denies any of this. Furthermore, I know of no participant who denies that "religious submission of mind and will must be shown in a special way to the authentic magisterium of the Roman Pontiff, even when he is not speaking *ex cathedra*," in the words of *Lumen Gentium*.

The reason it is nevertheless legitimate for Catholics to debate the revision to the Catechism is that the Church herself acknowledges a qualification on the duty to assent to non-infallible magisterial statements, and it is a qualification that clearly applies in this case. The qualification is recognized in the instruction *Donum Veritatis* issued during the pontificate of Pope John Paul II, and it has also been affirmed repeatedly in the tradition of the Church, including in the teaching of St Thomas Aquinas. Indeed, Pope Francis himself has acknowledged the legitimacy of certain kinds of critical discussion of magisterial statements.[4]

THE TEACHING OF ST THOMAS

I can't repeat here everything said in those earlier articles, but a few key points will suffice for present purposes. Let's begin with Aquinas's teaching on the matter, the most important sources for which are the *Summa theologiae* and his *Commentary on Saint Paul's Letter to the Galatians*. In *Summa theologiae* II-II, Q. 33, art. 4, Aquinas says:

---

4   I have discussed Aquinas's teaching on this matter at length in "Aquinas on St. Paul's correction of St. Peter," August 15, 2022; the teaching of *Donum Veritatis* and the rest of the tradition in "The Church permits criticism of popes under certain circumstances," May 20, 2018; and Pope Francis's statements in "Benedict XVI, Cardinal Pell, and criticism of Pope Francis," January 14, 2023.

It must be observed . . . that if the faith were endangered, a subject ought to rebuke his prelate even publicly. Hence Paul, who was Peter's subject, rebuked him in public, on account of the imminent danger of scandal concerning faith, and, as the gloss of Augustine says on Galatians 2:11, "Peter gave an example to superiors, that if at any time they should happen to stray from the straight path, they should not disdain to be reproved by their subjects."

Commenting on this passage, Fastiggi says:

This passage of Aquinas is widely used by papal critics to justify any resistance to the pope, his teachings, and decisions. They forget that Paul's correction of Peter had to do with Peter's behavior, not his teaching. In addition . . . this particular question of the *Summa* concerns fraternal correction in general. It is not focused on the correction of popes.

However, it is not difficult to show that these assertions are mistaken. First of all, Aquinas clearly takes Paul's rebuke of Peter to involve precisely his *teaching*, and *not* merely his behavior. He characterizes the episode of Paul's rebuke of Peter as a case where "*the faith* [was] *endangered*," and says that Peter brought "danger of scandal *concerning faith.*" In Chapter 2, lecture 3 of the Galatians commentary, he says that what Peter had done posed "danger *to the Gospel teaching,*" and that Peter and those who followed his example "walked not uprightly unto *the truth of the Gospel, because its truth was being undone*" (emphasis added). Peter failed to do his duty insofar as "*the truth must be preached openly* and *the opposite never condoned* through fear of scandalizing others" (emphasis added). Clearly, then, in Aquinas's view the problem was not merely that Peter *acted* badly, but that he seemed to condone *doctrinal error* and risked leading others to do the same.

Second, Aquinas is explicitly *not* commenting merely on fraternal correction in general. The *Summa* article is about *the correction of prelates, specifically.* Not only are popes prelates, but Aquinas uses the example of a pope (Peter) to illustrate the legitimacy in some circumstances of correcting prelates. Aquinas says that the episode of Paul's correction of Peter "gave an example *to superiors* . . . that they should not disdain to be reproved *by their subjects.*" He is not making a general point about the faithful correcting one another, but a specific point about the correction *of superiors by their subjects.* In the Galatians commentary, Aquinas says of Paul's rebuke of Peter:

Therefore from the foregoing we have an example: prelates, indeed, an example of humility, that they not disdain corrections from those who are lower and subject to them; subjects have an example of zeal and freedom, that they fear not to correct their prelates, particularly if their crime is public and verges upon danger to the multitude.

Contrary to what Fastiggi says, then, Aquinas clearly is teaching about *the correction of prelates, including popes*, rather than fraternal correction in general, and he is talking about correction *with respect to their teaching*, and not merely with respect to their behavior.[5]

Now, those who issued the appeal to the cardinals criticized the revision to the Catechism precisely because it is formulated in such a way that it might be read as conflicting with Scripture and Tradition. In other words, they believe that "the faith [is] endangered," that there is "imminent danger of scandal concerning faith." Accordingly, they are simply calling on the pope to reaffirm the teaching of Scripture and Tradition, just as Paul urged Peter to reaffirm the teaching that had been handed on to him.

Clearly, then, the appeal is perfectly in line with Aquinas's teaching about the possibility of subjects correcting prelates. Of course, Fastiggi would no doubt disagree with the judgment that the revision poses "imminent danger of scandal concerning faith." But *that is a different question.* If he wants to defend the revision, fine, but he should not speak as if the critics have no right to issue such an appeal. Rather, he should acknowledge that they *do* have such a right, and simply argue that in this case they were mistaken to think the right needed to be exercised.

At least, he should acknowledge this given that Aquinas's position is correct. But Fastiggi makes another remark that indicates that he thinks it is not correct. He says:

> What Aquinas says in this passage is offset by Pope Gregory XI's 1377 censure of various errors of John Wycliffe. Among these censured errors, number 19 reads: "An ecclesiastic, even the Roman Pontiff, can legitimately be corrected, and even accused, by subjects and lay persons" (Denz.-H., 1139).

But there are several problems with the assumption that this undermines Aquinas's teaching. First, as Aquinas himself emphasizes, "corrected" and related terms are ambiguous. They could be referring to correction of a juridical sort, which involves having the authority to direct another to do something and to punish him for disobedience. As Aquinas acknowledges, no one can "correct" a pope in that sense. But "correction" could mean instead the mere pointing out of an error, which Aquinas says amounts to a kind of fraternal assistance rather than the exercise of authority. For Pope Gregory's condemnation to conflict with Aquinas's teaching, he would have to have correction of the *second* sort in mind, not just the first. But Fastiggi gives us no reason to suppose that he does. Moreover, the other condemned propositions from Wycliffe involve juridical power of some sort or another. Context indicates, then, that Gregory is only condemning the thesis that subjects may *juridically* correct a pope, not the thesis that they may give *fraternal* correction of the kind Aquinas defends.

Second, if Gregory were condemning the latter sort of correction, he would not only be at odds with Aquinas. He would be at odds *with St Paul, and indeed*

---

5   There is a lot more to say about these passages from Aquinas. Again, see the article mentioned earlier for a fuller treatment.

with Scripture, which teach that Paul was within his rights to correct Peter, despite being his subject.

Third, as Fastiggi is well aware, blanket condemnations of large sets of propositions like the ones from Wycliffe need to be interpreted carefully. The condemnation does not necessarily imply that each proposition in the set is problematic in exactly the same way. In a single condemned set, one proposition may be heretical, another not strictly heretical but proximate to heresy, yet another simply badly formulated or otherwise misleading, and so on. So, the fact that the proposition from Wycliffe referred to by Fastiggi appears in the list condemned by Pope Gregory does not suffice to show that Gregory intended to condemn the position taught by Aquinas. Indeed, to my knowledge, no one before Fastiggi has even suggested that Gregory was condemning the position taken by Aquinas.

Fourth, if Gregory were intending to condemn that position, he would be contradicting the teaching of another pope, namely Pope Innocent III, who held that "only on account of a sin committed against the faith can I be judged by the church."[6] Since the rest of the Church is subject to the pope, this would be a case of a pope being "corrected . . . by subjects," to use the language condemned by Gregory. If we read Pope Gregory as condemning even fraternal correction of a pope, then, we will have a conflict between two popes. That is further reason *not* to read him that way.

THE TEACHING OF *DONUM VERITATIS*

A fifth point is that *Donum Veritatis* acknowledges that respectful criticism of magisterial statements can be legitimate, which it could not have done if Pope Gregory had been condemning all such criticism. So, let's turn to that document. Here are the relevant passages:

> The willingness to submit loyally to the teaching of the Magisterium on matters per se not irreformable must be the rule. It can happen, however, that a theologian may, according to the case, raise questions regarding the timeliness, the form, or even the contents of magisterial interventions . . .

> When it comes to the question of interventions in the prudential order, it could happen that some Magisterial documents might not be free from all deficiencies. Bishops and their advisors have not always taken into immediate consideration every aspect or the entire complexity of a question . . .

> Even when collaboration takes place under the best conditions, the possibility cannot be excluded that tensions may arise between the theologian and the Magisterium . . . If tensions do not spring from

---

6   Quoted in J. Michael Miller, *The Shepherd and the Rock: Origins, Development, and Mission of the Papacy* (Huntington, IN: Our Sunday Visitor, 1995), 292.

hostile and contrary feelings, they can become a dynamic factor, a stimulus to both the Magisterium and theologians to fulfill their respective roles while practicing dialogue ...

The preceding considerations have a particular application to the case of the theologian who might have serious difficulties, for reasons which appear to him well-founded, in accepting a non-irreformable magisterial teaching ...

If, despite a loyal effort on the theologian's part, the difficulties persist, the theologian has the duty to make known to the Magisterial authorities the problems raised by the teaching in itself, in the arguments proposed to justify it, or even in the manner in which it is presented. He should do this in an evangelical spirit and with a profound desire to resolve the difficulties. His objections could then contribute to real progress and provide a stimulus to the Magisterium to propose the teaching of the Church in greater depth and with a clearer presentation of the arguments ...

For a loyal spirit, animated by love for the Church, such a situation can certainly prove a difficult trial. It can be a call to suffer for the truth, in silence and prayer, but with the certainty that if the truth really is at stake, it will ultimately prevail ...

[T]hat public opposition to the Magisterium of the Church also called "dissent"... must be distinguished from the situation of personal difficulties treated above.

Note the following crucial points. First, *Donum Veritatis* acknowledges that while there is a strong presumption of assent even to non-irreformable magisterial statements, nevertheless it can in some cases be legitimate to "raise questions regarding the timeliness, the form, or *even the contents*" of such statements, since they "might not be free from all deficiencies." These deficiencies might concern "*the teaching in itself*, in the arguments proposed to justify it, or even in the manner in which it is presented." It can be that "*the truth* really is at stake." All of this makes it clear that it is not merely the behavior of magisterial authorities or the manner of their teaching that can in some cases legitimately be criticized, but *the teaching itself*.

Second, *Donum Veritatis* acknowledges that even in the best circumstances, such legitimate criticism may lead to "tensions" with the Magisterium, but that this is not necessarily a bad thing. The critic even "has the duty" to raise such objections, which "could ... contribute to real progress" insofar as they serve as a "stimulus" to the Magisterium to present its teaching in a more adequate way. And it can even be that in such a situation, it is the critic who undergoes "a difficult trial" and thereby "suffer[s] for the truth." *Donum Veritatis* thus makes it clear that it can happen that when a critic finds himself in some sort of conflict with magisterial authorities, that does not necessarily mean that he is the one who is in the wrong.

Third, *Donum Veritatis* explicitly states that what the critic in this sort of situation is engaged in "must be distinguished" from "dissent" from the Magisterium. It is possible, then, respectfully to criticize magisterial acts without thereby meriting the label "dissenter." How can this be? Wouldn't anyone who disagrees in some way with a magisterial statement *ipso facto* be "dissenting" from it and thereby count as a "dissenter"?

The answer is No, because "dissent" in this context does not connote mere disagreement, but has a narrower, technical meaning. *Donum Veritatis* goes on to identify several marks of "dissent." It involves "attitudes of general opposition to Church teaching," motivated by "the ideology of philosophical liberalism, which permeates the thinking of our age." For the dissenter, "freedom of thought comes to oppose the authority of tradition." The dissenter "aims at changing the Church following a model of protest which takes its inspiration from political society." In defense of his rejection of traditional teaching, he appeals to "the obligation to follow one's own conscience," the "weight of public opinion," "models of society promoted by the 'mass media,'" and the like. These sources of opinion lead the dissenter to conclude, for example, that "the Magisterium . . . ought to leave matters of conjugal and family morality to individual judgment." And so on. Obviously, then, "dissent" involves, specifically, *rejection of traditional Catholic doctrine*, of the kind associated with liberalism and modernism and represented by theologians like Hans Küng and Charles Curran.

Donum Veritatis does not say more about the precise nature of the legitimate sort of criticism that it distinguishes from "dissent." But it is clear that if "dissent" involves the *rejection* of traditional teaching, then a critic who *upholds* traditional teaching, and does so in the respectful manner demanded by *Donum Veritatis*, cannot justly be accused of "dissent." In particular, those who have respectfully criticized the revision to the Catechism for giving the appearance of a rupture with tradition cannot justly be accused of "dissent." That does not entail that Fastiggi cannot justifiably disagree with them. The point is just that, whatever one thinks of their position, it is *not* comparable to criticism of the Magisterium of the kind associated with the likes of Küng and Curran.

Sometimes it is claimed that *Donum Veritatis* does not allow the *public* expression of even legitimate criticism, on the basis of its remark—typically quoted out of context—that "the theologian should avoid turning to the 'mass media,' but have recourse to the responsible authority." But *Donum Veritatis* does *not* rule out public expression of such criticism, as is clear from several considerations. First, we need to consider the complete sentence from which this remark is quoted:

> In cases like these, the theologian should avoid turning to the "mass media," but have recourse to the responsible authority, *for it is not by seeking to exert the pressure of public opinion* that one contributes to the clarification of doctrinal issues and renders service to the truth.

Relevant, too, is *Donum Veritatis*'s other reference to mass media, in a passage characterizing the tactics of liberal dissenting theologians:

> The weight of public opinion when manipulated and its pressure to conform also have their influence. Often models of society promoted by the "mass media" tend to assume a normative value. The view is particularly promoted that the Church should only express her judgment on those issues which public opinion considers important and then only by way of agreeing with it.

With this context in mind, it is clear that what *Donum Veritatis* is criticizing is *not* the mere publication of criticism in journals, magazines, or other mass media as such. Rather, it is criticizing the tactic of using mass media *to stir up public opinion against the Magisterium*, as a means of trying to force the Church to conform to the values that prevail in such media.

Second, *Donum Veritatis* also says that the theologian who raises legitimate criticisms is obligated to "examine the objections which his colleagues might offer him." But the normal way in which such debate is conducted is in theological journals and the like, which entails publicizing one's criticisms. *Donum Veritatis* also states that "the theologian will refrain from giving *untimely* public expression" of his criticisms. So it is only *untimely* or *inappropriate* public expression that is ruled out, not all public expression as such.

Third, after *Donum Veritatis* was issued, Cardinal Ratzinger, as head of the Congregation for the Doctrine of the Faith, explicitly affirmed, when commenting on a hypothetical theologian who raises legitimate criticisms, that "we have not excluded all kinds of publication, nor have we closed him up in suffering."[7]

Now, in part 4 of his series, Fastiggi addresses the relevance of *Donum Veritatis* to the controversy over the revision to the Catechism. He does not accuse the critics of being "dissenters." Nevertheless, he does claim that those who issued the appeal to the cardinals did not satisfy the norms of *Donum Veritatis*. In particular, he objects that they "do not simply raise questions . . . [but] manifest a spirit of opposition to a papal teaching," that they are "so cock-sure of their position" that they "present as a non-arguable conclusion that their opinion of the Church's teaching on capital punishment is definitive and infallible," and so on.

One problem with such remarks is that they are aimed at a straw man. No critics of the revision to the Catechism hold that "*their opinion* of the Church's teaching on capital punishment is definitive and infallible." Rather, they claim that *the consistent teaching of Scripture and two millennia of tradition* is definitive and infallible. Fastiggi may disagree with his opponents about what Scripture and Tradition teach, but he should characterize their position accurately. Another

---

7   Quoted in Anthony J. Figueiredo, *The Magisterium-Theology Relationship: Contemporary Theological Conceptions in the Light of Universal Church Teaching Since 1835 and the Pronouncements of the Bishops of the United States* (Rome: Editrice Pontificia Università Gregoriana, 2001), 370.

problem with Fastiggi's remarks here is that they rest on a misreading of a further passage from *Donum Veritatis*. Addressing the manner in which respectful criticism of a magisterial statement should proceed, the passage in question says:

> In the dialogue, a two-fold rule should prevail. When there is a question of the communion of faith, the principle of the "unity of truth" (*unitas veritatis*) applies. When it is a question of differences which do not jeopardize this communion, the "unity of charity" (*unitas caritatis*) should be safeguarded. Even if the doctrine of the faith is not in question, the theologian will not present his own opinions or divergent hypotheses as though they were non-arguable conclusions. Respect for the truth as well as for the People of God requires this discretion.

Now, Fastiggi seems to think that the second paragraph here entails that when a theologian raises even a legitimate criticism, *everything* he says must be presented in a tentative way. But that is not what the passage says. What it says is that even if a theologian is not dissenting from a doctrine of the faith, that doesn't license him in treating what are really just matters of mere opinion or hypothesis as non-arguable conclusions. But it doesn't follow that he cannot treat *anything* as a non-arguable conclusion. For example, the theologian is perfectly within his rights to treat *the consistent teaching of Scripture and of the ordinary Magisterium over two thousand years* as a "non-arguable conclusion," because the Magisterium itself holds that teaching of that sort is infallible.[8]

Of course, Fastiggi may disagree with the claim that Scripture and the ordinary Magisterium really do teach that capital punishment is not intrinsically evil. The point for the moment, though, is that Fastiggi is mistaken in thinking that a lack of tentativeness is *per se* problematic.

Moreover, there are several historical cases where popes were legitimately criticized, and their critics rightly presented their criticisms in a non-tentative way. Paul's criticism of Peter was in no way tentative, but in fact extremely bold, and Scripture tells us that Paul was in the right. Pope Honorius's critics were not tentative in criticizing him for giving aid and comfort to the Monothelite heresy, and Pope John XXII's critics were not tentative in criticizing him for failing to uphold traditional teaching on the particular judgment.

Now, in part 3 of his series, Fastiggi addresses these sorts of examples, and says:

> Some critics of the revised teaching of the Church on the death penalty claim that they can oppose the teaching because popes have taught errors in the past, and they usually bring up cases such as Pope Honorius I (r. 625–638) and John XXII (r. 1316–1334). What these critics don't understand is that it was the Magisterium itself that resolved the doctrinal issues involved in these cases, not the critics. It is certainly

---

8   I have discussed the conditions under which the ordinary Magisterium is infallible in "Capital Punishment and the Infallibility of the Ordinary Magisterium," *Catholic World Report*, January 20, 2018.

permitted for scholars to raise questions about non-definitive papal teachings and to ask for clarifications. It is not permitted, though, for private scholars to assume the authority to correct the popes.

But the historical claims Fastiggi makes here are mistaken or at least misleading. Honorius was condemned by a council (three councils, in fact), and councils are subordinate to popes. It is true that popes then confirmed these councils, but the point is that the first of these councils condemned Honorius *before* papal approval was given, and was not accused of insubordination or the like for doing so.[9] John XXII was criticized by the theologians of his day, and while the Magisterium did settle the issue (beginning with John XXII himself, who recanted) it was prodded to do so *precisely because these critics pressed the issue.*

Fastiggi adds the remark that "if dissent from authoritative magisterial teachings can be justified because of alleged errors of prior popes, then any magisterial teaching can be rejected." But that does not follow at all. The reason these popes were criticized was only because they *failed to affirm traditional teaching*, and that is the only reason Pope Francis's revision to the Catechism has been criticized. The theological principles that justify such criticism would by no means entail that just "*any* magisterial teaching can be rejected." Rather, they would *only* justify criticisms of *failures to uphold traditional teaching.*

The problem with Fastiggi's position is that he treats all criticisms of magisterial statements as if they were of a piece, when they clearly are not. He fails to take account of the *teleology* of the Magisterium, the reason it exists in the first place, which is to *preserve the deposit of faith*, not to give popes and other churchmen carte blanche to teach whatever they feel like. And this is something that *the Church herself has constantly emphasized.* For example, the First Vatican Council teaches:

> For the Holy Spirit was promised to the successors of Peter not so that they might, by his revelation, make known some new doctrine, but that, by his assistance, they might religiously guard and faithfully expound the revelation or deposit of faith transmitted by the apostles.[10]

Similarly, the Second Vatican Council teaches:

> The living teaching office of the Church . . . is not above the word of God, but serves it, *teaching only what has been handed on*, listening to it devoutly, guarding it scrupulously and explaining it faithfully.[11]

And Pope Benedict XVI taught:

---

9 I have discussed the case of Honorius in detail: "The error and condemnation of Pope Honorius," October 4, 2022, and "Can Pope Honorius be defended?," October 6, 2022. See also chapter 12 below.

10 *Pastor Aeternus*, ch. 4, no. 6.

11 Second Vatican Council, Dogmatic Constitution on Divine Revelation *Dei Verbum* (November 18, 1965), ch. 2, no. 10.

The pope is not an absolute monarch whose thoughts and desires are law. On the contrary: the pope's ministry is a guarantee of obedience to Christ and to his Word. He must not proclaim his own ideas, but rather constantly bind himself and the Church to obedience to God's Word, in the face of every attempt to adapt it or water it down, and every form of opportunism.[12]

The development of Catholic doctrine is thus like a ratchet, which only goes one way. The body of teaching found in Scripture, solemn conciliar definitions, *ex cathedra* papal statements, and the ordinary Magisterium when it meets the conditions for infallibility, is locked in place forever. New implications can be drawn out of it (which is what "development" in the proper sense involves), but it *cannot* be *contradicted or reversed* (which would not be a true development at all, but rather a corruption of doctrine or failure to preserve the deposit of faith).

Now, it is precisely in order to assist the Magisterium in its function of preserving the deposit of faith that the teaching of Aquinas, of *Donum Veritatis*, and of the tradition more generally allows that there can be cases in which respectful criticism of magisterial statements is justifiable. Like the Magisterium, such criticism has precisely the function of *maintaining fidelity to tradition*, not of allowing the critics to say whatever they like. In short, and to oversimply, the teaching of Aquinas and of *Donum Veritatis* can never be used to justify "progressive" criticism of magisterial statements, but only certain kinds of "traditionalist" criticism. That is *not* to say that just anything of the latter sort goes. The point is that the principles underlying the teaching of Aquinas and of *Donum Veritatis* are not *neutral* between the different sorts of criticism theologians might want to raise. They favor those who want to preserve past teaching, and disfavor those who want to depart from it. Hence, again, Fastiggi is just mistaken to suggest that if you allow *any* criticism of magisterial statements, then *everything* is up for grabs.

THE TEACHING OF POPE FRANCIS

Let's turn finally to a statement from Pope Francis that is relevant to the issue at hand. As I've noted, he has on several occasions said that he welcomes respectful criticism.[13] One of his statements is especially important in this context. In the Apostolic Exhortation *Gaudete et Exsultate*, nos. 43–44, the pope writes:

In the Church there legitimately coexist different ways of interpreting many aspects of doctrine and Christian life; in their variety, they "help to express more clearly the immense riches of God's word." It is true that "for those who long for a monolithic body of doctrine guarded by all and leaving no room for nuance, this might appear as undesirable and leading to confusion." Indeed, some currents of gnosticism scorned

---

12   Homily of His Holiness Benedict XVI, Mass of Possession of the Chair of the Bishop of Rome, May 7, 2005.

13   See Feser, "Benedict XVI, Cardinal Pell, and criticism of Pope Francis."

the concrete simplicity of the Gospel and attempted to replace the trinitarian and incarnate God with a superior Unity, wherein the rich diversity of our history disappeared. In effect, doctrine, or better, our understanding and expression of it, "is not a closed system, devoid of the dynamic capacity to pose questions, doubts, inquiries . . ."

Now, those who have criticized the revision to the Catechism are doing *exactly what Pope Francis here acknowledges to be legitimate.* They are raising "questions, doubts, inquiries" about the formulation of the revision, on the grounds that it "leav[es] no room for nuance" and ignores "the rich diversity of our history" and "the immense riches of God's word." In particular, the revision focuses only on statements from the tradition that seem *unfavorable* towards capital punishment while entirely ignoring the mountain of statements from Scripture, the Fathers and Doctors of the Church, and previous popes that are clearly *favorable* to it. The revision also entirely ignores the empirical considerations favoring the judgment that there are at least some cases where public safety would best be served by keeping the death penalty on the books. The revision thereby gives the impression that capital punishment is intrinsically wrong, and that social scientists are in agreement that it is never needed in order to save lives — neither of which is true.

The critics of the revision to the Catechism thereby respectfully call upon the Magisterium to remedy these deficiencies. And they argue that reading the revision as a deficiently formulated prudential judgment rather than as a change in doctrinal principle ought to be among the "legitimately coexist[ing] different ways of interpreting" it (to use Pope Francis's words).

If Pope Francis's words in *Gaudete et Exsultate* apply to centuries of established Catholic teaching, it is hard to see how they can fail to apply also to a novel revision that is only five years old. Accordingly, those who accuse the revision's critics of "dissent" are not only at odds with the teaching of Aquinas and of *Donum Veritatis*; they are at odds with the teaching of Pope Francis himself.

As we have seen, Robert Fastiggi criticizes the critics of the revision. In the first part of this study I addressed what he has to say about the obligations of Catholics vis-à-vis the Magisterium of the Church. In this second part, I will address what he says about the teaching of Scripture, the Fathers, and previous popes on the topic of capital punishment.

In our book *By Man Shall His Blood Be Shed: A Catholic Defense of Capital Pun-ishment*,[14] Joseph Bessette and I assemble a mountain of evidence from Scripture, the Fathers and Doctors of the Church, two millennia of consistent papal teaching, and Catholic moral theology, in defense of the conclusion that the Church has taught irreformably that the death penalty can in principle be morally licit. In a follow-up article at *Catholic World Report*, I have also explained the conditions

---

14　San Francisco: Ignatius Press, 2017.

under which the ordinary Magisterium of the Church teaches infallibly, and have shown that the teaching that capital punishment is not intrinsically immoral meets these conditions.[15] In our book, Bessette and I also set out at length the social scientific arguments supporting the conclusion that keeping the death penalty on the books for the most heinous crimes is necessary for public safety.

One of the frustrating things about Fastiggi's series is that he leaves much of our argumentation unaddressed. Furthermore, many of the objections he does raise are ones I have already rebutted elsewhere — including in my previous exchanges with him — yet he does not acknowledge, much less answer, the responses I have already given. Yet Fastiggi's series nevertheless gives the false appearance of comprehensiveness, in part because of its sheer length, but also because he will sometimes belabor trivial points. For example, as we will see below, he tries vainly to read momentous significance into a passing allusion Pope Benedict XVI makes to Genesis 9:6 in an obscure speech on a topic unrelated to capital punishment. Meanwhile, major problems for Fastiggi's position go unaddressed. Many readers of a site like *Where Peter Is* will not only not have read our book, but are highly unlikely to follow up their reading of Fastiggi's articles with a look at our book to see if Fastiggi has represented it accurately, or if he really has answered all the difficulties facing the abolitionist case.

Yet another problem is that Fastiggi does not always carefully distinguish the issue of whether capital punishment is intrinsically wrong from the issue of whether it is merely better in practice not to inflict it. For example, he will often cite some critical remark that a Church Father or pope makes about capital punishment, as if it were damaging to the case Bessette and I make. But typically these are passages we have already addressed in our book. And typically they are passages that would be damaging to our position only if they asserted that capital punishment is intrinsically wrong, and they do not in fact do that. When the issues are disambiguated and formulated precisely, the passages in question do not have the force Fastiggi seems to think they have. Problematic ambiguities like this crop up again and again in Fastiggi's discussion.

SCRIPTURE AND THE CHURCH FATHERS

As Fastiggi notes, the Council of Trent teaches that "no one may dare to interpret the Scripture in a way contrary to the unanimous consensus of the Fathers." But as Bessette and I show at pp. 111–18 of our book, the Fathers of the Church are unanimous in teaching that Scripture allows for capital punishment, at least in principle. Fastiggi disputes this, writing:

> This position, though, has been rejected by Pope Francis in his October 3, 2020 encyclical, *Fratelli Tutti*, no. 265, when he correctly notes: "From the earliest centuries of the Church, some were clearly opposed to

---

15   Feser, "Capital Punishment and the Infallibility of the Ordinary Magisterium."

capital punishment," and he cites Lactantius (240–320), Pope Nicholas
I (c. 820–867), and Augustine (354–430) as examples.

But the problem with Fastiggi's argument here is that we need to distinguish (a)
the claim that capital punishment is wrong *intrinsically, or of its very nature,* from
(b) the claim that while it is *not* intrinsically wrong, it is still better not to use it.
As Bessette and I acknowledge, some of the Fathers, including the ones Fastiggi
mentions, do endorse claim (b), though there are also many Fathers who reject it.
But what is in question is whether any of the Fathers endorse claim (a). And in
fact, as Bessette and I demonstrate in our book, none of them endorses *that* claim,
and Pope Francis does not say that they do. Indeed, even E. Christian Brugger,
who is not only opposed to capital punishment but would like the Church to
go as far as condemning it as intrinsically immoral, admits that there is what he
calls a "patristic consensus" on the thesis that capital punishment is legitimate
at least in principle, even among those who opposed resorting to it in practice.[16]

In part 2 of his series, Fastiggi tries to make a big deal of the fact that Pope
Nicholas I was opposed to capital punishment—something Bessette and I explicitly acknowledge in our book. But Nicholas does not condemn it as intrinsically
evil. Fastiggi also suggests that Tertullian, Cyprian, and Lactantius are exceptions
to the patristic consensus. But he ignores quotations Bessette and I give in our
book that show otherwise. For example, in *A Treatise on the Soul,* Tertullian says
that "we do not account those to be violent deaths which justice awards, that
avenger of violence." Lactantius, in *The Divine Institutes,* acknowledges that a man
can be "justly condemned to [be] slain." In *Ad Demetrianum,* Cyprian indicates
that if Christianity really were a crime, the state would justly "put the man that
confesses it to death." These Fathers did indeed nevertheless oppose the use of the
death penalty in practice, but they do not teach that it is intrinsically wrong. Not
only Brugger, but also James Megivern, another prominent Catholic opponent
of capital punishment, acknowledge that the stronger thesis cannot be attributed
to these three Fathers.[17]

How desperate Fastiggi is to get around this difficulty is illustrated by the fact
that he even alludes in passing to David Bentley Hart's criticism[18] of *By Man
Shall His Blood Be Shed* as evidence that Bessette and I have somehow gotten the
Fathers wrong (though Fastiggi doesn't explain how). The first problem here is
that it is not hard to show that Hart's review was a dishonest hatchet job, as I
demonstrated when responding to it.[19] The second problem is that it is very odd
for an orthodox Catholic like Fastiggi to look to Hart, of all people, for sound

---

16   E. Christian Brugger, *Capital Punishment and Roman Catholic Moral Tradition* (Notre Dame, IN: University of Notre Dame Press, 2014), 95.

17   James J. Megivern, *The Death Penalty: An Historical and Theological Survey* (Mahwah, NJ: Paulist Press, 1997), 22–26.

18   David Bentley Hart, "Christians and the Death Penalty," *Commonweal,* November 16, 2017.

19   Edward Feser, "Hot Air vs. Capital Punishment: A Reply to Paul Griffiths and David Bentley Hart," *Catholic World Report,* November 28, 2017; idem, "A Hart that pumps bile," December 21, 2017.

exegesis. Hart is not Catholic and rejects Catholic norms for interpreting Scripture and the Fathers. Indeed, his view of Scripture is so far from a Catholic one that he is given to making remarks like this:

> Most of the Hebrew Bible is a polytheistic gallimaufry, and YHVH is a figure in a shifting pantheon of *elohim* or deities . . . [In] most of the Old Testament he is of course presented as quite evil: a blood-drenched, cruel, war-making, genocidal, irascible, murderous, jealous storm-god. Neither he nor his rival or king or father or equal or *alter ego* . . . is a good god. Each is a psychologically limited mythic figure from a rich but violent ancient Near Eastern culture . . . [The heretic] Marcion of Sinope . . . exhibited far greater insight than modern fundamentalists . . . in that he recognized that the god described in the Hebrew Bible—if taken in the mythic terms provided there—is something of a monster and hence obviously not the Christian God.[20]

Hart is also well-known for trying to reinterpret Scripture so as to make it compatible with universalism, which, from a Catholic point of view, is a heresy.[21] *This* is the exegete Fastiggi wants Catholics to trust to interpret Scripture and the Fathers on capital punishment?

A third problem is that Hart himself has conceded that "it is perhaps easier for me as an Orthodox Christian than it is for a Catholic to dismiss Feser's arguments."[22] For some reason, Catholics who cite Hart against me never quote this remark.

GENESIS AND THE DEATH PENALTY

Genesis 9:6 famously states: "Whoever sheds the blood of man, by man shall his blood be shed; for God made man in his own image." This passage has for millennia been understood by Catholic and Jewish commentators as sanctioning the death penalty, and as Bessette and I show at pp. 99–101 of our book, there is no plausible alternative way of reading it. In *De Laicis*, chapter 13, St Robert Bellarmine considers and rejects the claim that Genesis 9:6 is merely a prediction about what *will* happen to murderers, rather than a decree about what *should* happen to them. Among the points he makes is that such a reinterpretation is contrary to the traditional Jewish understanding of the passage. He points out that in the Targums, the passage is paraphrased as: "Whoever sheds men's blood before witnesses, *by sentence of a judge* his blood should be shed" (emphasis added). Bellarmine concludes that Genesis 9:6 "must be taken as an order and a precept." Even Brugger admits that attempts to reinterpret the passage are hard to defend, and concedes that it remains a "problem" for his radical abolitionist position.[23]

---

20   David Bentley Hart, "Good God? A Response," *Theopolis*, October 7, 2019.

21   Edward Feser, "Hart, hell, and heresy," July 22, 2020.

22   David Bentley Hart, "Further Reflections on Capital Punishment (and on Edward Feser)," *Church Life Journal*, December 19, 2017.

23   Brugger, *Capital Punishment*, 73.

Yet Fastiggi claims otherwise. He writes:

> This Scripture . . . can actually be used against the death penalty since the death penalty involves killing. In fact, Benedict XVI, in his 2012 Post-Synodal Exhortation, *Ecclesia in Medio Oriente*, no. 26 cites Genesis 9:6 as evidence that God forbids the killing of even those who commit murder: "God wants life, not death. He forbids all killing, even of those who kill (cf. Gen 4:15–16; 9:5–6; Ex 20:13)." In *Fratelli Tutti* 270, Pope Francis cites Gen 9:6 in his section against the death penalty, for this Scripture stands as a warning to "those tempted to yield to violence in any form."

But this line of argument is problematic in several ways. First, Pope Benedict's exhortation was not addressing the subject of capital punishment. As the reader can easily verify by looking at the text, the context in which he made the remark in question was a discussion of the idea of religious toleration. What the pope was saying is that the attempt to coerce others into adopting one's own religious point of view sometimes results in violence and even killing, and that God does not approve of this. The pope was not even addressing the topic of criminal justice, let alone the question of what sorts of punishments are appropriate for which crimes.

Now, it is standard methodology when interpreting papal texts to take such context into account, and to be very cautious about extrapolating momentous implications about a particular subject from papal remarks made in passing in a discourse devoted to a completely different subject. Fastiggi violates this methodological principle by insinuating that Benedict's remark implies some radical reinterpretation of Genesis 9:6 and, by implication, some revolutionary teaching vis-à-vis capital punishment.

Second, it is in any event highly misleading to imply, as Fastiggi does, that Benedict was "cit[ing] Genesis 9:6 as evidence that God forbids the killing of even those who commit murder." For one thing, the pope does not pinpoint Genesis 9:6 specifically and then make an explicit comment about how to interpret it. Rather, he simply includes it in a string of scriptural references that are implied to have some bearing—exactly *what* bearing, in the case of any of the individual Scriptural passages, is not specified—on God's will vis-à-vis killing. Benedict never explicitly makes, concerning Genesis 9:6, the claim that Fastiggi attributes to him.

For another thing, it is quite ridiculous on its face to suggest that Genesis 9:6 teaches that "God forbids the killing of even those who commit murder." Again, this passage has for millennia consistently been understood by Catholic and Jewish exegetes to be teaching the opposite. Even modern liberal exegetes who have tried to reinterpret it have only ever claimed that the passage is *neutral* about capital punishment, and they have had to strain credulity to go even that far (as, again, even Brugger concedes). To suggest, as Fastiggi does, that the passage is actually *condemning* capital punishment, is to imply that Jewish and Christian exegetes, traditional and liberal alike, have all been misreading it for millennia, and that its true import was revealed only a few years ago in a passing and oblique reference in a minor papal exhortation addressing an unrelated topic. With all due respect to Fastiggi, this doesn't pass the laugh test.

Nor is it remotely plausible to attribute such an interpretation to *Pope Benedict XVI*, of all people. Benedict's program was, famously, a "hermeneutic of continuity" that eschewed rupture with traditional Catholic teaching. It is absurd to propose that he intended radically to subvert the traditional reading of Genesis 9:6, and with it the Church's perennial teaching that the death penalty is not intrinsically immoral. It is doubly absurd to suppose that he would do so in a way that was so extremely subtle and inexplicit that no one even knew about it until Fastiggi drew our attention to it. Moreover, while head of the CDF, then-Cardinal Ratzinger stated in a 2004 memorandum that "it may still be permissible . . . to have recourse to capital punishment" and that "there may be a legitimate diversity of opinion even among Catholics about . . . applying the death penalty."[24] He could not have said such things if he believed that Genesis 9:6 absolutely forbade the execution of murderers. Once again manifesting a degree of intellectual honesty that too many Catholic opponents of capital punishment lack, Brugger acknowledges in the second edition of his book (2014) that in reality, Benedict XVI was "inclined to accentuate the continuity that exists between the tradition and the moves of his predecessor" vis-à-vis capital punishment, rather than to take John Paul II's teaching in a more radically abolitionist direction (p. xx).

To come to *Fratelli Tutti*, it is true that, in the context of criticizing the death penalty, Pope Francis includes Genesis 9:6 in a list of passages that he says warn of the consequences of violence. But he is not addressing, much less answering, exegetical questions about the precise meaning of the passage. And Pope Francis's habit of speaking with imprecision should make any responsible theologian wary of drawing momentous theological conclusions about some topic from remarks of his that are not directly aimed at that topic.

Consider, for example, Francis's remark in *Evangelii Gaudium* that "the first and the greatest of the commandments, and the one that best identifies us as Christ's disciples [is]: 'This is my commandment, that you love one another as I have loved you.'" What Scripture actually says is:

> When the Pharisees heard that he had silenced the Sadducees, they gathered together, and one of them tested him by asking, "Teacher, which commandment in the law is the greatest?" He said to him, "You shall love the Lord, your God, with all your heart, with all your soul, and with all your mind. This is the greatest and the first commandment." (Mt 22:34–38)

Should we conclude that we have somehow been misunderstanding Matthew 22 for two millennia, and that Francis has at last revealed what Christ actually taught

---

24 Joseph Ratzinger, "Worthiness to Receive Holy Communion: General Principles," www.ewtn.com/catholicism/library/worthiness-to-receive-holy-communion-general-principles-2153.

is the first and greatest commandment? That would be absurd. Quite obviously, the pope's remark is simply mistaken, and he was not speaking precisely. That would be enough of a reason to refrain from drawing some revisionary theological conclusion from his remark, but it is reinforced by the fact that he was not explicitly trying to settle a matter of scriptural exegesis in the first place.

The same thing is true of the remark in *Fratelli Tutti*. The pope simply gathers scriptural texts to illustrate the idea that violence has bad consequences. He does not say that his aim is to settle any exegetical controversy about the proper interpretation of Genesis 9:6.

THE MOSAIC LAW VERSUS THE GOSPEL?

Fastiggi points out in part 1 of his series that the Old Testament permitted slavery and polygamy, and that God even enabled the latter in the case of King David. Yet the Church has nevertheless rightly forbidden these things. He suggests that the case of capital punishment is similar. Even though the Old Testament allowed it, the Church can and should forbid it now in an absolute way.

But this is a false analogy. The first problem with it is that the Old Testament *merely* permits, but does not *require*, slavery and polygamy. The Israelites are not told that they must take slaves or marry more than one woman. They are told, at most, only that *if* they do these things, then there are certain conditions they must follow. By contrast, the use of the death penalty *is* positively commanded many times in the Old Testament. Moreover, these commands are not *ad hoc* in nature, directed to some specific temporary purpose (as are divine directives to the Israelites to destroy this or that pagan city, say). Rather, the Mosaic Law makes the death penalty a *standing and normal part of the everyday life of the nation of Israel.*

Hence, if capital punishment were *intrinsically* or *of its very nature* "an attack on the inviolability and dignity of the person," we would be left with the conclusion that Scripture not only *permitted*, but *positively commanded* the Israelites to set up the very structure of their society in a manner that was inherently and gravely contrary to the good of human beings. We would be left with the conclusion that Scripture thereby led the Israelites into grave moral error. But that is not possible given the Church's doctrine that Scripture *cannot* teach moral error.

Perhaps Fastiggi would acknowledge that it was not wrong for the Israelites to make use of capital punishment, but holds that it is nevertheless wrong to make use of it under the New Covenant, given the higher moral demands of the Gospel. Now, one problem with this is that the New Testament, too, explicitly affirms the legitimacy of the death penalty in some cases. For example, as Bellarmine pointed out, the deaths of Ananias and Sapphira in the Acts of the Apostles are essentially divine executions carried out at the behest of St Peter. In other words, *the first pope not only approved of capital punishment, but inflicted it himself.*[25]

---

25 I have discussed and defended Bellarmine's interpretation of this passage in "Bellarmine on capital punishment," March 23, 2018.

Romans 13:4 famously teaches that the governing authority "does not bear the sword in vain; he is the servant of God to execute his wrath on the wrongdoer." This has for two thousand years been understood by Catholic theologians to affirm the legitimacy of capital punishment. Church Fathers such as Tertullian, Origen, Ambrose, and Augustine read it this way, as do Doctors of the Church like Aquinas and Bellarmine. Even Brugger admits that there was a patristic and medieval "consensus" on this as the correct reading.[26]

Fastiggi makes a passing reference to a speech from Pope Pius XII that alludes to Romans 13:4, and suggests that Pius somehow distanced himself from the traditional interpretation. Fastiggi doesn't explain exactly how—nor could he have, since Pius says no such thing in that passage. Indeed, Pius isn't even addressing the topic of capital punishment at all in the passage. And in fact, as is well known, when Pius XII did discuss capital punishment, he clearly and firmly *endorsed* it.[27]

Bessette and I address Romans 13:4 and other relevant New Testament passages at pp. 103–11 of our book. I also address attempts to reinterpret Romans 13:4 in my response to Hart, mentioned earlier. Fastiggi offers no response to most of what we say.

But there is yet another problem with Fastiggi's suggestion that capital punishment, while permissible in Old Testament times, is immoral given the higher demands of the Gospel. The problem is that the Church for two millennia has taught the contrary. Indeed, on several occasions *the Magisterium directly addressed this thesis and explicitly rejected it*. For example, in 405, a bishop inquired with Pope St Innocent I about whether civil authorities had to refrain from using capital punishment after converting to Christianity. The pope answered in the negative, appealing to Romans 13 and suggesting that to forbid capital punishment would "overturn sound order . . . [and] go against the authority of the Lord."

In response to this, Fastiggi notes that Innocent begins his response to the bishop with the remark that "about these matters we read nothing definitive from the forefathers," and suggests that this somehow poses a problem for those who would appeal to Pope Innocent in defense of capital punishment. But there are two problems with Fastiggi's claim, whatever the significance of Innocent's remark (which isn't obvious). First, Fastiggi leaves out what Innocent immediately says next:

> For they [the forefathers] had remembered that these powers had been granted by God and that for the sake of punishing harm-doers the sword

---

26   Brugger, *Capital Punishment*, 112.

27   Fastiggi is likely borrowing here from John Finnis, who has vainly tried to make hay out of this passage from Pius XII. I refuted Finnis's flimsy arguments in two articles: "The Church Cannot Teach That Capital Punishment is Inherently Wrong: A Reply to John Finnis," *Public Discourse*, September 13, 2018, and "Unnatural Lawyering: John Finnis's Brief against Traditional Catholic Teaching on Capital Punishment," *Catholic World Report*, January 4, 2019.

had been allowed; in this way a minister of God, an avenger, has been given. How therefore would they criticize something which they see to have been granted through the authority of God?

Needless to say, that is pretty definitive. Innocent says that the power of execution was granted to the state *by God*, and that precisely for that reason, the forefathers would not criticize the death penalty. Second, whatever the forefathers had to say, what matters is that *Pope Innocent I's remark is itself definitive*. For whatever the forefathers thought, *he, as pope*, was being asked to make an authoritative decision by a bishop who wasn't sure what to think. And his response isn't to waver, but on the contrary, firmly to declare that to condemn capital punishment as inherently wrong would be "to go against the authority of the Lord."

But there is further papal teaching along these lines. For instance, in 1210, Pope Innocent III not only rejected the claim of the Waldensian heretics that Christians could not resort to capital punishment, but made repudiation of this thesis a condition of their reunion with the Church. Fastiggi alleges that in insisting that the death penalty could be inflicted "without mortal sin," Pope Innocent was merely making a point about the subjective culpability of public officials rather than the moral character of the act of execution itself. But Bessette and I answered this sort of dodge in our book (at pp. 124–25). The statement to which Innocent required the Waldensians to assent reads, in full, as follows:

> We declare that the secular power can without mortal sin impose a judgment of blood provided the punishment is carried out not in hatred but with good judgment, not inconsiderately, but after mature deliberation.

Furthermore, in an earlier letter to a Waldensian leader, Pope Innocent wrote:

> Let none of you presume to assert the following: that the secular power cannot carry out a judgment of blood without mortal sin. This is an error because the law, not the judge, puts to death so long as the punishment is imposed, not in hatred, nor rashly, but with deliberation.

Notice that the pope is not saying merely that a person might not be *culpable* for sin when inflicting the death penalty — as if inflicting it might still be intrinsically wrong, and it's just that the executioner doesn't know any better, or acts under the influence of strong emotion, and thus doesn't meet the conditions for mortal sin. No, the pope says instead that even when acting with "good judgment," "mature deliberation," "not in hatred, nor rashly," etc., one can in that case be blameless in inflicting the death penalty. And he says that "the law" itself requires this, not the fallible judgment of the individual. Once again, even Brugger admits that those who share his abolitionism do not have a strong case here, and that Pope Innocent did indeed intend to teach that capital punishment *itself* is licit, not merely that those who inflict it might lack subjective culpability.[28]

---

28   Brugger, *Capital Punishment*, 107.

Yet another relevant papal statement is Pope Leo X's condemnation of Luther's thesis that the execution of heretics is against the divine will. Then there is Pope St Pius V's promulgation of the *Roman Catechism*, which was, naturally, intended as a guide to living according to the principles of the Gospel, and directed to the Church universally rather than merely addressing some specific and contingent set of circumstances. This catechism enthusiastically endorses capital punishment for murderers, saying that "the just use of this power, far from involving the crime of murder, is an act of paramount obedience to this Commandment which prohibits murder." In the twentieth century, Pope Pius XII taught that "it is reserved . . . to the public authority to deprive the criminal of the benefit of life when already, by his crime, he has deprived himself of the right to live."

In our book, Bessette and I discuss these and other relevant papal statements on the subject of capital punishment at length. Now, if capital punishment really were *inherently* contrary to the demands of the Gospel, we would have to say that the Church has for two millennia consistently and gravely misled the faithful on a matter of fundamental moral importance. We would have to say that when directly addressing the question of whether the Gospel rules out capital punishment, popes Innocent I, Innocent III, and Leo X all got it wrong. Indeed, we would have to say that *the heretics whom Innocent III and Leo X were criticizing were right, and the popes were wrong*.

This is Fastiggi's idea of upholding the authority of the Magisterium?! Which is more likely to reinforce the Church's credibility: the view that Scripture and two millennia of magisterial teaching were right, and that Pope Francis's revision to the Catechism is badly formulated and should be revisited in order to make it more clearly consistent with the tradition; or the view that the Church has gotten things wrong for two millennia, and that only Pope Francis has somehow finally seen the truth? To ask these questions is to answer them.

There is a further irony here. Commenting on Pope Innocent I's affirmation of the legitimacy of the death penalty, Fastiggi claims that Innocent also allowed "torture," and suggests that this should lead us to reject what he says about capital punishment. One problem with this is that Fastiggi does not explain why the word he translates as "torture" should be understood to refer to torments intended to break the will (which would be torture, and immoral) as opposed to lesser corporal punishments (which would not be).

But leaving that aside, it is odd that Fastiggi, in order to defend one pope (Francis) against the charge of error, accuses another pope (Innocent) of error! If he is going to suggest that Innocent erred, then how can he consistently object to those who suggest that Francis has erred? Moreover, the cases are not parallel, because there is a clear and consistent tradition, from Scripture through two thousand years of magisterial teaching, in favor of the legitimacy in principle of capital punishment. But there is no such tradition with respect to torture. Hence, if Innocent can be wrong about torture, then, *a fortiori*, Francis can be wrong about capital punishment. Fastiggi thinks that his point about Pope Innocent helps his case, but in fact it *hurts* his case.

THE RATZINGER MEMORANDUM

During the 2004 U. S. presidential election, the question whether Catholic politicians who support abortion or euthanasia should be denied Holy Communion became a hot button issue. Some suggested that if these politicians were denied Communion, then Catholic politicians who supported capital punishment or the Iraq War should be denied it as well.

To clarify the matter, Cardinal Ratzinger, who was then Prefect of the Congregation for the Doctrine of the Faith, sent a memorandum titled "Worthiness to Receive Holy Communion: General Principles" (which I briefly referred to above) to then-Cardinal Theodore McCarrick, who was at the time the archbishop of Washington, DC (McCarrick has, of course, since been disgraced and defrocked, though that is irrelevant to the present issue). Ratzinger noted that the cases are not at all parallel, writing:

> Not all moral issues have the same moral weight as abortion and eutha-
> nasia. For example, *if a Catholic were to be at odds with the Holy Father on
> the application of capital punishment or on the decision to wage war, he would
> not for that reason be considered unworthy to present himself to receive Holy
> Communion.* While the Church exhorts civil authorities to seek peace,
> not war, and to exercise discretion and mercy in imposing punishment
> on criminals, it may still be permissible to take up arms to repel an
> aggressor or to have recourse to capital punishment. *There may be a
> legitimate diversity of opinion even among Catholics about waging war and
> applying the death penalty,* but not however with regard to abortion
> and euthanasia.

Notice several things about this teaching. As is well known, Pope John Paul II held that the cases where capital punishment is necessary to protect society are "very rare, if not practically nonexistent" (as the 1997 version of the Catechism puts it). Indeed, the pope made even stronger statements at other times, calling the death penalty "cruel and unnecessary" and calling for its outright abolition. All the same, Ratzinger acknowledged that "there may be a legitimate diversity of opinion even among Catholics about . . . applying the death penalty," and indeed that a Catholic in good standing could even be "at odds with the Holy Father" on the subject. He could not have said that if assent to the pope's position was obligatory. And notice that this is true even though the pope's prudential judgment concerned a matter of grave moral importance, and was put forward publicly, repeatedly, and in stern moralistic terms.

Note also the reference to "civil authorities," and how war and recourse to capital punishment can in some cases be permissible despite the fact that the Church urges such authorities to seek peace and exercise mercy on criminals. The clear implication is that it is ultimately *civil authorities* who have the responsibility to make a prudential judgment about whether capital punishment is necessary, just as they have the responsibility to determine whether war is necessary.

Some have claimed that the memorandum merely reflects Cardinal Ratzinger's personal opinion as a private theologian. But this is clearly not the case. Ratzinger was writing, not as a private theologian, but precisely in his official capacity as Prefect for the Congregation of the Doctrine of the Faith. And he was writing to a fellow bishop precisely to clarify for him a matter of Church doctrine and discipline.

Furthermore, the passage from the memo quoted above was incorporated almost verbatim into a USCCB document written by Archbishop William Levada (who would later succeed Ratzinger as head of CDF).[29] The purpose of this document was precisely to clarify for Catholics the same issues Ratzinger aimed to clarify in his memo. And the fact that a USCCB document incorporates the passage in question obviously indicates that it has doctrinal weight, and is not merely Ratzinger's personal opinion. It is worth adding that even Brugger acknowledges, in the second edition of his book, that the memo was written by Ratzinger "as prefect of the CDF."[30]

Now, keep in mind that as head of the CDF, Ratzinger's job was to be Pope John Paul II's doctrinal spokesman. Hence he was an authoritative interpreter of the pope's teaching on the issue of capital punishment. Since he explicitly said that there could be "a legitimate diversity of opinion" about the matter even among faithful Catholics — and indeed, that faithful Catholics could even be "at odds with" the pope on the matter — it follows that Pope John Paul II's position that capital punishment is no longer needed is not something Catholics are obligated to agree with.

How is this relevant to Pope Francis's revision of the Catechism? The main difference between John Paul's teaching and Francis's teaching is that the former allowed that there may still be rare cases where capital punishment is needed in order to protect society, whereas the latter denies that. Even Francis's appeal to the "dignity of the person" is not novel, because Pope John Paul II made the same appeal when criticizing capital punishment. For example, the 1997 edition of the Catechism says that non-lethal means of dealing with offenders are preferable because they are "more in conformity with the dignity of the human person."

Now, John Paul II's view that the cases where capital punishment is still needed to protect society are "very rare, if not practically nonexistent" was of its very nature a prudential judgment concerning matters of social science, law, criminology, etc. about which popes have no special expertise. For that reason, as Cardinal Ratzinger made clear, Catholics were not obligated to agree with that judgment. But Francis's view that non-lethal means are in every case sufficient

---

29   "Theological Reflections on Catholics in Political Life and the Reception of Holy Communion," June 13, 2004.

30   Brugger, *Capital Punishment*, xxviii.

to "ensure the due protection" of society is also, of its very nature, a prudential judgment concerning matters of social science, law, criminology, etc. about which popes have no special expertise. So, how can Catholics be obligated to assent to the latter view any more than they were obligated to assent to the former? What the Ratzinger memorandum says about John Paul's teaching applies *mutatis mutandis* to Francis's teaching.

In part 3 of his series, Fastiggi responds to those who argue that the Ratzinger memorandum supports the view that papal opposition to capital punishment amounts to a prudential judgment with which Catholics are not obligated to agree. Fastiggi concedes that "perhaps that argument could have been used prior to the 2018 revision" to the Catechism. However, he says, "it cannot be used now" because "that memorandum has been superseded by the change" to the Catechism, along with the CDF's explanation of the change. For one thing, says Fastiggi, "the revised text of the [Catechism] articulates a moral judgment that is not merely prudential." For another thing, the Ratzinger memorandum was in any case "never intended for publication, as Cardinal Ladaria [then prefect of the CDF] has explained" but was "just a private communication to some bishops."

Fastiggi supposes, then, that both the nature of the 2018 revision to the Catechism and Cardinal Ladaria's comments about the 2004 Ratzinger memorandum render that memorandum moot and undermine any argument based on it. But both of these suppositions are false.

First, it is easy to show that the revision to the Catechism, no less than John Paul II's position on capital punishment, *does* reflect merely prudential considerations. For the revised text appeals not only to human dignity, but also to the assumption that "more effective systems of detention have been developed, which ensure the due protection of citizens but, at the same time, do not definitively deprive the guilty of the possibility of redemption."[31] Similarly, in his letter to the bishops explaining the change to the Catechism, Cardinal Ladaria says that part of the reason for the change has to do with "the development of more efficacious detention systems that guarantee the due protection of citizens," with worries about "the defective selectivity of the criminal justice system and . . . the possibility of judicial error," with the judgment that "modern society possesses more efficient detention systems, [so that] the death penalty becomes unnecessary as protection for the life of innocent people," and so on.[32]

These are statements concerning *matters of empirical fact* about which churchmen have no more expertise than they have about stamp collecting, electrical engineering, or gardening. They are *inherently prudential* rather than doctrinal or moral in

31   "New Revision of Number 2267 of the *Catechism of the Catholic Church* on the Death Penalty—Rescriptum 'Ex Audientia Ss.mi,'" www.vatican.va/roman_curia/congregations/cfaith/ladaria-ferrer/documents/rc_con_cfaith_doc_20180801_catechismo-penadimorte_en.html.

32   "Letter to the Bishops regarding the new revision of number 2267 of the Catechism of the Catholic Church on the death penalty," www.vatican.va/roman_curia/congregations/cfaith/ladaria-ferrer/documents/rc_con_cfaith_doc_20180801_lettera-vescovi-penadimorte_en.html.

nature. And if these prudential judgments are mistaken (and in our book, Bessette and I argue that they are mistaken), then the justification for the conclusion that the death penalty ought entirely to be abolished is thereby undermined.

It is also worth noting that Ladaria's letter urges civil authorities "to *encourage the creation of conditions that allow for* the elimination of the death penalty where it is still in effect" (emphasis added). That implies that it may not in fact practically be possible to eliminate capital punishment everywhere. And it therefore implies in turn that abolishing capital punishment is *not* an imperative that follows from moral principle alone, but rather follows only *when* empirical conditions allow for it. But whether such conditions allow for it is, in the nature of the case, a prudential matter.

All things considered, then, while the *rhetoric* of the revision to the Catechism is certainly stronger than that of John Paul II, the actual *substance* of the teaching is essentially the same. Hence, as I argued above, if the 2004 Ratzinger memorandum applied to John Paul II's version of the Catechism, then why would it not apply as well to Francis's version?

Nor, contrary to what Fastiggi seems to think, do Cardinal Ladaria's comments about the Ratzinger memorandum show otherwise. These comments were made in a 2021 letter to Archbishop Gomez concerning the USCCB's intention of drafting guidelines for dealing with "Catholics in public office who support legislation allowing abortion, euthanasia, or other moral evils" yet want to receive Holy Communion.[33] Because the 2004 Ratzinger memorandum addressed precisely this issue, it comes up in the exchange between Gomez and Ladaria. As Fastiggi says, Ladaria does indeed note that the memorandum "was not intended for publication" but "was a private communication addressed to the bishops" (and Ladaria says "*the* bishops"—not, contrary to what Fastiggi implies, "*some* bishops").

Contrary to what Fastiggi insinuates, however, the fact that Ratzinger's memorandum was originally intended to be private is irrelevant to the issue at hand. For one thing, the memorandum was still not merely the private opinion of Cardinal Ratzinger; it was an official act *of the Prefect of the CDF*, acting to clarify *for the U. S. bishops* the bearing of Catholic doctrine on a matter of current controversy. The fact that the memorandum was meant for the eyes of the bishops rather than the general public doesn't change that fact or somehow magically render it irrelevant to understanding John Paul II's teaching on capital punishment.

Furthermore, Fastiggi fails to mention two crucial aspects of Ladaria's letter to Gomez. First, Ladaria does not say or in any way imply that the 2004 memorandum has been superseded or is otherwise irrelevant. On the contrary, he tells Gomez that the principles set out by Ratzinger in the memorandum "may be of assistance in the preparation of the draft of your document"! That is to

---

33   The letter may be found at https://wherepeteris.com/wp-content/uploads/2022/07/Ladaria-Letter-to-Gomez.pdf.

say, far from telling Gomez and the U. S. bishops that they should now ignore the 2004 memorandum, he explicitly says that they may make use of it.

Second, Ladaria in no way qualifies this advice in light of the 2018 revision to the Catechism. Indeed, *the topic of capital punishment is not mentioned at all* in Ladaria's letter to Gomez. If Fastiggi were correct, you would expect Ladaria to say that, in light of the revision, the U. S. bishops should no longer use Ratzinger's 2004 memorandum, or at least no longer use the part of it that deals with capital punishment. But not only does Ladaria not say that, he says that *they may* use the memorandum, while saying nothing at all about the topic of capital punishment. That would be a remarkable omission if the 2004 memorandum's teaching on capital punishment really were a dead letter in light of the 2018 revision to the Catechism.

If anything, then, Ladaria's 2021 letter supports rather than undermines the argument I've been defending. Once again, what Fastiggi supposes *helps* his case actually *hurts* his case.

ODDS AND ENDS

As I have noted already, I argue that the ordinary Magisterium of the Church has taught *infallibly* that capital punishment is not intrinsically wrong. Fastiggi does not answer those arguments, but in support of the claim that this has not been infallibly taught, he directs his readers to two articles by Brugger at *Public Discourse*.[34] But I answered Brugger in my own series of articles at *Public Discourse*.[35] Fastiggi also commends to his readers two articles by Finnis.[36] But I answered Finnis too.[37] And Fastiggi calls his readers' attention to two *Catholic World Report* articles wherein he has criticized my views.[38] But I have answered those articles as well.[39] I have also criticized Fastiggi's views in two further articles.[40] I urge

---

34 E. Christian Brugger, "Capital Punishment Is Intrinsically Wrong: A Reply to Feser and Bessette," *Public Discourse*, October 22, 2017; "Catholic Tradition, St. John Paul II, and the Death Penalty," *Public Discourse*, October 23, 2017.

35 Edward Feser, "Traditional Catholic Doctrine on Capital Punishment is Irreversible: A Reply to E. Christian Brugger," *Public Discourse*, November 19, 2017; "St. John Paul II Did Not Change Catholic Teaching on Capital Punishment: A Reply to E. Christian Brugger," *Public Discourse*, November 20, 2017.

36 John Finnis, "Intentional Killing Is Always Wrong: The Development Initiated by Pius XII, Made by John Paul II, and Repeated by Francis," *Public Discourse*, August 22, 2018; "The Church Could Teach That Capital Punishment Is Inherently Wrong," *Public Discourse*, August 23, 2018.

37 See the two mentioned earlier: Feser, "The Church Cannot Teach That Capital Punishment is Inherently Wrong" and "Unnatural Lawyering."

38 Robert Fastiggi, "Capital Punishment and the Papal Magisterium: A Response to Dr. Edward Feser," *Catholic World Report*, October 24, 2017; "Is There Really a Definitive Teaching of the Church on Capital Punishment?," *Catholic World Report*, November 10, 2017.

39 Edward Feser, "Catholic Theologians Must Set an Example of Intellectual Honesty: A Reply to Prof. Robert Fastiggi," *Catholic World Report*, October 30, 2017; "Yes, Traditional Church Teaching on Capital Punishment Is Definitive," *Catholic World Report*, November 21, 2017.

40 Edward Feser, "Prof. Fastiggi's pretzel logic," January 25, 2018; "Fastiggi on the revision to the Catechism (Updated)," September 20, 2019.

Fastiggi's readers to remember that there are two sides to every debate, and that they should read and consider *what I have actually said*, and not only what Fastiggi, Brugger, Finnis, Hart, et al. *claim* I have said.

In part 4 of his series, Fastiggi asks, rhetorically: "Is fidelity to the death penalty more important than fidelity to the Magisterium?" But this too attacks a straw man, because nobody claims in the first place that fidelity to the death penalty is more important than fidelity to the Magisterium. In reality, the critics of the revision to the Catechism are no less loyal to the Magisterium than Fastiggi is. But they insist that loyalty to the Magisterium involves more than loyalty to Pope Francis alone (even if it does, of course, involve that) – it involves loyalty to the consistent teaching of Scripture, the Fathers and Doctors of the Church, and all previous popes. And they insist too that loyalty to the Magisterium is perfectly consistent with the respectful criticism of problematic magisterial statements that *the Magisterium itself acknowledges to be permissible* in *Donum Veritatis*. Fastiggi has every right to criticize the views of the critics of the revision. But he has no right to pretend to be "more loyal than thou."

6

Power versus Authority in the Church[1]

ERIC SAMMONS

T
HE VATICAN DIRECTIVE THAT PARISHES CAN'T ADVER-
tise their scheduled traditional Latin Masses was met with widespread
mockery on social media. For anyone who has worked in a parish, the
idea of a curial bureaucrat in Rome trying to tell Mrs. Jones at St Joseph parish
in Des Moines what she can put in the bulletin is laughable and ridiculous. Heck,
some pastors can't even control what goes in the bulletin!

But behind the mockery is a deep insight into the differences between power
and authority, even though in today's world these two distinct ideas are often
muddled. This confusion has led to profound misunderstandings among Catholics
as to the nature of authority in the Church.

Unfortunately today, many Church leaders have power behind their commands,
but not authority. They know that they can command obedience from most
Catholics to their directives, and so they exercise power for their own sakes or for
the sake of their ideology, instead of for the common good. Thus, the German
bishops who want to normalize gay marriage might have the power to do so
among German Catholics, but they do not have the authority. The U. S. bishops
who allow pro-abortion politicians like Joe Biden to receive Communion might
have the power to do so, but they do not have the authority. Cardinal Cupich
might have the power to abolish *ad orientem* worship, but he does not have the
authority. Pope Francis might have the power to abrogate the Latin Mass, but he
does not have the authority.

We must always keep in mind this distinction between power and authority.
Former Cardinal Theodore McCarrick for decades had the support of high-ranking
Church officials, even though many knew of his monstrous misdeeds. Why?
Because he had immense *power* in the Church, even after he was retired and had
little to no *authority*. If Cardinal Cupich bans *ad orientem* worship, he might not
have that authority under Church (or divine) law, but he can make life miserable
to any priest who dares disobey. That's *power*.

Power comes from below—it is only possible if it has consent (whether forced
or given freely) from the people under control. Joseph Stalin had power in the
Soviet Union because no one below him dared resist him. Mikhail Gorbachev

---

1   First published at *Crisis Magazine* on December 30, 2021.

also had power, until the people of the Soviet Union no longer gave it to him. Authority, on the other hand, comes from above, ultimately from God. A father or a bishop or even a Catholic monarch has authority in certain spheres given to him by God for the common good of his family, diocese, or kingdom, respectively. Those under authority are obliged to follow the superior's commands, not because of their consent, but because the authority ultimately comes from the One who has true authority over all.

Due to the Fall, power can become virtually unlimited in this world, through force or influence. What could Stalin *not* do during his reign? A person with power also usually wants to acquire more power. As Lord Acton noted, "power corrupts; absolute power corrupts absolutely." Being able to tell people what to do can be intoxicating. Authority, on the other hand, is always limited in scope. Only God has unlimited authority, and He only delegates aspects of his authority to individuals as needed to bring people closer to Him.

It's important to note that this limitation applies to *everyone* with earthly—including ecclesial—authority, for only God Himself has full authority over man, as St Thomas Aquinas notes: "Man is subject to God simply as regards all things, both internal and external, wherefore he is bound to obey Him in all things. On the other hand, inferiors are not subject to their superiors in all things, but only in certain things and in a particular way." [2] Vatican I recognized these limitations in office of the papacy as well. It states:

> For the Holy Spirit was promised to the successors of Peter not so that they might, by his revelation, make known some new doctrine, but that, by his assistance, they might religiously guard and faithfully expound the revelation or deposit of faith transmitted by the apostles.

Legitimate papal authority, in other words, is exercised when the pope "religiously guards and faithfully expounds the revelation or deposit of faith transmitted by the apostles." But it's an illegitimate exercise of power when he tries to "make known some new doctrine." Even a pope has limited *authority* in the Church, although in modern practice he has almost unlimited *power*. And if a pope has only limited authority, then surely so do bishops and priests as well.

Problems arise when leaders mistake their God-given authority for power. They abuse their authority because they have the power to get away with it. So the abusive father is able to command his children far beyond his authority, because his children are unable to resist him. He has power over them. A bishop decides he can do whatever he wants—reassign priests he doesn't like, use diocesan funds for private jet trips—because he has the power to do so.

Our Lord strongly condemned this abuse of authority through the illegitimate exercise of raw power: "You know that the princes of the Gentiles lord it over them; and they that are the greater, exercise power upon them. It shall not be

---

2   *Summa theologiae* [hereafter *ST*] II-II, Q. 105, art. 5.

so among you: but whosoever will be the greater among you, let him be your minister: and he that will be first among you, shall be your servant" (Mt 20:25–27). True authority, which comes from God, is always put in the service of those under the ruler. St Gregory the Great well understood this, saying that "whoever calls himself universal bishop, or desires this title, is, by his pride, the precursor to the Antichrist" and instead called his role as pope "the servant of the servants of God."

It is also the lack of distinction between power and authority that often confuses today's debates over obedience. Most faithful Catholics instinctively know that obedience is an important and necessary virtue. But when a Church leader issues a questionable directive, the entire focus of discussion seems to be on those under his authority and their need to obey. But there is little to no discussion of whether the Church leader is exercising his authority or simply flexing his raw power. In fact, quiet obedience to false directives increases his power, leading to more false directives in the future.

How do we distinguish between commands given from legitimate authority and commands pushed through from the exercise of power? The line between authority and power comes in the nature of the command given. The father who tells his six-year-old son to eat his vegetables is exercising his legitimate authority as the provider of his family. But the father who tells his son he's actually a girl because he likes to dance is forcing his power over him. The first command is for the good of the son, the second is harmful. Thus, legitimate commands are those within the ruler's sphere of authority, and are issued for the good of those under his command. Anything else is an exercise of (mere) power.

The Catholic Church is suffering a crisis of authority today, not because she lacks legitimate authority, but because too many of her leaders are drunk with power. Instead of using their God-given authority for the common good — our salvation — they are enforcing their wills by raw power. Catholics need to accept the hierarchy's authority while rejecting its misuse of power. Only then will today's clericalist imbalance be restored to something more in line with Our Lord's desire that our leaders be servants who inspire and lead us, not dictators who revel in their own power.

7

The Catholic Church
and the Rule of Law[1]

JOHN LAMONT

T HE TERRIBLE CRIMES COMMITTED AGAINST MINORS by Catholic priests and religious have constituted a dreadful crisis for the Catholic Church over a period of many years. There is however one aspect of this crisis that has not attracted all the attention it should have.[2] This is the failure of the rule of law in the Church with respect to these crimes. Until November 27, 1983, the law in force in the Latin Church was the 1917 Code of Canon Law. Canon 2359 §2 of this code decrees that "if clerics have committed an offense against the sixth commandment of the Decalogue with minors under sixteen years of age . . . they shall be suspended, declared infamous, deprived of every office, benefice, dignity, or position that they may hold, and in the most grievous cases they shall be deposed." This canon declares that sexual abuse of minors must be punished by specific penalties. If it had been enforced, the grave crisis of sexual abuse in the Church would never have occurred, because the key to this crisis—the transferring of guilty priests to new locations where they could abuse again—was ruled out by the penalties imposed. But at some point after the Second World War, this canon ceased to be applied. Clerics who sexually abused minors were not canonically tried and punished, regardless of the severity of their crimes and the strength of the evidence against them. Nor were bishops ever punished for failing to enforce the canonical penalties against sexual abuse of minors, although such punishment was required by the 1983 Code.[3] A number of proximate reasons have been offered for this state of affairs—aversion to legalism, lack of understanding of canon law on the part of the responsible authorities—but none of these proximate reasons could have obtained without an underlying indifference to the enforcement of the law.

---

1 A revised version of a lecture given to the Society of St Hugh of Cluny in New York on Friday, April 4, 2014.

2 An exception to this lack of discussion is the *Report by Commission of Investigation into Catholic Archdiocese of Dublin*, November 29, 2009, commonly known as the "Murphy Report" as the commission was chaired by Justice Yvonne Murphy. The Commission asserted that "in practice, it appears to the Commission that, for a significant part of the period covered by the Commission, canon law was used selectively when dealing with offending clergy, to the benefit of the cleric and the consequent disadvantage of his victims. The Commission has not encountered a case where canon law was invoked as a means of doing justice to victims" (57–58).

3 See can. 1389 §2 in the 1983 Code.

It is true that the 1983 Code of Canon Law gravely weakened the law forbidding sexual abuse of minors, but it still required such abuse to be punished with a "just penalty." The weakening of the enforcement of canon law on pedophilia cannot be reasonably blamed on the 1983 Code, because the law had already ceased to be enforced by the time that code was promulgated. The law was weakened because Church authorities no longer wished or attempted to penalize the sexual abuse of minors; it was not that these authorities stopped penalizing pedophilia because of changes in the law.

Of course, no legal code is ever perfectly enforced. Every legal system suffers from inefficiencies, failures, and unjust favoritism for the powerful. It remains true however that the rule of law, in order to exist, must be universal. It requires at least some will and effort on the part of the ruling power to enforce the legal code *as a whole*. If the enforcement of an important law that is crucial for the well-being of the community is voluntarily and completely abandoned, this is not simply a matter of laws being broken, something that will always happen. It is rather a matter of there being no effort to stop them being broken on the part of authority; of no one in authority considering that the lack of enforcement of these laws is especially unusual, let alone a grave evil in itself; of there being no identification of the lack of enforcement of the laws as a principal reason for the flourishing of the evils they are designed to suppress; of there being no call for the enforcement of the law as the proper and indispensable path to the suppression of these evils. All these conditions obtained in the case of the lack of enforcement of canon law on sexual abuse, which is such a grave, widespread, and longstanding problem that it suffices on its own to establish that the rule of law does not exist in the Catholic Church. This does not mean that law is simply absent, a situation that is not really possible in any complex society. It means that law does not *rule*; it exists, but it is subject to the will of the people in charge of the society, rather than vice versa.

It would be possible to show that the same thing has happened in other areas of canon law, but that would take us too far afield; the gravity of this problem on its own suffices to establish that the rule of law does not exist in the Catholic Church.

In some cases, the process of corruption has gone so far that we can speak of a rule of criminals instead of the rule of law. In the case of the diocese of Ballarat in Australia, for example, there have been 130 claims and substantiated complaints of child sexual abuse since 1980. The Christian Brothers in Ballarat sexually abused 853 children, with an average age of thirteen, and at least thirty of their victims have since committed suicide. Fifty-eight monks and thirteen other personnel from the Benedictine abbey at Collegeville in Minnesota have been credibly accused of sexual abuse. The Norbertine abbey of St Norbert in Wisconsin has admitted that twenty-two of its members sexually abused minors. Every effort was made by these institutions to protect the criminal offenders and to silence or discredit their accusers. In cases like these, which are far from rare in the Catholic

Church, we are no longer dealing with religious associations, but with criminal associations passing themselves off as religious associations. The present discussion has the object of investigating how this extraordinary situation came into being.

The essence of the explanation that will be proposed is that the rule of law came to be abandoned because of the adoption of a tyrannical understanding of authority and a slavish understanding of obedience in the Latin rite of the Catholic Church. A tyrannical understanding of authority considers the rightful exercise of authority to lie purely in the will and command of the superior, and the corresponding servile understanding of obedience sees obedience as consisting purely in conformity to the will of the superior, rather than in obedience to the law and the underlying common good that produces, defines, and limits the power of a ruler. These understandings have rendered the idea of the rule of law in the Church undesirable and indeed incomprehensible for the clerics who have the charge of ruling the Church, and to some extent for all Catholics.

An external cause influencing the acceptance of a tyrannical notion of authority was the growth of absolutist conceptions of the state in the late Middle Ages and the Renaissance, a growth itself fostered by the revival of Roman law, with its absolutist conception of the supreme ruler as himself above the law. The need for the Catholic Church to ally itself with Catholic absolutist states during the Reformation impeded any criticism of such a conception of authority, and the formation of the outlook of Catholics by these states fostered acceptance of this conception.

The most important causes were however ones that were internal to the Church. These can be divided into philosophical and practical causes. The philosophical causes were the development of notions of law, freedom, justice, and authority that had their roots in the Middle Ages, but that came to be treated as undoubted axioms by the theologians of the Counter-Reformation. These notions and their consequences have already been discussed by scholars, most notably by M.-M. Labourdette, Michel Villey, and Servais Pinckaers.[4] An outline of the findings of these scholars is necessary for our topic, although unavoidably inadequate. Their basic finding is that St Thomas's modified Aristotelian understanding of these

---

4   M.-M. Labourdette's thought is to be found in his *Cours de théologie morale*, unfortunately unpublished due to his having fallen afoul of the leadership of his order because of his traditional theological views; the author of this paper was fortunate enough to come across a copy of this valuable work in a recycling bin in an underground car park. For an account of Labourdette's fate, see Aidan Nichols, "Thomism and the Nouvelle Théologie," *The Thomist* 64 (2000): 1–19. Michel Villey's main works are *La formation de la pensée juridique moderne* (Paris: Éditions Montchrestien, 1968; repr. Paris: Presses Universitaires de France, 2003); *Le droit et les droits de l'homme* (Paris: PUF, 1983; 3rd ed., 1998); *Seize essais de philosophie du droit, dont un sur la crise universitaire* (Paris: Dalloz, 1969); *Questions de saint Thomas sur le droit et la politique, ou, Le bon usage des dialogues* (Paris: PUF, 1987). His work has not been translated into English. For Servais Pinckaers, see *The Sources of Christian Ethics*, trans. Mary Thomas Noble (Washington, DC: Catholic University of America Press, 1995). For an account of the thought of these scholars on these topics, see John Lamont, "Conscience, Freedom, Rights: Idols of the Enlightenment Religion," *The Thomist* 73/2 (2009): 169–239, and "In Defence of Michel Villey," in *Truth and Faith in Ethics*, ed. Hayden Ramsay, St Andrews Studies in Philosophy and Public Life (Exeter: Imprint Academic, 2011).

notions was rejected, and replaced by quite different views that were largely of Sco-tist and nominalist origin. To understand these views and their shortcomings, we will proceed by describing them and contrasting them with St Thomas's positions.

It is somewhat paradoxical to say that the Scotist conception of freedom of the will as consisting in liberty of indifference was a fundamental basis for the development of a tyrannical notion of authority, but it is nonetheless true. In St Thomas's thought, a rational action or a voluntary action—the two expressions mean the same thing—is an action that proceeds from knowledge of the good sought in the action. Since the good is the ultimate motivating attraction behind such action, it follows that there is something that the will wills of necessity. This is the good—the final cause—of the agent, a final cause that corresponds to the agent's essential nature. All goods are sought for the sake of attaining the agent's final end. Of course, not all goods that are sought do really offer this attainment. Except in the case of rational beings who are enjoying the beatific vision, it is possible for the practical intellect to be ultimately directed towards a good or goods that do not in fact realize the agent's final end. However, even these goods are sought because the agent considers them to offer ultimate and complete satisfaction, and no good that does not have some relation to the actual final end of man can be sought voluntarily. So it is the case that the will wills something of necessity. It always wills to attain complete satisfaction; it always wills things that resemble to some extent what will actually satisfy; and if it enjoys the beatific vision, it always wills its real ultimate end, which is enjoyment of the vision of God.

Beginning with Duns Scotus, a different conception of freedom of the will came to be accepted by Catholic theologians. This is the conception of freedom as consisting in liberty of indifference. According to this conception, an act is free only if the agent has it in his power to either will or not will to do it. It follows from this account of freedom that there is nothing that the will wills of necessity. This means that obedience must necessarily involve some surrender of the will. Whenever a command is given, there must always be the possibility of the person commanded choosing to do otherwise; if this possibility is lacking, obedience to the command is not free, and thus is not really obedience.

The adoption of liberty of indifference led to a fundamental change in the understanding of law. St Thomas's claim that the good is willed necessarily is expressed by his description of the first principle of practical reason, which is "Do good and avoid evil." The practical reason is the rational faculty that gives rise to voluntary actions, as opposed to the theoretical reason which produces the beliefs assented to by the intellect. The first principle of practical reason is thus the principle that directs all voluntary action whatsoever. Because it directs all action to pursue good and avoid evil, it expresses the fundamental orientation of the will towards the good, and indeed defines what it is to have a will on St Thom-as's view. It does not suffice to direct all action towards objects that are entirely good, unless the agent has a direct and certain knowledge of the good for man, because such a direct and certain knowledge of the good is necessary to remove all attraction from options that are good in some respect but not good absolutely speaking. That is why the principle does not exclude the possibility of sin; only those who enjoy the beatific vision have the direct and certain knowledge of the good that can exclude wrongdoing. But it means that even sinful actions are not chosen because they are sinful, but for the sake of some good that is believed to characterize them.

However, if the will possesses liberty of indifference, St Thomas's account of the first principle of practical reason cannot be correct. Its directive to seek the ultimate good of man cannot be the principle for all voluntary action, because the will wills nothing of necessity, even the ultimate good of the agent. The meaning of this principle was therefore changed by the theologians of the Counter-Reformation. Instead of being the first principle for all voluntary action, it became the rule governing all moral action. As a result, the question of why we should obey this principle can arise. The answer can be found in Suárez; we should obey it because we are commanded to by our ultimate superior, God. Suárez did not go as far as William of Ockham, who held that God's command was the only feature that determined the goodness of good actions and the badness of bad actions. He thought that nature on its own determined what was good, but that this determination did not suffice for obligation. The fact that something is good provides a reason for doing it, in his view, but still leaves open the question "why do we have an obligation to do what is good?" Suárez thought that the only answer to this question—the extra factor needed to transform mere goodness into obligation—was a divine command. Because only God's authority creates an obligation to obey, all other authorities derive their right to obedience from a divine command to obey them. St Thomas held that we obey both human and divine authority because it is good to do so. This is impossible in Suárez's system.

We can see how in this scheme obligation, and hence obedience, are not ultimately rooted in the will of the individual obeying. Obedience cannot be an implementation of the fundamental orientation of the will towards happiness, as it is for St Thomas in the case of a good person who obeys as an act of justice. It must be an external imposition from some other will. Since rights consist in an entitlement to act freely within some sphere, obedience and rights become mutually exclusive—as do obedience and freedom, contrary to the idea that God's service is perfect freedom. We are in a universe where the will and freedom of man and God are by nature mutually exclusive—what God gains, man must lose. Admittedly the natural good is not denied in this system, as it is for Ockham, but the element of authority in this system—the element from which the duty of obedience emerges—is solely based on conformity to the will of the superior. Obedience thus essentially consists in submission to the will of another.

We can see the assumption of this fundamental antagonism between the divine and human wills in the famous ascetic counsel of St John of the Cross:

Strive always to prefer, not that which is easiest, but that which is most
   difficult;
Not that which is most delectable, but that which is most unpleasing;
Not that which gives most pleasure, but rather that which gives least;
Not that which is restful, but that which is wearisome;
Not that which is consolation, but rather that which is disconsolateness;
Not that which is greatest, but that which is least;
Not that which is loftiest and most precious, but that which is lowest
   and most despised;
Not that which is a desire for anything, but that which is a desire for nothing;
Strive to go about seeking not the best of temporal things, but the worst.

Literally interpreted, this spiritual counsel can only be suitable for devils and souls
in hell, who of course will not and cannot avail themselves of it. That is because
unless one's will is completely fixed on evil to the exclusion of any good at all,
as happens only with damned souls, on at least some occasions one will prefer
doing what is good to doing what is bad. Under such circumstances, doing what
is less pleasant rather than doing what is more pleasant will mean acting badly,
and following St John of the Cross's counsel will lead one to sin. The reason why
St John of the Cross ignores this obvious failing in his position—and why this
failing is scarcely ever given as an objection to his ascetic doctrine—is that he
and his readers have taken for granted the fundamental opposition between the
human and the divine will that is implied by liberty of indifference. His teaching
shows the influence of this conception of the will on the Counter-Reformation
outlook in general.

Connected with this transformation of the idea of obligation is the transformation of the understanding of rights that has been investigated by Michel
Villey. For St Thomas, the term *ius*—later to be translated as "right"—refers to
a thing; to a certain distribution of material or other goods and evils, which
conforms to the demands of justice. These demands are determined by the just
proportion set out by Aristotle in Book 5 of the *Nicomachean Ethics*, in which
members of a society receive the rewards and punishments that are due to them.
Human societies are natural entities with natural components—such as families, property, laws, religion—whose function is to cooperate in attaining their
good. The contribution of members of society to the whole whether for good
or for evil, a contribution constituted by their place and activity in these natural
structures, determines what is due to them. Justice is the virtue of rendering
to everyone their due—goods, obligations, or punishments, as the case may be;
and this due is a relation between persons and things, a relation that justice
preserves or brings into being.

This understanding of justice fell afoul of William of Ockham's nominalist metaphysics. Ockham held that only individual substances exist. In consequence he rejected the reality of relations, and the reality of entities that were

not substances, but had substances as their components. The objective right of
Aristotle and St Thomas is kind of relation, and the human society that founds
this objective right is a whole that is made up of substances but is not itself a
substance, so objective right could not be accommodated in Ockham's philosophy.
In its place he introduced what Villey calls a subjective right. This is a monadic
property of a single individual — a particular sphere of action in which a person
is entitled to act just as he pleases without interference from anyone. It is a scope
of action for the individual's liberty of indifference. Although Ockham's nomi-
nalism did not meet with complete acceptance, his understanding of subjective
right eventually achieved a complete victory — at least in theory — over the notion
of objective right. This meaning, which Villey terms "subjective right," came to
displace the older meaning of *ius* as objective right. With this displacement came
a fundamental redefinition of justice. This virtue came at first partially and then
completely to be understood as respect for the subjective rights of individuals.
Your rights are the area within which your will can operate freely; a constraint
on your range of choices, conversely, is a constraint on your rights. Suárez, who
was the principal Catholic legal theorist of the Counter-Reformation, defined
rights as subjective rights, and understood laws as limitations on these rights that
are based on the commands of the legislator. Here we have reproduced in the
sphere of law and justice the competition between two mutually exclusive wills,
that of the superior and that of the subordinate, in which what is gained by the
one is lost by the other. What has been contributed by the replacement of objective right by subjective right is the elimination of the competing understanding
of justice as based on desert, and as distinct from the command of a superior.

The Counter-Reformation understandings of will, freedom, authority, and
law thus both permitted and fostered the emergence of a tyrannical notion of
authority and a slavish notion of obedience, whereas St Thomas's understanding
of these things firmly excluded them.

However, in order for the tendencies of these philosophical positions to have a
deep effect on the Church, they needed to be embodied in practice. This embod-
iment took place in the conception of obedience that came to be adopted by the
Jesuits, and in the methods by which this conception of obedience came to be
inculcated and enforced. The source and best expression of this conception is to
be found in the writings of St Ignatius of Loyola, particularly in the Constitutions
of the Society and in his letter on obedience written to the Jesuits of Portugal in
1553. Its key elements are the following.

1. The claim that the commands of the superior have the force of divine
commands, and should be treated as divine commands — provided, of course,
that obeying them would not be manifestly sinful; this qualification should
always be understood as applying to the Jesuit conception of obedience. St Ignatius asserted: "The superior is to be obeyed not because he is prudent, or good,
or qualified by any other gift of God, but because he holds the place and the

authority of God, as Eternal Truth has said: He who hears you, hears me; and he who rejects you, rejects me [Lk 10:16]." "In all the things into which obedience can with charity be extended, we should be ready to receive its command just as if it were coming from Christ our Savior, since we are practicing the obedience to one in His place and because of love and reverence for Him."[5] This position seems to have received general acceptance in part because of acceptance of the fallacious inference from the premise that God commands us to obey the orders of our superiors, to the conclusion that the orders of our superiors are commandments of God.

2. The claim that the mere execution of the order of a superior is the lowest degree of obedience, and does not merit the name of obedience or constitute an exercise of the virtue of obedience.

3. The claim that in order to merit the name of virtue, an exercise of obedience should attain the second level of obedience, which consists in not only doing what the superior orders, but conforming one's will to that of the superior, so that one not only wills to obey an order, but wills that that particular order should have been given — simply because the superior willed it.

4. The claim that the third and highest degree of obedience consists in conforming not only one's will but also one's intellect to the order of the superior, so that one not only wills that an order should have been given, but actually believes that the order was the right order to give — simply because the superior (it is supposed) believes this himself. "But he who aims at making an entire and perfect oblation of himself, in addition to his will, must offer his understanding, which is a further and the highest degree of obedience. He must not only will, but he must think the same as the superior, submitting his own judgment to that of the superior, so far as a devout will can bend the understanding."[6]

5. The claim that in the highest and thus most meritorious degree of obedience, the follower has no more will of his own in obeying than an inanimate object. "Every one of those who live under obedience ought to allow himself to be carried and directed by Divine Providence through the agency of the superior as if he were a lifeless body which allows itself to be carried to any place and to be treated in any manner desired, or as if he were an old man's staff which serves in any place and in any manner whatsoever in which the holder wishes to use it."[7]

6. The claim that the sacrifice of will and intellect involved in this form of obedience is the highest form of sacrifice possible, because it offers to God the highest human faculties, viz., the intellect and the will.[8]

---

5   St Ignatius of Loyola, *Constitutions of the Society of Jesus*, part VI, ch. 1, in George E. Ganss SJ, *The Constitutions of the Society of Jesus* (St Louis: The Institute of Jesuit Sources, 1970), 247-48.

6   St Ignatius of Loyola, Letter 3304 to the members of the Society in Portugal (the "Letter on Obedience"), March 26, 1553, in *Letters of St Ignatius of Loyola*, trans. William J. Young, SJ (Chicago: Loyola University Press, 1959), 290.

7   *Constitutions*, part VI, ch. 1, in Ganss, *Constitutions*, 248-49.

8   St Ignatius of Loyola, *Letters*, 290-91.

Now because this disposition of will in man is of so great worth, so
also is the offering of it, when by obedience it is offered to his Creator
and Lord.... There are, however, many instances where the evidence
of the known truth is not coercive and it can, with the help of the will,
favor one side or the other. When this happens every truly obedient
man should conform his thought to the thought of the superior.

And this is certain, since obedience is a holocaust in which the whole
man without the slightest reserve is offered in the fire of charity to his
Creator and Lord through the hands of His ministers. And since it is a
complete surrender of himself by which a man dispossesses himself to
be possessed and governed by Divine Providence through his superiors,
it cannot be held that obedience consists merely in the execution, by
carrying the command into effect and in the will's acquiescence, but
also in the judgment, which must approve the superior's command,
insofar, as has been said, as it can, through the energy of the will,
bring itself to this.[9]

This claim is presented as following the tradition of the Church on obedience.
The innovation of St Ignatius can, however, be seen by contrasting his position
with that of St Gregory the Great. In his *Moralia*, St Gregory states that the merit
of obedience lies in sacrificing one's proud self-will. St Thomas makes a similar
point by describing the merit of obedience as consisting in sacrificing one's proper
will, i.e., one's will as functioning independently of God. St Ignatius, however,
makes it clear that it is not self-will, but the entire human faculty of will itself,
that is to be sacrificed; one's self-will could not be described as "of great worth."
This is a sacrifice in the sense of an abandonment and a destruction, since it
involves handing over one's will to the will of another human being. Underlying
this claim, of course, is the presumption of liberty of indifference, according to
which one's will necessarily functions independently of God. This presumption
is something that St Ignatius would have learned from his studies as a basic
axiom. His conception of the sacrifice of the will was simply an application of
this philosophical position to the religious life.

Some expositions of the Ignatian conception of obedience described obedience to an order that one suspects but is not certain to be illicit as an especially
high and praiseworthy form of obedience. This statement about the exceptional
merit of obeying orders that are morally dubious is made in St Ignatius's letter
150. The letter was in fact written for him by Fr Polanco, his secretary and close
collaborator who was responsible for composing much of the Constitutions; but
since it went out under St Ignatius's signature, it benefited from his authority.[10]

The character of the Society of Jesus was itself an important influence on the
Jesuit understanding of obedience. Monastic obedience had always been strict, and

---

9   Ibid.
10 See B. Lavaud, "L'obéissance religieuse d'après la correspondance de saint Ignace de Loyola,"
La vie spirituelle (October 1929): 87.

examples of monastic obedience were plentifully used by writers to illustrate the virtue of obedience as the Jesuits conceived of it. But these illustrations ignored the fact that monastic communities were governed by detailed Rules — those of St Basil, St Augustine, or St Benedict. The authority of a monastic superior was limited by the rule of the community, and had the purpose of bringing about the following of the rule. It was obedience to the rule, not to the superior as such, that was the fundamental tool of monastic perfection, and the object of monastic obedience. But the Society of Jesus had no rule. The decisions of the Jesuit superior were explicitly intended to take the place of the rule of life of the monastic community as the object of obedience and the path for spiritual perfection for the Jesuit. The primacy of law that was characteristic of monastic obedience was thus lost.

An obvious objection to the Jesuit conception of obedience was soon raised. It was remarked that acceptance of blind obedience would mean that heretical priests and bishops could easily lead their people into rejection of the faith. St Robert Bellarmine's response to this objection was that it was not a real possibility, because the preaching of heresy by bishops or priests would promptly be suppressed by the higher authority of the Holy See. This response of course required the pope himself to be incapable of heresy. The theory that the pope was not only infallible in his formal definitions of faith, but personally immune from heresy in virtue of his office, was accordingly first proposed in the Counter-Reformation, and argued for by Bellarmine. The claim that the pope was not only infallible in his formal definitions of faith, but personally immune from heresy in virtue of his office — first proposed by Albert Pighius in 1538 — was accordingly argued for by Bellarmine.[11] This claim met with opposition from sixteenth-century theologians, most notably Melchior Cano, Domingo de Soto, and Domingo Bañez, but in the seventeenth century it came to be widely accepted. Suárez upheld it, as did St Alphonsus Liguori, who denied that the pope could be a public or even an occult heretic.[12]

Bellarmine's position on this issue was discussed by Bishop Vincent Gasser in his official *relatio* to the First Vatican Council, in which he explained the sense in which papal infallibility was to be defined in the proposed dogmatic constitution *Pastor Aeternus*. Gasser asserted:

> As far as the doctrine set forth in the Draft goes, the deputation is unjustly accused of wanting to raise an extreme opinion, viz., that of Albert Pighius, to the dignity of a dogma. For the opinion of Pighius, which Bellarmine indeed calls pious and probable, was that the pope, as an individual person or a private teacher, was able to err from a type of ignorance but was never able to fall into heresy or teach heresy . . . . This is clear from the very words of Bellarmine . . . who, in book 4, chapter 6, pronounces

---

11   See St Robert Bellarmine, *De Romano Pontifice*, Bk. 4, ch. 6.
12   See *Dogmatic Works of St Alphonsus Maria de Liguori* (Turin, 1848), vol. 8, p. 720.

on the opinion of Pighius in the following words: "It can be believed probably and piously that the supreme Pontiff is not only not able to err as Pontiff but that even as a particular person he is not able to be heretical, by pertinaciously believing something contrary to the faith."[13]

Gasser's emphatic denial that a definition of the personal immunity of the pope from heresy was being proposed is worth quoting at length:

> Before I end this general *relatio*, I should respond to the most grave objection that has been made from this podium, viz., that we wish to make the extreme opinion of a certain school of theology a dogma of Catholic faith. Indeed this is a very grave objection, and when I heard it from the mouth of an outstanding and most esteemed speaker, I hung my head sadly and pondered well before speaking. Good God, have you so confused our minds and our tongues that we are misrepresented as promoting the elevation of the extreme opinion of a certain school of theology to the dignity of dogma?[14]

The *relatio* of Bishop Gasser provides the official interpretation of the meaning of the conciliar definition of papal infallibility. His disavowal of the thesis of the personal immunity of the pope from heresy thus had an official character. His characterization of this thesis as extreme was justified, since it was incompatible with the facts and the teaching of the Church—one pope, Honorius I, had actually been anathematized as a heretic by the third ecumenical council of Constantinople in 681. This official disapproval of the thesis did not however lead to its abandonment by theologians. Despite Bishop Gasser's sadly hanging his head, it continued to be endorsed as the most probable opinion by theologians and by standard Catholic works of reference, such as the *Dictionnaire de théologie catholique*.[15] The general adhesion to this thesis, in the face of the evidence and of its official disavowal at Vatican I, resulted from its necessity as an underpinning for the Jesuit conception of obedience. The Jesuit conception of obedience was thus at the root of later ultramontane excesses, which appealed to the belief that the pope could not err in any way in matters of faith—a superhuman privilege that was easily extended to the belief that the pope could not err in any way at all.[16] Papal cults of personality thus have their roots in the demands of this conception of obedience.

---

13   Bishop Vincent Gasser, in *The Gift of Infallibility: The Official* Relatio *on Infallibility of Bishop Vincent Gasser at Vatican Council I*, 2nd ed., trans. James J. O'Connor (San Francisco: Ignatius Press, 2008), 58–59.

14   Gasser, *Gift of Infallibility*, 58. Bishop Gasser attempts rather unconvincingly to exonerate Bellarmine from the charge of having upheld this thesis, on the basis of the fact that Bellarmine admitted that the common opinion of theologians was against Pighius's claim. The fact that the common opinion of theologians later changed to Bellarmine's side indicates the pressure of the Jesuit conception of obedience.

15   See the article "Infaillibilité du pape" by E. Dublanchy, in the *Dictionnaire de théologie catholique* (Paris: Letouzey et Ané, 1907–51), vol. 7, cols. 1716–17 [hereafter, *DTC*].

16   An example of ultramontane rejection of the possibility of papal error is given by Fr J. Steiger, in his article "Causes majeures," *DTC* 2:2039–40. Fr Steiger asserts that "rather than consider whether an arbitrary papal measure that would throw the Church into confusion would be invalid,

ᖰᘺ ᘿᖱ

To understand how the Jesuit conception of obedience departed from earlier conceptions, it is helpful to compare it with the teaching of St Thomas on obedience. The fundamental difference between the two is that St Thomas considers the proper object of obedience to be the precept of the superior.[17] Obedience that seeks to forestall the expressed will of the superior does not bear on what the superior wants or thinks in general, but only on what the superior intends to command. St Ignatius's lowest degree of obedience, which he does not consider to be virtuous, is thus what St Thomas considers to be the only form of obedience. St Thomas holds that St Ignatius's alleged higher forms of obedience do not fall under the virtue of obedience at all:

> For Seneca says (*De Beneficiis* iii): "It is wrong to suppose that slavery falls upon the whole man: for the better part of him is excepted." His body is subjected and assigned to his master but his soul is his own. Consequently in matters touching the internal movement of the will man is not bound to obey his fellow-man, but God alone.[18]

St Thomas's point here is that the limitation of the duty of obedience that is admitted by a pagan philosopher to belong to slaves *a fortiori* applies to the limitation of the duty of obedience in general. The contrast between Seneca and St Ignatius on this point is striking. St Thomas does not hold that his limitation on obedience applies only to obedience in natural matters, with religious obedience being excepted.

> Religious profess obedience as to the regular mode of life, in respect of which they are subject to their superiors: wherefore they are bound to obey in those matters only which may belong to the regular mode of life, and this obedience suffices for salvation. If they be willing to obey even in other matters, this will belong to the superabundance of perfection; provided, however, such things be not contrary to God or to the rule they profess, for obedience in this case would be unlawful.[19]

St Thomas does not consider obedience to involve the sacrifice of one's will as such. St Ignatius however makes it clear that it is not self-will, but the entire human faculty of will itself, that is to be sacrificed; one's self-will could not be described as "of great worth," the term that he applies to the will sacrificed by obedience.[20] This is a sacrifice in the sense of an abandonment and a destruction,

---

theologians have preferred to consider that Christ would never permit such a disaster; history has shown their position to be correct." This assertion would have been cleared by the editor of that standard work of reference. The fact that both these men could have forgotten St Paul's rebuke to St Peter (see Gal 2:11) is astonishing, and may be an indication of the strength of the servile mentality induced by their clerical formation.

17   *ST* II-II, Q. 104, art. 2, corp. and ad 3.
18   *ST* II-II, Q. 104, art. 5.
19   *ST* II-II, Q. 104, art. 5, ad 3.
20   As quoted above, he asserts in the "Letter on Obedience": "Because this disposition of will in man is of so great worth, so also is the offering of it, when by obedience it is offered to his Creator and Lord" (*Letters*, 289).

since it involves eliminating the operation of one's will and handing it over to the will of another human being. St Thomas, in contrast, describes the merit of obedience as consisting in sacrificing one's *proper* will (*propriam voluntatem*), i.e., one's will as functioning independently of God.[21] The virtue of obedience in his view only involves the sacrifice of one's self-will, which is defined by its adherence to objectives that are contrary to our ultimate happiness. Nor does he think of obedience as a virtuous form of personal asceticism. He does not hold that obeying a command we dislike is necessarily better than obeying a command we are happy to fulfil. Indeed, since a rightly directed will seeks the common good, a good person will be glad to carry out any suitable command, since such commands and obedience to them both exist for the sake of the common good.

Obedience does not for St Thomas occupy the central moral role that it does for Counter-Reformation theologians. He does not consider that all good acts are motivated by obedience to God, because he considers that there are virtues the exercise of which is prior to obedience – such as faith, upon which obedience to God depends. Nor does he consider that the essence of sin consists in disobedience to God, or even that all sin involves the sin of disobedience. All sin does indeed involve a disobedience to God's commands, but this disobedience is not willed by the sinner unless the sin involves contempt of a divine command – i.e., involves a will to disobey the command in addition to a will to do the forbidden act. He asserts that "when a thing is done contrary to a precept, not in contempt of the precept, but with some other purpose, it is not a sin of disobedience except materially, and belongs formally to another species of sin."[22] Obedience is simply an act of the virtue of justice, which is motivated by love of God in the case of divine commands and love of neighbor in the case of commands of a human superior. These loves are both more fundamental and broader than obedience.

In addition to his transformation of the traditional conception of religious obedience, St Ignatius was responsible for another innovation that revolutionized the relation of superior to inferior in the religious life. This was his introduction of a new conception of the manifestation of conscience. Opening one's heart to one's spiritual father, and revealing one's sins, trials, and tribulations, was an ancient practice in the monastic life: it was recommended by St Anthony himself.[23] This practice originally had three characteristics: it was a voluntary act on the part of the person manifesting his conscience, it was directed at a spiritual father who was chosen purely for his wisdom in guiding souls, and its purpose was the growth in holiness of the person making the manifestation.

St Ignatius rejected these characteristics. He not only encouraged but required the manifestation of conscience, and he required that the manifestation be made

---

21   See *ST* II-II, Q. 104, art. 3.
22   See *ST* II-II, Q. 105, art. 1, ad 1.
23   See Dacian Dee, OFMCap, *The Manifestation of Conscience* (Washington, DC: Catholic University of America Press, 1960), 2.

to the religious superior—he made no mention of manifestation to a spiritual father other than the superior. He required that such a manifestation be made every six months, and he directed that all superiors and even their delegates were qualified to receive these manifestations—in contrast to St Benedict, who limited the recipients of the manifestation of conscience to the abbot and a few selected spiritual fathers in the monastery. Finally, instead of restricting the purpose of the manifestation of conscience to the spiritual well-being of the manifestee, the superior was not only permitted but required to use the knowledge of his subordinates gained through the manifestation of conscience for the purposes of government.

The manifestation of conscience was much broader and more intrusive than the chapter of faults in monastic communities, which limited itself to external actions that contravened the rule, or even than the necessary extent of self-revelation in the confessional. It included "the dispositions and desires for the performance of good, the obstacles and difficulties encountered, the passions and temptation which move or harass the soul, the faults that are more frequently committed . . . the usual pattern of conduct, affections, inclinations, propensities, temptations, and weaknesses."[24] It should be underlined that the making of a full manifestation of conscience of this kind was impressed upon the inferior as a grave religious duty.

The overweening power that this practice gives to the superior needs no under-lining. The ancient religious orders (such as the Dominicans, Franciscans, and Carmelites) resisted the introduction of an obligatory manifestation of conscience on St Ignatius's model, but many modern religious institutes adopted it. The abuses of the practice were so severe that the Holy See eventually had to forbid it. Leo XIII's decree *Quemadmodum* banned the practice for lay institutes of men and all religious congregations of women in 1890, and it was banned for all religious by canon 530 of the 1917 Code of Canon Law (the Jesuits, however, were permitted to preserve it by a special decree of Pope Pius XI).[25] By this time, however, the practice had had several centuries to leave its mark on the understanding of authority and the psychology of superiors and subordinates within the Church.

There is probably a connection between liturgical practice and the Jesuit conception of obedience as well. The liturgical prayer of the Church is principally composed of the Psalms. Any reader of the Psalms will notice that they are full of what by Counter-Reformation standards is insubordinate language towards God; complaints, demands, criticisms, unsolicited advice, and reproaches. They are not compatible with a spirituality in which the Jesuit conception of obedience plays a central role. Accordingly the Counter-Reformation came to treat the recital of the Divine Office as important largely because it was a task that must be completed under pain of mortal sin. The actual content of the Office

---

24   These are descriptions given by the canonists Franco and Schaefer, quoted in Dee, *Manifestation of Conscience*, 49–50.

25   James F. Gill, SJ, "A Jesuit's Account of Conscience," *Studies in the Spirituality of Jesuits*, IX/5 (November 1977): 254.

was not put forward as a basis for spiritual development, because it was unsuitable for this purpose according to the standards of the Counter-Reformation. The spiritual life of laity and religious came to be focused on devotions, which did not pose this problem, instead of on the Office. It would be interesting to pursue the question of how far a tyrannical conception of authority influenced post-Counter-Reformation devotion and religious art. One may speculate that the feminized chinless portrayal of Christ, and the sickly sentimentality that characterized this period, were an attempt to balance the fear and aversion produced by the perception of Christ as a tyrant that would inevitably follow from belief in his supreme authority understood on nominalist lines.

The Counter-Reformation Church thus wholeheartedly adopted the Jesuit understanding of obedience, and extensively practiced the Jesuit method of manifestation of conscience. The effect of this scarcely needs explaining. The Jesuit understanding of authority was a tyrannical one, since it located authority in the will of the superior rather than in the law. Of course, the expositions of this understanding of authority always insisted that it did not extend to commanding sin, but this limitation did not have much practical import. The relevant understanding of a sinful command was more or less limited to grave and clear violations of the Decalogue, like murder and theft on a large scale, and the unjust commands of authority are rarely ones that insist on crimes of this sort; such crimes are not the sort of thing that unjust authorities usually have an interest in commanding. As noted earlier, some expositions of the Ignatian conception of obedience described obedience to an order than one suspects but is not certain to be illicit as an especially high and praiseworthy form of obedience.

To a tyrannical understanding of authority necessarily corresponds a servile understanding of obedience, where the object of obedience is not the law as understood by the reason, but the pure will of the superior untrammeled by the will or intelligence of the subject. Ignatian thought and practice not only upheld a servile understanding of obedience, but provided a uniquely effective method of producing such obedience. The follower's independent will and intellect are deliberately annihilated as far as is humanly possible, and this is done not only by external pressure, but also by a far more effective means—that of enlisting the follower's own will in the process, through getting the follower to believe that this annihilation is a religious duty, and indeed is the highest form of holiness. The Ignatian form of manifestation of conscience provided the perfect means of implementing this process. By leaving the subordinate with no thoughts or desires independent of the superior's will, it provided a means of thought control that surpassed anything described by George Orwell. It was no accident that totalitarian leaders such as Vladimir Lenin and Heinrich Himmler admired and emulated the Jesuits.

A number of objections are liable to be raised against this indictment of the Jesuit theory of obedience. Has not Jesuit spirituality in general, and the Constitutions of the Society of Jesus in particular, been given the authoritative approbation of the Church? Have the Jesuits not produced many saints and done great work for the Church, something that could hardly have been produced by a tyrannical and thus morally objectionable method of formation? Was St Ignatius himself not a great saint, and an outstanding leader whose methods were not in fact tyrannical ones? Have not Jesuits in the past shown a high level of ability and initiative, something that is incompatible with a method of formation that is a form of brainwashing and breaks the mind and will?

As far as the approbation of the Church goes, it can be pointed out that the essence of the spirituality of St Ignatius is contained in his *Spiritual Exercises*. These are distinct from the Constitutions of the Society and his other writings on obedience, and are the spiritual work of St Ignatius that has been singled out for approbation by the Church. They do not however contain the teachings of St Ignatius on obedience that are criticized here, and in fact lay stress on reflection and conscious action. The Constitutions of the Society have been approved by the Church as the basic regulations governing the structure and functioning of the Society. This approval thus bears on the Constitutions as a regulatory structure for the Society; the reflections on obedience in the Constitutions do not form part of this regulatory structure, and hence are not the objects of the approbation of the Constitutions by the Church.

When it comes to the achievements of the Society of Jesus, it should be remembered that notwithstanding the heroic witness of a number of Jesuit martyrs, the principal achievement of the Jesuits – the thing they were really good at, and that enabled them to make a decisive contribution to the Counter-Reformation – was running secondary schools. It was the Jesuit schools that enabled them to turn the tide in favor of the Church in a number of European countries. A defective understanding of authority and obedience did not have too much scope for action in these schools. For one thing, they were run according to a detailed and uniform program that did not leave much scope for tyrannical initiatives on the part of the superior. For another, they had the essential test of direct, immediate success or failure at their stated object, which is a main curb in practice on tyranny and servility. Educational success was immediately apparent, and meant the schools would flourish; educational failure was equally apparent, and meant that they would lose their pupils. Finally, the difficult and humbling side intrinsic to all successful teaching was not propitious for the characteristics that mark those who enjoy and practice tyranny or servility. Neither the servile nor the tyrannical have the qualities needed for success in teaching large numbers of adolescent boys. When it came to the main apostolic activity of the Jesuits, a literal understanding of St Ignatius's teachings on obedience was thus destined to remain largely a dead letter. Unfortunately this was not the case with other orders and other apostolic pursuits in the Church of the Counter-Reformation.

There are more considerations that need to be kept in mind when considering the successes of the Society of Jesus in general. The Society does seem to have ended up by attempting to train its recruits according to a servile conception of obedience, at least initially, but the caliber of Jesuit recruits led to this formation producing a result that was often different from its ostensible purpose. The Society was very selective in the men it admitted, insisting on ability and intelligence far above average, and the men admitted were generally given substantial tasks to do. Servile obedience is inculcated by subjecting the inferior to humiliating, pointless, and unpleasant tasks, to a degree intended to break their will and self-respect. With individuals of strong will and high intelligence, however, this process can fail of its purpose. In such a case, what it produces is great toughness and endurance, together with rigorous self-control and the capacity to disguise one's thoughts and emotions. Such a process is often used in the initial stages of military training, in order to produce just these qualities. When this toughness and self-control has been elicited, however, the character of military training is changed to foster the qualities of initiative and intelligence that are required for successful performance. The demand for success in important tasks requires subordinates to show initiative, and superiors to exercise actual leadership. Jesuits who lived up to the servile theory of obedience would thus tend to fail at the tasks required of them, and to suffer as a result. The need for success in the important tasks undertaken by the Society demanded a mitigation in practice of the tyrannical theory of authority.

It seems that the Jesuits in fact took this approach to obedience, appropriately so given St Ignatius's military background. Their training came to be valued not simply for its capacity to produce obedience, but even more for the traits of endurance, self-control, and dissimulation of the emotions that it inculcated — the Jesuits came to be recognized as distinguished above all others for their capacity to master anger. These traits are extremely useful in worldly activities, and explain much of the success of the Jesuits in worldly affairs, although their usefulness in producing holiness is open to question.

These mitigating factors depended however on the character of the Jesuits as a carefully selected elite. They could not obtain for the Church as a whole, and they did not do so. For the great majority of Catholic priests and religious, the Jesuit conception of obedience and the Jesuit method of manifestation of conscience tended to produce the result that was stated as their goal: subordinates who believed that they owed servile obedience to their superiors, that they should surrender their will and intelligence to the people above them, and that in so doing they were doing God's will and growing in holiness: and superiors who believed that their commands were the will of God, and that any resistance to these commands by their subordinates was rebellion against God himself.

It should also be recognized that the Jesuit approach to obedience was seen to have grave shortcomings, even when the Society of Jesus was still a faithful and useful organization. John Henry Newman made this point in somewhat startling terms, in the course of instructing his Oratorians on the Oratorian character:

Thus to shift for oneself, to depend on one's own resources, consideration, fellow feeling, knowledge of character, tact, good judgment are the characteristics of an Oratorian, whereas the Jesuit does not know what tact is, cannot enter into the minds of others, and is apt to blunder in most important matters from this habit of mechanical obedience to a Superior and a system.

Of course I am not speaking of certain gifted men among the Jesuits, such as St Francis Xavier, or the China Missionaries, or the Fathers at Paraguay — but take the run of Jesuits at this time, and I can't help thinking you will find, among a hundred high qualities, a want of sagacity and mental dexterity in meeting the age, and the men and difficulties belonging to it.... They are perfect as an organised body, but, as individuals, they are often little more than mechanical instruments, and are least of all men apt to deal with strangers or with enemies, not to say with friends....

There is a comparison between Athenians and Spartans in the celebrated funeral oration of Pericles, which illustrates what I would say: The point of the Orator's praise of the Athenians is this, that they, unlike the Spartans, have no need of laws, but perform from the force of inward character those great actions which others do from compulsion. Here the Oratorian stands for the Athenian, and the Spartan for the Jesuit.[26]

Newman goes on to cite Pericles' Funeral Oration at length, to rub in the contrast between the Oratorians and the Jesuits. One might suspect that some personal animosity was behind these remarks, but in fact Newman's relations with the Jesuits were cordial; the poet Gerard Manley Hopkins became a Jesuit on his advice.

As for the wisdom, sanctity, and achievements of St Ignatius, we should distinguish between the meaning of St Ignatius's writings on obedience when considered in abstraction from their original context, and the meaning that St Ignatius can be judged to have ascribed to them when we look at the context of his own purposes and actions. In the light of this context, it seems that what St Ignatius had in mind in his writings on obedience was the idea that the subordinate should not simply carry out explicit commands, but should grasp the plan of the superior that the commands were intended to implement, and should accept and enthusiastically carry out that plan. Such an approach to the superior's purposes was necessary for the tasks that he intended the Jesuits to carry out, because these tasks generally required independent action where regular recourse to the superior's instructions could not be available. It is in general the approach that subordinates must take to carry out any substantial task properly. However, in expressing this idea St Ignatius was handicapped by the deficient understanding of law that was accepted in his time. As we have seen, this understanding was not St Thomas's conception of a law as a rational plan to achieve

---

26 *Newman the Oratorian*, ed. Placid Murray OSB (Dublin: Gill and Macmillan, 1969), 209-10.

some good. Law was instead conceived of by the philosophers and theologians with whom St Ignatius was familiar as simply a set of commands. In his writings on obedience St Ignatius was trying to get across the idea that obedience to the law in this sense — obedience simply to the content of the explicit orders of the superior — was not sufficient, and that an understanding of and identification with the superior's purposes was necessary. He did not however have at his command an idea of a law that could exist in the superior's mind, be distinct from the superior's beliefs and purposes generally, and be rationally appropriated by the subordinate. He was therefore induced to convey his meaning by calling for an identification with the superior's personal intentions and beliefs, without making a satisfactory distinction between the superior's plan and general objectives as directed to the common good, and his other beliefs and goals.

We can draw a comparison here with St John of the Cross; just as St John would not have accepted the unreasonable conclusions that followed from his ascetical teaching, and did not put these conclusions into practice, so St Ignatius did not intend the unreasonable applications of his writings on obedience. He was simply betrayed into unreasonable positions, as was St John of the Cross, by the philosophical assumptions of his age, from which he was not able to emancipate himself. We might also see his personal struggles as an influence on his doctrine of obedience; originally vainglorious and ambitious, and always attracted to ruling and taking the initiative, he would have found the attempt at a total surrender of mind and will to another a useful tool for combating his dominant faults.

The problem was that St Ignatius's views on obedience in the context of his actions and purposes, and the meaning of his writings on obedience when considered on their own, were not identical; and it was the latter meaning, not the former, that was generally accessible to, and generally accepted by, the Church of the Counter-Reformation.

We find this, for instance, in the Jesuit Alonso Rodriguez's *Practice of Perfection and Christian Virtues*.[27] This work, the most widely read manual of ascetic theology of the Counter-Reformation, was published in Spanish in 1609, and went through many editions in many translations — over sixty in French, twenty in Italian, at least ten in German, several in English. It was required reading for Jesuit novices up to the Second Vatican Council. In his proposed examination of conscience, Fr Rodriguez requires the penitent

> II. To obey in will and heart, having one and the same wish and will as the Superior.

> III. To obey also with the understanding and judgment, adopting the same view and sentiment as the Superior, not giving place to any judgments or reasonings to the contrary.

---

27   The author, who lived from 1538 to 1616 and whose name is sometimes given also as Alphonsus, is frequently confused with his almost exact contemporary, St Alphonsus Rodriguez (1532–1617).

IV. To take the voice of the Superior ... as the voice of God, and obey the Superior, whoever he may be, as Christ our Lord, and the same for subordinate officials.

V. To follow blind obedience, that is obedience without enquiry or examination, or any seeking of reasons for the why and wherefore, it being reason enough for me that it is obedience and the command of the Superior.[28]

Rodriguez praises obedience — as he understands it — in illuminating terms.

One of the greatest comforts and consolations that we have in Religion is this, that we are safe in doing what obedience commands. The Superior it is that may be wrong in commanding this or that, but you are certain that you are not wrong in doing what is commanded, for the only account that God will ask of you is if you have done what they commanded you, and with that your account will be sufficiently discharged before God. It is not for you to render account whether the thing commanded was a good thing, or whether something else would not have been better; that does not belong to you, but to the account of the Superior. When you act under obedience, God takes it off your books, and puts it on the books of the Superior.... So the Religious, living under obedience, composes himself to sleep — that is to say, he has no trouble or care about what he is to do, but goes his way to heaven and perfection. Superiors see to that, they are the captains and masters of the ship.... This is the blessing which God has given to the Religious who lives under obedience, that all his burden is thrown on the shoulders of his Superior, and he lives at ease and without care whether this be better or that. This is one of the things that greatly move virtuous folk to live under obedience and enter Religion, — to be rid of the endless perplexities and anxieties that they have there in the world, and be sure of serving and pleasing God.... If I were there in the world and desired to serve God, I should be troubled and in doubt whether I eat too little or too much, sleep too much or too little, do too little or too much penance ... but here in Religion all these doubts are cleared away, for I eat what they give me, I sleep at the time appointed, I do the penance they assign me.[29]

Rodriguez adds that "not only in spiritual matters, but also in temporal, this is a life very restful and void of care. Like a passenger in a well-victualled ship, a Religious has no need to attend to his own necessities."

One could not give a plainer exposition of a servile notion of obedience. Rodriguez's position draws the logical conclusion from a literal understanding of St Ignatius's writings on obedience. If a subordinate entirely abandons the

---

28   Alphonsus Rodriguez, SJ, *Practice of Perfection and Christian Virtues*, trans. Joseph Rickaby, SJ (London: Manresa Press, 1929), tr. 21, ch. 10, pp. 385–86.

29   Rodriguez, *Practice of Perfection*, 529–31.

activity of his own mind and will when presented with the order of a superior, it is indeed the case that he surrenders all moral responsibility for the execution of the order, and the responsibility is transferred entirely to the superior who gives the order. That is because moral responsibility requires the functioning of one's intellect and will; if this functioning is legitimately abolished in the case of a superior's order, responsibility for the execution of the order is abolished as well. The fact that the abandonment of this functioning is presented as legitimate and indeed as obligatory is the key to this logical implication. If the functioning of one's mind and will is abandoned illegitimately, one does not lose all moral responsibility for the acts that one performs as a result of their abandonment. But if this abandonment is legitimate, as Rodriguez claims it is, moral responsibility is indeed necessarily suspended.

In drawing this conclusion, Rodriguez goes farther than St Ignatius. The absence of this conclusion in the writings of St Ignatius is what makes it possible to give a pious interpretation to his views on obedience, and to assert that his writings need not be read as an endorsement of a tyrannical understanding of authority and a servile understanding of obedience. With Rodriguez such an interpretation is ruled out, and these understandings of authority and obedience take undoubted possession.

Like other writers, Rodriguez makes the usual exception for obedience to commands that are manifestly contrary to the divine law. But this exception is not something that has much practical reality. Internalizing and practicing the Jesuit notion of obedience is difficult, and requires time, motivation, and effort. When it has been done successfully, it has a lasting effect. Once one has destroyed one's capacity to criticize the actions of one's superiors, one cannot revive this capacity and its exercise at will. Following the directive to refuse obedience to one's superiors when their commands are manifestly sinful then becomes psychologically difficult or even impossible.

There is an explicit appeal to the wisdom and goodness of superiors in this doctrine of obedience. This appeal however ignores the characteristic effects of the exercise of tyrannical authority, which are no less deep — perhaps deeper — than those of the practice of servile obedience. Such authority has an intoxicating effect, producing overweening pride and megalomania. Superiors in the grip of these vices become both prone to giving unjust orders, and incapable of conceiving of themselves as sinful or mistaken.

Rodriguez is especially interesting in his description of the principal appeal of a servile conception of obedience to the subordinate (its appeal to a superior needs no explaining). He states in the plainest terms that this appeal lies in the abdication of all adult responsibility, along with the worries that inevitably accompany it. The ruinous effects of attracting to the clerical state people who seek avoidance of adult responsibility, and the material security of passengers in a well-victualled ship, extend much farther than the overthrow of the rule of law in the Church.

An insidious feature of this conception of authority is that at the outset it seemed to be a success. It was used to put an end to the financial and sexual misbehavior of the clergy that had helped to produce the Reformation. By so doing, it contributed to the brilliant achievements of the Counter-Reformation. The situation of the Church was like that of Rome under Augustus or France under Louis XIV; the peace and order produced by absolute rule permitted a flowering of the talents produced by the free society that had existed prior to absolutism. When the inheritance of freedom was spent and the full effects of absolutism were felt, these talents withered. The brilliant constellation of saints and geniuses that illuminated seventeenth-century Catholic France was succeeded in the eighteenth century by failure and frequent capitulation in the face of the anti-Christian attacks of the Enlightenment.

The Jesuit conception of obedience did not remain a peculiarity of the Society, but came to be adopted by the Counter-Reformation Church as a whole. This was due to the prestige of the Society and the attractiveness to religious superiors of the nature of the obedience held up as a model, and also to the plausibility of the conception given the philosophical assumptions noted above. This conception of obedience was completely dominant in the many foundations of the Counter-Reformation, which, unlike the Benedictines, lacked traditions of their own to counteract a literal reading of St Ignatius. It was also prevalent in the new institution of the Counter-Reformation seminary. We can see a manifestation of this prevalence in the *Treatise on Obedience* of the Sulpician Louis Tronson, which gave St Ignatius's teaching and writings as the summit of Catholic teaching on obedience. The Sulpician adoption of the Jesuit conception was particularly important because of their central role in the training of priests in seminaries from the seventeenth century onwards. The seven years of seminary training meant that the tyrannical understanding of authority and the servile understanding of obedience conveyed by this training were deeply ingrained in those who went through it. An illuminating example of this tyrannical approach is given by Chris Geraghty, an alumnus of St Patrick's Seminary in Manly, Australia:

> My young sister was being confirmed just in a local parish at Neutral Bay, and I with my ears back, went up and asked for permission to go to this ceremony, which was important for the family and for the parish, and I was just refused, just no. No explanation given. And I thought that was pretty terrible until I was speaking recently to a member of the class who said that when he was at a seminary, his grandfather died and he wasn't allowed to go home for the funeral, and his brother, there were only three in the family, and two of them were in the seminary, so the brother who was not in the seminary was getting married; he wasn't allowed to go home for the wedding. And then in Springwood [the minor seminary for the archdiocese of Sydney, which Geraghty attended], I remember a student's father was

killed at Warragamba, and they didn't even mention it, say mass for
him or anything. Another student had his brother killed in the war,
they didn't celebrate mass for him either. They celebrated mass for
priests who died, people that we didn't know, but the people that we
did know, if they were lay people, they were passed over.[30]

Geraghty's account is the more informative because he makes it clear that the
seminary authorities were not generally bullies and sadists; they were putting
into practice a theory of authority and discipline.

The servile conception of obedience remained the standard one into the twentieth century. Adolphe Tanquerey, in his widely read and translated (and in many
ways excellent) work *Précis de théologie ascétique et mystique*,[31] could write that
perfect souls who have reached the highest degree of obedience submit their
judgment to that of their superior, without even examining the reasons for which
he commands them.[32] As a result of the general adoption of the Jesuit conception of obedience, this was the understanding conveyed to the laity. Its effect on
the laity was different from its effect on the clergy. The laity could never hope
to acquire authority, so the traits needed to rise in a tyrannical system were not
produced in them. What happened instead was that the laity were infantilized in
the religious sphere of their lives. This infantilization can be observed in religious
art and devotion, especially from the nineteenth century onwards, and in the willingness to give blind obedience to the clergy. It had of course a certain attraction;
there is a comfort in relapsing into childhood in some sphere of one's life, and
handing over deliberation, decisions, and adult responsibility to one's superiors.
This attraction is the basis of the appeal of religious cults and totalitarian states.
The Catholic laity did not have to endure tyrannical authority in every sphere of
their lives, so this comfort was all the more appealing to them; it did not have
the accompanying cost of total servility that the clergy had to pay.

It was thus the literal, tyrannical understanding of St Ignatius's writings on
obedience that had come to be accepted by the Counter-Reformation Church.
The enormous chaos that followed the Second Vatican Council is an indication
of this acceptance. It revealed a widespread alienation from Catholic teaching
and tradition among priests and religious, the majority of whom either gladly
rejected what they had been taught to consider true and holy or left the religious
life altogether. This was a consequence of identifying this teaching and tradition
with the tyrannical regime under which they had been formed. The resulting

---

30   Chris Geraghty, interview on Australian Broadcasting Corporation radio, July 6, 2003 at
6 pm; transcript at www.abc.net.au/radionational/programs/spiritofthings/priest-factory/3534652.

31   Adolphe Tanquerey, *Précis de théologie ascétique et mystique*, 7th ed. (Paris: Desclée et Cie,
1923); the book was translated into English as *The Spiritual Life: A Treatise on Ascetical and Mystical
Theology*, 2nd rev. ed., trans. Herman Branderis (Tournai: Desclée & Co., 1930). It is still in print.

32   Tanquerey, *Précis de théologie ascétique et mystique*, no. 1064, p. 668: "Les âmes parfaites font
plus encore; ils soumettent leur jugement à celui de leur supérieur, sans même examiner les raisons
pour laquelle il commande . . . . C'est ce qu'on appelle l'obéissance *aveugle*, qui fait que l'on est dans
les mains des supérieurs 'perinde ac *baculus* . . . perinde ac *cadaver*' (St Ignace, *Constit.*, VI, §1, reg. 36)."

hatred and alienation was greatly aggravated by the fact that this regime was largely incapable of communicating a real understanding of Catholic tradition in the first place, because such an understanding requires a mature exercise of intellect and will—precisely the things that religious formation was designed to extirpate. As a result there was little or no real grasp of the tradition to counteract the reaction against the generally accepted conception of it. Indeed such a real grasp often made a priest or religious suspect in the eyes of ecclesiastical authority, since it required this mature and independent exercise of thought and insight—as is the case with all substantial traditions.

As for the laity, their indoctrination in blind obedience made them willing and even proud to follow disaffected clergy when ordered to reject the liturgy and teachings that they had previously been told were sacred and inviolable. The lack of Catholic initiative by the laity in the preconciliar period is also to be explained by this infantilizing formation. It has long been noted that converts to the faith, at least in the English-speaking world, made a disproportionately large contribution to Catholic thought and culture. This was inevitable given the formation that cradle Catholics had received.

Formation in tyrannical authority and servile obedience inevitably fostered undesirable characteristics in the priests who exercised authority over the laity, and thus produced hostility to the clergy. It is significant that the term that came to be used for opposition to the Catholic Church in Europe was "anticlericalism." In its literal meaning, the word "anticlericalism" is quite distinct from opposition to Catholicism, since it simply means antipathy to the Catholic clergy. Such an antipathy does not imply rejection of the Catholic faith, and in some circumstances may be quite justified, or even required by fidelity to the Church. Its identification with anti-Catholicism as such was the result of an opportunistic exploitation by unbelievers of the widespread loathing of the clergy, a loathing caused by their practice of a tyrannical conception of authority, together with a genuine identification of the faith with the clergy—an identification fostered by the infantilization of the laity, which produced the impression that the faith was the property of the clergy as such.

There were of course many factors in the Church that counteracted the effects of the philosophical and practical forces described above: her intellectual traditions with their insistence on learning and philosophy, healthier traditions of spiritual teaching and practice, and the demands of reality itself in the form of the challenges and responsibilities faced by clergy and religious. In the twentieth century, however, the forces within the Church promoting a tyrannical understanding of authority and a servile understanding of obedience received decisive reinforcement from two factors.

The first was the promulgation of the Code of Canon Law in 1917. The basic idea of this codification—that of streamlining the canon law of the Latin Church, and making it easier to use—was well-meant, but the way in which this idea was implemented was fundamentally flawed. The problem with the 1917 Code was that it was a Napoleonic code, rather than a Justinian code. When the Emperor Justinian decided to codify Roman law for purposes similar to the ones that inspired St Pius X, the whole mass of previous Roman legal rulings and decrees were collected together, organized, and purged of obsolete and contradictory elements. They were not however ruled void of authority and replaced by an entirely new body of edicts. The great body of Roman legal tradition was preserved in Justinian's codification. In the Napoleonic code, in contrast, the previous legal tradition was abolished and entirely replaced by the new and much smaller collection of decrees that made up the code devised by Napoleon and his jurists. The Latin Code of Canon law of 1917 was deliberately designed on the Napoleonic rather than the Justinian model. The massive body of the Latin legal tradition, collected in the *Corpus Iuris Canonici*, was declared to be obsolete. From this point onwards the Latin Church had to operate largely without the benefit of its own legal tradition, on the basis of a legal system modeled on the legislation of a military dictator implementing Jansenist and Enlightenment ideas of law and authority.

In addition to the crippling of Catholic legal practice that this involved, the alleged abrogation of the entire *Corpus Iuris Canonici* was itself of dubious legality, since the canonical tradition of the Church has always been considered to contain substantial elements of sacred tradition. This is recognized by the Oriental Code of Canon Law, which states at its outset that "the canons of the Code, in which for the most part the ancient law of the Eastern Churches is received or adapted, are to be assessed mainly according to that law" (can. 2). It is paradoxical that the Oriental Code should recognize the authority of the Eastern canonical tradition, while the Latin Code should overthrow the Latin tradition — despite the fact that the Latin tradition is the one that contains most of the rulings of the pope, the highest legal authority in the Church. The 1917 Latin Code thus struck a severe blow at the rule of law in the Church.

The second factor in promoting a tyrannical understanding of authority was the abandonment of the Church's practical activities in the postconciliar period. The enormous involvement of clergy and religious in education and health was largely shut down along with the religious orders that carried out this involvement. The institutions that had carried out this involvement were handed over to governments or lay organizations, and became Catholic in name only (if that). The direct activity of the Church in preaching and administering the sacraments was also greatly reduced, as congregations shrunk after the Council and continue to decline. The expectation that priests and religious would succeed in carrying out serious work, and the accompanying need for competence and leadership, consequently declined along with the decline in serious work to carry out. The scope for tyrannical exercise of authority was correspondingly widened.

This last factor may seem to contradict the thesis about the dominance of a tyrannical conception of authority in the Church. Do not tyrants seek something to tyrannize over? If the importance and influence of Catholic activities declines steeply, does not their scope for tyranny decline with it?

To answer these questions, we need to understand the dynamics of an organization that has been dominated for a long time by a tyrannical conception of authority and a servile conception of obedience. The key point is that in a clerical system dominated by these conceptions, the leaders all start off as followers themselves. In this capacity, they learn the skills of the slave for survival and advancement; flattery, duplicity, bullying and humiliation of those beneath them, and concealment. Their promotion from subordinate to superior does not depend primarily on their competence at the tasks they are supposed to perform, but on their capacity to ingratiate themselves with their superiors. The leadership in such a system is thus not selected for its capacity to get things done, and is not generally motivated by a desire to get things done. The dominant motivation is desire to escape the servile position and enjoy the tyrannical position.

A collapse of the real activities of the institution does not get in the way of the fulfillment of this desire—if anything it makes it easier, by dispensing with the need for determination and intelligence in the personnel of the institution; these characteristics compete with the skills of the courtier as qualifications for promotion, and make the task of tyrannical leadership a lot more difficult. The deliberate destruction of the substantial activities of the Church that followed the Second Vatican Council was to a great extent motivated by the desire of religious leaders in the Church to free themselves of the encumbrance of real responsibilities, the better to have free range for the arbitrary exercise of their wills.

We have now seen how the members of the Church have been formed to accept a tyrannical understanding of authority and a servile understanding of obedience in religious affairs. This in turn explains why the rule of law does not obtain in the Catholic Church; its leaders do not consider themselves to be subject to the law, and their followers do not see the law as the source of their leader's authority or as a constraint upon the leaders' actions.

There are connections between these causes and the particular form of violation of the law mentioned at the outset of this chapter. Scandalous sexual activity on the part of priests is not new in Catholic history; it has occurred during every period in the past when zeal and fidelity in the Church has diminished. What is new, however, is the character of this activity. Previous scandal largely involved concubinage and casual fornication by priests. The scandals of the past sixty years, however, have been of a different character; involvement with adolescent boys has been much more significant than in any previous period of corruption on the part of the clergy. It is the main form of sexual vice among the clergy, which was not the case in previous periods. It is not of course that such involvement was absent in the past; it is that it was not the characteristic form that clerical sexual misbehavior took. This new development is a result of the fact that these forms of sexual abuse are closely connected with narcissistic personality types, and a social structure based on tyranny and humiliation both forms and selects for this type of personality.

Psychological maturity is needed in order to successfully resist sexual temptation. By attacking this maturity, the inculcation of a servile understanding of authority makes chastity very difficult. The warped and inadequate personalities of those who are attracted to perverse sexual activity will not be identified in a system of training that is based on inculcating servile obedience. Such persons are often good at servility and dissimulation. They will thrive in a system based on servile obedience, while men of intelligence and character will struggle under it.

Such activity will not be combated by the clerical leadership, because superiors will not think of their own authority as bound up with the authority of the law, and they will not be inclined to respect and obey the law as such. They will have a strong incentive to conceal sexual abuse, because the authority of the clergy over the laity rests on an infantilized conception of clerics as godlike father figures who can do no wrong. Such a conception is destroyed if serious wrongdoing by the clergy is made public. The laity who hold this conception will easily be persuaded or intimidated into silence about the cases of sexual abuse that they encounter. Both superiors and subordinates in a tyrannical system are taught to worship power and those who hold it, and to despise inferiors, the weak, and victims. As a result they will not tend to feel sympathy for victims of sexual abuse, especially children. Their sympathy will go to the abusers, who have been exercising tyrannical power in an extreme form. All the above phenomena have been observed time and time again in the cases of sexual abuse that have come to light.

The infantilization produced by this understanding of authority contributed to sexual abuse in several ways. An infantilized person cannot exercise independent judgment and is not able to stand up for himself or others. Infants are not able to comprehend evil, and they are not able to admit or even understand that their father figures are evil. Those priests who took the tyrannical understanding of authority seriously, rather than conforming to it in order to realize their ambitions and enjoy the pleasures of tyranny, were thus psychologically unable to speak out against sexual abuse and take risks to correct it. The ambitious did not do so because there was no percentage in it for them.

There is a connection between this understanding of authority and obedience and the approach taken by ecclesiastical authority to sexual abuse of minors. The almost universal strategy was to hush up the crime and move the offender somewhere else. This strategy was virtually given official sanction by canon 695 of the 1983 code, which required superiors to dismiss religious for living in concubinage and some other offenses, but permitted superiors to refrain from dismissing them for the offence of sexual abuse of minors. It does not seem satisfactory to explain this difference purely by postulating that ecclesiastical authorities considered sexual abuse to be a lesser offense than living in concubinage; sexual abuse of minors after all is a serious offense in criminal law, whereas living in concubinage has no consequences in civil law. The difference is more likely a consequence of the fact that living in concubinage, like kidnapping and other offences punishable (in theory) by mandatory dismissal according to canon 695, is a public act that is not susceptible of being hushed up. The tyrannical conception of authority will always mandate the concealment of a crime that has been committed by some-one holding authority in the Church, if such concealment is at all possible. The maintenance of authority of this kind requires that those under its sway should consider the holders of authority to be beyond all human failings. This is implicit in the very notion of (voluntary) servile obedience, which treats authority as godlike in nature. The acknowledgement and punishment of crime committed by a person in authority thus undermines the very basis of authority in a tyrannical regime – the opposite of its effect in a society ruled by law, where punishment of such a person strengthens the basis of authority by underlining that no one is above the law. Concealing rather than punishing the sexual abuse of minors was doubly attractive in a tyrannical system; the victims of this abuse were unable to stand up for themselves and prosecute their own cause, which made conceal-ment relatively easy, and the vile nature of these crimes made them particularly damaging to a tyrannical conception of authority.

As for the laity, the brutal truth is that much sexual abuse of children by priests occurred with the collusion of the parents of these children. Without this collusion, the sexual abuse of children and adolescents by priests could never have taken on the dimensions that it did. Witness this statement by "James," a boy repeatedly sexually abused by Cardinal McCarrick:

> James said he had tried to tell his father that he was being abused when he was 15 or 16. But Father McCarrick was so beloved by his family, he said, and considered so holy, that the idea was unfathom-able. . . . James says that as a boy, he had no safe place to discuss what was happening to him. "No place. No place. My father was just not going to hear it." . . . "I tried a couple of times with my mother, but she would say 'I think you're mistaken.' My father was born in 1918, my mother was born in 1920. They were raised in a way that the Catholic Church was everything. My father was a holy guy. He'd walk around with a rosary in his hand all day. My parents were very holy, and their parents were very holy. Their whole idea about life was that way." [33]

This erroneous conception of holiness was not only the result of the stupidity of this man's parents. It was what they had been taught by the clergy – following a tyrannical conception of authority. It meant that they were incapable of grasping that priests could be evil – and that they thought that this incapacity was virtuous and a religious duty.

The connection between the Jesuit understanding of obedience and the Second Vatican Council and its aftermath is a complicated one that needs exploring. That

---

33 Rod Dreher, "Uncle Ted's 'Special Boy,'" *The American Conservative*, July 25, 2018.

council was followed by a chaotic period in which Catholic practices and traditions were widely rejected, to an extent that was not mandated by the teachings of the council itself. This chaotic period, which saw the departure of a large proportion of priests and religious and the decline of many substantial religious orders, was probably in part a reaction against the tyrannical character of authority prior to the council — a reaction that was made possible by a weakening of this authority during and after the council.

This reaction did not however take the form of a move towards a legal understanding of authority, and the understanding of authority in the Church does not seem to have been fundamentally altered by conciliar or postconciliar developments; the absence of the rule of law in sexual abuse cases is sufficient evidence of this. Like other revolutions recorded by history, this revolt against tyranny did not lead to the triumph of freedom. Instead, it produced a more far-reaching and thorough tyranny, by destroying the elements of the *ancien régime* that had placed limits on the power of superiors. It did away with the factors listed above that had counteracted the influence of a tyrannical conception of authority in the Counter-Reformation Church.

The progressive faction that seized power in seminaries and religious orders had its own program and ideology that demanded total adherence and justified the ruthless suppression of opposition. The tools of psychological control and oppression that had been learned by the progressives in their own formation were put to most effective use, and applied more sweepingly than they had ever been in the past — the difference between the two regimes being rather like the difference between the Okhrana and the Cheka.[34]

Part of the progressive ideology was the falsity and harmfulness of traditional Catholic sexual teaching; the effect of this tenet on the sexual abuse crisis need not be labored. But it would be a mistake to think that progressivism as such is responsible for this crisis, and that its defeat would solve the problem. Deeply rooted assumptions and patterns of behavior in an institution persist with great tenacity, and can be reformed only when their deficiencies have been openly acknowledged and addressed. This has not happened in the Catholic Church, because the fundamental causes of the tyrannical exercise of authority in the Catholic Church have not been examined. Unless these causes are clearly displayed, an alternative, correct understanding of authority is proposed, and a serious and systematic attempt is made to reform the understanding of authority in the Church along proper lines, it is inevitable that the older understanding will be largely preserved.

---

34   The Okhrana were the secret police under Tsarist Russia and the Cheka were their replacement after the 1917 Bolshevik Revolution. Both organizations used the same immoral methods in pursuit of their objectives.

Examining the Deep Roots of the Abuse Crisis[1]

DARRICK TAYLOR

THE ONGOING SEXUAL ABUSE CRISIS IN THE CHURCH has left many good Catholics shaken, and like many I have tried to understand how this has happened. Obviously, homosexuality in the clergy plays a role, and the all-male nature of the priesthood provides opportunities for such abuse. But here I want to explore the larger historical forces that allowed abuse to flourish in the Church, which at least for me makes it somewhat more explicable in human terms, the irrational and mysterious nature of evil notwithstanding.

Perhaps the most insightful explanation I have encountered comes from the Canadian philosopher John Lamont, whose article "Tyranny and Sexual Abuse in the Church: A Jesuit Tragedy,"[2] identifies a warped idea of obedience which has influenced priestly formation since the sixteenth century. According to Lamont, a voluntarist conception of obedience, which made the will of a superior the necessary criterion for obedience, made its way into Jesuit training manuals and spread through post-Tridentine seminaries. This conception of obedience, he writes, departed from St Thomas Aquinas's conception of obedience according to law, whose source is in the nature of the good. According to Lamont, this new tyrannical idea of obedience inculcates a crippling dependence on those who internalize it, such that they can no longer critically assess the actions of those in authority. He cites statements from popular training manuals for priests which defined obedience as surrender of one's entire faculty of willing to their superior. Lamont argues that once clergy internalized this idea, it made appeals to any other authority null and void. This explains why canon law was no bar to sexual abuse, even though it provided remedies for it.

Clare McGrath-Merkle, in "Fallen Failsafes and a Revolutionary Modern Priesthood,"[3] identifies an exalted, quasi-idolatrous ideal of priesthood spread by French authors in early modern France. Focusing on the writings of Pierre de Bérulle, a seventeenth-century spiritual writer (and opponent of Cardinal Richelieu), she argues that in responding to critiques of clerical corruption, Bérulle promoted the idea that a priest loses his whole identity and becomes

---

1 First published at *Crisis Magazine* on May 18, 2021.
2 *Catholic Family News*, October 27, 2018. The article by Dr Lamont to which Dr Taylor refers is largely an excerpt from the essay published in the preceding chapter.
3 *The Regensburg Forum*, August 23, 2020.

one with the person of Christ upon ordination. Thus, he took the "step from affirming the perfection to which a priest is called, to affirming a perfection of his state of life, making the priest the source of all sanctity in the Church." By encouraging the priest to see himself as a "nullity" and identify himself wholly with Christ, she thinks Bérulle promoted the idea that it was the person of the priest rather than his office which mediates God's grace and holiness. Like Lamont, she thinks this idea would be spread in seminaries and teaching orders such as the Sulpicians, replacing older theologies of the priesthood found in the writings of St Gregory the Great and others.

In a very different vein, Bronwen McShea[4] claims that prior to the nineteenth century, European monarchs and nobility exercised influence over the Church, so that bishops didn't have as much power over clergy; lay leaders in Christendom were expected to play an active role in defending the Church from physical attacks and providing for its material needs. As a result, they would have had greater ability to intervene in cases of clerical abuse in the early modern period. But in the second half of the nineteenth century, in response to the revolutions of that period, the Church began asserting the authority of both pope and bishops to govern "immediately" the clergy and laity. While Vatican I established the immediate universal jurisdiction of the pope, Vatican II raised the episcopate to the status of a "College," elevating its importance above that of mere priests. Changes in canon law, its codification in 1917, and the growth of bishops' conferences after Vatican II, all gave greater freedom for bishops to remove pastors. These made it harder for lay men and women to seek answers if they thought their children were being abused, and it allowed bishops to move around priests accused of such crimes to avoid just such inquiries.

Changes in canon law seem to have been crucial, and nearly all the essays here mention the 1917 codification of canon law. According to canonist Edward Peters, this codification amounted to a "revolution" that gave bishops much more direct control over canon law, and as Lamont notes, it nullified laws contained in the old *Corpus Iuris Canonici*, whose provisions against sexual crimes were much stricter.

This is partly the subject of Kieran Tapsell's essay, "Canon Law on Child Abuse through the Ages."[5] Tapsell argues that from the time of Gregory XVI in 1842, popes made the handling of sexual crimes committed by clergy increasingly more secretive. The 1917 code dispensed with the requirement to notify and hand over the accused to secular authorities, and Pius XI's instruction *Crimen Sollicitationis* (1922) made the entire process a secret one from start to finish. Gone were public

---

4   See Bronwen McShea, "Bishops Unbound: The History Behind Today's Crisis of Church Leadership," *First Things*, January 2019, online at www.firstthings.com/article/2019/01/bishops-unbound. For a detailed study that brings out many of the same points, see the same author's *La Duchesse: The Life of Marie de Vignerot—Cardinal Richelieu's Forgotten Heiress Who Shaped the Fate of France* (New York: Pegasus Books, 2023).

5   *Journal of the Australian Catholic Historical Society* 36 (2015): 113–36; www.academia.edu/65995747/ Canon_Law_and_Child_Sexual_Abuse_through_the_Ages.

"degradations" of offenders, in which clerics were stripped of their status and handed over to the state for punishment.[6] Tapsell identifies fear of scandal in the face of rising anticlericalism during the nineteenth and twentieth centuries as the main reason for such changes, noting the fear of handing over priests to civic authorities in dictatorial regimes. Tapsell says the same idolization of priests noted by McGrath-Merkle played into the Church's fears, lest scandals harm the esteem of the priesthood (he cites as evidence of this the veneration of St John Vianney, beatified in 1905 and canonized in 1925, who said: "The priest is everything!").

What these essays suggest is that long-term causes of the abuse crisis originated in the Church's response to the two great cataclysms of the last half-millennium: the Reformation and the French Revolution. The Church certainly needed to reemphasize the sacrality of the priesthood in response to the Reformation, but in doing so she enshrined theological doctrines that made severe abuse possible. After the Reformation, nominalist ideas of obedience combined with a distorted view of priestly sanctity created psychological habits of dependence among the clergy and passed them on to the laity. In the case of the French Revolution, lay Catholics, becoming increasingly independent of clerical influence (due to growing literacy, industrialization, and other social changes), revolted against these notions of obedience and priestly superiority, which many clergy could only interpret as a rejection of their authority *as a whole*, given the type of obedience they were trained to expect. In turn, the Church responded to the liberal, anticlerical revolutions of that era by enacting legal reforms that shielded clergy from any attempt to undermine that authority.

Over the long term, these changes fostered an environment where sexual abuse could occur. As these authors indicate, canon law and other safeguards limited opportunities for abuse for several centuries. But by the mid-twentieth century, when the crisis began, these had been whittled away or otherwise undermined, so that they no longer acted as failsafes against abuse.

This does not mean that every priest was or is some kind of monster. But where such an idea of authority and obedience went unchecked, it must have created an atmosphere that drew abusive men to the priesthood. Moreover, if this narrative is correct—that the Church instilled an unhealthy idea of obedience in its clergy while later erecting barriers against exposing them to scandals that would undermine the belief that priests were "godlike father figures who can do no wrong," in Lamont's phrase—it would explain much about the contemporary Church.

That many Catholics view the pope as "an absolute monarch whose thoughts and desires are law" (as Benedict XVI put it, distancing himself from that false view), and that a papal adviser can publicly proclaim "in theology sometimes

---

6   See Thomas Doyle, OP, JCD, "The 1922 Instruction and the 1962 Instruction 'Crimen Sollicitationis,' Promulgated by the Vatican," October 3, 2008, www.awrsipe.com/doyle/2008/2008-10-03-Commentary-on-1922-and-1962-documents.pdf.

2 + 2 = 5," becomes explicable if the authors I have cited are correct. The rebellion against Church teaching on sexuality (and many other topics) in the 1960s must be related to the arbitrary exercise of authority experienced by priests who came of age in that era. It is not surprising that clergy and laity conflated the truth of doctrines they were taught with the corrupt use of authority they endured, and so they rejected both.

Conservative as well as traditional Catholics are apt to blame progressive ideas about sexuality for the abuse crisis, and while such ideas certainly contributed to the crisis, it seems likely that "clericalism" — at least as defined by the authors discussed above — did so as well, even if progressive Catholics may distort this notion in pursuit of their own agenda. Successfully addressing the causes of this calamity will require clergy and laity alike to foster a more healthy, mature notion of obedience, one which does not idolize the person of the priest, and to provide legal mechanisms that will protect the vulnerable in their care. If we do not, I fear the Church will wind up repeating this same history all over again.

❧ 9 ❧

What May Be Done about a Heretical Pope?[1]

A FRIAR OF THE ORDER OF PREACHERS

T HE QUESTION OF HOW THE CHURCH SHOULD respond if the Roman pontiff were to fall into heresy has been discussed at different times in her history. In our own day, it has been agitated again in several scholarly and semi-scholarly works, though without general agreement being reached.[2] In this article, I shall argue that the elements for a satisfactory response to this question exist within the Church's tradition, and shall propose how they may be synthesized.

"THE FIRST SEE IS JUDGED BY NO ONE"

We find statements of the judicial primacy of the see of Rome from a relatively early period in the history of the Church. The council of Serdica (c. 343) decreed the universal appellate jurisdiction of this see.[3] Pope Gelasius I stated in 495 in a letter to the bishops of Dardania that it is known to the universal Church that since this see "has jurisdiction over every church . . . no one may pass judgment on its verdict."[4]

The familiar phrase "the first see is judged by no one" apparently owes its origin to the so-called "Symmachian forgeries": various documents composed in the early sixth century to bolster the claim to the papacy of Symmachus against his rival Laurentius.[5] One of these documents, the *Gesta Marcellini*, purports to be an account of a synod of bishops meeting at Sinuessa in 303 to discuss whether Pope

---

1   Published here for the first time.

2   Laurent Fonbaustier, *La déposition du pape hérétique: Une origine du constitutionnalisme?* (Paris: Mare & Martin, 2016); John Salza and Robert Siscoe, *True or False Pope* (Winona: STAS Editions, 2015); Arnaldo Xavier da Silveira, *Can a Pope Be a Heretic? The Theological Hypothesis of a Heretical Pope* (Portugal: Caminhos Romanos, 2018); Cyrille Dounot, Nicolas Warembourg, and Boris Bernabé, eds., *La déposition du pape hérétique: Lieux théologiques, modèles canoniques, enjeux constitutionnels* (Sceaux: Mare & Martin, 2019); Lamont and Pierantoni, *Defending the Faith*. See also a proposal by Fr Aidan Nichols in a 2017 lecture to the Society of St Alban and St Sergius about the advisability of modifying canon law to deal with an erring pope, summarized online at catholicherald.co.uk/leading-theologian-change-canon-law-to-correct-papal-errors/, and Bishop Athanasius Schneider's "On the Question of a Heretical Pope," published in the following chapter.

3   DH 133–35.

4   PL 59:66.

5   Jeffrey Richards, *The Popes and the Papacy in the Early Middle Ages, 476–752* (London & Boston: Routledge & Kegan Paul, 1979), 81–82. The "council of Sinuessa" has long been universally regarded as a mere invention; see Charles Hefele, *A History of the Christian Councils*, trans. William Clark (Edinburgh: T. & T. Clarke, 1872), 127–28.

Marcellinus had been guilty of idolatry. This document relates that the bishops refused to reach a verdict, stating that "the first see is judged by no one" (*prima sedes non iudicabitur a quoquam*).[6] Another of the Symmachian forgeries, the *Constitutum Silvestri*, is a list of canons attributed to Pope Sylvester I (314-335). Among these are canon 3, "the supreme pontiff (*presul summus*) will not be judged by anyone, since it is written that a disciple is not above his master"; and canon 20, "no one will judge the first see, which itself desires to administer justice. For the judge will not be judged by the emperor, nor by any of the clergy, nor by kings, nor by the people."[7]

Although these two documents are today universally reckoned forgeries,[8] they nevertheless bear witness to the sentiment of the time when they were composed. Hence, when a genuine synod of bishops was held in Rome in 502 at the bidding of king Theodoric to consider the accusations made against Pope Symmachus by his rival, namely that he was guilty of unchastity, misuse of Church property, and keeping Easter on the wrong date, the bishops refused to pass a verdict, declaring that the bishop of Peter's see was not subject to the judgment of his inferiors (*nec antedictae sedis antistitem minorum subiacuisse iudicio*).[9] St Avitus of Vienne, writing after this gathering to the Roman senate on behalf of the bishops of Gaul, expressed their approval of the synod's statement, noting that "it cannot easily be understood on what grounds or by what law a superior may be judged by his inferiors," since "it does not belong to the flock to strike fear into their shepherd, but to the judge."[10]

The same position was taken three hundred years later, when Pope Leo III was accused of perjury and adultery. An assembly of bishops and abbots which had gathered to discuss the matter in the year 800 declared in the presence of both the pope and the emperor Charlemagne: "We dare not pass judgment on the apostolic see which is the head of all God's churches; it is all of us who are judged by it and its vicar; just as the custom was of old, it is judged by no one."[11] Alcuin of York had made the same assertion in a letter written the previous year to the bishop of Salisbury.[12] A little later, Pope Nicholas I would appeal to the

---

6   Mansi, *Sacrorum conciliorum nova et amplissima collectio*, vol. 1 (Florence, 1759), 1257. The phrase "*prima sedes*" was first used to refer to any metropolitan see, but had come by the fifth century to refer to that of Rome; James Moynihan, *Papal Immunity and Liability in the Writings of the Medieval Canonists* (Rome: Gregorian University Press, 1961), 4, n14.

7   Mansi, *Sacrorum conciliorum nova et amplissima collectio*, vol. 2 (Florence, 1759), 623; 632.

8   Richards, *The Popes and the Papacy*, 95.

9   Mansi, *Sacrorum conciliorum nova et amplissima collectio*, vol. 8 (Florence, 1762), 248; Richards, *The Popes and the Papacy*, 71-73.

10   Mansi 8:294: "Non facile datur intelligi qua vel ratione vel lege ab inferioribus eminentior iudicetur"; ibid., 295: "Non est gregis pastorem proprium terrere, sed iudicis." Avitus was himself a man of senatorial rank, and was thus a suitable spokesman for the Gallic bishops.

11   *The Eighth-Century Popes (Liber Pontificalis)*, trans. Raymond Davis (Liverpool: Liverpool University Press, 1992), 190. It is disputed whether the pope simply asserted his own innocence or took an "oath of purgation"; see Moynihan, *Papal Immunity*, 11-12.

12   *Monumenta Germaniae Historica. Epistolarum Karolini Aevi* [hereafter: MGH EKA], tom. 4 (Berlin: Weidmann, 1895), Letter 179, p. 297. Alcuin was unwilling that the pope should clear himself even by an oath, and quoted the words of St Paul: "To his own Lord he will stand or fall" (Rom 14:4).

Gesta Marcellini when writing to Emperor Michael III, quoting the phrase *prima sedes non iudicabitur a quoquam.* [13]

Accordingly, the principle of the judicial immunity and primacy of the see of Rome was incorporated by Gratian into his *Concordia* (or *Concordantia*) *Discordantium Canonum*, generally known as the *Decretum*, around 1140. [14] We find, for example, in the first of the three parts of this compilation, the relevant portion of the letter of Pope Nicholas to the emperor; [15] and in the second part, the letter of Pope Gelasius, mentioned above, [16] and a portion of a second letter of Pope Nicholas, written to the bishops of the western empire, which asserts the judicial immunity of the see of Rome as being of divine right, "having been divinely conferred by Christ's gift on blessed Peter." [17] Although of itself only a private collection, the *Decretum* became the chief point of reference for canonists for the next hundred years.

As we shall see, both Gratian himself and later authors discussed real or apparent exceptions to this judicial immunity of the popes. Nevertheless, it remained in theory and in principle a fundamental axiom of Christendom and the Church: the axiom that the first see is judged by no one was retained by the codification of 1917 as canon 1556, and is found in the current code as canon 1404.

THE POSSIBILITY OF A HERETICAL POPE

At the First Vatican Council, the *relator* of the commission *On the Faith*, Bishop Federico Zinelli, stated that God does not fail to provide necessary aid to the Church, and hence that if He permitted a pope to fall into heresy as a private person, "means will not be lacking to prevent the doctrine of the truly full and supreme power of the Roman pontiff from being undermined." [18] In accepting that a pope might fall into heresy, in acts that fall outside the scope of the infallibility defined by this council, Zinelli was simply continuing a long-established tradition.

The Third Council of Constantinople (680–681) named Pope Honorius in its list of those who had incurred the guilt of the Monothelite heresy, [19] and this conciliar decree was ratified by Pope Leo II. [20] While it is possible that Honorius may have incurred the guilt of this heresy by conniving at it rather than by holding it

---

13 MGH EKA, tom. 6 (Berlin: Weidmann, 1925), Letter 88, p. 466.

14 For collections before Gratian, including the *Dictatus Papae* associated with Gregory VII, see Moynihan, *Papal Immunity*, 15–21.

15 *Decretum Magistri Gratiani* (Leipzig: Tauchnitz, 1879), ch. 7, d. 21, pp. 71–72.

16 c. 18, C. IX, q. 3, p. 611.

17 c. 30, C. XVII, q. 4, p. 823. The relevant portion of the letter is given in MGH EKA, tom. 6, p. 606. We also find can. 20 of the so-called *Constitutum Silvestri*, attributed by Gratian to "Pope Innocent" at c. 13, C. IX, q. 3, p. 610; and a statement attributed to Pope Symmachus, contained in a *Libellus* written by Symmachus's contemporary Ennodius, to the effect that God has willed that the causes of other men should be decided by men, but has reserved judgment of the pope to Himself, at c. 14, C. IX, q. 3, p. 610.

18 Mansi, *Sacrorum conciliorum nova et amplissima collectio*, vol. 52 (Arnhem & Leipzig: Société Nouvelle d'Édition de la Collection Mansi [H. Welter], 1927), 1109.

19 DH 552.

20 DH 562–63.

(somewhat as a man may incur the guilt of theft by knowingly receiving stolen goods rather than by stealing them), Constantinople III itself did not draw this distinction.

Several popes after the time of Leo II have also mentioned the possibility that one of their number could be a heretic. At a Roman synod held in 869, Pope Adrian II noted that Honorius had after his death been declared anathema for heresy (*super haeresi*) by the rulers of all the churches; Adrian also sent his speech to be read at the Fourth Council of Constantinople.[21] Much later, Pope Innocent III made several references to the lamentable possibility of a heretical pope in sermons that he preached for the anniversary of his own episcopal consecration in 1198. It suffices for now to quote this passage: "The Roman Church could send away (*dimittere*) the Roman pontiff on account of fornication. I do not mean carnal fornication, but spiritual, that is, on account of straying from the faith (*propter infidelitatis errorem*), inasmuch as their union is not carnal but spiritual."[22] He added, however: "Yet I should not easily believe that God would permit the Roman pontiff to err against the faith (*contra fidem errare*)."[23]

I shall consider the position of the canonists when we see in what sense they treat heresy in a pope as removing his immunity: for now, we may note that the discussion of heresy in a pope entered the canonical tradition in the eleventh century,[24] and has formed part of that tradition ever since.[25]

The theologians came to the discussion somewhat later than the canon lawyers. The question of a heretical pope was apparently not broached by the scholastics of the high Middle Ages. However, an extended discussion about the consequences for the Church of a heretical pope is found in the *Summa de Ecclesia* of John de Torquemada (d. 1468).[26] By the time of the *Controversiae* of St Robert Bellarmine in the final decades of the sixteenth century, the preliminary question has come to be posed of whether it is in fact possible that a Roman pontiff could, as a "private person," ever be a heretic: the first author arguing that such a thing was impossible was Albert Pigghe (Pighius in Latin), in his *Hierarchiae Ecclesiasticae Assertio* of 1538. While Bellarmine himself thinks that a "pious and plausible" argument can be made for Pigghe's opinion, he does not suppose that it is binding on Catholics.[27] Francisco Suárez (d. 1617) adopted the same position as Bellarmine.[28]

---

21   "Third Allocution of Pope Adrian II, which was read by Peter the deacon," in Mansi, *Sacrorum conciliorum nova et amplissima collectio*, vol. 16 (Venice, 1771), 126.

22   Innocent III, Sermon III for the Consecration of the Pontiff, *PL* 217:665.

23   I leave aside the opinion of Pope Adrian VI, who in his *Commentary on the Sentences*, written as Adriaan Boeyens before his accession to the papacy but republished afterward, stated that several (*plures*) popes had been heretics. See Cyrille Dounot and Nicolas Warembourg, "Pontife et Souverain. L'inextricable souveraineté pontificale," in Dounot et al., *La déposition du pape hérétique*, 212.

24   Moynihan, *Papal Immunity*, 32.

25   Francisco Wernz and Peter Vidal, *Ius Canonicum ad Codicis Normam Exactum* (Rome: Gregorian University, 1937), no. 453.

26   *Summa de Ecclesia* (Venice, 1560), Bk. 4, pt. 2, chs. 18–20.

27   *De Romano Pontifice*, Bk. 4, ch. 6.

28   Francisco Suárez, *Opera Omnia* (Paris: Vivès, 1858), vol. 12, *De Fide*, disp. 10, sect. 6.11, p. 319: "To me it seems more probable that a pope could as a private person err from ignorance but not from

The principal point of discussion among the early modern scholastics, however, was not whether it was possible for a pope to fall into heresy, but whether in such a case he would lose the pontificate automatically or only after a sentence had been passed by the Church, and in the latter case, whether this sentence would be an act of authority or a bare declaration of fact.[29]

Among more recent ecclesiologists, both Charles Journet and Yves Congar have accepted that a Roman pontiff's falling into heresy is compatible with the dogmatic definition of Vatican I, the latter author stating that he knew of no theologian who accepted Pigghe's position.[30]

HERESY AND PAPAL IMMUNITY: SCRIPTURAL AND PATRISTIC BACKGROUND

Would a pope lose his judicial immunity if he were to lapse into heresy? By "heresy," here, we may understand both the sin and the crime: that is, both the deliberate doubt or denial of some revealed truth that must be believed by divine and Catholic faith, and the external manifestation of this denial or doubt.

While the scriptural and patristic sources do not discuss this question explicitly, they do contain the principles on which later discussion would build. Cajetan invokes various scriptural passages to establish the duty of separation from a heretical pope, including Galatians 1:8 ("even if we or an angel from heaven should preach to you a gospel contrary to the one we preached to you, let him be accursed"); 2 Thessalonians 3:6 ("we charge you, brethren, in the name of our Lord Jesus Christ, that you withdraw yourselves from every brother walking disorderly, and not according to the tradition which they have received of us"); and Titus 3:10: "A man that is a heretic (*hairetikon*), after the first and second admonition, avoid, knowing that he that is such a one, is subverted and sins, being self-condemned."[31] This last passage in particular will become a commonplace of the theological tradition.

Also of importance for later discussion was a principle laid down by Pope Celestine I (422–432). In speaking of the excommunications declared by Nestorius of Constantinople after he had begun publicly preaching against the divine maternity of Mary, Celestine asserted that denying the Catholic faith is incompatible with holding power to govern within the Church. In a letter to John, bishop of Antioch, the pope wrote:

---

contumacy. For although God could bring it about that a heretical pope would not harm the Church, still, a more fitting [*suavior*] disposition of divine providence would be for God to bring it about that a pope would never be a heretic, since He has promised that the pope would never err when defining."

29 See below for discussion.

30 Charles Journet, *The Church of the Word Incarnate*, vol. 1 (London: Sheed & Ward, 1955), 482–84; for Congar, see Cyrille Dounot, "Paul VI hérétique? La déposition du pape dans le discours traditionaliste," in Dounot, et al., *La déposition du pape hérétique*, 137. Louis Billot, on the other hand, affirmed that the promise of Christ to Simon Peter "seems absolutely to exclude" a defection from the faith on the part of St Peter's successor; he nevertheless considers what the legal consequences would be of notorious papal heresy: *Tractatus de Ecclesia Christi*, vol. 1 (Prato: Giachetti, 1909), q. 14, thesis 29, pp. 617–18.

31 Thomas de Vio (Cajetan), *De comparatione auctoritatis papae et concilii*, in *Opuscula omnia* (Lyons, 1525), ch. 20 (p. 21).

If anyone was excommunicated or cast from the episcopal or clerical rank by Bishop Nestorius, or by those who follow him, from the
time when [ex quo] they began to preach such things [sc. the denial of
the divine maternity], it is clear that this man has remained and still
remains in communion with Us, nor do We judge him to have been
deposed; for the judgment of someone who had already shown that
he should be deposed could not itself depose anyone.[32]

These words of Celestine were known to later authors, being quoted by Pope
Nicholas in his letter to the emperor in Constantinople,[33] and later by St Ivo of
Chartres, the preeminent canon lawyer of the generation before Gratian,[34] though
not in connection with the hypothesis of a heretical pope. Later still, Bellarmine
will quote them as decisive for determining the status of such a pontiff.[35]

Elphège Vacandard cited the allocution of Pope Adrian II sent to Constantinople
IV, as supporting the opinion that an ecumenical council may declare a pope to
be deposed for heresy.[36] The facts, however, hardly warrant this conclusion. The
relevant part of Adrian's message in 869 reads as follows:

We read that the Roman pontiff has given judgment about the prelates
of all the churches; we do not read that anyone has given judgment
about him: for although an anathema was pronounced against Honorius after his death by the Easterners, one should know that he had been
accused of heresy, for which cause alone it is permissible for subjects to
resist the acts of their superiors, or openly to reject their evil sentiments
(propter quam solam licitum est minoribus majorum suorum motibus resistendi,
vel pravos sensus libere respuendi); although even in that case it would
not have been lawful for any of the patriarchs or the other bishops to
pronounce judgment (proferendi sententiam) about him if the authority
of the consent of the pontiff of the same first see had not preceded.[37]

Far from holding, then, that an ecumenical council may find a reigning pope
guilty of heresy and declare him no longer pope, Adrian declares that no gathering
of bishops and patriarchs can presume to find even a deceased pope guilty, if the
current Roman pontiff disagrees with them. Subjects are allowed to resist their
superiors' acts and teachings, when these spread heresy, but not to bring these
superiors to trial and punish them. Accordingly, the bishops in Constantinople

---

32   Mansi, *Sacrorum conciliorum nova et amplissima collectio*, vol. 4 (Florence, 1760), 1050: "Si quis
vero, aut ab Episcopo Nestorio, aut ab his qui eum sequuntur, ex quo talia praedicare coeperunt,
vel excommunicatus vel exutus est seu antistitis seu clerici dignitate, hunc in nostra communione
et durasse et durare manifestum est; nec iudicamus remotum, quia non poterat quemquam eius
removere sententia qui se iam praebuerat ipse removendum."

33   MGH EKA, tom. 6 (Berlin: Weidmann, 1925), Letter 88, p. 462.

34   *Decretum*, pt. IV, ch. 58; *PL* 161:839.

35   St Robert Bellarmine, *De Controversiis*, vol. 2 (Paris: Vivès, 1873), *De Romano Pontifice*, Bk.
2, ch. 30, p. 609.

36   *DTC*, "Déposition et Dégradation des clercs, VI. Déposition des Papes."

37   Mansi, *Sacrorum conciliorum nova et amplissima collectio*, vol. 16 (Florence, 1771), 126.

decreed in their thirteenth canon: "If an ecumenical synod is gathered and some doubt or controversy should arise even about the holy church of the Romans, it is necessary to investigate the matter with due reverence and respect; to find out the truth and either to receive or to provide assistance but not boldly to pass judgment contrary to the supreme pontiffs of the elder Rome."[38] The canons of this council were placed into the collections made in the West before and after Gratian.[39]

We should however note that Pope Honorius, whose connivance with Monothelitism two centuries earlier is mentioned by Adrian II, was not condemned for professing a heresy that had been already condemned, but for supporting the formation of a new one: the relevance of this distinction will become apparent below.

Also prominent in the medieval discussion was a text from the *Sentences* of St Isidore of Seville. Having explained that bad ecclesiastical superiors are to be left to the judgment of God, Isidore adds an exception: "If the ruler departs from the faith, then he is to be rebuked by his subjects; but if his morals are evil, the people must bear with him and not punish him."[40] As the editor of Migne notes, Isidore's discussion was inspired by St Gregory the Great's treatment of the question in his *Commentary on Job*: Gregory had stated that "He [the Lord] judges the conduct of people by their rulers, but . . . he examines into the doings of rulers in his own person . . . . Therefore, provided the faith is not injured (*dum salva fide res agitur*), it is meritorious virtue to tolerate whatever pertains to a superior."[41]

Isidore's words were put into the decrees of the Council of Aachen in 816, and soon after into the "False Decretals" of Pseudo-Isidore, where they were presented as part of an epistle from Pope Clement I to St James. As Moynihan notes, they were thus transformed from a moral counsel to an authoritative norm.[42]

In speaking of the need to rebuke a ruler who departs from the faith, however, neither Isidore nor Pseudo-Isidore had referred to a *pope*. The first person known to use the text from Isidore's *Sentences* in the context of papal orthodoxy is a certain Auxilius, a Roman priest writing during the reign of Pope Sergius III (904–911). In his dialogue *Infensor et Defensor*, written to defend the validity of the ordinations of Pope Formosus (891–896), Auxilius asserts a right to speak if a pope acts against the faith or the Catholic religion, and even his imaginary opponent, quoting Isidore, allows that any pastor of the Church is to be corrected (*corrigendus*) if he deviates from the faith.[43]

---

38 DH 664.

39 Martin Jugie, *DTC*, "Constantinople, IVème Concile de."

40 Isidore, *Sententiae*: "Si a fide exhorbitaverit rector, tunc erit arguendus a subditis, pro moribus vero reprobis tolerandus magis distringendus [sic] a plebe est." *PL* 83:710.

41 *Moralia in Iob*, Bk. 25, ch. 36; *PL* 76:344-45. One English translation of the *Moralia* translates the first clause of this sentence as "Therefore whilst all is done in good faith": *Morals on the Book of Job*, trans. John Henry Parker (London: J. & J. Rivington, 1844). This seems strained, and there is nothing in the context to suggest it.

42 *Papal Immunity*, 28.

43 *PL* 129:1088-89, 1099. The speaker uses the word *corrigendus* ("due to be corrected") where St Isidore had said *arguendus* ("due to be accused or reproved"). For more details about this dialogue, see Moynihan, *Papal Immunity*, 35-37.

Neither "rebuke" nor "correct" need imply a judicial act, going beyond simple fraternal correction.[44] It is arguable that a further stage is reached around 1053, with the first letter written on behalf of Pope Leo IX to Michael Cerularius, patriarch of Constantinople. This letter has been generally attributed to Cardinal Humbert of Silva Candida.[45] Having set forth the preeminence and duties of the bishop of Rome, as well as the harm that he would do to himself and to others if negligent, Humbert continues: "No mortal presumes in this regard to rebuke (*redarguere*) him, since the one who is to judge all men is himself to be judged (*iudicandus*) by no one, unless perhaps he should be found straying from the faith (*nisi forte deprehendatur a fide devius*)."[46] The use of the word "judge" suggests an authoritative sentence; on the other hand, it is not clear that Humbert means it to be understood of a living pope, as opposed to Constantinople III's judgment of the deceased Honorius.

Humbert's text passed into the canonical collections: it appears, attributed to "St Boniface the martyr,"[47] in the *Collectio Canonum* produced around 1083 by Cardinal Deusdedit, an ally of Pope Gregory VII, and also in the *Liber Tarraconensis* (ca. 1085–1090).[48] It was included in the collection of canons produced by Ivo of Chartres a few years later,[49] and, crucially, in the *Decretum* of Gratian, where with trivial changes it appears as canon 6 of distinction 40, in the first of the three parts of that work. This canon generally came to be known as *Si papa*, from its opening words.[50]

A second canon relevant to the medieval discussion appears in the second part of the *Decretum*. Gratian writes: "Therefore if the bishop has fallen into a heresy that has already been condemned, he cannot condemn others, being himself condemned by the older excommunication. For an excommunicated man is not able to excommunicate others."[51] This recalls Pope Celestine's teaching that a heretical prelate cannot validly govern, although restricts it to the prelate who embraces a heresy that has been expressly condemned by the Church.

---

44   For the distinction between fraternal and authoritative correction, see St Thomas, *ST* II-II, Q. 33, arts. 1 and 3.

45   Brett Edward Whalen, however, writes: "There has been a misleading tendency in the past to ascribe all the key sources from the schism of 1054 solely to Humbert . . . . The body of texts related to the schism were a group effort, reflecting input by Pope Leo, Humbert, and others in their immediate circle" (*Dominion of God: Christendom and Apocalypse in the Middle Ages* [Cambridge, MA: Harvard University Press, 2009], 247). For further discussion, see Margit Dischner, *Humbert von Silva Candida: Werk und Wirkung des lothringischen Reformmönches* (Munich: Ars Una, 1996).

46   *Die Kanonessamlung des Kardinals Deusdedit*, ed. Victor Wolf von Glanvell (Paderborn: Ferdinand Schöningh, 1905), Bk. 1, ch. 306, p. 178.

47   The reason for this attribution is unknown. Moynihan takes it to be a simple error: *Papal Immunity*, 30.

48   For summary of the scholarship by which the text was traced back from Deusdedit to Humbert, see Moynihan, 29–30.

49   Ivo expressed the same opinion in a letter to several French bishops: "We are not willing to deprive of the highest keys of the Church him who holds the place of Peter unless he should manifestly depart (*manifeste . . . discedat*) from gospel truth." Letter 236, PL 162:240.

50   *Decretum Magistri Gratiani*, ch. 6, d. 40, p. 146.

51   ch. 3, C. XXIV, q. 1, pp. 965–66. In support of the canon, Gratian quotes judgments of Pope Gelasius I and Pope Felix I against Acacius.

HERESY AND PAPAL IMMUNITY: MEDIEVAL DISCUSSION

Gratian himself did not explain the meaning or mode of the judgment to be pronounced on a Roman pontiff who deviated from the faith. The "Decretists," the twelfth-century and early thirteenth-century canonists who commented on Gratian's work, proposed various accounts of what should be done. They understand the canon to be speaking of a living pope: hence, the first author known to have discussed the question, Rufinus of Assisi, says that the pope would have to be admonished a second and a third time before being condemned.[52]

The authors naturally asked whether and how *Si papa* could be reconciled with papal immunity. In answer to this question, two main schools emerged. The principal representative of the first school was Huguccio of Pisa, whose *Summa* was written around 1190.[53] Huguccio considered various cases. A pope might preach something which was certainly heretical and might contumaciously defend his position when admonished. In such a case he could be condemned (*condempnari*) for heresy.[54] The proper body to do this would be the college of cardinals, who would then elect a successor.[55] If, however, he repented when admonished, he could not be condemned. On the other hand, he might invent a new heresy: that is, an opinion that had not previously been condemned, but which some people wished to show was heretical.[56] In this case, says Huguccio, "I do not believe that they should be [judicially] heard."

According to this author, the reason that a pope can be condemned for preaching a known heresy is that otherwise the whole Church would be in danger. For the same reason, he supposes that a pope may be condemned when he committed any notorious crime, such as simony, concubinage, or sacrilege: "Is it not like committing heresy to scandalize the Church?" If heresy alone is mentioned in *Si papa*, he suggests, it is because this crime may be penalized as soon as it is public, even if it is not notorious.[57]

How does Huguccio reconcile his position with the judicial primacy of the pope,

---

52   Rufinus, *Summa*, commentary on d. 40, c. 6, quoted in Moynihan, *Papal Immunity*, 50. This *Summa* was written between 1157 and 1159.

53   Brian Tierney refers to this *Summa* as "the greatest achievement of twelfth-century Decretist scholarship." *Foundations of the Conciliar Theory: The Contribution of the Medieval Canonists from Gratian to the Great Schism* (Leiden: Brill, 1998), 236. Huguccio's commentary on *Si papa* is printed as appendix 1 of this work. See also Wolfgang Müller, *Huguccio: The Life, Works, and Thought of a Twelfth-Century Jurist* (Washington, DC: Catholic University of America Press, 1994); Kenneth Pennington and Wolfgang Müller, "The Decretists: The Italian School," in Pennington and Müller, eds., *The History of Medieval Canon Law in the Classical Period* (Washington, DC: Catholic University of America Press, 2008), 121–73.

54   Huguccio, *Summa*, commentary on d. 40, c. 6. The text is quoted both by Moynihan, *Papal Immunity*, 76, and by Tierney, *Foundations*, 227. The latter has "accused" (*accusari*) rather than "condemned" at this point. However, both authors quote Huguccio's opening summary of his position as *de heresi papa potest condempnari a subditis* ("the pope can be condemned by his subjects for heresy").

55   Huguccio, *Summa*, commentary on d. 63, c. 23, quoted in Moynihan, *Papal Immunity*, 82.

56   A good example of this is Pope John XXII's opinion that the souls of the saints will not receive the beatific vision until the last judgment.

57   For more on this distinction, see below.

and more generally with the well-established principle that a superior cannot be judged by his subjects? His answer is, in effect, that in the cases which he envisages, the pope has ceased to be a superior before being condemned: "When a pope falls into heresy, he is understood to be no longer superior but inferior to any Catholic (*minor quolibet catholico*)."[58] He insists, however, that this principle may only be applied when the crime is certain.[59] Here he is following a general principle also laid down by Gratian, that the laws requiring accusations by competent persons to precede judicial condemnations do not apply when crimes are manifest.[60]

Huguccio's most famous pupil was Lothar of Segni, the future Pope Innocent III. Innocent appears have shared his master's position that a heretical pope would automatically forfeit his rank without need for a trial in the proper sense. A pope "can be judged by men, or rather be shown to be judged (*potest ab hominibus judicari, vel potius judicatus ostendi*), if he loses his savor by way of heresy; for he who does not believe is already judged."[61] On the other hand, Innocent does not follow Huguccio in broadening the concept of heresy to include other obstinate and notorious crimes liable to scandalize the whole Church.

The representative of the second main school of thought among the Decretists is "Alan the Englishman" (Alanus Anglicus). In his *Apparatus Ius Naturale*, written around 1210, Alan held that in defining questions of faith, the pope possessed less authority than a council or the college of cardinals: for this reason, either body might try a pope on a question of heresy against his will, even when it concerns a point of doctrine not previously defined.[62] The pope cannot take away this right from a council, for doing so could lead to the ruin (*perniciem*) of the Church. On the other hand, Alan denied that a council was superior over a pope in other matters, and hence held that it is not competent to try or to depose a pope for any crime save heresy.[63]

Alan thus appears as a forerunner of the conciliarist movement. Unlike Huguccio, he admits a true exception to papal judicial immunity, with a man who is still pope being liable to a trial in the proper sense of the word for a charge of heresy. This opinion tended to prevail among the canonists of the later Middle Ages, with Huguccio's position, of a papal loss of office *ipso facto*, being mostly neglected.[64] On the other hand, even those authors who followed Huguccio assume the existence of a body that would judge that such a loss of office had in fact occurred.

---

58   *Summa*, commentary on d. 21, c. 4, quoted in Tierney, *Foundations*, 57.

59   *Summa*, commentary on C. 6, q. 1 *post* c. 21, quoted in Tierney, *Foundations*, 57.

60   c. 14–15, C. 2, q. 1, p. 445. Gratian quotes here a dictum attributed by him to St Ambrose, that "obvious matters do not require an accusation" (*manifesta accusatione non indigent*).

61   Pope Innocent III, Sermon IV for the Consecration of the Pontiff, PL 217:670.

62   *Apparatus Ius Naturale*, commentary on d. 40, c. 6, quoted in Moynihan, *Papal Immunity*, 96: "*De sola heresi invitus potest papa iudicari . . . . Hoc ideo in hoc crimine quia circa ea quae ad fidem pertinent minor est collegio cardinalium vel concilio generali episcoporum*" ("A pope can be judged against his will only for heresy. . . . This is so in this crime because in matters of faith, he is less than the college of cardinals or a general council of bishops").

63   Moynihan, *Papal Immunity*, 100–102.

64   Moynihan, 141–43.

According to Vacandard, writing in the *Dictionnaire de théologie catholique*, the doctrine that "heresy constitutes a crime for which a pope can be deposed by a general council . . . was received and confirmed by the whole of the Middle Ages."[65] We can see that this description must be qualified in several important ways: the heresy must be one that the Church has already established to be such; "depose" must be taken in a broad sense to include "registering a self-deposition"; and the college of cardinals must be mentioned as an alternative to a general council. Likewise, the "Middle Ages" must be taken as beginning in the middle of the twelfth century.

In 1234, Pope Gregory IX published the *Decretals*, the first collection of laws to be papally promulgated. This was not intended to replace all earlier law, but was rather a collection of the decrees published by the popes between the time of Gratian and that of Gregory's own predecessor, Honorius III: it therefore left intact earlier laws insofar as they were compatible with these.[66] Accordingly, later canonists and theologians continued to treat *Si papa* as an authority: Bellarmine cites it as his first piece of evidence for the Church's right to take action about a manifestly heretical pope.[67]

THEOLOGICAL ASSESSMENT

No law of purely ecclesiastical origin would be sufficient for dealing with the problem of a pope who fell into heresy, since the Roman pontiff would be able to exempt himself from its scope. *Si papa* is thus of interest to the theologian today only if, and insofar as, it embodies a provision of divine law. The fuller articulation of divine law achieved since the Middle Ages, and especially at Vatican I, shows that neither of the two main Decretist schools may be followed exactly. The position of Alanus Anglicus, and of the later conciliarist school, that a man who was still a true pope might be put on trial on a count of heresy and deposed if found guilty cannot stand against the dogmatic definition of universal papal jurisdiction pronounced in 1870 by *Pastor Aeternus*.[68] Alanus's instinct, however, that heresy in a pope was a crime unique in its consequences was partially sound, as we shall see.

---

65   Vacandard, "Déposition et Dégradation des clercs," VI. Déposition des Papes, col. 519.

66   Moynihan, *Papal Immunity*, 112. Charles Duggan notes that "the *Decretum* remained the first book of the corpus of canon law until the early twentieth century" ("Decretal Collections from Gratian's *Decretum* to the *Compilationes antiquae*," in Pennington and Müller, *History of Medieval Canon Law*, 247).

67   Bellarmine, *De Romano Pontifice*, Bk. 2, ch. 30, p. 608.

68   DH 3064: "If anyone, then, shall say that the Roman pontiff has the office merely of inspection or direction, and not the full and supreme power of jurisdiction over the universal Church, not only in things which belong to faith and morals, but also in those which relate to the discipline and government of the Church spread throughout the world; or assert that he possesses merely the principal part, and not all the fullness of this supreme power; or that this power which he enjoys is not ordinary and immediate, both over each and all the Churches and over each and all the Pastors and the faithful; let him be anathema." Cf. *Codex Iuris Canonici* [hereafter: *CIC*], canon 1372: "A person who makes recourse against an act of the Roman pontiff to an ecumenical council or the college of bishops is to be punished with a censure."

Huguccio was therefore correct to argue that no one who was still a pope could be tried for heresy or for any other crime. His explanation, however, of why heresy renders a pope "less than any Catholic" and hence liable to trial, namely, that otherwise great scandal would be given to believers, is inadequate. We have seen that his logic led him to consider that notorious simony or concubinage also effected papal self-deposition. In fact, any public, mortal sin in a pope would be a scandal, but it is contrary to Scripture and Tradition to claim that he would thereby lose his office. If the steward begins *to strike the menservants and maidservants, and to eat and to drink and be drunk*, it is not they but the lord of that steward who is to separate him from them and put him with the unbelievers (see Lk 12:45–56). On the other hand, Huguccio was on surer ground when he denied to the cardinals the right to determine whether a pope had already lost office by upholding a doubtful opinion whose heretical nature had not previously been determined. Without its papal head, no synod may define doctrine.[69]

The true reason why heresy, when openly professed, renders a pope or anyone else to be less than any Catholic is simply that it causes him to be not a Catholic. If a pope were to say: "I am fully persuaded that there was [a time] when the Son was not; he is not God in the same sense as the Father," and if it were to prove on investigation that he was not joking or intoxicated or speaking under grave duress, then he would be rightly judged to have ceased to profess the Catholic faith, and thus to have ceased to be a member of the Church, and hence to have made himself unable to hold any office within it. In recognizing the last fact, a Catholic would no more be sitting in judgment over a pope than would the papal chamberlain who announces his death. This analogy also indicates that the proper body to take legal cognizance of the fact of a papal self-deposition for heresy is the college of cardinals, since according to the present law of the Church, this is the body that must elect a bishop of Rome when the see is vacant.[70] If many early modern theologians spoke of an "imperfect" ecumenical council as necessary to recognize the fact of a papal self-deposition, this seems a sign of the long shadow cast upon the Church by conciliarism.[71]

Hence St Robert Bellarmine, commenting on the position of Juan de

---

69   See the Vatican II, *Lumen Gentium* 22: "The order of bishops . . . is also the subject of supreme and full power over the universal Church, provided we understand this body together with its head the Roman pontiff and never without this head. This power can be exercised only with the consent of the Roman pontiff."

70   *CIC* 349. In the preamble to his 1996 apostolic constitution *Universi Dominici Gregis*, Pope John Paul II nevertheless affirmed that "it seems to be an indisputable principle that it pertains to the Roman pontiffs to define and adapt to changing times the manner of designating the person called to succeed Peter in the Roman See."

71   Cajetan had spoken of such a headless council as "perfect according to the present state of the Church," *De comparatione auctoritatis papae et concilii*, ch. 16. Bellarmine calls it more simply "imperfect": *De Controversiis*, vol. 2 (Paris: Vivès, 1873), *De Conciliis*, Bk. 1, ch. 9, pp. 206–7. Suárez allows that many local councils might in these circumstances take the place of a (so-called) imperfect ecumenical one; and while not legally necessary, the holding of such councils would seem wise given the gravity of the affair (*De Fide*, disp. 10, sect. 6.7, pp. 317–18).

Torquemada, notes that the correct opinion on the loss of the papacy for heresy follows from the correct opinion about membership of the Church. Whereas Torquemada considered that a Catholic was placed outside the Church by even private heresy, Bellarmine maintained that such a person remains a member of the Church, albeit a dry and dead one: "It is certain that, whatever this or that person may have thought, a hidden heretic, if he were a bishop or even the supreme pontiff, would not lose jurisdiction, nor rank, nor the name of head in the Church, until either he himself publicly separated himself from the Church, or being convicted of heresy he was separated against his will."[72] In other words, it is not the fact of heresy but the profession of it that causes loss of office. Otherwise, as he remarks in understated fashion, "all acts that require jurisdiction would become uncertain, which would unsettle the universal Church not a little."

Bellarmine's position also follows from the account of the visible Church given by the Second Vatican Council: "The bonds which bind men to the Church in a visible way are profession of faith (*professionis fidei*), the sacraments, and ecclesiastical government and communion."[73] Hence, someone who by publicly professing heresy ceased to profess the faith would cease to belong to the visible Church, and so could hold no office within her. Since also we must believe by divine and Catholic faith not only matters already defined by the Church's solemn judgment but also those "proposed as divinely revealed . . . by her ordinary and universal magisterium,"[74] membership of the Church would be lost by publicly contradicting not only a defined dogma but also anything manifestly taught in this latter way. If, for example, Nestorius lost his office from the time that he began publicly to preach against the Theotokos, this must be because the divine maternity plainly formed part of the Church's ordinary and universal magisterium.[75]

"NOTORIOUS" HERESY

Naturally, given the unique importance of the matter, the profession of heresy must be entirely certain in order to produce its effect. Later canonists, developing Bellarmine's account, expressed this by using the term "notoriety." "Notorious," in this developed canonical language, is a stronger term than "public." Thus the 1917 Code of Canon Law declared a crime to be public "if it has already been made

---

72 Bellarmine, *De Conciliis*, Bk. 3, ch. 10, pp. 338–39. He notes that Torquemada may have only meant that no one could be said to be united inwardly to the body of Christ if he lacked faith.

73 *Lumen Gentium* 14. Cf. Pope Pius XII, Encyclical *Mystici Corporis* (June 29, 1943), no. 22: "Only those are to be included as actually members of the Church who have been baptized and profess the true faith (*veramque fidem profitentur*), and who have not been so unfortunate as to separate themselves from the unity of the Body, or been excluded by legitimate authority for grave faults committed."

74 Pope John Paul II, Apostolic Letter *Ad Tuendam Fidem* (May 18, 1998), no. 4, modifying can. 750 §1.

75 In explaining why those who followed Nestorius's opinion were culpable, St Thomas Aquinas wrote: "The man who follows the opinion of some master against the plain witness of Scripture or against what is held publicly according to the authority of the Church cannot be excused from the fault of error" (*Quodlibetal Questions*, III, 4, 2). Another example of such an opinion would be the denial that Christ's tomb was empty on Easter Day.

widely known (*divulgatum*), or if it happens in such circumstances that it can be prudently judged that it will easily become widely known"; it declares a crime to be notorious "if it is publicly known and was committed in such circumstances that it cannot be concealed by any subterfuge (*tergiversatione*) or excused by any legal opinion (*suffragio iuris*)."[76] Accordingly, a celebrated commentary on this code, adopting Bellarmine's position, restates it thus: "Through *heresy notoriously* and *openly* expressed (*divulgatam*), the Roman Pontiff, should he fall into such, is by that very fact and before any declaratory sentence of the Church, deprived of his power of jurisdiction."[77]

The distinction between crimes that are "occult," "public," and "notorious" has not been retained in the current code, which simply states in canon 1330 that "a delict which consists in a declaration or in another manifestation of will, doctrine, or knowledge must not be considered completed if no one perceives the declaration or manifestation."[78] This fact is not however of direct importance for our present question, which, as we have seen, depends by nature on divine law: and again, a pope who lost office for notoriously professing a heresy would lose it not exactly as a punishment for a crime but for having put himself in a state that is, like death, intrinsically incompatible with holding the papacy, namely, being a non-Catholic.[79] Hence, commentators on the current code take the same position as their predecessors.[80]

Wernz-Vidal's statement that the loss of office would happen "before any declaratory sentence of the Church" alludes to a well-known controversy between theologians. Cajetan had held that a pope who became a manifest heretic would not be *ipso facto* deposed, but would have to be deposed by the Church. His

---

76   1917 *CIC*, can. 2197 § 1 and § 3. A standard commentary explains the latter phrase as meaning that there must be no extenuating circumstances that would reduce imputability: Charles Augustine Bachofen, OSB, *A Commentary on the New Code of Canon Law*, vol. 8 (St Louis, MO: Herder, 1918), 17. A crime is said to be notorious by notoriety of law, rather than of fact, if it is confessed by a defendant at his trial or once the judge has found him guilty: 1917 *CIC*, can. 2197 § 2.

77   Wernz and Vidal, *Ius Canonicum*, no. 453, p. 517, emphasis in original. Another standard commentary on this code, teaching the same doctrine as Wernz-Vidal, explains that the code is silent about the case of a heretical pope because law provides for what easily happens and not for what happens very rarely: Guido Cocchi, *Commentarium in Codicem Iuris Canonici* (Turin: Marietti, 1930), Bk. II, part 1, p. 26.

78   In his commentary on this canon, Thomas Green notes that it "raises questions which need to be resolved in the practical working-out of penal discipline." See James Coriden, Thomas Green, and Donald Heintschel, eds., *The Code of Canon Law: A Text and Commentary* (London: Geoffrey Chapman, 1985), 906.

79   I therefore do not quite agree with John Lamont, when he speaks of the loss of the papacy as a punishment inflicted by divine law on a publicly heretical pope (see Lamont and Pierantoni, *Defending the Faith*, 360–61). Under the new covenant, divine law does not specify temporal punishments for specific offences; the only punishment specified by divine law for unrepentant heresy in a pope (or in anyone else) is damnation.

80   Lawrence Wrenn states: "Canon 1404 is not a statement of personal impeccability or inerrancy of the Holy Father. Should, indeed, the pope fall into heresy, it is understood that he would lose his office. To fall from Peter's faith is to fall from his chair." See Coriden et al., *The Code of Canon Law*, 951. See also Edward Peters, "A canonical primer on popes and heresy," *In the Light of the Law*, December 16, 2016, https://canonlawblog.wordpress.com/2016/12/16/a-canonical-primer-on-popes-and-heresy.

attempt, by introducing a distinction between "authority over the pope" and "authority over the bond between a man and the papacy," to deny that the pope would therefore have a human superior, was doomed to failure, being a distinction without a difference. John of St Thomas would later refine Cajetan's position by arguing that the Church would simply judge the fact of heresy, without claiming to penalize the man, whereupon Christ would Himself depose His vicar.[81] But this refinement is unnecessary: having ceased to be a Catholic by a notorious profession of heresy, he would already have ceased to be pope. Like the man mentioned by St Paul to St Titus, he would be "self-condemned" (*autokatakritos*). The role of "the Church" — in modern times, the college of cardinals — would be to note that the office had become vacant and to proceed to fill it.

Francisco Suárez offers two objections to the Bellarminian position.[82] The first is that no punishment is incurred except either in virtue of the law itself or as a result of a judicial sentence. Since loss of the papacy is so grave a punishment, divine law would need to state explicitly that manifest heresy causes this loss, which it does not; and hence the loss of the papacy must require a declaratory sentence of heresy by the Church, at which point Christ would depose the man. But this argument rests on the false premise that loss of the papacy would occur by way of *punishment*.

Suárez's other argument is that Catholics would dispute among themselves about whether or not the necessary notoriety had been reached, whereupon "schisms would follow, and all things would become confused."[83] The reply to this is that notorious things by definition require no discussion among men of good faith. While some of the cardinals might well not act in good faith and thus begin a schism, this would not show that the principle that they were guiltily ignoring or fraudulently invoking — that of the loss of office for professing heresy — is not a part of divine law. One may also retort Suárez's argument by pointing out that the requirement for a declaratory sentence to be passed could lead equally easily to schism, since nothing in divine law tells us what majority of voters would be necessary for the sentence to be valid.

Since the purpose of the "first and second admonition" mentioned in the letter to Titus is to establish that a person enunciating a heresy is "pertinacious," that is, aware of what he is doing,[84] many authors do not consider these admonitions to

---

81 John Poinsot, *Cursus Theologicus*, IIa IIae, qq. 1-7 (Paris: Vivès, 1885), disp. II, art. III, no. XXff., pp. 259ff. John did not suppose that Christ would intervene visibly; he held that after the fact of papal heresy had been declared, it could simply be declared also that Christ had deposed him. Charles Journet followed this opinion.

82 *De Fide*, disp. X, sect. 6, nos. 3-10. Charles Journet strangely describes Suárez as sharing Bellarmine's opinion (*The Church of the Word Incarnate*, 1:483). He gives no reference, and so this may arise from a habit of dividing theological controversies along Dominican-Jesuit lines.

83 *De Fide*, disp. X, sect. 6, no. 4.

84 Cocchi notes that pertinacity exists as soon as a person chooses to hold an opinion that he knows to contradict a doctrine proposed by the Church: *Commentarium in Codicem Iuris Canonici*, Bk. III, part 4, p. 23.

be necessary if pertinacity is otherwise obvious.[85] There would clearly be a great difference between a parishioner without theological training who said in a conversation "Christ had only one will" and a supreme pontiff who repeatedly denied the virginity of Mary while preaching at Midnight Mass. Nevertheless, should a pope profess even so blatant a heresy, it would seem useful for the cardinals to administer the admonitions as a way of determining if he were of sound mind.

A REMAINING PROBLEM

It may be objected that I have made things too easy for myself by speaking of a pope who would deny some defined dogma, or other well-known truth of the faith, in set terms. What if there were a pope who avoided a notorious profession of heresy but who spoke or acted in such a way that it could be reasonably judged, or even judged beyond reasonable doubt, that he denied or doubted some revealed truth, and thus was guilty of the crime of heresy? The classical treatises of theology and canon law hardly seem to allow for this case, distinguishing as they do simply between the crime of occult heresy, understood as heresy manifested by some external act but known to few or even none,[86] and the crime of notorious heresy. The case that we are now considering, by contrast, is that of a pope who frequently used words naturally understood as expressing some heresy, though susceptible to being bent into orthodoxy by a strained interpretation, and who favored those who openly professed the heresy in question, while disfavoring those who resisted it. John Lamont has pointed out that at a certain point the laws of probability will oblige even the most benign observer to judge that a person acting in such a way has rejected the revealed truth at stake.[87]

A pope who acted thus would not however cease to be a member of the Church, for as long as he expressed in general terms his wish to hold the Church's teaching, and for as long as he avoided any individual declaration or action that was an unequivocal profession of heresy. He would therefore not lose the papacy by ceasing to be capable of holding office in the Church. Moreover, though he could be judged informally to have committed the crime of heresy, the immunity attaching to the first see would prevent him from being tried for this crime. Nor would the commission of the crime cause him to lose the papacy *ipso facto*, since we have seen that such loss does not occur by way of punishment for a crime committed.

John Lamont, again, has argued that in such a case, the bishops of the Church should ask the pope to abjure the heresy, following the procedure mentioned in Titus 3:10, and that should he refuse to do so, they could formally announce the fact of his heresy to the rest of the faithful, whereupon divine law itself would separate him from the Church and the papal office: "The role of this judgment would be to give the public fact a juridical force; it would not be an exercise of

---

85   For references, see Silveira, *Can a Pope Be a Heretic?*, 204–5.
86   For example, a signed statement kept locked in a drawer and shown to no one.
87   Lamont and Pierantoni, *Defending the Faith*, 359; see chapter 47 below.

authority that would create this fact or its consequences."[88] This view seems to be materially identical to that of John of St Thomas, though applied to a more complex case than the seventeenth-century Dominican envisaged.

However, since the bishops even as a body lack jurisdiction over the pope, there seems no reason why their judgment about him, more than anyone else's, would give a juridical force to this public fact. To say "we are not punishing him, only determining a fact" would not seem enough to rebut the charge of usurping authority: for before a body can determine a fact about some person by a legal judgment that will cause him to be deposed even by an independent authority—in this case, by God himself—this body must first possess some jurisdiction over him. Hence the bishops are not competent to pass a sentence in virtue of which divine law would remove such a man from the papacy. Nor could the bishops free the Church from this evil in virtue of the principle mentioned in *Lumen Gentium 22*, according to which they may initiate a collegiate act which a pope may afterwards "freely accept" (*libere recipiat*) and thus validate.[89] The putatively heretical pope could hardly ratify the bishops' initiative by deposing himself, nor could a man elected to replace him do this, since he would not be a true pope, the former one having *ex hypothesi* not yet been deposed.

How then should the Church respond to such a calamity? Each rank would have its proper role, in accordance with the words of Pope Adrian II to the Fourth Council of Constantinople that in a case of heresy it is permissible for subjects to resist the acts of their superiors, and openly to reject their evil sentiments.[90] Since each bishop is by "divine institution and the obligation of his apostolic office responsible for the Church (*Ecclesiae sponsor*), together with the other bishops,"[91] each one a vicar of Christ within his own diocese and not a vicar of the Roman pontiff,[92] the principal task must fall to them. They would be obliged to admonish such a pope, even in public.[93] They could assemble to do this with greater effect, perhaps by province or by bishops' conference.[94] It could not be excluded that wider assemblies might also be held, though in an

---

88   Lamont and Pierantoni, 360.

89   This is the suggestion of Dounot and Warembourg, "Pontife et Souverain," in Dounot et al., *La déposition du pape hérétique*, 216.

90   See p. 116 above. For his part, Suárez wrote: "If a pope were to employ physical force, by aggression or unjust war, he could be resisted by an act of defense though not by one of offence. And if the violence were spiritual, commanding evil things, or profaning or destroying sacred ones, then he could be resisted in a proportionate way." Francisco Suárez, *Omnia Opera*, vol. 24 (Paris: Vivès, 1859), *Defensio Fidei Catholicae*, Bk. 4, sect. 6.18, p. 383.

91   Second Vatican Council, Decree Concerning the Pastoral Office of Bishops in the Church *Christus Dominus* (October 28, 1965), no. 6.

92   See the *Collective Declaration of the German Bishops* of January–February 1875, approved by Pope Pius IX in the apostolic letter *Mirabilis Illa Constantia* of the same year (*DH* 3112–17).

93   St Thomas, *ST* II-II, Q. 33, art. 4, ad 2: "If the faith were endangered, a subject ought to rebuke his prelate even publicly."

94   See *CIC*, cann. 439-59 and Code of Canons for the Oriental Churches, 84 and 152. Particular councils and bishops' conferences cannot issue binding decrees against the will of the first see (*CIC* cann. 446, 455–56), but nothing prevents them from issuing public statements.

informal manner.[95] While their first concern should be to reaffirm the revealed truths under threat, they could hardly do so with the necessary force unless they were also to warn their people that these truths were being undermined by the man occupying the papacy. At the same time, they ought to remind them of the respect necessary for one who still held the highest office on earth,[96] and carefully explain the meaning and limits of papal infallibility.[97] If the bishops neglected these tasks, the burden would seem to devolve upon lower clergy and theologians. The rulers of Catholic states, should any then exist, might withdraw their ambassadors from the Holy See.

If none of this proved sufficient, then in union with their priests, the bishops could organize public prayers, that the erring pope should repent or else be removed by God. The lay faithful should join in them, with the prayers of children being especially solicited. Fathers and mothers of families should instruct their children about the crisis in the Church, in proportion to their capacity to understand it without being scandalized; and all should intensify their own spiritual life, while governing themselves according to the letter and spirit of canon law.[98] All of this would constitute a unique way, suited to the unique circumstances, of fulfilling St Paul's instruction to "avoid" (*paraitou*) a heretical man.[99] If it were done, the trial would be short-lived: "And will not God vindicate his elect, who cry to him day and night? Will he delay long over them?" (Lk 18:7).

---

95   St Robert Bellarmine asserted that one of the reasons for holding an "imperfect" ecumenical council is the suspicion of heresy in a Roman pontiff: *De Controversiis*, vol. 2, *De Conciliis*, Bk. 1, ch. 9, pp. 206-7. Since no kind of ecumenical council can be held against the will of the Roman pontiff, it seems better to avoid the phrase. But no law prevents the bishops of the world from assembling to discuss such suspicions or even opinions and certainties outside a council.

96   Our fathers in the faith enjoyed a robust sense of the distinction between the man and the office. In the middle of the sixth century, many Romans were disgusted with Pope Vigilius, for having, as they supposed, brought about the death of his predecessor Silverius. When the pope was obliged to leave Rome for the imperial city at the bidding of the emperor Justinian, a crowd assembled to see him off. "Justinian ordered Vigilius to be brought to Constantinople. He was seized in the Church of St Cecilia and put on board a ship. The crowd asked his blessing, to which they cried 'Amen.' Then they pelted him with stones and sticks and crockery, shouting: 'Thy famine be with thee: thy plague be with thee: thou hast done evil to the Romans. Mayest thou find evil where thou goest'"; Dom John Chapman, *Studies on the Early Papacy* (Port Washington and London: Kennikat Press, 1928), 229.

97   An indispensable tool for so doing is John P. Joy's *Disputed Questions on Papal Infallibility* (Lincoln, NE: Os Justi Press, 2022).

98   See especially *CIC* 212 §3: "In proportion to the knowledge, competence, and eminence that they possess, [the Christian faithful] have the right and even at times the duty to manifest to the sacred pastors their judgment about matters pertaining to the good of the Church, and to make this judgment known to the rest of the Christian faithful, without prejudice to the integrity of faith and morals, with reverence toward their pastors, and being attentive to the common benefit and to the rank of persons."

99   The verb *paraiteomai*, followed by an accusative of the person, commonly has the senses "reject" or "refuse," though "avoid" is also a possible sense of the word. See W. Bauer, F. Gingrich, F. Danker, *A Greek Lexicon of the New Testament and Other Early Christian Literature* (Chicago and London: University of Chicago Press, 2000), 764. The Vulgate has *devita* ("avoid"), though the nuance of difference between this and "reject" does not appear to have influenced the theological discussion of our question.

⫷ 10 ⫸
On the Question of
a Heretical Pope[1]

BISHOP ATHANASIUS SCHNEIDER

T HE ISSUE OF HOW TO HANDLE A HERETICAL POPE, in concrete terms, has not yet been treated in a manner which approaches anything like a true general consent in the Catholic tradition. So far, neither a pope nor an ecumenical council has made relevant doctrinal pronouncements nor have they issued binding canonical norms regarding the eventuality of how to handle a heretical pope during the term of his office.

There is no historical case of a pope losing the papacy during his term of office due to heresy or alleged heresy. Pope Honorius I (625–638) was posthumously excommunicated by three ecumenical councils (the Third Council of Constantinople in 681, the Second Council of Nicaea in 787, and the Fourth Council of Constantinople in 870) on the grounds that he supported the heretical doctrine of those who promoted Monothelitism, thereby helping to spread this heresy. In the letter with which Pope St Leo II (d. 683) confirmed the decrees of the Third Council of Constantinople, he declared the anathema on Pope Honorius ("*anathematizamus Honorium*"), stating that his predecessor "Honorius, instead of purifying this Apostolic Church, permitted the immaculate faith to be stained by a profane treason."[2]

The *Liber Diurnus Romanorum Pontificum*, a miscellaneous collection of formularies used in the papal chancery until the eleventh century, contains the text for the papal oath, according to which every new pope, upon taking office, had to swear that he "recognized the sixth ecumenical council, which smote with eternal anathema the originators of the heresy (Monothelitism), Sergius, Pyrrhus, etc., together with Honorius."[3]

In some Breviaries until the sixteenth or the eighteenth centuries, Pope Honorius was mentioned as a heretic in the lessons of Matins for June 28, the feast of St Leo II: "*In synodo Constantinopolitano condemnati sunt Sergius, Cyrus, Honorius, Pyrrhus, Paulus et Petrus, nec non et Macarius, cum discipulo suo Stephano, sed et Polychronius et Simon, qui unam voluntatem et operationem in Domino Jesu Christo dixerunt vel praedicaverunt.*" The persistence of this Breviary reading through many centuries shows that it was not considered scandalous by many generations of Catholics

---

1   First published at *Rorate Caeli* on March 20, 2019.
2   Denzinger-Schönmetzer, no. 563.
3   *PL* 105:40–44. Hans Foerster prepared a critical edition of the *Liber Diurnus Romanorum Pontificum* (Bern: Francke Verlag, 1958).

that a particular pope, and in a very rare case, was found guilty of heresy or of supporting heresy. In those times, the faithful and the hierarchy of the Church could clearly distinguish between the indestructibility of the Catholic faith divinely guaranteed to the Magisterium of the See of Peter and the infidelity and treason of an individual pope in the exercise of his teaching office.

Dom John Chapman explained in his book *The Condemnation of Pope Honorius* that the same Third Ecumenical Council of Constantinople that declared anathema on Pope Honorius made a clear distinction between the error of a particular pope and the inerrancy in faith of the Apostolic See as such. In the letter asking Pope Agatho (678–681) to approve the conciliar decisions, the Fathers of the Third Ecumenical Council of Constantinople say that Rome has an indefectible faith, which is authoritatively promulgated to the whole Church by the bishops of the Apostolic See, the successors of Peter. One can ask: How was it possible for the Third Ecumenical Council of Constantinople to assert this and yet in the same breath to condemn a pope as a heretic? The answer is clear enough. Pope Honorius was fallible, he was wrong, he was a heretic, precisely because he did *not*, as he should have done, declare authoritatively the Petrine tradition of the Roman Church. To that tradition he had made no appeal, but had merely approved and enlarged an erroneous doctrine. But once disowned by his successors, the words of Pope Honorius I were harmless against the fact of the inerrancy in Faith of the Apostolic See. They were reduced to their true value, as the expression of his own personal view.

Pope St Agatho did not let himself be confused and shaken by the lamentable behavior of his predecessor Honorius I, who helped to spread heresy. In spite of this, Pope Agatho kept his supernatural view of the inerrancy of the See of Peter in teaching the faith, as he wrote to the emperors in Constantinople:

> This is the rule of the true faith, which this spiritual mother of your most tranquil empire, the Apostolic Church of Christ (the See of Rome), has both in prosperity and in adversity always held and defended with energy; which, it will be proved, by the grace of Almighty God, has never erred from the path of the apostolic tradition, nor has she been depraved by yielding to heretical innovations, but from the beginning she has received the Christian faith from her founders, the princes of the Apostles of Christ, and remains undefiled unto the end, according to the divine promise of the Lord and Savior himself, which he uttered in the holy Gospels to the prince of his disciples: saying, "Peter, Peter, behold, Satan hath desired to have you, that he might sift you as wheat; but I have prayed for thee, that thy faith fail not. And when thou art converted, strengthen thy brethren."[4]

Dom Prosper Guéranger gave a short and lucid theological and spiritual explanation of this concrete case of a heretical pope, saying:

---

4   Ep. *"Consideranti mihi" ad Imperatores.*

> What exultation rang through the abyss, when one sad day saw [Pope Honorius] the representative of Him who is essential Light appear to side for a moment with the powers of darkness in bringing on a cloud which would interpose itself betwixt Heaven and those mountains of God, where He dwells with His Vicar; it is but too probable that the social aid of intercession was weaker just then than it should have been.[5]

There is, furthermore, the weighty fact that during two thousand years there was never a case that a pope during the term of his office was declared deposed because of the crime of heresy. Pope Honorius I was anathematized only after his death. The last case of a heretical or semi-heretical pope was the case of Pope John XXII (1316–1334) when he taught his theory that the saints would enjoy the beatific vision only after the Last Judgment in the Second Coming of Christ. The treatment of that particular case in those times was as follows: there were public admonitions (University of Paris, King Philip VI of France), a refutation of the wrong papal theories made through theological publications, and a fraternal correction on behalf of Cardinal Jacques Fournier, who eventually became his successor as Pope Benedict XII (1334–1342).

The Church in the very rare concrete cases of a pope committing serious theological errors or heresies could definitely live with such a pope. The practice of the Church until now was that she left the final judgment about a reigning heretical pope to his successors or to a future ecumenical council, such as in the case of Pope Honorius I. The same would probably have happened with Pope John XXII, if he had not retracted his error.

Popes were deposed several times by secular powers or by criminal clans. This occurred especially during the so-called Dark Ages (tenth and eleventh centuries), when the German emperors deposed several unworthy popes, not because of their heresy, but because of their scandalous immoral life and their abuse of power. However, they were never deposed according to a canonical procedure, since that is impossible because of the divine structure of the Church. The pope gets his authority directly from God and not from the Church; therefore, the Church cannot depose him, for any reason whatsoever.

It is a dogma of faith that the pope cannot proclaim a heresy when teaching *ex cathedra*. This is the divine guarantee that the gates of hell will not prevail against the *cathedra veritatis*, which is the Apostolic See of the Apostle St Peter. Dom John Chapman, an expert in investigating the history of the condemnation of Pope Honorius I, writes:

> Infallibility is, as it were, the apex of a pyramid. The more solemn the utterances of the Apostolic See, the more we can be certain of their truth. When they reach the maximum of solemnity, that is, when they are strictly *ex cathedra*, the possibility of error is wholly eliminated. The

---

5   Dom Prosper Guéranger, OSB, *The Liturgical Year*, trans. Dom Laurence Shepherd, OSB (Great Falls, MT: St. Bonaventure Publications, 2000), *Time After Pentecost*, Bk. 3, vol. 12, p. 429.

authority of a pope, even on those occasions when he is not actually infallible, is to be implicitly followed and reverenced. That it should be on the wrong side is a contingency shown by faith and history to be possible.[6]

If a pope spreads doctrinal errors or heresies, the divine structure of the Church already provides an antidote: in such a case, the substituting ministry of the representatives of the episcopacy and the invincible *sensus fidei* of the faithful step into the breach. In this issue the numerical factor is not decisive. It is sufficient to have even a few bishops proclaiming the integrity of Faith and correcting thereby the errors of a heretical pope. It is sufficient that bishops instruct and protect their flock from the errors of a heretical pope; their priests and the parents of Catholic families will do the same.

Furthermore, since the Church is also a supernatural reality and a mystery, a unique supernatural organism, the Mystical Body of Christ, bishops, priests, and lay faithful — besides corrections, appeals, professions of faith, and public resistance — necessarily also have to do acts of reparation to the Divine Majesty and acts of expiation for the heretical acts of a pope.

According to the Dogmatic Constitution *Lumen Gentium* (no. 12) of the Second Vatican Council, the entire body of the faithful cannot err in matters of belief, when from the bishops down to the last of the lay faithful they show universal agreement in matters of faith and morals. Even if a pope is spreading theological errors and heresies, the faith of the Church as a whole will remain intact because of the promise of Christ concerning the special assistance and permanent presence of the Holy Spirit, the Spirit of the truth, in His Church (Jn 14:17; 1 Jn 2:27).

When by an inscrutable permission of God, at a certain moment of history and in a very rare instance, a pope spreads errors and heresies through his daily or ordinary non-infallible Magisterium, Divine Providence awakens at the same time the witness of some members of the episcopal college, and also of the faithful, in order to compensate for the temporary failures of the papal Magisterium. One has to say that such a situation is very rare, but not impossible, as Church history has proven. The Church is indeed one single organic body, and when there is a failure and lack in the head of the body (the pope), the rest of the body (the faithful) or eminent parts of the body (the bishops) supply for the temporary papal failures. One of the most famous and tragic examples of such a situation occurred during the Arian crisis in the fourth century, when the purity of faith was maintained not so much by the *ecclesia docens* (pope and episcopate) but by the *ecclesia docta* (faithful), as St John Henry Newman has stated.

The theory or opinion that the papal office may be lost by deposition or declaration of the *ipso facto* loss implicitly makes the pope identical with the entire Church or manifests the unhealthy attitude of a pope-centrism. The representatives of such an opinion (especially some saints) were those who manifested an

---

6   Dom John Chapman, *The Condemnation of Pope Honorius* (London: Catholic Truth Society, 1907), 109.

exaggerated ultramontanism or pope-centrism, making the pope a kind of half-god who cannot commit any errors, not even in the realm outside the object of papal infallibility. Thus, a pope committing doctrinal errors, which theoretically and logically includes also the possibility of committing the gravest doctrinal error, i.e., a heresy, is for the followers of that opinion (deposition of a pope and loss of his office because of heresy) unbearable or unthinkable, even if the pope commits such errors in the realm outside the object of papal infallibility.

The theory or theological opinion that a heretical pope can be deposed or lose office was alien to the first millennium. It originated only in the High Middle Ages, in a time when pope-centrism arrived at a certain high point, when unconsciously the pope was identified with the Church as such. This was already in its root the mundane attitude of an absolutist prince according to the motto: *"L'État, c'est moi!"* or in ecclesiastical terms: "I am the Church!"

The opinion that a heretical pope *ipso facto* loses his office became a common opinion starting with the High Middle Ages. To this day it remains a theological opinion and not a teaching of the Church and therefore it cannot claim the quality of a constant and perennial teaching of the Church as such, since no ecumenical council and no pope has supported such an opinion explicitly. The Church condemned a heretical pope, but only posthumously and not during the term of his office. Even if some Doctors of the Church (e.g., St Robert Bellarmine, St Francis de Sales) held such an opinion, it does not prove its certainty or the fact of a general doctrinal consensus. Even Doctors of the Church have been known to err; such is the case with St Thomas Aquinas regarding the question of the Immaculate Conception, the matter of the sacrament of Orders, or the sacramental character of the episcopal ordination.

There was a period in the Church where there was, for instance, an objectively wrong common theological opinion that asserted that the handing over of the instruments was the matter of the sacrament of Orders — an opinion that could not invoke antiquity and universality, even though such an opinion was for a limited time supported by a pope (by the decree of Eugene IV) and for a limited period of time by liturgical books. This common opinion was, however, later corrected by Pius XII in 1947.

That a heretical pope may be deposed or that he loses his office *ipso facto* because of heresy is only a theological opinion, one that does not fulfil the necessary theological categories of antiquity, universality, and consensus (*semper, ubique, ab omnibus*). There have been no pronouncements of the universal ordinary Magisterium or of the papal Magisterium that would support the theories of the deposition of a heretical pope or of the loss of his office *ipso facto* because of heresy. According to a medieval canonical tradition, which was later collected in the *Corpus Iuris Canonici* (the canon law valid in the Latin Church until 1918), a pope could be judged in the case of heresy: *"Papa a nemine est iudicandus, nisi deprehendatur a fide devius,"* i.e., "the pope cannot be judged by anyone, unless he has been found deviating from the faith."[7] The Code of Canon Law of 1917, however, eliminated the norm of the *Corpus Iuris Canonici*, which spoke of a heretical pope. Neither does the Code of Canon Law of 1983 contain such a norm.

The Church has always taught that even a heretical person, who is automatically excommunicated because of formal heresy, can nevertheless validly administer the sacraments, and that a heretic or formally excommunicated priest can in an extreme case exercise even an act of jurisdiction by imparting to a penitent sacramental absolution. The norms of the papal election that were valid up to and including Paul VI admitted that even an excommunicated cardinal could participate in the papal election and he himself could be elected pope:

> No cardinal elector may be excluded from active and passive partici-
> pation in the election of the Supreme Pontiff because of or on pretext
> of any excommunication, suspension, interdict or other ecclesiastical
> impediment. Any such censures are to be regarded as suspended as far
> as the effect of the election is concerned.[8]

This theological principle must be applied also to the case of a heretical bishop or a heretical pope, who in spite of their heresies can validly perform acts of ecclesiastical jurisdiction and therefore do not lose *ipso facto* their office because of heresy.

The theory or theological opinion allowing the deposition of a heretical pope or the loss of his office *ipso facto* because of heresy is in practice unworkable. If it were applied in practice, it would create a situation similar to that of the Great Schism, which the Church already experienced disastrously at the end of the fourteenth and the beginning of the fifteenth centuries. Indeed, there will be always a part of the cardinals' college and a considerable part of the world's episcopate and also of the faithful who will not agree in classifying a concrete papal error/errors as formal heresy/heresies and consequently they will continue to consider the current pope as the only legitimate pope.

A formal schism, with two or more pretenders to the papal throne — which will be an inevitable consequence of even a canonically enacted deposition of a pope — will necessarily cause more damage to the Church as a whole than a relatively short and very rare period in which a pope spreads doctrinal errors or heresies. The situation of a heretical pope will always be relatively short in comparison with the two thousand years of the existence of the Church. One has to leave an intervention, in this rare and delicate case, to Divine Providence.

The attempt to depose a heretical pope at any cost is a sign of all too human behavior, which ultimately reflects an unwillingness to bear the temporal cross of a heretical pope. It may also reflect the all too human emotion of anger. It will, in any case, offer a far too human solution, and as such is somewhat similar to behavior in politics. The Church and the papacy are realities which are not purely

---

7   *Decretum Gratiani, Prima Pars*, d. 40, c. 6, pt. 3.
8   Paul VI, Apostolic Constitution *Romano Pontifice Eligendo* 35.

human, but also divine. The cross of a heretical pope—even when it is of limited duration—is the greatest imaginable cross for the entire Church.

Another error in the intention or in the attempt to depose a heretical pope consists in the indirect or subconscious identification of the Church with the pope or in making the pope the focal point of the daily life of the Church. This means ultimately and subconsciously a yielding to unhealthy ultramontanism, pope-centrism, and papolatry, i.e., a papal personality cult. There were indeed periods in the history of the Church when for a considerable period of time the See of Peter was vacant. For instance, from November 29, 1268, to September 1, 1271, there was no pope and in that time neither was there any antipope. Therefore, Catholics should not make the pope and his words and actions their daily focal point.

One can disinherit children of a family. Yet one cannot disinherit the father of a family, however guilty or monstrously he behaves himself. This is the law of the hierarchy which God has established even in creation. The same is applicable to the pope, who during the term of his office is the spiritual father of the entire family of Christ on earth. In the case of a criminal or monstrous father, the children have to withdraw themselves from him or avoid contact with him. However, they cannot say, "We will elect a new and good father of our family." It would be against common sense and against nature. The same principle should be applicable therefore to the question of deposing a heretical pope. The pope cannot be deposed by anybody; only God can intervene and He will do this in His time, since God does not fail in His Providence (*Deus in sua dispositione non fallitur*). During the First Vatican Council, Bishop Zinelli, *relator* of the conciliar commission on Faith, spoke in these terms about the possibility of a heretical pope: "If God permits so great an evil (i.e., a heretical pope), the means to remedy such a situation will not be lacking."[9]

The deposition of a heretical pope will ultimately foster the heresy of conciliarism, sedevacantism, and a mental attitude similar to that which is characteristic of a purely human or political community. It will also foster a mentality similar to the separatism of the Protestant world or to autocephalism in the commonwealth of the Orthodox churches.

The theory or opinion allowing deposition and loss of office is revealed furthermore to be in its deepest roots—though unconsciously—also a kind of "Donatism" applied to the papal ministry. The Donatist theory identified the sacred ministers (priests and bishops) almost with the moral holiness of Christ Himself, demanding therefore for the validity of their office the absence of moral errors or misconduct in their public life. The mentioned theory in a similar way excludes the possibility of a pope making doctrinal errors, i.e., heresies, declaring by that same fact his office invalid or vacant, as the Donatists did, declaring the priestly or episcopal office invalid or vacant because of errors in the moral life.

---

9   Mansi 52:1109.

One can imagine that in the future the supreme authority of the Church (pope or ecumenical council) could stipulate the following or similar binding canonical norms for the case of a heretical or a manifestly heterodox pope:

• A pope cannot be deposed in whatsoever form and for whatever reason, not even for the reason of heresy.

• Every newly elected pope on entering upon his office is obliged in virtue of his ministry as the supreme teacher of the Church to take the oath of protecting the entire flock of Christ from the danger of heresies and avoiding in his words and deeds any appearance of heresy in compliance with his duty of strengthening in faith all the shepherds and the faithful.

• A pope who is spreading obvious theological errors or heresies or helping in the spread of heresies by his actions and omissions should be obligatorily corrected in a fraternal and private form by the Dean of the College of Cardinals.

• After unsuccessful private corrections, the Dean of the College of Cardinals is obliged to make his correction public.

• Together with the public correction, the Dean of the College of Cardinals must make an appeal for prayer for the pope that he may regain the strength to confirm unambiguously the entire Church in the faith.

• At the same time the Dean of the College of Cardinals should publish a formula of a Profession of Faith, in which there would be rejected the theological errors that the pope teaches or tolerates (without necessarily naming the pope).

• If the Dean of the College of Cardinals should omit or fail to make the correction, the appeal to prayer, and the publication of a Profession of Faith, any cardinal, bishop, or group of bishops should do this and, if even the cardinals and bishops omit or fail to do this, any member of the Catholic faithful or any group of Catholic faithful should do this.

• The Dean of the College of Cardinals or a cardinal, a bishop or a group of bishops, or a faithful Catholic or a group of Catholic faithful who published the correction, appeal to prayer, and the Profession of Faith cannot be subjected to any canonical sanctions or penalties or accused of disrespect towards the pope for this reason.

In the extremely rare case of a heretical pope, the spiritual situation of the Church can be described with the words that Pope St Gregory the Great (590–604) used, calling the Church in his time "an old ship woefully shattered; for the waters are entering on all sides, and the joints, buffeted by the daily stress of the storm, are growing rotten and herald shipwreck."[10]

The episodes narrated in the Gospel about Our Lord calming the stormy sea and rescuing Peter, who was sinking in the water, teach us that even in the most dramatic and humanly desperate situation—that of a heretical pope—all the shepherds of the Church and the faithful should believe and trust that God in His Providence will intervene and Christ will calm the raging storm and restore

---

10   *Registrum* I, 4, *Ep. ad Ioannem episcopum Constantinopolitanum.*

to the successors of Peter, His Vicars on earth, the strength to confirm all the shepherds and faithful in the Catholic and Apostolic Faith.

Pope St Agatho, who had the difficult task of limiting the damage that Pope Honorius I caused to the integrity of the faith, left vivid words of ardent appeal to each successor of Peter, who must always be mindful of his grave duty to guard unspoiled the virginal purity of the Deposit of Faith:

> Woe is me, if I neglect to preach the truth of my Lord, which they [viz., my predecessors] have sincerely preached. Woe is me, if I cover over with silence the truth which I am bidden to give to the exchangers, i.e., to teach to the Christian people and imbue it therewith. What shall I say in the future examination by Christ himself, if I blush — which God forbid! — to preach here the truth of his words? What satisfaction shall I be able to give for myself, what for the souls committed to me, when he demands a strict account of the office I have received? [11]

When the first pope, St Peter, was materially in chains, the whole Church implored his liberation: "Peter was kept in prison. But prayer was made without ceasing by the church unto God for him" (Acts 12:5). When a pope is spreading errors or even heresies, he is in spiritual chains or in a spiritual prison. Therefore, the entire Church has to pray without ceasing for his liberation from this spiritual prison. The entire Church must have a supernatural perseverance in such a prayer and a supernatural trust in the fact that it is ultimately God who governs His Church and not the pope.

When Pope Honorius I (625-638) adopted an ambiguous attitude towards the spreading of the new heresy of Monothelitism, St Sophronius, Patriarch of Jerusalem, sent a bishop from Palestine to Rome, saying to him the following words: "Go to the Apostolic See, where are the foundations of holy doctrine, and do not cease to pray till the Apostolic See condemn the new heresy."

In dealing with the tragic case of a heretical pope, all the members of the Church, beginning with the bishops, down to the simple faithful, have to use all legitimate means, such as private and public corrections of the erring pope, constant and ardent prayers and public professions of the truth in order that the Apostolic See may again profess with clarity the divine truths that the Lord entrusted to Peter and to all his successors. "For the Holy Spirit was promised to the successors of Peter not so that they might, by his revelation, make known some new doctrine, but that, by his assistance, they might religiously guard and faithfully expound the revelation or deposit of faith transmitted by the apostles." [12]

Each pope and all members of the Church must be reminded of the wise and timeless words that the Ecumenical Council of Constance (1414-1418) pronounced about the pope as the first person in the Church who is bound by the faith and who must scrupulously guard the integrity of the faith:

---

11 Ep. *"Consideranti mihi" ad Imperatores.*
12 First Vatican Council, Dogmatic Constitution *Pastor Aeternus*, ch. 4.

Since the Roman Pontiff exercises such great power among mortals, it is right that he be bound all the more by the incontrovertible bonds of the faith and by the rites that are to be observed regarding the Church's sacraments. We therefore decree and ordain, in order that the fullness of the faith may shine in a future Roman pontiff with singular splendor from the earliest moments of his becoming pope, that henceforth whoever is to be elected Roman pontiff shall make the following confession and profession in public. [13]

In the same session, the Council of Constance decreed that every newly elected pope had to make an oath of faith, proposing the following formula, from which we quote the most crucial passages:

I, N., elected pope, with both heart and mouth confess and profess to almighty God, that I will firmly believe and hold the Catholic Faith according to the traditions of the Apostles, of the General Councils and of other Holy Fathers. I will preserve this faith unchanged to the last dot and will confirm, defend and preach it to the point of death and the shedding of my blood, and likewise I will follow and observe in every way the rite handed down of the ecclesiastical sacraments of the Catholic Church.

How timely is such a papal oath and how urgent it is to put such on oath into practice, especially in our days! The pope is not an absolute monarch, who can do and say what he likes, who can change doctrine or liturgy at his own discretion. Unfortunately, in recent centuries — contrary to the Apostolic tradition in ancient times — the behavior of the popes as absolute monarchs or as half-gods became so commonly accepted that it shaped the theological and spiritual views of the prevailing majority of the bishops and the faithful, and especially among pious people. The fact that the pope must be the first in the Church who has to avoid novelties, obeying in an exemplary manner the tradition of the faith and of the liturgy, was sometimes blotted out from the consciousness of the bishops and the faithful by a blind and pious acceptance of a kind of papal absolutism.

The papal oath from the *Liber Diurnus Romanorum Pontificum* considered as the main obligation and the most distinguished quality of a new pope his unshakeable faithfulness to the Tradition as it was handed down to him by his predecessors:

Nihil de traditione, quod a probatissimis praedecessoribus meis servatum reperi, diminuere vel mutare, aut aliquam novitatem admittere; sed ferventer, ut vere eorum discipulus et sequipeda, totis viribus meis conatibusque tradita conservare ac venerari. (To change nothing of the received Tradition, and nothing thereof that I have found before me guarded by my God-pleasing predecessors, to encroach upon, to alter, nor to permit any innovation therein; with glowing affection as her truly faithful student and

---

13   Thirty-ninth session from October 9, 1417, ratified by Pope Martin V.

successor, to safeguard reverently the passed-on good, with my whole strength and utmost effort.)

The same papal oath named, in concrete terms, fidelity to the *lex credendi* (the Rule of Faith) and to the *lex orandi* (the Rule of Prayer). With regard to the *lex credendi*, the text of the oath says:

> *Verae fidei rectitudinem, quam Christo auctore tradente, per successores tuos atque discipulos, usque ad exiguitatem meam perlatam, in tua sancta Ecclesia reperi, totis conatibus meis, usque ad animam et sanguinem custodire, temporumque difficultates, cum tuo adjutorio, toleranter sufferre.* (I promise to keep with all my strength, even to the point of death and the shedding of my blood, the integrity of the true faith, whose author is Christ and which through your successors and disciples was handed over up to my humble self, and which I found in your Church. I promise also to bear with patience the difficulties of the time.)

With regard to the *lex orandi*, the papal oath says:

> *Disciplinam et ritum Ecclesiae, sicut inveni, et a sanctis praecessoribus meis traditum reperi, illibatum custodire.* (I promise to keep inviolate the discipline and the liturgy of the Church as I have found them and as they were transmitted by my holy predecessors.)

In the last hundred years, there were some examples of a kind of papal absolutism concerning changes in the liturgical tradition of the Church. Drastic changes were made in the *lex orandi* by Popes Pius X, Pius XII, and Paul VI, and in the *lex credendi* by Pope Francis.

Pius X became the first pope in the history of the Latin Church who made such a radical reform of the order of the psalmody (*cursus psalmorum*) that it resulted in the construction of a new of Divine Office regarding the distribution of the psalms. The next case was Pope Pius XII, who approved for liturgical use a radically changed Latin version of the millennia-old and melodious text of the Vulgate Psalter. The new Latin translation, the so-called "Pian Psalter," was a text artificially fabricated by academics and was, in its artificiality, hardly pronounceable. This new Latin translation, aptly criticized with the adage *"accessit latinitas, recessit pietas,"* was then *de facto* rejected by the entire Church under the pontificate of Pope John XXIII. Pope Pius XII also changed the liturgy of Holy Week, a millennia-old liturgical treasure of the Church, introducing partially *ex novo* invented rituals. Unprecedented liturgical changes, however, were executed by Pope Paul VI with a revolutionary reform of the rite of the Mass and of the rites of all other sacraments — a liturgical reform that no pope before had ever dared to do with such radicalness.

A theologically revolutionary change was made by Pope Francis insofar as he approved the practice of some local churches of admitting in singular cases sexually active adulterers (who are cohabitating in so-called "irregular unions") to Holy Communion. Even if these local norms do not represent a general norm in the Church, they nevertheless signify a denial in practice of the divine truth of the absolute indissolubility of a valid and consummated sacramental marriage. His other alteration in doctrinal questions consists in the change of the biblical and the constant bimillennial doctrine regarding the legitimacy of the death penalty. The next doctrinal change is found in the interreligious document of Abu Dhabi of February 4, 2019, approved by Francis, which states that "the pluralism and the diversity of religions, color, sex, race, and language are willed by God in His wisdom." This formulation needs an official papal correction, as a natural reading of it contradicts the first commandment of the Decalogue and the unmistakable and explicit teaching of Our Lord Jesus Christ, hence contradicting Divine Revelation.

Against this background stands the impressive and thought-provoking episode narrated in the life of Pope Pius IX, who, requested of a group of bishops to make a slight change in the Canon of the Mass (introducing the name of St Joseph), answered: "I cannot do this. I am only the pope!"

The following prayer of Dom Prosper Guéranger, in which he addresses Pope St Leo II and praises him for his strenuous defense of the integrity of faith in the aftermath of the crisis caused by Pope Honorius I, should be assiduously prayed by the pope himself and all of the faithful, especially in our time:

> Uphold, in every age, the Pastor who rules Christ's Church, that he may keep himself aloof from the darkening mists that earth exhales; keep ever alive in the hearts of the faithful flock that strong prayer, which should continually be made without ceasing for him by the Church (cf. Acts 12:5): and then Peter, were he even chained in the depths of the darkest dungeon, will be reached by the Sun of Justice and clearly see his way in that pure ray; then will the whole body of the Church be lightsome. For Jesus hath said, "the light of the body is the eye: if the eye be single the whole body will be lightsome" (Mt 6:22). By thy teaching we realize more fully the strength of the rock whereon the Church stands; we know that the gates of hell shall never prevail against her (Mt 16:18). For surely the efforts of the spirits of darkness never went to such lengths as they did in that sad crisis [of Pope Honorius] to which thou didst put an end: nor was their success, however great in appearance, contrary to the divine promise; for it is to the teaching of Peter, not to his [Honorius's] silence [and his support of heresy], that the unfailing assistance of the Holy Ghost is guaranteed.[14]

The extremely rare case of a heretical or of a semi-heretical pope must ultimately be endured and suffered in the light of the faith in the divine character and in the indestructibility of the Church and of the Petrine office. Pope St Leo the Great formulated this truth, saying that the dignity of St Peter is not abated

---

14   Guéranger, *The Liturgical Year*, 12:429.

in his successors, however unworthy they may be: *"Cuius dignitas etiam in indigno haerede non deficit."* [15]

There could be a truly extravagant situation of a pope who practices sexual abuse of minors or subordinates in the Vatican. What should the Church do in such a situation? Should the Church tolerate a papal sexual predator of minors or subordinates? For how long should the Church tolerate such a pope? Should he lose the papacy *ipso facto* because of sexual abuse of minors or subordinates? In such a situation there could originate a new canonical or theological theory or opinion of allowing the deposition of a pope and the loss of his office because of monstrous moral crimes. Such an opinion would be a counterpart of the opinion allowing the deposition of a pope and the loss of his office because of heresy. However, such a new theory or opinion (deposition of a pope and the loss of his office because of sexual crimes) would surely not correspond to the perennial mind and practice of the Church.

The tolerance of a heretical pope as a cross does not mean passivity or an approval of his wrongdoing. One should do all that is possible to remedy the situation of a heretical pope. To bear the cross of a heretical pope under no circumstances means consenting to his heresies or being passive. It is comparable to the way in which people have to bear, for instance, an iniquitous or atheist regime as a cross (how many Catholics lived under such a regime in the Soviet Union and were bearing this situation as a cross in the spirit of expiation!), or as parents have to bear as a cross an adult child who became an unbeliever or immoral, or as members of a family have to bear as a cross for instance an alcoholic father. The parents cannot "depose" their errant child from membership in their family, just as the children cannot "depose" their errant father from membership in their family or from the title "father."

The surer way — not deposing a heretical pope — reflects a more supernatural view of the Church. Such a way with its practical and concrete countermeasures and counteractions under no circumstances means passivity or collaboration with the papal errors, but a very active commitment and a true compassion with the Church, which, in the time of a heretical or semi-heretical pope, experiences her Golgotha hours. The more a pope spreads doctrinal ambiguities, errors, or even heresies, the more luminously will shine the pure Catholic Faith of the little ones in the Church: the faith of innocent children; the faith of religious sisters; the faith of the hidden gems of the Church, the cloistered nuns; the faith of heroic and virtuous lay faithful from all social conditions; the faith of individual priests and bishops. This pure flame of Catholic Faith, oftentimes nurtured by sacrifices and acts of expiation, will burn more brightly than the cowardice, infidelity, spiritual rigidity, and blindness of a heretical pope.

The Church is of such a divine character that it can exist and live for a limited period of time notwithstanding a reigning heretical pope, exactly because of the

---

15   *Serm.* 3, 4.

truth that the pope is not synonymous or identical with the Church. The Church is of such a divine character that even a heretical pope is not able to destroy the Church, for even though he heavily damages the life of the Church, his action has only a limited duration. The Faith of the entire Church is greater and stronger than the errors of a heretical pope and this Faith cannot be defeated, not even by a heretical pope. The constancy of the entire Church is greater and more durable than the relatively short-lived disaster of a heretical pope. The true rock upon which resides the indestructibility of the Church's Faith and holiness is Christ Himself, the pope being only His instrument, just as every priest or bishop is only an instrument of Christ the High Priest.

The Church's doctrinal and moral health does not depend exclusively on the pope, since by divine law the Church's doctrinal and moral health is guaranteed, in the extraordinary situation of a heretical pope, by the fidelity of the teaching of the bishops and ultimately also by the fidelity of the entirety of the lay faithful, as St John Henry Newman said and as history sufficiently demonstrates. The Church's doctrinal and moral health does not depend to such an extent on the relatively short-lived doctrinal errors of a single pope that it renders thereby the papal See vacant. As the Church can support a popeless time, as already occurred in history for a period even of several years, so the Church is by divine constitution so strong that she can also support a short-lived heretical pope.

The act of deposition of a pope because of heresy or the declaration of the vacancy of the papal chair because of the loss of the papacy *ipso facto* by its heretical occupant would be a revolutionary novelty in the life of the Church, and this regarding a highly important issue in the constitution and the life of the Church. One has to follow in such a delicate matter—even if it is of practical and not strictly of doctrinal nature—the surer way (*via tutior*) of the perennial sense of the Church. Notwithstanding the fact that three successive ecumenical councils (the Third Council of Constantinople in 681, the Second Council of Nicaea in 787, and the Fourth Council of Constantinople in 870) and Pope St Leo II in 682 excommunicated Pope Honorius I because of heresy, they did not even implicitly declare that Honorius I had lost the papacy *ipso facto* because of heresy. In fact, the pontificate of Pope Honorius I was considered valid even after he had supported heresy in his letters to Patriarch Sergius in 634, since he reigned after that for another four years until 638.

The following principle, formulated by Pope St Stephen I (d. 257), although in a different context, should be a guideline in treating the highly delicate and rare issue of a heretical pope: "*Nihil innovetur, nisi quod traditum est,*" i.e., "Let there be no innovation beyond what has been handed down."

11

On Papal Resignation
and Papal Heresy[1]

BISHOP ATHANASIUS SCHNEIDER

T HE HYPOTHESIS OF THE POSSIBILITY OF A HERETI-
cal pope derives from the Decree of Gratian (dist. XL, cap. 6, col. 146)
from the twelfth century. According to the opinion expressed in this
decree, the pope cannot be judged by any human authority, except if he has
fallen into heresy (*a nemine iudicandus, nisi deprehendatur a fide devius*). Basing themselves on this spurious decree erroneously attributed to St Boniface
(d. 754) and accepted by Gratian, the medieval theologians and theologians of
the subsequent centuries maintained as possible the hypothesis—but not the
certitude—that a pope could fall into heresy. The eventual condemnation of a
pope in the case of heresy by a so-called imperfect council of bishops corresponds
to the thesis of mitigated conciliarism. The heretical thesis of conciliarism holds
that a council is superior to the pope.

Even if—according to the opinion of the automatic loss of the papacy for heresy—the judgment of the loss of the papal office is pronounced by the heretical
pope upon himself, and he automatically falls from office without any judgment
by the Church, such an opinion contains a contradiction and reveals a hint of
crypto-conciliarism. For according to this opinion, the College of Cardinals or a
group of bishops would have to issue an official declaration about the fact of the
automatic loss of the papal office. According to another opinion, the automatic
loss of the papal office for heresy would be tantamount to a renunciation of
the papal office. However, one has to bear in mind the inevitable possibility of
disagreement among members of the College of Cardinals or of the episcopacy
regarding whether or not a pope is guilty of heresy. Hence, there will always be
doubts regarding the automatic loss of the papal office.

The pope as pope cannot fall into formal heresy in the sense that he would
pronounce a heresy *ex cathedra*. But according to renowned traditional theologians
he can favor heresy or fall into heresy as a private doctor or also as pope, but
only in his non-defining and non-definitive Magisterium, which is not infallible.

St Robert Bellarmine's opinion is that "a pope who is a manifest heretic ceases
in himself to be pope and head, just as he ceases in himself to be a Christian and
member of the body of the Church: whereby, he can be judged and punished by

---

1   First published at *LifeSiteNews* on February 28, 2020.

the Church."[2] The opinion of St Robert Bellarmine and other similar opinions on the loss of the papal office for heresy are based on the spurious decree of Gratian in the *Corpus Iuris Canonici*. Such an opinion has never been approved explicitly by the Magisterium or supported by an explicit teaching about its doctrinal validity by the Roman Pontiffs. In fact, this matter has not been decided by the Church's Magisterium and does not constitute a definitive doctrine pertaining to the universal and ordinary Magisterium. This opinion is supported only by theologians, and not even by all the Fathers of the Church from antiquity. This opinion was not taught unanimously and universally by the bishops in their constant Magisterium. Neither Gratian nor St Robert Bellarmine, nor St Alphonsus, nor other renowned theologians asserted with their opinions a doctrine of the Magisterium of the Church. Even some interventions of individual Fathers of the First Vatican Council, which seem to support the opinion of the automatic loss of the papacy for heresy, remain their personal opinion, but not a formal teaching of the First Vatican Council. And even if some few popes seemed to support such an opinion (as, e.g., Innocent III or Paul IV), this does not constitute a proof of the constant teaching of the universal and ordinary Magisterium. One also cannot cite Pope Gregory XVI to support the opinion of the automatic loss of the papal office for heresy. For he supported this thesis in his book *The Triumph of the Holy See and the Church Against the Attacks of the Innovators* before he became pope, hence not in his papal Magisterium.

The automatic loss of the papal office by a heretical pope touches not only on the practical or juridical aspects of the life of the Church, but also on the Church's doctrine — in this case, on ecclesiology. In such a delicate matter, one cannot follow a mere opinion, even if it has been supported by renowned theologians (such as St Robert Bellarmine or St Alphonsus) for a considerable period of time. Instead, one must wait for an explicit and formal decision by the Magisterium of the Church — a decision which the Magisterium has not yet issued.

On the contrary, the Magisterium of the Church, since Popes Pius X and Benedict XV, has seemed to reject such an opinion, as the formulation of the spurious decree of Gratian was eliminated in the 1917 Code of Canon Law. The canons that address the automatic loss of an ecclesiastical office for heresy in the 1917 Code of Canon Law (can. 188 §4) and in the 1983 Code of Canon Law (can. 194 §2) are not applicable to the pope, because the Church deliberately eliminated from the Code of Canon Law the following formulation taken from the previous *Corpus Iuris Canonici*: "unless the pope is caught deviating from the faith (*nisi deprehendatur a fide devius*)." By this act, the Church manifested her understanding, the *mens ecclesiae*, regarding this crucial issue. Even if one does not agree with this conclusion, the matter remains at least doubtful. In doubtful matters, however, one cannot proceed to concrete acts with fundamental implications for the life of the Church,

---

2   Bellarmine, *De Romano Pontifice*, II, 30.

such as, e.g., not to name an allegedly heretical or an allegedly invalidly elected pope in the Canon of the Mass or preparing for a new papal election.

Even if one supports the opinion of the automatic loss of the papal office for heresy, in the case of Pope Francis the College of Cardinals or of a representative group of bishops has not issued a declaration regarding the automatic loss of papal office, specifying the concrete heretical pronouncements and the date when they happened.

According to the opinion of St Robert Bellarmine, a single bishop, priest, or lay faithful cannot state the fact of the loss of papal office for heresy. Consequently, even if a single bishop or priest is convinced that Pope Francis has committed the crime of heresy, he has no authority to eliminate his name from the Canon of the Mass.

Even if one subscribes to the opinion of St Robert Bellarmine, in the case of Pope Francis doubt still remains, and there is still no statement by the College of Cardinals or a group of bishops affirming the automatic loss of the papal office and informing the entire Church about this fact.

Faithful Catholics can morally (but not canonically) distance themselves from erroneous or evil teachings and acts of a pope. This has occurred several times in the course of the Church's history. However, given the principle that one ought to give the benefit of the doubt regarding the position of one's superior (*in dubio pro superiore semper sit præsumendum*), Catholics should also consider the correct teachings of the pope as part of the Magisterium of the Church, his correct decisions as part of the Church's legislation, and his appointments of bishops and cardinals as valid. For even if one subscribes to the opinion of St Robert Bellarmine, the necessary declaration of the automatic loss of the papal office has still not been issued.

A moral and intellectual "distancing" of oneself from erroneous teachings of a pope also includes resisting his errors. However, this should always be done with due respect for the papal office and the person of the pope. St Bridget of Sweden and St Catherine of Siena, both of whom admonished the popes of their times, are fine examples of such respect. St Robert Bellarmine wrote: "Just as it is licit to resist the Pontiff who attacks the body, so also is it licit to resist him who attacks souls or destroys the civil order or above all, tries to destroy the Church. I say that it is licit to resist him by not doing what he orders and by impeding the execution of his will." [3]

Warning people about the danger of a pope's wrong teachings and actions does not require convincing people that he is not the true pope. This is required by the nature of the Catholic Church as a visible society, in contrast to the Protestant understanding and to the theory of conciliarism or semi-conciliarism, where the convictions of an individual or of a particular group inside the Church are considered as having an effect upon the fact of who is the true and valid shepherd in the Church.

The Church is strong enough and possesses sufficient means to protect the faithful from the spiritual damage of a heretical pope. In the first place, there is

---

3   Bellarmine, *De Romano Pontifice*, II, 29.

the *sensus fidelium*, the supernatural sense of the faith (*sensus fidei*). It is the gift of the Holy Spirit, by which the members of the Church possess the true sense of the faith. This is a kind of spiritual and supernatural instinct that makes the faithful *sentire cum Ecclesia* (think with the mind of the Church) and discern what is in conformity with the Catholic and Apostolic faith handed on by all bishops and popes, through the universal ordinary Magisterium.

One should also remember the wise words that Cardinal Consalvi spoke to a furious Emperor Napoleon, when the latter threatened to destroy the Church: "What we [i.e., the clergy] tried to do and did not succeed in doing, you for sure, will not succeed in doing." Paraphrasing these words one could say: "Even a heretical pope cannot destroy the Church." The pope and the Church are indeed not totally identical. The pope is the visible head of the Militant Church on earth, but at the same time he is also a member of the Mystical Body of Christ.

The *sentire cum Ecclesia* requires from a true son or daughter of the Church that he or she also praise the pope when he does right things, while asking him to do still more and praying that God enlightens him so that he may become a valiant herald and defender of the Catholic Faith.

The former Pope Benedict XVI is no longer the pope. It suffices to reread the core of Pope Benedict XVI's declaration of renunciation to realize what it meant. The following affirmations of the former Pope Benedict XVI eliminate any reasonable doubts about the validity of his abdication, and about his recognition of Pope Francis as the only true pope: "Among you, in the College of Cardinals, there is also the future pope to whom today I promise my unconditional reverence and obedience."[4] "I have taken this step with full awareness of its gravity and even its novelty, but with profound interior serenity."[5] "There is not the slightest doubt about the validity of my renunciation of the Petrine ministry. The only condition of validity is the full freedom of the decision. Speculation about the invalidity of renunciation is simply absurd."[6] During a conversation with a journalist from the Italian newspaper *Corriere della Sera*, the former Pope Benedict XVI said: "The pope is one, he is Francis." These words of Benedict XVI were reported in the written edition of *Corriere della Sera*, June 28, 2019 and anticipated in the Italian version of *Vatican News* on June 27, 2019.[7]

The Church is a visible society. Therefore, what was essential for the fulfillment of Benedict XVI's resignation was not his possible internal thought but what he externally declared, for the Church does not judge about internal intentions (*de internis non iudicat Ecclesia*). Pope Benedict XVI's ambiguous acts, like wearing a white cassock, keeping his name, imparting the apostolic blessing, etc., do not

---

4   *Farewell Address to the Cardinals*, February 28, 2013.
5   *Last General Audience*, February 27, 2013.
6   Letter from February 18, 2014, to Andrea Tornielli, published in *La Stampa*, February 27, 2014.
7   This last statement, attributed to the pope emeritus, has been disputed by some. See Dorothy Cummings McLean, "No evidence Pope Benedict said 'the Pope is one; it is Francis,'" *LifeSiteNews*, July 4, 2019.

affect the unequivocal meaning of his act of renunciation. Many of his demon-strable and unequivocal words and actions after his resignation also confirm that he considers Pope Francis, and not himself, to be the pope.

Declaring Pope Francis to be an invalid pope, either because of his heresies or because of an invalid election (for reasons of alleged violations of the con-clave norms or for the reason that Pope Benedict XVI is still the pope because of his invalid renunciation) are desperate and subjectively taken actions aimed at remedying the current unprecedented crisis of the papacy. They are purely human solutions and betray a spiritual myopia. All such endeavors are ultimately a dead end, a cul-de-sac. Such solutions reveal an implicit Pelagian approach to resolving a problem with human means; a problem, indeed, which cannot be resolved by human efforts, but which requires a divine intervention.

One need only examine similar cases of the deposition of a pope or declaration of the invalidity of his election in Church history to see that they provoked rival and contentious claimants to the papal office.

Such situations caused more confusion for the Church than did tolerating a heretical or doubtfully elected pope with the supernatural vision of the Church and trust in Divine Providence.

The Church is not a solely human reality but a divine-human reality. She is the Mystical Body of Christ. Attempts to resolve the current crisis of the papacy which favor the opinion of St Robert Bellarmine with its concrete solution, or take refuge in the unproven theory of Benedict XVI still being the only true pope, are doomed to fail from the start. The Church is in the hands of God, even in this most dark time.

We must not be lax in proclaiming Catholic truth, warning and admonishing when papal words and actions clearly harm the faith. But what all true sons and daughters of the Church ought to do now is launch a serious worldwide crusade of prayer and penance to implore a divine intervention. Let us trust in the Lord's words: "Will not God give justice to his elect, who cry to him day and night? Will he delay long over them?" (Lk 18:7).

ADDENDUM[8]

There is no authority to declare or consider an elected and generally accepted pope as an invalid pope. The constant practice of the Church makes it evident that even in the case of an invalid election this invalid election will be de facto healed through the general acceptance of the one elected by the overwhelming majority of the cardinals and bishops.

Even in the case of a heretical pope he will not lose his office automatically and there is no body within the Church to declare him deposed because of heresy. Such actions would come close to the heresy of conciliarism or episcopalism. The

---

8 First published as "Bishop Athanasius Schneider on the Validity of Pope Francis" at *OnePe-terFive* on September 19, 2023.

heresy of conciliarism or episcopalism says basically that there is a body within the Church—be it an ecumenical council, a synod, the college of cardinals, the college of bishops—that can issue a legally binding judgment over the pope.

The theory of the automatic loss of the papacy due to heresy remains only an opinion, and even St Robert Bellarmine noticed this and did not present it as a teaching of the Magisterium itself. The perennial papal Magisterium never taught such an opinion. In 1917, when the Code of Canon Law (*Codex Iuris Canonici*) came into force, the Magisterium of the Church eliminated from the new legislation the remark of the *Decretum Gratiani* in the old *Corpus Iuris Canonici*, which stated that a pope, who deviates from right doctrine, can be deposed. Never in history has the Magisterium of the Church admitted any canonical procedures for the deposition of a heretical pope. The Church has no power over the pope formally or judicially. The surer Catholic tradition says that the members of the Church can avoid a heretical pope, resist him, refuse to obey him—all of which can be done without requiring a theory or opinion that says that a heretical pope automatically loses his office or can be deposed.

Therefore, we must follow the surer way (*via tutior*) and abstain from defending the mere opinion of theologians (even they be saints like St Robert Bellarmine), which says that a heretical pope automatically loses his office or can be deposed by the Church.

The pope cannot commit heresy when he speaks *ex cathedra*; this is a dogma of faith. In his teaching outside of *ex cathedra* statements, however, he can commit doctrinal ambiguities, errors, and even heresies. And since the pope is not identical with the entire Church, the Church is stronger than a singular erring or heretical pope. In such a case one should respectfully correct him (avoiding purely human anger and disrespectful language), resist him as one would resist a bad father of a family. Yet the members of a family cannot declare their evil father deposed from fatherhood. They can correct him, refuse to obey him, separate themselves from him, but they cannot declare him deposed.

Good Catholics know the truth and must proclaim it; they must offer reparation for the errors of an erring pope. Since the case of a heretical pope is humanly irresolvable, we must implore with supernatural faith a divine intervention, because that singular erring pope is not eternal, but temporal, and the Church is not in our hands, but in the almighty hands of God.

We must have enough supernatural faith, trust, humility, and the spirit of the Cross in order to endure such an extraordinary trial. In such relatively short situations (in comparison to two thousand years) we must not yield to a too human reaction and to an easy solution (declaring the invalidity of his pontificate), but must keep a cool head and at the same time a true supernatural view, trusting in divine intervention and in the indestructibility of the Church.

12

Is There a Charism
of Infallible Safety?[1]

JOHN P. JOY

A S WE KNOW, THE POPES ARE INFALLIBLE UNDER
certain conditions. According to Vatican II (repeating the teaching of
Vatican I), the Roman Pontiff is infallible when, "as the supreme shepherd and teacher of all the faithful, who confirms his brethren in their faith, by
a definitive act he proclaims a doctrine of faith or morals."[2] But what about papal
teaching that falls short of these conditions? In other words, what about the
non-definitive teaching of the authentic papal magisterium?

I have argued elsewhere that such teaching is not infallible and so could occasionally contain error in matters of faith or morals.[3] But could it be infallibly *safe*
even if it's not infallibly *true*? What would that mean? Some Catholic theologians
have put forward a thesis that the Holy Spirit, even though he does *not* protect
non-definitive (or merely authentic) papal teaching from *all* kinds of error (and
so it would not be infallibly *true*), does nevertheless prevent it from containing
anything *so erroneous* that it would be harmful to souls to embrace it (hence it would
be infallibly *safe*). In other words, according to the infallible safety thesis, the pope
may teach *some* errors in his non-infallible magisterium, but not *dangerous* errors.

What would be excluded by this view? Certainly, heresy would be out of the
question. If all papal teaching is infallibly safe, then no pope would ever be able
to teach heresy, which is the most dangerous form of error. Proponents of this
view might admit that a pope could personally believe heresy, or even teach it
as a private theologian, but they would necessarily deny that he could ever teach
heresy in his authentic magisterium.

What else? Any teaching that would contradict preexisting infallibly taught
Catholic doctrine would also have to be excluded, since it could never be "safe"
for a Catholic to deny a doctrine that he has a prior obligation to accept.

WHAT CAN BE SAID IN FAVOR OF THIS VIEW?

In the first place, we should admit that the infallible safety thesis has an initial plausibility and appeal as an argument from fittingness. It would sure make
life easier for Catholics if we could simply accept everything every pope teaches

---

1   First published at *OnePeterFive* on December 27, 2023.
2   *Lumen Gentium* 25.
3   See my *Disputed Questions on Papal Infallibility*, 3–41.

without fear of any possibility of dangerous error. And if the pope is supposed to be the rock of faith and the center of unity for the Church, why wouldn't God preserve more of his teaching from more kinds of errors? Wouldn't it be better if the popes were more infallible rather than less?

When we look for support for this thesis in the documents of the magisterium, however, we do not find much. To be sure, Pope John Paul II spoke about a charism of divine assistance that extends beyond the infallible teaching of the pope to his entire magisterium. In a General Audience of March 24, 1993, he said, "Alongside this infallibility of *ex cathedra* definitions, there is the charism of the Holy Spirit's assistance, granted to Peter and his successors so that they would not err in matters of faith and morals, but rather shed great light on the Christian people. This charism is not limited to exceptional cases, but embraces in varying degrees the whole exercise of the magisterium."[4]

However, John Paul II makes it clear in the very same General Audience that he does not intend this charism to be understood as a kind of infallibility, for he explicitly says that the pope is infallible "*only* when he speaks *ex cathedra*."[5] If the difference between definitive and non-definitive papal teaching consisted merely in a distinction between *kinds* of infallibility (i.e., "infallibly true" vs. "infallibly safe"), it would be odd for teaching that is supposedly infallibly safe to be described simply as "non-infallible" without any qualification. Yet this is how Pope John Paul II described it in an address to the bishops of the United States, saying: "The *non-infallible* expressions of the authentic magisterium of the Church should be received with religious submission of mind and will."[6] The official notes of the Theological Commission at Vatican II similarly use the word "non-infallible" without qualification to describe this kind of teaching.[7]

The Instruction of the Congregation for the Doctrine of the Faith *Donum Veritatis* is another magisterial text that speaks of a "divine assistance," which is said to guide "magisterial decisions in matters of discipline, even if they are not guaranteed by the charism of infallibility."[8] Such a text is far from conclusive, however, since it can easily be understood as asserting a special grace that protects the Church from *frequent errors* in the exercise of the authentic magisterium rather than from *dangerous errors*. As *Donum Veritatis* itself goes on to say, "It would be contrary to the truth, if, proceeding from some particular cases, one were to conclude that the Church's Magisterium can be *habitually* mistaken in its prudential judgments, or that it does not enjoy divine assistance in the integral exercise of its mission."[9]

---

4   Pope John Paul II, General Audience, March 24, 1993.

5   Ibid.

6   Pope John Paul II, Address to the Bishops from the United States of America [of New York] on Their *Ad Limina* Visit, October 15, 1988.

7   *Acta Synodalia Sacrosancti Concilii Oecumenici Vaticani Secundi* (Rome: Typis Polyglottis Vaticanis, 1970-99), II/1, 255; III/1, 250.

8   CDF, *Donum Veritatis* 17.

9   *Donum Veritatis* 24.

Finally, there is support for the infallible safety thesis in the theological tradition going back to such eminent theologians as Johann Franzelin and Louis Billot in the late nineteenth and early twentieth centuries. Good scholastics that they were, however, they would certainly insist that the arguments for and against the thesis be argued on their own merits rather than by appeal to their authority as theologians.

OBJECTIONS TO THE IDEA OF "INFALLIBLE SAFETY"

When we examine the arguments, there are a number of serious objections to this thesis, which I find much more persuasive (in fact, conclusive).

In the first place, the thesis necessarily posits a distinction between errors that are dangerous to believe and errors that are safe to believe. But in matters of faith and morals, how could it be safe to embrace any error at all? That some errors are more dangerous than others is easy to concede, but that some errors are "safe" is hard to accept. Presumably, the reason why popes and councils in past centuries took the trouble to issue solemn condemnations of propositions that were not heretical but merely "offensive to pious ears," "evil sounding," or "captious" is because they believed that even such slight deviations from correct teaching constituted a danger to the faithful.

Second, it is not at all easy to square the idea of infallible safety with the historical case of Pope Honorius (625–638), who was condemned as a heretic by a whole series of ecumenical councils (Constantinople III, Nicaea II, Constantinople IV), whose acts, including their condemnations of Honorius as a heretic, were confirmed and ratified by later popes. This poses a real dilemma, or in fact a trilemma, for the infallible safety thesis.

The trilemma is this: there are only three possible ways to interpret these condemnations of Honorius as a heretic. Either (1) he really taught heresy in his letters to Sergius, the Patriarch of Constantinople, and was rightly condemned for it; or (2) he did not teach heresy and was wrongfully condemned; or (3) he did not teach heresy, but was nonetheless rightly condemned because his teaching, although technically orthodox, contributed to the spread of the Monothelite heresy by appearing to provide support for it through its ambiguous formulations.

On the first interpretation, the infallible safety thesis clearly falls apart, for that would be a case of a pope teaching heresy, which is the most dangerous kind of error. On the second interpretation, Honorius is off the hook, but we are then confronted with the problem of multiple ecumenical councils, confirmed and ratified by multiple popes, that would all be guilty of an egregious error in having wrongfully condemned Honorius as a heretic. Apart from how this would require us to abandon the long-held and well-established tradition that the solemn condemnations of ecumenical councils are infallible (no small price to pay), what would it say about *their* infallible safety? If popes are infallibly safe even in their non-infallible teaching, then surely ecumenical councils are as well; and how could it be safe to follow their teaching if they committed an error like this? Would it have been "safe" for Catholics for centuries to be anathematizing a pope as a heretic if he were not one? If popes are protected by the Holy Spirit from ever teaching heresy, it would not seem very safe for Councils to be condemning popes as heretics.

Finally, on the third interpretation, which I think the most likely one historically, even though Honorius would not have actually taught heresy, he would have been rightly condemned by the Councils for exercising his magisterium in such a way as to incur the guilt of heresy through the support he provided for it in his letters, which is sure proof that his teaching was not a safe guide for the faithful to follow.

A third objection to the infallible safety thesis is that it depends primarily on theological speculation, which reasons *a priori* and without reference to historical facts. Speculative theology is valuable in itself, but the theologian who practices it must be willing to take into account the evidence of history. If things occur (or have occurred) in the history of the Church that don't fit with a particular theory, then the theory has to be reevaluated.

One consequence of this is that purported instances of dangerous error in non-infallible papal teaching cannot be brushed aside by appeal to the idea of infallible safety without begging the question. If the thesis is true, then it would follow that there could be no true instances of popes teaching dangerous error; but when the truth of the thesis is the point at issue, then purported instances of such dangerous teaching have to be taken seriously as potential evidence against the thesis.

A speculative theological position like "infallible safety" may have seemed more plausible in the late nineteenth and early twentieth centuries when the popes were thundering orthodox teaching with great clarity. But the list of perplexing things said by Pope Francis continues to grow. Even if every statement could be carefully (if laboriously) explained in an orthodox fashion, we would at least have to concede, based on the facts, that the papal magisterium is not protected from ambiguous formulations that insinuate or suggest dangerous errors, or from which dangerous errors might be taken away by reading texts at face value or in their natural meaning. For example, to believe that certain passages of Scripture are no longer materially true or teachable — a position Pope Francis recently espoused in one of his responses to *Dubia*[10] — at least suggests a dangerous error because of its implications for the truth of Scripture in general, even if the particular Scripture passages alluded to might not seem to be of great importance.

This fact, in and of itself, undermines the foundational speculative argument for the infallible safety thesis, which can be summarized as follows:

1. God must provide a means of preserving faithful Catholics from falling into dangerous error.
2. If the popes are able to teach dangerous error in their non-infallible magisterium, many Catholics will fall into dangerous error.

---

10   Contained in the responses to the first set of *Dubia* submitted by five cardinals on July 10, 2023, a text found below on pp. 432–33, together with John Lamont's critique.

3. Therefore, God must prevent the popes from teaching dangerous error even in their non-infallible magisterium.

But consider a parallel argument:

1. God must provide a means of preserving faithful Catholics from falling into dangerous error.
2. If the popes are able to lend support to dangerous error in their non-infallible magisterium, many Catholics will still be led astray.
3. Therefore, God must prevent the popes from lending support to dangerous error even in their non-infallible magisterium.

This is contradicted not only by the example of Honorius but also by recent history, so there must be a flaw in it. What could it be? Certainly, it is not the first premise; the problem must be in the second premise, which asserts that *the means by which* God preserves faithful Catholics from falling into dangerous error *must be* a charism of infallible safety. But if God has provided *another* means of preserving Catholics from falling into dangerous error, then this premise would fail.

Let's begin with the lesser problem of papal teaching that lends support to dangerous error, which we know is indeed possible, because it has happened historically. What means does God provide to protect the faithful from being led astray by such teaching? There are two options here:

Option 1. If the obligation of the faithful to accept non-infallible teaching with a religious submission of will and intellect is *unconditional*, then they will need to know—for every magisterial statement—how to resolve every possible ambiguity by detailed knowledge of context, original language, theological nuance, etc., or at least they must have access to the explanations offered by professional apologists of potentially problematic papal teaching.

Option 2. If the obligation of the faithful to accept non-infallible teaching with a religious submission of will and intellect is *conditional* (meaning that it must be accepted only on the condition that it does not contradict the established contents of the faith), then all that the faithful will need in order to protect themselves from falling into dangerous error is a knowledge of the faith such as is found in Scripture and in every traditional catechism. When confronted with a papal teaching that seems to provide support for dangerous error, an ordinary Catholic who knows his faith would be able to withold assent on the basis of what is already publicly known and well-established Catholic doctrine rather than be forced to suffer constant crises of faith while waiting for someone to provide an explanation of how the teaching doesn't quite technically violate the faith.[11]

---

11 In this case, it would not even be necessary for an ordinary Catholic to assert that he knows that a particular papal teaching is in fact erroneous or incapable of being defended; rather, if the new teaching appears to him incompatible with something to which he is already bound, such as the Ten Commandments or the Nicene Creed or any other longstanding authority, he will abstain from accepting the new teaching, keeping his judgment in suspension. He would be not so much rejecting it as refraining from accepting it.

The latter option seems not only simpler and more effective, but also more in keeping with the wisdom of God's Providence, since the knowledge required to protect the faithful from dangerous ambiguities or insinuations of error is, on this telling, the same knowledge that *all* Catholics are already *required* to have in any case—the basic knowledge of the faith—rather than an additional technical knowledge available only to a few.

If this, then, is how God protects his faithful from being led astray by dangerous ambiguities or insinuations of dangerous error in official papal teaching, then there is no need to posit an additional mechanism, such as the "infallible safety" thesis, to protect the faithful from being led astray by plain assertions of dangerous error, or even heresy, in the official (but non-infallible) teaching of the pope.[12]

The whole solution to this question, therefore, hinges on the nature of the obligation Catholics have to accept non-infallible teaching with a religious submission (*religioso obsequio*) of will and intellect: Is it conditional or unconditional? If unconditional, then the teaching of the authentic magisterium must be infallibly safe, completely protected from heresy and all dangerous error, since otherwise the faithful would have no choice but to accept such teaching. If conditional, however, then it could very well be possible for dangerous errors or even heresies to be taught by the authentic magisterium. And there is conclusive proof that this obligation must be conditional, for in *Lumen Gentium*, the same response of "religious submission of the mind" (*religioso animi obsequio*) is said to be owed to the teaching of individual bishops, who we know can teach heresy (one need only name Nestorius): "In matters of faith and morals, the bishops speak in the name of Christ and the faithful are to accept their teaching [*in sui Episcopi sententiam* refers to "their bishop" in the singular] and adhere to it with a religious assent."[13] The same text goes on to say, "This (*Hoc*) religious submission of mind and will must be shown in a special way to the authentic magisterium of the Roman Pontiff,"[14] indicating that the religious submission owed to individual bishops and to the pope is the same in kind even though the latter is greater in degree.

If the same kind (even if not the same degree) of religious submission is owed to one's bishop, whose teaching is certainly not infallibly safe, as is owed to the authentic magisterium of the pope, then there is no reason to conclude that his teaching must be infallibly safe either. Peter is the rock on which Christ founded the Church. But the faithful are ultimately preserved from dangerous error not by every word that proceeds from the mouth of the pope, but by his judicious use of the keys of the kingdom, entrusted to him by Christ, when he binds and looses the minds of the faithful by his infallible judgments and definitions *ex cathedra*.

---

12   One enormous benefit of this conclusion is that it shows how it could be possible for Divine Providence to allow a pope to fall into heresy and even to teach heresy non-definitively, without the indefectibility of the Church being undermined. For, on this view, the Church is indefectible in the public profession of faith to which all are bound, from the least to the greatest.

13   *Lumen Gentium* 25.

14   Ibid.

On Non-infallible Teachings of the Magisterium and the Meaning of *Obsequium Religiosum*[1]

JEREMY R. HOLMES

POPE FRANCIS'S MANY CONTROVERSIAL STATEMENTS have brought with them a new interest in how Catholics should respond to non-infallible teachings of the Magisterium. The pope's infallibility was solemnly defined only in the late nineteenth century, so it is no surprise that careful reflection on non-infallible-but-still-authoritative teachings is a fairly recent thing. Vatican II's constitution *Lumen Gentium* tackles the topic head-on, but even there it just says that we owe the pope's non-infallible statements a religious *obsequium* of mind and will. This language was picked up in the *Catechism of the Catholic Church*, the Code of Canon Law, the CDF's Instruction on the Ecclesial Vocation of the Theologian *Donum Veritatis*, the *Professio Fidei*, and the CDF's doctrinal commentary on the concluding formula of the *Professio Fidei*, so it appears to be the Church's phrasing of choice for describing a Catholic's proper response to non-infallible magisterial teaching in general.

But what does it mean? Sometimes "religious *obsequium*" is translated "religious assent," at other times "religious submission," and at other times "religious respect." What exactly are we being asked to do? Taking into account everything said in the above-mentioned documents, and looking a bit deeper for a theological account of what they say, let's unpack the key term *obsequium*.

THE DICTIONARY MEANING OF THE WORD

The Latin word *obsequium* is not a mystery in itself. Its basic meaning is compliance or a readiness to comply.[2] So, for example, the Roman army would bring a people back to *obsequium* — that is, subjugate them — by force of arms. Or a lover would show *obsequium* — a readiness to, erm, "comply" — with her man. In English we have an old-but-not-quite obsolete word "obsequy" to signify the same thing. In the context of theology, the meaning of *obsequium* is admirably captured by the English word "submission."

---

1   First published at *Catholic World Report* on December 30, 2017; also included as an appendix to Joy's *Disputed Questions on Papal Infallibility*.

2   So the Oxford Latin Dictionary, which also offers as extended meanings "assiduous service or attention," "deference," or "solicitude."

As the above examples show, to call something *obsequium* is a fairly outward description of what is going on: the interior motivation behind the *obsequium* could be almost anything. One complies with one's lover out of amorous love. One has a readiness to comply with the Roman army because they kill disobedient people. One complies with the commands of one's parents out of respect for them as parents — or perhaps for fear of a spanking. One complies with the government's laws both because they are the custodians of the common good (reverence) and because they can punish (fear). In some of these cases the *obsequium* is a moral obligation, while in others it is just a fact arising from the situation. When someone's readiness to comply is driven by flattery, such that he changes with every slightest perceived whim of his master, we call him "obsequious."

The *obsequium* we give to the Magisterium is specified as "religious": it does not arise from fear for our lives, nor from amorous love, but from reverence.

Reverence for what? For the office, bestowed on certain men by God, of protecting the Church's common good, a common good that includes the truth of the faith. We meet a teaching from the Magisterium with an act of submission (*obsequium*) inspired by reverence for the Magisterium's God-given office (*religiosum*). It is like the reverence one has for a sacred place: one would not carry out a non-religious activity in a Church without a pressing reason; one would be even more reluctant to transgress the sanctuary itself except in a case of great necessity; one would never in any situation agree to strike a monstrance or a tabernacle or do anything else that would endanger the Eucharist; and one could not conceive of disrespecting the Eucharist itself. The reverence due to the sacred forbids it.

To refuse assent to a magisterial teaching is to transgress the Magisterium's sacred office, while to assent is to act with reverence toward it. This is why some translations of *Lumen Gentium* render the word *obsequium* as "respect." Although this is a decent attempt to describe the nature of the act, the English word "respect" seems to fall somewhat short of the strong reverence that is due to a sacred office, and it reaches for one of the more extended lexical meanings of the Latin word *obsequium*. For the purposes of this article, I will continue to render *obsequium* as "submission," as better capturing the natural species of the act, while pursuing the idea of "reverence" as expressing the moral species of the act.

DEGREES OF ENGAGEMENT OF THE MAGISTERIUM'S AUTHORITY

While I compared reverence for the Magisterium to reverence for a church or a tabernacle, there is a key difference between reverence for inanimate sacred things and reverence for a sacred person. The sacred thing is simply there, more or less sacred as the Church has made it so. But a person holding a sacred office can choose to bring the sacredness of his office more or less to bear on a situation. So while a church is only as sacred as it is, and the sanctuary inevitably more so, and the tabernacle even more so, a person holding the magisterial office can engage his office to a lesser degree, a greater degree, or a maximal degree, depending on his judgment.

There is nothing mystical about this. Every moral authority works the same way. For example, a child should obey his father out of piety, and the father can invoke his God-given role as father to a greater or a lesser degree. Sometimes the father only interposes his paternal office slightly, and the child knows that a slight reason would be enough to justify transgressing his father's request. At other times the father interposes his paternal office more significantly, so the child knows that it is unlikely any reason would justify disobedience. And sometimes, in rare cases, the father can lay his entire paternal office between the child and a given deed, as though to say: If you do this, you utterly disrespect my paternity. The child who goes ahead with the deed at that point estranges himself from his father.

The same thing is true of governmental authority. While the government has power to punish those who are not motivated by anything more noble than fear, a good citizen obeys the law out of reverence for the office of the lawgiver. And the government indicates the greater and lesser degrees to which it interposes the dignity of its office between a citizen and a given deed by assigning greater and lesser penalties. For something trivial, like a speeding violation, the penalty is trivial. For something that defies all the demands of reverence for lawful authority, like treason, the penalty can even be death.

Notice that neither of these cases depends on the particular expertise of the one who holds the office. It helps if one's father is wise, but piety makes demands even toward a mediocre parent; no one in his right mind presumes the government knows best, but every good citizen intuitively obeys laws promulgated by the legitimate authorities.

INVOKING THE OFFICE OF THE MAGISTERIUM TO VARYING DEGREES

So it comes as no surprise that those entrusted with guarding the Church's common good, the truth of the faith, can interpose the sacredness of their office between believers and a given path to a greater or lesser degree, even to the point of putting their entire office at stake. When the Magisterium only partially interposes its office between believer and deed, we have non-infallible yet magisterial teachings. When the Magisterium entirely interposes its office between believer and deed, it makes a difference who does this and how:

• If an individual bishop completely interposes his office and the believer goes ahead anyway, he is estranged from that bishop, although not necessarily from the Church. One might have to do this sometimes, if the bishop in question has himself betrayed the office he invokes. This is like the case when a child simply must disobey an abusive father, who has made a mockery of his paternity.

• If the bishops all together, or the bishop of Rome acting as their head, completely interpose their office—not just this man's episcopacy, but the episcopacy as a whole—and one goes ahead, then one is estranged from the Church. Because

God gave the episcopacy to the Church, breaking ties with the episcopacy as such can never be a good idea.

• If the bishops all together declare that statement X is in the deposit of revelation, then the case is more serious still. When a person begins to consider whether he should adopt the Christian faith, he hears many different voices: the Bible says things, this or that preacher says things, bishops say things, and even his own experience and random books he picks up. But when he makes the decision that is the act of faith, what he commits to is this: All these many voices were but one voice, the voice of God inviting me to Him. The act of faith is an act of hearing the voice of God in obedience. And when the bishops all together, or the pope speaking as their head, declares that a given statement is in the deposit of revelation, their statement merges into the many voices that the believer originally heard and accepted as the voice of God. The believer's response is no longer one of reverence for the office of the Magisterium but of trust in God. To withhold assent at this point would be to void the act of faith itself, to undo one's original commitment. It would no longer be a sin of irreverence toward the Magisterium but a sin of heresy. In the analogy of respect for sacred things given above, this would be like desecrating the Eucharist, the very reason why everything around it is sacred.

Each of the above-mentioned levels of authority has a distinct term to describe it. As regards non-infallible magisterial statements, i.e., lesser interpositions of the office, normal people normally do not have any sufficient reason to transgress the interpositions. So the normal outcome of reverence for the Magisterium is compliance, i.e., assent. This assent does not take the form of saying "I know X is true" — this is for acts of faith or of compliance with the definitive magisterium — but of saying "I think that X is true," using the language of firm opinion. Even though the Magisterium can invoke its office more and less here, yielding varying degrees of moral obligation to comply, the responses to these various degrees do not differ *in kind* and so are all described by the same terms.

When the magisterium completely interposes its office, i.e., hands down a definitive teaching, the response is not in any way uncertain. So the response is not described here as *obsequium religiosum*, but *firmiter tenere*, to "hold firmly," saying not "I think" but "I know."

The response to God's voice is *credo* — I believe.

OBSEQUIUM RELIGIOSUM IN CASES OF DISAGREEMENT

With regard to the lesser interpositions of the Magisterium's office, people can find themselves in a hard situation where a good reason for withholding compliance presents itself. However, the reverence given to non-infallible acts is always the same for the same degree of interposition of the office, even though how one acts on that reverence will depend on other factors like one's academic training, one's responsibility for instructing others, the harmony of the teaching with other magisterial teachings, etc. Disagreeing with a non-infallible teaching does not mean withdrawing that which makes the *obsequium religiosum* a meaningful act: in a given case one may not comply, and yet the reverence that normally drives compliance is still present.

The reverence still present is not an empty form, either, because it still imposes certain limits on one's actions. If necessity forced a soldier to move through a church sanctuary with a rifle, for example, he still would not spit chewing tobacco or write on the walls: his reluctant violation of the space would not eliminate his reverence. And similarly, even when we must disagree with magisterial statements — e.g., when they disagree with other magisterial statements — we do so with sorrow at the necessity and with respect for the office and its holder.

It might seem as though the fact that magisterial statement A disagrees with greater magisterial statement B voids the reverence due to A, because reverence for the magisterium itself outweighs what would have been given to A. But this is not so. Suppose for example that a Catholic saw the Eucharist in danger of desecration in the sanctuary and ran pell-mell through the church and through the sanctuary to prevent the desecration: his religious reverence for the church and the sanctuary would not be diminished by his apparently disrespectful behavior. Quite the contrary: he could reverence the sanctuary *only* by rushing to save the Eucharist, the reality which makes the sanctuary sacred.

And again, none of this is mysterious: it is the way moral authority normally works. If a father has repeated command X time and again, in the most serious terms, and then later gives command Y only once, casually, as the child leaves for school, what does the child do if he finds that obeying Y conflicts with obeying X? He understands that his father has substantially invested his paternal office in X and only slightly in Y, and consequently to obey command Y would be to disrespect his father's very fatherhood, and therefore would constitute "obedience" only in an outward and physical way.

The difference in authority levels is also crucial from the parent's point of view: the father expresses some things more seriously and other things more casually precisely because he wants his child to know which things give way in a crisis and which things do not. Imagine the pressure on a father if he knew that every statement he uttered put his entire paternity at stake. Imagine the constraint he would feel if he knew that every command he gave his child, no matter how small, absolutely bound that child in all circumstances. It would be practically unworkable.

The Magisterium is no different in this regard. Sometimes the Church speaks infallibly, putting her entire office at stake and forcing a Catholic to choose: union with the Church or estrangement? Sometimes the Magisterium invests its office not entirely, but substantially. At other times, the Magisterium puts its office behind a given statement only in a small way. These differing levels of authority are there both for the faithful and for the Magisterium itself, to make its moral

authority workable. The pope does not have to suffer the intolerable burden
of intending to speak infallibly or of being seen as speaking infallibly in every
circumstance, no matter how casual his utterance. And in hard circumstances,
when choices must be made between teachings of higher authority and teachings
of lesser authority, the faithful can know that only assent to those teachings in
which the Magisterium's office is more invested is true *obsequium religiosum.*

14

The Magisterium of
the iPhone Church[1]

DARRICK TAYLOR

PETER KWASNIEWSKI'S RECENT ESSAY[2] ON THE MAG-
isterial quandary of Catholics today articulates well the situation of orthodox Catholics in our day and age, when so much of Church teaching
seems up for grabs. I think I have a partial explanation of why there is such a
magisterial crisis at the moment.

Kwasniewski has written eloquently on the nature of obedience and authority. And in the current crisis, the whole nature of authority has become a hot
topic, as those who defend Pope Francis's papacy have adverted to the same
"hyperpapal" stance that many in the reign of John Paul II did over moral questions, only this time on a different side of the dispute. But the debate over papal
authority is actually a proxy for deeper questions, namely about the nature of
the Church itself.

Let me explain what I mean by quoting at length from the late Pope Benedict,
from his Christmas address to the curia in 2005. This speech is famous for his
explanation of two "hermeneutics" of Vatican II: that of rupture, and that of
continuity. The passage concerns the proponents of "rupture," for whom Vatican II

> is considered as a sort of Constituent Assembly that eliminates an old
> constitution and creates a new one. However, the Constituent Assembly
> needs a mandator and then confirmation by the mandator, in other
> words, the people the constitution must serve. The Fathers had no
> such mandate and no one had ever given them one; nor could anyone
> have given them one because the essential constitution of the Church
> comes from the Lord and was given to us so that we might attain
> eternal life and, starting from this perspective, be able to illuminate
> life in time and time itself.

I think Benedict hit upon the key issue. What he is saying here is that the Church
has a nature, or form, which is in its essence unchangeable because it is given
by a divine sovereign. Dissenters in the reigns of John Paul II and Benedict XVI,
turned hyperpapalists under Francis, clearly don't believe this. They care less

---

1   First published at *Crisis Magazine* on April 25, 2023.
2   Peter Kwasniewski, "Conundrums about Interpretation: What Is a Catholic to Do?," *Crisis Magazine*, March 30, 2023, now incorporated into idem, *Bound by Truth*, 11–17.

about the type of government the Church assumes (monarchical, democratic), and far more that its "constitution" be understood as alterable. That is why they are consistent when they praise Francis and revile Benedict; for them, Vatican II was the moment when the Church gave up *semper eadem* and admitted that reality was dynamic rather than static. Benedict told them no, while Francis indulges them in this idea.

This doesn't mean these dissenters-turned-hyperpapalists don't care about authority, but it means something vastly different for them than for orthodox Catholics. For the orthodox, that authority is meant to preserve what Christ gave to the Apostles and to safeguard it. The purpose of authority appears quite otherwise if you don't believe in unchanging truth, or if you believe that truth is ultimately unknowable. If that is the case, authority's primary role is to ratify changes, to verify that the Church is up-to-date; reality is dynamic, and we have no choice but to keep up with it.

Where did they get this idea from? I suppose it is a result of the influence of modernism, but there is a reason why they find such ideas plausible in the first place. People respond to what they see in their daily lives, not to abstract theological ideas. Modern Westerners have lived for quite a while now in a humanly constructed, technologically driven society that caters nonstop to human desires.

The progressive idea of authority echoes this. Despite all the talk about "the Spirit" and "the spirit of Vatican II," the controlling metaphor for their vision of the Church is mechanistic rather than organic or spiritual. The whole notion of "updating" (*aggiornamento*) is fundamentally a technological one, one that presumes the sort of continuous progress one finds in technology. For these people, the Church needs constant updating as if it were an iPhone—Church 1.0, 2.0, and so forth—to keep up with the demands of "reality," i.e., of its customers.

Incredulous Catholics rightfully respond with skepticism and indignation when prelates like Cardinal Jean-Claude Hollerich, SJ, proclaim that the Church can contradict itself by ordaining women. To them, such $2 + 2 = 5$ logic is incomprehensible. But for Hollerich and his supporters, such arbitrariness is no problem because the world they inhabit simply *is* an arbitrary human construction, as that is what twenty-first-century society has become. For them, authority is that which enables them to adapt and flourish accordingly. God, and therefore Christ, is to them less a lawgiver or Savior than a sort of cosmic Steve Jobs, delivering TEDx Talks to empower them to be their best selves. The Church is simply a form of technology they use to achieve this.

On this view, the Church is an instrument, not the divine community in which they encounter Christ. As absurd as it sounds, this idea is one possible response to the confusion about magisterial authority Kwasniewski identified. The Church is so ancient, and has issued so many formal declarations of belief, that it is quite impossible for any one person to keep them straight in his head. (The Church can even "forget" doctrine, as Joseph Shaw once pointed out.[3]) Hyperpapalism saves one from the mental work of trying to determine which elements in this body of teaching are authoritative by assuming they are all provisional and treating the papacy like some oracular dictatorship, unbound by logic or consistency.

Naturally, this does not solve the problem. If you believe that the basic teachings of the Christian faith are givens, it is possible *in principle* to discern which ones are definitive and which ones are not, since they do not constantly change. But if you believe formal pronouncements of Church doctrine are merely jumping off points for the next "evolution" of faith, the very meaning of what "authority" demands loses all stability. Trying to follow the pronouncements of someone who actually believes this dynamic view becomes almost impossible — rather like trying to follow the contradictory statements of Pope Francis.

I do not, however, presume that every theologian or prelate who talks a certain way actually believes what he is saying. Far from it. I have learned from painful experience that it is dangerous to presume every bishop or cardinal believes the things he claims publicly about Church teaching. The sexual abuse scandals should have taught us about this disconnect, if nothing else. I recall reading an unnamed cardinal (a liberal one) express admiration for Cardinal Burke around the time Francis removed him from the Roman Rota, because Burke seemed to *believe* what he was *saying*.

You know why: several figures who were "conservatives" under his predecessors have toed the line on pretty much everything in the reign of Francis. I had never heard of Cardinal Hollerich before the "Synod on Synodality," but I imagine the lure of the spotlight for a bishop of Luxembourg, previously of Japan, must be pretty tempting for an otherwise undistinguished prelate in a dying European Church. Unbelief and a desire for advancement is just as good an explanation for people making these incredible statements as actual belief in absurdities.

But there is clearly a core of people who do, and not all of them are intellectual nonentities. The eminent Church historian Francis Oakley has argued for conciliarism while maintaining that the Church's dogmatic definitions are by definition changing and therefore cannot bind the faithful in perpetuity.[4] Likewise, Cardinal Walter Kasper wrote, back in the 1960s, that

> the God who is enthroned over the world and history as a changeless being is an offence to man. One must deny him for man's sake, because he claims for himself the dignity and honor that belong by right to

---

3 See Joseph Shaw, "Can the Church forget doctrine?," *LMS Chairman*, June 12, 2018. Thomas Pink has argued the same: the "official doctrine" of a certain period of time can be discerned not only in what is said, but in what is left unsaid and then largely forgotten, except perhaps by a few scholars. See above, pp. 24–26.

4 Francis Oakley, "Authoritative and Ignored: The Overlooked Council of Constance," *Commonweal*, October 11, 2014.

man . . . . We must resist this God, however, not only for man's sake, but also for God's sake. He is not the true God at all, but rather a wretched idol. For a God who is only alongside of and above history, who is not himself history, is a finite God. If we call such a being God, then for the sake of the Absolute we must become absolute atheists. Such a God springs from a rigid worldview; he is the guarantor of the status quo and the enemy of the new. [5]

This is not merely an attitude toward authority; it is a conviction about the nature of reality itself.

Which is why, to bring us full circle, Benedict XVI's depiction of the divisions in the Church as a matter of interpretation doesn't capture the radical incompatibility of the visions that fuel them. It is not a matter of mere interpretation but of violently opposed ideas of what the Catholic faith is. Confusion about what the Magisterium requires in terms of assent will not soon abate, until the Church's leaders recognize that its "constitution" does indeed come from the Lord and is not the protean chimera of their imaginations.

---

5   Walter Kasper, "Gott in der Geschichte," in *Gott heute: 15 Beiträge zur Gottesfrage*, ed. Norbert Kutschki (Mainz: Matthias-Grünewald-Verlag, 1967), cited in Fr Franz Schmidberger, SSPX, "Kasper's New Pastoral Approach to Marriage," March 25, 2014, https://sspx.org/en/news-events/news/kaspers-new-pastoral-approach-marriage-3886.

{ PART II }
Ultramontanism
True and False

15

Let Be Be Finale of Seem[1]

STUART CHESSMAN

EDWARD GIBBON WROTE HIS MASSIVE *DECLINE AND Fall of the Roman Empire* in the era of the late Enlightenment, a time of profound spiritual change in Europe. More recently, some notable authors have applied Gibbon's framework of "decline and fall" to Christendom and the Roman Catholic Church itself. Noteworthy examples are *The Decline and Fall of the Roman Church* by Malachi Martin (1981) and *The Decline and Fall of the Catholic Church in America* by David Carlin (2003). Just in this year, Michel Onfray has contributed *Decadence: The Life and Death of Judeo-Christianity*. On closer inspection such works describe three distinct historical phenomena.

The first "decline and fall" is the secularization of the West, eventually culminating in the disintegration of "Christendom" as a cultural, religious, and political reality. Loss of faith was accompanied by the evaporation of papal political power. We perhaps can place the beginnings of this development around 1300. By the time (1799) Novalis wrote *Christendom or Europe* in the wake of the French Revolution, this phase could be considered over. Even the pope died that very year in exile, as a prisoner of the French.

After the collapse of Christendom, however, the Roman Catholic Church was able to reorganize itself internally under the leadership of the ultramontane papacy. Ultramontanism in the nineteenth-century sense contested the growing hegemony of liberalism yet also depended on it. The renewed stature of the papacy presupposed liberalism's eliminating or weakening other competing centers of material and spiritual power in the Church (especially the absolute monarchies, but also the landed contemplative monasteries, the state churches of France and the Holy Roman Empire, etc.). What emerged by 1870 was a rigidly centralized Church organized around the clergy and the pope. All authority in matters of doctrine, liturgy, and to some extent politics was reserved to the pope and Vatican. The Church strived for uniformity in worship, music, philosophy, and theology. Obedience to authority was elevated to an almost mystical value.

The second decline (and fall) dates to the Second Vatican Council and its aftermath. As a consequence of the Council and contemporary secular cultural revolutions, the uniform, centralized structure perfected between 1870 and 1958 collapsed. A great diversity of ecclesiastical organizations, "theologies," and liturgies

---

1 First published at the blog of the Society of St Hugh of Cluny on November 11, 2017. The title is a quotation from Wallace Stevens's poem "The Emperor of Ice-Cream."

emerged among the more "engaged" members of the church. As Malachi Martin perceptively remarked, these new forms of "doing Church" were not just *autocephalous* but *autozoic*: not just autonomous in regard to Rome but having fundamentally different structures, practices, and philosophies. What resemblances existed, for example, between the Catholic Church of the Netherlands (with its *Dutch Catechism*) and that of Poland; the Jesuit order and Opus Dei; the Catholic University of Louvain in Belgium and Thomas Aquinas College in California? Over all this chaos, the centralized administrative structure of the Vatican and the hierarchy remained intact — but the pope hardly dared take action against the (progressive) centrifugal forces even if he wanted to do so. The result, as to the mass of Catholics, was continued erosion of religious belief and practice — not only among the laity but even among the clergy and religious.

With the election of Pope John Paul II, however, the Church experienced a "Wojtylian Restoration" with a renewed focus on the pope and the Vatican. The pope reoccupied the center of attention, even if stylistically now more as a secular political leader than as a religious figure. The journeys, public appearances, and media interviews of Pope John Paul II were the defining characteristics of his renewed papacy.

Yet the ultramontane revival of John Paul II remained only a "great façade" (in the phrase of Christopher Ferrara). Aside from insisting on a limited external conformity and firing warning shots at the most egregious progressive offenders, the Vatican made no attempt to recreate the uniformity of doctrine and morals that existed in the preconciliar years. At all times in the papacy of John Paul II, Catholic hierarchs, religious orders, and schools embraced and agitated for the most diverse and contradictory positions. The Vatican's solution to mounting massive problems — like declining numbers of clergy and religious, clerical sexual abuse, financial corruption, and above all the decline in the West of belief and religious practice among Catholics — was to sweep them under the rug.

Now the start of the third "decline and fall" can be placed in the reign of Pope Benedict XVI. Pope Benedict had continued in most respects the regime of his predecessor. He departed from it, however, by taking a marginally more conservative teaching line and implementing significant legislative changes in the field of liturgy. This naturally aroused a storm of opposition both within and outside the Church, both in public and behind the scenes. Pope Benedict was utterly incapable of mastering the powers challenging his papacy: the establishment religious orders, the Vatican bureaucracy, the mass of Catholic "academics" and "scholars," the Western European episcopates (especially that of Germany!). These more or less open opponents had no intention of yielding the positions of power they had acquired over the Church since the Second Vatican Council. Moreover, they acted in the closest alliance with the secular media and to some extent even the secular political powers. They rendered the Church almost unmanageable for Pope Benedict, whose ultimate answer was capitulation. Pope Benedict's resignation was a staggering blow to papal authority.

In Pope Francis, the Catholic progressive forces finally established a man of their own as the supreme power in the Church. There followed an unprecedented outpouring of progressive words, gestures, and deeds — often in direct contradiction to what had been considered settled (at least on paper) in morality, theology, and philosophy. The supposed bastions of Wojtyłian conservatism, like the Italian and United States hierarchies or the Knights of Malta, fell almost overnight. Supposedly "Wojtyłian" bishops, publicists, and scholars (like Cardinal Marx of Munich) quickly became bellicose advocates of the new order.

A "cult of personality" around Pope Francis arose dwarfing anything in the past. The pope also employed authoritarian, not to say crudely manipulative, means in furthering his agenda. Indeed, Francis and his clique have sought to address the rising number of critics of Bergoglian policies by reviving ultramontane rhetoric in its most extreme form. The pope himself talks of his "magisterial authority" and of the "irreversible" reforms of Vatican II. The canonization or beatification of every pope since 1958 — excluding Pope Benedict — also fits into this pattern. The paladins of Team Francis accept as (at least de facto) infallible every document of Pope Francis; even his uncontrolled ramblings in planes, interviews and, daily, in the Casa Santa Marta acquire in their eyes magisterial force. Substantive criticism of the current regime is triumphantly countered by accusations of "criticizing the pope," of "disloyalty to the Holy Father," and, of course, "creating scandal."

It's all a delirious and previously unimaginable alliance of dissent and ultramontanism, of the *National Catholic Reporter* and *L'Osservatore Romano*, of the Jesuit order and the Knights of Columbus. We believe, though, that this novel Bergoglian ultramontanism is inherently unstable. The notion of a "progressive," "dissenting," or even "heretical" pope is simply too outrageous and contradictory for too many people. The sudden reversal of principles — like those of marriage — that only yesterday were proclaimed immutable will prove even more destabilizing than the changes of the 1960s. And just a cursory look reveals that Pope Francis can be authoritarian and decisive only when conforming to the dogmas and expectations of modern Western civil society.

At least as of this moment, hardly anyone in the Catholic establishment will take on Pope Francis. Yet outside of the mainstream institutions, the Bergoglian revolution has aroused a storm of criticism. It's quite a contrast to the initial unopposed implementation of Vatican II, which built on the legacy of centralized ultramontane control. The main effect so far of the reign of Francis is to compound the already existing fractures and chaos of the postconciliar Church. Pope Francis professes to endorse such "diversity" as a positive development conducive to ongoing change. We already see the quantifiable results in the free fall of vocations and of the practice of the faith. Truly this is the third "fall" of the Catholic Church since 1789!

But out of this seemingly inevitable tragedy may come at least one advantage: the truth. For far too long the Catholic Church has continued to take refuge in fantasies of stability and success, of secular standing and influence. You need look only at any of the official Catholic media to confirm this — isn't the Al Smith Dinner in New York the incarnation of this self-deception? Even the supposedly hard-nosed liturgical traditionalists remained to some extent in thrall to these mirages. The poison of dishonesty has eroded the faith more surely than any persecution or loss of worldly advantages could do. Moreover, in addition to obscuring reality, the culture of ultramontanism also inculcated habits of spiritual torpor, passivity, and blind deference to authority (by extension, also to secular authority!) that have left Catholics ill-equipped to navigate the unprecedented postconciliar crisis.

Let be be finale of seem! Jettisoning the Catholic culture of pretend is the first, most necessary step towards reform. To that extent we owe Pope Francis a debt of gratitude. Does not the shipwreck of a mythical centralized day-to-day magisterium make possible a return to the Catholic spiritual "basics" of prayer, penance, and evangelization? And doesn't the Tradition of the Church — present before us in the Fathers and Doctors, in history and art, and above all in the liturgy as it is lived every day — remain to us as a surer guide?

16

Face-to-Face with Romanism[1]

STUART CHESSMAN

T HE ENTIRE TRADITIONALIST WORLD SEEMS TO BE
waiting with trepidation for whatever Pope Francis will be doing to *Summorum Pontificum* and the celebration of the Latin Mass worldwide. It's
noteworthy that the entire process has been conducted in secrecy by the Vatican
and certain episcopal initiates. That those reported to be in the forefront of the
anti-*SP* effort—such as Cardinal Parolin or, for that matter, the pope himself—do
not necessarily enjoy the best of reputations or authority at this very moment is no
hindrance to their ability to initiate global liturgical changes. And on *this* issue—as
opposed to, let's say, the agenda of the German Synodal Way—papal power in the
eyes of the European Church establishment is unlimited. Consider the statements
of Prof. Georg Bier in the online publication of the German Catholic Church:

> As a matter of principle it is possible for the pope to completely abolish
> again this form of the Mass [the traditional Mass]. The pope as supreme
> legislator can always decree whatever he deems to be most beneficial
> for the Church . . . [According to Bier, however, for tactical reasons
> simple abolition of the traditional Mass is unlikely. —SC] There will be
> at most moderate restrictions—but as a matter of principle the pope
> has all possibilities.[2]

In Bier's view, both *Summorum Pontificum* and the document Pope Francis is
crafting are governed entirely by material and political considerations and tactical
expediency. The passage in *Summorum Pontificum* which seems to expressly limit
the authority of the Church to abolish the traditional Mass is dismissed by Bier as
a "dodge" or "trick" by Benedict to preserve continuity with his predecessor—no
theological issue here.

Reading these words today, I was struck once again by the link between centralized ultramontane absolutism and liturgical, moral, and theological experimentation (the latter, of course, taking in 2021 a reactionary, defensive form!).
The totally arbitrary and unlimited papal authority described in the quotation
above contrasts with the historical role and self-understanding of the papacy

---

1 First published at the blog of the Society of St Hugh of Cluny on July 14, 2021. Of course,
only two days after this article was published, the rumored document about which Chessman speaks
was released: *Traditionis Custodes*.

2 Georg Bier, Professor for Canon Law and the History of Canon Law at the University of
Freiburg, as interviewed by Christoph Hartmann, "Wie der Papst die Feier der vorkonziliaren Messe
einschränken könnte," *Katholisch.de*, July 14, 2021; translation by Chessman.

in the "greatest of centuries" (the thirteenth) or in the Counter-Reformation. In my view, the Catholic Church's dysfunctional structures and organizational principles continue to exercise a highly negative influence, blocking true reform and spiritual development.

Two recent articles, dealing with issues arising in unrelated contexts, have neatly identified this highly problematic situation for the Church. First, Joseph Shaw, the chairman of the Latin Mass Society, has this to say in his review of Leo Darroch's *Una Voce: The History of the Foederatio Internationalis Una Voce 1964-2003*:

> The first [episode Shaw considered] is the interview and associated correspondence which took place between de Saventhem [then head of Una Voce International] and Archbishop (later, Cardinal) Giovanni Benelli, then Prefect of the Congregation for Divine Worship, in 1976 . . . . De Saventhem summarized Benelli's position in a letter to him following the meeting:
>
> "Your Excellency has urged us to espouse as a matter of conscience the new forms of the Church's public cult . . . Although the character of irreformability only attaches to definitions, promulgated *ex cathedra* in matters of faith and morals, [you asserted that] the assent due to the acts of the Sovereign Pontiff ought equally to express itself in humble obedience to those of his acts which merely concern the discipline or other nondoctrinal aspects of the government of the Church. For there also, you said, it is the same one and indivisible charisma which guarantees that all these acts cannot but be ordered towards the true and certain good of the Church. Consequently, you could only consider as reckless and irreconcilable with a proper ecclesiology all demands or initiatives which implied that the utility of such and such an act of government duly promulgated by the reigning Pontiff or under his authority could be a subject of discussion or even contestation."
>
> Cardinal Benelli did not dispute the accuracy of this summary. What it amounts to — as Dr de Saventhem goes on to explain at some length, though not in these terms — is an extreme ultramontanism, the view that imbues the reigning pope's prudential decisions with something close to infallibility, and his wishes with a force approaching that of Divine Law. The prevalence of such attitudes in Rome is part of the explanation of why things were so difficult for Una Voce in the 1970s and later.[3]

Second, Bronwen McShea considers a case of excessive Vatican intervention in local artistic issues in the 1920s but draws broader conclusions:

> The new generation of churchmen [after the Council], once in power, redirected the Church toward a warm embrace of the modern world. The irony is that in doing so, through the decrees of Vatican II and in the Council's aftermath, they preserved and strengthened centralized

---

3   The review may be found at the website of the International Una Voce Federation: www. fiuv.org/p/book.html.

mechanisms of ecclesiastical control, not just over doctrine and worship, but also over cultural judgments and sensibilities. Rome and the clerical hierarchy were suddenly airing out a Church that supposedly had been stifling and stale inside for many centuries. Now, "openness" was not optional: dialogue became the order of the day. The modernized engines of ecclesiastical governance were revved up for *aggiornamento*, which the laity and lower clergy would get, whether they wanted it or not. Even Maritain, late in life in *The Peasant of the Garonne*, would rue this turnabout.

Much as they had with theology and the liturgical reform, the bishops oversaw a rushed, coordinated aesthetic revolution. Old-fashioned crucifixes, paintings, statues, stained-glass windows, and even sacred vessels were cast aside for modern ones—beautiful, well-crafted, and elegant in some cases, but ugly, kitschy, and blasphemous in countless others. Vatican-issued and chancery-stamped statements, more revisions of canon law, and conferences paved the way. Ordinary Catholics stood by—bewildered, often—as the styles of art that had been forcefully opposed by their mitered shepherds just a few years before were now promoted by them. All manner of Expressionist, Cubist, Fauvist, and Abstract works began to populate cathedrals and small-town churches. Sacred spaces were bulldozed, whitewashed, and reconstructed. And a great deal of fine artwork—crafted lovingly and donated by the laity of past eras—disappeared overnight . . . .

In view of the complex history of which Servaes [the Belgian artist referenced by McShea's article] was a part, it is worth considering whether more mature modern approaches to sacred art would have developed organically, in creative dialogue with the wider culture and ancient traditions, had Vatican bureaucrats and their defenders in the early twentieth century behaved more, not less, like their Tridentine-era predecessors. Vatican I and Vatican II both effected highly centralized, Rome-driven reform. They may appear in some respects antithetical, but they ran on the same rails. The centralizing impulse of the age seduced Rome into censoring experimental artists in ways that Tridentine and medieval Church officials had not imagined necessary or even possible. Then, by the mid-twentieth century, mortified by the Church's cultural marginalization, the hierarchy tried to reverse it with an even heavier hand—foisting a sloppy and destructive aesthetic revolution on the Church to accompany the dramatic liturgical and theological reorientations.[4]

---

4   Bronwen McShea, "When Rome Policed Art," *First Things*, August 2021, online at www.firstthings.com/article/2021/08/when-rome-policed-art.

17

Understanding True Ultramontanism[1]

JOSÉ A. URETA

O NE CAN ONLY AGREE WITH THE EDITORIAL POSI-tion published on *OnePeterFive* about uniting the clans in a single crusade to rebuild Christendom and "restore all things in Christ." I join the editorial team in lamenting the catastrophe of some representatives of traditional Catholicism who "argue among themselves over minutiae while heretics triumph against dogma."

It is not in this quibbling spirit that I accept the invitation to present a guest submission. Rather, I hope to contribute to the core of this new focus: the correct attitude a faithful Catholic must adopt toward the errors promoted by Pope Francis and numerous bishops.

I fully agree with the rejection of two false solutions: sedevacantism and any favoring of the Greek Orthodox schism. However, I would like to share my reservations on using two new labels: the "false spirit of Vatican I" and "extreme ultramontanism." Both are used incorrectly to describe the reprehensible attitude of those who would rather be wrong with the pope than right and against him.

I denounced the false concept of obedience that paralyzes many conservative Catholics in my book, *Pope Francis's Paradigm Shift: Continuity or Rupture in the Mission of the Church? An Assessment of His Pontificate's First Five Years.* I called it "magisterialism." This error crept in over the last few decades among admirers of John Paul II and Benedict XVI. Magisterialists criticized neo-modernists not because they rejected traditional Church teaching but because they attacked the magisterium of the reigning pope.[2]

With *OnePeterFive*'s editorial team, I reject as false the idea that "the whole of Catholic life must revolve around the pope who is, as it were, some kind of de facto oracle at Delphi, whose every whim becomes a binding law in the Church." This notwithstanding, I believe it is dangerous to attribute this error to a "false spirit of Vatican I" and "extreme ultramontanism." I can see how it is tempting to draw a simple parallel between the two councils, insinuating that some people distorted their documents in the postconciliar period.

---

1   First published at *OnePeterFive* on October 12, 2021.
2   See, in this line, the insightful article of Fr Chad Ripperger, "Operative Points of View," *Christian Order*, March 2001, https://christianorder.com/features/feature_2001-03.html.

However, I see three problems with this approach:

(1) it suggests an impossible approval for the Second Vatican Council — just as magisterialism would have stemmed from a "false *spirit* of Vatican I," the current Church crisis would be due to "the *spirit* of Vatican II" supposedly being in contradiction with that council's texts;

(2) it unfairly casts a pall of suspicion over the nineteenth century's ultramontane movement, placing it on the same footing as the progressivism responsible for the Second Vatican Council;

(3) it distorts the historical record because papolatry is not a poisoned fruit of ultramontanism but the distorted progeny of its opponents, the liberal Catholics. The latter used it during the pontificate of Leo XIII, trying to force traditional Catholics to accept his misguided policy of *ralliement* — rallying around the Masonic French Republic.

To their credit, the ultramontanes were the great defenders of the two dogmas of faith regarding the pope that were solemnly defined at the First Vatican Council. These were (a) the pope's full, supreme, immediate, and universal jurisdiction (papal supremacy) and (b) his infallibility. The ultramontanes' spirited defense of these truths triggered the false accusation back then that they were "theologians of absolutism" and had immolated truth "as a sacrifice to the idol they have erected for themselves in the Vatican."[3] Their accuser was the well-known liberal Catholic writer, Count Charles de Montalembert.

Did the ultramontanes love these two privileges of the Vicar of Christ in an exaggerated, distorted way? Nothing of the sort. An overview of the thought and action of His Eminence Louis-Édouard Cardinal Pie, bishop of Poitiers, demonstrates this.

At the First Vatican Council, then-Bishop Pie was a major figure along with Henry Edward Cardinal Manning. I use Cardinal Pie as an example because I live a good part of the year in France, and thus I am more familiar with his life. France was also the intellectual center of the ultramontane movement. Finally, the bishop of Poitiers was the great defender of the social kingship of Christ and inspired St Pius X's motto, which *OnePeterFive* has also adopted to define its editorial position: *Instaurare omnia in Christo.*

Let us begin with Montalembert's false accusation that the ultramontanes had some sympathy for absolutism. It is completely baseless concerning both the temporal and the religious sphere. The ultramontanes — and especially the future Cardinal Pie — were legitimist monarchists. They rejected Bonapartist imperial centralism and defended a tempered monarchy. "Christian royalty, especially French royalty" — wrote Bishop Pie in a royalist program at the request of the Count of Chambord, heir to the French throne — "has never been an arbitrary or even absolute royalty. This temperament is in the dynasty's very marrow, as seen in the

---

3 Édouard Lecanuet, *L'Église et le Second Empire (1850–1870)*, vol. 3, *Montalembert*, 4th ed. (Paris: Ancienne Librairie Poussièlgue, 1912), 467.

existence of various orders of the kingdom, the provincial assemblies, the Estates General, the Parliaments, the local liberties, and, above all, in Christian morals."[4]

Bishop Pie applied the same vision of tempered authority to the Church. He was a great defender of the prerogatives of what were called *particular* or *provincial* councils back then. He worked to have them held in his ecclesiastical province, executed their decrees, and, following the spirit that had inspired them, drafted the rules they elaborated. About a letter from Pius IX to the Austrian bishops urging them to hold a provincial council, Bishop Pie commented that it was an "unanswerable rejoinder to those rash accusations of monopolizing all areas of responsibility and of a tendency to a boundless centralization, which some people have not been afraid to raise in recent times against the Roman Church." He added:

> Particular councils are an element and a guarantee of freedom and nationality for the various provinces of the Catholic world; several ecumenical councils have given them this character. Now, far from taking offense at the holding of these provincial meetings, the head of the Church himself asks for their resumption, regrets their abandonment, and highlights their benefits.[5]

Which benefits?

> As long as there remain diversities of origin, language, government, I would even say climate . . . the existence of a common law, an absolute, uniform legislation without modifications and dispensations will be impossible on a rather large number of points of ecclesiastical discipline . . . . [A common law] admits as an element of the law itself the principle of exceptions, derogations, modifications, provided they are made in normal conditions. Now, the tribunal that offers the most guarantee . . . is the hierarchy of the province assembled canonically, conciliarly, subordinating their decrees to apostolic review.[6]

Elsewhere Bishop Pie wrote: "Never has the Apostolic See insisted more [than under Pius IX] on the periodic holding of particular councils, in which the bishops nevertheless fulfill in common that function of judges, which Rome is accused of disputing."[7]

Let me digress for a moment. The Second Vatican Council's fathers were ill-advised when accusing the First Vatican Council of having "unbalanced" the structure of the Church. It addressed this non-problem by introducing a "collegiality" unknown to tradition, borrowing from Eastern schismatics. It borrowed

---

4   Louis Baunard, *Histoire du cardinal Pie: Évêque de Poitiers* (Poitiers: H. Oudin, 1886), 2:488. All translations are the author's.

5   *Lettre pastorale* (July 14, 1866), in *Oeuvres de Monseigneur l'évêque de Poitiers*, 5th ed. (Poitiers: Librairie Henri Oudin, 1876), 2:442.

6   Ibid., 2:443.

7   *Oeuvres de Monseigneur l'évêque de Poitiers*, 9th ed. (Poitiers: Librairie Religieuse H. Oudin, 1887), 6:67.

even the word, a poor translation of the Russian term *sobornost*.[8] Contrary to *Lumen Gentium* (no. 22) and the Preliminary Note added by Paul VI, the college of bishops united to the pope does not exercise a permanent supreme power over the universal Church. The Catholic Church is not two-headed. She has only one head: the successor of Peter. Unless the pope convenes the bishops into a council, their authority is ordinarily limited to the single diocese where they have jurisdiction, as its shepherd. They can meet in provincial councils, however, under the supervision of the Holy See, which must watch over the unity of the Church. The Holy See refuses to exercise this oversight today regarding the German Synodal Path, even though this assembly of the German Church usurps a doctrinal power that the old provincial councils never had. These were limited to legislating on disciplinary matters.

However, let us return to our subject and go to the heart of the matter: were the ultramontanes papolaters who wanted to make the Successor of Peter a kind of Pythia who delivered Apollo's oracles at Delphi? Not at all!

In this respect, the attitude of Bishop Pie before and during the First Vatican Council is very enlightening. Having been appointed consultor by Pius IX even before the council was publicly announced, Bishop Pie wrote a plan for the preparatory commission on the current topics that, in his opinion, the future council should address. He was convinced that the great problem of the moment was secularism's denial of the social kingship of Christ. Thus, his proposed plan focused especially on the errors of rationalism and naturalism, which the Dogmatic Constitution *Dei Filius* addressed.

Papal infallibility was not included in his plan. Although an ardent advocate of papal infallibility, Bishop Pie was not fixated on this unproclaimed dogma. He even proposed as conciliar consultor Arthur-Marie Le Hir, a priest of St-Sulpice and professor of Sacred Scripture at the famous Parisian seminary, which was the bulwark of Gallicanism.

After the council's official inauguration, it was the liberals who stirred up a controversy about infallibility, which was not yet on the agenda. Pressed by several friendly bishops to enter the arena of this controversy, Bishop Pie refused. In a letter to his diocese, he explained his reasons:

> We resolved from now on to avoid dealing in our own name with the capital questions that impose themselves on this holy assembly. It seemed to us that the respect due to our venerable colleagues in the episcopate, as well as the respect we owe to ourselves, commanded this reserve. We should neither anticipate the judgment of others, nor formulate in advance our personal judgment, disposed as we are to profit from the exchange of thoughts, from the fruit of discussions,

---

8   See Albert Kallio, OP, "Collegialità nel Vaticano II: una nuova dottrina?," *Chiesa e post concilio*, June 26, 2018, https://chiesaepostconcilio.blogspot.com/2018/06/collegialita-nel-vaticano-ii-una-nuova.html.

and especially to obey the lights and movements of the Holy Spirit, whose assistance will not fail us at the proper time.[9]

The bishop of Poitiers was not disturbed by the fierce media polemic between the two camps on this burning subject:

> Let individual writers, under their personal responsibility, form sup-positions and engage in discussions in this regard. The Church, which is very liberal in its procedures and gives free rein to the expression of all thoughts and feelings during the duration of the conciliar sessions, is not alarmed or offended by these public debates when contained within just limits. As long as false liberalism does not claim a monopoly on freedom, as has happened before, and, in its habit of practical absolutism, it does not repress opinions and cry scandal because of the freedom given to its opponents. (331–32)

One would say that that he speaks prophetically about our days!

The future Cardinal Pie did not abandon his reserve until Bishop Henri Maret, dean of the Sorbonne University, published two volumes. In them, Bishop Maret dubbed the supposed "omnipotence" that would be created by the definition of the pope's personal infallibility (unsubordinated to any approval by the college of bishops) as *absolutism*. Instead, the Gallican prelate argued that the bishops should ordinarily participate in the Church's general government. This would occur through ecumenical councils held every ten years! (If alive today, Bishop Maret would be a loud promoter of Pope Francis's inverted-pyramid Synodal Church.) On the twentieth anniversary of his episcopal consecration, Bishop Pie affirmed in his sermon that to subordinate the popes' doctrinal decisions to the positive or silent assent of the world's hierarchy would insult the promise of Our Lord Jesus Christ to St Peter. True to custom, however, he hastened to add that he did not intend "to provoke or prejudge in any way a conciliar definition, whose timeliness first, and then the form, must be entirely reserved to the judgment of the great synodal assembly and the Holy Spirit's supreme will" (340). Conforming actions to words, he published Bishop Maret's reply in the diocesan weekly, adding that, "In any fair polemic, it is the rule that a defense can be presented where an attack has occurred" (341).

Bishop Pie's reserve continued when Bishop Félix Dupanloup, the liberal champion, published two polemical writings on the eve of the council's opening. In asserting the unseasonableness of a solemn definition of the Roman pontiff's magisterial power, Bishop Dupanloup made a full-scale attack on infallibility itself. In response, the bishop of Angoulême, Most Rev. Antoine-Charles Cous-seau, pronounced the famous words: *Quod inopportunum dixerunt, necessarium fecerunt*: those who say that the proclamation of the dogma is inopportune have

---

9 Baunard, *Histoire du cardinal Pie*, 2:330–31. Subsequent references to this volume will be in parentheses after the quotations.

made it necessary. Dom Prosper Guéranger, abbot of Solesmes, commented that Bishop Dupanloup's intervention was what was missing to conclude that the time had come to define papal infallibility. Nevertheless, Bishop Pie limited himself to reaffirming, in a confidential letter to his mother, that, "Despite all this, we are resolved to remain silent. The council will gain from it" (355).

On December 8, 1869, feast of the Immaculate Conception, the council was solemnly opened. On December 14, with 470 out of 700 votes, Bishop Pie was the second council father elected to the Commission of Doctrine and the Faith. This first victory for the ultramontane doctrines that he represented found him as respectful to the liberal minority as before. In a letter to Fr Gervais, the Vicar General of the Bordeaux archdiocese who had remained in France, he said: "It would have helped if some theologians from the other side, as the bishop of Grenoble [Most Rev. Jacques Ginoulhiac], had been appointed to the first commissions." By *first*, he meant those on doctrine and discipline (357).

He was the rapporteur on the schema on "Faith and Reason." He confided to his mother that the general congregation had received his presentation well, "bishops of almost all shades complimented me" (365). Small wonder that the Dogmatic Constitution *Dei Filius*, which contained this schema, was approved unanimously by the assembly.

On the day of this approval, April 24, 1870, a worsening international situation and threats of war prompted 150 council fathers gathered by the future Cardinal Manning, archbishop of Westminster and the great leader of the ultramontane current in English-speaking countries, to present to Pope Pius IX a *postulatum* requesting the prompt discussion of the Roman pontiff's infallibility. Contrary to what some might think, Bishop Pie was not among the petition's signatories, although he was the French-speaking ultramontane champion. His moderation stands out in the explanation he later gave to his priests. While recognizing the question's importance, he believed that "not every council must settle every controversy and define every doctrine" (375). He reasoned further that it was not yet the turn for papal infallibility in the council program's logical order. This, because the second part of the schema *De Fide* on grace, original sin, and redemption, almost entirely written by then, had not yet been discussed. He thought that only after finishing this great dogmatic synthesis should the council fathers tackle the chapter on the Church and the supreme pontiff. That is where the question of papal infallibility would find its natural place.

Finally, he believed that his position on the Commission of Doctrine and the Faith demanded this reticence "since I was likely to be called on to intervene personally in the official introduction of the cause, which indeed happened" (377).

A comment from his biographer is interesting for this essay's purpose:

> It was surprising that he did not belong to any militant group and that, accessible to all, he usually met with many people of various opinions, studying each one of them, avoiding shocking them with

absolute partisanship and bias, but immediately becoming very firm
in the eyes of the bishops who had made themselves leaders of the
opposition. His entourage and friends would have liked him to lead
the majority, but he avoided any personal intervention for he saw it
as misunderstanding the spirit of the Church. (377–78)

This notwithstanding, Bishop Pie was quick to recognize the urgency of addressing papal infallibility so as not to leave it in the state of turmoil in which it had
been placed by the polemics triggered by the Gallican-liberal minority. The latter
hurriedly protested through the voice of sixty-seven bishops against any possible
change to the council's program.

On May 9, 1870, seeing that five hundred bishops had now joined the request
to deal with the question, Pius IX ordered the distribution of the outline on papal
infallibility. The Commission of Doctrine and the Faith commissioned Bishop
Pie to report on this new topic. He did so four days later, before the general
congregation. In the commission's name, he apologized for presenting an outline
that was out of place but said it was imposed by the passion with which public
opinion was grappling with the subject. He explained the first three chapters on
pontifical power. In the fourth, he addressed infallibility, the logical and obligatory
corollary of the pope as supreme and universal judge. He concluded with these
reassuring words to the council fathers: "Undoubtedly, the schema proposed to
you has not been perfected. That is why the commission you have entrusted to
prepare it has no greater desire than to see its sketch perfected by you" (384).

In thirty-four general congregations in the mornings and particular ones
in the afternoons, both "infallibilist" ultramontanes and the "anti-infallibilist"
and "inopportunist" party thoroughly discussed the topic. Gallicans continued
to maintain that the infallibility of the Church could not rest on the person of
the pope alone but required the agreement of pope and council. On the other
hand, liberal Catholics did not oppose the thesis of the personal infallibility
of the pope but considered it inappropriate to proclaim this dogma because
its *absolutist* character could offend the democratic spirit of the modern world.
They also feared that the ultramontanes would extend papal infallibility ret-
roactively to the *Syllabus*, which had condemned their plans for a "Christian-
ization of liberalism."

Benefiting from his influence, Bishop Pie received copies of all speeches, especially those of his opponents, and took notes to adjust his positions. Sometimes
he let his sadness show: "One is astonished to see how even men of the Church
judge things exclusively from the human point of view" (388).

The liberal-Gallican minority tried filibustering, prolonging the debates indef-
initely. On July 4, 1870, a telegram was sent from Paris to a council father. It read,
"Hold on for a few days. Providence is sending you unexpected help." It was the
war. Recognized as inevitable in the upper echelons of the French government,
it would cause the council's postponement to an unspecified date.

The telegram had arrived too late, though. On that July 4 and the day before, a total of fifty-six speakers relinquished their time to speak. The discussion was now closed. Several minority leaders left Rome. On July 13, the general congregation approved the whole schema. The votes were 451 *placet*, 88 *non placet*, and 62 *placet juxta modum*, i.e., a yes vote, but suggesting improvements. Some of the majority wanted an even clearer definition. Those in opposition proposed inserting that, to be infallible, the pope had to rely on the testimony of the Churches: *nixus testimonio Ecclesiarum*, which subordinated papal infallibility to the bishops' assent.

The result was the opposite. "Thus, the majority improved the meaning of the contested phrases," says Bishop Pie,

> and, in the face of these threats from within and without, the Church affirmed its constitution. In canon IV, it was added that not only did the pope have the greater part—*potiores partes*—but the entire fullness of the supreme power. Likewise, these words were added to the dogmatic paragraph of the fourth chapter: "Therefore, such definitions of the Roman Pontiff are of themselves, and not by the consent of the Church, irreformable." (392)

Thus clarified, papal infallibility was solemnly proclaimed on July 18, 1870, by the unanimity of the council fathers present minus two, one of whom went to lay his act of faith before Pius IX that same evening, and the other on the following morning. Most of the dogma's opponents abstained from the session. On July 19, as the mysterious telegram from Paris had foreseen, the Franco-Prussian War broke out. Two months later, the Piedmontese invaded Rome, making Pius IX a prisoner in the Vatican. He was unable to continue the conciliar assembly, which was interrupted *sine die*.

Bishop Xavier de Mérode gave eloquent testimony of Bishop Pie's harmonizing temperament. That former soldier, hailing from a Belgian princely family, had organized the famous Zouaves for the defense of the Papal States. Although a friend of the bishop of Poitiers, he was Montalembert's brother-in-law and came from a liberal background. In the council, he had joined the minority. The day after the proclamation of the dogma, and when Bishop Pie was already on the train, Bishop de Mérode went to his carriage. After asking the entourage to give them some time alone, the two doctrinal opponents had a long conversation in which Bishop de Mérode shed many tears. Bishop Pie showed the same benevolence toward all the members of the minority and had the Poitiers diocesan weekly register the adhesions and submissions they addressed to the sovereign pontiff.

Through his charitable efforts, Bishop Pie also obtained the submission *in articulo mortis* of Fr Alphonse Gratry. This priest's anti-infallibility writings had been one of the most powerful weapons the liberal press used against ultramontane doctrines. Bishop Pie's charitable dispositions had a doctrinal source. Contrary to the Jansenist tendencies of the Gallicans, he had helped the cardinal-archbishop of Rheims, Archbishop Thomas Gousset, to import *Liguorism* from Italy. Instead of the concept of a terrible God, the moral doctrine developed by St Alphonsus Liguori promoted the idea that our God was a God of love and confidence.

Having achieved the victory of truth over liberal and Gallican errors, was the French ultramontane champion led to exaggerate the scope of the conciliar definition? Did he consider the pope infallible even in his *ordinary* magisterium? And was he infallible in matters that did not touch on faith and morals?

The future Cardinal Pie would have been astonished if anyone had asked him such questions. He was well aware of human weakness and knew that divine assistance had been promised to the pope only under very restrictive conditions:

> The assistance guaranteed to him [the pope] from above is not inspiration or infused science. Therefore, his duty is not to neglect any natural and supernatural elements that can help the triumph of truth and the work of grace. Some of these elements are study, advice, discussion, the collecting of all insights and experiences. . . . Before pronouncing himself, there are examples of how the head of the Church has asked in writing for the opinion of his brothers worldwide and encouraged discussion among those he could gather around him. It was under these conditions that Pius IX published the dogmatic bull that defines the Immaculate Conception of Mary.[10]

Hence also the appropriate role of good counsel: "What more modern theological language calls the pope teaching *ex cathedra*, was called in previous ages the pope speaking with counsel: *papa loquens cum consilio*."[11]

Bishop Pie was also conscious that infallibility did not extend to the Holy Father's *ordinary* magisterium, and in his *extraordinary* teaching, only the dogmatic judgment itself demanded the assent of the faithful. "Indeed, theology admits that if the most solemn doctrinal acts of the teaching Church impose themselves on the intelligence and faith of Christians as far as their final decision is concerned, the preliminaries and considerations of the decision remain in the realm of controversy." Therefore, "the supreme supernatural magisterial power . . . strengthened by its infallibility regarding the essence of things, safely delivers to a proper and respectful examination all that is not the object of this privilege."[12]

Bishop Pie was called in his time "the hammer of liberalism." A fitting tribute, seeing how his distant predecessor in the same see, St Hilary of Poitiers, was known as "the hammer of Arians" (*Malleus Arianorum*).

If this leader, of such edifying intellectual and moral stature, was the great and undisputed leader of the French ultramontane bishops at the First Vatican Council, the natural conclusion is that the "spirit of Vatican I" was imbued with a supernatural love for truth and, therefore, it was objective, prudent, balanced,

---

10   *Lettre pastorale et mandement* (May 24, 1869), in *Oeuvres*, 6:408-9.
11   Ibid., 6:408.
12   Allocution of December 1861, in *Oeuvres*, 4:338-39.

and nuanced even in the heat of controversy. Therefore, there is nothing to fear from an "extreme ultramontanism" since it would only represent that same Christian faith and wisdom in greater perfection. The First Vatican Council's ultramontane spirit is far from the caricature sketched by its liberal or Gallican opponents and which, due to a misunderstanding, some traditionalists today are redrawing.

Neither the "false spirit of Vatican I" nor ultramontanism is responsible for the subsequent drift to the fixation on the reigning pope's person and magisterium to the detriment of truth and tradition. This *magisterialism* is the progeny of the liberal-progressive movement within the Church, and it started in the pontificate of Leo XIII. Liberals used it to bolster the pope's misguided policy of "rallying around the [French Masonic] Republic," a folly that the ultramontanes opposed. I will take up this topic in the next chapter.

18

Leo XIII: The First Liberal Pope Who Went Beyond His Authority[1]

JOSÉ A. URETA

I N THE ESSAY PUBLISHED AS THE PRECEDING CHAPTER, I cleared up the misunderstanding that has led some traditionalists to blame ultramontanes and a so-called spirit of Vatican I for the "papolatry" exhibited by some Catholics who believe that the pope must be obeyed even when acting against the Church's traditional teaching. I will now demonstrate that it was not the ultramontanes but liberal Catholics who pushed the limits of papal infallibility far beyond those set by Vatican I's dogmatic constitution *Pastor Aeternus*.[2]

This drift toward absolutism began with the *ralliement* (1884), a papal policy of rallying around the Republic that Pope Leo XIII imposed on French Catholics. Liberal Catholics, eager to reconcile the Church with revolutionary modernity, enthusiastically welcomed this course of action. On the contrary, ultramontane Catholics emphasized the limits of the pope's magisterial power and opposed his undue intrusion in France's temporal affairs.

The episode was masterfully analyzed by Prof. Roberto de Mattei in his book *Leo XIII's Ralliement—The Failure of a Pastoral Project*.[3] To avoid separation between the Church and the French State, Pope Pecci urged Catholics to unite with the Republic and fight anticlerical laws from within the system. Vatican diplomacy sought to obtain the French government's goodwill to recover the territories that the Kingdom of Italy had taken from it.

Leo XIII's new policy had two major difficulties. First, it challenged the monarchical convictions of a majority of the French clergy and laity. Second, French elections had brought Masonic and secularist governments to power. These governments had introduced divorce, expelled the Jesuits, forbidden priests and religious to teach in public schools, abolished religious instruction in schools, and imposed military service on clerics.

---

1   First published at *OnePeterFive* on October 19, 2021.

2   "Liberal" in the nineteenth century meant Catholics who wanted to compromise with the Liberal world created by the Masonic French Revolution. This terminology and its meaning is similar to but also different from the term "liberal" as used in English to refer to churchmen alive today. — *Ed.*

3   Published in French as *Le ralliement de Léon XIII—L'échec d'un projet pastoral* (Paris: Éditions du Cerf, 2016).

Pope Leo XIII was an intellectual with solid principles, but he was a liberal at heart. He naively believed that republican anticlericalism could be defused by convincing liberals that the Church did not oppose the Republic but only its secularism. Unlike the pope, the French faithful clearly saw that the de-Christianization of France was not an accessory element but the very *raison d'être* of the republican regime. For these Catholics, accepting the Republic meant acquiescing to the "republican spirit," that is, the egalitarian and antireligious bias of the revolutionary ideology of 1789 that would then be allowed to permeate society as a whole.

Leo XIII chose Cardinal Charles Lavigerie (1825–1892), archbishop of Algiers, as the "authorized intermediary" between Paris and the Vatican to implement the *ralliement* policy. Making a toast at a reception for officers of the French Mediterranean war fleet gathered in Algiers in 1890, he urged them to accept the republican form of government, arguing that the union of all good citizens was France's supreme need and "the first wish of the Church and her Pastors."

Leo XIII joined the fray a few months later, granting an interview (the first ever by a pontiff) to a pro-government Parisian daily, *Le Petit Journal*. He stated, "Everyone can keep his personal preferences, but in the field of action, there is only the government that France has given itself. A republic is a form of government as legitimate as any other." His encyclical *Au Milieu des Sollicitudes* on the Church and State in France came out three days later, soon followed by the apostolic letter *Notre Consolation*. In the latter, the pope insisted on his idea of "accepting the civil power as it actually exists without ulterior motive and with that perfect loyalty which befits a Christian."

For Catholics accustomed to fighting the Masonic Republic, this about-face posed a problem of conscience. It is similar to that raised by Cardinal Joseph Zen and the Catholics of the underground Church in the face of the ominous agreement signed between the Holy See and the Chinese Communist regime.

At the time, the majority of the French episcopate gave a cold reception to the *ralliement* policy. Some prominent ultramontane figures, such as Bishop Charles-Émile Freppel of Angers, openly opposed it. Cardinal Lavigerie let loose the first salvo of "magisterialism"—the error of giving more importance to a pontiff's teachings and gestures than to that of Tradition. Lambasting those "intransigent" Catholics who claimed to follow Pius IX in order to oppose Leo XIII, the cardinal declared, "The only rule of salvation and life in the Church is to be with the pope, with the living pope. Whoever he may be."[4]

The same instruction soon came from the pope's own pen. The occasion was a letter from Cardinal Jean-Baptiste Pitra, one of the prominent representatives

---

4   de Mattei, *Le ralliement de Léon XIII*, 95. Further references to this work will be given in parentheses. In an interesting echo of this sentiment, Archbishop Charles Scicluna stated on January 25, 2017, concerning *Amoris Laetitia*: "Whoever wishes to discover what Jesus wants from him, he must ask the Pope, *this* Pope, not the one who came before him, or the one who came before that. This present Pope." See Edward Pentin, "Archbishop Scicluna: We Are Following the Pope's Directives," *National Catholic Register*, January 30, 2017.

of the *"partito piano"* (party of Pius IX) to a Dutch correspondent. The recipient promptly published the text he had received from the cardinal. Its most crucial passage defended ultramontane journalists and praised the Catholic expansion that had taken place under Pius IX, without saying a word about his successor. A press campaign was then unleashed against the old cardinal, accusing him of seeking to oppose Leo XIII's policy with his own. A Belgian newspaper even accused him of being "the schismatic leader of a small church that wants to lecture the pope, posing as more papal than the pope." The secular press joined with liberal Catholic newspapers demanding that the cardinal be punished.

At the instigation of Cardinal Lavigerie, the pope published a letter in *L'Osservatore Romano* addressed to the cardinal archbishop of Paris.[5] The missive demanded that the faithful obey him in an exclusively political matter that had nothing to do with faith, morals, or ecclesiastical discipline. It would be much like Pope Francis making mandatory his beliefs on immigration or climate change. The abuse of magisterial power manifested in Leo XIII's letter deserves a thorough analysis, yet that would be beyond the scope of this chapter. Thus, I will cite only its most significant parts (with my comments in italicized square brackets).

> It is not difficult to see that, perhaps because of the misfortune of the times, there are some Catholics who, not content with the submissive role the Church has assigned to them, believe they can take up a role in government. At least they imagine they are allowed to examine and judge the acts of authorities according to their own way of seeing things. That would be a serious disorder if allowed to prevail in the Church of God, where, by the express will of its divine Founder, two distinct orders have been established most clearly: the teaching Church and the taught Church, the pastors and the flock, and among the pastors, one who is the head and supreme pastor for all. Pastors alone have been given the full power to teach, to judge, to direct; on the faithful has been imposed the duty to follow these teachings, to submit with docility to these judgments, to allow themselves to be governed, corrected, and led to salvation. [*Yes, indeed, this is true in matters of faith, morals, and Church discipline; but regarding everything else, the faithful are free to have personal opinions.*]
>
> And to fail in such a sacred duty, one need not make an act of open opposition to the bishops or to the head of the Church: it suffices to make opposition in an indirect manner, which is all the more dangerous as people seek to hide it more with contrary appearances. [*This is a reference to the ultramontanes, who were the champions of papal infallibility within its proper sphere.*]
>
> It is also a proof of insincere submission to establish an opposition between one Supreme Pontiff and another Supreme Pontiff. [*Sounds*

---

5 *Epistola Tua*, dated June 17, 1885; an alternative translation may be found at https://novusordowatch.org/leo13-epistola-tua/.

familiar...] Those who, [choosing] between two different directions, reject the present one and stick to the past do not show obedience to the authority that has the right and duty to direct them. In some respects, they resemble those who, after a condemnation, would like to appeal to a future council or a better informed pope. [*This is another attack on the ultramontanes, which accuses them of being conciliarists.*]

Displaying a centralism and authoritarianism hitherto unknown, Leo XIII added:

What one must hold on this point, then, is that in the general government of the Church, apart from the essential duties of the apostolic ministry imposed on all pontiffs, it is up to each of them to follow the rule of conduct which he deems best according to the times and other circumstances. In this, he is the sole judge, having in this matter not only special insights but also a knowledge of the general situation and needs of Catholicity, according to which his apostolic solicitude should be regulated. [*But is the pope infallible in everything he does? If not, one can legitimately have a contrary opinion.*] It is he who must procure the good of the universal Church, with which the good of its various parts is coordinated. All others subject to this coordination must assist the action of the Supreme Director and serve his purposes. [*Not if they believe in conscience that he is mistaken.*] As the Church is one, as her head is one, so is her government, to which all must conform. [*The present canon law recognizes the right of the faithful to express their disagreement with due respect to pastors.*]

Six days later, one leading parish priest in Paris described the new climate in the Church as follows:

The bishops must recognize and proclaim that the pope is always right. The parish priests must proclaim and acknowledge that their bishop is always right. The faithful must recognize and proclaim that their parish priest, united to his bishop and united to the pope, is always right. It is like the gendarmerie, but it is not very practical, and history testifies that it has not been very practical. (111–12)

For his part, Cardinal Lavigerie congratulated Leo XIII for resisting the winds of discontent from the faithful and ultramontane newspapers: "By this act of truly pontifical vigor, Your Holiness has condemned a new kind of tyranny, which was trying to impose itself on the Catholic hierarchy" (111).

After publishing the encyclical *Au Milieu des Sollicitudes*, the pope further hammered the nail into the coffin. While recognizing that his policies dealt with a temporal matter, he wrote to the bishop of Grenoble:

There are some, We regret to say it, who, while claiming to be Catholics, believe they have the right to oppose the direction given by the head of the Church under the pretext that it is a political direction. Oh well! Facing their erroneous claims, we maintain each of the acts that previously emanated from Us in all their fullness and continue to say: "No, undoubtedly, We do not seek to enter politics; but when politics is closely connected with religious interests, as is happening in France at present, if anyone has the mission to determine the conduct that can effectively safeguard religious interests, of which the supreme end of things consists, it is the Roman Pontiff." (322)

As soon as the encyclical appeared, Mr Émile Ollivier — a former minister of Emperor Napoleon III, who was far from being ultramontane — wrote in a column in the daily *Le Figaro*:

> While waiting for the future to decide between Pius IX and Leo XIII, one can freely choose between two opinions; for, like our forefathers, we can say: *non de fide* — it is not of faith. As for those who consider the papal letter an *ex cathedra* definition, it would be a waste of time to argue with them. One must send them back to school. (164)

The former Bonapartist minister was not exaggerating. After moral theology professors concluded that papal directives obliged on pain of mortal sin, two liberal Catholic newspapers wrote that those who continued to publicly support the monarchy were committing a grave sin. It was reported that some faithful had been denied absolution for having committed the "sin of monarchy." In his memoirs, Cardinal Domenico Ferrata, the former nuncio to Paris, commented that the apostolic letter *Notre Consolation* "henceforth excluded all equivocation: one had to accept it or declare oneself a rebel to the word of the pope" (170).

The ultramontanes avoided both pitfalls. They neither rallied to the Masonic Republic as Leo XIII wanted nor rebelled against his authority. They simply resisted him as St Paul had resisted St Peter "to his face" (Gal 2:16) or, *mutatis mutandis*, as Plinio Corrêa de Oliveira resisted Paul VI's *Ostpolitik*.[6]

Between October 1891 and February 1894, a small group of religious and laity met monthly in an *ad hoc* association called Our Lady of Nazareth. Its aim was to "act on the next conclave and obtain that the present pope not be given a successor who continues his liberal and political erring ways, so disastrous for the Church." In July 1892, the group's main leader, Fr Charles Maignen, released a study "whose conclusions [were] likely to allay concerns of French Catholics who, for reasons of conscience, refuse to adhere to a government that persecutes the Church." He stated, "Leo XIII did not act by virtue of the spiritual power that the Supreme Pontiff can exercise indirectly in the temporal order [*ratione peccati*], and consequently, his teachings, advice, or even orders, do not bind French Catholics in conscience." In another study that was never published, entitled *Un pape légitime, peut-il cesser d'être pape?* (Can a legitimate pope cease to be the pope?), Fr Maignen addressed the delicate problem of a pope-heretic (248–49).

---

6   See "The Vatican Policy of Détente with Communist Governments — Should the TFPs Stand Down? Or Should They Resist?," September 1, 1974; text at www.tfp.org/vatican-policy-detente-com-munist-governments-tfps-stand-resist/.

Therefore, we can conclude without hesitation that exaggerated devotion and submission to the pope to the point of believing oneself obliged to obey him in matters unrelated to the faith or when he teaches or commands error does not come at all from exaggerated "ultramontanism" or a supposed "spirit of Vatican I." On the contrary, it comes from the liberal Catholic current.

What was the result of the policy of "rallying" around the republic? As Leo XIII himself recognized, it was a complete failure. At an audience shortly before his death, he said to Jules Méline, former President of the French Council:

> I have sincerely attached myself to the Republic, and that has not prevented the current government from recognizing my feelings and ignoring them. They unleashed a religious war that I lament and which harms France even more than the Church. (223)

If Pope Francis is sincere, like his predecessor, he will soon have to say the same thing about his agreement with Xi Jinping. And acknowledge that Cardinal Zen was right.

19

Ultramontanism: Its Life and Death[1]

STUART CHESSMAN

T HE ACTIONS OF PRESENT POPE HAVE PUT INCREDIBLE
stress on the Church's constitution, the papal absolute monarchy. I'd like
to offer some reflections on this system of government: *ultramontanism*.
To understand it, though, we have to go back in history, starting with the reign
of Pius IX when the ultramontanist regime received its "classic" form. I will focus
on history—what actually happened—as opposed to theological considerations.

1. ORIGINS OF ULTRAMONTANISM

In the wake of the French Revolution the Church seemed to have collapsed
when the pope died in French captivity in 1799. She survived—but never attained
again the identification of the Catholic Faith with state, culture, and society that
had existed prior to 1789 in Catholic Christendom. The Church was henceforward
a minority component of European society—even if one that remained enormously
influential. The new mission was thus clear: the Church needed to *re-evangelize*
Europe and the world—to rebuild the faith and her own institutions.

By the conclusion of the First Vatican Council in 1870, the face of the Catholic
Church had indeed been renewed. What were the features of the new regime?

The Vatican Council of course was most famous for defining the infallible
authority—under certain defined circumstances—of the pope. But in practice
(the "spirit of Vatican I") the pope was henceforward treated as de facto infallible
in all his decisions, at least in the sense that no Catholic could question them.
Any kind of discussion, let alone criticism, of the pope was strictly prohibited.
The pope's immediate jurisdiction was extended directly to the entire world.
All authority in matters of the faith, organization, and liturgy was centralized
in the Vatican. It was expected that normally the pope should have sole right
to appoint bishops. Obedience to ecclesiastical authority was elevated to a central position in the Catholic faith. The Church's independence from secular
authority at every level was likewise proclaimed. Obviously, ultramontanism
required adjustments to previously existing structures within the Church that
had other organizational principles. For example, Leo XIII established in 1893

---

1   First published in four installments at the blog of the Society of St Hugh of Cluny on December
20, 23, 27, and 31, 2021, then *in toto* at *Rorate Caeli* on January 7, 2022.

a Benedictine Confederation under an Abbot Primate, headquartered in Rome, that embraced the previously autonomous Benedictine congregations. Going beyond these rules of governance, the pope assumed the position of chief spiritual leader and teacher of the Catholic Church. His image and personality were made known to Catholics throughout the world. It was expected that devotion would be paid to him. Bishop Josip Juraj Strossmeyer (one of the opponents of ultramontanism at Vatican I) summarized the effects of Vatican I: "I went in a bishop and came out a sacristan."

The ultramontane regime was a reaction to the historic Gallicanism of the French Church and to the recent clashes over state interventions in the governance of the Church (e.g., in Prussia, Spain, and Russia). To this was added the perceived weakness of national hierarchies and individual bishops in confronting secular governments. Loyalty to the pope was cemented by the fierce antipapal attitude of most of the avowed adversaries of the Church — and their subjection to the powers of this world. For example, much of the opposition to Pius IX was clearly dependent on support from Prussia (a predominantly Protestant state), on the German secular universities, etc.

But other developments which, at first glance, might have seemed hostile to the Catholic Church, encouraged ultramontanism as well. For example, the French Revolution and its successor, nineteenth-century liberalism, had overthrown or drastically weakened rival regimes, such as the French monarchy, that previously had claimed a role in the government of the Church. It had expropriated or destroyed vested clerical institutions across Europe. By default, the papacy stood alone. Of course, in the days of Pius IX the Church rejected such theories (like Cavour's "free Church in a free state"). Do we not also detect in ultramontanism the influence of another nineteenth-century development: the Napoleonic regimes? Under Napoleons I and III all power in France had been concentrated in one absolute, charismatic leader — originally, as a bulwark against revolutionary excesses.

Now ultramontanism was not achieved in a day. The system took many decades to perfect. Did not the Austrian emperor's veto of Cardinal Rampolla's candidacy for the papacy — an extreme un-ultramontane action — take place as late as 1903? The pope himself was still surrounded and framed by the elaborate ritual trappings of the past: the noble guards, the fans, the *sedia gestatoria*. For the first sixty years after the First Vatican Council, the pope remained a "prisoner of the Vatican." Yet, as the years went on, the ultramontane elements of Catholicism increased. Pius X, whose election was likely facilitated by the monarchical veto, abolished it. The last state in Europe that could even remotely be considered a Catholic monarchy, the Austro-Hungarian empire, was dissolved in 1918. In 1929, a new peace agreement was signed with Italy, giving the Holy See once more possibilities of freedom and independence. And as formerly mission territories such as the United States grew in importance the ultramontane element of the

Church also increased. Developments in technology and communications (such as radio) also assisted in spreading the message of the Vatican and the pope throughout the Catholic world and beyond.

Between 1846 and 1958, the Church accomplished many great things. First and foremost she did not disintegrate under the hammer blows of liberalism in the second half of the nineteenth century and she survived the far more violent attacks of anticlerical, communist and national socialist regimes in the first half of the twentieth century. Aided by the spread of European colonial regimes, the Catholic Church now became truly universal. Did not the United States, a former colony, advance between 1840 and 1960 from the status of an outlying mission territory to one of the strongest and wealthiest national churches in the world? Analogous progress occurred throughout the then vast British empire. Innumerable new congregations and orders sprang up, mostly devoted to an active apostolate of some kind: education, health care, the missions, etc. In the Catholic world entire nations sought a new, closer link between Church and state (Ireland, Spain, and Portugal).

By the reign of Pius XII a new level of respect also seemed to have been achieved, at least in that part of the world dominated by the United States and its allies. Catholic politicians were playing a key role in many of the nations on the continent of Europe. In the United States itself, a new era of harmony with the non-Catholic world seemed to have been established. Concrete evidence of this is the vast number of churches and schools that were built in the twenty years after the end of the Second World War. Did this not demonstrate the great success of the Church—as reformed under Pius IX?

And the successes of the Church were not merely material or measured by numbers. New devotions such as Lourdes and Fatima, new saints such as St Thérèse of Lisieux exercised a worldwide influence. A whole new galaxy of apologists testified to their Catholic faith, often using the literary forms of the novel or poetry. Many individual artists (e.g., Gaudí, Bruckner) devoted their efforts to the Catholic Church. Furthermore, the Church rediscovered its treasures of chant and of medieval philosophy. She developed Catholic positions in regard to the totally new economic situation that had arisen in the course of the nineteenth century. Finally, the twentieth century produced legions of new martyrs—in Mexico, Spain, the Soviet Union, after World War II throughout Eastern Europe and, during this entire era, across the colonial/developing world (e.g., China).

But there was another side of the coin. Despite all the successes and the relentless whirlwind of activity, there was a palpable narrowing of the Church after Vatican I. The Church seemed to have less and less relevance to the secular world, to be more and more remote and turned in on itself. The great hopes in the immediately preceding period of a grand Catholic recovery and of the reconversion of Europe—such as those of the Oxford movement, led by Newman, or of

German Romanticism culminating in the regime of King Louis I of Bavaria—had evaporated. A great uniformity of belief and practice was achieved—among the believers. But if we expanded the definition of the Church to include the entire baptized population, the results in key Catholic countries were less impressive. Didn't communists play a tremendous political role in France and Italy post-1945? And the cultural influence—even dominance—of these Stalinist parties in those years was even more impressive.

Perceptive observers noted problems early on in the seemingly solid framework of ultramontane culture. For example, Joris-Karl Huysmans asked why most of the prominent Catholic apologists of his age were converts—not the products of the Catholic educational system. He saw the ugliness of much of the art and architecture of the Church of that time as a truly satanic influence. Huysmans also had reservations about the products of Catholic seminaries in France, and early on spotlighted certain abuses that would become all too obvious towards the end of the twentieth century.

These "spiritual" and "cultural" deficiencies seemed to increase as time went on, even though ever-greater material resources became available. As evidence, compare the 1967 edition of the *Catholic Encyclopedia* in the US (nearly all the entries of which had been finished before the Council ended) with its predecessor of 1907–13, or the Basilica of the National Shrine of the Immaculate Conception in Washington with the 1918 church of St Vincent Ferrer in New York City. That eminent university president Robert Maynard Hutchins (who had enabled the teaching of neoscholastic philosophy at the University of Chicago) is reported to have frankly told the assembled presidents of the Catholic colleges of the United States what a mediocre job they were doing. And, as we know now, many individuals of doubtful faith or morality—and sometimes both—entered the priesthood and the religious life in the last great wave of expansion after the Second World War.

Aside from its spiritual problems, ultramontanism entailed a number of practical difficulties. By centralizing all authority in the pope, the entire Catholic Church now became involved in the issues of any one particular church. Grand, centrally directed papal initiatives such as the reform of Church music under Pius X also created very negative side effects—attributable in part to the difficulty of attempting detailed management of local affairs from the Vatican. The very nature of the ultramontanist regime tended to advance the careers of bureaucrats, builders, and administrators rather than spiritual leaders among the bishops.

The claims of papal authority created expectations that could never be fulfilled. There was disappointment—unspoken or not—at the *ralliement* under Leo XIII, the reaction of the Church to the French secularization decrees in 1905, the papal disavowal of *Action Française*, and the Vatican's management in Germany of the relations of the Catholic Church and the Catholic political party with the Nazi regime, among other actions. Sometimes this criticism came from the left and sometimes from the right. But a common thread was the expectation that in the twentieth century the Church needed to make heroic gestures in opposition to the forces of the world. The cautious and perhaps prudent reserve of the Vatican seemed to contrast with its grand claims of omnipotence.

Characteristic of the last years of ultramontanism under Pius XII was a circa-1960 study that compared the management structure of the Catholic Church with an American business corporation — General Electric, I believe. The comparison, according to most reports I have seen, was favorable to the Church. Yet in this analysis, the Church explicitly assumes the role of a minority participant in the ruling secular "civil society" of the West. Similarly, around the same time, the popular Catholic historian Henri Daniel-Rops affected to discern, from the perspective of ultramontanism, a positive side even to events like the separation of Church and State in France in 1905:

> It marked the end of Gallican tendencies, which was a notable contribution towards Pius X's effort to strengthen the hierarchy and centralize ecclesiastical government. Henceforward there would be no intermediary between the pope on the one hand and the clergy and Christian people of France on the other. The bishops would be chosen directly by Rome . . . [2]

Late ultramontanism thus was now reaching political conclusions almost the opposite of those of Pius IX.

By 1930, at the latest, there was also a revival of progressive Catholicism. As always, leftism proceeds from the existence of very real problems and issues. There was a real sense that it was inadequate for the Church to remain a society within a society, separate from the world. What was necessary was the reconversion of the entire world to Christianity. But almost from the beginning, less wholesome views mingled with these aspirations. What started as frustration with the timid "bourgeois" nature of ultramontanist Catholicism and the Church's excessive conformity to this world, developed into at first admiration and then uncritical acceptance of twentieth-century secular regimes. Initially there was undisguised jealousy of the alleged successes of totalitarian movements, especially communism, in inspiring their followers and in "solving the problems" of modern man. Dorothy Day is a case study in this. Later, with Jacques Maritain, the focus of these feelings of Catholic inferiority switched to the United States and the democratic society.

During the reign of Pius XII a pervasive culture of internal criticism emerged within the Church. Given the restrictions on Catholic discourse, it often took the disguised form of historical, liturgical, philosophical, or artistic studies. By

---

2   Henri Daniel-Rops, *A Fight for God 1870-1939*, vol. 1, trans. John Warrington (Garden City: Image Books/Doubleday, 1967), 221.

1959 all aspects of Catholic tradition were routinely depicted as corrupt and purely arbitrary products of historical circumstance. It seemed the entire Church had taken the wrong direction even as early as the fourth century (the famous "Constantinian" transformation). A truly revolutionary situation was emerging, at least within the Western European churches, when Pope John XXIII succeeded to the papacy. And the actors in this budding revolution weren't representatives from the fringes, but the official intellectuals and clerical bureaucrats of the Catholic Church herself. It was a revolution from above, by the establishment, that was in the making. The regime of ultramontanism at the Vatican itself seemed completely incapable of discerning what was going on even among its own protégés.

2. THE PERIOD FROM 1958–2013

In the foregoing part, I reviewed the triumph and maturity of "ultramontanism" in the Catholic Church. Fundamentally a defensive strategy, it aimed at blocklike unity, centralized control, and absolute subordination to superiors. Especially up to 1945, its catalogue of achievements was remarkable. Yet, like all defensive stances, it could not be prolonged forever. At some point a counterattack must be undertaken — for otherwise the enemy, having familiarized himself over time with a static opponent, will find a path to break through . . .

The Second Vatican Council convened in 1962. In no prior council had both the freedom from overt secular control and papal dominance over the proceedings been so assured.[3] The course and outcome of the council were determined by a new alliance of the papacy with internal progressive forces. Paul VI enjoyed almost unlimited scope of action in implementing the council throughout the Catholic world.

The management of the Council and its subsequent implementation were truly the greatest triumph of ultramontanism. No previous pope had radically and systematically changed the liturgy and the forms of Catholic piety (e.g., the rules governing fasting, the architecture and decoration of churches) virtually overnight. Paul VI found active supporters for his mission of change. A whole legion of clergy was inspired to forcefully drag into the modern Church the benighted sectors of the laity and their own less "enlightened" fellow clergy and religious. But, on the whole, resistance was minimal — so effective had been the inculcation of ultramontane obedience over the generations. The customs and traditions of the Church had likely lost their grip on much of the Catholic world through the ultramontane understanding of obedience to authority and adherence to legal rules as the source of their legitimacy.

---

3   With the exception of any understandings that may have been reached prior to the Council with the Soviet Union. But in avoiding a specific critique of the Communist world the Council was only following the lead of the Western secular establishment which, by that time, had largely committed to an ideology of "peaceful coexistence."

But even while still in session, the Council had unleashed forces that shattered the closed ultramontane world. For the progressive clergy, empowered by Paul VI, undertook to directly reverse the theology, teachings on personal morality, and the governing structures of the Church — all the things that hindered complete reconciliation with the world. Internally, the Council and its aftermath may have been revolutionary, but viewed from outside, these changes were completely conformist, as the Church adopted the worldview, vocabulary, and even the dress of the secular world of the 1960s. The guiding conciliar principles of *aggiornamento* and "reading the signs of the times" had in fact subordinated the Church to secular society far more thoroughly than had been conceivable under the European monarchies of the eighteenth century, the Holy Roman Empire of Gregory VII's day, or the Roman empire in the fourth century. None of these historical powers had at its disposal means (such as news media in the modern sense) capable of reaching into the life of each individual Catholic. Truly, it was a new, monumental "Constantinian shift"! And it was in these very years of the Council that the Western establishment's attitude to the Church began to progressively change from a politically dictated posture of respect to an overt, intensifying hostility: starting with Rolf Hochhuth's 1963 drama *The Deputy* and culminating in an across-the-board critique of "retrograde" Catholicism — above all, the Church's teachings on sexual morality.

These developments came to a head with the storm over Paul VI's 1968 encyclical on contraception, *Humanae Vitae*. The pope could not obtain obedience to his decree — not only from the "rebels" but also from the religious orders, Catholic universities, and even entire episcopal conferences. For Paul VI found himself confronting not only internal opponents, but also modern "civil society" and its media, which stood behind the rebellious elements. It was a previously unthinkable breach in ultramontane discipline. Truly, the Council, which had marked the high water mark of ultramontanism, had now administered to it its greatest defeat.

As to papal authority, the result was deadlock. Paul VI would not withdraw his encyclical — but neither did he attempt to insist on its enforcement. The same impasse was true of many other doctrines and rules of the church. A state of permanent, unacknowledged "civil war" from now on prevailed in a Church in which a substantial part of the Catholic establishment either denied or understood in a new non-literal way what had been previously fixed and certain doctrine. To give just one example, papal infallibility, a foundation stone of ultramontanism, met with two new responses: either it was denied outright (Hans Küng's *Infallible? An Inquiry*, 1971), or, more subtly, its origins were called into question (Hubert Wolf's *The Nuns of Sant'Ambrogio*, 2013). The progressives did not necessarily see any need of respecting the "views" (Eamon Duffy) of the Vatican.

Of course, some leaders of the Church — and not just those resident in the Vatican — continued to resist these interpretations and tried to preserve Catholic doctrine as traditionally understood. Popes John Paul II and Benedict XVI took numerous actions and made frequent statements on the liturgy, Catholic education, sexual morality, etc. Like *Humanae Vitae*, these were mostly ignored. Disciplinary measures to impose order on the Jesuits (under John Paul II) or on American religious sisters (under Benedict) ended in capitulation by the Vatican. For there was very little the popes could do. To directly confront the progressive establishment would in short order draw the media into the fray. That would reveal clearly that the alleged conciliar reconciliation of the Church with the modern world had failed. Moreover, I suspect the popes feared that a large portion of the laity would follow the media.

This reluctance of the popes during this period (1970–2013) to act against the progressive forces and their institutions was not just dictated by tactical considerations. All these popes shared at least to a limited extent the opinions and goals of the progressives. And they were also desirous of a favorable presentation by the media. Peter Seewald's biography of Pope Benedict reveals this obsessive concern of the Vatican with the pope's image in the press.

There was no longer any question of recreating the preconciliar unity of belief and practice. At most, the popes could achieve a "tilt" in the direction of Catholic tradition—mainly through episcopal appointments. Even here the results were erratic. Yet, within the constraints outlined above, under John Paul II there was an "ultramontane revival." John Paul II gained prestige from his role in the collapse of communism and his charismatic public persona. He adopted to a great extent the style of secular politicians and regimes. That even extended to features imported from the repertoire of the totalitarian states of the Eastern bloc (e.g., youth days and festivals; massive orchestrated public appearances). The result was a renaissance of the papal image—appealing to so many at the time. The cult of "John Paul the Great" was born.

The "neo-ultramontane" wave generated an immense amount of activity on the part of the partisans of the "Polish pope"—especially in the United States and mostly among those outside the clerical establishment. Papal infallibility was reemphasized by these activists and now extended far beyond the 1870 definitions. The election of the pope was now "God's choice."[4] The articles contained in *Civiltà Cattolica*, because they were cleared by the Vatican Secretary of State, took on an aura of infallibility. The infallibility of *Humanae Vitae* was proposed. The stalemate of the postconciliar Church was recast as a struggle between papal authority and "dissenters." Although such positions remained unofficial, they are indicative of the pro-papal surge under John Paul II.

The new papalism, however, had to account for the tolerance of John Paul II for the progressive forces. The explanation that was found was the pope's need

---

4   The title of a book by Weigel. See Peter Kwasniewski, "Games People Play with the Holy Spirit," in *Illusions of Reform: Responses to Cavadini, Healy, and Weinandy in Defense of the Traditional Mass and the Faithful Who Attend It* (Lincoln, NE: Os Justi Press, 2023), 134–50.

to avoid "schism." This is, of course, a degenerate ultramontane understanding, in which preserving the external appearance of unity takes precedence over ensuring its actual substance.

Another aspect of the neo-ultramontane era — sparked by the style and restless activity of John Paul II — was the obsession with the political aspects of the papacy and the Vatican. A whole legion of reporters, "information entrepreneurs," and, later, internet personalities concerned themselves with the internal affairs of the Vatican. In considering any issue of Catholicism it became usual to include speculation on Vatican personnel moves. Actions having the greatest importance for each individual Catholic were portrayed as the product of changes in the leadership of, and even within, Vatican dicasteries. Do I need to mention all the Vatican novels published in this era? — some of them informative, others ludicrous. Whatever might be the Vatican's actual authority over the Church, this focus on Rome demonstrated that an unhealthy ultramontanism was alive and well.

We should mention at this point the ever-growing bureaucratization of the Church after the Council. Despite all the disorders within the Church, offices, "apostolates," and administrators increased. As the ranks of clergy and religious declined in the postconciliar chaos, the number of lay employees grew exponentially. The clergy were also assimilated to bureaucrats. A retirement age was now set for bishops, and they increasingly were moved about from diocese to diocese. At the local level, term limits began to be imposed on pastors. Added to this mix was an extreme degree of legalism. The result was an increased perception of the Church as a secular organization like the United Nations, a governmental agency, the EU headquarters, or, later, a very large NGO (non-governmental organization).

Towards the end of John Paul II's papacy, and during the whole of Benedict XVI's reign, the Church and in particular the Vatican had to face ever increasing difficulties. The fundamental issue of the decline of belief and practice of the faith within the Church herself had not been resolved. The Vatican bureaucracy became a cesspool of careerism, incompetence, and financial corruption. The documentation that has been disclosed on the career of Cardinal McCarrick reveals how little John Paul II understood of the appointments he was charged with making. The scandals of sexual abuse, the conduct of the leaders of the Legionaries of Christ, and financial misdeeds at the Vatican opened up new fronts for relentless secular attack on the Church from 2002 to the present day. Pope Benedict was utterly unable to contend with either the media or his own Vatican bureaucracy. Indeed, the pope's enemies in the latter organization resorted to outright treason to block Benedict's initiatives.

Faced with a rising tide of challenges, these popes seem to have slipped into a fantasy world — at least if popular biographies are any guide. According to George Weigel's *Witness to Hope* (1999), John Paul II seems to have been of the opinion that his innumerable voyages thorough the world were having major political effects (only in Poland was that conclusion perhaps justified). In Seewald's biography, *Benedikt XVI: Ein Leben* (2020), Pope Benedict is reported to have thought, upon ascending the papal throne, that all issues of the Church already had been favorably resolved by his predecessor. To quote another example, at several Vatican-sponsored conferences it was proposed that excess priests be shifted from the developed to the third world—this, at a time when the churches of these "advanced" countries were in fact relying more and more on imported African, Asian, and Latin American priests.

In the same vein, as the popes' real power within the Church declined, papal visions of global leadership grew. The bishop of Rome was now described as the "pope of all mankind," a sort of worldwide spiritual advocate. Thus, John Paul II presided over interfaith assemblies at Assisi. Pope Benedict lectured in abstract terms on the relationship of faith and reason to the unbelieving German parliament.

Most importantly, the need for a renewed evangelization—now primarily within the Church herself—still had not been met. The opening to the world had been a one-way street in which the world instructed the Church. The marriage of the Council with ultramontanism had produced a culture that was far more provincial than the ghetto of 1958 so derided by the advanced Catholic circles of that time. The art and music of the Church by 2013 was either kitsch or uninspired copies of modern aesthetic orthodoxy. The increasing lack of funds limited even that activity.

The papacy had indeed survived the turmoil it had itself created in the wake of the Council. But the conciliar papacy had not preserved the Church's unity in doctrine and practice—the reason ultramontanism had been advocated in the first place. The Vatican increasingly functioned as a mere administrative center, while all kinds of developments, heterodox or not, proceeded autonomously. In 2013, Pope Benedict resigned. It was a crushing blow to the papacy and absolutely unimaginable under preconciliar ultramontanism.

3. THE PERIOD FROM 2013 TO THE PRESENT

By 2013—the year of Pope Benedict's resignation—the stalemate that had arisen at the end of the 1960s had lasted for forty-five years. The popes had not dared to force a showdown with the progressive forces on a significant issue. That would have called into question the Council. But neither would they accede to progressive demands to explicitly adapt Catholic theology and morality to the dictates of the modern world, which would render dubious the Church's claims of continuity with its perennial tradition. The result was that the Vatican's authority declined to a merely administrative role, while the pressure of secular society on the Church steadily increased. The Church disguised this process through the activity of John Paul II's papacy and otherwise strove to maintain an image of infallibility, omnipotence, harmony of past and present, and agreement among all elements of the Church. The result is best described as "managed decline."

Pope Francis's election brought a recommitment to the progressive agenda of the 1960s along with a radical revival of ultramontane authoritarianism. Thus, his regime strongly resembles the reign of Paul VI—at least as it existed up to 1970. In one extreme recent example, if Paul VI had imposed on the entire Church radical changes in liturgy, so Pope Francis has now undertaken to compel the traditionalist Catholics to adopt the Novus Ordo. An entire population of Catholics—priests, religious orders, monasteries, schools, and laity—previously in official good standing with the Church, have been reduced overnight to outcasts. Prior papal legislation, commitments, and agreements to the contrary—such as the regimes established for the *Ecclesia Dei* communities—have been revoked or stand in constant danger of revocation. The Vatican has published a set of implementation measures that have centralized authority to an unheard-of degree—regulating even the content of parish bulletins!

And this anti-traditionalist "crusade" is but one example among many. From the first day of his pontificate, Pope Francis rejected the application to himself of any of the customs, laws, and rules of the church. He routinely disregards the rulings and statements of his own Vatican officials. A whole series of Catholic congregations and orders (like the Order of Malta) have been placed under the rule of papal commissioners. The same is now true of the entire Italian church in regard to Francis's legislation on divorce. The pope has received the resignation of one entire country's episcopate (Chile) and later of individual bishops in other countries (Germany and France). A class of bishop emerged that, after proffered resignation, continues in office only at the discretion of the pope. The Vatican has asserted centralized control over contemplative religious monasteries and orders, over the establishment of any new religious congregation, and, most recently, over the term of office of the leadership of the so-called movements. In the United States, Francis has intervened directly and repeatedly in the affairs of the national bishops' conference and even in American domestic politics (e.g., the management of USCCB meetings, the status of politicians who promote abortion, the recognition of New Ways Ministry).

Pope Francis has added to his 1960s progressivism publicity techniques borrowed from the repertoire of John Paul II. Gigantic papal events and voyages continue. Papal statements, interviews, and books proliferate. A vast papal public relations apparatus has come into being at the Vatican and beyond—often in league with the secular press (e.g., *Vatican Insider, Crux, Rome Reports*). Francis has progressively refined this system over the years to focus it ever more closely on its designated role as a vehicle for propagating his image and thoughts.

The centralizing tidal wave at the Vatican has been reproduced down to the lowest level of the Church. The existence of the Catholic Church's traditional organizational form at the base—the parish—was increasingly called into question. The archbishop of New York has openly speculated about a reorganization in which all Church property would be vested in the Archdiocese—a step that would, when combined with the current term limits on pastors, effectively transform all New York parishes into chapels. In dioceses in Germany and in the United States (such as the Cincinnati and Hartford archdioceses), plans are being implemented that provide for radical reductions in the number of parishes. In response, the Vatican has feebly tried to uphold parish rights under canon law.

The changes in rhetoric and style are as significant as the concrete measures. The pope has divided the Church into friends and enemies. For example, in the American context, the pope has made absolutely clear what he thinks the role of Catholic media should be—by singling out for praise the eminently conformist *Catholic News Service* while accusing its competitor, the "conservative" EWTN, of doing the work of the devil. His publicists carry on this campaign further, denouncing those who "criticize the pope" and, in the last month or two, speculating on how Francis can neutralize "rogue" prelates (his critics in the hierarchy). They also explain that Francis really shouldn't care about those in the Church he hurts or "leaves by the wayside."

The pope often employs against his conservative opponents the language and techniques of ultramontanism. In *Traditionis Custodes*, for example, the pope sets up Church unity and the inviolability of the Council as absolute values. Indeed, the Second Vatican Council (and its implementing decrees) are described as "dictated by the Holy Spirit." The pope has canonized representatives of Catholic modernity (like Pope Paul VI!) thereby seeking to invest their polices with an aura of infallibility. Pope Francis himself claims to teach "with magisterial authority." One often gets the sense Francis is mocking the legalistic and traditional diction of certain of his enemies, as when he titles his motu proprio seeking to abolish traditionalism *Traditionis Custodes* ("Guardians of Tradition")!

The culture of the Catholic Church under Francis has been rightly described as *Orwellian*. The great advocate of dialogue never communicates with those who question his policies or who are the recipient of his attacks. Effeminate rhetoric (tenderness; accompaniment) contrasts with brusque commands and coarse denunciations. Advocacy of a "synodal" church proceeds hand-in-hand with extreme centralization. The apostle of unity within the Church excludes whole sections of believers without a second thought. Truly the regime of Francis can be called *totalitarian ultramontanism*!

Yet the pope's totalitarian ultramontanism has a radically limited scope. The most obvious constraint on Francis is the power of the Catholic progressives, the media, and the institutions of Western civil society. Francis is absolutely dependent on their support. But their backing is not at all unconditional; it depends on the pope continuing to advance their agenda. Whenever Francis's Vatican has been perceived as wavering in this mission, the progressive powers, like the German church, have summarily rejected its (and his) authority. Just recently, Francis and the leadership of his upcoming synod on synodality have had to abjectly apologize to the progressive New Ways Ministry in the US.

In his direct interactions with the institutions governing the Western world, the pope pursues policies that are both totally secular and largely identical with the positions advocated by the media. So, Pope Francis precisely implemented the dictates of the establishment regarding suspension of religious services because of Covid-19. I should add that the relationship—often scandalous—between the Vatican and the Western financial powers has never been closer.

Resistance within the Church to Pope Francis has, however, also emerged from the other end of the spectrum, even if it is, in contrast to the progressive challenges, most often not publicly disclosed. Only a few prelates from this quarter—generally retired or previously removed from their positions—criticize the pope openly. Nevertheless, the publication of a book by the "pope emeritus" and Cardinal Sarah helped to derail Francis's push for a married clergy. The pope's acceptance of divorce in *Amoris Laetitia* and his accompanying measures have by no means been received enthusiastically everywhere. Indeed, it took blatant manipulation by the Vatican to obtain in the first place from the synods on the subject something that Francis could call approval of his marriage policies. Francis has had to publicly employ strong-arm tactics with the American hierarchy to block their policies on opposition to abortion. Finally, bishops throughout the world generally have been slow in signing on to Francis's war against traditionalists.

Thus, in the opinion of certain progressives, the organizational deadlock that existed prior to Francis's papacy has reemerged. The tug-of-war continues between the advocates of radical change and the upholders of some form of Catholic tradition. The debate on synodality in Rome and in Germany—which really often is about other substantive issues such as married and female priests—may well bring this conflict to a head.

What a strange fate for ultramontanism! A set of policies that was supposed to secure the doctrine of the Church from internal enemies and preserve her independence from secular control has instead facilitated the greatest crisis of belief in the Church's history along with her most abject subjection to the "temporal power"—not that of monarchs as in the past, but that of the media, banks, NGOs, universities and, increasingly, "democratic" governments (including China!). The most extreme assertions of ultramontanism (such as those by Pope Francis) coincide with today's total humiliation of the Church. Is it failure caused by trying to achieve spiritual objectives through the application of organizational techniques? In any case, the need for evangelizing the world that arose after the religious collapse of the French Revolution remains unmet even today, as a whole, by the institutional Church.

4. CONCLUDING THOUGHTS

During the papacy of Pius IX the theory and, to a great extent, the practice of the modern ultramontane regime were perfected. This system did secure internal unity and stability, leading the Church through one of the most pivotal periods of world and European history. Yet the lead-up to the Second Vatican Council, the course of the Council itself, and the implementation of its decisions revealed all too clearly the deficiencies of ultramontanism. The extreme centralized structures and absence of any real exchange of ideas in the Roman Catholic Church privileged the influence of "experts," cliques, and behind-the-scenes intrigue. At the pope's command, the bishops, clergy, and laity, unable to think for themselves, accepted blindly the destruction or relativization of that which, only yesterday, they had held sacred and immutable.

But the "conciliar Church" itself bore the hallmarks of the ultramontane past that it affected to despise — provincialism, authoritarianism, pervasive bureaucracy, and remoteness from the life of men and women today. The hundreds of pages of conciliar decrees and the literary productions of the conciliar champions (Rahner, Ratzinger, Küng, Schillebeeckx, etc.) made, outside of the clerical bureaucracy, little impression in the Church — and none on the world outside it. Indeed, far from being an avenue for establishing new communication with the world and the laity, Vatican II — its interpretation and defense — became just one more burden on the Church establishment.

Within the Church itself, however, all the institutions so carefully built up since the 1830s — the schools, seminaries, monasteries, religious congregations, hospitals, universities — experienced a more or less universal existential crisis. Entire national churches (e.g., the Netherlands, Quebec) collapsed virtually overnight, while most others in the developed world commenced a continuous decline of religious practice. Conflict within the ecclesiastical establishment itself broke into the open, as the Vatican and the Church's dominant intellectual leadership fell out on a broad spectrum of issues.

It became increasingly apparent that the positions of the progressives were irreconcilable with Catholic doctrine and morality, at least as previously understood. The postconciliar popes up to Francis, however, could not face the consequences of either adopting the progressive agenda or condemning it. The result was a deadlock between the progressive institutions and the Vatican which lasted for the next forty-five years. In the actual practice of ruling the Church, the ultramontane papacy more and more assumed a merely administrative role.[5]

---

5   The situation of the Church under John Paul II and Benedict thus recalled that of Austria-Hungary in the years 1866 to 1918. It was a monarchy that had progressively lost its prior spiritual or ideological *raisons d'être* (such as being ruler of the Holy Roman Empire, the advocate of Catholicism in Central Europe, and the leader of an embryonic German national state). What remained in the central authority were the cult of the house of Habsburg-Lorraine (Emperor Franz Josef) and ongoing administrative responsibilities. Meanwhile, ideologies that called into question the very existence of

In the midst of the postconciliar conflicts over the faith, Catholic tradition-alism was born. The new conciliar model was manifestly not working; a return to—or preservation of—the past recommended itself. Contrary to what Pope Francis asserts, the attitudes of the traditionalists to the authority of the Council varied greatly—as did their understanding regarding ultramontanism. Clearly the establishment of the SSPX and their consecration of bishops in 1988 were utterly contrary to the ultramontane system. By placing Catholic doctrine and tradition above obedience to authority, Archbishop Lefebvre in effect challenged ultramontanism's foundational assumptions. I am not sure, however, that the SSPX (and later the FSSP) fully grasped what was happening. I get the sense they adhered to a paradigm that all was perfect in the Church prior to Vatican II—that the Church's afflictions were attributable to infiltrators and dissenters. And, after achieving reconciliation with the Vatican, the FSSP certainly labored to project an image of alignment with an authoritarian and infallible papacy.

To the traditionalists could be added the "conservatives"—which the progressive establishment hardly distinguishes from the traditionalists. From the late 1960s onward they espoused a radical ultramontanism, understanding the progressives primarily as "dissenters" from authority. For the conservatives, just like their nineteenth-century predecessors, the papacy is a defender of Christian morality in the secular world, and the omnipotent guardian of doctrinal purity within the Church. This was often juxtaposed to the feebleness of the national hierarchies, which the conservatives usually viewed as ineffectual bureaucracies. Yet in fact, the papacy itself, not just the episcopacy of the local churches, was usually reluctant to be directly drawn into conflict with either the liberal forces in the Church or the governing powers of the Western secular world.

Pope Francis has attempted to revive progressive conciliarism and make it final and irreversible. To do this, he has made the most extreme assertions of ultramontane authority in history. So far, his most salient "achievements" *de jure* in ruling the Church have been the attempted institutionalization of divorce within Catholicism and the launching of a campaign of repression of Catholic traditionalism. He has also adopted or tolerated the policy positions of the ruling secular powers on a broad range of issues—totally in harmony with the Catholic liberals. His actions are very often accompanied by intemperate language denouncing perceived adversaries—similar to the rhetorical style of many progressives.[6]

---

the Austro-Hungarian state—e.g., liberalism; socialism; Hungarian, Czech, Polish, and even German nationalism; religious unbelief in general—proliferated, unchallenged and unrefuted.

6   In the many volumes of Ludwig Pastor's *History of the Popes* one certainly finds, particularly in the period between 1294 and 1559, papal utterances and deeds that are violent, extreme, or even insane. These, however, occur most often in the context of papal secular political ambitions, with an audience of political rivals, officials, and ambassadors. Moreover, and crucially, papal words were not broadcast all over the world, let alone published at the parish level. Nor were the popes of those years holding themselves out as spiritual leaders of all the laity everywhere. They seemed most intent on dominating laterally or upwardly, not downwardly.

Yet, after eight years, the pope's actions still fall short of the demands of his progressive allies. Further papal initiatives — to introduce married and female clergy, to regularize homosexuality, to explore a "synodal" system of governance — have stalled. The hierarchs of the Catholic Church remain, in general, extremely unwilling to criticize Pope Francis publicly. We do not fully know what is going on behind the scenes. Whatever its source, however, internal Church resistance has obviously slowed the progressive onslaught. Once again, in the eyes of the progressives, the stagnation of the post-*Humanae Vitae* Church has returned. In places like Germany they therefore feel empowered to take matters into their own hands — with, so far, a feeble public reaction from the Vatican.

We must remember, after all, that the Catholic Church rests on the voluntary adherence of the faithful throughout the world. National and family support for remaining Catholic continues to erode — even in Poland. In most places, the Church also lacks the resources to offer the valuable patronage of an establishment (like that of the Church of England). In the aftermath of the Council, the majority of the Catholic laity in the developed world have ceased to practice their faith. In some places many have gone further and declared their public exit from the Church (Germany) or become evangelical Protestants (throughout Latin America and to some extent in the United States). Even the remaining practicing Catholics often have little understanding of Catholic doctrine; their adherence to the rules of the faith regarding sexual morality is also limited.

Thus, just as it was after the French Revolution, the fundamental challenge to the Church — evangelizing the modern unbelieving world — still remains outstanding. Now, however, the majority of the Catholic clergy and faithful stand in need of evangelization as well! Ultimately this is a spiritual problem — a crisis of faith. A spiritual challenge can only be addressed by spiritual answers. Such a need cannot be met by a return to ultramontane centralization, strong-arm tactics, and publicity tricks. Let us think also of our duty of evangelization to non-Catholics and non-Christians. For those outside the Church, ultramontanism is like "preaching to the choir" — absolutely incomprehensible. Endlessly reiterating conciliar and progressive platitudes of the 1960s and '70s that are themselves derived from prior secular ideologies will have just as little success. These policies have been imposed for decades in one way or another and have failed.

In my opinion traditionalism is this answer, the real path of reform, the way out of the ultramontane/progressive dead end. That is because it rests not on the authority of the clergy or the support of the secular world, but on the individual commitment of the laity — not to some self-constructed worldview or to an image of the Church as it appeared in any one era, but to the fullness of Catholic tradition as it exists in every age. The traditionalists of the last twenty years or so — priests, religious, and families — have become such because they experienced and then voluntarily lived the traditional Mass. Thus, Catholic traditionalism fully respects the freedom of conscience of the individual believer and even presupposes it. It is not a sect, a cult, a "group" (Pope Francis), or an ideology; it is a way of life and of faith that is freely available to all. Yet its practice so often works a total transformation of those who fully undertake to live according to its precepts. The traditional Catholic faith is thus the spiritual answer that believers and nonbelievers are secretly awaiting in this age of unbelief. It is now up to us who have lived it to make it available to the whole world.

FIGURE 1. Mural in the church of St. Francis Xavier, New York. On September 25, 1534, the wretched papacy of Clement VII came to an end. Just over a month earlier in that year, before dawn on August 15, the first Jesuits had taken their vows (before Peter Faber, the only priest among them): a force of renewal emerging at the tail end of a long period of papal misgovernance.

FIGURE 2. Pope Clement XIV (1769–1774) was a spineless individual who labored to please the powers of this world—in his day, the absolute monarchies—by abolishing the Jesuit order and imprisoning its leaders. After his death, his sympathizers handsomely financed a great monument by Canova that disingenuously depicts this pope as a grandly authoritarian, Caesar-like monarch.

FIGURE 3. The Art of Ultramontanism: At the Shrine of Our Lady of Pompeii (also known as the Shrine of Our Lady of the Rosary) in Italy, one finds, in the corridors outside the church, a series of paintings with ex-votos, illustrating the relationship between Pope Leo XIII and the lay founders of this shrine. In this painting, the pope is enthroned in the heavens, holding pen and paper as if waiting for divine inspiration, while angels carry his words to the four corners of the earth.

FIGURE 4. From the Shrine of Our Lady of Pompeii. Leo XIII is borne aloft on the *sedia gestatoria*, wearing his tiara, blessing with one hand and pointing commandingly with the other. This is the "god-king" papacy that paved the way for the more extravagant public gestures of Pius XII.

FIGURE 5. From the Shrine of Our Lady of Pompeii. An allegorical scene in which Leo XIII defends the Church by banishing the demons into the deep. The art is not very good, but the sentiments are conveyed with total effectiveness: the pope, like Christ, rules over all of God's creatures.

FIGURE 6. The Cathedral of Covington, Kentucky, contains an unusual series of windows illustrating dogmatic and administrative decrees of popes and councils—at a time when none of the popes depicted in the windows had been beatified or canonized. The windows are evidence of the central role that the pope and the Vatican had assumed in Catholic culture by 1914. Here is Pius IX proclaiming the dogma of the Immaculate Conception.

FIGURE 7. A window in Covington Cathedral depicting the 1903 reform of church music by Pope Pius X. Window by Mayer, Munich, c. 1910.

FIGURE 8. This unusual photo shows Pope Pius XII standing before his gestatorial chair as he is carried into one of the Vatican's apostolic halls to bless crowds gathered there. Pilgrims in great numbers are presently crowding the Vatican to be blessed before the pontiff retires to his summer palace shortly. (Original caption.)

Figure 9. Ultramontane window in the Church of Our Saviour, New York, contemporary with the proto-progressive encyclical *Mater et Magistra* of Pope John XXIII (1961), which it parallels with Christ teaching in the temple. William F. Buckley's public disagreement with the pope's conclusions (on economics) — as captured in his pithy phrase "Mater, si, Magistra, no" — was, up till then, virtually unheard of.

FIGURE 10. September 8, 1963: a young boy kissing Pope Paul VI's ring during a ceremony to celebrate the Holy Mass at the Church of Genazzano.

FIGURE 11. A plaque commemorating Pope Paul VI's visit to the United Nations (*not* to the American Church) — reminiscent of Pope Francis's trip to Marseilles (but not officially to France). This plaque, and the one featured in the next Figure, are in the Church of the Holy Family, New York, built by Cardinal Spellman, one of the last arch-ultramontanists.

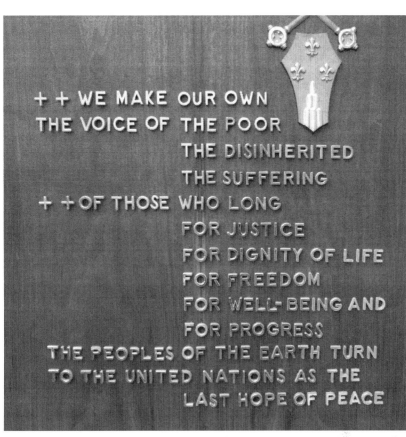

Figure 12. A quotation from Pope Paul VI from the same visit to the UN. The reader may judge for himself.

FIGURE 13. Ultramontanism 2021: a German-language "conservative" website regularly carries the messages and homilies of Pope Francis—which, as often as not, contradict the editorial polices of the same site.

FIGURE 14. Ultramontanism on the parish level. Screenshot from the website of St. Stanislaus parish, New Haven, showing the extensive coverage given to Pope Francis. The Vincentians in charge of this Polish-language parish were not long ago summarily dismissed. This parish was well-known for its Latin Mass, for which music and ceremonial support was offered for thirty-seven years by the St. Gregory Society. On Sunday, December 31, 2023, a decree from Archbishop Leonard Blair, read out just before the start of the Latin Mass, informed the faithful that this Mass would be discontinued in mid-January, in spite of the community of the faithful that had formed around it at St Stanislaus for decades. Such contempt for the faithful is typical of the reign of Francis and his apparatchiks.

FIGURE 15. Ultramontanism on the parish level (continued). A well-attended Latin Mass was arbitrarily terminated at this parish in Danbury, CT, just after *Traditionis Custodes* was issued.

20

Modernism, Not Ultramontanism, Is the "Synthesis of All Heresies"[1]

JOSÉ A. URETA

I N AMERICAN TRADITIONALIST CIRCLES, IT IS BECOMING fashionable to blame "ultramontanism" for the ills affecting Catholicism today. Supposedly, Pope Francis is able to impose a revolutionary agenda on the Church because of the actions of ultramontanes during the First Vatican Council. Detractors admit that ultramontanes turned traditional Church teaching on papal infallibility and universal jurisdiction into dogma. They go on to claim, falsely, that ultramontanes corrupted the faithful's obedience to the pope into obsequiousness, having enveloped his person in an aura of exaggerated venerability. This development supposedly resulted in a centralization and consequent abuse of power in the Church. To avoid ultramontane-fostered "papolatry," some authors suggest rethinking the papacy in terms of the first millennium, before St Gregory VII, concerning the appointment of bishops and the exercise of the pope's magisterial power.[2]

This accusation appeared in Stuart Chessman's "Ultramontanism: Its Life and Death."[3] According to the author, a certain "spirit of Vatican I" led people to interpret that Council's dogmatic definitions far beyond the limits imposed by their text. That inaugurated an "ultramontane regime" in which "all authority in matters of the faith, organization, and liturgy was centralized in the Vatican," and "obedience to ecclesiastical authority was elevated to a central position in the Catholic faith" with a corresponding decrease in episcopal authority. A bishop of the anti-infallibilist minority ironically commented, "I went in a bishop and came out a sacristan."

The Lateran Treaty and the creation of the Vatican State, as well as new communication technologies, allegedly increased the importance of this "ultramontane" element in the life of the Church. That had some advantages — "a great uniformity of belief and practice was achieved" — but also serious drawbacks, primarily the bureaucratization of the Church and its inevitable consequence: mediocre manager-bishops who ceased to be "spiritual leaders" capable of converting the

---

1 First published at *Rorate Caeli* on January 25, 2022.
2 See Eric Sammons, "Rethinking the Papacy," *Crisis Point Live* (video), September 28, 2021.
3 See the preceding chapter.

world. This "defensive strategy," "aimed at blocklike unity, centralized control, and absolute subordination to superiors," resulted in "a revival of progressive Catholicism." The latter would have originated "as [a feeling of] frustration with the timid 'bourgeois' nature of ultramontanist Catholicism and the Church's excessive conformity to this world," and as a reaction to "restrictions on Catholic discourse."

As per Mr Chessman's narrative, "ultramontanism" later allied with "internal progressive forces" that materialized at the Second Vatican Council. He goes so far as to state: "The management of the Council and its subsequent implementation were truly the greatest triumph of ultramontanism." The revolutionary changes imposed by Paul VI met little resistance because "the customs and traditions of the Church had likely lost their grip on much of the Catholic world through the ultramontane understanding of obedience to authority and adherence to legal rules as the source of their legitimacy."

Due to the growth of the progressive current—the story continues—ultramontanists failed to consolidate the authority of the Roman Pontiff in the aftermath of Vatican II and particularly after the rejection of *Humanae Vitae*. However, John Paul II undertook a "neo-ultramontane revival" that emphasized papal infallibility and transformed the pope into a "worldwide spiritual advocate." Domestically, however, and particularly under Benedict XVI, "the Vatican increasingly functioned as a mere administrative center," taking the bureaucratization of the Church even further and transforming it into a "cesspool of careerism, incompetence, and financial corruption."

Pope Francis's election entailed "a recommitment to the progressive agenda of the 1960s along with a radical revival of ultramontane authoritarianism." Using "the language and techniques of ultramontanism," the Argentine pope "sets up Church unity and the inviolability of the Council as absolute values" to silence and oppress traditionalists. Hence, "truly the regime of Francis can be called totalitarian ultramontanism!"

In short, for such traditionalist critics, all the evils under which the Church now suffers result from ultramontanists, whose great mistake was to have sought "to achieve spiritual objectives through the application of organizational techniques." Paradoxically, ultramontanism ultimately achieved the opposite of its goal:

> A set of policies that was supposed to secure the doctrine of the Church from internal enemies and preserve her independence from secular control has instead facilitated the greatest crisis of belief in the Church's history along with her most abject subjection to the "temporal power"—not that of monarchs as in the past, but that of the media, banks, NGOs, universities and, increasingly, "democratic" governments (including China!).

From the above, one could almost say that the Church's "mysterious process of self-demolition," due to the infiltration of the "smoke of Satan" of which Paul VI spoke, originated, developed, and attained its apex thanks to ultramontanism, the new synthesis of all evils! What could be the way out of this crisis? The author says "the way out of the ultramontane/progressive dead end" requires an anti-ultramontane traditionalism because it does not stand "on the authority of the clergy" but "on the individual commitment of the laity" to the "fullness of Catholic tradition," with due respect to "the freedom of conscience of the individual believer."

Mr Chessman's intellectual construction suffers from two defects. First, he attributes the origin of the current crisis of Faith to purely natural factors — the way papal power is structured and exercised. The truth is that it stemmed from a moral and religious crisis that escalated throughout the West since the Renaissance and Protestantism, as Prof. Plinio Corrêa de Oliveira sharply analyzed in *Revolution and Counter-Revolution.*[4] Second, Mr Chessman's theory is unhistorical.

In recent articles, I have briefly dealt with the error that consists in attributing to the ultramontane current and a so-called "spirit of Vatican I" the expansion of the pope's magisterial and disciplinary authority beyond the limits set by the dogmatic constitution *Pastor Aeternus.*

In the first article,[5] I showed how the top representative of ultramontanism, Cardinal Louis-Edouard Pie, had a perfectly balanced and non-absolutist concept of the papal monarchy and was a great supporter of provincial plenary councils. In the second article,[6] I showed that Pope Leo XIII — orthodox in doctrine but liberal in policy — was the one who began demanding that lay Catholics adhere to his "*Ralliement*" unconditionally, supporting France's republican and Masonic regime. The ones who applauded the imposition of unconditional obedience in political matters were representatives of the liberal current who had opposed the dogmatic definitions of Vatican I. One of those liberal prelates, Cardinal Lavigerie, went so far as to state: "The only rule of salvation and life in the Church is to be with the pope, with the living pope. Whoever he may be." I further showed that the representatives of ultramontanism were the ones who resisted that abusive extension of papal authority and obedience beyond their defined limits. They were so keenly aware of those limits that, still in the nineteenth century, one of them raised the question of the theological possibility of a heretical pope.

St Pius X was an ultramontane pope and a great admirer of Cardinal Pie. The French prelate's writings inspired him to choose "*instaurare omnia in Christo*" as the motto of his pontificate. True, Pius X demanded full obedience in matters of faith and was very firm in denouncing and repressing heresy. He excommunicated modernist leaders and imposed the Anti-Modernist Oath. However, he did not abuse papal authority or seek to impose uniform thinking in matters where Catholics are entitled to form a personal opinion. He even excused the Scotton brothers, owners of an antimodernist newspaper, for their zeal opposing Cardinal

---

4   Plinio Corrêa de Oliveira, *Revolution and Counter-Revolution*, 3rd ed. (Spring Grove, PA: The American Society for the Defense of Tradition, Family, and Property, 1993).

5   See chapter 17.

6   See chapter 18.

Andrea Carlo Ferrari, the archbishop of Milan. He said they employed excessive language because "to defend themselves, they are using the same weapons with which they were struck."[7]

To the applause of the liberal current, non-ultramontane popes subsequently required the faithful to obey their agenda of strict appeasement of revolutionary political powers. That started with Benedict XV. In his first encyclical (*Ad Beatissimi Apostolorum*), he silenced those who defended unreserved adherence to Church teachings and their validity in society, labeling them "integrists." He did so "to quell dissension and strife of any kind among Catholics and prevent new ones from arising, so all may be united in thought and action."

To achieve that, everyone had to align with the Holy See:

> Whenever legitimate authority has once given a clear command, let no one transgress that command, because it does not happen to commend itself to him; but let each one subject his own opinion to the authority of him who is his superior, and obey him as a matter of conscience. Again, let no private individual, whether in books or in the press, or in public speeches, take upon himself the position of an authoritative teacher in the Church. All know to whom the teaching authority of the Church has been given by God: he, then, possesses a perfect right to speak as he wishes and when he thinks it opportune. The duty of others is to hearken to him reverently when he speaks and to carry out what he says.[8]

Divergent opinions were allowed in matters other than faith and morals such as lay Catholic political action or the journalistic approach to be taken to modernism, provided that the pope has not given his own line: "As regards matters in which without harm to faith or discipline—*in the absence of any authoritative intervention of the Apostolic See*—there is room for divergent opinions, it is clearly the right of everyone to express and defend his own opinion."[9] A practical application of this restriction on debate was placing the newspaper owned by the Scotton brothers under the strict control of the bishop of Vicenza, reversing the freedom of opinion that St Pius X had defended.[10]

Benedict XV's successor, Pius XI—who belonged to the same non-ultramontane current—went so far as to excommunicate the subscribers of the monarchist newspaper *Action Française* because of its director Charles Maurras's agnostic

---

7   *Romana beatificationis et canonizationis servi Dei Papae Pii X disquisitio circa quasdam obiectiones modum agendi servi Dei respicientes in modernismi debellationem*, ed. Card. Ferdinando Antonelli (Vatican City: Typis poliglottis Vaticanis, 1950), 178, in Roberto de Mattei, "Modernismo e antimodernismo nell'epoca di Pio X," in Michele Busi, Roberto de Mattei, Antonio Lanza, Flavio Peloso, *Don Orione negli anni del modernismo* (Milan: Jaca Book, 2002), 60.

8   Benedict XV, Encyclical *Ad Beatissimi Apostolorum* (November 1, 1914), no. 22.

9   Ibid., no. 23.

10   Giovanni Vian, "Il modernismo durante il pontificato di Benedetto XV, tra riabilitaziioni e condanne," note 23, https://iris.unive.it/retrieve/handle/10278/3691556/113213/Il%20modernismo%20 durante%20il%20pontificato%20di%20Benedetto%20XV%20-%20testo%20atti%20Bologna.pdf.

opinions.[11] (It would be as if Pope Francis excommunicated *Breitbart* or *Fox News* readers for supporting anti-immigration policies.) He even removed the cardinal's hat from the Jesuit Louis Billot, one of the twentieth century's greatest theologians, for having expressed opposition to that measure.[12] The same non-ultramontane Pius XI approved the agreement between Mexico's liberal bishops and the Masonic government that was negotiated by the US ambassador, which pressured the Cristeros to lay down their arms. As is well known, the government failed to honor the agreement, executed thousands of Catholic fighters, and upheld most of its anticlerical laws.[13] Within the Church, Pius XI centralized the lay apostolate worldwide into Catholic Action, an organization infiltrated by liberal and secular leanings. He gave it preeminence over all the traditional and autonomous lay apostolate movements such as Third Orders, Marian Sodalities, and the Apostleship of Prayer.

Pope Pius XII was a figure full of contrasts. Before making Fr Augustin Bea, SJ (later created a cardinal) his confessor, he held a traditional position close to that of the heirs of ultramontanism. He condemned emerging progressive errors, particularly in the area of liturgy. Later, inspired by Fr Bea and helped by then-Fr Bugnini, the same Pius XII revolutionized Holy Week's liturgical rites and allowed the use of the historical-critical method (of Protestant origin) for biblical studies.

The one who warned about the danger of an "instrumentalization" of the Magisterium was no anti-ultramontane liberal but a leading figure of the Roman school (the stronghold of what remained of ultramontanism in academia). In an article published in *L'Osservatore Romano* on February 10, 1942, Msgr Pietro Parente denounced "the strange identification of Tradition (source of Revelation) with the living Magisterium of the Church (custodian and interpreter of the Divine Word)."[14] If Tradition and Magisterium are the same, then Tradition ceases being the unchanging deposit of the faith and varies according to the teaching of the reigning pope.

All this proves that blaming ultramontanism for the errors of identifying Tradition with the living Magisterium and imposing uniform thinking in non-dogmatic matters is historically flawed. It was the liberal-progressive current that did these things. Those who claimed to be the heirs of ultramontanism *resisted* the attempts to force them to accept the pope's liberal policy of an extended hand to the world throughout that period.

---

11   "Taming the *Action* – II. The Decree," *Rorate Caeli*, January 21, 2012, https://rorate-caeli.blogspot.com/2012/01/taming-action-ii-decree.html.

12   See Peter J. Bernardi, SJ, "Louis Cardinal Billot, SJ (1846–1931): Thomist, Anti-Modernist, Integralist," *Journal of Jesuit Studies*, 8.4 (2021): 585–616, https://doi.org/10.1163/22141332-08040004.

13   See Brian Van Hove, SJ, "Blood-Drenched Altars," *EWTN*, www.ewtn.com/catholicism/library/blooddrenched-altars-4082.

14   Pietro Parente, "Supr. S. Congr. S. Officii Decretum 4 febr. 1942 – Annotationes," *Periodica de Re Morali, Canonica, Liturgica* 31 (February 1942): 187 [originally published as "Nuove tendenze teologiche," *L'Osservatore Romano*, February 9–10, 1942].

The centralism and authoritarianism now blamed on ultramontanism were not a fruit of Vatican I or its so-called "spirit." They were the fruit of liberalism infiltrating the Church. As Plinio Corrêa de Oliveira explains: "Liberalism is not interested in freedom for what is good. It is solely interested in freedom for evil. When in power, it easily, and even joyfully, restricts the freedom of the good as much as possible. But in many ways, it protects, favors, and promotes freedom for evil."[15] Just as liberals denounced "the Bastille" before the French Revolution but imposed the Terror once in power, Catholic liberals and modernists denounced the supposed authoritarianism of Bl. Pius IX and St Pius X. However, as soon as they seized the highest positions in the Church, they imposed rigid obedience to their world-embracing agenda even in strictly political affairs not involving matters of faith and morals.

Another of Mr Chessman's historical inaccuracies is the supposed alliance between ultramontanism and progressivism at the Second Vatican Council. Giuseppe Angelo Roncalli was no ultramontane but a sympathizer of modernism in his youth. When opening the conciliar assembly, John XXIII excoriated the "prophets of doom," meaning the ultramontanes. All of that Council's historians reckon there was a clash between the progressive and conservative minorities, with the former gradually managing to pull the vast moderate majority to its side. The handful of prelates with an ultramontane spirit, gathered as the *Coetus Internationalis Patrum*, were the ones who worked the most to include in the Council's texts traditional truths opposed to modernist novelties. Bl. Pius IX must have turned in his grave as Vatican II approved the introduction of a "dual" supreme authority in the Church, implicit in the theory of collegiality. How can anyone pretend that "the management of the Council and its subsequent implementation were truly the greatest triumph of ultramontanism"?

There is no doubt that the pontificate of John Paul II was a first attempt to give the Council's novelties a moderate interpretation along the lines of what was later dubbed a "hermeneutic of continuity." His supporters defended this moderate position mainly by appealing to the Roman pontiff's celebrity media image (Fr Chad Ripperger called it "magisterialism"[16]). However, it makes no sense to characterize this moderate offensive as an "ultramontane revival." John Paul II is the author of *Ut Unum Sint*. This encyclical intended "to find a way of exercising the primacy which, while in no way renouncing what is essential to its mission, is nonetheless open to a new situation" by seeking to meet "the ecumenical aspirations of the majority of the Christian communities."[17] This ambition was precisely the opposite of what the ultramontanes achieved at the First Vatican Council: the dogma of the pope's primacy of jurisdiction — which heretical and schismatic Christian communities reject.

---

15   Corrêa de Oliveira, *Revolution and Counter-Revolution*, 52.

16   Ripperger, "Operative Points of View."

17   John Paul II, Encyclical *Ut Unum Sint* (May 25, 1995), no. 95.

As mentioned before, one of the errors in Mr Chessman's article is to attribute the origin of the current crisis of Faith to a purely natural factor: the bureaucratic and centralized exercise of papal authority. The growing centralization of papal power in the hands of non-ultramontane and even anti-ultramontane popes (Leo XIII, Benedict XV, Pius XI, and the conciliar popes) is not the reason why the crisis of Faith worsened in the late nineteenth century and throughout the twentieth century. The crisis stemmed from and was aggravated by the penetration of the world's putrefying liberal miasmas into the Catholic Church. Modernity's mentality was born of the anti-Christian Revolution and started dominating the West's cultural, intellectual, and political life from the Renaissance onward. The Church was pressured to adapt to the new emerging world, mainly from the nineteenth century. "It is not a matter of choosing between the principles of 1789 and the dogmas of the Catholic religion," exclaimed Duke Albert de Broglie, one of the leaders of the liberal Catholic bloc, "but to purify principles with dogmas and make both walk side by side. It is not a question of confronting each other in a duel but of making peace."[18]

Such infiltration of revolutionary errors in the Church reached its climax with modernism, which professes that the dogmas of Faith must adapt to humanity's evolving religious experience and that worship should evolve according to each era's uses and customs. Pius IX and Pius X issued explicit condemnations against any attempt to reconcile the Church with modern errors. They urged Catholics to courageously confront what St Pius X called "the synthesis of all heresies." This opposition made them models of an ultramontane papacy. However, their successors were less energetic and even conciliatory. With John XXIII and the opening of the Second Vatican Council, the ultramontane, anti-liberal position of combat against modernity and its errors was officially abandoned and replaced with an attitude of benevolent dialogue with and submission to the modern world.

Like the twentieth-century modernists, Pope Francis openly seeks to adapt the Church to "anthropological and cultural changes." According to him, the divine impulse present in humanity's progress justifies today's changes. He attributes these impulses and new dynamics in human action to divine action: "God manifests himself in historical revelation, in history. . . . God is in history, in the processes,"[19] he asserts. Eugenio Scalfari, the agnostic founder of *la Repubblica*, was right when he titled his article on *Laudato Si'*: "Francis, the Pope-Prophet Who Meets Modernity."[20] The applause of modern leaders for the present pope's statements and initiatives confirms that assessment.

---

18   Albert de Broglie, *Questions de religion et d'histoire* (Paris: Michel Lévy Frères, 1860), 2:199.

19   Antonio Spadaro, SJ, "A Big Heart Open to God: An Interview with Pope Francis," *America*, September 30, 2013, www.americamagazine.org/faith/2013/09/30/big-heart-open-god-interview-pope-francis.

20   Eugenio Scalfari, "Francesco, papa profeta che incontra la modernità," *la Repubblica*, July 1, 2015, www.repubblica.it/cultura/2015/07/01/news/francesco_papa_profeta_che_incontra_la_modernita_-118048516/.

The current pope and some previous ones have abused papal authority to advance the modernist agenda of reconciling the Church to the revolutionary world. This does not make them ultramontane popes. The careerist prelates who ran their dioceses as mediocre public servants and ignored the infiltration of modernist errors among the faithful — errors with which they sympathized — were not ultramontanes either. The clerics and faithful who espoused modernist errors did not do so because of a false notion of obedience. They did it because they were imbued with the liberal and revolutionary spirit of the world.

During this long apostasy from the faith, a small ultramontane minority of clergy and laity strove to counter the infiltration of heresy and defend traditional Church teaching. If some of them did not do more or even shrank from the fight, it was because of cowardice, not an excessive ultramontane reverence for the papacy. Blaming ultramontanism for the current crisis of the Church and ignoring the fundamental role of modernism in its gestation and journey toward paroxysm is like blaming a dam for being unable to resist a flood while exonerating the foaming and churning waters that overran it.

Ultramontanes have always admired and respected the hierarchical order in the universe, society, and the Church, especially in the papacy, the highest authority on earth. The same love for the hierarchical order led them to venerate and obey the Creator and Sovereign Lord of the world and the Divine Founder of the Church. They thus reject any error or transgression of the divine Law: "one must obey God rather than men." Because of their well-ordered love of the principle of authority, those who most love the papacy are also better prepared to staunchly, albeit respectfully, resist any deviation from Tradition. No one had a more ardent love for the primacy of Peter than St Paul, who "went up to Jerusalem to meet Cephas" (Gal 1:18) and returned there fourteen years later to expound the Gospel he preached to the Gentiles "in order not to run in vain" (Gal 2:2). No one, however, was firmer than St Paul in "resisting [Peter] to his face" "because he was blameworthy" (Gal 2:11).

In the short run, the proposal to "resize" the papacy to avoid abuse could lessen the problems of conscience created by a series of popes who have promoted the self-demolition of the Church. However, in the long run, it would help Church self-demolishers, bent on destroying or at least weakening the Rock on which she is built. Paradoxically, both ultra-progressives and new "anti-ultramontane traditionalists" propose to stop calling the pope the "Vicar of Christ," as did the editor of *Crisis Magazine*. He claimed that this title lends itself to excessive veneration if applied to the pope alone, whereas it could also apply to all bishops.

Paradoxically, an article denouncing "ultramontane totalitarianism" first appeared on the blog of a society established to honor St Hugh of Cluny. He was the great adviser to popes St Leo IX, Nicholas II, and especially the great St Gregory VII. The latter, his Cluniac confrere, raised papal authority to an apex.

He reestablished the Church's internal discipline with the Gregorian reform. Concerning the investiture of bishops and abbots, he victoriously affirmed papal supremacy over civil authority. St Hugh was with St Gregory VII at the famous episode in Canossa, which revolutionary historians consider the starting point of ultramontanism.

Undiplomatic attitudes by St Leo IX's legate angered the Greeks and favored the Eastern Schism. The scandalous lifestyles of Renaissance popes angered the Germans and favored Luther's heresy. Today, Pope Francis's blatantly erroneous teachings and egregiously unpastoral actions must not arouse emotional anger in his victims. While Catholics may legitimately harbor doctrinal reservations about and resist a wayward occupant of the throne of Peter, they must never succumb to reservations about the papacy itself. These are always illegitimate. Let us imitate the French monarchists during the Restoration, who, despite Louis XVIII's liberal policy—which favored Bonapartists and republicans and persecuted defenders of the throne—shouted, *"Vive le roi, quand même!"* ("Long live the king anyway!").

The papacy's present eclipse is probably the most dramatic in the Church's two-thousand-year history. The crisis requires us to increase our love for this holiest of earthly institutions. Jesus Christ established it as the keystone of His Church and endowed it with the power of the keys, the most tremendous and sacred power binding Heaven and Earth.

21

The Synthesis of Ultramontanism and Progressivism[1]

STUART CHESSMAN

I AM GRATEFUL TO MR JOSÉ A. URETA FOR HIS RESPONSE (chapter 20) to my essay "Ultramontanism: Its Life and Death" (chapter 19). Here I should like to indicate why I still disagree with his position.

My brief overview of ultramontanism attempted to describe what occurred in historical fact. I wrote of ultramontanism as a system of governance of the Church that had achieved its basic form under Pius IX. Its first characteristic was the centralization in the papacy of all authority in governance, theology, liturgy, etc., with rights of intervention even on the local level. Ultramontanist practice recharacterized the role of the clergy of the Church as bureaucrats of a vast administrative structure. Any criticism of the hierarchy and especially of the pope was prohibited. The scope of *de facto* papal infallibility increasingly extended to cover even the day-to-day decisions of the pope. Authority and obedience to it became overriding principles of the Church. Finally, Catholics began to develop a personal relationship with the pope as a supreme spiritual leader.

These characteristics of the actual practice of the ultramontane system were not necessarily fully supported by theology or canon law. They developed unevenly and over the decades. I am grateful to Mr Ureta for a reference that shows that at least a minority had perceived theological difficulties with ultramontanist practice early on:

> In an article published in *L'Osservatore Romano* on February 10, 1942, Msgr Pietro Parente denounced "the strange identification of Tradition (source of Revelation) with the living Magisterium of the Church (custodian and interpreter of the Divine Word)."

In the same vein, hadn't Jaroslav Pelikan (certainly not a witness hostile to Catholicism) wondered in 1959 whether "the magisterium has virtually suspended the authority of tradition"?[2]

Mr Ureta, however, seems to define ultramontanism much more narrowly than I do—as a special subcategory of Catholic ecclesiastical politics and thought. He seems to admit as ultramontanists only those popes and prelates who espoused policies with which he agrees, especially those antagonistic to social and intellectual

---

1 First published at the blog of the Society of St Hugh of Cluny on February 16, 2022.
2 Jaroslav Pelikan, *The Riddle of Roman Catholicism* (New York: Abingdon Press, 1959), 83.

revolution. This produces the strange result that, for Mr Ureta, only two popes, Pius IX and Pius X, seem to have been "true" ultramontanes! Thus the ultramontanes (using Mr Ureta's definition) appear to have been singularly unsuccessful in convincing even their superiors in Rome of the merits of their policies. All the other popes of the last 170 years are described by Mr Ureta as non- or even anti-ultramontanes.

Further, it seems these "authentic" Roman ultramontanes were utterly unable to argue effectively against the progressives at Vatican II. Regardless of their at times eloquent objections to what was unfolding before their eyes, they all conformed to the postconciliar changes — with the conspicuous exception of Archbishop Lefebvre. Thus in their majority, they testified in true ultramontane fashion to the priority of obedience to papal authority and the preservation of external unity over their doctrinal and liturgical convictions.

I also find a lack of historical awareness in Mr Ureta's remarks. So, for example, he triumphantly points to St Gregory VII as a pope who "raised papal authority to an apex" and "victoriously affirmed papal supremacy over civil authority." But the world of Gregory VII was not at all that of Pius IX — the historical context was entirely different! Gregory VII reigned as Christendom was reaching its first maturity. By Pius IX's day, Christendom had already collapsed. Under Gregory VII, the Church was beginning to consolidate her temporal power. Ultramontanism crystallized in 1870 — precisely when the pope's temporal power disappeared. Now Gregory VII sought both much less and much more than the nineteenth-century ultramontanes. He had no idea of imposing some kind of centralized administrative regime governing all aspects of the Church's life (which in any case would have been physically impossible in the eleventh century). For example, Mr Ureta's own reference to Cluny calls to mind that in the tenth and eleventh centuries the liturgical restoration of the Church proceeded on its course entirely outside of Rome. (By the way, Gregory VII was most probably not a "confrere" of St Hugh of Cluny.)

On the other hand, as Mr Ureta points out, Gregory VII fought not only for the freedom of the Church from secular control — laudably enough — but also for the supremacy of the Church over secular authority. Those latter claims — and the spiritual weapons utilized to enforce them — had problematic aspects. The Church has avoided raising them in more recent eras. And I don't think that today anyone sane would want to return temporal authority to the Church. The Vatican's management of the limited secular affairs remaining to it is just as abysmal as the exercise of its spiritual responsibilities.

I never said that ultramontanism was the root of all evils in the Church. Clearly, the loss of faith that spread from the eighteenth century onward has been the Church's main challenge. Vatican II is critical both as the product of that loss of faith and an immense accelerant of it. Finally, the formless liturgy of the conciliar Church is both a further symptom and cause of Catholic decline.

What I *did* write was that the essentially defensive regime of ultramontanism had achieved mixed results even during its heyday of 1870–1958. I described how the overthrow of most aspects of Catholic practice and liturgical life during and after Vatican II was inconceivable without ultramontane liturgical centralization and the habits of absolute deference to authority. Further, I pointed out that the conservative heroes John Paul II and Benedict XVI had been unable to do more than preserve the "great façade" of unity despite relentless pro-papalist propaganda.

Finally, with the regime of Pope Francis, we witness the synthesis of extreme ultramontane centralization with progressive revolutionary content. Just in the last year, Pope Francis has intensified his control of the Knights of Malta. He has personally intervened to endorse a small movement in the United States (New Ways Ministry) that had been subject over the years to various ecclesiastical censures. He has similarly endorsed one political figure (President Biden) who was potentially coming into conflict with the United States Catholic hierarchy over his aggressive support of abortion. Irrespective of their formal ecclesiastical position, confidantes of Francis like Cardinals Cupich (Chicago) and Hollerich (Luxembourg) by reason of their blatant political connection enjoy an inordinate influence in the Church. Finally and most extraordinarily, in *Traditionis Custodes* Francis has condemned an entire sector of the Catholic clergy, religious, and laity to second-class status, parochial exclusion, and eventual elimination. To carry out this mission of annihilation, Francis has endorsed rules implementing the anti-traditionalist campaign even on the parish level. All these initiatives are buttressed by ultramontane acts and rhetoric — from the canonization of the conciliar popes to the positing of external Church unity as an absolute goal, mantled in grandiose claims of "magisterial authority."

Yet while the scope of Francis's papal power seems to grow endlessly, in fact the far greater power of the left and the secular establishment confines it within narrow limits. The Church is increasingly playing the role of a mere agency of the secular power elite of the West on matters such as Covid-19, interreligious relations, and "migrants." The German church is proceeding on its progressive synodal path regardless of what the Vatican says. All Francis can do is talk of unity and attempt to co-opt the German synodal ideas and rhetoric. The same is true for the Church on the local level. For example, in our area, the LGBT parishes of Manhattan proceed on their chosen path — publicly and explicitly — no matter what Cardinal Dolan says. In the Bridgeport diocese, an attempt by the principal of an exclusive girls school to restrain pro-Planned Parenthood manifestations (with Bishop Caggiano's backing) ended in total capitulation — by the Church. Thus, the great growth of bureaucratic ultramontane power coincides with the greatest weakness of the Church in the face of both secular society and the Church's own internal progressives.

Catholic traditionalism had in fact coexisted within the Church alongside the Vatican II establishment, and did so even for about eight years of Francis's reign.

For hadn't Pope Benedict with *Summorum Pontificum* summoned Catholics to set aside their earlier resentments and animosities in the interest of liturgical peace? This was the course followed by most traditionalists. Indeed, some went further and in order to ingratiate themselves with bishops and mainstream religious orders were willing to disguise and censor their own opinions.

Yet Francis has now revoked that peace. Moreover, beyond the liturgical realm, he has either made or is fostering drastic changes to fundamental Catholic practices and even the basic rules of morality. All of this is justified as an exercise of papal authority—resting on the arbitrary decision of Francis. And this is largely accepted, at least publicly and at least by the clergy. Yet, for others, a stark choice now presents itself. One must choose between the will of Francis and, not just traditionalism, but even Catholicism as such. And really, between the current papal regime and one's sanity. For as in any totalitarian regime, not even the rules of logic are allowed to restrict the arbitrary will of absolute authority. As a Francis favorite, Cardinal Jean-Claude Hollerich (a Jesuit drawing on Asian "wisdom") puts it:

> The Japanese do not think as in the European logic of opposites. If we say a thing is black, it means it is not white. The Japanese, on the other hand, say: "It is white, but perhaps also black." In Japan opposites can be combined without changing the point of view.[3]

It is in this disturbing context that I feel compelled to reexamine the role of ultramontanism in the Church.

---

3   Sandro Magister, "If the Conclave Wants a Second Francis, Here Is the Name and the Program," *Settimo Cielo*, February 10, 2022.

22

The Failure of the Ultramontanist Hermeneutic of Continuity[1]

VICTOR CLEMENS OLDENDORF

I
T IS RATHER DIFFICULT TO UNDERSTAND THE MOTIVES
that induced the Renovamen publishing house to present the book *Tradition
and Living Magisterium* at the end of last year [2021], of all times, as a new
publication, namely, the German translation (*Tradition und lebendiges Lehramt*) of a
text whose Portuguese original—as can be concluded from internal criteria—must
have appeared around 2007.[2] Its author is Bishop Fernando Rifan, who presides
as Ordinary of the Apostolic Administration of the Holy Curé of Ars, whose territory coincides with that of the Brazilian diocese of Campos, and to whom the
liturgical books of the Roman Rite as it was in force in 1962 (according to *Traditionis
Custodes*, we must be formally correct and precise) were granted as a proper rite.

Apart from a new preface by the German Cardinal Gerhard Müller and an
addendum on *Traditionis Custodes* spanning not even three pages, no updating of
the text has been attempted.

Thus, at its best, the book is a testimony and document of the mood and
expectations of conservative and traditionalist circles in the phase of the beginning
of the Ratzinger pontificate (that was a long time ago . . .). Three examples may
illustrate this: on page 20, there is talk of Pope Benedict XVI having "just" given
"worldwide freedom to the traditional form of celebrating Mass" with *Summorum
Pontificum*, while in fact it is Pope Francis who has just taken back this freedom
worldwide with *Traditionis Custodes*. Referring to the 1990 Instruction *Donum*

---

1   The following book review, which appeared in German at *kathnews.de* on January 4, 2022 and
was then published in English at *OnePeterFive* on January 12, 2022, is illuminating for many reasons. In
describing the oddity of a 2021 translation of a work published around 2007 *yet not updated* to take into
account what has happened between 2007 and 2021, the reviewer paints a portrait of the serious internal
flaws of the "hermeneutic of continuity" school, which still wishes to pretend—even after a decade of
Pope Francis—that some kind of Hegelian synthesis of preconciliar and postconciliar remains possible,
and that the instrument of its accomplishment is an all-powerful papacy. One wonders what it would
take to awaken such people from their pleasant dreams. One wonders how soon
the bishop and clergy of Campos will be asked by Rome to "accompany" their flocks to the so-called
"unique expression of the *lex orandi* of the Roman Rite." If sustained by a theology as flimsy as Bishop
Rifan's, Campos will fall like a house of cards in a brisk wind. Moreover, Bishop Rifan, born in 1950,
will soon turn 75. Unless something changes dramatically in Rome, Campos may not see a successor
consecrated according to the old pontifical, nor a man who is of the same mind as Rifan about the value
of the authentic *lex orandi* of the Roman Church. The version of the review presented here, which differs
in some respects from the German original, has received approval in *forma specifica* from the author. — *Ed.*

2   The publication year for the German first print run is 2022, but the book was actually
delivered at the end of 2021.

Veritatis, page 42 states that it "recently recalled" the need for a fundamental loyalty to the Magisterium. If one did not know that Cardinal Ranjith has been archbishop of Colombo since the summer of 2009 and, by the way, opportunistically has long since discontinued—or, at least, no longer articulates—any commitment in favor of the traditional liturgy or of a tradition-oriented *ars celebrandi* in postconciliar worship, one would think after reading (p. 54) that he had "recently" been appointed Secretary of the Congregation for Divine Worship. However, that was the case on December 10, 2006.

It is a great shortcoming in a publication if such things are not updated and left unremarked on in a translation of whatever book that is so much delayed. What is frequently done in other contexts could have been done here, too: the translator might at least have included supplementary footnotes to indicate the changed circumstances.

ANACHRONISTIC IN SEVERAL RESPECTS

These more external weaknesses of the German version, however, do not constitute the most serious deficiency of *Tradition and the Living Magisterium*. For not only does it give the impression that one continues to be in a climate of hope for a "reform of the reform" or for the hermeneutics of "reform in continuity" in the interpretation of the Second Vatican Council, as presented by Benedict XVI at the Christmas audience on December 22, 2005 to the cardinals—no, even the most positive optimist sees by now that these approaches were never concretely and effectively implemented even during the past pontificate of Benedict XVI and are now, in the area of liturgy since (at the latest) *Traditionis Custodes*, unmistakably erased.

CORRECT PERCEPTIONS AND ARGUMENTS

This is not to say that every argument or observation of Bishop Rifan is false or mistaken. For example, there is undoubtedly still a traditionalist tendency to want to surpass one another in holding a stricter or more extreme position, or in taking up an ever-older version of the Tridentine rite. Likewise, there is a real danger of radicalization and embitterment that can go so far as to occasion the abandonment of any practice of the faith or even the loss of the faith altogether. However, it is questionable whether one can, as Rifan does, accuse anyone who, for example, holds or considers the position of sedevacantism or sedeprivationism as a possible theological position (Rifan does not differentiate between the two variants) of being extreme or radical simply on this account.

Sedevacantism is a theological theory and opinion that differs from the present position of both the Fraternity of St Peter and the Society of St Pius X. It is a different position, a different attempt to understand, explain, and deal on a day-to-day basis with the enormous problem of the postconciliar crisis that has existed since Vatican II—a crisis all Catholic traditionalists agree exists; an attempt, we may say, to solve it above all in practical terms. Sedevacantism and sedeprivationism are thus not automatically extreme or fanatical, and there are some theologians, especially in the USA, who hold these positions in an objective, moderate, and even conciliatory manner, without any danger of embitterment. It is not my purpose here to either endorse or critique such views.

ONLY THE CONCLUSIONS DIFFER

Rather, I emphasize the point for the reason that Bishop Rifan conspicuously advocates the same magisterial positivism and follows the same ultramontanist narrowing of a certain current of nineteenth-century neoscholastic theology that remained a guiding force in Rome until about the middle of the last century and, in our day, enables the sedevacantists, who follow it out in a particularly stringent manner, to reach their conclusions. While the sedes think that, because of their ultramontanist presuppositions, the postconciliar popes could not be legitimate popes or, in any case, could not exercise the authority of a legitimate pope in an effective and binding way, Bishop Rifan, with a certain overextension or almost apotheosis of the pope (as was not unusual in the nineteenth century), thinks that the postconciliar popes are legitimate. And thus, because they are popes, he thinks there can be nothing to object to in the Second Vatican Council and in the postconciliar magisterium as well as in the liturgical reform of Paul VI.

In this sense, Rifan approvingly and exclusively quotes preconciliar theologians up to the immediate eve of the Second Vatican Council, who, however, obviously do not know and are not engaging with the nature and extent of Paul VI's post-conciliar liturgical reform and, possibly due to ultramontanist bias, could never have *imagined* a development initiated and authorized by the pope such as the one that took place during and after Vatican II.

On the basis of experience since then, it is clear how important it is to under-stand not only the jurisdictional primacy of the pope but also his personal, indi-vidual infallibility in the context of the larger tradition and theological endeavor that preceded the First Vatican Council for centuries and not just in the immediate run-up to it. This point must be made, of course, in response not only to Rifan, but to many others who, with sometimes quite contradictory consequences, tend to take refuge in a supposedly ideal world of the pontificates of Pius XII or Pius X.

WHY WAS AND IS THE TRADITIONAL LITURGY ADHERED TO AT ALL?

Another weakness of such formalistic, positivistic argumentation as presented by Rifan is that it ignores the fact that the Roman Liturgy, in the form given to it by Paul VI, is *not* usually celebrated on the basis of its *editio typica*; and not even in this case — in its Latin version, at a high altar, with male altar servers and the classical form of receiving Communion — would the "renewed" rite of Mass be flawless. Moreover, the liturgy that actually exists out in the world is very different from what might be called the "theoretical liturgy" of Paul VI. Such a discrepancy *never* existed with regard to the preconciliar liturgical books that the preconciliar voices to whom Rifan refers had taken for their object of reflection, and whose judgment he now simply transfers to Paul VI's liturgical reform of 1969.

Incidentally, if the author were truly consistent, he would have to concede that there was consequently no room to privilege the old liturgy or to retain it on the basis of a preference. In that case, he should have long since moved his Apostolic Administration to adopt, after all, the *editiones typicae* of the postconciliar liturgical books (even if we might say, for the sake of argument, in their most conservative interpretation and employment in worship). And anyone who agrees or does not strongly disagree with Rifan's papalist reasoning would also have to accept the same conclusion for himself.

Actually, he would have to open himself up even further if he were to agree with Cardinal Müller, who writes in the Preface: "To a genuinely Catholic mind, it must seem absurd that a dispute over dogmatic truth should be ignited by the two forms of the one Mass, which differ only in some external rites, including the direction of celebration and the language of celebration in Latin or the vernacular, which do not belong to their substance."

This preface was already out of date when it was penned on November 4, 2021, because, according to *Traditionis Custodes*, there are no longer two forms of the Roman Rite, and, before *Summorum Pontificum*, there were many variants of Gregorian-Latin liturgy in the Western Church, but not an "ordinary" and an "extraordinary" use of the Roman Rite that differed as much from each other as do the Roman Tridentine and the postconciliar Pauline Rite, the latter of which is now established by positivism as the sole expression of the *lex orandi* in the Roman Rite.[3]

AN ABSTRACT-THEORETICAL INTERPRETATION OF THE COUNCIL AS A FORM OF DENIAL OF REALITY

Bishop Rifan is similarly out of touch with reality, not only in his almost compulsive pressure to justify himself with regard to the postconciliar liturgical reform—from which, however, his Apostolic Administration has so far remained exempt in principle—but also in his handling of the texts of the Second Vatican Council. What is the use, one might ask, of the possible application of a hermeneutic of continuity supported here or there by documents of the Magisterium, when in reality (as Rifan says) "the ecclesiastical public has allowed itself to be impressed in part [*recte*: dominantly] by modernist interpretations or Protestant expressions of opinion," and when these interpretations continue to be the ones that practically prevail? It doesn't seem to have much more use than a theoretical rite of Paul VI, as we have sketched it above, when it barely exists anywhere—and which, moreover, would only hide for a time the losses and deficiencies that are still inherent in it, compared to the Gregorian rite codified after the Council of Trent.[4]

---

3   See Fr. Laurent Jestin, ICKSP, "The End of Conciliation Efforts," *Rorate Caeli*, January 10, 2022.

4   It would also be consistent here to distinguish the original, somewhat moderate, liturgical reform up until 1965 from the subsequent, more radical Pauline reform that crystallized in the missal of 1969.

A SINGLE POSITIVE ASPECT OF THE BOOK AND A POSSIBLE POSITIVE EFFECT

Of course, the Magisterium is alive (inasmuch as those who can wield it are alive), and one advantage of the book reviewed here, albeit very critically, is when it speaks in its title of a "living Magisterium"[5] and not of "the living character of Tradition."[6] The Tradition has stability, and those who exercise the Magisterium can fail in their non-definitive judgments. Thus, anyone who recognizes the incumbent popes and bishops as legitimate can, in principle, strongly criticize what they have taught and decreed from a certain point in time, and basically fade it out or ignore it for himself and his environment.[7]

Yet if Bishop Rifan were right, any traditionalist reaction to the Second Vatican Council and especially to the new rite of Mass of 1969 would have been illegitimate from the beginning. Indeed, the occurrence of such a crisis as the traditionalists perceive would have been excluded from the outset by the assistance of the Holy Spirit.

That nearly nothing is excluded and impossible in the Church can be seen now (at the latest) with Pope Francis and *Traditionis Custodes*; after all, the pope with his *motu proprio* simply endeavors to return us to the original situation immediately after Vatican II and after the introduction of the Pauline *Novus Ordo Missae*.

If the book *Tradition and the Living Magisterium*, in the form in which it is presented in a German translation at the present moment, is to have any meaning at all for the Church and to be of any use, it will be by inducing the realization that rolling backwards accomplishes nothing. One can neither remain mentally in the pontificate of Benedict XVI and in the projections and hopes that were not fulfilled in that pontificate, nor roll backwards into the immediate postconciliar period with all that Pope Francis wants to do and prescribe, since the exaggerated magisterial and papal optimism characteristic of Paul VI's era was only a rather short-term phase and tendency, already breaking down in his day, and all the more in ours.

The experience of the immediate postconciliar period and the adherence that spontaneously arose especially for the liturgical tradition under attack intuitively proved, already at that time, that this ultramontanist current is inapplicable and unable to carry on the tradition. This hard-won insight remains valid now and in the future. Possibly it even becomes clearer thanks to the contrast of Bishop Rifan's naïve remarks; otherwise, the reading of his book would be dispensable, given how weak and disappointing was its statement on *Traditionis Custodes*.

---

5   Bishop Rifan also correctly refers here (*Tradition und lebendiges Lehramt*, 33, n19) to the Second Vatican Council and *Dei Verbum* 10.

6   As occurred, spinning the Council text further, in the motu proprio *Ecclesia Dei*, where in 4 and 5b there are unsustainable references to *Dei Verbum* 8.

7   Cf. the well-chosen contrast between a "signpost" and a "companion": *Tradition und lebendiges Lehramt*, 27ff.

⟨ 23 ⟩
Papolatry and Ultramontanism Are Not the Same[1]

ROBERTO DE MATTEI

I N RECENT MONTHS, A DEBATE ON ULTRAMONTANISM has opened on *Rorate Caeli* and elsewhere, with interesting interventions by Stuart Chessman, Clemens Victor Oldendorf, and José Antonio Ureta.[2] I know these authors personally and I have esteem and friendship for them, but to be faithful to the Latin adage *Amicus Plato, sed magis amica veritas* (Plato is my friend, but truth is a greater friend), I will stick to what seems to me to be the truth.

In this respect I must say that I share the doctrinal position of José Antonio Ureta, although perhaps what divides Ureta and me from the other authors is above all a semantic problem, relating to the use of the term "ultramontanism." This is why I would like to explain, on a historical level, who the ultramontanes were and why I consider myself an admirer and intellectual heir to them.

The term "ultramontanism" was created and used with negative connotations in the nineteenth century, to designate the faithful attitude of Catholics "beyond the Alps" to the doctrines and institutions of the papacy.[3] Ultramontanes were opposed to the doctrines of Gallicanism, Febronianism, and Josephinism, which advocated for the restriction of the power of the papacy in favor of that of the episcopate. More generally, ultramontanes fought against liberal Catholics who rejected opposition to the French Revolution and tried to establish forms of accommodation with the modern world. Exponents of this ultramontane or counterrevolutionary school were the French political philosopher Count Joseph de Maistre (1753–1821) and the Spanish statesman Juan Donoso Cortés, Marquis of Valdegamas (1809–1853) and many others.

Joseph de Maistre is author of the book *Du Pape* (1819), a work which had hundreds of reprints, and which anticipated the dogma of papal infallibility. Donoso Cortés denounced the absolute antagonism between modern society and Christianity in his *Ensayo sobre el Catolicismo, el liberalismo y el socialismo* (Madrid, 1851). I recall also the good influence during the nineteenth century of the monumental twenty-eight-volume *Histoire universelle de l'Église catholique* by René François Rohrbacher (1789–1856), which went through seven editions

---

1   First published at *Rorate Caeli* on February 10, 2022.
2   Found in chapters 19, 22, 17, and 20, respectively.
3   Fr Richard Costigan, SJ, explained this concept well: *Rohrbacher and the Ecclesiology of Ultramontanism* (Rome: Gregorian University, 1980), xiv–xxvi.

between 1842 and 1901 and was translated into Italian, English, and German. This work influenced nineteenth-century Catholic thought no less than the works of Joseph de Maistre and Juan Donoso Cortés.

The struggle between ultramontane Catholics and liberal Catholics developed above all in France in the second half of the nineteenth century. The champions of the liberal front were Count Charles Renée de Montalembert (1810–1870), with his magazine *Le Correspondant*, and Félix-Antoine Philibert Dupanloup (1802–1878), bishop of Orléans. The ultramontane leaders were Cardinal Louis Pie (1815–1880), bishop of Poitiers, called "the hammer of liberalism," and Louis Veuillot (1813–1883) with his journal *L'Univers*. Pope Pius IX supported the ultramontane movement and condemned Catholic liberalism with the encyclical *Quanta Cura* and the *Syllabus Errorum* or summary of the principal errors of the time published on December 8, 1864, the tenth anniversary of the promulgation of the doctrine of the Immaculate Conception. Bishop Pie, Veuillot, and Donoso Cortés were consulted during the development of these documents. From that point on, the *Syllabus* would become the manifesto of "ultramontane" or "integral" Catholics against the relativism of liberal Catholics.

Five years after, when Pius IX announced the Vatican Council, liberal Catholics decided to come out into the open. The first to engage battle was Dupanloup, who published a short work on infallibility, saying that it was "inopportune" to proclaim it. In Germany Ignaz von Döllinger (1799–1890), rector of the University of Munich, accused Pope Pius IX of preparing "an ecclesiastical revolution" which would impose infallibility as a dogma. In England the theses of Döllinger and Dupanloup were spread by Lord John Emerich Acton (1834–1902).

The ultramontane Catholics fought for the approbation of the dogma of the primacy of Peter and of papal infallibility. In the vanguard was Cardinal Henry Edward Manning (1808–1892), archbishop of Westminster, who occupied a position in the Council comparable to that of St Cyril at the Council of Ephesus. A few years earlier, together with Ignaz von Senestrey (1818–1906), bishop of Regensburg, he had made a vow, drawn up by Fr Matteo Liberatore (1810–1892), to do everything in his power to obtain the definition of papal infallibility. They were flanked by eminent personalities, such as the Jesuit father, later cardinal Johann Baptist Franzelin (1816–1886), papal theologian in the Council, Dom Prosper Guéranger (1805–1875), the founder of the French Congregation of Solesmes which reestablished Benedictine monastic life in France, and St Anthony Marie Claret (1807–1870), archbishop of Trajanópolis, spiritual leader of the Spanish bishops, the "the Pope's Imperial Guard" at Vatican I.[4]

The liberals, echoing the conciliarist and Gallican theses, held that the authority of the Church did not reside in the Pontiff alone, but in the pope united to the bishops, and judged the dogma of infallibility to be erroneous, or at least inopportune. Claret was one of the four hundred Fathers who on January 28,

---

4   See Letter to Mother María Antonia París, Rome, June 17, 1870.

1870, signed a petition asking for the definition of the dogma of infallibility, as being not only opportune, but *sub omni respectu ineluctabiliter necessaria*, and on May 31, 1870, delivered a moving address in defense of papal infallibility.

Bl. Pius IX, on December 8, 1870, with the constitution *Pastor Aeternus*, defined the dogmas of the primacy of Peter and of papal infallibility (*DH* 3050-75). Today, these dogmas are for us a precious benchmark on which to found true devotion to the Chair of Peter.

Liberal Catholics were defeated by the First Vatican Council, but after a century they became the protagonists and winners of Vatican II. Gallicans, Jansenists, and Febronianists openly held that the structure of the Church must be democratic, led from the bottom, by priests and bishops, of whom the pope would be only a representative. The constitution *Lumen Gentium*, promulgated by the Second Vatican Council, was (like all the Council documents) an ambiguous one, which recognized these tendencies, but without bringing them to their final outcomes.

On December 9, 1962, Fr Yves Congar (1904-1995) wrote in his diary: "I believe that all that is done to convert Italy from its ultramontane political, ecclesiological, and devotional attitude toward the Gospel will also be a gain for the universal Church. So, at this time, I have accepted many commitments in this regard."[5] The Dominican theologian added: "Ultramontanism really exists .... Rome's colleges, universities, and schools distil all of it in different doses: the highest, almost deadly one, is the dose currently being administered at the Lateran [University]"; "miserable ultramontane ecclesiology," Congar writes again on February 5.[6] He regarded his struggle against the theologians of the "Roman school" as a "mission." The theological Roman school was the heir of the ultramontane movement: Cardinal Alfredo Ottaviani, Cardinal Ernesto Ruffini, but also Archbishop Marcel Lefebvre were representative of this school.

Michael Davies (1936-2004), who attributes part of the conciliar disaster to a false papal obedience, reminds us that Cardinal Manning said: "Infallibility is not a quality inherent in any person, but an assistance attached to an office."[7] The First Vatican Council doesn't teach that the charism of infallibility is always present in the Vicar of Christ, but simply that it is not absent in the exercise of his office in its supreme form, that is, when the Sovereign Pontiff teaches as universal shepherd, *ex cathedra*, in matters of faith and morals.[8] Michael Davies himself can be considered an ultramontane traditionalist, like all those who resisted Vatican II and the Novus Ordo with respect and love for the papacy. This is the position I uphold in my book *Love for the Papacy and Filial Resistance to the Pope in the History of Church*.[9]

---

5 *Diario del Concilio 1960-1966*, in 2 vols. (Cinisello Balsamo: San Paolo, 2005), vol. 1, p. 308.
6 Respectively, vol. 1, p. 201; vol. 2, p. 20.
7 In *Pope John's Council* (Chawleigh, Chulmleigh: Augustine Publishing Company, 1977), 175.
8 *Pope John's Council*, 175-76.
9 New York: Angelico Press, 2019.

In 1875, in their opposition to Chancellor Bismarck, the German bishops declared that the Magisterium of the pope and bishops "is restricted to the contents of the infallible Magisterium of the Church in general, and it is restricted to the contents of the Holy Scripture and Tradition" (*DH* 3116). Pope Pius IX gave his full support to this declaration with his letter *Mirabilis Illa Constantia* to the bishops of Germany on March 4, 1875 (*DH* 3117). I agree entirely with this ultramontane statement which can constitute the basis of a respectful resistance to the unjust decisions of the Holy See.

"Papolatry" and "Magisterialism" were born after the Second Vatican Council: an extreme cult of the person of the pope that developed in parallel to the humiliation of the papacy. This has nothing to do with ultramontanism.

I hope I have explained why I am proud to be an ultramontane and why I am worried about the criticisms of ultramontanism.

⟨ 24 ⟩

Defending Ultramontanism[1]

JOSÉ A. URETA

T HE EDITOR OF *ONEPETERFIVE* WAS KIND ENOUGH TO invite submissions regarding the origin of the excessive submissiveness of many Catholics to Pope Francis's manifestly erroneous teachings and measures. He says such attitude stems from "a false spirit of Vatican I" and what he calls *hyperüberultramontanism*. This seemingly humorous expression appears to be an antipolemical hedge. Yet the masthead of the article displays a pontifical tiara superimposed with the series heading "Ultramontanism and the False Spirit of Vatican I." The absence here of the precautionary prefix *hyperüber-* was perhaps an oversight, but it is revealing nonetheless.

I accept the invitation and begin by saying that I agree with Peter Kwasniewski's observation in a recent article that restricting oneself to the "Magisterium of the moment" is contrary to Church teaching.[2] It means ignoring Scripture and Tradition and accepting non-infallible novelties from the current pope and bishops as the only way to know the truth. I fully agree with his use of *magisterial* and *hyperpapalist* to designate those Catholics who adopt this adulterated obedience. While he used "ultramontanism" to refer to such Catholics in the past,[3] he did not do so now.

Last year, I wrote three articles to address the traditionalist mischaracterization of ultramontanism.[4] In them, I demonstrated three things:

(1) the future Cardinal Edouard Pie, the most prominent leader of the French ultramontanes during the First Vatican Council, had a very balanced concept of papal monarchy and the limits of the Roman pontiff's magisterial and governing authority;

(2) the abusive demand that the faithful adhere unrestrictedly to a reigning pope's non-infallible teachings and acts of government came from the Liberal current during the papacy of Leo XIII, who demanded that Monarchist French Catholics accept their country's secular Masonic Republic; and,

(3) the popes closest to the Liberal current—Benedict XV, Pius XI, and the conciliar popes—aggravated that abuse throughout the twentieth century. The process culminated with the current pontiff's totalitarianism, which led Henry Sire to call him, quite adroitly, *The Dictator Pope*.

---

1   First published at *OnePeterFive* on June 20, 2022.
2   See "The Three Pillars of Christianity," in Kwasniewski, *Bound by Truth*, 3–10.
3   See, for example, his essay "My Journey from Ultramontanism to Catholicism," in *The Road from Hyperpapalism to Catholicism: Rethinking the Papacy in a Time of Ecclesial Disintegration*, vol. 1, pp. 1–27.
4   See chapters 17, 18, and 20.

In his turn, Prof. Roberto de Mattei wrote an article providing the context of the controversy between ultramontanes on the one hand and Gallicans and Liberals on the other.[5] He showed how Bl. Pius IX fully supported ultramontanism. He cited two examples showing how balanced the ultramontane current was. The first was a declaration by German bishops. They pointed out how the Magisterium of the pope and bishops "is restricted to the contents of the infallible Magisterium of the Church in general, and it is restricted to the contents of the Holy Scripture and Tradition" (*DH* 3116). The second was a statement by Cardinal Manning, which was quoted by Michael Davies: "Infallibility is not a quality inherent in any person, but an assistance attached to an office."[6]

Finally, Prof. de Mattei highlighted the paradoxical adoption by some sectors of traditionalism of the hostility toward ultramontanism shown by Dominican theologian Yves Congar. He was one of the main architects of the Second Vatican Council, and, in his Council diary, he railed against what he called the "wretched ultramontane ecclesiology."[7] On December 9, 1962, he wrote, "everything that is done with a view to converting Italy to the Gospel from political, ecclesiological or devotional ultramontanism, is that much gained for the universal Church as well."[8]

Only if the historical data furnished in the well-known historian's article and my trio of articles is false would it be legitimate to continue blaming the ultramontane current for the unjustifiable acceptance of the current pope's errors in teaching and governing the Church. However, it is wrong to do so if the facts are true. Therefore, those who attribute today's hyperpapalist obsequiousness to the ultramontanes must first refute Prof. de Mattei's and my articles. They should provide more conclusive historical data than what we presented.

That has not happened so far. No one has refuted what Prof. de Mattei and I have written. I draw attention to this incoherence and ask *anti-hyperüberultramontanes* to be intellectually honest. They must either refute what Prof. de Mattei and I wrote or stop mischaracterizing ultramontanism. Moreover, they should admit that history shows that *magisterialism* and *hyperpapalism* are the spurious fruits of the Liberal Catholic current, which resorts to authoritarianism to impose its errors. I invite our anti-ultramontane traditionalist friends to a more elevated debate.

---

5   See chapter 23.

6   Davies, *Pope John's Council*, 175.

7   Yves Congar, *My Journal of the Council*, trans. Mary John Ronayne and Mary Cecily Boulding (Adelaide: ATF Press, 2012), 485.

8   Congar, 247.

25

A Psychological Approach to Treating the Disease of Ultramontanism[1]

ROBERT W. KEIM

CHESTERTON AFFIRMED THAT GREAT WRITERS AND artists are seekers and purveyors of symbols whether they are aware of it or not. I would go further and say that human beings in general are symbolists without knowing it. Mountains represent a liminal space between heaven and earth, between divinity and mortality, and hence, I see more in the term "ultramontanism" than a reference to the man beyond the Alps. I see a yearning, a quest—a primal need—for the *theios aner*, the godlike man, who dwells somewhere among the misty peaks, or beyond them . . . perhaps even at the threshold of the heavens.

Here I speak not of Christ, the God-Man, who ascended into a celestial and supramaterial realm. The godlike man is visible, tangible, audible; his home is a palace, his raiment is authority, his voice is law. One can believe in him, honor him, *trust in him*—without recourse to supernatural faith. And when the Son of Man returns, will He find faith upon the earth?

The great mountaintops of Greek mythology: here we traverse a land of gods and heroes. On Mount Olympus, we find Zeus and his anthropomorphic entourage. On Mount Pelion, the mortal king Peleus marries the goddess Thetis. On Mount Ida, the infant Paris defeats death, like-to-the-gods Achilles attacks Aeneas, and the next generation of heroic men learn courage and self-mastery.

The ancient Greek mind searched these summits for some sense of resolution to the fundamental and relentless paradox of human life: man is mortal like the beasts, but aspires to the immortality of the gods; he is an animal that dies, and a spirit that lives. His very existence is liminal—threatened by the roving evils of the material world and burdened by the passage of time, yet excluded from Elysian bliss and incompatible with atemporality.

The certainty of death and the tragic ambiguity of the human condition are, of course, perennial themes in mythologies and religions from all times and places. The Greeks responded with epic tales of heroes and demigods, with mystery cults that aspired to ecstatic self-transcendence, and with vague notions of afterlife

---

1 First published at *OnePeterFive* on July 11, 2022, under the pen name Robert V. Newman.

in an underworld. They had not the ineffable gift of the Catholic faith, which supplies the comprehensive and definitive response — the only truly satisfying response — to these harsh realities.

THE RESURGENCE OF PRIMAL FEAR

For Europeans living in the Age of Faith, Christian soteriology moderated and regulated the persistent and sometimes convulsive antagonism between human beings and the human condition. Medieval pilgrims at Montserrat could sing the song "We Hasten to Death" (*Ad Mortem Festinamus*) to a melody that is buoyant and almost celebratory, and this was not mere flippancy — the lyrics refer also to repentance, conversion, judgment, and the horror of damnation.

This fascinating song is emblematic of a healthy psychological attitude toward vulnerability and mortality, and though this attitude was certainly not universal in medieval Europe, I do believe it was generalized to a degree that is exceedingly rare in the history of the world's cultures, both primitive and developed.

But healthy psychology requires a healthy psyche, and the optimal nourishment for the human psyche is truth. Medieval culture eventually yielded to the more anthropocentric ethos of the Renaissance, and as the Renaissance degenerated into Protestant subjectivism, Enlightenment rationalism, and scientific positivism, the gloriously harmonious doctrines of the Catholic faith were increasingly diluted, distorted, and discarded.

When Western civilization approached the dismal terminus of systematic skepticism and widespread religious indifference, modern man rediscovered the cognitive dissonance and gnawing, protean fears that were endemic in pre-Christian cultures. And given that he lacked the support and consolation even of tribal ritualism or a socially consecrated mythos, the conditions were ripe for neurosis. Indeed, Freud and his followers in the psychoanalysis movement had no shortage of neurotic patients for their case studies.

Catherine of Siena was a saint, a mystic, and a brilliant psychologist, insofar as psychology is the science of the human mind and soul. In a letter to the cardinal of Ostia, she explains that "as soon as a rational creature loves himself egotistically, he immediately falls into fear."[2] She declares: "O how dangerous is this [servile] fear! It cuts off the arms of holy desire, blinds man and does not permit him to know or see the truth, because this fear proceeds from the blindness caused by self-love."

Catherine is offering a crucial insight into the psychological nexus of egocentricity, servile fear, and alienation from truth. The general course of modernity, beginning with Renaissance humanism and descending asymptotically toward nihilistic humanism and the cult of self, has led Western societies back into the stormy waters of primal fear and existential anxiety. The infiltration of

---

2 Angelo Belloni recently translated St Catherine's letters from fourteenth-century Tuscan into modern Italian. These quotations are my literal translations of his Italian text.

primal fear is a psychological burden in itself, but as Catherine suggests, fear also renders us insensitive to truth; in the absence of transcendent truths, fear escalates, and the cycle continues. Something must be done, or the effects upon the psyche could be devastating.

ULTRAMONTANISM AND THE THEORY OF TRANSFERENCE

Disoriented and apprehensive amidst the spiritual and ideological wreckage of the nineteenth century, modern man regressed to his instinctive defenses against existential ambiguity and the terror of anticipated annihilation. Prominent among these defenses is a process known to modern psychology as transference, which the twentieth-century German psychologist Erich Fromm explains as follows:

> In order to overcome his sense of inner emptiness and impotence, [the neurotic patient] chooses an object on to whom he projects all his own human qualities . . . . By submitting to this object, he feels in touch with his own qualities; he feels strong, wise, courageous, and secure. To lose the object means danger of losing himself. This mechanism, idolatric worship of an object, . . . is the central dynamism of transference . . . . The transference phenomenon is . . . found in all forms of idolization of authority figures, in political, religious, and social life.[3]

It is perfectly understandable that for Latin-rite Catholics, the preferred transference object—the preferred candidate for idolization—is the pope of Rome.

Transference is a natural human response to the subtle yet potentially traumatizing fears that circulate in the human psyche: fear of freedom, fear of the unknown, fear of death and annihilation, fear of an encroaching abyss, the immense and formless abyss that the Greeks called *khaos*. Man's psychological instinct is to transfer these fears, and the cosmic power that engenders them, to some object or person, such that they become localized, comprehensible, survivable, perhaps even controllable.

This instinct serves us well when the recipient is Almighty God, for we thereby do exactly what Our Savior exhorted us to do: *be not afraid, cast your cares upon the Lord.* Our heavenly Father becomes the locus of the various traumatic and oppressive fears that accompany the human condition, and from His divine Heart they emerge as the one fear that exalts, enlightens, and liberates: the fear of God, *principium sapientiae.*

This instinct does *not* serve us well when weakened faith—abetted by exaggerated piety, misguided fervor, or religious realpolitik—directs the gaze of transference to a fallible mortal, especially one who is surrounded by malign influences and subject to the corrupting effects of fame and power. The pope is the successor of St Peter, the vicar of Christ, the patriarch of the West, and

---

3   Erich Fromm, *Beyond the Chains of Illusion: My Encounter with Marx and Freud* (London: Abacus, 1980), 49–50.

the sovereign of the Vatican City-State. He is the supreme human authority in the Church. But he is not God, and he is not dogma, and he is not sacred Tradition. Rather, he is *custos traditionis*: the guardian of ecclesiastical realities that utterly transcend him.

The Austrian psychologist Alfred Adler linked neurosis to a failure of courage, and he remarked that transference seems to promise us "an easy and immediate satisfaction of unfulfilled desires."[4] The modern world's scorched-earth war of attrition against the Church and the faith is an unprecedented crisis, but ultramontanism is a facile and ultimately self-destructive response. Catholics have no need to idolize or heroicize the pope. We worship the One God, and His Son is the divine Hero, and His words will not pass away: *Fear not, take courage — I have overcome the world.*

THE DIVINE PHYSICIAN

In the title of this essay I refer to the *disease* of ultramontanism. This is not intended to be sensationalistic or pejorative but rather a precise diagnosis. Ultramontanism is quite literally a source of grievous dis-ease, of systemic dis-order, in the Mystical Body of Christ. In a clinical setting one might speak of *popitis*, for it resembles an inflammatory condition: the papacy is swollen and throbbing with lifeblood drawn from other portions of the Church. Inflammation is a healing mechanism, not inherently harmful, and indeed, ultramontanism has been promoted or reinforced by many well-intentioned Catholics who love the Church. But the Francis pontificate has demonstrated, in most compelling fashion, that popitis is inflammation of the autoimmune variety: chronic, unproductive, self-destructive. Let us invoke the divine Physician on behalf of His Mystical Body, and search *diligently* — the word derives from *diligere*, to love — amidst the Church's bimillennial treasury for remedies of proven efficacy.

---

4 *The Individual Psychology of Alfred Adler: A Systematic Presentation in Selections from His Writings* (New York, Basic Books, 1956), 343.

26

The Tower, and the City, of Babel: A Warning against Ultramontanism[1]

ROBERT W. KEIM

B EHOLD, SAITH THE LORD IN THE APOCALYPSE, *I MAKE all things new*. The Eternal Wisdom thus reveals—*apokalypsis* means disclosure, unveiling—the hermeneutical path that leadeth unto life. And though the gate be strait, and the way narrow, the destination is broad indeed: we seek the celestial Heart of the One who telleth the number of the stars and calleth them all by their names.

The geometer knows that a regular polygon with countless sides is indistinguishable from a circle. At once an infinitely faceted jewel and a sphere of ineffable perfection and unity, Holy Writ scintillates with new insights, perpetually refracting, in Dante's imagery, the divine Point of Light into literal, moral, allegorical, and anagogical meanings.[2] The Scriptures are waiting to be made new, but modern scholarship all too often inserts the wrong subject into this action. *I make all things new*: this is God speaking, not the exegete. The Magisterium—God's indescribably beneficent gift of knowledge and certainty to mankind—circumscribes both the scriptural cosmos and the reader who has entered, prayerfully and humbly, therein. Thus liberated by the magisterial enclosure, the reader passes from *ego*centric innovation to *theo*centric instruction, manifestation, revelation: *apokalypsis*. We aspire merely to be good instruments and true; Holy Scripture is ancient, immutable, and its Author makes it ever youthful, ever new.

REVISITING THE TOWER OF BABEL

Textual study of any kind—indeed, language itself—is subject to ossification and even fossilization. Sometimes a particular message or thematic element gains ascendancy in the popular or scholarly mind, to the occlusion of other interpretive possibilities. I believe that something of this nature has occurred with the account of the Tower of Babel (Gen 11:1-9). I say nothing against any interpretation

---

1 Published here for the first time.
2 *Paradiso*, Canto XXVIII (Longfellow translation): "A point beheld I, that was raying out / Light so acute, the sight which it enkindles / Must close perforce before such great acuteness . . . . My Lady, who in my anxiety / Beheld me much perplexed, said: 'From that point / Dependent is the heaven and nature all.'"

consecrated by the wisdom of the Church as expressed by her priests, saints, and theologians. I will, however, propose a reading that seems to me rigorous yet often overlooked, and which serves as a potent and ominous warning against the dread disease of ultramontanism.

Even in these days of abysmal catechesis and generalized religious indifference, a large proportion of people living in post-Christian countries will recognize the term "Tower of Babel." How many, I wonder, have heard teachers or clerics discuss the *city* of Babel? Relatively few, I suspect, and yet the Scripture is clear: "And they said: Come, let us make a city and a tower, the top whereof may reach to heaven" (Gen 11:4). At this point one could argue that the city is incidental, especially given the dramatic description of the tower.[3] However, the following verse demonstrates that Adonai was concerned about both: "And the Lord came down to see the city and the tower, which the children of Adam were building" (Gen 11:5). Even more significant is the *omission* of the tower in verse 8: "And so the Lord scattered them from that place into all lands, and they ceased to build the city."

In my experience, the standard explanation of the Babel narrative foregrounds the tower and the deplorable pride that fueled its construction. Wicked men, striving once again to be "as gods" (Gen 3:5), are determined to build a tower that will elevate them to the realm of divine power. The Lord punishes their impious pride, and abolishes their iniquitous project, by confounding their shared language and "scatter[ing] them abroad upon the face of all countries" (Gen 11:9).

I will not claim that this reading is "incorrect" in any way. I do, however, consider it incomplete and unsatisfying. First of all, it attends almost exclusively to the tower and does not account for the prominence of the city. Furthermore, the Babel pericope makes no explicit reference to pride and no explicit or implicit reference to punishment. Verse 4 relates the builders' desire to "make [their] name famous," but this bespeaks worldly, perhaps imperialistic, ambition more than pride as a grievous sin directed principally toward God. The Hebrew says literally "let us make for us a name," suggesting a rather terrestrial vainglory instead of a pride that "imitates God inordinately . . . and wishes to usurp His dominion over our fellow-creatures."[4]

THE CITY OF BABEL

Let us examine the narrative more closely, beginning with the city. As argued above, the text per se — that is, the biblical passage shorn of cultural accretions — indicates that the construction of the city is no less important than the construction of the tower. This captures my attention for two reasons. First, "city" is a marked word in the Book of Genesis. Its first appearance is saturated with

---

3   Syntactic analysis of the English text does not establish unequivocally that "top whereof" refers to "tower" rather than "city" or "city and tower," but in the Hebrew text "top" has a singular masculine possessive suffix and therefore cannot refer to עִיר, which is feminine when it denotes a city or town.

4   Augustine, *City of God*, quoted in Aquinas, *ST* II-II, Q. 162, art. 1, ad 2.

villainy and disgrace — saturated, in fact, with human blood: "And Cain . . . built a city" (Gen 4:17). The Bible makes no allusion to the notion of a city until the murderer decides to build one. An inauguration this infamous leaves a stain that is not easily effaced, and I am inclined to agree with literature scholar Dr Ricardo Quinones:

> Josephus . . . found the city to have been the product of a curse on Cain . . . . The city is a place of violence. It cannot seem to escape its blood-beginnings. Those pagan rituals of blood sacrifice that seemed so propitiatory were to Augustine accurate metaphors of an inescapable reality: the city, founded in blood, continues to live by blood.[5]

Second, any city, but especially one deliberately founded and built by ambitious men, is more than a densely populated settlement. It signifies commerce, wealth, secularity, politics, control; it is a symbol of, and a tool for, the centralization and consolidation of power.

THE RETURN OF THE UNIVERSAL LANGUAGE

Years ago I came across the following anecdote written by Solange Strong Hertz:

> I remember once confiding my difficulties in mastering Spanish to a Spanish friar having trouble with English. "But child," he consoled me, raising eyes and arms to heaven, "languages are a *ponishment* from God!"[6]

Perhaps they are, and I certainly sympathize with the bouts of discouragement experienced by language learners. But I say again that the Babel pericope makes no explicit or implicit reference to punishment. God's intention, it seems to me, is communicated quite clearly:

> And he said: Behold, it is one people, and all have one tongue: and they have begun to do this, *neither will they leave off from their designs*, till they accomplish them in deed. Come ye, *therefore*, let us go down, and there confound their tongue, *that they may not understand one another's speech*. And so the Lord scattered them from that place into all lands, *and they ceased to build the city*. (Gen 11:6–8, emphasis added)

The Lord divided the common tongue into mutually unintelligible languages or dialects in order to *frustrate their designs* — more specifically, to prevent the construction of the city.

Languages are certainly a source of travail and inconvenience, but so are food, clothing, shelter, families, education, and many other things that I would not

---

5   Ricardo Quinones, *The Changes of Cain: Violence and the Lost Brother in Cain and Abel Literature* (Princeton, NJ: Princeton University Press, 1991), 41.

6   I am sure that I read this in *Latin Mass Magazine*, but currently I can find it only in the online archives of *The Remnant*: www.remnantnewspaper.com/Archives/archive-2005-0731-bring_on_the_clowns.htm.

describe as a punishment from God. I propose that the plurality of languages is first and foremost a gift whereby our Heavenly Father protects us from an innate urge to congregate, consolidate, and dominate. This plurality undermines socio-political systems that conduce to oppression, exploitation, homogenization, and dehumanization. It counteracts the universal tendency of postlapsarian culture to drift toward carnality, materialism, megalomania, and idolatry. It inevitably promotes subsidiarity and impedes its antithesis: centralization in the political realm, hyperpapalism in the ecclesiastical realm.

In the Western Church, Latin was once the ideal complement to the plurality of tongues: a shared, sacred language that uplifted and united without encroaching upon local customs, folk culture, ethnic identity, and the judicious distribution of political and spiritual authority. But Latin is increasingly *persona non grata* in the postconciliar Church, and the Babelian tongue has returned with a vengeance: the language now spoken at the Vatican, a fusion of bureaucratese and Newspeak, has infiltrated every diocese on earth. Proclaimed *ad nauseam* from the high tower of papal authority, it promises to amalgamate the peoples of God into a formless mass of mediocrity and ambiguity. Having buried Christendom under six feet of vacuous teachings, sentimental palaver, and appallingly prosaic liturgies, Vaticanspeak has become the official language of the *civitas pontificis*, the vast ecclesiastical city built around the decadent postmodern papacy. Let us pray that the language of the Church regain its commitment to conviction, reality, beauty, and Truth. Let us pray that the good God will scatter the neo-Babelian empire of dissimulation, sophistry, and insufferable prolixity. *Let your speech be yea, yea: no, no: and that which is over and above these, is of evil.*

WITH ARMS OUTSTRETCHED

I am certainly not the first person who has discerned precepts against central-ization and worldly ambition in the Babel narrative. The eminent biblical scholar Charles Ellicott, for example, states that the construction project represents

> what is now called centralisation, by which the individual sacrifices his rights to the nation, the provinces to the capital, and small nations are bound together in one empire, that the force of the whole body may be brought to bear more rapidly and effectually in carrying out the will of the nation or of the ruler.... The Deity affirms that this central-isation is injurious to man's best interests, and must be counteracted by an opposite principle, namely, the tendency of mankind to make constant changes in language, and thereby to break up into different communities.... At Babel the first attempt to bind the human family into one whole came to an ignominious end.[7]

Probably not many readers have interpreted this message as a cataphoric condem-nation of ultramontanism, but principles that apply to secular sociology apply a

---

7   Charles Ellicott, *A Bible Commentary for English Readers*, vol. 1 (London: Cassell, n.d.), 53–54.

fortiori to the Catholic Church, which is and will always be the most important society in the world.

After so many years of ultramontane ecclesiology and spirituality, the alternative seems hopelessly distant. For instance, how many of us, when thinking about St John Vianney, would naturally imagine him offering not the traditional Latin Mass as we know it, but rather Mass according to the rite of the archdiocese of Lyon?

Too many Catholics have learned to look at Rome and see the Church, and to look at the pope and see the *theios aner*, the "godlike man." There is no need; the Church is all around us, and we can look at God Himself:

> All his life [the Curé d'Ars] followed the peculiar rite of the Church of Lyons. According to that rite, after the elevation the celebrant stands still for a while with outstretched arms. M. Vianney prolonged this ceremony; the beholders were impressed by it. In 1827 a little schoolboy, himself destined to become a priest, used to assist him in the capacity of altar boy. "I was impressed," he relates, "when I saw how, after the Consecration, he lifted both his eyes and hands and remained for nearly five minutes in a kind of ecstasy. We used to say, my comrades and I, that he saw the good God."[8]

---

8   François Trochu, *The Curé d'Ars: St Jean-Marie-Baptiste Vianney* (Charlotte: TAN Books, 2007), 344.

27

Have Modern Media Created the Ultramontane Papacy?[1]

DARRICK TAYLOR

THERE IS MUCH DEBATE THESE DAYS IN CONSERVATIVE and traditional Catholic circles about papal authority. Francis's pontificate has produced concern about the uses of papal power, driven by Francis's apparent contradiction of what have been understood as settled doctrines on moral questions as well as the teachings of his immediate predecessors. What has undoubtedly flummoxed Catholics concerned with orthodoxy is how many ordinary Catholics don't seem to understand that the pope can't simply will whatever he wants with regard to doctrine. How did things get this way?

Much of this discussion has centered around "ultramontanism." The term ultramontane literally means "beyond the mountains." It was first used during the Investiture Controversy of the eleventh and twelfth centuries, when opponents of the German Emperor Henry IV appealed to the pope "beyond the mountains" in Italy. With the Reformation, theologians made increasing appeal to papal authority in debates with Protestants. According to Thomas Pink, it was during this period that theologians such as Francisco Suárez and St Robert Bellarmine began to link the Church's infallibility with its canonical authority—insinuating that its infallibility in teaching the faith extended to its disciplinary legislation, as a means of opposing the claims of absolute monarchs over the Church.[2]

But ultramontanism as we now know it took shape during the nineteenth century, when the Church rallied European Catholics around the banner of the papacy in the face of anticlerical governments, culminating in the declaration of papal infallibility by the First Vatican Council. Since then, the term "ultramontanism" has become a shorthand for absolute papal supremacy.

In this process, modern media played a large role. Many have noted that, in the past, few ordinary Catholics would have concerned themselves with the off-hand comments of popes, and they rightly point to the influence of news media on attitudes toward the papacy.

The rise of the popular Catholic press was crucial to the development of ultramontane sentiment on a popular level in the nineteenth century. In France, during the 1830s, journalists like Louis Veuillot and his daily *L'Univers* began attacking

---

both anti-Catholic republicans and liberal Catholics like the Abbé de Lamennais who wanted to compromise with them.

Beginning with Pius IX, popes encouraged popular writers like Veuillot and the Jesuit paper *La Civiltà Cattolica*, founded in 1853. This popular ultramontane press, in return, exalted the pope's authority as never before. This went hand in hand with the centralization of church government under Pius IX. Thus, the Vatican embraced a kind of populist authoritarianism in terms of apologetics and approach to governance, which has characterized it to this day.

This was a major shift for the Vatican, which since the Reformation had seen the press as the invention of the devil and tried to curb its influence. But the Vatican had little choice at that point. The French Revolution and Napoleonic wars had threatened the very existence of the papacy, and it found itself increasingly at the mercy of hostile modern states whose financial and bureaucratic powers dwarfed its own, a reversal of the conditions that had made the papacy a formidable power in European life for centuries. The Holy See needed the "masses" on their side in order to resist the encroachments of liberal states.

The emergence of a popular Catholic press was made possible by technological advancements in printing that occurred during the nineteenth century. Until 1811, printing presses were operated by hand, which limited their production capacity. A German, Friedrich Koenig, invented a steam-driven cylinder press that could produce copies at ten times the speed of earlier presses, and these began to proliferate around the world by the 1830s.

This technology appeared just as modern states were dissolving regional cultures across Europe, attempting to establish modern, national identities in place of local ones. This process turned the European peasantry into "masses" that needed a focus of loyalty. In this is the key to understanding "ultramontanism": it is not a formal doctrine (there are no encyclicals on "ultramontanism" that I am aware of) but a sentiment or species of rhetoric used to mobilize the faithful around the pope. This rhetoric, though intended to deal with hostile threats from outside the Church, inevitably became involved in intraecclesial disputes. This, in turn, led to an inflation of ultramontane rhetoric with long-term consequences.

In the run-up to Vatican I, adulation of the pope became so egregious that historians have dubbed this later phase "neo-ultramontane" to distinguish it from the earlier variety, and for good reason. Its proponents attributed to the pope the direct inspiration of the Holy Spirit and much more.

Among these was the British convert and theologian W. G. Ward, editor of the *Dublin Review*. According to Ward, the pope's infallibility meant "his every doctrinal pronouncement is infallibly guided by the Holy Ghost," and amounts to "a new inspiration." The 1864 *Syllabus of Errors* he regarded "as the Word of God." Veuillot rivaled him in this, claiming that "the infallibility of the pope is the infallibility of Jesus Christ Himself." Others referred to the pope as "the Vice-God of mankind" and the "Permanent Word Incarnate." One French monsignor wrote of the "three incarnations of the Son of God" — in the womb of Mary, in the Eucharist, and in "the old man in the Vatican." And the Jesuits at La Civiltà Cattolica, ever helpful, informed their readers that "when the Pope meditates, it is God who is thinking through him."

These writers must have known these egregious exaggerations were not true, but they also wanted to use loyalty to the pope as a club against their opponents. Secular governments were afraid Vatican I would reassert Church prerogatives over areas such as marriage and family life, and opponents of the definition tried to inflame those suspicions, hoping to get those governments to intervene. In response, Veuillot and company ratcheted up their rhetoric, as one of his opponents put it, with the intention "to declare the pope infallible in matters of faith in order to give him the appearance of infallibility in other matters as well."

This brainless propaganda had its intended effect, demonizing anyone who objected to it and destroying any resistance in the Church to the definition of infallibility. This is what caused John Henry Newman to balk at the definition initially, and it led Ignaz von Döllinger, previously a supporter of infallibility, to violently oppose it and incur excommunication.[3] It also contributed to the schism of the Old Catholics who refused to accept the definition after the council. Doubtless many of the opponents of defining papal infallibility couldn't separate the hyperbole of its defenders from the conciliar definition itself.

Of course, the actual definition of papal authority in Pastor Aeternus is much more restrained and nuanced. And Pius IX seconded the German bishops when, in reply to criticism from the German government, they averred that the pope was not "a perfectly absolute sovereign" over the Church. But it is difficult to imagine that such nuanced scholastic qualifications had much impact on the popular Catholic imagination.

Writers such as Newman and others repeated these qualifications, but it is doubtful how much they penetrated the average Catholic's mind, as opposed to the image projected by a vernacular Catholic press that must have often dispensed with them. Certainly, such sentiments remained widespread. For virtually all of the popes since Pius IX have exploited this popular image to bolster the standing of the papacy, including the current pope.

It seems clear enough now that supporters of Pope Francis have been using the same strategy as their ultramontane predecessors: to insinuate that his infallibility extends further than it truly does and to demonize their opponents for opposing his designs. The difference, of course, is that the ultramontanes were orthodox and advocated positions consistent with previous Church teaching and tradition, whereas "Team Francis," as Damian Thompson has called Francis's Anglophone journalistic supporters, has cheered every novelty Francis has proposed, no matter how at variance with the historic teaching of the Church.

---

3   See chapter 39.

It is not surprising that this strategy has had some success. Appeals to personal loyalty are hard to dispel, personal loyalty being a natural emotion. That's why the ultramontane press took up that cudgel in the first place. Loyalty needs no long explanations for a mass audience. Conversely, explaining to the average Catholic the reasons why the pope can't dispense with natural or divine law when they become inconvenient is a much more difficult matter in any age.

However, it has clearly not been as successful as its backers would prefer, and this is due primarily to the media climate which is so different than it was fifty or a hundred years ago. The invention of the internet has broken any sort of monopoly on information or news. In the 1870s, a few men like Veuillot could dominate print media and drown out their opponents. But no such dominance is possible today. A quick Google search can reveal what the Church's teaching has been, and even with the support of a friendly secular media (another major difference from the 1870s), Francis still cannot completely marginalize his critics. This is probably one reason why he does not like conservative American Catholics very much: they have made greater and more effective use of the internet and social media to oppose his agenda than any other part of the Church has been able to do.

The fact is that modern media make distorting the teaching of the Church much easier, even when wielded by orthodox writers, if they are not careful with their words. It is worth recalling that Vatican II was, in part, an attempt by the Church to change its image as an authoritarian monolith to better communicate with "modern man." The irony is that the caricature it attempted to overcome was at least partly the making of its own ultramontane supporters. Even more ironic is that, despite the council's admonitions to the contrary, and all the talk of the "spirit of Vatican II," the power of the papacy has only grown since the council ended. For all of Francis's assertions about the necessity of following Vatican II, his actual reforms and interventions have largely strengthened and centralized the papacy at the expense of the bishops.

None of this means that either ultramontanism or modern media are evil in and of themselves. As I stated above, the Church had little choice in the nineteenth century but to lean into the papacy and its aura of authority. However, they are both powerful instruments, and there is a saying in international relations that there are no such things as defensive weapons, only weapons. In that sense, there is a perfect symmetry between the modern media and ultramontanism as a rhetorical device: what they build up and defend, they can also destroy.

28

Ultramontanists: Godfathers of the Traditionalist Movement[1]

ROBERTO DE MATTEI

THE CRISIS THE CHURCH IS EXPERIENCING TODAY IS certainly unprecedented in its characteristics, but it is neither the first nor the last in history. Think, for example, of the attack suffered by the papacy in the years of the French Revolution.

In 1799 the city of Rome was invaded by General Bonaparte's Jacobin army. Pope Pius VI was taken prisoner to the city of Valence, where he died on August 29, his death hastened by ill-treatment. The town hall of Valence notified the Directory of Pius VI's death, adding that the last pope in history had been buried.

Ten years later, in 1809, Pius VI's successor, Pius VII, old and infirm, was also arrested and, after two years of imprisonment in Savona, was taken to Fontainebleau, where he remained until the fall of Napoleon. Never had the papacy appeared so weak before the world. But ten years later, in 1819, Napoleon had disappeared from the scene and Pius VII was back on the papal throne, recognized as the supreme moral authority by European rulers. In that year 1819, *Du Pape*, the masterpiece of Count Joseph de Maistre (1753–1821), was published in Lyon, a work that had hundreds of reprints and anticipated the dogma of papal infallibility, later defined by the First Vatican Council.

DE MAISTRE: ULTRAMONTANE COUNTERREVOLUTIONARY

Joseph de Maistre is a great defender of the papacy, but it would be wrong for anyone to make him an apologist for the despotic pope or dictator. Today there are some traditionalists who blame ecclesiastical abuses of power on intransigent Catholics of the nineteenth century. These ultramontanes and counterrevolutionaries, we are told, attributed excessive power to the pope, enthusing beyond measure about the dogma of infallibility. This overreaction results in sympathy with those Gallican Catholics who denied infallibility and the universal primacy of the pope, and with those liberal or semi-liberal Catholics who, while not denying in principle the dogma of infallibility, considered its definition inappropriate.

Gioacchino Pecci, pope under the name Leo XIII, was in fact the first modern pope to rule in a centralizing manner, imposing as almost infallible the political and pastoral choice of *ralliement* with the French Third Republic.

---

1 First published at *OnePeterFive* on July 28, 2022. Translated by Kennedy Hall.

The dogma of infallibility proclaimed by Pius IX accurately defines the limits of this extraordinary charism, which no religion possesses, outside of the Catholic religion. The pope in the Church cannot do whatever he wants, because the source of his power is not his will. The pope's task is to transmit and defend, through his Magisterium, the Tradition of the Church. Alongside the pope's extraordinary Magisterium, which has its source in *ex cathedra* definitions, there is an infallible teaching that flows from the conformity of the ordinary Magisterium of all the popes to the Apostolic Tradition. Only by believing with the Church and its unbroken Tradition can the pope confirm his brethren in the faith. The Church is not infallible because she exercises authority, but because she transmits a doctrine.

"I AM TRADITION"

The words attributed to Bl. Pius IX, "I am Tradition," sometimes arouse scandal. However, these words must be understood in their correct meaning. What the pope means is not that his person is the source of Tradition, but that there is no Tradition outside of him, just as there is no *sola scriptura* independent of the Magisterium of the Church.

The Church is based on Tradition, but it cannot continue without the pope, whose authority cannot be transferred to either an ecumenical council, a national episcopate, or a permanent synod.

THE PRIORITY OF HIERARCHY OVER DOGMA

There is a statement by Joseph de Maistre in his "Lettre à une dame russe sur la nature et les effets du schisme," which may be as astonishing as that of Pius IX, but which is also profoundly true: "If it were permitted to establish degrees of importance among things of divine institution, I would place hierarchy before dogma, so indispensable is it to the maintenance of the faith."[2]

This sentence encapsulates the capital problem of the *regula fidei* in the Church. Fr Giovanni Perrone (1794–1876), founder of the Roman theological school, develops this theme in his work *Il protestantesimo e la regola di fede*.[3] The two sources of Revelation are Tradition and Sacred Scripture. The former is divinely assisted, the latter divinely inspired. "Scripture and Tradition fertilize each other, illustrate each other, strengthen each other, and complete the ever one and identical deposit of Divine Revelation."[4]

But in order to preserve this deposit of faith, which is always one and the same until the end of the ages, Christ entrusted it to an ever-living and speaking authority: the authority of the Church which consists of the universal body of bishops united with the visible head of the Church, the Roman Pontiff on whom Christ conferred

---

2   Joseph de Maistre, "Lettre à une dame russe sur la nature et les effets du schisme et sur l'unité catholique," in *Lettres et opuscules inédits* (Paris: A. Vaton, 1863), vol. 2, pp. 267–68.

3   Rome: Civiltà Cattolica, 1953, in three volumes.

4   Perrone, *Il protestantesimo*, 1:15.

fullness of power over the universal Church. Sacred Scripture and Tradition constitute the remote norms of our faith, but the proximate *regula fidei* is represented
by the teaching and judging authority of the Church, which has its apex in the
pope. Hierarchy comes in this sense before dogma. But even if we were to give
dogma primacy over hierarchy, we should remember that, of all dogmas, the one
that in a certain sense underpins all others is precisely the dogma of the infallible
authority of the Church. The Church enjoys the charism of infallibility, although
she exercises it in an extraordinary way only intermittently. But the Church is
always infallible, and has been so not since 1870, but since Our Lord transmitted
to his Vicar on earth St Peter the power to confirm his brethren in the faith.

The apostolic succession on which the Church's authority is based is a fundamental element of its divine constitution. The Council of Trent, in defining
the truth and rules of the Catholic faith, states that they are contained "in the
written books and unwritten traditions which, received by the Apostles from the
mouth of Christ himself, or from the Apostles themselves, under the inspiration
of the Holy Spirit, transmitted as it were from hand to hand, have come down to
us" (*DH* 1501). "Only the Tradition that rests on the Apostolic Tradition is true,"
reiterates contemporary Roman theologian Msgr Brunero Gherardini (1925–2017).[5]
This means that the Roman Pontiff, successor of Peter, prince of the Apostles, is
the guarantor par excellence of the Church's Tradition. But it also means that
under no circumstances can the object of faith exceed what is given to us by the
testimonies of the Apostles.

SOLA SCRIPTURA AND SOLA TRADITIO

Protestants denied the authority of the Church in the name of *"sola scriptura."*
This error leads from Luther to Socinianism, which is the religion of modern
relativists. But the authority of the church can also be denied in the name of *"sola
traditio,"* as the Orthodox do and as some traditionalists are in danger of doing.
The separation of Tradition from the authority of the Church leads in this case
to autocephaly, which is the condition of those without a visible and infallible
authority to relate to.

What the Protestant proponents of *sola scriptura* and the Greek Orthodox
proponents of *sola traditio* have in common is the rejection of the infallibility of
the pope and his universal primacy: the rejection of the Roman Chair. This is
why, according to Joseph de Maistre, there is no radical difference between the
Eastern Schism and Western Protestantism:

> It is a fundamental truth in all religious matters that every church that
> is not Catholic is Protestant. Attempts have been made — in vain — to
> draw a distinction between schismatic and heretical churches. I know
> well what is meant, but in the end all difference lies only in words,

---

5   Brunero Gherardini, *"Quod et tradidi vobis": La Tradizione, vita e giovinezza della chiesa* (Frigento:
Casa Mariana, 2010), 405.

and every Christian who refuses the Holy Father's communion is a Protestant or soon will be. What is a Protestant? He is a man who protests; and what does it matter whether he protests against one or more dogmas, against this or against that? He may be more or less Protestant, but he always protests ... Once the bond of unity is broken, there is no longer a common tribunal, nor consequently an invariable rule of faith. Everything is reduced to the particular judgment and civil supremacy that constitute the essence of Protestantism.[6]

In the Catholic Church, the authenticity of Tradition is guaranteed by the infallibility of the Magisterium. Without infallibility there would be no guarantee that what the Church teaches is true. The understanding of God's word would be left to the critical inquiry of individuals and the gates of relativism would be opened wide, as happened with Luther and his followers. By denying the authority of the pope, the Protestant Revolution condemned itself to constant variation in a whirling doctrinal becoming. But in the East, after the schism of 1054, the Orthodox Church—which in the name of *sola traditio* accepts only the first seven ecumenical councils—condemned itself to sterile immobility.

Those under the spell of Orthodoxy should be reminded of Joseph de Maistre's words: "All these Churches separated from the Holy See at the beginning of the twelfth century can be compared to frozen corpses whose forms have been preserved due to the cold."[7]

A theologian of the Assumptionists, Fr Martin Jugie (1878–1954), developed this theme in a book published in 1923 called *Joseph de Maistre et l'Église greco-russe*, which I recommend reading.

> For many centuries, the East has been accustomed to regard revealed doctrine as a treasure to be guarded, not as a treasure to be exploited; as a set of immutable formulas, not as a living and infinitely rich truth, which the spirit of the believer always seeks to understand and assimilate better.[8]

The Church was not founded by Christ as an institution, already rigidly and irrevocably constituted, but as a living organism, which—like the body, the image of the Church—was to have a development. This development of the Church, its growth in history, takes place through contradiction and struggle, fighting especially against the great heresies that attacked it internally. De Maistre again:

> When we consider the trials that the Roman Church has undergone through the attacks of heresy and the mixing of barbarous nations that took place in her bosom, we stand in admiration as we behold that, in the midst of these terrible revolutions, all her titles are intact and go back to the Apostles. If the Church has changed some things

---

6   Joseph de Maistre, *Du Pape* (Lyon-Paris: H. Pélagaud, 1878), 401; 405.
7   de Maistre, *Du Pape*, 406.
8   Martin Jugie, *Joseph de Maistre et l'Eglise greco-russe* (Paris: Maison de la Bonne Presse, 1923), 97–98.

in her external forms, it is a proof that She lives, for everything that lives in the universe changes, according to circumstances, in everything that does not have to do with essences. God, who reserved them for Himself, gave the forms to time to arrange them according to certain rules. The variation of which I speak is even the indispensable sign of life, because absolute immobility belongs only to death.[9]

The First Vatican Council, quoting Vincent of Lérins, explains that the understanding of the truths of faith must grow and progress with the succession of ages and centuries in understanding, knowledge, and wisdom, but only "in the same dogma, meaning, and judgment" (*Commonitorium*, 23, 3). Progress of faith does not in fact mean alteration of faith. Condemnation of the alteration of faith, however, does not mean the rejection of all organic development of dogma, which is accomplished through the Magisterium of the Church, under the influence of the Holy Spirit, and is guaranteed by the charism of infallibility. But if the Church is infallible there must be a subject that exercises this charism. This subject is the pope and it cannot be anyone other than he. In belief in the infallibility of the pope lie the roots of belief in the infallibility of the whole Church.[10]

The Constitution *Pastor Aeternus* of the First Vatican Council clearly states what the conditions of papal infallibility are. The infallibility of the pope in no way means that he enjoys, in matters of government and teaching, unlimited and arbitrary power. While the dogma of infallibility defines a supreme privilege, it sets its precise boundaries, admitting the possibility of infidelity, error, and betrayal.

For the papolater, or "hyperpapalist," the pope is not the Vicar of Christ on earth, whose job it is to transmit intact and pure the doctrine he has received; instead, he is a successor of Christ who "improves" the doctrine of his predecessors, adapting it to the changing times. Gospel doctrine is in perpetual evolution because it coincides with the Magisterium of the reigning Pontiff. The perennial Magisterium is replaced by the "living" Magisterium, expressed by pastoral teaching, which changes from day to day, having its *regula fidei* in the subject of the authority and not in the object of the truth transmitted.

TRADITIONALISM AND THE PAPACY

One does not need specialized theological knowledge to understand that, in the unfortunate case of contrast—true or apparent—between the "living Magisterium" and Tradition, primacy can only be attributed to Tradition, for a simple reason: Tradition, which is the "living" Magisterium considered in its universality and continuity, is in itself infallible, while the so-called "living" Magisterium, understood as the current preaching of the ecclesiastical hierarchy, is so only under certain conditions.[11] Indeed, in the Church, the ultimate "rule of faith"

---

9   de Maistre, 410.
10   Michael Schmaus, *Dogmatica cattolica* (Casale Monferrato: Marietti, 1963), vol. III/1, p. 696.
11   Roberto de Mattei, *Apologia della Tradizione* (Turin: Lindau, 2011), 146.

in times of defection from the faith is not the contemporary living Magisterium and its non-defining acts, but Tradition, which constitutes, with Sacred Scripture, one of the two sources of the Word of God.

What happens when those who govern the Church cease to guard and transmit Tradition, and, instead of confirming their brethren in the faith, create confusion in their minds and cause bitterness and resentment in their hearts?

When this happens it is time to increase love for the Church and the pope. But the answer to hyperpapalism is not the neo-Gallicanism of certain traditionalists, nor the *sola traditio* of the Greek-Russian schismatics. The man of Tradition is not an anarchotraditionalist, but a Catholic who repeats with Joseph de Maistre:

> O holy Church of Rome, as long as the word is preserved for me, I will use it to celebrate you. I salute you, immortal mother of science and holiness! Hail, *magna parens* . . . In the midst of all imaginable upheavals, God has constantly watched over you, O Eternal City! All that could destroy you has rallied against you, and you have stood; and as you were once the center of error, you have now for eighteen centuries been the center of truth.[12]

Love for the Roman Pontiff, his prerogatives and rights, has characterized authentically Catholic spirits throughout twenty centuries of history, because, as Plinio Corrêa de Oliveira states, "after love for God this is the highest love taught to us by religion."[13]

However, one should not confuse the Roman primacy with the person of the reigning pope, just as one should not confuse the so-called living Magisterium with the perennial Magisterium, or the private and non-infallible teaching of the pope with the Tradition of the Church. The error, as Chilean scholar José Antonio Ureta has well pointed out, lies not in ultramontanism but in neo-Gallicanism, which today comes in two versions: that of the German synodalists and that of some neotraditionalists, especially from the Anglo-Saxon area.

The only hope in the future lies not in the diminishment of the papacy, but in the exercise of its supreme authority to solemnly and infallibly condemn the theological, moral, liturgical, and social errors of our time. It is useless to discuss who will be the next pope. It is important to discuss what the next pope should do and to pray that he will do it.

---

12   de Maistre, *Du Pape*, 482; 483.
13   Roberto de Mattei, *Il crociato del secolo XX. Plinio Corrêa de Oliveira* (Casale Monferrato: Piemme, 1996), 309.

⸬ 29 ⸬
One Year Later[1]

STUART CHESSMAN

WHAT HAS HAPPENED?

More than a year has passed since Pope Francis issued the motu proprio *Traditionis Custodes* (hereafter, *TC*) on July 16, 2021, in which he declared war on Catholic traditionalism. He aimed to isolate the traditionalist faithful—priests and laity, young and old—from the rest of Church, to penalize and eventually eliminate them. *TC* was followed by regulations issued by close allies of Francis—whatever their ecclesiastical position might be—Archbishop Roche, Cardinal Cupich, and Rome's Cardinal De Donatis (although the latter, like some other former "friends of Francis," is reported to have very much fallen out of favor). These edicts radicalized the provisions of *TC*, imposing new and onerous burdens on clergy and laity. All these actions, like *TC* itself, were couched in contemptuous and hostile language. It is a campaign of unprecedented violence in recent Church history.

Yet the celebration of the Old Mass and the other sacraments continued unmolested and uninterrupted in so many places. Traditionalists celebrated Holy Week this year [2022]—even in dioceses like Rome and Chicago where the most stringent anti-traditionalist measures had been first implemented. Traditionalist priests and deacons continued to be ordained. Traditional Catholic pilgrimages, events, and conferences in Chartres, San Francisco, and elsewhere have proceeded on schedule. Many bishops were understandably reluctant to unleash a liturgical war in their dioceses, regardless of the pope's urging.

Already last February the *TC* onslaught experienced its first official reverse when Pope Francis announced the exemption of the FSSP from *TC*'s restrictions on the celebration of the traditional Mass and the other sacraments. There were even vague indications that this decision would be incorporated into canon law—whatever meaning that has in today's Church—and extending it to the other *Ecclesia Dei* communities. This was a clear about-face for the Vatican. Let us recall that the opening shot of Pope Francis's war against Catholic Tradition—even before the promulgation of *TC*—was the dissolution of an FSSP apostolate in Dijon, France.

That "break in the action," however, appears to me to have been a temporary tactical move on the part of the pope. A confrontation with the *ED* congregations this Eastertide was simply too early on the schedule. More recently the Vatican has resumed its attack on traditionalism with redoubled intensity. Several American dioceses this year have restricted or even abolished the traditional Mass, in

---

1   First published at the blog of the Society of St Hugh of Cluny on August 5, 2022.

some cases reversing previous statements, either delegating the "dirty work" to subordinates or, in one case (Savannah), to the Vatican itself.

Most significantly, the antitraditionalist campaign has now invaded dioceses where traditionalists have had a longstanding presence. Cardinal Cupich has ended the apostolate of the Institute of Christ the King Sovereign Priest in Chicago (the location of their American headquarters!). Cardinal Wilton Gregory—like Cupich, a special protégé of Pope Francis—has terminated the traditional Masses at the six parishes of his archdiocese at which it was celebrated. And now, the neighboring Arlington diocese, with one of the most significant traditionalist presences in the United States, has also imposed similarly drastic restrictions. We hear ominous muttering regarding restrictions in our immediate area as well.

It is reliably reported that Francis's nuncio in Washington is directly involved in these actions, even threatening bishops with deposition if they are recalcitrant. We have heard that every request by priests to celebrate the Old Mass, forwarded to Rome pursuant to *TC*, has been rejected with Francis's personal participation. The pope continues to conduct an aggressive publicity campaign against traditionalists—exemplified by the rabid, insulting denunciations in several interviews during his just-concluded visit to Canada. The war against traditionalism preoccupies the pope and, increasingly, the entire Roman Catholic leadership.

Of course, the Vatican's war is not confined to liturgical "traditionalism" but extends, in varying degrees, to the entirety of Catholic Tradition. For the pope's denunciation of "restorers" and "restorationism" is by no means limited to adherents of the Old Mass. And the progressive forces in the Church have been quick to seize the advantage of Pope Francis's favor. The so-called "German" synodal path with its deviations from Catholic theology, sacramental discipline, and morality is now spreading to France, Ireland, Italy, and beyond. "Abuses" in the celebration of the Novus Ordo continue unchecked. A confrontation is ongoing between large sections of the American episcopate and Catholic progressive forces—both in secular society and in the institutional Church—regarding concrete, not verbal, opposition to abortion. Most recently, building on the precedent of *Amoris Laetitia*, there is agitation emanating from the Vatican itself for "revising" *Humanae Vitae*. In all these cases Pope Francis either explicitly condones the progressive developments, says nothing about them, or offers nebulous, contradictory, and non-binding guidance.

WHAT IS THE MEANING OF THIS?

It has been asserted that opposition to "The Council," the new Mass, and the authority of the pope prompted the pope's motu proprio. By "The Council" I mean the totality of the changes made between 1962 and 1978, whether found in the conciliar documents themselves, in the texts of implementing legislation (like the Novus Ordo), or in the officially sponsored or tolerated practice of the Church. I think Pope Francis has the same understanding of these words. Let us examine what the turmoil unleashed by *TC* reveals about each of those pillars of the Catholic establishment.

Starting with the Novus Ordo: to judge from the need the pope feels for a war against traditionalism as well as from the available public data on Catholic participation in the sacraments throughout the Western world, the Novus Ordo liturgy has clearly and completely failed to revitalize or even stabilize Catholicism. Periodic attempts to combat "abuses" have not gained general acceptance. Well before *TC*, Pope Francis had expressly prohibited even the term "reform of the reform." Indeed, the *TC* war against traditionalism includes measures designed to confirm the Novus Ordo as a break with the past. So, for example, contrary to the liturgical rubrics and laws, in several dioceses priests now need permission to say the Novus Ordo *ad orientem*, or celebrating *ad orientem* has simply been banned. In other places the interpolation of older elements in the Novus Ordo has been specifically prohibited. Of course, from the first days of his pontificate Francis has arbitrarily disregarded liturgical rubrics, thus himself establishing a clear "hermeneutic" of the new liturgy.

Second, *TC* and its implementation enable a whole new generation of Catholics to experience what "The Council" was in actual practice. Just as in the 1960s, the Church is coercing liturgical changes, tolerating and even encouraging doctrinal confusion, denouncing her own allegedly corrupt past and the recalcitrant lay faithful, and finally initiating the friendliest dialogue with the avowed enemies of the Church (such as the Communist regimes). Passages of Francis's documents are virtually identical to those of Pope Paul VI. In both eras the papacy and clergy pose as the enlightened leaders guiding the Church out of a dark past.

Traditionalists and especially conservative Catholics have tended very much to underestimate this aggressive, destructive ideological thrust behind "The Council." The self-understanding of "The Council" was that of a break with a corrupt and antievangelical past—in liturgy, in government, in discipline, and even to some extent in theology. If internally "The Council" was revolutionary, externally it was completely conformist to the culture of the modern Western world. These have remained the ideological constants of "The Council"—even if the conciliar advocates subsequently diverged greatly on what form the "conciliar" Church would take. To believe that these convictions would dissipate with time, or that some type of lasting peace could be achieved with such an ideological movement, was in retrospect wishful thinking. Similarly, in arguing for traditionalism it is useless to point to the youth of traditionalist congregations, their new apostolates, their many vocations or just the financial contributions they make to parishes or dioceses. Against ideological thought, appeals to reality are without effect.

From the 1960s onward, the Catholic educational institutions, mainstream religious orders and, depending on the diocese, the hierarchy and a great percentage of the lower clergy as well absorbed this vision of "The Council" regardless of what was in fact happening. So, although over the decades traditionalists, even with papal support, were expanding their presence in churches and parishes and celebrating more and more splendid Masses, this met with a continuing, relentless opposition – often fanatical – from the established religious orders (especially but not only the Jesuits), the Catholic colleges and news media, much of the hierarchy (especially in Europe), and the more ideologically committed among the clergy and the laity. I could tell of a whole series of unpleasant encounters with such forces just in our little apostolate in the New York area over the last fifteen years.

It is revealing that, even though only a minority of the clergy actively desires to become persecutors in Francis's war, *TC* has nevertheless achieved some significant early results, compared, let us say, to *Humanae Vitae*, *Ex Corde Ecclesiae*, *Ecclesia Dei*, or *Summorum Pontificum*. For *TC*, in contrast to these previous papal actions, is aligned with the above vision of "The Council," the institutional Church, and indeed the demands of the "modern" world.

Third, none of this would be possible without the ultramontane constitution of the Roman Catholic Church. For *TC* rests entirely on the authority of Francis. He has made no attempt to convince traditionalists or anyone else of the correctness of his course – instead offering only slogans ("there's no turning back!") and personal invective.

Pope Francis is doing exactly what previous critics of the Catholic Church – Protestant, Orthodox, and agnostic – had always claimed the ultramontane papacy would do. Francis has sought to manage the Catholic Church in the United States, if necessary even down to the parish and individual level. He intervenes directly in the American political process with "Catholic" politicians (although these earlier critics could hardly have imagined the direction the pope's interventions have taken!). The pope has substituted his magisterium for Catholic Tradition, including the notion that this magisterium or "living tradition" can reverse the treatment of matters already settled by Tradition or prior magisterium. Francis-friendly commentators explain that the pope, after all, can do whatever he wants.

But the most reprehensible aspect of *TC* is that the Catholic Church is once again resorting to coercion in spiritual matters. We hear of "reeducating" traditionalists, of subjecting them to lectures, of requiring statements of adherence to the Council and the new Mass from congregations and individual priests. Rights and institutions of many years' standing have been summarily revoked. As for those who may drop out of the system, one establishment commentator explains that Francis does not necessarily need to show concern for those he harms or "leaves by the wayside." Recent utterances of the pope betray a truly paranoid fear of traditionalists infiltrating the Church. A pervasive dishonesty dominates Church documents and the official Catholic media. The regime of *TC* obviously resembles more and more the spirit of past and present totalitarian societies – the last two decades of the Soviet Union come to mind.

The current regime of the Catholic Church gives the lie to the endlessly repeated statements, in the Vatican II documents and elsewhere, regarding lay participation, dialogue, freedom of conscience, subsidiarity, etc. I certainly hope no one in the Catholic Church is laboring under the illusion that *TC* will increase the prestige of the papacy or the Catholic Church in this unevangelized world! Especially since this is occurring while the practice and understanding of the Catholic faith among the laity are at an all-time low, the number of priests, religious, and Catholic institutions continues its downward plunge, corruption of all kinds at the Vatican and elsewhere is rampant, and the Church appears totally confused and conflicted about her Faith and mission. The results of *TC* for the institutional Catholic Church will be dire.

WHAT ARE THE TRADITIONALIST FAITHFUL DOING — AND WHAT OF THE FUTURE?

More important than any protests, publications, or hierarchical (in)action, traditionalist priests and laity must continue to celebrate the Mass and the other sacraments. If I can trust the evidence of my own eyes — and some local data recently released — participation at traditional Masses in my immediate neighborhood has *increased* since *TC* — as indeed has been the case ever since Francis ascended the papal throne.

Courage has not been universal among traditionalists, however. Some have despaired of the institution under the current circumstances. The Canons Regular of St John Cantius in Chicago (who do *not* benefit from *ED* protection) immediately ceded to the demands of Cardinal Cupich. Their pastor wrote, as they prepared to celebrate this year's Holy Week in the Novus Ordo: "This year, things may appear to be different. But the marvel is beheld not merely in what we see, nor how the liturgy is celebrated." If that statement is true, why did they ever embrace celebrating the traditional Mass in the first place?

Yet most traditionalists have strived to preserve their liturgy and the other sacraments. In dioceses where bishops have forcefully implemented *TC*, public protests are beginning (these have already been underway in Paris for a year). And after some initial waffling last summer in France, it seems the *ED* communities are insisting on the rights granted to them in their founding charters. Depending on the course of events, traditionalists will have to organize more effectively and build up networks within and outside of the official Church. I already read of clandestine Masses being celebrated. Experience gained negotiating official restrictions during the Covid-19 panic will help here. The SSPX, which providentially rejected a Vatican offer in 2012, will also necessarily play an important role.

Catholic traditionalists must continue to speak out forcefully for the truth and against the pope's actions. *TC* has triggered an unending stream of articles and books. Going well beyond recycled polemics, this outpouring of commentary should help traditionalists understand better who they are and what they stand for. In this search for understanding they are assisted by many non-traditionalists and even non-Catholics. Many intelligent nonbelievers are horrified by the self-destructive cultural movement initiated by Francis and seek to comprehend what is going on in the Catholic religion. Similarly, many non-traditionalists — the "Catholic conservatives" — are dismayed by the wholesale assault on all aspects of Catholic Tradition, and especially on the legacy of Popes John Paul II and Benedict XVI. As in the case of the SSPX, in the face of this crisis it is time for all of us to set aside the grudges and rancor of the past.

Catholic traditionalism is the voluntary dedication of the ordinary faithful to the fullness of Christian truth. They understand that the objective truths of the Catholic Faith are more completely and precisely embodied in the traditional liturgy. They are not individualistic or charismatic but follow an objective discipline. Their motivation is not aestheticism or sentimentality, nor is it the product of some personal "attachment"; it is the preservation of the Faith for themselves, their families, and ultimately the whole Church. That is why they have sacrificed so much: the long journeys many must make to attend a traditional liturgy; the burdens they must assume to homeschool their children or educate them at independent Catholic schools; the sustaining of the disfavor and repression directed at them in dioceses, parishes, and schools.

The institutional Roman Catholic Church, which thinks only in secular political, ideological, and materialistic terms, cannot understand such dedication. Pope Francis and his friends talk of "ideological" and "rigid" laity and young priests, of traditionalists who "follow fashions," and of "restorationism" (itself a secular political concept). For a further example of this materialistic outlook, consider Bishop Michael Burbidge of Arlington, who implicitly justifies his restrictions on traditionalists by claiming that "approximately 2.5% of local, Mass-attending Catholics . . . prefer this liturgical form" (evidently forgetting about the One who said: "Where two or three are gathered together in My name . . ."). But it will be exactly from among such minorities that, God willing, the future recovery of the Church will proceed.

30

Distinguishing Ultramontanisms[1]

TIMOTHY FLANDERS

SINCE THE PUBLICATION OF OUR [*ONEPETERFIVE*] EDI-torial stance a little over a year ago,[2] I have been pleased to read the contributions to the fraternal debate about ultramontanism at *OnePeterFive* as well as at *Rorate Caeli*. Reflecting on the year's contributions, I intend in this and subsequent articles to reply to the debate in general and to a few men in particular, namely Mr José Antonio Ureta, Prof. Roberto de Mattei,[3] and most recently, Mr Luiz Sérgio Solimeo.[4] In accordance with the spirit of our editorial stance, we have published critical essays like theirs, written by our friends and allies in the traditional movement, in the hopes of further sharpening our analysis of ultramontanism and the problems facing the Church. I am grateful for the work of these good men and offer this treatment in a spirit of fraternal debate and zeal for truth.

THE GODFATHERS OF THE TRADITIONALIST MOVEMENT

In response to the new regime of Iconoclasm unleashed by *Traditionis Custodes*, our editorial stance sought to reignite the zeal of our forefathers in the traditionalist movement, as Kwasniewski has powerfully exhorted us to do.[5] Our forefathers already fought the fight we now face and won a critical (albeit incomplete) victory in *Summorum Pontificum*. Thus we must revisit our forefathers and emulate their zeal, their erudition and, by the prayers of Our Lady, their piety.

At the same time, we sought to contextualize post-Vatican II traditionalism as one part of an overall Catholic counter-revolutionary movement in response to the Liberal revolution of modernity. We seek to "unite the clans" not just to restore the Latin Mass that stands at the heart of Latin-rite Catholicism, but, by God's grace, to rebuild Christendom in souls and society. So we revere and honor the counter-revolutionaries who have gone before us.

---

1   First published at *OnePeterFive* on September 9, 2022.

2   See "Unite the Clans to Rebuild Christendom!," *OnePeterFive*, August 31, 2021.

3   See chapters 24 and 28.

4   Luiz Sérgio Solimeo, "Against Traditionalist Neo-Gallicanism," *OnePeterFive*, August 25, 2022; cf. the same author's "One Cannot Destroy the Papacy to Save the Church: True Ultramontanism and the Right to Resist," *The American Society for the Defense of Tradition, Family, and Property*, January 16, 2020, www.tfp.org/one-cannot-destroy-the-papacy-to-save-the-church-true-ultramontanism-and-the-right-to-resist/.

5   See Peter Kwasniewski, "It's Time to Imitate Our Forefathers: Never Give Up!," *OnePeter-Five*, July 28, 2021, and "The Primacy of Tradition and Obedience to the Truth" in idem, *Bound by Truth*, 82–101.

This seems to be among the chief concerns raised by Messrs Ureta, de Mattei, and Solimeo. The Comte de Maistre and Louis Veuillot were counter-revolutionaries fighting with the pen while the Ninth Crusaders fought with the temporal sword. As such they are indeed our godfathers in the modern traditionalist movement against Liberalism and we do well to study their lives and imitate their virtues. They were men of God fighting against the machinations of the fallen angels in their time. These counter-revolutionaries were ultramontanes. So it is true that we cannot dismiss the ultramontane movement as a whole, nor should we disparage it or these great men. We see in the discussion and sources from Mr Ureta an important theological consideration from some of the leading figures of the ultramontane movement such as Cardinal Edouard Pie. He was no precursor of today's hyperpapalism but advocated a true and orthodox ultramontanism which passed into the dogmatic definitions of Holy Church with the Vatican Council of 1870.

ULTRAMONTANISM AS AN HISTORICAL TERM

At the same time, as Mr Stuart Chessman noted in his initial reply[6] to Mr Ureta, there seems to be a difference of definition evinced in the usage of the term "ultramontanism." Here I wish to introduce a few distinctions into the definition of the term which I hope will help us move into a deeper territory in this conversation.

For ultramontanism, broadly understood, is primarily a *historical* term, as Dr Kwasniewski notes on the first page of the first volume of his work *The Road from Hyperpapalism to Catholicism*. The term used in a historical sense simply means the movement that arose in the nineteenth century to defend, promote, and rally around papal monarchy and centralization.

The term used in a historical sense would include everyone from de Maistre and Veuillot to Cardinal Pie and Bl. Pius IX, as well as the common lay faithful who were affected by the Ninth Crusade. But the broad historical use of the term would also include Leo XIII's hyperpapalism — well critiqued by Mr Ureta — as well as that of Félicité de Lamennais, who "insist[ed] on a highly exaggerated ultramontane concept of papal infallibility" even in opposition to reason itself.[7]

Ultramontanism used in a historical sense would simply include all those who exalted papal authority in the nineteenth century. This emphasizes the fact that history is filled with numerous factors of causality. A single idea promoted by this or that man can have all sorts of effects in this or that context, or upon this or that person. When we are thinking historically, we can attribute layers of causality to a phenomenon like ultramontanism, saying it became the cause, *historically speaking*, of both good and bad results, according to its application in any given context by any given man.

---

6   See chapter 21.

7   Michael D. Greaney, "New Things," Foreword to Thomas P. Neill, *They Lived the Faith: Great Lay Leaders of Modern Times* (originally published 1951; repr. Post Falls, ID: Mediatrix Press, 2020), xvi.

Yet we can also *narrow* the historical use of the term ultramontanism to refer *only* to the *faithful* Catholic counter-revolutionaries. This usage would include Veuillot and exclude de Lamennais. We might then add an adjective and call this "counter-revolutionary ultramontanism."

But in the mess of history, this counter-revolutionary ultramontanism is not unrelated to the broader historical term ("ultramontanism" without a modifier), which encompasses all papal centralization whatsoever as a historical, interconnected mass movement of the times.

In the tumultuous and bloody century in which it arose, counter-revolutionary ultramontanism was a mass movement using mass media and fiery rhetoric, *with good reason*, in order to combat the violence of the Liberals and Communists destroying souls and society. Our forefathers were fighting a war, and collateral damage does not make their cause unjust, but illustrates the bitterness of the struggle, the glory of the combat, and the nobility of the fighting men. Not all collateral damage is the fault of the soldier, nor can all collateral damage be prevented. But all collateral damage is lamentable, no matter what the cause. We shall return to this in a moment.

ULTRAMONTANISM AS A THEOLOGICAL TERM

As we noted above, ultramontanism can also be understood in view of dogma, and herein it acquires a far more *strict sense*. Hence we introduce here the term "theological ultramontanism," which refers specifically to: (1) the *theological party* at the Vatican Council promoting the definition of papal monarchy *before the definition*, and (2) *after* the solemn promulgation of *Pastor Aeternus*, the *theological definition itself* of papal monarchy to which all Catholics are bound to assent with the assent of faith. It is in this *strict sense* that we can say truthfully that every pious Catholic is a *theological* ultramontanist.

When we consider "ultramontanism" as *theological terminology*, we cannot ascribe to it (or equate with it) hyperpapalism, since the latter would of course be nothing other than a *perverse use* of the orthodox doctrine of the papal monarchy for the sake of Modernism, Liberalism, or whatever else the hyperpapalists may be trying to achieve. It is a trick of the Devil to use what God has established in order to discredit the papacy itself, as is being done acutely in our day, and that is the serious concern here.

THEOLOGICAL ULTRAMONTANISM AGAINST GALLICANISM

When used theologically and not historically, the term comprises the condemnation of certain articles of Gallicanism, which were formally condemned at Vatican I: namely, the denial of the universal jurisdiction of the papacy and the heresy that infallible definitions obtain their infallible status only via the consent of the Church (as well as conciliarism and its associated heretical propositions).

These narrower *sententiae* were anathematized at Vatican I.

Yet we must be careful here too, because Gallicanism can also be understood either historically or theologically, and *not* all theological positions forwarded by such groups were condemned at Vatican I.

For example, if a Catholic were to say that the temporal authority of the Church (emperors, kings, princes, and nobility) has some role in ecclesiastical governance as the vicar of Christ's kingship in the Christian world (as Mr James Bogle recently argued),[8] he is merely repeating the traditional doctrine of the Two Swords (a doctrine which is, at most, *de fide non definita*).[9] He is not a Gallican. By no means was this view condemned at Vatican I.[10]

Gallicanism can be charged only to a Catholic who has proposed one of the condemned propositions excluded by the definitions of ecclesiastical authority. All other questions (to which we will return in a subsequent chapter) have yet to be resolved, and hence remain open for discussion and debate. It is indeed clear from the work of such scholars as Bronwen McShea[11] that something has gone seriously wrong in the progressive denaturing and exclusion of temporal authority and lay co-responsibility in the modern Church. Even the corrupt clericalist clergy of our day are forced to hand over abusers to the lay, temporal sword, as they themselves promulgate policies to report abuse to the lay authority (that is, the police).

THE INTERPLAY BETWEEN HISTORICAL AND THEOLOGICAL

Here we must return to the subject of "collateral damage." For the great counter-revolutionary men of letters and the heroes of the Ninth Crusade who shed their blood in the defense of the papal monarchy are indeed a "grace like the Counter-Reformation," as Mr Solimeo contends.

Aye, brother! *Deus vult!*

Yet in our zeal for truth, let us ask a historical question of these great lay heroes of counter-revolutionary ultramontanism: did they all understand papal monarchy in the strict orthodox sense given by Vatican I and enunciated by Cardinal Pie? Probably not. Did Louis Veuillot's invocation of Bl. Pius IX with the words used liturgically to hymn the Holy Spirit achieve the theological precision necessary for a definition of doctrine? Of course not. It was a rhetorical device employed by a lay fighter in the ultramontane counter-revolution. Yet this rhetoric had consequences (perhaps unintended).[12]

---

8   James Bogle, "Is the Pope Really the 'Head of the Catholic Church?,'" *Inside the Vatican* (no date given), https://insidethevatican.com/magazine/is-the-pope-really-the-head-of-the-catholic-church/.

9   This doctrine was enunciated by Pope Gelasius (*Famuli Vestrae Pietatis*, AD 494), Gregory VII (Letter to Bishop Hermann of Metz, March 15, 1081), and Boniface VIII (*Unam Sanctam*, November 18, 1302), among many others (see *The Josias* Library at https://thejosias.com/library/), but has never been formally defined, and hence *de fide non definita*.

10   We refer the reader to the opening chapters of Charles Coulombe's *Blessed Charles of Austria: A Holy Emperor and His Legacy* (Gastonia, NC: TAN Books, 2020), in which the doctrine of Christian kingship is well articulated.

11   See McShea, "Bishops Unbound."

12   John C. Rao has an important contextualization of this rhetoric in "Louis Veuillot and

In the mess of history a single cause can have multiple layers of effects. And that brings us to the most difficult conversation.

THE INCORRUPT, SAINTLY ULTRAMONTANE POPES

We must soberly evaluate Bl. Pius IX's statement "I am Tradition!" Was this truly meant as a nuanced theological statement, or was it an outburst of rage, or both, or more? We are obliged to interpret him as sympathetically as possible, but if the historical data convincingly shows us he lost his temper and said something dangerously imprecise, there is a limit to how much can be explained, and that limit is the same that reason affords us. As Kennedy Hall wrote, "Piously thinking the best about the pope [and, *a fortiori*, a saintly pope] can turn to excess which goes beyond reason."[13]

What about when the saint broke with tradition by refusing to invite lay nobility to Vatican I? In so doing, he broke with fifteen centuries of custom and helped to create the clericalist imbalance in the Church that we suffer under today. French prime minister Émile Ollivier said, quite rightly I fear, that by this act the pope *formalized* the separation of Church and state, which he had formerly condemned.[14] This was as bad as, if not worse than, Leo XIII contradicting his anti-Liberal writing by his pro-Liberal stance vis-à-vis Third Republic France.

Yet the saint also formally confirmed the *nuanced* interpretation of Vatican I, against a hyperpapalist distortion. The German bishops clarified that "the opinion according to which the pope is 'an absolute sovereign because of his infallibility' is based on a completely false understanding of the dogma of papal infallibility" and that the pope "is restricted to the contents of Holy Scripture and Tradition and also to the dogmas previously defined by the teaching authority of the Church."[15] Pope Pius IX called this "the true meaning of the Vatican decrees" and approved the same for the Swiss bishops.[16]

Catholic 'Intransigence,'" in idem, *Catholic Christendom versus Revolutionary Disorder* (Waterloo, ON: Arouca Press, 2023), 26–53.

13   Kennedy Hall, "The Pope that Broke the Camel's Back," *OnePeterFive*, August 12, 2021.

14   Sir Rowland Blennerhassett, "The Hohenlohe Memoirs," *The Eclectic Magazine*, vol. 148 (University of Iowa, 1907), 236.

15   Gerhard Ludwig Müller, "By What Authority: On the Teaching Office of the Pope," *First Things*, January 16, 2018. See also idem, "Statement on the Limits of Papal Authority," in *Roman Encounters: The Unity of the Faith and the Holy See's Responsibility for the Universal Church*, trans. Susan Johnson (Irondale, AL: EWTN Publishing, 2019), 230–31.

16   Olivier Rousseau, "Le vraie valeur de l'épiscopat dans l'Église d'après d'importants documents de 1875," *Irénikon* 29 (1956): 121–42, in Patrick Granfield, *The Limits of the Papacy: Authority and Autonomy in the Church* (New York: Crossroad, 1987), 116, n21. Granfield references *DH* 3112–17 which also has Pius IX's letter to the German bishops. Cf. Congar, *My Journal of the Council*, 97, n3. The Swiss bishops said that Christian dogma "in no way depends upon the caprice of the pope or upon his good pleasure, to make such and such a doctrine the object of a dogmatic definition: he is tied up and limited to the Divine Revelation, and to the truths which that revelation contains; he is tied up and limited by the Creeds already in existence, and by the preceding definitions of the Church; he is tied up and limited by the divine law and by the constitution of the Church." The pope "wrote to the Swiss Bishops that nothing could be more opportune or more worthy of praise, or cause the

But can we say that some of the Pontiff's actions nevertheless led to some of these distortions? Or some of the rhetoric of the ultramontanes? Indeed, it would be reasonable to think that this climate created these distortions, and this is the false spirit of Vatican I, to which we will return in a subsequent chapter.

St Pius X, another incorrupt saint, confirmed the clericalist Church and the *de facto* suppression of the traditional Two Swords doctrine by revoking the right of papal veto for the Holy Roman Emperor. He himself proclaimed hyperpapalism by promoting blind obedience to the pope (which Rafael Cardinal Merry del Val had to qualify), and created a break with Tradition by his radical breviary reform.[17] Pius X's treatment of the Eastern Catholics in the United States by way of Latinization directly contradicted Leo XIII's explicit assurances of safeguarding the rites of the East, and his breviary reform created a dangerous precedent of papal power over the rights of Tradition in the liturgy—a precedent that was acted on with ever-greater audacity, culminating in the creation of an entire body of new rituals, and, more recently, in an attempt to deprive the most venerable of Christendom's historic rites of its status as an "expression of the *lex orandi*" of the Roman Rite.[18]

Yet whatever faults may have been the result of acts or omissions by Bl. Pius IX and St Pius X, intended or unintended, it is certain that they not only achieved a great degree of holiness (evidenced by their incorrupt relics and miracles), but their pontificates were among the greatest in the post-Tridentine period, and indeed the whole of Church history.[19] Perhaps in our own day, where copious historical data is readily available for the saints in a way almost unheard-of in history, we have the lamentable burden of finding these faults in the saints since we cannot deny our reason and the investigation of history and theology. But faults such as these

---

truth to stand out more clearly." Dom Cuthbert Butler, *The Vatican Council (1869–1870): Based on Bishop Ullathorne's Letters*, ed. Dom Christopher Butler (Westminster, MD: The Newman Press, 1962), 464–65.

17   See the passage given as one of the epigraphs to this volume. Meanwhile, his secretary of state, Cardinal Merry del Val, said this: "Great as our filial duty of reverence is towards whatever he may say, great as our duty of obedience must be to the guidance of the Chief Shepherd, we do not hold that every word of his is infallible, or that he must always be right. Much less do we dream of teaching that he is infallible, or in any degree superior to other men, when he speaks on matters that are scientific, or historical, or political, or that he may not make mistakes of judgment in dealing with contemporary events, with men and things." *The Truth about Papal Claims* (Boonville, NY: Preserving Christian Publications, 2012), 19.

18   On the danger of papal precedents, see chapters 2 and 3. Writes Dom Alcuin Reid: "That a pope could discard ancient liturgical tradition by sole virtue of his own authority is found nowhere in liturgical history before Saint Pius X . . . . Lamentably, in a period where the prevalent ultramontanism led to the assumption that even the prudential judgments of popes were unquestionably correct, Saint Pius X contravened that part of the principle of liturgical reform that obliges even popes to respect objective liturgical Tradition and to develop it organically" (*The Organic Development of the Liturgy*, 2nd ed. [San Francisco: Ignatius Press, 2005], 77–78).

19   On the incorrupt relics of Bl. Pius IX, see the witness of Madre Pascalina in Charles Theodore Murr, *The Godmother: Madre Pascalina, A Feminine Tour de Force* (2017), 75–80. She also relates a story—which at the time impeded his beatification—about how Pius IX lost his temper when he was fleeing from the Freemasons and swore at his secretary who could not break through a locked door (67–74).

do not cancel out the great good these popes and the other aforementioned men did to combat the Revolution in their day. Counter-revolutionary ultramontanism was indeed a movement of grace.

DR PLINIO'S STATEMENT ON THE PAPACY

Now let us turn to another godfather of the traditionalist movement, the "crusader of the twentieth century," Dr Plinio Corrêa de Oliveira. As Prof. de Mattei relates:

> Love for the Roman Pontiff, his prerogatives and rights, has charac-terized authentically Catholic spirits throughout twenty centuries of history, because, as Plinio Corrêa de Oliveira states, "after love for God this is the highest love taught to us by religion [*dopo l'amore per Dio questo è il più elevato amore insegnatoci dalla religione*]."[20]

This statement may initially seem fitting for the Catholic veneration of the office and the man. But at closer inspection, it appears rather dangerous as well as theologically imprecise. For the Catholic Faith teaches us that after God, Our Lady receives *hyperdulia*, and St Joseph receives *protodulia*, and then all the angels and saints follow. When speaking about our obligations of veneration to the per-sons of the Church Militant, it would seem to be an open theological question whether the fourth commandment binds us to venerate our parents before any other person of the Militant Church, or the Sovereign Pontiff before our parents. If some theological authority has resolved this question, I am not aware of it. But I venerate with all my heart Our Lady directly after God, and then St Joseph, and no human person will take their place after God.

Therefore I ask: what was the context of Dr Plinio's statement? Was it merely a rhetorical hyperbole, as occurs with M. Veuillot? Or was it a dangerously impre-cise statement which, taken out of context, could lend itself to an unrestrained hyperpapalism? Prof. de Mattei is also translating this statement presumably from Portuguese to Italian, and this article was then translated by Kennedy Hall into English. Might there be a translation difficulty here? There may well be an orthodox interpretation of the statement. As it stands, however, it seems, at very least, a prudentially inappropriate thing to say. In any case, if it is true that Dr Plinio spoke imprecisely here, we would—using the same piety with which we forgive or excuse the excesses of saints and the godfathers of the traditionalist movement—not forsake Dr Plinio or foolishly dismiss his entire movement, but recognize the grace that raises up and sustains the movements of Tradition in every place, and venerate our forefathers and their zeal.

Thus the streams of ultramontanism—stretching back to the Europe-wide ven-eration of the Servant of God Pius VII, that pope who withstood the tyrant—are indeed grace-filled and good movements against the Revolution.

---

20   See chapter 28.

THE GRACE-FILLED MOVEMENT AND THE PROVIDENCE OF GOD

Yet like the Counter-Reformation, even this grace-filled movement had certain unintended consequences or blind spots that may or may not be attributable to individuals in the movement but that are clearly visible in hindsight.[21] Further, no man can foresee how his words or actions — sometimes perfectly executed for the time — will have consequences in history. Noting and correcting some excess into which our forefathers fell or which they did not foresee is not any dishonor to their memory, but rather a taking up of the same mantle for the new generation. In heaven, these forefathers look down on us to urge us into battle; they are not concerned about any faults that we reluctantly find in them, if only we join them in the heavenly Kingdom. The grace which raises up a movement does not endow the same with infallibility or impeccability, for "we have this treasure in earthen vessels, that the excellency may be of the power of God, and not of us" (2 Cor 4:7). If the Blessed Apostle said these words of himself and his ministry, how much more is this true concerning the rest of us sinners?

With this reflection on ultramontanism in the broadest historical sense, we can see deeper roots of our current problems, and the grace that raised up men of God like Veuillot and Bl. Pius IX will also fortify us sinners to fight the same fight against the fallen angels in our day, better equipped with the harmonizing of truths that the Devil seeks to twist and oppose into excess and heresy. In a theological sense, we know that the Holy Spirit is working and guiding the Church, and leading her *into all truth* according to the infallible promise of His Majesty (Jn 16:13). At the same time, in a historical sense, we can see certain issues arising in the nineteenth century that are connected to our own problems today. In the next two chapters, we will discuss the *dubia* of Vatican I and the "false spirit" of the same.

---

21 Among other things, we can point to the harm of Latinizations in the Eastern Rite and the failure to resolve the *De Auxiliis* controversy as possible harmful blind-spots in the Counter-Reformation.

31

The *Dubia* of Vatican I[1]

TIMOTHY FLANDERS

T HE LAST CHAPTER DISCUSSED DIFFERENT TERMINO-
logical aspects of ultramontanism. The primary dichotomy I am attempting to emphasize here is the distinction between *historical meaning* and
theological meaning. I believe this is where many of us get confused or start talking
past each other whether we are discussing the First Vatican Council or the Second.

Elsewhere,[2] we brought up the importance of the theological notes, which
we term "Theology 102." This is because after Vatican II especially, owing to an
existing decline in theology which had been ongoing since 1773,[3] theology suffered
an unprecedented collapse: many official theologians and bishops no longer know
Latin and the vast body of Tradition communicated in that language ("Theology
101") nor the "norms of theological interpretation known to all" (appendix to
Lumen Gentium), especially the theological notes ("Theology 102"). That collapse
complicates our discussion of this whole modern period. In this chapter, we will
attempt to apply the norms of theological interpretation to the First Vatican
Council, and in the chapter that follows, we will discuss further the *historical*
ramifications of the Council, in the form of the "False Spirit of Vatican I."

Before we begin let me emphasize again that I am not a theologian in the full-
est sense, for a theologian is traditionally understood to be a man of prayer who
gains wisdom by his holiness first and his knowledge second. Although I am not a
theologian, I know enough to understand that many "theologians" out there are
merely academics falsely claiming the title theologian. I am merely an educated
lay leader who am attempting to imitate in some small way my lay forefathers, the
great noblemen of Christendom — St Constantine the Great, Emperors Sigismund
and Charles V. These men entangled themselves in "clerical" theological questions
only in order to help the theologians do their own job. These *dubia* of Vatican I
will be resolved by theologians. As a layman, I don't want to shoulder the burden
of the spiritual sword, yet due to the circumstances I must do something according
to my state in life. This is meant to be a form of the "mutual help" between the
Two Swords of Christendom. Therefore I offer these reflections to laity so that
they can grasp some of the elements of this debate, which I hope will help us
move into a higher and more productive area of conversation.

---

1   First published at *OnePeterFive* on September 15, 2022.
2   See Timothy Flanders, "The Post-Vatican II Decline of Theology," *OnePeterFive*, June 13, 2022.
3   See Timothy Flanders, "The Pre-Vatican II Decline of Theology," *OnePeterFive*, June 7, 2022.

HISTORICAL AND THEOLOGICAL MEANING

Before we delve into the theological meaning of Vatican I, let's apply our distinctions to ecumenical councils in general. The layers of reality in which we deal with these questions — theological and historical — are related, but they are not the same. When we are dealing with an ecumenical council, we need to remember that on a *historical level* a great deal of evil machinations can exist at such a council, and even good men and saints can fall into this — and this can have all sorts of bad fruit on the historical level — yet nevertheless the *theological meaning* of the council can be protected and guided by the Holy Spirit, bringing forth good fruit.

The first seven ecumenical councils offer many examples: there was violence, even bloodshed — and the "good guys" at the council were by no means uninvolved. History forgets these evils but remembers the theological achievements.

Take the Council of Ephesus (431). St Cyril, Doctor of the Church, bribed the officials and terrorized the Council Fathers with an army of violent monks until the orthodox definition of faith was established.[4] Thus the theological meaning of the Council was safeguarded, but the saint's actions produced immediate bad fruit by threatening a schism with the Antiochian catechetical school. Showing his saintliness, however, St Cyril won over his theological enemies in the reconciliation with John of Antioch in 440.[5] Without such saintliness, the *historical effects* of the Council of Ephesus could have obscured the *theological fruit* of the Council. (Indeed, the Greek schisms hardened in the next century precisely due to a loss of such holiness before and after the Fifth Ecumenical Council.)[6]

Why is this the case — why does God allow such evil to be mixed with the good? It is because, in His Providence, He allows men to produce evil by an abuse of their freedom. Yet God always brings good out of evil: He allows error *in order to bring about a greater truth*. It is within the power of the omnipotent God's Providence to work out these difficult matters, even with the machinations of evil at work to undermine His purposes. And can there be any doubt that the fallen angels work their hardest to undermine God's work specifically when churchmen gather at an ecumenical council?

THE HISTORICAL AND THEOLOGICAL MEANING OF VATICAN I

Thus when we say "the false spirit of Vatican I" we are speaking about some of the harmful *historical* effects of certain aspects of historical ultramontanism as well as of *the historical event* of Vatican I. This does not and cannot truly undermine

---

4   Timothy (Kallistos) Ware, *The Orthodox Church* (London: Penguin, 1993), 34; John Meyendorff, *Imperial Unity and Christian Division: The Church 450-680* (Yonkers, NY: St Vladimir's Seminary Press, 2011), 165.

5   DH 271-73.

6   That is, the Second Council of Constantinople. On this, see Timothy S. Flanders, *City of God vs. City of Man: The Battles of the Church from Antiquity to the Present* (N.p.: Our Lady of Victory Press, 2021), 141-61.

the acts of God's Holy Spirit at Vatican I in defining the dogmas of papal primacy and infallibility (as well as those on God, revelation, faith and reason, in the other decree of the Council, *Dei Filius*).

However, in the mess of history, the theological meaning can become *obscured* merely in a historical sense — in other words, some people might become confused or there might be some problematic inferences or extrapolations that need to be corrected. Since theological and historical meanings are connected in the mess of reality (theological definitions occur *in history* — at a given time and place), these things can become garbled after a Council, and hence a "false spirit" can arise in which the Devil attempts to use the very acts of God against the Church.

After a Council's anathemas inevitably foil the Devil's plots, the fallen angels quickly turn to twisting and abusing those very definitions in order to undermine what God has built.

Having said all this, let us first abstract our analysis from the realm of history and focus solely on the theological achievements of Vatican I, and discuss some of the *dubia* that remain. In the next chapter we will look into some of the historical happenings at the Council and afterwards in order to distinguish the theological achievement from the false spirit.

THE BASIC DOCTRINE OF PAPAL MONARCHY

We can summarize Vatican I's doctrine of papal monarchy in two basic points:

1. *Ex cathedra* definitions on faith or morals are infallible and irreformable *ex sese, non ex consensu ecclesiae* [from themselves, not from the consensus of the Church].
2. The Roman Pontiff enjoys ordinary and immediate jurisdiction over every bishop and every member of the faithful.

The definitions of these two dogmas, accompanied by anathemas, are contained in the decree *Pastor Aeternus*, and are best reviewed in the current edition of Denzinger[7] together with the associated *relatio* brought into English (with commentary) by James T. O'Connor and published by Ignatius Press.

WHY ARE THERE AMBIGUITIES IN VATICAN I?

The points above resolve any *dubia* concerning whether or not the pope can ever be infallible, and the extent of his jurisdiction. In other words, it resolves these questions under the strict parameters of the definitions and anathemas, excluding certain errors of Gallicanism which now, due to this definition, have been anathematized as heresy.

However, certain ambiguous phrases remain in the documents of Vatican I — for example, that the pope enjoys the "gift of truth and never-failing faith" and that the "See of St Peter always remains unblemished by any error" (*Pastor Aeternus*).

---

7   *DH* 3050–75.

It is important to note that these phrases seem to have a clear meaning *prima facie*, but are actually *theologically ambiguous*. This is because they do not use technical theological language so as to exclude propositions to the contrary, as the above two points do. The Holy See is indeed unblemished by any error, but does that mean that no pope has ever sinned against doctrine? Does that mean that the pope has never made a prudential error? What about a magisterial error in the realm that came to be called the ordinary (papal) magisterium? As an aside, and descending again to the historical plane, it is indeed possible that ambiguous phrases may turn up in an ecumenical decision due to the machinations of enemies (as has been amply demonstrated in regard to Vatican II),[8] but they can also arise due to the fact that *the Council Fathers do not wish to resolve a certain question at that time*.

Thus ambiguous phrases may be the result of a compromise between two theological parties at a Council: the Fathers conclude that they do not intend to resolve such questions and agree upon an *equivocal* phrase so that a vote will be able to advance the *pressing* dogma against the important error or heresy.

It is important to see that the question at Vatican I was not the infallibility and jurisdiction of the pope *per se*—as we now discuss it—but rather the assertion of the Revolution that the Church had lost its own charism of truth at all (as well as the secular State's power over bishops, condemned in #2 above). The Revolution asserted that the Church of Christ had ceased to have any power of truth over souls and society (thus Napoleon's taunt of Pius VI as "Pius the Last"). Further—and not unrelated—it had asserted that monarchy itself was *per se* tyranny, and thus Liberalism (or else its ugly daughter, Communism) was going to "liberate" the world from Monarchy by "revolution" (read: bloodshed).

Thus ultramontanism defended the papal monarchy in order to safeguard the most basic truths of the *infallibility of the Church as a whole*, as we see when the definition contextualizes papal infallibility as an *organ* of the Church's infallibility: "When the Roman Pontiff speaks *ex cathedra* . . . he possesses, by the divine assistance promised to him in Blessed Peter, that infallibility which the divine Redeemer *willed his Church to enjoy* in defining doctrine concerning faith or morals."[9] Thus the overall purpose of *Pastor Aeternus* is to defend the Church's infallibility in general by means of the papal infallibility in particular. The second point of doctrine regarding the universal jurisdiction was meant to combat the takeover of the bishops by the revolutionary regimes, as had happened in France with the clerical oath (a question made acute by Pius VII's ambiguous Concordat of 1801). The Council was not seeking to resolve other ancillary questions debated among theologians for centuries (and that we continue to debate today, with a renewed intensity). This is why ambiguities remain on other questions that do not directly bear upon the issues raised by the Revolution.

---

8 See Roberto de Mattei, *The Second Vatican Council: An Unwritten Story*, trans. Michael J. Miller et al. (Fitzwilliam, NH: Loreto Publications, 2012).

9 DH 3074.

Notice what the ambiguous phrases mentioned above do *not* say: they do not address the question of whether Pope Honorius was validly declared a heretic. They do not address the extent to which a pope can err outside of exercising *ex cathedra* authority (what about John XXII?). They merely repeat honorary phrases that have always been attributed to the Holy See, but do not resolve *dubia* that remained unanswered at the Council due to their irrelevance in answering the hubris of the Revolution.

THE *DUBIA* OF VATICAN I

Therefore let us list the *dubia* which have not yet received an answer but have become more pressing in the period following Vatican I (1870–present):

1. Is it possible for the pope to teach any error? (Or: does infallibility extend beyond *ex cathedra* determinations?)
2. Is it possible for the pope to become a heretic?
3. Does the pope have absolute authority over the liturgy? (Or: is the pope in modifying the liturgy bound to any Tradition other than the form and matter of the sacrament?)
4. Can we ever disobey or resist the pope on a matter not manifestly sinful?

All of these questions were left unresolved by Vatican I, notwithstanding strong statements which seem to resolve them *prima facie*. These questions have numerous precedents in history, as Prof. Roberto de Mattei shows in *Love for the Papacy and Filial Resistance to the Pope in the History of the Church*, and as Dr Kwasniewski discusses in the first volume of his two-volume *The Road from Hyperpapalism to Catholicism*. The Fathers of Vatican I were not unaware of these numerous historical questions. They merely chose to pass over them to resolve the more pressing issues of papal monarchy. However, the historical effect of this approach was to allow a false spirit of Vatican I to arise after the Council. We shall return to that point later.

THEOLOGICAL SCHOOLS FOLLOWING VATICAN I

For now we will outline four general schools of thought surrounding the Vatican Council, and show where each of these generally falls in answering the *dubia* of Vatican I, together with an approximate theological note.

1. *Hyperpapalist*: the pope can never be in error or heretical, and his will is equivalent to the will of the Holy Spirit, and thus anything less than blind obedience to him is schismatic. (*Tolerated opinion*.)
2. *Papal Maximalist*: the pope's infallibility extends beyond *ex cathedra* statements, but he can be disobeyed *if and only if* he commands something that is manifestly and intrinsically sinful (which is possible, as history shows). Therefore, he enjoys *absolute* power over the liturgy, keeping only the form and matter of the sacrament intact. Public resistance to

ecclesiastical authority is a scandal to the faithful and *per se* leads to schism. (*Pious opinion.*)

3. *Papal Minimalist*: the pope can become a heretic and err outside of his *ex cathedra* statements (although this will happen only rarely, due to the general protection of the Church by the Holy Spirit). The pope is bound to Tradition in his liturgical acts. He can be disobeyed even in things not manifestly sinful, but *only* according to a well-formed conscience. Public resistance to ecclesiastical authority can be justified only for a *manifestly grave cause*. (*Probable opinion.*)

4. *Neo-Jansenist*:[10] the pope (and the Magisterium in general) can be ignored, dismissed, and disobeyed in all their acts which fail to achieve infallible authority, and the faithful possess *carte blanche* to mock, ridicule, and insult ecclesiastical authority publicly. (*Rash, dangerous, contrary to Catholic teaching.*)

These four schools of thought mix with each other, and an individual Catholic may fall into different categories depending on different questions he might raise on this or that matter. We might note that the Hyperpapalist position is *tolerated*, and would seem to find support in certain hyperbolic statements of the saints (and even modern, informal statements of the Pontiffs),[11] but has never enjoyed magisterial authority in definitive statements. This is partially the *sententia* of Albert Pighius (asserting that the pope can never be even a *private heretic*), which was shared by St Robert Bellarmine, but which the *relatio* of Gasser expressly states is not the doctrine of Vatican I.[12]

The Maximalist stance is seen to arise especially after Trent with its anathema against those who say the Church does not have authority to change the liturgy "saving only its substance," and especially after Vatican I in the papacies of Bl. Pius IX, Leo XIII and St Pius X. It enjoys authority based mostly on papal precedents[13] and honorific, ambiguous statements, but not on definitive magisterial texts, notwithstanding strong statements obliging the faithful to obedience.[14]

---

10 I term this attitude "Neo-Jansenist" as opposed to "Neo-Gallicanist" because Jansenism was a dispute with papal authority about the Faith taught by the Fathers (specifically St Augustine) whereas Gallicanism was a dispute with papal authority about the role of the Catholic temporal authority. Further, the attitude cannot be called "Old Catholic," since Old Catholics rejected Vatican I and are thus formally heretics. Given that no traditionalists today claim Catholic temporal authority in their dispute with the Magisterium or refuse assent to Vatican I, it seems this impious attitude is more properly compared to Jansenism's bad-faith dealings with ecclesiastical authority.

11 See the last chapter.

12 See above, pp. 87–88.

13 See chapter 2.

14 *Pastor Aeternus* again: "Both clergy and faithful, of whatever rite and dignity, both singly and collectively, are bound to submit to this power by the duty of hierarchical subordination and true obedience, and this not only in matters concerning faith and morals, but also in those which regard the discipline and government of the Church throughout the world." What is the nature of this "true obedience"? Does it extend to obeying a sinful command? Does it extend to obeying but violating a well-formed conscience? Does it extend to obeying in prudential matters? These

However, the Minimalist St John Henry Newman would seem to counter this by presenting a view of Tradition (and thus of the liturgy) contained in the Church Fathers which emanates first from the "ordinary Magisterium" of the *regula fidei* and what St Basil says was "handed on to us in mystery."[15] Both Vatican Councils assert that the Magisterium is given authority to *safeguard Tradition*, making Tradition itself *more authoritative*.[16] Still, this position has not been clarified by any explicit magisterial texts, outside of CCC 1124–25, *Summorum Pontificum*, and certain ambiguous statements from Cardinal Ratzinger.[17] The limiting factors conceded by Bl. Pius IX mentioned in the last chapter seem to accord with this school, but that has not prevented the popes from asserting absolute power over the public liturgy (in the form of the Divine Office) within a generation of Vatican I, and later over Holy Week (Pius XII) and over all the sacramental rites (Paul VI).

Finally, some traditionalists unfortunately fall into the final camp, that of Neo-Jansenism, which is what Fr Ripperger characterizes as "disrespect of authority and the Magisterium" which is, according to him, one of the "ten problems in the traditional Catholic movement."[18] There is really no room to assert a Neo-Jansenist position since it comes from theological ignorance at best, and sinful impiety at worst (the latest *Professio Fidei* explicitly rejects this course of action by obliging the faithful to *obsequium religiosum* to non-infallible magisterial acts, notwithstanding this phrase's ambiguous nature).[19] Nevertheless, in response to the extremes of the Hyperpapalists, sometimes people react by embracing a *de facto* sedeprivationism, or worse. This tends toward making oneself one's own Magisterium and falling into the trap of prideful, private judgment.

As we can see, Vatican I allows the first three theological opinions and does not bring closure. The pontificate of Pope Francis has thrown open all of these questions as pressing matters which theologians have been trying to resolve.[20]

We should note here that those who castigate fellow Catholics for falling into one of the first three schools must beware lest they set themselves up as their own magisterial authority. At *OnePeterFive* we condemn *hyperpapalism* as a false doctrine, but we must also acknowledge that these our condemnations must be submitted to ecclesiastical authority and authoritatively adjudicated, as only a living and traditional Magisterium can do.

In recent years, thanks to the work of Joseph Ratzinger and because of the traditionalist movement in general, hyperpapalism is becoming a much weaker

---

are left unanswered by this ambiguous phrasing. For extensive commentary, see Kwasniewski, *Bound by Truth*.

15   *De Spiritu Sancto*, ch. 27.

16   See *Pastor Aeternus* 6; *Dei Verbum* 10.

17   See "Best Quotes on the Liturgy by Joseph Ratzinger/Benedict XVI," *New Liturgical Movement*, January 2, 2023.

18   See his lecture of that title, a transcript of which is available at www.tumblarhouse.com/blogs/news/problems-in-the-traditional-catholic-movement.

19   See chapter 13.

20   See Lamont and Pierantoni, *Defending the Faith*, for a particularly impressive attempt to do so.

theological position. Perhaps the pontificate of Francis has had this silver lining: that more and more mainstream theologians and bishops are moving away from the hyperpapalist position, and landing more in the spectrum between Maximalism and Minimalism. However, this process has only just begun under Francis, and we may have generations to go before hyperpapalism is condemned or these *dubia* are resolved.

In the next chapter, we will discuss further the historical fallout of Vatican I, and define its "false spirit."

32

What is the False Spirit of Vatican I?[1]

TIMOTHY FLANDERS

I N THE LAST CHAPTER, WE DISCUSSED FURTHER SOME of the interplay between theological and historical meaning at an ecumenical council. In particular, using the example of the Council of Ephesus (431), we observed that God can bring good out of evil even when a Council is filled with controversial actions which become a scandal to good men. In this way the Holy Spirit can protect and guide an ecumenical council to a *theological achievement* against heresy, while *at the same time*, the historical circumstances and actions of individuals can obscure this theological achievement *on a historical level*.

In other words, the historical confusion or "bad fruit" after any given council does not (and cannot) negate the good fruit of the proclamation of orthodoxy. The best that the devil can do is obscure this good fruit in the minds of many, but he cannot undo what has been wrought by God.

"THE FALSE SPIRIT" OF A COUNCIL

Here is where we find the phenomenon of a "false spirit" of a council. Let us discuss again the machinations at the Council of Ephesus. The *historical actions* of St Cyril at the Council of Ephesus provoked schism from orthodox churchmen in Antioch, even though his *theological achievements*—confirmed by the Holy See and protected by the Holy Spirit—still proclaimed the ineffable glory of the Theotokos against Nestorius. The "false spirit" that resulted from Cyril's excesses at the Council was a bitterness among the followers of St Cyril (the so-called *miaphysites*) against their theological rivals in the Antiochian school (the so-called *dyophysites*). Had it not been for the holiness of St Cyril restraining his own followers and forcing a reconciliation with John of Antioch, the "false spirit" of Ephesus—again, speaking *only* in regard to its historical unfolding and ripple effects, not to the crystal-clear theological achievement in itself—could have solidified the lamentable Greek schisms then and there.

It is beyond the scope of this essay to tell the sorry tale of the hardening Greek schisms between the Syriac Christians, Miaphysites, and Dyophysites.[2] To make a sad and bloody story short, the *historical events*—the actions of individual men

---

1   First published at *OnePeterFive* on October 3, 2023.
2   For a detailed treatment, see Flanders, *City of God vs. City of Man*, 141–61.

and the context of those actions—which surrounded the third through the fifth ecumenical councils helped to precipitate the first lasting schism in Christendom between these three Greek parties, weakening the eastern front in the face of the Sassanians, and later the Muhammadans.

The point is that these councils are indeed ecumenical and achieved infallible pronouncements against heresy (particularly at Chalcedon, with its harmony of orthodox Latin, Greek, and Syriac traditions),[3] yet "bad spirits" arose, *historically occasioned* by these councils, and based *not* on the action of the Holy Spirit but rather on the excesses of zealous orthodox and the sinful machinations of heretics. A "false spirit" of a council therefore refers to the *effects* of that council as an historical event, *not* to the council's teaching considered as a theological achievement. When we speak of the "false spirit of Vatican I," we are addressing the historical aftermath of that council, which can be distinguished from its theological achievements.

HINDSIGHT IS ALWAYS 20/20

Yet more, we can say that in the unfolding of history, sometimes even good, measured actions by good churchmen can have effects in a few generations that were not (and could not have been) foreseen. As we discussed in our first essay (chapter 30), it is no dishonor to our holy fathers to frankly recognize some misstep here or there that produced some unpredictable bad fruit generations later.

To take an easy example, it would be foolish to blame Calvinism on St Augustine, since St Augustine was a great Father of the Church battling heresy in his own time. If some of St Augustine's strong statements about grace were twisted by heretics later on, this is no fault of the great Doctor of Hippo; indeed, they furnished the opportunity for men of Calvin's age to defend Augustine's orthodoxy and refute its heretical distortions. It is no dishonor to the great Augustine to concede that some of his statements were imprecise on this matter. As we say in the States, "hindsight is always 20/20." If the saint would have known how his words would be abused by heretics, he would have rephrased them.

We should feel the same way about the counter-revolutionary ultramontanes,[4] who fought the Revolution and the fallen angels manfully in their own age, and whose mantle we pray to be worthy to pick up. Nevertheless we can see now, generations later, how some of their words and actions helped to produce a "false spirit of Vatican I."

Before we turn to even more conspicuous changes occasioned by Vatican I, let us briefly look at how the ordinary Catholic teaching office was traditionally practiced by our forefathers since the Apostles. For the overall historical movement of ultramontanism (with other factors) helped to produce a dramatic shift away from this *status quo ante*.

---

3   Jaroslav Pelikan, *The Christian Tradition: A History of the Development of Doctrine*, vol. 1: *The Emergence of the Catholic Tradition (100–600)* (Chicago: University of Chicago Press, 1971), 263.

4   See chapter 30.

SUBSIDIARITY OF THE ORDINARY TEACHING OFFICE:
THE FAMILY AND THE PARISH

Before Vatican I, the papacy issued universal decrees only in *extraordinary circumstances*, i.e., rarely and for the gravest of situations. This is because the ordinary teaching office of the Church was exercised primarily by the local bishop, whose title of *episkopos* indicates that he "watches over" the *depositum fidei* and its transmission, which is *ordinarily and primarily* taught and passed down by bishops to their clergy, by parish priests to their faithful, and by parents to their children.

So let us note this first of all: the *primary teacher of the faith* for most Catholics is the parent, and then the parish priest. The local bishop would be involved in a typical Catholic's life at Confirmation (in the Latin rite) or if that Catholic attended pontifical events or processions. That local bishop might write a pastoral letter to his diocese, but that's it. Tradition was passed down in a local village around the village or municipal church. It was seen in all the monuments built by parents and priests down the ages in a community — the parish church, the statuary, the processional paths, the customs, cuisine, dancing, etc. All of these things were passed down and taught by parents and priests. This cannot be overemphasized: the *normal teaching office* was the parent's first, the priest's second, and, rarely, the local bishop's. Only *in extreme cases* would the pope himself be involved in a normal Catholic's life.

Thus the doctrine of the Two Swords was most commonly seen in the cooperation and mutual help between the parents (lay power — temporal sword) and the local priest (clerical power — spiritual sword). But this might also involve in extraordinary cases the local noblemen and princes (lay power — temporal sword) with the local bishop (spiritual sword), and only in extreme cases the king or emperor cooperating with the bishop of Rome.

This began to change dramatically with Trent, since the universal crisis of the Protestant Revolt shook Latin Christendom to its foundations. Still, even the papally-promulgated *Roman Catechism*, taught by local priests, was simply an *augmentation* of the existing structure of the ordinary Tradition handed down through parents and priests. The pope increasingly began to intervene in various nations and in more extreme cases on the universal (Latin) level, *but with the caveat* that local custom and the local bishop would *trump* the pope (except for grave cases). The stipulations of *Quo Primum* allowed the local and tradition rites to prevail in all cases; only that which was relatively new (under two hundred years' duration) had to be given up.

The office of the pope was primarily *reactive*, for *answering questions that could not be resolved on the local level*. In other words, the papacy functioned to support the subsidiarity of the local teaching office of the bishop, who was merely "watching over" — not directly intervening unless necessary! — the passing down of the Tradition by parent first and priest second. This was the normal, ordinary Catholic life of Tradition for centuries and centuries. The papacy simply was never the universal teaching office it is today.

THE PAPACY REPLACES THE FAMILY AND PARISH CULTURE

In reaction to the French Revolution, the popes began to write more nationwide or universal encyclicals. This was an unprecedented innovation of the papal office, but was deemed necessary for the times. To take another phrase from the States, "desperate times call for desperate measures." As Pius V had done with *Quo Primum* at the time of the Protestant Revolt, later popes felt the need to act in a new and desperate way to address a new and desperate situation. Due to the concurrent First Industrial Revolution in Western Europe and North America (c. 1760–1840), families had been displaced from the traditional catechetical environment of local traditions and customs tied to the village community. The normal teaching office of the parents and the priests was severely weakened. Local bishops often couldn't build churches quickly enough to keep up with the rapid urbanization of the faithful.[5] Meanwhile, the Liberal and Communist wolves pounced on the faithful, spreading their poisonous doctrines and destroying Christian culture. Thus the pope, as a good father, filled this vacuum, defending the flock from the wolves and teaching the faith when the local, ordinary teaching office was weakened. But it seems he did not foresee certain negative consequences.

The "nuclear family" was invented by the industrial urbanization, which stripped the family of aunts, uncles, grandparents, cousins, etc.[6] With this reductionism of the family and loss of parish culture, with the constant bloody revolution of Liberalism, it makes complete sense why our forefathers the counter-revolutionary ultramontanes rallied around the papal teaching office. The result, however, especially after Vatican I, was to move the center of gravity of normal Catholic catechetical life away from the local family and parish to the universal teaching office of the pope.

Notice that nowhere in the documents of Vatican I is such a process promulgated, much less suggested—but it transpired nonetheless. It is one of many manifestations of a "false spirit of Vatican I," not contained in its decrees but occasioned by historical forces.

PAPAL VOLUNTARISM AND THE LOSS OF TWO SWORDS

Depending on how you count it, Leo XIII wrote eighty-eight encyclicals in his twenty-five year pontificate, amounting to an average of 3.52 per year. This set the precedent for the post-Vatican I papacy. Note, as well, that the majority of these encyclicals are *ordinary* teaching documents—not responses to specific questions with precise theological notes or censures. Because of the *dubia* of Vatican I,[7] it was easy enough for ordinary Catholics to think that everything contained in an encyclical is infallible. This matter became acute, as Mr Ureta

---

5   Owen Chadwick, *The Secularization of the European Mind in the Nineteenth Century* (Cambridge: Cambridge University Press, 1975), 97.

6   David Popenoe, *Families without Fathers*, new ed. (New Brunswick: Transaction Publishers, 2009), 81.

7   See the last chapter.

shows (drawing on Prof. de Mattei's work),[8] when Leo XIII *de facto* reversed the position of Bl. Pius IX regarding the French Third Republic. Leo XIII himself seemed to support hyperpapalism in his handling of this situation, leading to the hyperpapalist doctrine: "The sole rule of salvation is to be with the living pope."

Was this axiomatic simplism really invented *ex nihilo* under Leo XIII with *no causal* relationship to events in the pontificate of Bl. Pius IX? Surely not. As we mentioned in chapter 30, Bl. Pius refused to invite lay noblemen to Vatican I, breaking about fifteen centuries of Tradition, an action which received criticism as "formalizing the separation of Church and state."[9] The effect of Pius's action was the *de facto* suppression of the Two Swords doctrine, by negating the *office of the lay, temporal sword* represented at councils by emperors, kings, princes, and noblemen, who were not judges of doctrine, yet also not mere spectators. As well-formed Christian noblemen, they would encourage and enable the bishops to do their job.[10] Thus the lay temporal order, *de facto* stripped of its rights by Pius IX, was vulnerable to the clericalist hyperpapalism of Leo XIII in his dealings with the Third Republic. St Pius X then revoked the right of lay veto over the pope, further stripping the lay order of its traditional rights.

Note, again, how none of this is found stated in or is necessarily implied by the documents of Vatican I. It is nevertheless occasioned by the historical event of the Council.

THE FIRST "MEDIA COUNCIL" IN WARTIME

Another critical point to seize upon is that Vatican I was the first council in which the newspapers churned out public opinion at an unprecedented rate. For the mass of the faithful, without any theological erudition to understand the nuances of true theological ultramontanism (as Mr Ureta elucidates it), the fiery rhetoric of the Comte de Maistre and Louis Veuillot—both of them laymen without theological training—seems to have produced a mass-media enthusiasm for defending the Holy See and elevating the pope as high as possible.[11] Since Catholic families throughout the world were sending their sons to die in the Ninth Crusade defending the pope from the Masonic revolutionaries, this was not a time for a nuanced theological presentation.

---

8   See chapter 18.

9   This is a paraphrase of the comments made by French prime minister Émile Ollivier as quoted in Blennerhassett, "The Hohenlohe Memoirs," 236.

10   Take, for example, this lay involvement at Lateran V: "Towards the close of the council (1517) the noble and highly cultured layman, Gianfrancesco Pico della Mirandola, delivered a remarkable speech on the necessity of a reform of morals; his account of the moral condition of the clergy is saddening, and reveals the many and great difficulties that stood in the way of a genuine reform. He concluded with the warning that if Leo X left such offences longer unpunished and refused to apply healing remedies to these wounds of the Church, it was to be feared that God Himself would cut off the rotten limbs and destroy them with fire and sword. That very year this prophetic warning was verified [when Luther began the Protestant revolt]." Klemens Löffler, "Pope Leo X," in *The Catholic Encyclopedia* (New York: Robert Appleton Company, 1910), www.newadvent.org/cathen/09162a.htm.

11   See chapters 17 and 27.

The media furor certainly did not help to provide the patient, nuanced analysis necessary to disentangle "theological ultramontanism" (a terminology that can be used to describe the dogma of Vatican I) from hyperpapalism (that "false spirit" we are treating). But we need sympathetically to understand why our forefathers chose at times not to bother with achieving the utmost conceivable or desirable theological precision. In wartime, bodies are needed to take up their weapons—the Rosary and/or the musket—to defend the clergy and our wives and children from Liberalism's prideful bloodshed. That is the main concern, and it is an urgent one. Coming into the council, we have the mighty wave of a generations-long media campaign pushing ahead a war that is being waged only a few miles from the Vatican. As we know, the Masonic revolutionaries finally made it to the Vatican later in 1870, stopping the council in its tracks. The Fathers of the First Vatican Council were fighting the fallen angels on a theological level, while our counter-revolutionary forefathers were *losing ground* to the revolutionaries who were slowly taking more territory and marching closer and closer to Rome. This revolutionary wartime historical context is essential for understanding the intense media campaign of the counter-revolutionary ultramontanes and the *urgency* of the theological ultramontane party at Vatican I.[12] It is easy for us in peacetime to judge harshly the missteps or excesses of our forefathers in wartime. You and I are now living in the ruins of that world that our forefathers nobly but unsuccessfully defended, bled, and died for. We should pay them our respect and honor, even if we criticize the unintended consequences of their haste and zeal.

THE "COUP" AT THE COUNCIL INCREASES THE EXCESS

With this context we can understand why the theological ultramontanes at the council fought zealously to have their party's doctrine dogmatized. They were opposed by the moderate "inopportunists" like St John Henry Newman (who wrote against them as a priest observer) or Eastern bishops like Chaldean Joseph VI Audo. These men believed in the dogma of papal infallibility but warned that, given the historical context, the dogma would lead to a false exaggeration of papal power.[13] Meanwhile, a third party, sympathetic to Liberalism, did not believe in the doctrine, considering it historically untenable. In this camp were observers like Lord Acton and Ignaz von Döllinger, who began manipulating the press with a view to undermining the council in any way they could.[14] They were, incidentally, aided by Dr Georg Ratzinger, the great uncle of Joseph Ratzinger.[15] Owing to the excessive enthusiasm sparked by wartime and the temptation of

---

12   Read Roberto de Mattei's summary of recent scholarship: "The 'Ninth Crusade' of the Papal Zouaves," *The Remnant* online, April 1, 2020.

13   R. Rabban, "Chaldean Catholic Church (Eastern Catholic)," *New Catholic Encyclopedia* (2003), vol. 3, p. 369, cited from Encyclopedia.com.

14   See John O'Malley, SJ, *Vatican I: The Making of the Ultramontane Church* (Cambridge, MA: Belknap Press of Harvard University Press, 2018), 149.

15   Peter Seewald, *Benedict XVI: A Life*, vol. 1: *Youth in Nazi Germany to the Second Vatican Council 1927–1965*, trans. Dinah Livingstone (London: Bloomsbury, 2020), 374.

theological triumphalism as a defiant response to modernity, the theological ultramontanes seized control of the council to produce what their critics termed a "coup," as Kwasniewski has treated in another place.[16]

It is fitting to recall St John Henry Newman's candid and perspicacious observations. Shortly after the definition of papal infallibility was promulgated, but before the Freemasons seized Rome, he wrote to his friend these prescient words about the false spirit of Vatican I:

> I have various things to say about the Definition . . . . To me the serious thing is this, that, whereas it has not been usual to pass definition except in case of urgent and definite necessity, this definition, while it gives the pope power, creates for him, in the very act of doing so, a precedent and a suggestion to use his power without necessity, when ever he will, when not called on to do so. I am telling people who write to me to have confidence — but I don't know what I shall say to them, if the pope did so act. And I am afraid moreover, that the tyrant majority is still aiming at enlarging the *province* of Infallibility. I can only say if all this takes place, we shall in matter of fact be under a new dispensation. But we must hope, for one is obliged to hope it, that the pope will be driven from Rome, and will not continue the Council, or that there will be another pope. It is sad he should force us to such wishes.[17]

This was Newman's opinion of the theological ultramontanes at the Council: a "tyrant majority." And to an Englishman especially, the accusation of "tyranny" means an unlawful, seditious act which does great harm and is against tradition.

Further historical events augmented the false spirit about which Newman was concerned. For, like St Cyril's Council of Ephesus, it seems — at least to "Minimalists" like Newman — that the actions of the theological ultramontanes created an aftermath that proved harmful to the Church. The ultramontane party at the Council felt that they had "won," even though, as Newman insinuates, they did not get all that they wanted. But, as mentioned above, the very next pontificate indeed churned out a flood of encyclicals that seemed to be cases of "us[ing] his power without necessity, when ever he will, when not called on to do so."

THE END OF EPISCOPAL SUBSIDIARITY

Newman's words indicate that there were hyperpapalist churchmen among the theological ultramontane party, and it seems that these contributed to the unprecedented papal centralization after Vatican I. For the dogmatic definition of papal jurisdiction declared that the pope has universal jurisdiction — but does that mean that the whole world should function as his personal diocese, to be

---

16   See "The 'Spirit of Vatican I' as a Post-Revolutionary Political Problem" in Kwasniewski, *Bound by Truth*, 18–29.

17   Newman to Ambrose St John (August 21, 1870), in Charles Stephen Dessain and Thomas Gornall, eds., *The Letters and Diaries of John Henry Newman* (Oxford: Oxford University Press, 1973), vol. 25, cited by Kwasniewski, *The Road from Hyperpapalism to Catholicism*, 9.

regulated by an army of nuncios or auxiliaries who, as it were, report back to him to ensure the implementation of his personal "vision for the company"?

In practice, local bishops became vicars of the Roman Pontiff, who appointed bishops throughout the world without local participation or confirmation by the temporal ruler (both of which were traditionally approved by the Church, within due limits). The modern idea that Pope Francis should regulate what is contained in a parish bulletin is a complete loss of subsidiarity for the local bishop. But this drift was already happening under Pius X, at least in the perception of some observers. The liturgical, historical, and linguistic scholar Adrian Fortescue said these words about that pope:

> You know, we have stuck out for our position all our lives . . . unity, authority, etc., Peter the Rock and so on. I have, too, and believe it. I am always preaching that sort of thing, and yet is it now getting to a *reductio ad absurdum*? Centralisation grows and goes madder every century. Even at Trent they hardly foresaw this kind of thing. Does it really mean that one cannot be a member of the Church of Christ without being, as we are, absolutely at the mercy of an Italian lunatic? . . . Give us back the Xth century Johns and Stephens, or a Borgia! They were less disastrous than this deplorable person.[18]

And later, in a passing comment in 1919: "I never cared a tinker's curse for what the Congregation of Rites may have decided about the order in which the acolyte should put out the candles at Vespers."[19] This, from the author of some of the most detailed liturgical manuals we have. He appreciated the delicate balance between local customs, universal laws, and areas of discretion or adaptability.

Christ constituted the Church with *subsidiarity* so that the Rock of Peter need not take on the near-impossible task of governing the whole world as his diocese. He willed to begin with twelve apostles, not one alone, so that they could divide among themselves the demanding missionary work of establishing local churches after Pentecost. God did not, moreover, endow the machination of Vatican bureaucracy with infallibility, and the lack of sufficient awareness of curial limitations can lead and has led to serious missteps due to centralization, like the silencing of Padre Pio or the betrayal of the Cristeros. The universal jurisdiction of the pope cannot and should not make the whole world his diocese, nor can this result be logically extrapolated from what Vatican I teaches.

CREATING A PUBLIC LITURGY *EX NIHILO*

As the loss of the local bishop's authority has led to our imbalanced ecclesial environment, the radical redesign of the breviary under Pius X is a direct

---

18   Letter, November 5, 1910, quoted in Alcuin Reid's Introduction to Adrian Fortescue's *The Early Papacy* (San Francisco: Ignatius Press, 2008), 12.

19   Letter to S. Morison (November 24, 1919), in Aidan Nichols, *The Latin Clerk: The Life, Work, and Travels of Adrian Fortescue* (Cambridge: The Lutterworth Press, 2011), 287.

precedent for the Holy Week of Pius XII and the modern rite of Paul VI. The pope "radically altered the ancient arrangement of the Roman psalter" with the "summary abolition" of pious tradition.[20] "That a pope could discard ancient liturgical tradition by sole virtue of his own authority," writes Reid, "is found nowhere in liturgical history before St Pius X."[21] Here was the creation of a new liturgy according to the "signs of the times," and imposed on the entire Church by the pope. Because of the loss of the local bishop's authority (at least *de facto* if not *de jure*), the bishop could not veto this universal legislation, which made no room for local or regional exceptions (as *Quo Primum* had done) and recognized no independent weightiness in the bishops' opinion (as when the fathers assembled in Trent rejected Paul III's experimental breviary). As a result, Pius X has the unenviable distinction of abolishing, throughout the Catholic Church, the Laudate Psalms as Jesus Himself prayed them.[22]

Again, that the pope can do such a thing is found nowhere in the Vatican I decrees, but rather is occasioned by this false spirit.

CANON LAW

Along with the loss of local subsidiarity is another unprecedented act not contained in the decrees of Vatican I: a universal code of canon law. Before this, a centuries-old body of canons existed, but there was no single "code" for everyone; the local bishop handled canonical matters according to canonical traditions and local customs. By promulgating a universal code, the local bishop's authority to legislate for his own diocese was again undermined. Thankfully, even in our current (1983) code the bishop has authority, in certain situations, to dispense with universal legislation at his discretion; but as we have seen, Pope Francis and his curia have taken steps to prevent individual bishops from invoking canon law in order to dispense from the observance of *Traditionis Custodes* — so urgent a priority has the extinction of the Church's memory and heritage been deemed to be by the progressives who have usurped the highest positions in the hierarchy.

Along with this, an important omission was made in the 1917 code and repeated in the 1983 code, as related by Bishop Schneider:

> According to a medieval canonical tradition, which was later collected in the *Corpus Iuris Canonici* (the canon law valid in the Latin Church until 1918), a pope could be judged in the case of heresy: "*Papa a nemine est iudicandus, nisi deprehendatur a fide devius*," i.e., "the pope cannot be judged by anyone, unless he has been found deviating from the faith"

---

20 Reid, *Organic Development of the Liturgy*, 74–78.

21 Ibid., 78.

22 Reid quotes Anton Baumstark: "Down to the year 1911 there was nothing in the Christian Liturgy of such absolute universality as this practice in the morning office, and no doubt its universality was inherited from the worship of the Synagogue. . . . Hence to the reformers of the *Psalterium Romanum* belongs the distinction of having brought to an end the universal observance of a liturgical practice which was followed, one can say, by the Divine Redeemer Himself during His life on earth" (*Organic Development of the Liturgy*, 75–76).

(*Decretum Gratiani, Prima Pars,* dist. 40, c. 6, 3. pars). The Code of Canon Law of 1917, however, eliminated the norm of the *Corpus Iuris Canonici,* which spoke of a heretical pope. Neither does the Code of Canon Law of 1983 contain such a norm.[23]

Notice this gives the false impression that Vatican I dogmatized the opinion of Pighius, when in fact the *relatio* of Gasser explicitly contradicted that notion.[24] Nevertheless, such a notable omission in canon law, and the false impression on which it is based, is fully in keeping with the false spirit of Vatican I.

I remember talking to a sedevacantist once who told me that because the Church canonized St Robert Bellarmine and made him a Doctor shortly after Vatican I, therefore his opinions about the papacy are the doctrine of the Church. This is a prime example of the false spirit of Vatican I. Bellarmine may have agreed with Pighius concerning the hypothesis of a heretical pope — namely, that a pope cannot become a heretic, even privately, a view Bellarmine calls "pious and probable" — but (forgive me for repeating it again) this was not taught at the Council. The false spirit of Vatican I is at work here too, creating a false impression that seems to be rather widespread.

THE PAPAL ORACLE

All of these historical factors and more have contributed to a situation in which traditionalists and other Catholics are accused of "schism" for confirming the faith we all learned in First Communion catechism[25] or for acting upon the principle enunciated by Benedict XVI: "What earlier generations held as sacred, remains sacred and great for us too, and it cannot be all of a sudden entirely forbidden or even considered harmful." It is a situation in which bishops are removed from their dioceses based on the arbitrary will of the pope, as if they were mere "vicars of the Roman Pontiff," in spite of *Lumen Gentium* 27 rejecting this view by name. It is a situation in which the pope has become a "Delphic oracle" who is believed to hold the power to change white to black, and lies into truth. This historical situation was certainly occasioned by Vatican I, but the opinions underlying it were not taught by Vatican I. Therefore we may justly identify and repudiate the "false spirit of Vatican I." These historical factors must be faced if we want to overcome hyperpapalism and successfully transmit the faith to our children and our children's children.

The false spirit of Vatican I is a mighty engine that drives the false spirit of Vatican II, and with it, the current "synodality" that was the dream of arch-Liberal, Cardinal Martini.[26]

---

23   See chapter 10.

24   See Gasser's words, quoted above on pp. 87–88.

25   See the statement dated September 16, 2022, signed by four bishops and many priests and scholars: "The Teaching of the Catholic Faith on the Reception of the Holy Eucharist," published at *Rorate Caeli,* September 17, 2022.

26   See Julia Meloni, "The Weapon of the St. Gallen Mafia Is Synodality," *OnePeterFive,* September 20, 2021.

33

The Pope Needs Reform, Not the Papacy[1]

JOSÉ ANTONIO URETA

HENRY SIRE'S BOOK *THE DICTATOR POPE* IS APTLY titled, for it is not difficult to see that Pope Francis behaves like a true despot.[2] At the end of August (2022), he finally organized a consistory of cardinals but, in practice, muzzled them by dividing them into language groups. He allowed only a rapporteur from each group to speak at the plenary session—and only to summarize the group's discussion. Then, in early September, he imposed a new constitution on the Order of Malta, bypassing internal debates on amendments to its governing statutes. Simultaneously, he removed the Order's authorities and appointed interim leadership until a new head is elected under his constitution.

From a strictly juridical perspective, he perhaps had the authority to do both things. The cardinals are his advisers, so he can listen to them or not. As for the Order of Malta, despite being sovereign in the temporal order, it is essentially a religious order, so the pope has the power to intervene in its canonical structuring.

However, the Catholic Church is not a government department coldly ruled by decrees. Instead, she is a living reality whose administrative laws serve as a skeleton supporting immemorial customs that vivify and smoothen their application. Furthermore, neither the cardinals nor the Order of Malta's religious and laity are the pope's slaves; they are brothers and sons.

Ignoring the ancient customs governing the relationships between the pope and cardinals and between him and religious orders (or Catholic movements, for the Order of Malta is a mixed entity) is equivalent to governing the Church with that *dirigisme* with which Enlightenment despots ended organic medieval monarchy.

Paradoxically, this papal despotism is used to equalize and democratize the Church. In a March 2015 interview with a Mexican television station, Pope Francis stated, "I think this [the Curia] is the last court that remains in Europe. The others have been democratized."[3]

By appointing cardinals "from the periphery," Pope Francis is effectively demolishing the College of Cardinals, an eminently elite institution whose members

---

1 First published by *The American Society for the Defense of Tradition, Family, and Property*, September 19, 2022.

2 See chapter 46.

3 "Pope Francis Speaks with Mexican Television," *America*, March 13, 2015.

have held the protocol rank of "princes of the Church" since Boniface VIII (1294–1303). By intervening in the Order of Malta, Pope Francis seeks to end an aristocratic institution inherited from the Crusades—two aberrations, in his mind, for which the Church must do penance.

Pope Francis wants "a Church with an Amazonian face"[4]—desacralized, vulgar, and pauperized after the Amazon natives' "good living." The latter will be granted their own rite in the Church, incorporating ancestral pagan superstitions. At the same time, the Catholic faithful who love the traditional Latin rite are persecuted for their alleged backwardness (*indietrismo*).

Pope Francis feels entitled to change Church teaching on adultery, conditions to receive Communion, the death penalty, and just war while eyeing changes on artificial contraception and homosexual relations. His dictatorial behavior has shocked the *sensus fidei* of millions of Catholics and legitimately drawn reaction and resistance from dozens of prelates and hundreds of intellectuals and lay leaders worldwide. For my part, I wrote an article on the motu proprio *Traditionis Custodes* stating that "The Faithful Are Fully Entitled to Defend Themselves Against Liturgical Aggression—Even When It Comes from the Pope."[5]

However, some intellectuals who have publicly resisted Pope Francis's doctrinal deviations and abuses of authority have raised the possibility of recasting the papacy *per se*. They attribute the current pope's tyranny and the passivity of the overwhelming majority of the hierarchy to an inflated role of the papacy throughout the twentieth century. In their view, this so-called hyperpapalism results from a permanent imbalance that the proclamation of the dogmas of papal supremacy and infallibility by the First Vatican Council unwittingly introduced into the life of the Church.

Some argue that the exaggeration of papal authority started in the Middle Ages with the affirmation of papal power in the pontificate of St Gregory VII (1073–1085).[6] For them, the relationship style between the pope and the local churches should return to how things were in the first millennium, before the Eastern schism (1054).

Although these authors do accept the First Vatican Council's dogmas of papal supremacy and infallibility, they say it is necessary to correct abuses in their exercise and, consequently, in how the faithful view the papacy. Thus, they reexamine complaints of supposedly excessive meddling by the popes in the election of bishops and the direction of local churches as if the grousing were legitimate. In so doing, they recycle false beliefs first expressed by Orthodox schismatics and later by supporters of Gallicanism.

---

4   Pope Francis, Apostolic Exhortation *Querida Amazonia* (February 2, 2020), no. 61.

5   The article was published at *The American Society for the Defense of Tradition, Family, and Property*, July 25, 2021, www.tfp.org/the-faithful-are-fully-entitled-to-defend-themselves-against-liturgical-aggression-even-when-it-comes-from-the-pope/.

6   See chapter 2.

Paradoxically, this erroneous proceeding by some writers in the traditionalist camp to reevaluate the exercise of the papacy coincides with earlier proposals by leading progressives. Suffice it to mention the well-known 1996 lecture at Campion Hall, Oxford, by Most Rev. John R. Quinn, the controversial archbishop emeritus of San Francisco, titled "The Claims of the Primacy and the Costly Call to Unity."[7]

True, the motivations of both currents are very different. By proposing to change the way the pope exercises the papacy, progressives strive to realize the Second Vatican Council's ecumenical dream of uniting all churches and Christian denominations without any of them converting to Catholicism proper. The proposal of these traditionalists aims to protect the faith and the Church's traditional rites from the conciliar novelties that Pope Francis enforces *manu militari*.

Nevertheless, both evaluations of the papacy's performance are similar, as are the practical proposals for rectification. Both currents take the first millennium as their model and guide. They call for a diminished role for the Roman Curia, a devolutionist return of authority to local bishops, changes in how the latter are chosen, a more decentralized Church, and a greater application of the principle of subsidiarity. Both progressives and neo-Gallican traditionalists manifest the same antipathy for the papacy as the Church's "full and perfect monarchy."[8]

Progressivism is sheer Revolution within the Church. Therefore, it is not surprising that its leaders—moved by their "liberty, equality, fraternity" ideals—seek to reduce the pope's attributes as much as possible or to have him use them to transform the Church into an egalitarian democracy. What is strange, however, is to see traditionalist writers spreading opinions contrary to counterrevolutionary principles, advocating a recasting of the papacy into something akin to what progressives suggest. Unwittingly perhaps, they fall into the defect denounced by Joseph de Maistre—an author they dislike for being at the origin of nineteenth-century ultramontanism. He wisely warned that the counter-revolution should not be a "contrary revolution" but rather "the opposite of the Revolution."[9]

There is no denying the merit of these traditionalist writers in denouncing Pope Francis's errors and abuses. However, they make the same mistake as promoters of the German Synodal Way, who blame the Church's traditional structure and doctrine for clerical sexual abuses when they should rather blame sinful clerics. The solution to clergy sexual abuse, some Germans claim, lies in suppressing priestly celibacy and the hierarchical differences between clergy and laity. Likewise, neo-Gallican traditionalists advocating a reinterpretation of the papacy maintain that Pope Francis's many abuses and the passivity of

---

7   John R. Quinn, "The Claims of the Primacy and the Costly Call to Unity" (June 29, 1996), item 5301 at CatholicCulture.org.

8   Louis Billot, *Tractatus de Ecclesia Christi* (Rome: Aedes Universitatis Gregorianae, 1927), 1:535.

9   Joseph de Maistre, *Considérations sur la France*, in *Œuvres*, ed. Pierre Glaudes (Paris: Robert Laffont, 2007), 276.

bishops and faithful toward them result from a hypertrophied papal authority and "ultramontanism," unwittingly encouraged by the dogmas of papal supremacy and infallibility.

As is well known, clerical sexual abuse is not due to priestly celibacy or the Church's hierarchical structure but to dissolute morals among the clergy. That is particularly true of those allowed to enroll in seminaries and unwisely ordained priests by complacent bishops despite their homosexual orientation.

Likewise, Pope Francis's doctrinal deviations and abuses of authority do not result from the hypertrophy of papal authority but from his modernist convictions and the dictatorial character denounced by Henry Sire in his aforementioned book.[10] The passivity of bishops and faithful who disagree with the pope but dare not resist him does not stem from any diminished role in Church life. Indeed, at least doctrinally, their role was increased by the Second Vatican Council's dogmatic constitution *Lumen Gentium*, which introduced two novelties: episcopal collegiality and the notion of the Church as the People of God. Rather, in most cases, such passivity stems from careerism, cowardice, fear of going against the grain, and a lack of supernatural spirit.

There is no need to change Church discipline on priestly celibacy or her teaching on the clergy's superiority over the laity to solve the sexual abuse crisis. Similarly, to address today's papal tyranny, there is no need to redefine the papacy or its ordinary ways of exercising the Petrine ministry. What is needed is a profound conversion of the pope, bishops, and faithful. That conversion will help the pope act truly as the Vicar of Christ, not His almighty replacement. For their part, a converted people, filled with faith and fidelity to Tradition, will know how to distinguish between the voice of a true shepherd and one that leads the flock over a cliff.

If a hypertrophied papal authority resulted from excessive veneration of the papacy by the faithful, the ultramontanes and their successors would have been the staunchest defenders of pontifical errors and abuses after the First Vatican Council. After all, they were the advocates of defining papal prerogatives as dogmas of the faith. However, what happened was precisely the opposite, as I have demonstrated previously.[11] From the time of Leo XIII to the Second Vatican Council, followers of the ultramontane current rose against the errors and abuses committed by individual popes. It was liberal Catholics—whose party had deemed those dogmatic definitions "inopportune"—who sought to impose those errors and abuses on all Catholics. With Cardinal Charles Lavigerie, such liberal Catholics claimed: "The only rule of salvation and life in the Church is to be with the pope, with the living pope. Whoever he may be."

Plinio Corrêa de Oliveira, the twentieth century's leading counterrevolutionary among the laity, gave a shining example of ultramontane fidelity. In a harrowing

---

10   See also chapters 45 and 46.
11   See chapter 18.

and humiliating moment, the Brazilian Catholic leader expressed his veneration for the papacy in touching terms. In 1968, the TFPs of Brazil, Argentina, Chile, and Uruguay collected 2,038,112 signatures in the streets of those countries' prominent cities on a petition asking Pope Paul VI to take action against communist infiltration in the Church. The several thousand sheets containing the signatures (some stained with blood as communist activists attacked young TFP volunteers) were delivered to the Vatican Secretary of State. However, the Holy See failed even to acknowledge receipt. In contrast, a few weeks later, a delegation of progressive priests took a challenging document to the Vatican, and Paul VI quickly promised to study their demands. The Brazilian TFP founder used his weekly column in *Folha de S. Paulo* to call out the pope's unworthy behavior, using the literary device of a letter from an imaginary Protestant reader, Jeroboam Cândido Guerreiro, as his point of departure:

> Don't you realize, Dr Plinio, that Vatican doors and the Pope's heart are open to all currents and opinions except to ideological tenets and voices blowing from your end of the spectrum?
>
> Frankly, I am astonished at how easily, in your articles, you pretend to see none of this and manifest yourself as a fervent and intransigent Catholic as if today's Pope were not Montini but Sarto ("Saint" Pius X), the cruel hammer of heretics from the beginning of the century.
>
> I am not writing this to mortify you, Dr Plinio, but the truth must be said: Open your eyes. The modernized papacy and the New Church reject you and your confreres more than anyone else in the world . . . .
>
> Yet, despite having the door shut in your face, you present yourself in public as a papist, as fanatical as when you were a young member of the Marian Sodalities hollering the hymn: "Long live the Pope, may God protect him, the Shepherd of Holy Church!". . .
>
> Have the courage to explain to the public your contradictory position.

In his article, Plinio Corrêa de Oliveira answers this fictitious letter with a hymn of love for the papacy:

> It is not with the enthusiasm of my early youth that I stand before the Holy See today. It is with even greater, much greater enthusiasm. The more I live, think, and gain experience, the more I understand and love the pope and the papacy. That would be true even if I found myself in the circumstances Mr Jeroboam Guerreiro depicts.
>
> I still recall the catechism lessons explaining the papacy: its divine institution, powers, and mission. My young heart (I was then about nine years old) was filled with admiration, rapture, and enthusiasm. I had found the ideal to which I would dedicate my entire life. From then until now, my love for this ideal has only grown. And I pray to Our Lady that she increase it in me until my dying breath. May the last act of my intellect be an act of faith in the papacy. I want my final act of love to be an act of love for the papacy. I would die in the peace of

the elect, well united to Mary, my Mother, and through her to Jesus, my God, King, and excellent Redeemer.

My love of the papacy, Mr Guerreiro, is not abstract. It includes a special love for the pope's sacrosanct person yesterday, today, and tomorrow. It is a love of veneration and obedience.

I insist: It is a love of obedience. I want to give every teaching of this pope, and those of his predecessors and successors, the full measure of adherence that Church doctrine prescribes to me, holding as infallible what She says is infallible, and as fallible what She teaches is fallible. I want to obey the orders of this or any pope to the full extent the Church commands me to. That is, by never placing my will or the might of any earthly power above them, and by refusing obedience to a pope's order only when it involves sin. In that extreme case, as the Apostle Paul and all Catholic moral theologians teach, one must obey the will of God instead.

That is what my catechism classes taught. That is what I read in the treatises I studied. That is how I think, feel, and am with all my heart.[12]

Plinio Corrêa de Oliveira's love of the papacy showed in his tremendous esteem for pontifical ceremony. At a meeting with younger members of the Brazilian TFP in January 1976, they projected the film *Vatican City Under Pius XII*. It showed Pope Pacelli wearing the tiara and carried in the *sedia gestatoria* surrounded by *flabella* and the papal guard. After the screening, Dr Plinio improvised this explanation of pontifical pomp:

All these scenes are deduced directly from what theology teaches us about the papacy and from the Church's wise teachings on how to organize life.

The papacy is the highest institution on Earth. It is higher than any temporal power because what concerns the spirit is worth more than what concerns matter. What concerns the supernatural is worth more than what concerns the natural. And the pope has universal power over all peoples everywhere, whereas all other sovereignties in the world are limited. There is no king or president of the world, but the pope is the shepherd of the whole world and has jurisdiction over souls throughout the globe. He is the representative of the supreme supernatural power—God's power on Earth—and it behooves him to exercise to the highest degree the transcendent powers proper to the Catholic Church of teaching, guiding, and sanctifying. He is the highest hierarch of the whole Church and thus must also be surrounded by the most extraordinary manifestations of respect that can be paid to a man.

It follows from all this that life around the pope must be organized to correspond to three ideas: respect, love, and strength. Respect: the pope must be venerated. Love: the pope being the representative of

12   Plinio Corrêa de Oliveira, "A perfeita alegria," *Folha de S. Paulo*, July 12, 1970, www.plinio-correadeoliveira.info/1970_236_CAT_A_perfeita_alegria.htm.

Christ on Earth, all of humanity's love for Our Lord Jesus Christ must apply immediately to the pope, His representative on Earth. Strength: the pope is a shepherd, and no shepherd can be weak because he must defend the sheep and thus use force against wolves; the power to fight wolves is part and parcel of the power of governing the sheep.

So you see around the pontiff religious pomp and, at the same time, paternal and visible force, represented by the three pontifical guards that defend the Vatican palaces: the Swiss Guard, the Palatine Guard, and the Noble Guard (composed of members of the Roman patriciate who took turns, serving for free in the Guard). They guaranteed the pontiff's integrity and the safety of the Vatican's colossal art treasures, in addition to controlling the enormous flow of people there. But its primary significance is that, as the case may be, the pope has the right and duty to use force to defend the faith. And in these guards, whose uniforms are so distant from [those of] the Crusades, there's a reminiscence of the Crusades.

The Church wisely organized things so everyone who went to see the pope could carry their devotion and love to the highest degree and their respect and fear in the face of strength. A visit to St Peter's Basilica and the Vatican Palace was a spiritual exercise from which the faithful left with their souls more united to the pope than before.

Pay attention to people's faces when they talk to the pope, but especially when he moves on. It's almost the face of someone who has just received Holy Communion. Someone receives just a short word from the pontiff, but what a word! He will forever keep the timbre of the pope's voice, his smile, the temperature of his hand, how he shook it or did not, and the imponderables surrounding the pope. The person keeps all that for a lifetime and even unto death.

I experienced it myself. I took several objects to be blessed by Pius XII, including some of the candles sold on Via della Conciliazione. They were beautifully worked, with reliefs, figures, etc. He blessed them. As I returned to the hotel, I thought: "When I die, I want to hold the candle blessed by the Vicar of Christ. In this way, I will remain united to the See of Rome until I am unconscious, hanging between life and death, and my intellect no longer articulates any thought. My hand will cling to this candle that represents what I love most on Earth: the pope, with whom everything on Earth is worthy of love, without whom nothing is worthy of love but only contempt, marked by original sin and under the devil's dominion.[13]

A superficial or biased person would deduce from these exclamations of love for the papacy that Plinio Corrêa de Oliveira was a victim of "papolatry," someone incapable of objectively analyzing the pope's teachings and gestures, let alone resisting their enforcement. That person would be deeply mistaken because Dr

---

13   "Saint of the Day," January 10, 1976, adapted for this essay from spoken to written style.

Plinio's admiration for the papacy was an acute expression of love for the Holy Church and, in short, for Our Lord. Therefore, if the reigning pope taught or did anything contrary to the Church's perennial teaching and action, that very love of God led him to oppose it with the quickest and strongest reactions.

As early as 1965, five years before writing the imaginary reply above to Jeroboam Guerreiro, Plinio Corrêa de Oliveira closely followed the studies of Arnaldo Xavier da Silveira on the theological hypothesis of a heretical pope. He participated in a three-day symposium to discuss the matter along with Bishops Geraldo de Proença Sigaud and Antônio de Castro Mayer.

Since October 1969, nine months before the *Folha* article, he had followed Xavier da Silveira's studies on the *Novus Ordo Missae* of Paul VI and participated in two symposia in the presence of Bishop Mayer. They resulted in the book concluding that the new Mass was unacceptable in conscience for a well-educated Catholic.

Six months before his *Folha*'s Jeroboam article praising the papacy, Plinio Corrêa de Oliveira had written another in the same daily, titled "The Right to Know."[14] In it, he informed the Brazilian public of a letter to Paul VI by Cardinals Ottaviani and Bacci, authors of *A Brief Critical Study of the New Order of Mass*, and a letter addressed to Fr Annibale Bugnini from the St Anthony Maria Claret Association of Priests and Religious (with a membership of 6,000 priests). The Association's letter concluded: "We Catholic priests cannot celebrate a Mass which Mr Thurian, of [the] Taizé [community], declared he could celebrate without ceasing to be a Protestant. Obedience can never impose heresy (on us)."

Just as significantly, almost two years before his enthusiastic comments on the *Vatican City Under Pius XII* film, Plinio Corrêa de Oliveira wrote "The Vatican Policy of Détente with Communist Governments – Should the TFPs Stand Down? Or Should They Resist?" The document denounced the wrongheaded policy of détente, which is continued today by Pope Francis in his criminal agreement with Red China subjecting the Underground Church in China to the whims of Xi Jinping. Addressed to Paul VI, the TFP's "Declaration of Resistance" was published as a paid ad in thirty-seven Brazilian newspapers and fourteen more in other countries. It stated: "Our soul is yours; our life is yours. Order us to do whatever you wish. Only do not order us to do nothing in the face of the assailing Red Wolf. To this, our conscience is opposed."

Plinio Corrêa de Oliveira recalled this paragraph in the first of a two-article series in December 1983 and January 1984. They were titled "Luther, Absolutely Not!"[15] and "Luther Thinks He Is Divine."[16] Both reacted to John Paul II's benevolent letter to Cardinal Johannes Willebrands, in charge of the Vatican's

---

14   Plinio Corrêa de Oliveira, "O direito de saber," *Folha de S. Paulo*, January 25, 1970, www.pliniocorreadeoliveira.info/FSP_700125_direito_de_saber.htm.

15   December 27, 1983: text at www.tfp.org/luther-absolutely-not/.

16   January 10, 1984: text at www.tfp.org/luther-thought-he-was-divine/.

office of ecumenism, on the 500th anniversary of Luther's birth and dated October 31, the anniversary of his revolt. His reaction to John Paul II's participation in a festive act of love and admiration for the heresiarch in a Protestant temple in Rome was even stronger: "Dizzying, frightening, groaned my Catholic heart at this. However, my faith and veneration for the papacy redoubled." [17]

In January 1977, writing an update to his work *Revolution and Counter-Revolution*, Dr Plinio made a highly critical assessment of the Second Vatican Council with the same clarity and courage:

> Using "*aggiornamento'*d" tactics (about which the least that can be said is that they are contestable in theory and proving ruinous in practice), the Second Vatican Council tried to scare away, let us say, bees, wasps, and birds of prey. But its silence about Communism left full liberty to the wolves. The work of this Council cannot be inscribed as effectively pastoral either in history or in the Book of Life. It is painful to say this. But, in this sense, the evidence singles out the Second Vatican Council as one of the greatest calamities, if not the greatest, in the history of the Church. [18]

I could give many more examples of resistance, but that would exceed the limits of this essay. Those given suffice to show that Plinio Corrêa de Oliveira, inflexible ultramontane defender of the Vicar of Christ's attributes on Earth, decisively resisted the Second Vatican Council, Paul VI, John Paul II, and their erroneous teachings and actions — perhaps even before the birth of some of these traditionalist writers calling for a reinterpretation of the papacy. He did this energetically because his legitimate resistance sprang from his deep veneration for the papacy.

Someone may wonder: How can we extricate ourselves from this stalemate if it is unacceptable to recast the papacy or change how it is exercised even in the face of Pope Francis's abuses?

In my 2018 book, *Pope Francis's "Paradigm Shift": Continuity or Rupture in the Mission of the Church?* I mentioned Plinio Corrêa de Oliveira's 1976 conclusion to the Chilean TFP's book, *The Church of Silence in Chile*. It is to recognize the authority that Pope Francis and diocesan bishops have but to interrupt routine daily coexistence with the demolishing prelates, just as a wife and children can interrupt cohabitation under the same roof with an abusive husband and father without breaking the marital and filial bonds. [19]

Finally, I believe that what I wrote four years ago is even more valid today. I thus repeat it at the end of this essay:

---

17 Corrêa de Oliveira, "Luther, Absolutely Not!"

18 Plinio Corrêa de Oliveira, *Revolution and Counter-Revolution* (York, PA: The American Society for the Defense of Tradition, Family, Property, 1993), 145.

19 See José A. Ureta, *Pope Francis's "Paradigm Shift": Continuity or Rupture in the Mission of the Church?*, trans. José Aloisio Schelini (Spring Grove, PA: The American Society for the Defense of Tradition, Family, and Property, 2018), 166–71.

In the present confusion, which threatens to worsen very soon, one thing is sure: Catholics faithful to their baptism will never break the sacred bond of love, veneration, and obedience that unites them to the Successor of Peter and the successors of the Apostles. This is true even when these may eventually oppress them in their attempt to demolish the Church. If in the abuse of their power and seeking to coerce the faithful into accepting their deviations those prelates condemn them for their fidelity to the Gospel and for legitimately resisting abusive authority, it is those shepherds, not the faithful, who will be responsible for the rupture and its consequences before God, the rights of the Church, and history. St Athanasius is a case in point. Although he was a victim of the abuse of power, he remains a star in the Church's firmament forever.[20]

When Divine Providence decides to put an end to the apocalyptic crisis the Holy Church is going through, and a holy pope comes to govern her, as prophesied by numerous saints and privileged souls, the stains now disfiguring the papacy will shine with the same supernatural splendor as the wounds of the Passion shone on our Divine Redeemer's resurrected Body. At that hallowed hour, the holy hands of the Successor of Peter will bless particularly those who behaved like the good sons of Noah[21] in today's days of upheaval with unfaithful popes. Holding fast to the *sensus fidei*, they increased their veneration for the papacy, without falling into the trap of pretending to reform by human hands that which divine hands established: "Thou art Peter; and upon this rock I will build My Church" (Mt 16:18).

Yes, indeed! The pope needs reform, not the papacy.

---

20 Ureta, *Pope Francis's "Paradigm Shift,"* 170–71.
21 See Gen 9:20–27.

{ 34 }
Continuities[1]

STUART CHESSMAN

W E READ MUCH ABOUT THE "SYNODAL PATH," THE "Synodal Church," the "Synod on Synodality" and "synodality" itself. Few, however, seem to have noted the remarkable agreement among all the actors involved in these events. The German Synodal Path supposedly was the product of the unique nature of the German Church: bureaucratic, historically antagonistic to "Rome," and enjoying the benefits of the Church Tax. Yet similar recommendations were soon forthcoming in France and Ireland. Then, the allegedly "conservative" Church of the United States issued its own "national synthesis" which has a surprising resemblance to the positions taken by the Germans. For example, the USSCB summary found among the main issues facing the Church:

> Closely related to the wound of polarization is the wound of marginalization:
>
> Those who experience marginalization, and thus a lack of representation in the Church, fall into two broad groups. The first includes those marginalized who are made vulnerable by their lack of social and/or economic power, such as immigrant communities; ethnic minorities; those who are undocumented; the unborn and their mothers; people who are experiencing poverty, homelessness, or incarceration; those people who have disabilities or mental health issues; and people suffering from various addictions. Included also in this group are women, whose voices are frequently marginalized in the decision-making processes of the Church: "women on parish staff said they felt underappreciated, underpaid, not supported in seeking formation, worked long hours, and lacked good role models for self-care." The second group includes those who are marginalized because circumstances in their own lives are experienced as impediments to full participation in the life of the Church. Among these are members of the LGBTQ+ community, persons who have been divorced or those who have remarried without a declaration of nullity, as well as individuals who have civilly married but who never married in the Church. Concerns about how to respond to the needs of these diverse groups surfaced in every synthesis.
>
> Persons who have been divorced, whether remarried or not, often feel unwelcome within the Church.

---

1 First published at the blog of the Society of St Hugh of Cluny on October 19, 2022.

The hope for a welcoming Church expressed itself clearly with the desire to accompany with authenticity LGBTQ+ persons and their families. . . . In order to become a more welcoming Church there is a deep need for ongoing discernment of the whole Church on how best to accompany our LGBTQ+ brothers and sisters.

There was a desire for stronger leadership, discernment, and decision-making roles for women — both lay and religious — in their parishes and communities.

Synodal consultations identified that more work is necessary to welcome diverse cultural and ethnic communities. [2]

This consensus extends not just across borders but up and down the chain of authority in the Church. The archdiocese of Philadelphia, for example, produced its own statement pf priorities completely in accord with those mentioned above. Artwork arising out of those sessions in Pennsylvania was subsequently republished by the Vatican. In Rome, Cardinal Mario Grech has defended the German Synodal Path against its critics in other hierarchies.

Finally, the continuity extends across time as well as space. In 1976 the famous Call to Action conference was held in Detroit with the support and participation of senior members of the American hierarchy. In substance, its characterization of the issues facing the Church resembles closely those of the synodal reports of today. [3] In Germany, the Würzburg Synod held between 1971 and 1975 anticipated in many respects the current Synodal Path.

The number and specificity of the demands or proposed actions vary among these declarations, conferences, and "processes." But the underlying issues that are identified are generally the same. How can we account for this extraordinary unanimity? After all, hasn't the Church throughout the world and over recent decades been characterized by tensions between conservatives and progressives, traditionalists and liberals? Yet, when the Church undertakes a project to "listen" to its base, only one perspective emerges, only one set of priorities is deemed worthy of comment.

One obvious fact is that in all these meetings, conferences, and sessions the same people and the same institutions are involved. They are the bureaucrats who in fact run the Catholic Church, regardless of postconciliar talk of an empowered laity, subsidiarity, or synodal government by the bishops. They include the teachers and administrators at the Catholic educational institutions, the journalists of the Catholic press, the members of the mainstream religious orders, the administrators of dioceses, the staffs of national episcopal conferences, and the leadership of Catholic organizations of every kind. The Roman curia, along with its related

---

2   National Synthesis of the People of God in the United States of America for the Diocesan Phase of the 2021–2023 Synod, www.usccb.org/resources/US%20National%20Synthesis%202021-2023%20Synod.pdf.

3   Vincent P. Miceli, SJ, "Detroit: A Call to Revolution in the Church," item 4544 at Catholic Culture.org; originally published in *Homiletic & Pastoral Review*, March 1977.

and subordinated entities, is itself one of the foremost examples. Note that the administrators of the Church include (or form close alliances with) many not officially in the Church's employ. Members of the "engaged" or "activist" laity, for example, can be counted among the partners of the bureaucracy. Other allies have found a home as teachers or students at secular universities and divinity schools. The publication perhaps most representative of the views of the Roman Catholic bureaucracy—the *National Catholic Reporter*—was specifically founded in the 1960s outside the formal perimeter of the Church.

The makeup of the bureaucracy has shifted over the years—there are far fewer priests and nuns today in comparison to 1976 or 1966—but that has hardly diminished its role. Most of the few religious sisters that remain no longer serve in schools or hospitals but as administrators of one kind or another. Jesuits today rarely are able to staff their own schools and universities but direct and decisively influence their lay disciples who manage these places.

The actual number of administrators has undoubtedly steadily increased. Many bishops and diocesan priests also have come to understand their function to be links in a bureaucratic chain. Moreover, the bureaucratic tide is daily conquering new territory. Pope Francis has just decreed that laymen and women can lead Vatican congregations and dicasteries. A woman has just been appointed as a kind of "deputy vicar general" in a German diocese.[4]

These bureaucrats and their hangers-on are the ones who select the issues to be addressed in the synodal process and formulate the "solutions" for them. Not even the "1%" supposedly surveyed in the synodal process has had any real say in the matter.

This institutional stability is linked with ideological uniformity. The ascendancy of the ecclesiastical bureaucracy, although its roots reach much further back, is really the product of Vatican II. For it was in the wake of the Council that the functionaries were empowered to assume the direction of the Church. They internalized and perpetuated the basic twofold nature of the Council: a revolutionary reaction against all forms of the past in Catholicism, combined with total openness to the norms of contemporary society. It's easy to see how seductive such a message is for modern administrators. As against the laity and "reactionary" elements of the clergy they could pose as bold innovators in an ongoing, endless process of change. In relation to the powers of secular society—both in and outside of the state—they could appear as accommodating fellow citizens of modernity. Therefore, at all times the Church bureaucracy has remained the guardian of the progressive vision.

These continuities in structure and belief within the Catholic Church reflect the consolidation of the modern *civil society* of the West and of its ideology. As in the case of the Church, the cultural and structural unity of the secular world extends

---

4   Luke Coppen, "Rome silent on German diocese's appointment of lay 'vicar general representative,'" *The Pillar*, October 14, 2022.

over all Western societies (see Thomas Molnar's *The Emerging Atlantic Culture*).[5] Moreover, just like the Church bureaucracy, the secular *power elite* includes both state (governmental) and private institutions and players. The Church operates within this society, and after the Council explicitly has looked to it for guidance. In secular society too, there has been continuity in ideology since the 1960s, even if developments steadily assume a more and more extreme form. The "woke" ideology dominant today would have exceeded the expectations of all but a fringe of extreme radicals fifty years ago. But on such issues as support of unrestricted abortion the secular establishment has been consistent over the decades.

Now the controlling influence of secular society is evident not only in the political and moral positions adopted by the Church administrative entities, but also in the very fact of the bureaucratic ascendancy within the Church. For is not the introduction of the *managerial revolution* one of the hallmarks of the contemporary world? Political conservatives have long lamented the *deep state*, impervious to political control and following its own agenda. A whole literature has arisen on these developments in the American educational system, where at every level the rate of growth of administrative staffs far exceeds that of both students and teachers.

Continuities of institutions, people, and ideology, all embedded in a supportive secular society, explain why the progressive Catholic vision has been so resistant to change — and why it now directs the synodal process. Catholic conservatives and traditionalists have been slow to understand or acknowledge these facts. Years ago, James Hitchcock wondered why conservative priests turn "middle of the road" or even progressive on becoming bishops. Others were amazed at how little headway the ideas of Popes John Paul II and Benedict seemed to make in the Church. The fact of Catholic bureaucratic continuity helps to clarify the situation. For those who dispute the consensus expressed in the synodal documents it will be insufficient to write grand speeches and articles and otherwise engage in intellectual debate. They must accept the necessity of relentless conflict with a concretely existing establishment holding all the power. It's a struggle that, in the short term, has no immediately foreseeable resolution.

In the long term, as we know, the outcome will be quite different.

---

5   New Brunswick, NJ: Transaction Publishers, 1994.

35

Papal without a Pope:
Recent Manifestations of
Conservative Catholicism[1]

STUART CHESSMAN

A S THE NATURE OF THE POLICIES OF POPE FRANCIS became clear, American conservative Catholicism quickly found itself in a grave dilemma. No other subculture within the Church had placed so much weight on loyalty to the papacy as the ultimate criterion of Catholicity. Yet the new pope, while insisting on absolute loyalty to his person, systematically rejected or reduced to a nebulous ideal everything for which the conservatives had fought: "life issues" (especially opposition to abortion); alliances with evangelical Christianity; opposition to socialism, liturgical abuses, "LGBT" and the entire progressive Catholic agenda. The pope regularly coarsely denounces revered conservative champions (EWTN, for example, is claimed to be "doing the work of the devil"). And in the greatest humiliation of all for the conservatives, a hail of disparaging remarks and insinuations continued to shower down from Francis's entourage on the Catholic Church in America and on the United States in general. All this commenced, of course, years before Francis launched his war on traditionalist Catholics. But even amid this campaign, in word and deed, Francis and his sycophants continue to make clear that all of the Left's adversaries are also their targets.

The conservative movement has been searching for a response. To their credit, few were able to follow the example of clerical institutions like Opus Dei and celebrate the steps the pope is taking against them. Instead, some conservatives simply withdrew into silence. Others surreptitiously shifted into a quiet alignment with the positions of the traditionalists, their erstwhile adversaries. Still others denounced the ever-increasing number of outrages in the Church while avoiding mentioning the pope's role in them. I myself considered that, in view of this, conservative Catholicism had reached the end of the road, that from now on the landscape of the Catholic right would be dominated by traditionalism.

Indeed, the drift to traditionalism — or at least the openness to traditionalist thought — among conservatives has continued to progress. But I was a bit hasty

---

1 First published at the blog of the Society of St Hugh of Cluny on October 21, 2022.

in my expectations regarding the demise of the entire movement. After more than nine years of the reign of Francis, conservative advocates have returned to the secular media — *as conservatives, but without the pope.* They champion conservative Catholic issues — sometimes now even including the right to attend the traditional Mass. But they are forced to argue without the benefit of reliance on authority. Let us look at some of their recent products.

Michael Warren Davis speaks of "us trads."[2] He writes of the beauty of the Latin Mass. But what exactly is his position? Although Davis claims to be a "trad," his positions resemble much more closely those of a Catholic conservative. According to Davis:

> As many of you know, there is a powerful clique of Catholic bishops who oppose the traditional Latin Mass . . . . Last year, Pope Francis published his apostolic letter *Traditionis Custodes*. It gave those anti-TLM bishops the excuse they needed to begin shutting down their Latin Mass parishes in their dioceses.

That is the last reference to Pope Francis in Davis's article. I don't think many people would characterize the relationship between *Traditionis Custodes* and the subsequent actions of the bishops in this manner. The bishops' enforcement actions are clearly the intended result of *Traditionis Custodes* and indeed reflect some coordination with the Vatican. Of course, Davis earlier had propagated the utterly erroneous notion that Pope Francis had once been indifferent or even favorable to the traditional Mass.

Naturally, Davis thinks whatever is happening now is largely the fault of the traditionalists themselves:

> No doubt they [the anti-traditional Mass bishops] would cite the army of bloggers, vloggers, and Twitter trolls who devote themselves to castigating the hierarchy. And it's true: some of these traditionalists say things about the pope that would make Martin Luther blush. So, if your only exposure to traditionalist Catholics came via the internet, you might agree that the TLM is a bad influence.
>
> Look: I'm the first to admit that there are problems in the Latin Mass community . . . I've bent over backwards to give our bishops the benefit of the doubt.
>
> I even have a soft spot for Cardinal Gregory . . . I have to believe that he truly loves Jesus Christ and His holy Church.

Why does Davis "have to" believe that? Is he Gregory's confessor? As he has done in the past, Davis is denouncing those he is claiming to defend — and whose rights have been violated — while "bending over backwards" to excuse the establishment.

---

2 Michael Warren Davis, "Politics of Reason and Beauty," *The American Conservative*, September 29, 2022.

> So why does Archbishop Gregory do what he does? There's only one
> answer that makes any sense. Cardinal Gregory doesn't understand
> the desire for beauty in worship.

So, you see, Gregory is just aesthetically challenged. Davis has a profound misunderstanding of Catholicism if he thinks all these people who sacrifice so much
to attend traditional Masses do so *primarily* because of the aesthetic experience.

George Weigel, the grand old man of Catholic conservatism, argues in *The
Wall Street Journal* for the "necessary" Second Vatican Council.[3] However, he also
signals his dissent from the views of the circle of the bishop of Rome:

> Contrary to the claims of those votaries of Pope Francis who claim that the
> Council instituted a "paradigm shift" in the Church's self-understanding,
> John XXIII did not convoke Vatican II to reinvent Catholicism.

Pope Francis's views on the subject are not explored further in this article. Weigel
devotes paragraph after paragraph to the claimed original vision of John XXIII.
But how then did the problems of today's Church arise? Weigel does, after all,
frankly acknowledge the current catastrophic situation. According to Weigel, this
is the fault of those (unnamed) individuals who abandoned John XXIII's original intent to embrace secular modernity uncritically. In fact, much of Weigel's
article is a covert critique of the interpretations and policies emanating from the
Vatican today. In this regard, it's remarkable that Weigel does not mention the
name of Paul VI.[4]

The traditionalists are, nevertheless, still utterly mistaken:

> The more radical Catholic traditionalists of our day seem to imagine
> that the Catholic bastion of the mid-twentieth century could have
> sustained itself indefinitely. . . . Thoughtful assessments of Vatican II
> and its legacy must acknowledge that the pre-conciliar Catholic past was
> more brittle and frailer after two world wars and more vulnerable to the
> cultural tsunami of the 1960s than some nostalgic traditionalists imagine.

Weigel's "thoughtful assessment" is just the usual list of calumnies against "radical"
and "nostalgic" traditionalists as well as gratuitous assertions about the past. I
don't think anyone on the traditionalist side today imagines that the preconciliar
Church was perfect. But to make the claim—as George Weigel does—that the
problems after the Council are (at least in large part) attributable to the debility
of an already feeble structure seems to contradict empirical studies[5] and, in the

---

3   George Weigel, "What Vatican II Accomplished," *The Wall Street Journal*, September 30,
2022; also in the anthology *Sixty Years After: Catholic Writers Assess the Legacy of Vatican II*, ed. Peter
A. Kwasniewski (Brooklyn, NY: Angelico Press, 2022), 154–60.

4   On the convenient absence of Paul VI from many conservative narratives, see Gregory DiPippo, "Paul VI Did Not Exist: A 'Nostalgic' Response to George Weigel on Vatican II,"
OnePeterFive, October 24, 2022.

5   Such as those of Guillaume Cuchet in *Comment notre monde a cessé d'être chrétien: Anatomie
d'un effondrement* (Paris: Seuil, 2018) in chapters 2 ("Le tournant de 1965") and 3 ("Les causes de la

case of some of us, the evidence of our own eyes. George Weigel seeks to disassociate himself from the "votaries" of Francis yet his rhetoric here is virtually indistinguishable from theirs.

In Weigel's view, what are the points of light in postconciliar Catholicism? Where has John XXIII's vision been realized sufficiently to support Weigel's claims that the Council has been, at least in some places, a success? Weigel cites the progress of the African Church. But Africanization and the growth of the Church on that continent had been underway well before the Council—didn't a certain traditionalist archbishop have a key role in that? And under Francis hasn't the African Church been regularly portrayed as an "adversary" of the conciliar establishment? Then, Weigel speaks of the movements within the Soviet bloc and the emergence of John Paul II in Poland as fruits of the Council and specifically, of the Declaration on Religious Freedom *Dignitatis Humanae*. But Poland under Cardinal Wyszyński was viewed in the Cold War years as one of the most retrograde churches, *not* as an exemplar of implementation of the Council. John Paul II was after all the product Poland's conservative, nationalist, even clerical Catholic culture.[6] And when Weigel writes of the "self-liberation" of the Eastern bloc from communism, I think that is more than a little exaggerated. Overall, Weigel can only assemble a highly selective and factually questionable historical summary to back up his narrative.

We have covered elsewhere a third example of conservative journalism: the announcement of the new Institute of Human Ecology at Catholic University—also published in *The Wall Street Journal*.[7] The author, Andrea Picciotti-Bayer, however, focuses not on conflicts within the Church but on the Church's potential role in politics and the secular world (a subcategory of Catholic conservative thought). In this article, too, the current pontiff and the hierarchy (except for Archbishop Gomez of Los Angeles) are noticeable by their absence. Apparently the "dazzling intellectual tradition of the Church," supposedly offering so much potential benefit to our world, is not necessarily best represented by the Church's current leadership.

Finally, Ross Douthat has written the most interesting of the pieces we are considering—dealing with the anniversary of Vatican II.[8] Douthat expressly claims for himself the title of "conservative." His contribution, however, compared

---

rupture"). For a summary, see John Pepino, "Anatomist of the Catholic Collapse in France and Beyond," *Catholic World Report*, September 13, 2022.

6   A sign of this fact is that Poland has, in recent decades, progressively liberalized its liturgical life under the influence of Western European "experts" who have gone forth on charitable missions, as it were, to set straight the benighted Eastern Europeans with their too-rigid pieties. Thus, communion in the hand, which was unheard-of before the fall of Communism, is now standard in urban locations.

7   Andrea Picciotti-Bayer, "Counterfeit Catholicism, Left and Right," *The Wall Street Journal*, September 23, 2022. My review is "The 'Dazzling Catholic Intellectual Tradition'—The Institute for Human Ecology at Catholic University," Society of St Hugh of Cluny blog, September 26, 2022.

8   Ross Douthat, "How Catholics became Prisoners of Vatican II," *The New York Times*, October 12, 2022; also in Kwasniewski (ed.), *Sixty Years After*, 63–67.

to those of his peers, shows the greatest understanding of reality and departs farthest from prior conservative orthodoxy. He freely concedes that the Council has been, on its own terms, a failure. He acknowledges the problematic nature of the reign of Francis. Indeed, the very existence of Pope Francis illustrates the failure of the conservative Catholics' attempts over the years to contain the Council to a restricted and fixed set of provisions. Yet, like Weigel, he declares that the Council was "necessary." Furthermore, it is " irreversible." I believe, though, that Douthat has an understanding of that word very much more nuanced than the Vatican's. (Historical events, of course, can *never* be "undone.") Neverthe-less, these two terms serve to remove the Council from all rational inquiry. It is transformed into a scientific fact or even an article of faith—much like Pope Francis's statement in his letter accompanying *Traditionis Custodes* that to doubt the Council is to doubt the Holy Spirit. Thus, whatever Douthat's reservations about the current state of the Church and its leadership may be, at the end of the day he defers to the irrational authority of the Council—even in the face of its failure. There is no way out.

This brief review shows that conservative Catholicism lives on even if deprived of what once was its most essential feature: reverence for papal authority. These conservatives of today acknowledge, to a greater or lesser extent, the postconciliar disasters and losses. They can regret the persecution of traditionalists. Whether openly or not, they diverge in many respects from the current party line of the Vatican and do not rely on (current) papal authority. And, at least in the case of Ross Douthat, they can even admit the failure of the Council itself. Yet despite all these insights, the traditionalists remain adversaries for them. Instead of seeking further reconciliation with the defenders of Tradition, these conser-vative authors inevitably take refuge in dogmatic assumptions which allow a return to the principle of institutional authority, at least in some attenuated form: Davis's bishops acting in good faith; Weigel's necessary Council as defined in the era of Pope John XXIII; the "dazzling Catholic intellectual tradition" of Picciotti-Bayer; and finally, Douthat's necessary and irreversible, even if failed, Council. Regardless of the continuing rapprochement between the two parties under the relentless pressure of Pope Francis's regime, the divergence between traditionalists and Catholic conservatives regrettably remains intact.

36

Ultramontanism:
A Means, Not an End[1]

CHARLES A. COULOMBE

THE EXCITEMENT OF RECENT MONTHS OVER THE CAM-
paign against the Latin Mass and its adherents, waged by the highest
levels in the Catholic Church, is both tragic and ironic. Tragic, of course,
because of the souls lost and the lives blighted—the re-expulsion of the Benedictine
monks from Glastonbury, England, over their attachment to the Mass of their
predecessors in that holy spot featured the current bishop of Clifton in the role
of Henry VIII.

But it is ironic because, prior to the current pontificate, no hardier partisans
of ultramontanism were to be found than in the ranks of traditional Catholics—although since 2013 many a figure in the Catholic world who happily disregarded the teachings of John Paul II and Benedict XVI have transformed into
virtual papolaters.

Of course, ultramontanism itself—the hailing of the reigning pontiff as Supreme
Leader of the faithful, whose every utterance must be accepted unquestioningly—is
a relatively recent phenomenon in the life of the Church, reflected triumphantly
in many a late nineteenth-century church, such as Paris's Sacre Coeur, or London's
Brompton Oratory. Before examining our present situation in any detail though,
we need to look at how we got here.

From the time Emperor Theodosius the Great passed the Edict of Thessalonica
in AD 380, which made baptism the passage into Roman citizenship as well as
membership in the Church, the Catholic Church and the Catholic State were
seen as distinct aspects of one Catholic body. In this edict, the emperor declared:

> It is our desire that all the various nations which are subject to our
> Clemency and Moderation should continue to profess that religion
> which was delivered to the Romans by the divine Apostle Peter, as it
> has been preserved by faithful tradition, and which is now professed
> by the Pontiff Damasus and by Peter, bishop of Alexandria, a man of
> apostolic holiness. According to the apostolic teaching and the doctrine
> of the Gospel, let us believe in the one deity of the Father and of the Son
> and of the Holy Spirit, in equal majesty and in a holy Trinity. We order

---

1   First published at *Crisis Magazine* on March 10, 2023. This article was published shortly after
the release of the infamous "Roche's Rescript" dated February 20, 2023.

the followers of this law to embrace the name of Catholic Christians; but as for the others, since in our judgment they are foolish madmen, we decree that they shall be branded with the ignominious name of heretics, and shall not presume to give to their conventicles the name of churches. They will suffer in the first place the chastisement of the divine condemnation and in the second the punishment of our authority which in accordance with the will of Heaven we shall decide to inflict.

After the Christological controversies of the fourth and fifth centuries—which successive emperors took their part in either exacerbating or settling (doing the latter finally)—Pope St Gelasius I wrote to Emperor Anastasius the following description of the two powers:

There are two, august Emperor, by which this world is chiefly ruled, namely, the sacred authority (*auctoritas sacrata*) of the priests and the royal power (*regalis potestas*). Of these, that of the priests is weightier, since they have to render an account for even the kings of men in the divine judgment. You are also aware, most clement son, that while you are permitted honorably to rule over humankind, yet in divine matters you bend your neck devotedly to the bishops and await from them the means of your salvation. In the reception and proper disposition of the heavenly sacraments you recognize that you should be subordinate rather than superior to the religious order, and that in these things you depend on their judgment rather than wish to bend them to your will. If the ministers of religion, recognizing the supremacy granted you from heaven in matters affecting the public order, obey your laws, lest otherwise they might obstruct the course of secular affairs by irrelevant considerations, with what readiness should you not yield them obedience to whom is assigned the dispensing of the sacred mysteries of religion?

A century later, Emperor Justinian would write to the pope:

We have exerted Ourselves to unite all the priests of the East and subject them to the See of Your Holiness, and hence the questions which have at present arisen, although they [i.e., the answers to them] are manifest and free from doubt, and, according to the doctrine of your Apostolic See, are constantly firmly observed and preached by all priests, We have still considered it necessary to bring to the attention of Your Holiness. For we do not suffer anything which has reference to the state of the Church, even though what causes the difficulty may be clear and free from doubt, to be discussed without being brought to the notice of Your Holiness, because you are the head of all the Holy Churches, for We shall exert Ourselves in every way (as has already been stated), to increase the honor and authority of your See.

This relationship between Church and Empire—and the various kingdoms into which the latter was divided, in much the same fashion (theoretically) as the

Church was divided into dioceses—would continue until the Protestant Revolt; this was so with the Byzantines, and with the Western or Holy Roman Empire revived for Charlemagne by Pope St Leo III in 800. Against this backdrop, the papacy's own temporal sovereignty culminated with the birth of the Papal States.

But it was not a relationship without difficulties. As the Investiture controversy and the Guelph and Ghibelline struggle showed, while both the popes and the emperors (and kings) agreed on basic principles about their relationship, conflict often arose regarding the concrete application of these principles. Nevertheless, such opponents of papal politics as Dante could not be considered as other than faithful Catholics, regardless of their stances in these areas.

Indeed, if various popes chastised wayward monarchs such as England's Henry II and the Holy Roman Emperor Henry VI, it took Emperor Otto I to end the century-long pornocracy in Rome, and Emperor Sigismund to end the Great Schism. If popes had to approve the choice of Holy Roman Emperor, he (and the kings of France and Spain) had the right to veto any one candidate for the papacy they thought inappropriate for the job.

As mentioned, this rocky but ultimately successful marriage began to unravel as a result of the Protestant Revolt, whereby the Catholic Church was forcibly separated from several Christian States, whose rulers created substitute ecclesiastical bodies to replace the Church on the one side and to act as departments of state on the other. The great power politics of the sixteenth and seventeenth centuries led to the seemingly undying enmity between the kings of France and the Habsburgs, during which the papacy would support first the former (hence Urban VIII's backing the Swedes against Emperor Ferdinand II in the Thirty Years' War, and the latter's famous comment that he would "be the champion of the Church despite the pope") and then the latter (which resulted in the pope chanting the *Te Deum* when news of the Battle of the Boyne came in 1690).

In the eighteenth century, a more integrally Catholic policy prevailed at Rome, whereby the popes tried to reconcile Bourbons and Habsburgs and encouraged both to support Stuart restoration in the British Isles. Eventually, this would bear fruit in 1755, when the two dynasties did ally—an alliance sealed with the marriage of the future Louis XVI with Marie Antoinette. Unfortunately, it was two centuries too late to end the Protestant or the Muslim menace to Christendom.

The revolution of 1789 began the creation of the secular State we know today, in which religion of any kind exists purely at the whim of the temporal rulers of a given country—as exhibited during the Covid-19 lockdown. But as nation after nation through the course of the nineteenth century found its Catholics pitted against their temporal rulers, a very different attitude toward the papacy arose among them. Before, if there was a conflict between a Catholic ruler and the pope, believing Catholics did not automatically presume the pope was right; moreover, in any such dispute, the temporal ruler would attempt to show that he was actually working harder for the good of the Church than his pontifical opponent. Bishops, priests, and laity would have to try to make sense of the situation on that basis.

But now, from Portugal to Poland and throughout the Americas, the nineteenth century saw papacy and national Churches together in conflict with liberal regimes who made no secret of their opposition to the Church as such — and to its Faith. Under such conditions, the pope went from being the religious head of the Church who might or might not be correct in the political arena, to being the beleaguered religious *and* political leader of the faithful across the globe. This was a role particularly suited to Bl. Pius IX, who not only had to offer moral support to his embattled children in foreign lands but was directly attacked by the forces of Liberalism in the persons of Cavour and Garibaldi.

In response, he called for volunteers from all over the Catholic world to defend him. These truly gallant and heroic young men — the Papal Zouaves — rallied to Pius's banner. From across the planet, they came; often enough, they and/or their families were veterans of the Church's struggles against the revolution in their own homelands. They saw their service in the Papal States as a continuation of those struggles and, indeed, as a latter-day Crusade.

From all of the political and military conflicts besetting the Church in this era arose *ultramontanism*. Capped by the definition of papal infallibility at Vatican I, followed almost immediately by the definitive (so far!) loss of the Papal States, this in turn gave the Holy Father a redoubled moral authority. The multiplication of Catholic Parties in various countries (forerunners of the now defanged and secularized Christian Democratic parties) under Leo XIII, as well as his timely and useful writings on social issues, reinforced the high repute of the Vicar of Christ.

World War I and the ruin of Austria-Hungary — the last great Catholic power — ushered in the interwar Catholic Revival, when the lack of Catholic temporal power was seen in many quarters as an advantage, and when, if anything, Catholic politics became even more clerical. Certainly, the direct leadership of the clergy in the Catholic parties in the Netherlands, Belgium, Austria, Slovenia, Czechoslovakia, and elsewhere was seen as a very good thing indeed (although the same tendency in the United States pitted Fr Coughlin against Msgr John Ryan).

World War II propelled the almost ghostly figure of Pius XII into interstellar heights in the general Catholic imagination — heights which he clambered even higher, if possible, as a result of his postwar advocacy of the persecuted Church in the newly Communist Captive Nations and his patronage of De Gasperi, Schuman, and Adenauer (themselves all being considered for beatification). This prestige was duly passed on to John XXIII.

Perhaps only someone of Pius XII's sterling reputation could have put through the liturgical changes he oversaw (alterations in Holy Week, abolition of most octaves, etc.) with barely a note of dissent. So, too, with John XXIII's tinkering with the calendar. Indeed, it was the widespread view of the pope as virtually the Oracle at Delphi that initially allowed Paul VI to alter so much with relatively little adverse reaction—although for those who did so react, the full force of Roman power was brought to bear.

Nevertheless, it did not escape those of us alive then that the Holy Father happily pounced upon traditionalists but was unable to do anything about the dissent of even national bishops' conferences from *Humanae Vitae*. For many, this was the beginning of the loss of belief in papal impeccability that had grown up since the French Revolution.

John Paul II's partial freeing of the Tridentine Mass, his opposition to Communism, and his revitalizing of nearly moribund Eucharistic and Marian devotions did a great deal to recover some of the ground lost. Benedict XVI seemed to go from strength to strength—although his apparent flight from the wolves ended his pontificate on a decidedly sour note. Nevertheless, from 1978 to 2013, ultramontanism was easy to hold for a great many.

The arrival of Pope Francis certainly strained the concept for those who held the same religious views as, say, Bl. Pius IX or Leo XIII. Those who dissented from *Humanae Vitae* and found Francis's immediate predecessors retrograde and confining, on the other hand, became latter-day Papal Zouaves—and never more so than when Francis directly contradicted Benedict over liturgical and doctrinal matters.

So now it must be said: apart from the religious loyalty the papal office commanded even from its political opponents like Dante and Emperor Ferdinand II, our deference to a reigning pontiff must somehow be commensurate with his manner of conducting himself in that effort—even as filial loyalty is still owed to a drunken father but must be tempered according to his actual behavior.

There is, of course, no earthly authority higher than the pope; we, his subjects, are rather limited in what we can do—but not in what, as history shows us, we must sometimes endure. We must pray very hard for him—and that he will do what God wants him to. Pope Francis's time in office will end with his having to account for his actions to Him Whose Vicar he is. May it go well for him—and for all of us, when our time comes.

37

Centripetal Governance and the Loss of Coherence[1]

STUART CHESSMAN

THE BY NOW DAILY OUTRAGES OF POPE FRANCIS, IN word and deed, have maintained the focus on the governance of the Roman Catholic Church. What is the interaction of the constitution of the Roman Catholic Church with the developments—or aberrations—in liturgy, morality, and organization of the last sixty years? The most salient aspect of this constitution is the dominant role of the papacy in all aspects of the life of the Roman Catholic Church. In other words, ultramontanism.

I prefer ultramontanism as the historically accurate term for the governing structure of the Roman Catholic Church that was finalized in 1870. I don't think neologisms like papolatry, papalism, or hyperpapalism are really adequate substitutes. Of course, there is inevitably some degree of definitional confusion. So, for example, Martin Mosebach's collection of essays titled (in English) *Subversive Catholicism* has the original title *Der Ultramontane*. Yet reading this book it's clear that the author intended by the title to describe his adherence to the worldwide Catholic Church as opposed to the schismatic tendencies of his homeland or the totalitarian secular trends of this age. The content of the book, however, is clearly critical of ecclesiastical ultramontanism.[2]

Ultramontanism is not just a set of doctrinal definitions promulgated by Vatican I regarding papal authority and its infallibility. It is a constitution, a system of government, and a culture that eventually pervaded the Roman Catholic Church. Ultramontanism was not confined merely to the papacy and the episcopacy but gradually had ramifications throughout the Church.

What were the characteristics of this new, post-1870 order? All legal and doctrinal authority throughout the Church was centralized in the pope. The ideal of the Church was absolute unity in organization and rite under the pope. The papacy (and the entire Church) was declared independent from the influence of any secular power. Hand in hand with the extension of papal jurisdiction was the proclamation of papal infallibility. In actual practice, any definitional limits in the

---

1   Published here for the first time.
2   Martin Mosebach, *Der Ultramontane: Alle Wege führen nach Rom* (Augsburg: Sankt Ulrich Verlag, 2012), especially, at 102, "Er ist ja nur der Papst." The English edition: *Subversive Catholicism: Papacy, Liturgy, Church*, trans. Sebastian Condon and Graham Harrison (Brooklyn, NY: Angelico Press, 2019); see pp. 15–23: "He Is, After All, Only the Pope."

original texts of Vatican I were set aside in favor of a broad charism of infallibility, the scope of which steadily grew over the years. The role of authority—and obedience to authority—was elevated to central importance within the Church. In a less clearly defined but eventually equally important development, the pope was established as a popular religious "leader," who at least in theory entered into a direct, personal relationship with individual Catholics throughout the world.

Closely associated with the triumph of papal ultramontanism were two additional phenomena: legalism and clericalism. By legalism we mean the pervasive extension of legal norms to all aspects of the Christian life. Fulfilling precisely enumerated duties became characteristic of Catholic practice: for example, what parts of the Mass did the Catholic have to attend to fulfill his "Sunday obligation"? In 1917 a new code of canon law was promulgated, modeled after secular codes.[3]

Clericalism is the establishment of the clergy as the leaders and directors of Catholic life in all respects. However, what is often meant by clericalism is in reality bureaucracy. That is, the reconfiguration of every office in the church from the bishop down to the parish priest as a bureaucratic position ultimately subordinated to the central direction of the pope. Any lay initiatives (including, in Europe, the newly emerging Catholic political parties) at least in theory had to submit to such clerical direction. This distinction between the clerical and the bureaucratic was perhaps at first not overt since, after the crisis of the French Revolution and its aftermath, almost all leadership positions in the Church were filled by clerics anyway.

Developments in the Church always take place in a certain historical context. The ultramontane response to the nineteenth century resembles in many respects that of Napoleons I and III in France to revolutionary movements there—the concentration of all power in one absolute ruler, the development of bureaucracy, the promulgation of legal codes and other reforms. A Napoleonic regime, moreover, was not exactly that of a "legitimate" monarch of the Restoration but had charismatic and popular aspects. The "liberal" regimes of nineteenth-century Europe also shared the same passion for perfecting centralized law and bureaucracy—only, in their case, subject to ultimate control by a parliament or constitutional monarchy.

THE CULTURE OF ULTRAMONTANISM

The post-1870 Catholic world is depicted by recent, totally dishonest, Catholic historiography as a nightmarish period of oppression and reaction. But this is absurd, and focuses solely on the travails, real or imagined, of successive generations of scholars. After Vatican I, in contrast to Vatican II, there was no massive defection of Catholics, no institutional collapse anywhere. Yes, the "Old Catholics" in Germany and adjacent countries regrettably split off, but this was an exceedingly minor group, blatantly in league with non-Catholic powers. Also

---

3   See McShea, "Bishops Unbound."

relatively minor were the casualties under Pius X among the Modernists and
the various nationalist schisms around the same time among Greek Catholics,
Poles, and in the Philippines.

In fact, after 1870 the Church continued her nineteenth-century expansion and
in many respects improved her situation. This was widely recognized outside the
Church. For example, in the 1930s Ezra Pound wrote of the immense advances
achieved by the Roman Catholic Church: "The Church today is a far different
affair from what it was in the days when Pio IX slithered down and Cardinal
Antonelli was the chief power."[4] By this he meant not only the improvement in
the condition and morality of the clergy but also the development of the social
doctrine of the Church since the papacy of Leo XIII. New examples of holiness
inspired the faithful (St Thérèse of Lisieux, the apparitions at Fatima) and even
the entire world (Fr Damien of Molokai). The innumerable religious congregations, particularly of women, founded in the nineteenth century, continued their
growth. Formerly mission territories also reached maturity during this age, notably the United States, which by 1914 had become a major factor in the Catholic
Church worldwide. Then there were the notable works of art, literature, music,
and science created especially in the 1870–1920 era: Gaudí, Bruckner, Dvořák,
Mendel, Huysmans, Hopkins, Péguy, Chesterton . . . the list is endless. What is
remarkable is not only the number but the individuality of these participants and
their multifaceted contributions to the final days of a Christian culture.

Of course, some of this creativity is attributable to the slow penetration of
ultramontane ideals. The ultramontane system had been imposed on the Church
only in 1870. Although there was widespread popular support for Pius IX in the
Catholic community, in no way did ultramontanism become an exclusive force
in the Catholic Church. This is evident when we consider the limited success of
the first ultramontane attempts to centralize and direct the Church's spiritual life.
Leo XIII had privileged scholastic philosophy in 1879 (Aeterni Patris) but never
could achieve unanimity among Catholic philosophers. To direct attention to the
achievements of medieval philosophy was a very great benefit, but to impose a
variant of this philosophy by decree was not conducive to its acceptance.

Similarly, Pius X mandated the use of chant in 1904 (Tra le Sollecitudini) and
imposed other restrictions (for example, on women singing in church). By no
means, however, did chant actually become the prevalent musical idiom at the

---

4   Ezra Pound, Guide to Kulchur (New York: New Directions, 1970; originally published in 1938).
Cardinal Giacomo Antonelli was the notorious first minister of Pius IX. Pound says elsewhere in
the same book: "The immeasurable ascent of the Church of Rome between the time of Cardinal
Antonelli and our time [our time here being the time of the Concordat] very nearly proves Cavour's
contention as to the effect of the Temporal Power" (76). "I cannot over-emphasize the assertion
that the Catholic Church rotted when the hierarchy ceased to believe its own dogma. Cavour was
the best XIXth century friend of the Church. The Church rises with the rise of civilization around
it. There is an infinite gulf between the Italian Church in our time and what it was in Cardinal
Antonelli's" (164). Of course, Pound was a partisan of Mussolini, which must be taken into account
in reading such remarks.

parish level throughout the Catholic Church. Indeed, the exercise of centralized control had the detrimental side-effect of cutting the Catholic Church off from its own immediate musical heritage and musical developments in the contemporary world. Pius X's campaign against modernism also seemed to be an initial victory of the papacy, but the use of administrative measures alone did not totally exorcise the demons the pope had sought to combat.

Even at the level of the papacy itself no purely ultramontane culture existed. The Church's social doctrine recognized the principle of subsidiarity, which doesn't seem to harmonize with the ultramontane ideal of centralized control. As the twentieth century advanced, the Church gave greater heed to the value of the Eastern rites (after several disastrous experiences). Again, this deviates from the ultramontane ideal of liturgical uniformity. The same was true of the intellectual life. Some liturgical texts were revised to emphasize the unique status of the papacy—and to tidy up some detrimental legacies of the past (e.g., the legend of Pope Marcellinus). Yet Ludwig Pastor was able to write his great history of the popes with the direct cooperation of the Vatican. At certain points, such as his discussion of Savonarola, ultramontane restrictiveness was admittedly evident. However, on the whole, Pastor produced an extremely fair depiction of the era—one that, where necessary, was unsparing in the criticism of the Renaissance papacy, however unpopular that frankness was among certain prelates in the Vatican.

Other developments, however, revealed tensions within the ultramontane order—such as the early appearance of so-called "movements," a series of seemingly wildly unconnected phenomena on the fringes of the Church. Perhaps the first to appear was the Schoenstatt Movement in 1914. We next had Eric Gill's succession of distributist villages, and the Catholic Worker movement of Dorothy Day. The 1930s saw the beginnings of Opus Dei in Spain. All these and subsequent organizations differed in their membership, structure, and objectives. But what they had in common was a way of life centered not around a rule (as in the case of a traditional order or religious community), but a charismatic, visionary leader whose word was law. These movements both reflected and reacted against ultramontane culture. Their culture of blind obedience to a charismatic leader mirrored a popular view of the role of the pope in the Roman Catholic Church. As within nineteenth-century ultramontanism itself, the more recent movements exhibited a certain blurring of the roles of the laity and of the clergy. Indeed, in Opus Dei, a class of celibate lay members became subject to quasi-religious discipline.

These new organizations either explicitly, in the case of the Catholic Worker, or implicitly, like Opus Dei, offered a critical commentary on the inherited constitution of the Catholic Church. A common thread was activating or energizing a supposedly passive laity in pursuit of objectives to be realized in the secular world (living the economy of distributism, advocating workers' rights and social change, giving Christian witness in the working world). Now some of these organizations were so tied to the unique person of the leader (in Gill's case), or incorporated such contradictory elements (like anarchism in the case of the Catholic Worker), that they never acquired a leading role within the Church. The great exception here was Opus Dei, which from the beginning possessed a strong organization that enabled it to continue its development.

We also possess literary testimony of the limitations of ultramontane culture as it was practiced at the level of the ordinary faithful. These situations, real or fictional, involved a confrontation between the mentality of a convert or would-be convert — enthusiastic, taking doctrines at their literal value, and ready for sacrifice — and that of the clergy or the "homegrown" lay Catholics. Simone Weil famously stated in 1942 that:

> I love God, Christ, and the Catholic faith . . . I love the saints through their writings and what is told of their lives . . . . I love the six or seven Catholics whom chance has led me to meet in the course of my life. I love the Catholic liturgy, hymns, architecture, rites, and ceremonies. But I have not the slightest love for the Church in the strict sense of the word, apart from its relation to all these things I do love.[5]

What does this mean? There certainly are a number of things going on here regarding Weil's state of mind. But had not Weil formed an impression that the Church, "in the strict sense of the word," was not among the things she loved, but an organization, an institution, with a defined set of beliefs (a catechism) and an entry requirement (baptism)? The entirety of Catholic tradition had been withheld from her. Moreover, already at that time, it apparently was hinted to her that some of the beliefs she had a hard time accepting could be ignored . . . [6]

The novel *Judith's Marriage* by Fr Bryan Houghton (written in the 1980s but describing events in the 1950s and 1960s) depicts the unacknowledged tension between the Catholic Faith in its tradition and doctrine, and the ultramontane cult of the institution and obedience to authority. In 1962, the convert Judith, enthusiastic about the teaching and life of the Catholic Church, is now troubled by the first tremors emanating from the Vatican Council. Her husband, a born and bred Catholic, has a different perspective:

> I can well understand how these bishops annoy you. As a convert you are in love with the Church as she stands. . . . Not only are you wedded to the Church's faith, but to every detail of its external expression, since you could only get to know the Faith by how the Church manifested it. That seems to me absolutely fair. But myself, as a cradle Catholic, do not look at things quite in that light. . . . My first and natural reaction is to bow to the Church's visible authority. . . . If the visible authority in the Church wishes to change the expressions in which the Faith is formulated, there are two possible reactions. The

---

5 Simone Weil, *Waiting for God*, trans. Emma Craufurd (New York: Capricorn Books, 1959), 49–50.
6 See the perceptive analysis by Cristina Campo: "Introduzione a Simone Weil, Attesa di Dio" (1966), in *Sotto falso nome* (Milan: Adelphi Edizioni, 1998), at 170–72, 178–79.

first is yours: what must be preserved at all costs is the Faith . . . . The second is mine: what must be preserved at all costs is the authority of the visible Church . . . . [7]

THE PAPACY OF PIUS XII

All these simmering issues came to a head in the reign of Pius XII. No pope before had enjoyed such secure power over the Church. His confrontations with various totalitarian regimes added to the prestige of the Church in the eyes of her own members and (apparently) of the secular world. In certain corners of the Church, like the United States, there was a spectacular new wave of vocations, church and school construction, and overall Catholic expansion. At least in the part of the world dominated after 1945 by the United States, the position of the Church seemed stronger than ever, and the conflicts of the past seemed eliminated or at least reduced to a manageable level (for example, the relations with the communist parties in France and Italy).

In the Church itself, ultramontane exaltation of the institution of the papacy and its authority reached new heights; Pius received extravagant personal praise as well. It seemed like a golden age of the Church marred only by the advances of the totalitarian forces in Europe and Asia. It was in these years that the Catholic Church was compared with a successful American multinational business corporation. It was the final flower of ultramontanism: the pope as the chief executive officer with the bishops and religious orders as his branch managers transmitting his directives all the way down to the local parishes.

All was not perfect. In purely Catholic countries a large portion of the laity continued to dissent from Catholic teaching in their practice of the faith and especially in their politics, regardless of their formal membership in the Church. The hostile secular forces seemed to be able to regroup and advance with ever greater ruthlessness: from the liberals of the mid-nineteenth century to the Freemasons in France, Spain, and Latin America to the Communists and the National Socialists of the twentieth century, these adversaries seemed to show inexhaustible vitality. Their success, or apparent success, aroused envy on the part of "advanced" Roman Catholics.

Under Pius XII, Catholic life, especially among the laity in the parishes, remained vigorous. At a higher level, however, there had been a narrowing. Pre-ultramontane visions of a general Catholic recovery — such as the ideals of the Tractarian movement in nineteenth-century England — had dissipated. By the 1950s the average art and music of the Church were obviously a far cry from that of earlier ages — not only the Middle Ages, but even the era immediately before World War I. The growing ranks of the clergy and the religious included, as it later turned out, many very superficially formed and educated people. The same

---

7 Bryan Houghton, *Judith's Marriage* (Brooklyn, NY: Angelico Press, 2020; originally published 1987), 84–85.

could be said of the intellectual and spiritual life of the multitude of Catholic educational institutions formed or expanded during this time.

But the most momentous development of all was the coming to maturity in Pius XII's papacy of a progressive Catholic culture among the clergy and their lay adepts. In philosophical, theological, liturgical, patristic, and historical studies, the entire scope of Catholic culture was subjected to forceful critique and found wanting. The Catholic world which ultramontanism had fought so hard to preserve was now decried as a "ghetto." The progressive activity was by no means restricted to words, but above all in Europe inspired the construction of a new multitude of modernistic churches, built well before the Council—and liturgical experimentation had already begun.[8]

The progressive movement advanced from strength to strength and in certain places, like France and Germany, attained almost a dominant position among the intellectually engaged clergy. Much of this activity was invisible to the laity—particularly in the United States, but also in the countries in which the progressive forces were most active. By the end of the reign of Pius XII a frankly revolutionary situation had developed in Western European clerical and intellectual circles. In contrast to his predecessors, Pius XII and the ultramontane, neoscholastic theologians of the Vatican seemed completely incapable of grasping the depth of the developing challenge and of responding effectively to it. Pius XII reprimanded a few of the bolder champions of the movement; articles were written against the most egregious positions of the progressives. However, these measures were too late and incomplete.

THE VATICAN COUNCIL

Between 1962 and 1965 Vatican II revolutionized the Catholic Church. The Council and, later, its implementing decrees, changed the entire face of the Church: her liturgy, her sacraments, the dress and rules of the religious orders, her art, and, above all, her self-understanding. The Council initiated a tumultuous upheaval of Catholic life at every level. A large percentage of the faithful immediately ceased practicing the faith. The active religious orders that had expanded so greatly in the last phase of the Church of Pius XII now entered into an irreversible decline. We cannot say, however, that Vatican II stood in total contradiction to its immediate past. History in any case would tell us that that was unlikely. Previous revolts such as the Protestant Reformation in 1517 or the French Revolution in 1789 repudiated the old order—but in each case the old regime was instrumental in facilitating their rise and even instigating their actuation. Vatican II was no different.

Recent events have once again helped us focus on the personal role that John XXIII and Paul VI played in initiating the Council, managing it, and implementing

---

8   For examples, see Peter Kwasniewski, "Cathedrals of Mordor and Zen-like Meditation Rooms: Some Churches That Fail as Churches," *New Liturgical Movement*, May 23, 2022.

it. In no way was the Council contrary to ultramontane papal rule. Rather, like the contemporary Cultural Revolution in China, the Council depended on the supreme authority for its existence. There was, however, one fundamental distinction. The Cultural Revolution, like the student revolts of 1968, involved groups outside the mainstream that were mobilized against the managers of society. In the case of the Second Vatican Council, it was the leading caste of the Church, the clergy and religious themselves, who assumed the role of revolutionaries. Ultramontane obedience assured that any resistance to the Vatican reforms would be marginal at best.

In theory, ultramontanism was one of the aspects of the old regime that the proponents of the Council set out to demolish. The Council championed the rights of the bishops, instead of centralized Roman government; empowerment of the laity, instead of clericalism. But in practice and even in certain conciliar texts, the Council did not at all curtail ultramontanism and clericalism but instead exacerbated them. What greater exercise of papal power could be conceived than the replacement of the entire Roman Rite by papal decisions assisted by committees of experts?

As for the clergy, the charismatic style of leadership pioneered by the "movements" of the 1920s and '30s now became almost the rule. The priests could pose as leaders of a benighted laity. Liturgical changes also facilitated this exaltation of the clergy: the priests, now facing the people, needed at each Mass to extemporize a lengthy dialogue with them as their leader in prayer. And in fact, only the clergy were in possession of (and disposed of) information on the ever-changing liturgical rules.

But the role of ultramontanism in the creation of the "conciliar Church" was not limited to that of an efficient bureaucratic tool that efficiently implemented the decisions of the Council and overrode any opposition. The transformation of the Catholic Church into a centralized bureaucracy had created a spiritual affinity between the self-understanding of the Church establishment and the conciliar agitation for rationalism, didactic clarity, and simplicity. As in the previously mentioned comparison of the Catholic Church to an American business corporation, one bureaucracy (the Church) was reaching out for inclusion to her secular sisters. A defining characteristic of the industrial or permissive society was the expansion and perfection of governing bureaucratic structures: legal, educational, business, and governmental—the institutions that actually ruled the developed democracies. After "razing the bastions," the Church no longer understood itself to be a separate society but was integrated into the modern world. And the media, the ever more powerful ruler of this world, now assumed the same powerful role in the Church.

Changes to canon law over the decades facilitated the evolution of a formless class of functionaries within the Church. Bishops and cardinals now had "retirement" ages. Bishops were much more frequently transferred now from one see to another. On a lower level, the pastor or parish priest was subject to a term limit (twelve years in the case of New York). Later, more and more frequently, parishes could be entrusted outright to lay leadership.

Thus, postconciliar clericalism did not depend on the status of the clergy as "ordained ministers" but related rather to their function as bureaucrats and "experts." It was a new golden age of clerical bureaucracy. Because of the postconciliar inability to recruit new members of the religious orders and clergy, the ranks of these administrators were more and more filled with religious sisters (whose own foundations were disintegrating) and laypeople. These new initiates became and remained fanatical advocates of continuing change.

These two developments—the growing influence of the authority of the secular media within and over the Church and the consolidation of a progressive clerical bureaucracy—came to a head only three years after the end of Vatican II in the dramatic reactions to Pope Paul VI's encyclical *Humanae Vitae*. Pope Paul VI shrank from confronting these new powers who had openly revolted against his magisterium. From now on, the progressive forces could operate to a great extent independent of Catholic moral principles and papal authority as well. Ultramontanism had experienced its first great check, albeit one it had itself birthed. An undeclared civil war raged in the Church, between those who wanted to retain to a great extent the tradition of the Church and those who wanted complete assimilation with modernity. Catholic unity of belief had collapsed.

THE "CONSERVATIVE" POPES' RESPONSE: JOHN PAUL II AND BENEDICT XVI

Popes John Paul II and Benedict tried to stabilize the situation, to reassert principles of Catholic morality and liturgy, to restore some balance to the system. They in no way sought to challenge the revolutionary forces by now entrenched in the Catholic religious orders, educational institutions, and a large percentage of the clergy and hierarchy. Indeed, at times they offered them further concessions, such as the Assisi interreligious conferences. The papal plan was to manage the conflicting forces within the Church and project an image of stability and unity.

Pope John Paul II pursued these policies by means of a greatly expanded personal media presence. Strangely similar in strategy to Pius IX, the Polish pope sought to rally Catholics around his person. But his techniques were radically different from those of the "prisoner of the Vatican." Massive rallies and events, interviews with the secular media, endless journeys to all corners of the world—it was all taken from the playbook of secular politicians (including those of authoritarian states). A degree of success was undeniably achieved; there quickly developed a cult of "John Paul the Great." Pope Benedict decidedly lacked the charismatic gifts of his predecessor, but nevertheless continued these policies.

The "movements," whose beginnings we have described, suddenly attained an unheard-of prominence under John Paul II. They were transformed from a fringe element to a central feature of the Church. Perhaps the growing influence of charismatic Protestantism on the Catholic Church from the 1970s onward played a role in this. And certainly, the image of a charismatic, dominating papacy that Pope John Paul II projected was replicated in the new movements. While their structure, theology, and membership differed greatly, the movements universally shared two characteristics: an autonomous life separate from that of traditional parishes and blind obedience to a charismatic leader.

The movements' success in securing ecclesiastical recognition concealed a dark side. The unlimited power of the absolute leaders of such communities often led to great abuses; in fact, it is hard to find one of these movements that has not suffered a crippling scandal – the most notable example being the Legionaries of Christ. And, except perhaps in parts of the Latin world, the movements never acquired a general leadership role or offered a real alternative to the inherited Catholic structure of bishops, priests, and laity.

In reality, the new ultramontanism of John Paul II – John Rist calls it "celebrity autocracy" – was but a shadow of the regime that prevailed up to the 1960s. Neither John Paul II nor Benedict dared to directly challenge the progressive Church bureaucracy which during the entire duration of both papacies conducted an effective guerrilla war against the popes' policies (it goes without saying that both of them continued to appoint liberals as bishops and cardinals, in addition to more conservative candidates). In this they were aided by the secular media which, as we have seen, had become a central, even a dominant force within the Catholic Church since the time of Paul VI. The media's task was made easier by the gradual emergence, since the 1980s, of the sexual abuse scandal that eventually put the Church on the strategic defensive throughout the world. When the popes did attempt action against the most aggressive dissenters, they either completely failed (as with the Jesuits or the Leadership Conference of Women Religious) or, in effect, had to accept a compromise (Hans Küng). Similar lack of success greeted attempts to rein in the liturgical abuses of the Neocatechumenal Way, and it would take much longer before the corruption in the Community of St John, in L'Arche, and in other hallowed groups was identified and targeted for reform.

We cannot avoid mentioning in this context the total lack of any systematic control over episcopal and cardinalatial appointments, a weakness characteristic of both John Paul II and Benedict. Startling evidence of this was the case of Cardinal McCarrick. It was uncertain whether the Vatican had any real understanding of what was going on in the Western world or even in the Vatican itself. Reports tell us of rampant corruption at the Vatican throughout the reigns of both popes. Indeed, in the case of Benedict XVI, Vatican dysfunction developed into outright treason. The result in the case of Benedict was abdication. It was mute testimony to the popes' loss of control over a chaotic Church – including their own immediate bureaucracy.

POPE FRANCIS: TOTALITARIAN ULTRAMONTANISM

In 2013 Benedict was succeeded by Pope Francis. In every respect the papacy of Francis has returned to the chaos of the 1960s. Francis belongs, of course, to the Jesuits—the order which has been most aggressive in advancing the progressive agenda and challenging the policies championed (at least verbally) by John Paul and Benedict. The means by which Francis seeks to turn the clock back to the era of Paul VI is the renewed exercise of papal authoritarianism. But Francis also draws on the publicity techniques of John Paul II. And although Francis is not at all an enthusiast for most of the "movements," his regime exceedingly resembles their style of "formless despotism"(Spengler): a charismatic leader demanding loyalty and blind obedience from an unstructured and undifferentiated mass of followers. Francis acts in the name of an astonishingly crude ideology. The Council and the new Mass are ordained by the Holy Spirit—so to resist them is to resist God. You must go forward, you must change, you cannot go back. Obedience to irrational authority is thus the foundation of his regime.

Just by selecting the name Francis, Bergoglio emphasized his role as a charismatic spiritual leader rather than a link in an apostolic succession of popes. Francis has assumed the role of a spiritual guide for all the world's Catholics. The pope relentlessly expounds his views in all kinds of contexts: formal documents and decrees but also innumerable interviews with the media. The media, both Catholic and non-Catholic, talk of the pope's personal "vision" and of his reforming plans for the Church. His image and his daily thoughts are reprinted in many parish bulletins in the United States. The Vatican would even like to see the message of Francis brought directly into each Catholic home in the world.

No aspect of doctrine, no previously recognized right or institution is free from a potential change dictated by Francis. Francis routinely disregards canon law. He routinely disavows the decisions and statements of his own subordinates. Thus, the Church becomes totally lawless: the only doctrine, the only law of the Roman Catholic Church is what Francis wills at any one time. The only ruling principle is loyalty to him as a leader.

The pope constantly exercises an unlimited, arbitrary authority. He has set aside all customs and traditions restraining in one way or another the pope's absolute freedom of choice in appointments (and dismissals) within the Church. Heads of Vatican congregations and even sitting bishops are summarily dismissed without any reason being given. In intervention after intervention, Pope Francis has imposed his personal direct control over religious orders, congregations, dioceses, and Vatican departments. A whole class of bishops exists who have tendered their resignations—which have not yet been accepted. Even more so than their colleagues, these bishops continue in office at the discretion of Francis. The college of cardinals has been reduced to a virtual nullity—its only function now will be to vote in the next conclave.

The pope works through his own Vatican bureaucracy—which he has transformed into a mere conduit for his views. But he also operates outside it when it serves his purposes to use "unofficial" channels. The critical fact for a higher-ranking Catholic cleric today is not his legal position but his personal relationship to Francis. The list of the "friends of Francis" continues to change because individuals rise to prominence through papal favor and then are summarily cast aside.

So far, Francis's most radical measure was *Traditionis Custodes* and its follow-up. For here he repudiated the solemn commitments of his two immediate predecessors. He created within the Church an officially segregated class of believers and he announced his intention to coerce traditionalists into the Novus Ordo, regardless of Vatican II's commitment to freedom of conscience. He established direct supervision of parish life by the Vatican in order to implement *Traditionis Custodes*, abandoning any pretense of respecting episcopal authority or "synodality." He has implicitly called into question the future of the vocations of hundreds of priests and religious who have entered religious life in traditional communities since 1988 in the *Ecclesia Dei* institutes based on the assurances of Pope John Paul II. In one act, Francis has repudiated Catholic tradition, the rights and assurances given to traditionalists by his two predecessors, and even key alleged advances of the sacrosanct Council! And all this without any real consultation with the hierarchy or even, at first, an explanation. It is an amazing assertion of arbitrary, unlimited authority.

But this is just one example among many. *Amoris Laetitia*, after all, is hardly reconcilable with previous Catholic teaching on divorce and on the sixth commandment generally. An initiative is now underway in the Church—with Francis's support—to expand the recognition of the so-called LGBT movement and towards that end redefine Christian morality. And by now Francis has involved the whole Catholic world in the "synodal path" and its offspring, the "synod on synodality."

I have called the regime of Francis totalitarian ultramontanism. Going far beyond any mere autocracy, it "liquefies" (Aldo Maria Valli)[9] or renders irrelevant (John Lamont) all structure, norms, and authority of whatever kind and focuses all attention on the leader. In that respect, it closely resembles the regime that formerly existed in the Soviet Union, especially under Stalin himself. But the later Third Reich and the China of Mao were similar examples. Even Massimo Faggioli (a bona fide supporter of both Francis and the progressive cause) has written that it's sad that one needs to rely on the experience of the Soviet Union to interpret the goings on in the Catholic Church day-to-day.[10]

---

9   The expression is used in the pages of Aurelio Porfiri and Aldo Maria Valli, *Uprooted: Dialogues on the Liquid Church* (Hong Kong: ChoraBooks, 2019).

10   Indeed, Faggioli recently pointed out: "Francis has also marginalized the institutional filters that are meant help craft his message and protect his authority. This is happening at time when a certain type of hyper-papalism is defining certain sectors of Catholicism, where the Church's voice on public issues is reduced to the dissemination or interpretation of whatever the pope says or does not say, and whatever he does or chooses not to do, and also how the wider public applauds

A final noxious aspect—and product—of ultramontane totalitarianism is the dishonesty that now pervades all aspects of Catholic life. The pope and the bishops routinely make statements and then contradict them. The pope has indeed made statements against abortion and euthanasia—but then honors abortionists and those politicians working relentlessly to preserve and expand the scope of abortion laws. The official Catholic news media (to the extent that they are not already progressive) are totally dishonest. Crimes continue to be covered up, and ecclesiastical criminals are declared guilty and then not guilty without any apparent change in circumstances. Religious orders in terminal decline pretend there is nothing wrong with them or the Church. "Catholic" universities describe themselves as Catholic or secular depending on the expectations of a given audience. Those with any familiarity with the old Soviet regime can testify that it was that system's pervasive dishonesty, not its repression or brutality, that eventually was fatal to the morale of the socialist states. The Church of today may be no different.

After ten years, Francis has demonstrated that he can say or do anything he wants without arousing public opposition in the hierarchy. We cannot say that all or even a majority of the hierarchy and the clergy are totally aligned with a regime of this kind. Certainly, there seems to be reluctant support or even passive resistance by many bishops in relation to *Traditionis Custodes* and *Amoris Laetitia*. If we may credit Roman rumors, behind-the-scenes pressure has been exerted by some in the Vatican and the episcopate against the pope's more radical appointments and proposed actions. Only a miniscule minority, however, will publicly voice disagreement with Francis's regime. And some institutions, like Opus Dei or the Knights of Malta, continue to declare their praise of Francis and devotion to him even as he tears them apart.

I recognize that applying the label "totalitarian" to the Catholic Church today is inexact in some very important respects. The essence of the totalitarian regimes of Hitler, Stalin, and Mao, after all, was the absolute freedom of the leader from all constraints including those of his own party and ideology. In the case of Francis, however, that freedom definitely does not exist. First, Francis is absolutely dependent on the support of the secular news media. Throughout his ten-year pontificate they have steadfastly supported him and have extracted him from crisis after crisis: the ongoing clerical abuse disclosures, endless Vatican intrigues

---

or criticizes his words and actions. In the higher echelons of the Church's hierarchy, it has become rare for a cardinal or a bishop to express an opinion different from the pope's without being seen as an enemy or a traitor" ("Pope Francis' fog of war," *La Croix*, November 20, 2023). Fellow *La Croix* journalist Robert Mickens, as liberal as the day is long, makes a similar observation about a pope who is very freely "using the institutional levers at his disposal": "He has issued numerous decrees, set up untold numbers of protocols for dealing with a variety of issues, but—again—he is seen to apply them unevenly and indiscriminately, or to not even apply them at all. According to the Church's law, he is under no obligation to justify this, but it is troubling for many (or it should be) that a pope who is now in the process of making synodality the legacy of his pontificate, should act in such a . . . non-synodal way" ("How Pope Francis' unorthodox governing style is likely to impact the next conclave," *La Croix*, December 2, 2023).—*Ed.*

and scandals, the Cardinal McCarrick affair, and most recently, Fr Rupnik and the Centro Aletti. Francis, of course, is ideologically aligned with these news media — his policies almost uniformly reflect theirs. In addition, Francis also knows that were he to diverge in any important way from their party line, this happy (for him) situation would change overnight. Just consider the recent slaps on the wrist administered to Francis by the media for his uncertain support for Ukraine in the present war. In that case, Francis or the Vatican had to quickly retract (or explain away) some of his more nonconformist utterances.

This media domination over his papacy also requires Francis to defer to the progressive forces in the Church. For if Francis would have a major conflict with them — in the unlikely event that he would seek this out — they would certainly call on their friends in the secular media. The Catholic progressives after all are loyal not to Francis personally but to their vision of the world and of the Church. Both they and the secular media continue to direct salvos against the Catholic Church, the hierarchy, and Vatican offices, but almost never against Francis himself. Thus, the would-be totalitarian Francis has in fact a restricted scope of authority, boxed in by his own supporters. We see this in the German "synodal path" and in the "synod on synodality," in which the international Catholic bureaucracy — which by now primarily consists of lay employees — has recommenced its mission of changing Catholic doctrine and morality, with Francis providing encouragement in the background.[11]

The media and the bureaucracy are the leading forces of modern societies. The autocratic authority of Francis thus exists solely within the constraints of the modern liberal world. The policies of Francis — as opposed to some of the verbiage — do not deviate at all from the expectations of the ruling forces of that world. Thus, the most extreme triumph of ultramontanism has culminated in the greatest subjection of the Church to the "world." It is a "Babylonian Captivity" of the papacy beyond anything imaginable in the Middle Ages.

ULTRAMONTANE AUTHORITY, THE CONSERVATIVES, AND THE TRADITIONALISTS

What is the future of ultramontanism? According to the Church establishment and the Catholic progressives (which by now are virtually identical), it has been superseded; it's a relic of the past. After all, are we not heading down the synodal path? Progressive publications still advocate further dismantling of the authoritarian papacy. At the same time, Pope Francis, the Church bureaucracy, and the

---

11 It cannot be said that the various slaps administered by the Vatican to the wrists of German bishops amount to much. No serious ecclesiastical penalties have been threatened or administered; the Germans themselves keep going in the same direction, in spite of the admonitions; and we have seen that when Francis does take something seriously, he acts decisively, as he did in removing, without (and against) canonical process, Bishop Daniel Fernández Torres and Bishop Joseph Strickland, and in sidelining Cardinal Burke. Actions speak louder than words, and nowhere is this more true than with a Peronist.

progressives all assert the full force of unlimited ultramontane control when it suits their purposes, regardless of any "synodal" considerations. Once again, we encounter the culture of official Catholic dishonesty.

But what has been the reaction of traditionalists and conservatives to developments since 1965? They were shocked, of course, by the Council and its aftermath. But as early as 1968, when Paul VI issued *Humanae Vitae*, there was an effort to recover ultramontanism, to rally to the pope against so-called dissenters. These tentative initiatives became much more real under John Paul II and his cult of personality. Loyalty to the pope now became the watchword of the conservative forces. The gap between the blind loyalty to the papacy that the conservatives espoused and the actual policies of the Wojtyła papacy grew to monumental proportions.

The conservatives could not have foreseen the papacy of Francis. Francis specifically rejected every point of the conservatives' policies: their alliance with conservative evangelicals, defense of capitalism, hostility to Communism, and advocacy of Catholic moral and social teaching "in the public square." The reaction of the conservatives varies. Some have loudly criticized the pope's policies and even demanded a rethinking of papal power. Others dissent from the substance of these policies but never challenge the institution or Pope Francis himself. Only a minority continue, while remaining in substance conservatives, to declare their full support for Pope Francis (Opus Dei, *The Pillar*).

Regarding traditionalists, many have sought to distance themselves from the ultramontane papacy. Some have not. José Ureta and Roberto de Mattei have both sharply criticized Pope Francis yet at the same time firmly advocate the strictest ultramontanism. They understand ultramontanism as a set of theological definitions adopted in 1870 that are closely tied with the *Syllabus of Errors* and the struggle against secular revolutionary forces of that time. (Catholic progressives usually offer a similar definition.) Yet Ureta asserts that most popes after 1870 did not follow ultramontanism, as he defines it, at all. In fact, after 1962 the popes specifically rejected it. Ureta and de Mattei do not explain how, under ultramontane theory, this is even possible. We must conclude from the evidence of these very writers that the exercise of ultramontane authoritarianism is indeed severable from the content of Church policy. They also do not explain how years later the "true" ultramontanes were utterly unsuccessful in maintaining intellectual control of the Catholic Church and even, at Vatican II, of the papacy.

The ultramontane defenders (Ureta and de Mattei) have further sought to distinguish the authoritarian papal actions taken during Vatican II and its aftermath — and now those of Pope Francis — from the "true" ultramontanism of Pius IX and Pius X. As noted, they would also distinguish the ultramontanism of Pius IX and Pius X from the policies of all other post-1870 popes. Yet this is a totally arbitrary position — there is no such distinction. As John Rist and Cardinal Gerhard Müller have pointed out, there is even institutional continuity between the ultramontane supporters of Pius IX and those of Francis. The Jesuit order played a decisive role in Vatican I—and is doing the same today under Pope Francis. In support of their position, Ureta and de Mattei adduce Cardinal Pie, Joseph de Maistre, and Louis Veuillot as authoritative exponents of "true" ultramontanism. For good reasons, they don't mention Félicité de Lamennais or Josef Kleutgen, SJ—personalities as important as the others (or perhaps even more important than they) in formulating papal supremacy.

The continuity between nineteenth-century ultramontanism, even in its very infancy, and that of today is evident from the sources cited by the ultramontane traditionalists themselves. Roberto de Mattei favorably quotes Joseph de Maistre, writing decades before Vatican I, for the propositions that:

> If it were permitted to establish degrees of importance among things of divine institution, I would place hierarchy before dogma, so indispensable is it to the maintenance of the faith . . . . It is a fundamental truth in all religious matters that every church that is not Catholic is Protestant. Attempts have been made—in vain—to draw a distinction between schismatic and heretical churches. I know well what is meant, but in the end all difference lies only in words, and every Christian who refuses the Holy Father's communion is a Protestant or soon will be.[12]

I do not think that the Catholic Church has ever adopted such doctrinal assertions. But these are classic statements of an essential aspect of ultramontanism: the substitution of subordination to authority for a shared common faith. De Maistre's words, however, have proved uncannily prescient—in a way he could not possibly have foreseen. For after the Council, the Church was indeed divided into mutually exclusive factions, with different doctrines, liturgies, and even lifestyles. Yet these groups on the whole remained "in the Church"—thus ultimately subject, at least nominally, to papal authority. Have we not read praise of John Paul II and even of Paul VI for "avoiding schism" by refraining from insisting on Catholic doctrine? Essential after Vatican II was the avoidance not of heresy but of schism. Truly, after Vatican II, hierarchy, however feeble, did take precedence over the now totally conflicted realm of dogma! Of course, Pope Francis and his team approach de Maistre even more closely with their insistence on personal loyalty to Francis as the decisive criterion of Catholicity.

THE END OF "CATHOLICISM"?

Throughout the entire papacy of Francis, the institutions of the Church have continued to crumble and the practice of the faith of the Roman Catholic Church has continued its radical decline. This does not trouble the Catholic establishment nor that minority of the Catholic laity that continues to practice its faith (according to the rules of the establishment) and to contribute, or pay taxes, to the Church.

---

12 See chapter 28 above.

Yet for the Vatican and the Church bureaucracy, the problem remains that, at the end of the day, the existence of the Roman Catholic Church depends upon to the voluntary commitment of the faithful to the Catholic faith. The Church no longer has major benefices, sinecures, and other significant economic advantages to bestow. Even in Poland there hardly exists anymore a direct nationalist link between Church and people. To the extent any automatic membership in a "Catholic milieu" ever existed in modern times, it is either gone or in the process of disappearing. Therefore, as the practice of the faith declines, the Church, as an institution, will at some point face a crisis. But when that will happen we do not know. To insiders, the Communist world seemed to be on the brink of collapse for decades, yet it soldiered along up to 1989/1991. Institutions can continue for a long time after their inner substance has gone.

I do believe that at some point the Catholic Church will have to face the issues raised by the ultramontane papacy if it is to survive in anything like its current form. Many have written of the need to bind the papacy more closely to tradition and the Scriptures. Privately making proposals for ecclesiastical reform is of limited utility. No forum exists in the Church today to facilitate the objective consideration of reforms or even of facts. The "synod on synodality" is the best evidence of that. And this too is a legacy of ultramontanism. Accordingly, such a restructuring, or rather refocusing, of the papacy will come about through the force of historical events—or should I say divine providence? The Church will endure, but where it will exist, and what dimensions it will have, are unknown to us. What we can do, however, is to continue to give witness to Catholic tradition in its totality.

38

The Hyperinflation of the Papacy[1]

ERIC SAMMONS

I F YOU READ THE *CATECHISM OF THE CATHOLIC CHURCH* from front to back, you'll note that at least 98% of the content has nothing to do with the papacy. Creation, Original Sin, the Incarnation, hypostatic union, the Resurrection, moral commands against killing and lying, the inspiration of Scripture, sacramental grace, the all-male priesthood: none references the pope. In fact, the subject "pope" doesn't even get its own entry in the subject index; instead, it reads, "Pope: see Apostolic Succession; Church: structure: hierarchical constitution."

The absence of extensive references to the pope is also the case when you peruse Catholic liturgical texts and the myriad Catholic devotions: very few even mention the pope, and none are intrinsically connected to the papacy.

Likewise, the Niceno-Constantinopolitan Creed, which was written in the fourth century as the fundamental synopsis of Catholic belief—and which is still recited every Sunday at every Catholic Mass—does not mention the pope. When it describes the Church, it calls it "one, holy, catholic, and apostolic"—no mention of "papal" (although of course the papacy is part of the "apostolic" mark of the Church, as the *Catechism* properly notes).

And yet, when debates occur related to Catholic belief and practice either online or in real life today, usually the pope and the papacy dominate the discussion: "the pope said," "Pius XII commanded," "according to John Paul II . . ."

This dichotomy is stark and reflects a variety of historical factors, including nineteenth-century European political debates[2] and the long run of good and effective pontiffs after the Council of Trent. The most important factor, however, is that we all live in a post-Reformation world, in which a large section of Christianity decided to chuck the papacy to the curb. Because of this, Catholics realized they needed to defend the pope and the papal office, for fear of falling into the same individualist errors of Protestantism.

Yet, as the contrast I highlighted above indicates, that laudable goal has morphed into a papacy-dominated religion in the minds of most Catholics (and non-Catholics). Even though the vast majority of Catholicism is not directly connected to the papacy, many Catholics today reference the papacy in almost every aspect of Catholic life.

---

1 First published at *Crisis Magazine* on November 8, 2023.
2 See "The 'Spirit of Vatican I' as a Post-Revolutionary Political Problem," in Kwasniewski, *Bound by Truth*, 18–29.

This is most apparent in the area of morality. Catholicism has a rich moral tradition, in which a multitude of virtues form a symphony of a saintly life. Fortitude, justice, prudence, and temperance are the hinges on which these virtues hang, and in concert with the gifts of the Holy Spirit, all the virtues work together for our salvation.

You wouldn't know it by listening to many debates about morality today, however. Now, almost every moral issue is reduced to one virtue: obedience. And typically this single virtue is reduced even further to obedience to the pope. That is the only virtue that matters; the only thing required of the Catholic to live a moral life.

If the pope says that artificial contraception is wrong, then you need to avoid that practice out of obedience to the pope. Not because artificial contraception violates human sexuality in so many ways, and fundamentally undermines the purpose of marriage, the procreation and education of children. No, it's because the pope said so.

The problem with this distortion of Catholic teaching is that it places the entirety of morality on the shoulders of one man. If a pope rightly condemns artificial contraception, fine. But if a pope suggests (or even his advisors suggest) that perhaps there are "exceptions" to the moral law in this area, then a debate opens about what should be an undebatable topic — at least if you understand the reasoning behind the prohibition.

This problem of course isn't just hypothetical these days. Pope Francis's frequent condemnation of the death penalty (and his rewriting the *Catechism* to that effect) has led many modern Catholics to believe the death penalty is always immoral, in contradiction to thousands of years of Catholic teaching. There is no discussion of the virtue of justice or the importance of protecting the common good. Instead, it's just "we have to obey the pope on this."

That's not conformity to Catholic moral teaching; that's cult-like obeisance.

And to be clear, this is not just true of Catholic progressives under Pope Francis. Excessive focus on the papacy was also the case with conservatives under Pope John Paul II. In fact, such an unbalanced view goes back more than a century; since Vatican I the dominance of obedience to the pope as the *sine qua non* of Catholic morality has been pervasive.

The twentieth century, in fact, could be called the "Papal Century" in Church history. While the papacy has always been an important aspect of Catholicism, and over time became the direct driving force in the Church, in the twentieth century that reality reached an apex.

One reflection of papal dominance can be seen in the *Credo of the People of God*, written by Pope Paul VI as a modern summary of our faith. First, the very fact that a new creed was created not by a council, but individually by a pope speaks volumes. And within the new creed we also see the papal focus. The role of the pope is mentioned three separate times, and in the very first line on the Church, it states, "We believe in one, holy, catholic, and apostolic Church, built by Jesus Christ on that rock which is Peter." Now the papacy is front-and-center in the definition of the Church, not a corollary of her apostolic nature.

While there is nothing false in Pope Paul VI's creed, and in fact it makes sense to at least once mention the papal role in modern, post-Reformation times, the change in emphasis we see when it comes to the papacy reflects what has become an unhealthy distortion of authentic Catholic teaching.

Simply put, the role of the papacy in the minds of too many Catholics has morphed from being the *center* of Church unity to the *source* of Church teaching. He is seen as hand-picked by the Holy Spirit and guided every minute by that same Holy Spirit. Thus his opinions on various social and political matters are seen as quasi-revelations from God. It's as if God reveals things to us through the pope, and only the pope. To question the pope's views is to question God Himself.

The proper Catholic understanding, on the other hand, puts the pope at the end of the line of revelation, so to speak, not the beginning.

First, God revealed truths about Himself and about this world both through natural revelation (reason) and Divine Revelation. He did this particularly through His Chosen People, as we see throughout the Old Testament. From both natural revelation and Divine Revelation, we come to know truths about God and about how we are to worship and live.

Then, in the fullness of time, God sent His Son to reveal Himself fully. Everything we need to know for our salvation is complete in Jesus Christ: there is no need for any new revelation beyond Him.

Jesus Christ shared this full revelation—the deposit of faith—with His apostles, both directly and after His Ascension through the Holy Spirit. The apostles received this revelation and were charged with proclaiming it to the nations.

After the death of the apostles, their successors the bishops were then given a different task. While they are also charged with proclaiming the deposit of faith, they receive no new revelation, but instead must protect the deposit of faith handed on to them by the apostles. Further, they then hand it on to the next generation of bishops.

So far, there is no mention of the pope, which might seem odd to modern Catholics convinced that the papacy is the only office that matters. It is only in that last step—the role of the bishops—that the pope is involved.

First, he has the same task as the other bishops; after all, he himself is a bishop. He is to proclaim and protect the deposit of faith and faithfully hand it on to his successors.

Unlike the other bishops, the pope does have a second role. He is also to "strengthen the brethren" (Lk 22:32). When there is a dispute among the bishops, he is there to help resolve it. He is the final court which decides among debating bishops. This is the reason, in fact, for his gift of infallibility. It ensures that debates can end and doctrine be declared in a definitive way. This gift of infallibility is not an invitation to make new declarations, or, heaven forbid, change existing teachings.

Note then how many Catholics today put the cart before the horse: rather than the pope manifesting his own revelation from God, he is actually at the end of the process, receiving what has been given to him by his predecessors, protecting it, and, if necessary, settling disputes that arise among the episcopate. He is not creating new teachings or even charged with "developing" them.

It might appear from what I've written thus far that I don't think the papacy is important or vital to the life of the Church. That's not true; if that were the case, I'd still be Protestant, or perhaps become Eastern Orthodox. The papacy, properly understood, *is* vitally important. It's the "fail-safe" in the system; it keeps the Church from diverging from the deposit of faith when the bishops as a whole fail to defend it properly. As can be seen by the multitudinous and contradictory teachings of the Protestants and the failure of the Eastern Orthodox to maintain certain orthodox teachings, the papacy is necessary.

But the most dangerous heresies are not those that reject the truth; they are the ones that *distort* the truth. By keeping some of the truth, they are more attractive. It's true that the papacy is important, even necessary, but it's not true that it is the most important aspect of Catholicism. It's true that the pope must protect the faith, but it's not true that he creates it. The pope should not dominate the faith, but should be its humble servant. Catholics then must thread the needle between a rejection of the papacy and a hyperinflation of it.

39

Can We Learn Anything from the Critics of Vatican I?[1]

DARRICK TAYLOR

JUST BEFORE THE FIRST VATICAN COUNCIL, A CRITIC warned what would happen if the council defined papal infallibility as its ultramontane supporters wished. "Ultramontanism, he wrote, "is essentially Papalism," and for its adherents

> the power of the pope over the Church . . . neither knows nor tolerates any limits. He is to be sole and absolute master, and all beside him are his plenipotentiaries and servants, and are, in fact, whether mediately or immediately . . . On Ultramontane principles the Church is in a normal and flourishing condition in proportion as it is ruled, administered, supervised, and regulated, down to the minutest details . . . from Rome.

The consequence of defining the pope's infallibility would be that it "will extend its dominion over men's minds . . . till it has coerced them into subjection to every Papal pronouncement," for it would encompass any subject. After theologians had abandoned their "adherence . . . to the ancient tradition," then "every pope, however ignorant of theology, will be free to make what use he likes of his power of dogmatic creativeness, and to erect his own thoughts into the common belief, binding on the whole Church."[2]

For traditionalists, this might sound like an apt description of the Church under Pope Francis, and their situation under *Traditionis Custodes*. Several figures in the traditionalist sphere have questioned the wisdom of ultramontanism and even the definition of papal authority enshrined by the First Vatican Council, as having been the origins of the current tyrannical exercise of papal authority. However, they might balk at the author of the above quotation: Ignaz von Döllinger, the German theologian excommunicated for rejecting papal infallibility.

Döllinger became a heretic when he rejected the anathemas of Vatican I. But in what was said in the above quotation, was Döllinger right? Is there a link between Vatican I and the papacy of Francis, who has governed in an authoritarian manner, often at the expense of Tradition? In this essay, I will examine the arguments made by opponents of infallibility leading up to and during the Council, as well

---

1   First published at *OnePeterFive* on November 13, 2023.
2   Ignaz von Döllinger, *The Pope and the Council* (London, Oxford, and Cambridge: Rivington's, 1869), 40–41.

as the conciliar definition. By understanding them in their context, I hope to shed light on the current plight of the Church, and what traditionalists in particular might learn from these critics.

THE PAPACY IN A STATE OF EMERGENCY

First we must set the context. Ultramontanism was a nineteenth-century movement within the Church which pushed for the centralization of authority in the papacy, as a response to the upheavals of the time. It gained strength as the *Risorgimento* (the unification of Italy) advanced, the Papal States dwindling to the area around Rome in 1860 when Italy became a unified kingdom. Both the Vatican and the ultramontanist press thought the Church was in a death struggle with the godless modern nation-state, and their solution was to concentrate power in Rome's hands, as a means of shielding the episcopate from the various states that seemed to threaten them. Moreover, popular acclaim for the papacy in an age of mass media drove Romanization and centralization of papal authority as much as papal initiative did.[3]

Internally speaking, the major target of the ultramontanes were the remaining Gallicans. Gallicanism was a set of beliefs, largely French, which upheld the "liberties" of local churches and monarchs against papal authority; these beliefs had persisted since the Middle Ages.[4] Ultramontanes benefited from the fact that the Revolutions of the nineteenth century swept away many of the old Gallican settlements in places like France, making Rome's authority over bishops much more direct. Unsurprisingly, those of Gallican sentiments were prominent among the critics of papal infallibility and of centralization, both before and during the Council.

Such centralization predated the Council. Pius IX actively promoted centralizing authority into papal hands. While promoting Dom Guéranger's efforts at renewing Gregorian chant, he gave impetus to the campaign against the neo-Gallican rite in France, ensuring that it died out there (this was one of several initiatives whose origins were popular and didn't come from the papacy). Pius IX revived *ad limina* visits from bishops, which had fallen into abeyance, and took greater control over their appointment, often ignoring candidates from cathedral chapters. He imposed greater control over the selection of Eastern Catholic bishops with the bull *Reversurus* (1867). Pius defined the Immaculate Conception as a dogma (1854), taking advantage of popular piety, and canonized a much greater number of saints than his immediate predecessors—both highlighting papal authority.[5]

---

3   O'Malley, *Vatican I*, 82–83, 101–2; Roger Aubert, "Ultramontane Progress and Final Gallican Resistance," in *History of the Church*, vol. 8: *The Church in the Age of Liberalism*, eds. Roger Aubert, Johannes Beckmann, Patrick J. Cornish, Rudolf Lill (New York: Crossroad Publishing Co., 1981), 304–7; Marvin O'Connell, "Ultramontanism and Dupanloup: The Compromise of 1865," *Church History*, vol. 53, no. 2 (June 1984): 201–5.

4   O'Malley, *Vatican I*, 26–40; cf. Charles Berthelot du Chesnay and J. M. Gres-Gayer, "Gallicanism," *New Catholic Encyclopedia*, 2nd ed., vol. 6 (Detroit: Gale, 2003), 73–78.

5   O'Malley, *Vatican I*, 76–79; O'Connell, "Ultramontanism and Dupanloup," 203; Aubert, "The Vatican Council," in Aubert et al., *The Church in the Age of Liberalism*, 308–9.

This extreme support for papal authority in the 1860s is sometimes called neo-ultramontanism by historians, as it drew on older strands of thinking on papal authority going back to the Reformation and, indeed, to the High Middle Ages. As Thomas Pink has noted, many theologians in the nineteenth and twentieth centuries believed that the Holy Spirit prevented the pope from erring in his legislation, such that canon law could be said to be covered by infallibility. Such an idea was never given formal, magisterial approval but was widely held. It appalled Döllinger, who thought it based on beliefs in the so-called Decretals of Pseudo-Isidore, a medieval forgery.[6]

However, canonists in the High Middle Ages never saw these texts as relating to any idea of papal infallibility. Dominican theologians qualified the idea up through the fifteenth century, but in the sixteenth, with the trauma of the Reformation, such qualms were cast aside. The assurance that papal legislation would be guided by the Holy Spirit was a key part of Bellarmine's apologetic. To be sure, by the nineteenth century, most acknowledged the decretals that espoused such ideas to be forgeries, but many theologians still believed this about papal legislation. Some did not, such as John Henry Newman, but it remained part of the "official theology" of the Church and definitely influenced the fathers at Vatican I.[7]

The Vatican naturally drew upon this exalted notion of infallibility, facing what they saw as an emergency situation, a rebellion against the Church (the *Risorgimento* was popular among many priests in Italy, for example). Beyond its theologians, popular opinion amplified by an ultramontane press went even farther in exalting papal authority, encouraging Pius IX to see a formal definition of his infallibility as a natural response to this emergency. How did critics of this exaltation of papal authority respond?

GALLICANS, HISTORIANS, AND "INOPPORTUNISTS"

The controversy among Catholics on the eve of the council largely pitted the ultramontanists (or neo-ultramontanists) against the Catholic Liberals, led by Döllinger. One should not exaggerate the level of criticism directed toward the pope, however; all of the critics under discussion accepted papal primacy, and nearly all accepted the doctrine of papal infallibility or would come to accept the definition after the council.[8]

The old-style Gallicanism that denied papal infallibility in favor of councils was nearly dead by the 1860s; only Döllinger would go so far as to deny it altogether. "Theological Gallicanism" by then mostly meant the belief that the

---

6   See Thomas Pink's treatment of this question in chapter 3; cf. Thomas Albert Howard, *The Pope and the Professor: Pius IX, Ignaz von Döllinger, and the Quandary of the Modern Age* (Oxford: Oxford University Press, 2017), 123–27.

7   Brian Tierney, *Origins of Papal Infallibility, 1150–1350: A Study on the Concepts of Infallibility, Sovereignty, and Tradition in the Middle Ages* (Leiden: Brill, 1972), 12–13; Pink, "Papal Authority" (chapter 3 above); Klaus Schatz, SJ, *Papal Primacy: From Its Origins to the Present* (Collegeville, MN: Liturgical Press, 1996), 132–33.

8   Howard, *Pope and Professor*, 117–30; Butler, *The Vatican Council*, 85–91.

pope could not make dogmatic pronouncements on his own without the consent of the Church, meaning the bishops, and that "the exercise of Apostolic power is . . . regulated by the canons of the Church."[9] This appeal to the canon law and disciplinary legislation of the Church as a limit on papal power would be put forth by, among others, the French-born American bishop Augustin Vérot (1805–1876) during the conciliar debates, one of the few true Gallicans at the council. Many who were not Gallicans feared that proclaiming papal infallibility to be a dogma would virtually abolish the episcopate.[10]

Another powerful criticism came from historians, especially from Germany. History came into its own as an academic subject in the nineteenth century, and the primary criticism of men like Döllinger and Lord Acton was that the idea of papal infallibility was historically incredible. Especially in Germany, influenced by secular and Protestant trends, a powerful current arose that depicted the neoscholastic approach to theology favored by Rome as ahistorical and out of step with contemporary emphasis on historical context. In fact, Döllinger and Acton were deeply influenced by German philosophical trends, including what they called *Historismus*, the idea that "all human beliefs and ideas are historically conditioned and subject to change."[11]

The leading figure in this group was unquestionably Döllinger, supported by Acton. Both appeared to have thought of the issue of infallibility as purely a matter of the historical record, which in their minds disproved it. We have already seen that Döllinger thought the idea was based on medieval forgeries, but others without his philosophical baggage were quite aware of more substantial historical difficulties with the idea. Several cited the case of Honorius I, condemned by three ecumenical councils and a pope, as proof against the doctrine, though most did not hold the historicist views of Döllinger. This included the distinguished Church historian of Tübingen, Karl Joseph von Hefele, whom Pius IX made bishop of Rottenberg just before the council and who would (along with many others) cite the case of Honorius during conciliar debates.

But the critics of the definition also had to contend with the ultramontane press, whose rhetoric practically made the pope out to be a demigod. To give one example, Louis Veuillot (1813–1883), editor of the ultramontane newspaper *L'Univers*, rewrote the sequence *Veni Creator Spiritus* with Pius IX as its subject: "To Pius IX, Pontiff King, / Father of the Poor, / Giver of Gifts, / Light of lights, / Send forth thy beam of Heavenly Light!"[12] It needs to be repeated that defining papal infallibility was very popular with most Catholics, and centralization of the

---

9   Butler, *The Vatican Council*, 31.
10   Butler, 113–14; Aubert, "The Vatican Council," 320.
11   Perez Zagorin, "Lord Acton's Ordeal: The Historian and Moral Judgment," *The Virginia Quarterly Review*, vol. 74, no. 1 (Winter 1998); Aubert, "The Backwardness of Religious Studies and the Controversy about the 'German Theologians,'" in *History of the Church*, 8:239; George Iggers, "Historicism: The History and Meaning of the Term," *Journal of the History of Ideas*, vol. 56, no. 1 (1995): 133. Zagorin notes that Acton used the term "historicist" to describe his own views.
12   O'Malley, *Vatican I*, 87. For more examples, see chapter 27.

papacy turned it into what is still today very much a populist institution. This populist dimension of support for infallibility partially explains why Döllinger and Acton went so much farther in their critique than many with similar concerns.

Both Döllinger and Acton believed that knowledge of the Church's tradition could only be acquired by rigorous historical examination. Writing in 1864, Acton wrote that when it came to dogmas, "every decree . . . requires a preliminary examination" by historians.[13] Likewise, Döllinger would later claim that ecumenical councils were only "free" when they followed "the rules required by the ascertainment of tradition," presumably by historians like himself.[14] They feared that on papal infallibility, the bishops were parroting the common folk's corruption of tradition and ignoring historical experts who alone could make the Church's beliefs credible to modern society.

The near blasphemous rhetoric of the ultramontanes fueled another critique by those who feared the definition would be imprudent, whom history has dubbed the "inopportunists." These critics believed defining infallibility was "inopportune" because the governments of Europe and modern society more broadly would use it as an excuse to further shackle the Church. This name derives from a group of fourteen German bishops that met at Fulda in 1869, and issued a public letter in which they argued that because of "the actual state of things in Germany, the definition would be inopportune." The bishops (which included Hefele) were responding to the furor that Döllinger's articles in the newspaper *Allgemeine Zeitung* caused and which he issued as a book, *The Pope and the Council*, in July 1869.[15]

The "inopportunists" included perhaps the most famous of those opposed to the definition, John Henry Newman. Newman thought the definition unnecessary because it countered no heresy, unlike dogmas and anathemas pronounced in past councils. It would encourage the pope to act alone without the bishops more frequently, resulting in a practical "alteration of the elementary constitution of the Church." He particularly feared a definition might result in an enlarged domain of infallibility that, combined with ultramontane sentiment, could give to the pope an "enormous power . . . *not restrained even by the Depositum.*"[16]

Newman also feared it would be a "retrospective doctrine," meaning it would lead to scrutiny of past papal teachings and raise questions about them, such that it could throw "religion into confusion, make skeptics, encourage scoffers, and throw back enquirers." Newman, like many critics, including Döllinger, feared the definition would prevent reunion with other Christian bodies such as the Anglicans and the Orthodox. He also suspected that Archbishop Manning's

13   *Lord Acton on Papal Power*, ed. H. A. MacDougall (London: Sheed and Ward, 1973), 91.

14   Ignaz von Döllinger, *Declarations and Letters on the Vatican Decrees, 1869-1887* (Edinburgh: T&T Clark, 1891), 97.

15   Butler, *Vatican Council*, 91-92; O'Malley, *Vatican I*, 123-25; Howard, *Pope and Professor*, 129-37.

16   John Henry Newman, *Letters and Diaries of John Henry Newman*, vol. 24: *A Grammar of Assent: January 1868 to December 1869*, ed. Charles Stephen Dessain and Thomas Gornall, SJ (Oxford: Clarendon Press, 1978), 327, italics in original; Ian Ker, *John Henry Newman: A Biography* (Oxford: Clarendon Press, 1988), 633; 635.

disregard for the possible difficulties it might cause Catholics in the future was motivated by Manning's conviction that "the world is soon coming to an end."[17]

Finally, critics worried the definition might cause conflict with the civil authorities in countries like Germany, England, and France. In addition to concern about the authority of bishops (with regard to papal primacy), this political concern animated many of the minority bishops at the council. Such fears were well founded: on their way to the meeting at Fulda, the bishops who issued the letter were insulted and nearly attacked by an angry mob, and the German *Kulturkampf* was in some ways a direct response to Vatican I.[18]

That civil governments threatened the Church across Europe played into ultramontane hands; they saw in a definition of infallibility a weapon to use against them. Newly formed nation-states like Italy and Germany feared the possible subversion of tenuous national unity by a united Catholic bloc, following directions from the pope. (It is noteworthy that Vatican I did not include representatives from any civil government.) Opponents feared that extreme ultramontanes wanted to define the pope's infallibility so they could insinuate that it extended to his actions in the temporal sphere. Some feared it was their "intention to declare the pope infallible in matters of faith in order to give him the appearance of infallibility in other matters as well."[19]

This concern made Döllinger apoplectic about papal infallibility. He accepted papal primacy, but feared proclaiming the pope infallible would naturally apply to his governance of the Church. Döllinger's research on the history of the papacy convinced him that the idea the pope could not err in his legislation, as many believed, was false. As Acton wrote, "the history of Church government was the influence which so powerfully altered his position."[20] Until the 1860s, Döllinger publicly supported papal infallibility, but his studies in history and the unhinged rhetoric of the ultramontanes turned him against the doctrine, making him its most vocal critic.

THE DEBATES AT THE COUNCIL

Even before debates on *Pastor Aeternus* commenced, the bishops had several exchanges concerning infallibility. A public exchange between Archbishop Manning and Bishop Dupanloup just before the council centered on Manning's assertion that the pope could define doctrine "apart from the episcopal body," but also with Archbishop Deschamps over the broader question of "separate infallibility." Dupanloup and others criticized those who wanted infallibility defined for making the pope separate from the rest of the Church, particularly the bishop.

Deschamps' reply anticipated the definition in *Pastor Aeternus*, claiming that the pope could never separate himself from "the faith of all centuries," and that

17   Newman, *Letters*, 25:377–79; Ker, *Newman*, 635.
18   Butler, *Vatican Council*, 92.
19   Aubert, "The Vatican Council," 321.
20   Howard, *Pope and Professor*, 128.

his infallibility only served to preserve the deposit of the faith and not promulgate "new revelations."[21] Deschamps' notion of infallibility was the moderate one, and during the council, those in the majority made clear they rejected the much more extreme ideas circulating in ultramontane circles.

On the "infallibilist" side were Archbishop Deschamps of Malines, Archbishop Manning of Westminster, Cullen of Dublin, and Donnet of Bordeaux. Most of these were opposed to the inanities of Veuillot and the press, but a handful, led by Manning, were more extreme, regarding their opponents as "heretics . . . to be heard and condemned." Pius IX proclaimed neutrality, but as the council proceeded, he made clear his support for the majority and his hostility to the minority.[22]

Most critics hailed from Germany, France, and Eastern Europe, the latter being keen on reconciliation with the Orthodox and opposing the definition as a stumbling block to that end. Almost all of these were "inopportunists." The most important were Archbishops Melchers of Cologne and Hefele of Rottenberg; two Austrian bishops were also prominent in opposing the definition, Schwarzenberg of Prague and Rauscher of Vienna. Among the French, the outstanding members of the Minority were Archbishop Darboy of Paris, who was murdered by Communists during the Paris Commune in 1871, and Dupanloup of Orléans, a favorite of Pius IX despite his opposition because of his support for the Papal States.[23]

But it was the ultramontanes who determined the course of the council. The council opened on December 8, 1869, and debates began in deputations over the nature of the documents to be presented to the bishops. These would be scrutinized by the bishops and then revised for final debate. This meant electing members to staff the deputations that drafted the documents was crucial. The most important of these was the congregation *de Fide*. The "infallibilists," led by Cardinal Manning, organized an informal committee to draw up a list of candidates to fill the *de Fide*. All of twenty-four of them (save one by mistake) were strong supporters of infallibility. All twenty-four were elected.

This meant that the topic of infallibility, which was not originally supposed to be dealt with early on, and might not have been discussed before Italian troops besieged Rome in 1870, now became one of the first topics to be debated. Manning's political maneuvering hardened the divisions already present, and led Döllinger to claim the council was not "free." That a definition would be promulgated became an inevitability because of this maneuvering.[24] (The reader should

---

21 "Why then do people speak of 'separate infallibility,' as if the faith of the successor of Peter could ever be exclusively personal or separate itself from the faith of all centuries? . . . It has for object only the preservation of the deposit of faith and to declare when necessary its content; and it is not by new revelations or by inspirations that the supreme doctrinal authority preserves the faith and declares it, but by the fidelity divinely promised to the employment of the means necessary to preserve and declare it." Butler, *Vatican Council*, 127–28.

22 O'Malley, *Vatican I*, 154.

23 Butler, *Vatican Council*, 112–17.

24 O'Malley, *Vatican I*, 156, 185; Butler, *Vatican Council*, 140–44; Aubert, "The Vatican Council," 321–22.

note the parallel between what the ultramontanes did at Vatican I and what the European "progressives" did at Vatican II, changing the schema and committees at the outset. It is highly likely, in my opinion, that the progressives at Vatican II had in mind the precedent Manning and company set in 1870.)

Initial debates began on December 28 for the document on the Catholic Faith (that would become the constitution *Dei Filius*). While the deputation finalized it for the final debate, the Fathers debated disciplinary issues from January to March. The minority criticized several aspects of Roman centralization. Several Eastern bishops pleaded for the customs of their churches that had become Latinized recently, particularly their manner of choosing bishops, which the Vatican reversed in the Bull *Reversurus* of 1867. Pius IX gave the Latin-rite cardinal who spoke in their name a personal dressing down as a result. Another schema dealt with a proposal for a universal catechism for the whole Church. Several bishops objected to this, partly on account of their attachment to local catechisms, but the proposal passed. It was never promulgated, however, subsumed by debates on the primacy and infallibility.[25] *Dei Filius* was promulgated on April 24, and five days later, the presidents of the deputations announced that decrees on primacy and infallibility would be debated next, to the consternation of the minority. Debates on *Pastor Aeternus* began on May 13.

Debates on the primacy were not as fierce as those on infallibility but did bring out notable tendencies. Critics were more historically sensitive than their counterparts who favored the definition. In opposition to the idea that the pope possessed a *plenitudo potestas* they raised the specter of Pope Honorius I, mentioned earlier, to argue otherwise. Much criticism focused on the way the definition construed papal jurisdiction, particularly the phrase "immediate, universal, and episcopal." Some bishops, especially the Germans, feared the terms would be misconstrued as a sort of papal absolutism, which men in modern society would reject. But on the whole, "there was no disposition on their part to minimize the nature and extent of the jurisdiction and powers inherent in the primacy."[26]

Some bishops, especially the more "Gallican" sort such as Vérot of St Augustine and the Eastern bishops, argued that the pope had supreme power in the Church but that he had to "govern according to the canons." But such a tainted, "Gallican" idea was interpreted as disloyalty to the pope — especially by Pius IX, who despite assurances of neutrality very much pushed for the definition of infallibility, denouncing members of the minority in private and deprecating them in public as the debate turned toward that subject.[27]

The debates on infallibility largely mirrored the divisions that had opened up prior to the council. The majority defended infallibility as necessary to shore up the crumbling authority of society and reassure the faithful of the unchanging nature

25   Butler, *Vatican Council*, 190–98; O'Malley, *Vatican I*, 189; Aubert, "The Vatican Council," 323–24.
26   Butler, *Vatican Council*, 333–34, 336–37; O'Malley, *Vatican I*, 192.
27   Butler, *Vatican Council*, 338; O'Malley, *Vatican I*, 188, 209–10.

of the faith. The minority, by contrast, thought that modern society abhorred any kind of "absolutism" and argued that the exercise of the pope's infallibility must take into account the "witness of the whole Church." By this they meant consultation with the bishops of the world, a suggestion flatly rejected by the majority, who thought that in a time of emergency the pope could not wait to take the pulse of the entire Church, but must be able to act freely and quickly to squash heresy and restore the unity of the Church.[28]

Most bishops in favor were not as extreme as Cardinal Manning (perhaps because, as Dom Cuthbert Butler pointed out, Manning, unlike many in the majority, was not trained as a dogmatic theologian), and many made several efforts to find a compromise that would satisfy the minority. Famously, Cardinal Filippo Maria Guidi, a Dominican, argued for a more moderate definition of infallibility, derived from St Antoninus of Florence (1389-1459) — one that stipulated that the pope, while not bound legally in any way by the opinions of the bishops, must consult them, as his power was not arbitrary and willful.

This speech, which many on both sides of the debate received favorably, led Pius IX to scold Guidi in private that evening (June 18). Pius accused of him of siding with the enemies of the Church, and when Guidi pleaded that before a pope issued a definition he must study the tradition of the Church, Pius IX responded with his famous reply: "I, I am the Tradition! I, I am the Church!" (*Io, io sono la tradizione! Io, io sono la chiesa!*).[29] Debate went on till July 4, but after the Guidi affair, it was clear no compromise would emerge, and the document became *Pastor Aeternus* on July 18 virtually unchanged.

Its final definition of papal authority looks different in significant ways when considering the primacy as opposed to infallibility. The definition of the primacy was fulsome, with hardly any sense of the limits of the pope's authority to govern the life of the Church. By contrast, even though the minority did not get the clarity they wanted in terms of *how* exactly the pope was infallible, the definition is much more narrow and limited than that on the primacy.

Moreover, even though *Pastor Aeternus* does not explicitly state that the pope's authority is limited by tradition, it can be said to have stated it implicitly. In the preamble, it says the institution of the primacy must be believed "in accordance with the ancient and unchanging faith of the whole Church," while the chapter on infallibility stipulates that the popes exercise infallibility "not so that they might, by his [the Holy Spirit's] revelation, make known some new doctrine, but that by His assistance, they might religiously guard and faithfully expound the revelation or deposit of faith, transmitted by the apostles."[30]

Even in the chapter on the primacy, the minority managed to have the text state that bishops have their authority "by the Holy Spirit," an important qualification

28   O'Malley, *Vatican I*, 203-4; Schatz, *Papal Primacy*, 158-61; Aubert, "Vatican Council," 319.

29   Butler, *Vatican Council*, 352-56, 378; O'Malley, *Vatican I*, 208-14.

30   *Decrees of the Ecumenical Councils*, vol. 2: *Trent to Vatican II*, ed. Norman J. Tanner, SJ (Washington, DC: Georgetown University Press, 1990), 816.

given the absolute-sounding definition of papal primacy, and providential considering that the planned schema on episcopal authority was permanently shelved
after the Italian army captured Rome on September 20.[31] Even if one has concerns about the misuse of the definition itself, one has to say that it is not nearly
as problematic as it might have been. This owes something to the efforts of the
minority, as well as the more moderate among the majority.

WHAT HATH THE COUNCIL WROUGHT?

Did Vatican I lead to the exaltation of papal authority we see today? The
answer is a complicated one. At least in part, the answer is yes. Much like the
documents of Vatican II, *Pastor Aeternus*, when properly interpreted, doesn't allow
for something like the destruction of the entire liturgical tradition prior to 1970.
Yet taken in isolation, the conciliar definitions of primacy and infallibility don't
appear this way. As critics at Vatican I pointed out,[32] they can lead to grievous
abuses when torn out of the context of the Church's larger tradition, because
they do not clearly specify limits to papal authority, especially in regard to the
pope's primacy. Without the context of tradition, the definition of the primacy
allows people to infer that it extends far beyond the actual terms of the definition itself. I suspect this was the hope of the more extreme ultramontanists: to
ensure obedience by making disobedience as psychologically costly as possible.
Pairing an expansive definition of papal primacy with a less broad but still not
completely circumscribed infallibility allows one to believe (or to convince others) that the pope is some sort of spiritual dictator. As one bishop at Vatican I
warned, "no matter how careful the decree was in its wording, ordinary people
would conclude the council had made the pope a despot."[33]

And for obvious reasons, the Vatican has rarely bothered to clear up the matter.
The practical purpose of issuing the definition was to boost papal authority, not limit
it. Ultramontanes hoped to frighten hostile governments with it, and critics feared
it would provoke them. They were both right. In 1875, German bishops responded
in a letter to the German government's criticisms of the council, insisting the pope
was "not a perfectly absolute monarch." Pius IX gave his public approval to their
missive in an apostolic letter, *Mirabilis Illa Constantia*, and that letter is the only
magisterial document I am aware of that acknowledges limits on papal primacy. 1875
was the nadir of the *Kulturkampf*, with bishops being imprisoned or exiled. Perhaps
this pressure helped the post-Vatican I papacy admit limits to its governing power.[34]

---

31   *Decrees*, 814.
32   O'Malley, *Vatican I*, 203.
33   The bishop was William Clifford of England (O'Malley, *Vatican I*, 205).
34   For the German bishops' letter and Pius IX's letter, see *DH* 3112-17. The only other document
that clearly states such limits comes from the Theological Commission at Vatican II. During the Second
Vatican Council, the Theological Commission rejected an amendment to *Lumen Gentium* proposed
by none other than Paul VI, which, in effect, said the pope was accountable to God alone; because,
said the Commission, "the Roman pontiff is also bound to revelation itself, to the fundamental
structure of the Church, the sacraments, to the definitions of earlier councils, and other obligations

Having said this, Vatican I only partially explains our current imperial papacy. The centralization Döllinger bemoaned would likely have happened without the council. The rise of modern media, the collapse of the Papal States, the elimination of Gallican settlements and royal privileges (which meant there were fewer intermediary bodies between Rome and the bishops) — all would have happened with or without the council. By the end of World War I, the Vatican became like a modern state, whose sovereignty runs unimpeded by mediating bodies, as witnessed by the compilation of the first universal code of canon law, promulgated in 1917. Vatican I was a product of centralization and Romanization, not its cause.

Moreover, belief in the near godlike powers of the papacy long preceded *Pastor Aeternus* and was a source for it. The belief, noted by Pink, that the pope was infallible as a legislator long predated Vatican I. The role of the Jesuits should also be mentioned here. They of course were active in promoting infallibilism at Vatican I, but it was the Jesuits, and St Robert Bellarmine in particular, who first popularized this idea in the post-Reformation era. Bellarmine was one of the first to suggest the pope was not only infallible when proclaiming dogmatic definitions, but personally incapable of heresy. Bellarmine's influence can be glimpsed in the conciliar debates on infallibility, as all sides appealed to his authority.[35]

The critics of Vatican I were correct that it was inopportune to define the pope's infallibility in 1870. They recognized, as Newman did, that the Tradition was not clear on how the pope's infallibility should be exercised. They were also right about its potential for misunderstanding and abuse. Though to be fair to the "infallibilists," no one in 1870 could have dreamed that a pope would even hint his approval of the blessing of same-sex "couples," or that one might micromanage parish bulletins. The papacy of Francis is truly unprecedented.

Still, Francis has not dared to issue any dogmatic definitions to accomplish his agenda. One reason why is that *Pastor Aeternus* is clear that popes cannot formulate dogmatic definitions for novel purposes. The ultramontanist gambit has so far worked in that regard. Instead, Francis has exploited his powers as primate of the Church, governing in opposition to Tradition in the most "absolutist" manner possible. As several historians have noted, the pope's primacy is a bigger problem for the Church than his infallibility.[36]

The difficulties with *Pastor Aeternus* are real, but the issue of what limits there might be to the pope's authority, if only in moral rather than juridical terms, has still not been settled. Despite being treated unjustly, traditionalists can contribute

---

too numerous to mention." See Avery Cardinal Dulles, SJ, "Authority in the Church," in *Civilizing Authority: Church, State, Society*, ed. Patrick McKinley Brennan (Lanham, MD: Lexington Books, 2007), 44. In rejecting the amendment, the Commission noted the concerns of Eastern Christians regarding papal authority, but also alluded to the debate at Vatican I over the phrase which declares papal definitions to be binding "of themselves and not by the consent of the Church" (*Pastor Aeternus*, ch. 4 — another point of heated debate during that council). See *Acta Synodalia Sacrosancti Concilii Oecumenici Vaticani II: Periodus Tertia, Pars I* (Rome: Typis Polyglotis Vaticana, 1973), 247.

35 On the Jesuit notion of obedience, see John Lamont's essay in chapter 7.

36 Butler, *Vatican Council*, 330; Schatz, *Papal Primacy*, 162–63.

to this development in the long run, as did the critics of Vatican I, even if they were not entirely successful. God may be using this pontificate for that very purpose, though I claim no insight into the plans of the Almighty.

They should learn from the example of Döllinger, with whom we began this essay. If one could not tell, I have some sympathy for Döllinger, as did Newman. Döllinger was a fine historian and defender of the Church for many decades before the 1860s, and a man of exemplary character. His downfall began when ultramontane newspapers attacked him as a heretic and a traitor, well before his opinions became heresy. He did not deserve such treatment from fellow priests, who should have acted toward him as his "true brethren," in Newman's phrase.[37]

Döllinger was correct that history disproves the infallibility of papal governance, but he conflated ultramontane exaggerations with the more modest claims of *Pastor Aeternus* regarding the pope's teaching authority. The modern hyperpapalists make the same conflation. But Catholics are bound, under pain of mortal sin, to accept with the assent of faith only the minimum interpretation of Vatican I, not the extremist or even the maximum interpretation.[38]

Döllinger allowed his justifiable anger at his treatment to poison his view of the Church's authority, a product of the modern press and its genius for conflict (which is now many times more toxic in the age of Twitter and TikTok). But more than this, his implicit assertion that only historians could determine what the Church's Tradition allowed doomed him. As Acton put it, "it was said of him that he set the university in the place of the hierarchy."[39]

Even if traditionalist critics of the Church are correct, most still have no authority to make good on their criticisms. They have every right to point out what is wrong, and should go on doing so, but they should do this in a way that does not consume them. They should heed the scholarly, prayerful, and trustful example of Newman, and not act as if their forays in print or online will somehow decide controversies that God will in time bring to an end. (We should also note that whatever faults Pius IX had in dealing with this issue, God Almighty vindicated his personal sanctity, as he is an incorrupt saint whom John Paul II beatified.)[40]

Powerlessness in the face of injustice may be agonizing, but it also might be providential. As Thomas Pink has written, critics of *Traditionis Custodes*, *Amoris Laetitia*, and other papal misdeeds have nothing but their integrity and the truth of their criticisms to justify themselves, rather than law or power. If they are one day vindicated, as I believe they will be, it will only be because their criticisms are true: "One must ultimately appeal to truth . . . and in a Church founded on truth, it must be truth that matters."[41]

---

37   Newman, *Letters*, 25:308.
38   On this important theological truth, see chapters 31 and 32.
39   Howard, *Pope and Professor*, 127.
40   See the comments of Madre Pascalina in Charles Murr's *The Godmother*, 67–85.
41   See above, p. 41.

{ PART III }
Francis against Tradition

Can a Pope Abolish the Traditional Latin Mass?[1]

MATT GASPERS

I N THE ERA OF *TRADITIONIS CUSTODES*, WHEN STILL FUR-
ther restrictions are rumored, possibly up to and including the attempted
total abolition of the Roman Rite in its immemorial form, Catholics would
do well to ask a very basic question: Does the pope have the authority to abolish
what the Council of Trent calls "the received and approved rites of the Catholic
Church"? Other pertinent questions include: How have popes since the Council of Trent understood and applied Trent's teachings? Is the pope bound to
faithfully preserve and hand on what he himself has received? Does the pope
have unlimited power to change (or even abolish) the Church's "received and
approved rites" in whatever ways he thinks best, without regard for apostolic
and ecclesiastical traditions?

These are the questions we will address in this chapter. Along the way, we
will review some common proof-texts to which hyperpapalists appeal in favor
of their erroneous position that the pope has virtually absolute power over the
Church's liturgical rites.

LEX ORANDI, LEX CREDENDI: IMPORTANCE OF LITURGICAL STABILITY

Even from apostolic times, liturgical stability has played a vital role in maintaining unity and integrity of faith for the universal Church. The reason for this
is summed up by the ancient axiom *lex orandi, lex credendi* — "the law of prayer
is the law of belief." In other words, the Church's liturgy (public worship and
prayer) shows forth and gives expression to the Deposit of Faith.

All throughout Church history, heretics have sought to change the Church's
lex orandi in order to accommodate and propagate their heretical *lex credendi*. St
Robert Bellarmine cites an example from "the times of the Emperor Constantine,"
during which "Catholics and Arians were customarily distinguished because the
former would sing *Gloria Patri, et Filio, et Spiritui Sancto* at the end of the Psalms
[during Mass], whereas the latter used: *Gloria Patri, per Filium* [through the Son], *in
Spiritu Sancto* [in the Holy Ghost]."[2] The purpose of the Arian *Gloria Patri* was, of
course, to deny that the Son and the Holy Ghost are consubstantial with the Father.

---

1   First published at *Catholic Family News* on March 3, 2023.
2   St Robert Bellarmine, *On the Most Holy Sacrifice of the Mass*, trans. Ryan Grant (Post Falls, ID:
Mediatrix Press, 2020), Bk. 2, ch. 16, p. 247.

As it was during the Arian crisis (fourth century), so it was also during the Protestant revolt (sixteenth century). Liturgical scholar Adrian Fortesque (d. 1923) observes in his classic work *The Mass: A Study of the Roman Liturgy*:

> The Protestant Reformers naturally played havoc with the old liturgy. It was throughout the expression of the very ideas (the Real Presence, Eucharistic Sacrifice and so on) they rejected. So they substituted for it new Communion services that expressed their principle but, of course, broke away utterly from all historic liturgical evolution [development].

In response to these attacks, the Council of Trent (1545–1563)

> wished the Roman Mass to be celebrated uniformly everywhere. The medieval local uses [i.e., variations of the Roman Rite as celebrated in particular cities or regions] had lasted long enough. They had become very florid and exuberant; and their variety caused confusion. It would be better for all Roman Catholics to go back to an older and simpler form of the Roman Rite. In its eighteenth session (February 16, 1562) the Council appointed a commission to examine the missal, to revise it and restore its earlier form. . . . They accomplished their task very well. It was not to make a new missal, but to restore the existing one "according to the custom and rite of the holy Fathers" [Pope St Pius V, *Quo Primum*], using for that purpose the best manuscripts and other documents.[3]

Thus, the Roman Missal prepared by the Tridentine liturgical commission and promulgated by Pope St Pius V in 1570 exemplifies a true liturgical reform, that is, a restoration and codification of the "received and approved" Roman Rite. Regarding the permanent value of this traditional rite, Michael Fiedrowicz explains near the end of his scholarly work on the subject:

> The traditional rite of the Mass proves itself to be a clear and complete testimony of the central truths of the Faith, a demonstration of the true Faith, so that the rule of prayer (*lex orandi*) at the same time presents an authentic rule of faith (*lex credendi*). Not a single core element of the *depositum fidei* is concealed, diminished, or ambivalently formulated. Unambiguous and unabbreviated, the traditional form of the Mass manifests that which the Church believes, has ever believed, and ever will believe. Accordingly, this liturgy is referred to [by Dom Prosper Guéranger] as "tradition in its most powerful and solemn form," and [by Bishop Jacques-Bénigne Bossuet] as "the most important instrument of tradition."

---

3   Adrian Fortesque, *The Mass: A Study of the Roman Liturgy* (Fitzwilliam, NH: Loreto Publications, 2003), 205–6, emphasis added. Here Fortescue exaggerates somewhat, as *Quo Primum* strongly shored up the rights of all regional liturgical traditions of over 200 years' standing, and made it difficult for such uses to be replaced by requiring, for the adoption of the Roman Rite, the unanimous vote of the bishop and his entire chapter.

> The celebration of the liturgy in its traditional form thus constitutes an effective counterweight for all levelings, reductions, dilutions, and banalizations of the Faith.[4]

TRENT'S DECREES ON LITURGICAL MATTERS

This brings us to the specific decrees of the Council of Trent with respect to liturgical development and the extent of the Church's power over liturgical rites. During Session VII (March 3, 1547), convened under Pope Paul III (r. 1534–1549), the Fathers of Trent issued a decree on the sacraments and several sets of related canons (anathemas), among which we find the following:

> If anyone says that the received and approved [*receptos et approbatos*] rites of the Catholic Church that are customarily used in the solemn administration of the sacraments may be despised or omitted without sin by the ministers as they please or that they may be changed to other new rites by any pastor in the Church: let him be anathema.[5]

Liturgical rites are obviously "approved" by the Church (and the pope, in particular), but what does it mean for them to be "received"? St Basil the Great (d. 379) provides some helpful insights:

> Of the beliefs and practices whether generally accepted or publicly enjoined which are preserved in the Church, some we possess derived from written teaching, others we have received delivered to us in a mystery by *the tradition of the Apostles*; and both of these in relation to true religion have the same force.... What writing has taught us to turn to the East at the [Eucharistic] prayer? Which of the saints has left us in writing the words of the invocation at the displaying of the bread of the Eucharist and the cup of blessing? For we are not, as is well known, content with what the Apostle or the Gospel has recorded, but both in preface and conclusion we add other words as being of great importance to the validity of the ministry, and these we derive from unwritten teaching.[6]

In short, a "received" liturgical rite is one that is rooted in "the tradition of the Apostles" and, as such, has been "preserved by the [Church] Fathers," to quote St Athanasius (d. 373).[7] The approval and preservation of a given liturgical rite is a consequence of its having been "received" from apostolic tradition — it is "approved" and preserved precisely because it is "received."

---

4 Michael Fiedrowicz, *The Traditional Mass: History, Form, and Theology of the Classical Roman Rite*, trans. Rose Pfeifer (Brooklyn: Angelico Press, 2020), 301. Fiedrowicz is a priest of the Archdiocese of Berlin and, since 2001, has served as Professor of Early Church History, Patrology, and Christian Archeology at the Theological Faculty of Trier.

5 Can. 13 on the Sacraments in General (*DH* 1613).

6 St Basil the Great, *On the Holy Spirit*, ch. 22, 66 (www.newadvent.org/fathers/3203.htm).

7 St Athanasius, *Four Letters to Serapion of Thmuis* 1, 28, in William A. Jurgens, *The Faith of the Early Fathers* (Collegeville: The Liturgical Press, 1970), vol. 1, no. 782, p. 336.

Now, those who tend to overinflate papal authority point to other passages from the Council of Trent as "proof" that the Church and her visible head have tremendous discretionary power over the liturgy. They cite, for example, the following text from Session XXI (July 16, 1562), over which Pope Pius IV (r. 1559–1565) presided:

> Furthermore, [the holy council] declares that, in the administration of the sacraments — provided their substance is preserved — there has always been in the Church that *power to determine or modify* what she judged more expedient for the benefit of those receiving the sacraments or for the reverence due to the sacraments themselves — according to the diversity of circumstances, times, and places.[8]

What hyperpapalists fail to mention, however, is the *context* of this statement, namely, an explanation of why Communion under the species of bread alone is sufficient (since Christ is wholly present under either species), which had been the custom of the Roman Church for many centuries by the time of Trent's decree. It has *nothing* to do with making radical changes to the order or texts of the Mass.

Hyperpapalists will also quote from Session XXII (September 17, 1562), likewise held during Pius IV's reign:

> And as human nature is such that it cannot easily raise itself up to the meditation of divine realities without external aids, Holy Mother Church has for that reason *duly established certain rites*, such as that some parts of the Mass should be said in quieter tones and others in louder; and she has provided ceremonial such as mystical blessings, lights, incense, vestments, and many other rituals of that kind from *apostolic order and tradition*, by which the majesty of this great sacrifice is *enhanced* and the minds of the faithful are aroused by those visible signs of religious devotion to contemplation of the high mysteries hidden in this sacrifice.[9]

They focus on the affirmation that "Holy Mother Church has . . . *duly established certain rites*," reasoning that the Church can abolish what she herself has established, while neglecting that the aforementioned ceremonies come "from *apostolic order and tradition*." The above passage, far from proving a power to suppress, actually demonstrates the principle that liturgical development results in *enhancement* (growth) over time, not *reduction* (minimalism).

Moreover, the same decree's teaching on the Roman Canon testifies to the Church's deep concern for preserving not only "apostolic traditions" (those which derive from the Deposit of Faith) but also ecclesiastical traditions (those established after the death of the Apostles):

---

8   Decree on Communion under Both Species and the Communion of Young Children, ch. 2 (*DH* 1728, emphasis added).

9   Decree on the Sacrifice of the Mass, ch. 5 (*DH* 1746, emphasis added).

Holy things must be treated in a holy way, and this sacrifice [the Mass] is the most holy of all things. And so, that this sacrifice might be worthily and reverently offered and received, the Catholic Church many centuries ago instituted the sacred canon. It is so free from all error that it contains nothing that does not savor strongly of holiness and piety and nothing that does not raise to God the minds of those who offer. For it is made up of the words of Our Lord Himself [Scripture], of apostolic traditions [Tradition], and of devout instructions of the holy pontiffs [ecclesiastical traditions].[10]

And to drive home the seriousness of the subject matter, the Fathers of Trent anathematized anyone who would dare to say that "the canon of the Mass contains errors and therefore should be abolished."[11]

IS THE POPE BOUND TO PRESERVE "RECEIVED AND APPROVED RITES"?

Following the Council of Trent, the popes themselves have understood that the duty to faithfully preserve and hand on the Church's "received and approved rites" applies, first and foremost, to the Supreme Pontiff.

Roughly a year after Trent had concluded, Pope Pius IV included the following in his Tridentine Profession of Faith (November 13, 1564):

I most firmly accept and embrace the apostolic and ecclesiastical traditions and all other observances and constitutions of the same [Catholic] Church.... I also profess that there are truly and properly speaking seven sacraments of the New Law, instituted by Jesus Christ our Lord and necessary for the salvation of the human race.... I also admit and accept the rites received and approved in the Catholic Church for the solemn administration of all the sacraments mentioned above.[12]

The same pope who approved Trent's decrees which recognize the Church's "power to determine or modify" how the sacraments are administered (Session XXI), as well as her power to duly establish "certain rites" (Session XXII), clearly saw himself as being bound to "admit and accept the rites received and approved in the Catholic Church," thus acknowledging his duty to preserve and hand them on.

A little over three hundred years later, towards the beginning of the First Vatican Council (Session II), Pope Pius IX repeated his predecessor's words nearly verbatim:

Apostolic and ecclesiastical traditions and all other observances and constitutions of that same [Catholic] Church I most firmly accept and embrace.... I profess also that there are seven sacraments of the new law, truly and properly so called, instituted by our Lord Jesus Christ and necessary for salvation.... I likewise receive and accept the rites

---

10   Decree on the Sacrifice of the Mass, ch. 4 (*DH* 1745).
11   Can. 6 on the Sacrifice of the Mass (*DH* 1756).
12   Bull *Iniunctum Nobis* (*DH* 1863–64, emphasis added).

of the Catholic Church which have been received and approved in the solemn administration of all the aforesaid sacraments.[13]

Note well: The same Pontiff who defined papal infallibility and reaffirmed the pope's "full and supreme power of jurisdiction over the whole Church, not only in matters that pertain to faith and morals, but also in matters that pertain to the discipline and government of the Church throughout the whole world,"[14] also clearly recognized that he himself was bound to "firmly accept and embrace" not only "apostolic and ecclesiastical traditions" — including "the rites . . . which have been received and approved" — but also "all other observances and constitutions" of the Church.

Those who claim that the pope has virtually absolute power over the Church's liturgical rites must reckon with these solemn professions made by Pius IV (1564) and Pius IX (1870), both of whom adhered to the Council of Trent's teaching that the Church's "received and approved rites" must be preserved and handed on.

While it is true that popes have added, removed, or modified various liturgical prayers and ceremonies over the centuries, such changes were introduced with great reverence and care to preserve the substance of the rite as a whole (and obviously never to appease heretics). Moreover, there eventually came a time (relatively early, in the grand scheme of Church history) when significant alterations ceased. On this point, Fortescue notes:

> The reign of St Gregory the Great (590–604) marks an epoch in the history of the Mass. He left the Roman liturgy practically in the state in which we still have it [referring to the traditional Latin Mass]. . . . There is moreover a constant tradition that St Gregory was the last to touch the essential part of the Mass, namely the Canon. . . . From, roughly, the time of St Gregory we have the text of the Mass, its order and arrangement, as a sacred tradition that no one ventured to touch except in unimportant details.[15]

Popes are indeed guardians of tradition (*traditionis custodes*). They are *not* absolute monarchs "whose thoughts and desires are law," as Pope Benedict XVI bore witness at the beginning of his pontificate.[16]

WHAT ABOUT PIUS XII'S TEACHING IN *MEDIATOR DEI*?

Let us now turn to Pope Pius XII's landmark Encyclical *Mediator Dei* on the Sacred Liturgy (November 20, 1947). Before surveying some key passages, it is crucial to understand the historical context and impetus behind the document.

---

13   Pope Pius IX, Profession of Faith (January 6, 1870) (www.papalencyclicals.net/councils/ecum20.htm).

14   Vatican I, *Pastor Aeternus*, ch. 3 (*DH* 3064).

15   Fortescue, *The Mass*, 172–73.

16   Pope Benedict XVI, Homily for the Mass of Possession of the Chair of the Bishop of Rome, May 7, 2005.

Simply put, Pius XII issued *Mediator Dei* (hereafter, *MD*) to affirm all that was good in the Liturgical Movement, which began in the late 1800s and was encouraged by Pope St Pius X (r. 1903–1914), while also condemning Modernist errors which had crept into the movement closer to the time of his pontificate (r. 1939–1958).[17] This context puts Pius XII's teachings into proper perspective, including his statement that "the Sovereign Pontiff alone enjoys the right to recognize and establish any practice touching the worship of God, to introduce and approve new rites, as also to modify those he judges to require modification" (*MD* 58). In other words, the pope's unique power is always in the service of guarding the Church's liturgical patrimony against those who are "over-eager in their search for novelty" and end up "straying beyond the path of sound doctrine and prudence" (*MD* 8).

Below are some key passages from *Mediator Dei* in which Pius XII discusses the nature of the Church's liturgical rites and the scope of her power over them, interspersed with some brief commentary (emphasis added throughout):

> From time immemorial the ecclesiastical hierarchy has exercised this right [to express her faith] in matters liturgical. It has organized and regulated divine worship, *enriching it* constantly with new splendor and beauty, to the glory of God and the spiritual profit of Christians. What is more, it has not been slow—keeping the substance of the Mass and sacraments carefully intact—to modify what it deemed not altogether fitting, and to add what appeared more likely to *increase* the honor paid to Jesus Christ and the august Trinity, and to instruct and stimulate the Christian people to greater advantage. (*MD* 49)

Note that Pius XII did *not* say the ecclesiastical hierarchy has the right to abolish "the received and approved rites of the Catholic Church" (Council of Trent). Notice, also, how he mentions that the hierarchy's role over the centuries has been to *enrich*, not impoverish, the Church's liturgical rites. Note, furthermore, that changes are for *increasing* the honor to Christ and the Trinity—certainly not for decreasing them.[18]

> The sacred liturgy does, in fact, include divine as well as human elements. The former, instituted as they have been by God, cannot be changed in any way by men. But the human components admit of various modifications, as the needs of the age, circumstance and the good of souls may require, and as the ecclesiastical hierarchy, under guidance of the Holy Spirit, may have authorized. This will explain the marvelous variety of Eastern and Western rites. Here is the reason

---

17   For additional background, see Fr Didier Bonneterre, SSPX, *The Liturgical Movement* (Kansas City: Angelus Press, 2002).

18   For a full defense of this thesis—that development tends in the general direction of amplification, explicitation, and glorification—see Peter A. Kwasniewski, *The Once and Future Roman Rite: Returning to the Traditional Latin Liturgy after Seventy Years of Exile* (Gastonia: TAN Books, 2022).

for the *gradual addition*, through *successive development*, of particular religious customs and practices of piety only faintly discernible in earlier times. (*MD* 50)

Again, his description of "various modifications" over the centuries underscores the fact that additions have been "gradual" and "development" has been slow and measured, not characterized by abruptness or eagerness for novelty. Moreover, the phrase "under guidance of the Holy Spirit" means that the rites *already* "received and approved" may be confidently attributed to His guidance, which it would be impious to repudiate by canceling out those rites or modifying them past recognition.

> The Church has further used her right of control over liturgical observance to protect the purity of divine worship against abuse from *dangerous and imprudent innovations* introduced by private individuals and particular churches. Thus it came about—during the sixteenth century, when usages and customs of this sort had become increasingly prevalent and exaggerated, and when private initiative in matters liturgical threatened to compromise the integrity of faith and devotion, to the great advantage of heretics and further spread of their errors—that in the year 1588, Our predecessor Sixtus V of immortal memory established the Sacred Congregation of Rites, charged with the defense of the legitimate rites of the Church and with the prohibition of any spurious innovation. (*MD* 57)

This is a crucial passage. Pius XII specifies that the Church's "right of control over liturgical observance" is *directly tied* to her duty "to protect the purity of divine worship against abuse from dangerous and imprudent innovations," which heretics invariably seek to introduce. Thus, the Church's power over the liturgy is primarily one of preserving and defending her "legitimate rites," that is, her "received and approved rites" (Council of Trent).

> The Church is without question a living organism, and as an organism, in respect of the sacred liturgy also, she grows, matures, develops, adapts and accommodates herself to temporal needs and circumstances, *provided only that the integrity of her doctrine be safeguarded.* This notwithstanding, the temerity and daring of those who introduce novel liturgical practices, or call for the revival of obsolete rites out of harmony with prevailing laws and rubrics, deserve severe reproof. (*MD* 59)

This is a clear rebuke of Modernists within the Liturgical Movement, who sought to "introduce novel liturgical practices" and revive "obsolete rites," and who already expressed hesitations about or desired revisions of that "doctrine" the integrity of which it is the pope's duty to safeguard. It is also a prophetic indictment of the radical reforms which began in earnest just twenty years later under Pope Paul VI.

The liturgy of the early ages is most certainly worthy of all veneration. But ancient usage must not be esteemed more suitable and proper, either in its own right or in its significance for later times and new situations, on the simple ground that it carries the savor and aroma of antiquity. The more recent liturgical rites likewise deserve reverence and respect. They, too, owe their inspiration to the Holy Spirit, who assists the Church in every age even to the consummation of the world. They are equally the resources used by the majestic Spouse of Jesus Christ to promote and procure the sanctity of man. (*MD* 61)

Commenting on this passage (a favorite of hyperpapalists), Dr Kwasniewski explains that it

is often quoted out of context, as if it amounts to blanket endorsement of any and all "recent liturgical rites." Yet this encyclical was published in 1947, prior to any major changes that would be made to the Roman Rite in the years thereafter; the noble Roman Rite was still very much intact. Pius's mention of "more recent liturgical rites" refers to everything medieval and Baroque—that is, everything *subsequent* to that ancient period of which the Liturgical Movement tended to be enamored.... By the time we reach the pontificate of Pius XII, this collective body of liturgy—which was simultaneously ancient, medieval, and Baroque, as an organic reality that had passed through all of these periods and had acquired elements from each of them—was already highly stabilized and consistent for four hundred years.[19]

Kwasniewski further notes: "The liturgy in its diachronic totality—a treasure of great perfection and beauty, a living reality born of the Holy Ghost in the womb of the bridal Church—was lovingly kept and handed down by the ordering of Divine Providence, which no pope dared disturb or oppose .... Indeed, this passage from *Mediator Dei* [n. 61] reads rather like a commentary on the famous Canon 13 of the Seventh Session of the Council of Trent"[20]—the canon to which we have referred repeatedly throughout this article.

It is neither wise nor laudable to reduce everything to antiquity by every possible device. Thus, to cite some instances, one would be straying from the straight path were he to wish the altar restored to its primitive table form; were he to want black excluded as a color for the liturgical vestments; were he to forbid the use of sacred images and statues in churches; were he to order the crucifix so designed that the Divine Redeemer's Body shows no trace of His cruel sufferings; and lastly, were he to disdain and reject polyphonic music or singing in parts, even where it conforms to regulations issued by the Holy

---

19 Kwasniewski, *Once and Future Roman Rite*, 63.
20 Kwasniewski, 63–64.

See.... This way of acting bids fair to revive the *exaggerated and sense-less antiquarianism* to which the illegal Synod of Pistoia gave rise.[21]

Is this not an indictment of the manifold errors and abuses we have witnessed since the advent of Paul VI's radical liturgical reform? And all of them, including the *Novus Ordo Missae* itself, are rooted in the same "exaggerated and senseless antiquarianism" which Pius XII rightly condemned.

For some final background to *Mediator Dei* and the pope who issued it, let us recall the startling comments made by Cardinal Eugenio Pacelli (the future Pius XII) in 1931:

> I am worried by the Blessed Virgin's messages to little Lucia of Fatima. This persistence of Mary about the dangers which menace the Church is a divine warning against *the suicide of altering the faith, in her liturgy, her theology and her soul* .... I hear all around me *innovators* who wish to dismantle the Sacred Chapel, destroy the universal flame of the Church, reject her ornaments and make her feel remorse for her historical past ....
>
> A day will come when the civilized world will deny its God, when the Church will doubt as Peter doubted. She will be tempted to believe that man has become God. In our churches, Christians will search in vain for the red lamp where God awaits them. Like Mary Magdalene, weeping before the empty tomb, they will ask, "Where have they taken Him?"[22]

In light of these comments, does anyone honestly believe that Pius XII would have approved of Paul VI's attempt to replace the traditional Latin Mass with what Cardinal Ratzinger famously called "a banal product of the moment"?[23] On the contrary, Pius XII would surely have agreed with Cardinals Ottaviani and Bacci, who warned Paul VI that "the Novus Ordo represents, both as a whole and in its details, a striking departure from the Catholic theology of the Mass as it was formulated in Session XXII of the Council of Trent."[24]

PREPARE FOR LEGITIMATE RESISTANCE

Based on the sources we have covered in this article, it is clear that the answer to our basic question — *Does the pope have the authority to abolish "the received and*

---

21   Pius XII, *Mediator Dei*, nos. 62, 64.

22   Msgr Georges Roche, *Pie XII devant l'Histoire* (Paris: Editions Robert Laffont, 1972), 52, 53. Quoted by Christopher Ferrara in *False Friends of Fatima* (Pound Ridge, NY: Good Counsel Publications, 2012), 9, emphasis added. Interesting to note that he speaks of "reject[ing] her ornaments," i.e., rejecting that continual process of enhancement of public worship that we have seen repeatedly mentioned in magisterial documents.

23   See "Translation of Ratzinger's Preface to the French [1992] Edition of Klaus Gamber" (referring to Msgr Gamber's book *The Reform of the Roman Liturgy: Its Problems and Background*), *New Liturgical Movement*, February 8, 2023.

24   Letter to Pope Paul VI, September 25, 1969, attached to the *Brief Critical Study of the New Order of Mass* prepared by a group of Roman theologians (https://lms.org.uk/ottaviani-intervention).

approved rites of the Catholic Church"? — is a resounding *no*. Hence, if Pope Francis tries to abolish and forbid the traditional Latin Mass, Catholics will be well within their rights to resist such an abuse of power. Indeed, one may and must go further: it would be their duty and privilege to resist this abuse in defense of so great a good as the Church's liturgical tradition, which abides while popes come and go.

As Dr Kwasniewski states in his work *True Obedience in the Church*:

> The postconciliar liturgical reform, its subsequent ruthless implemen-
> tation, and Pope Francis's renewed efforts to extinguish the preceding
> tradition are unreasonable, unjust, and unholy, and therefore cannot
> be accepted as legitimate or embraced as the will of God. As St Thomas
> Aquinas famously says: unjust laws "are acts of violence rather than
> laws ... Wherefore they do not bind in conscience." A repudiation
> of our Catholic liturgical patrimony is tantamount to disobedience to
> God; and we will be obedient to God through our "disobedience" to
> the revolutionaries.[25]

May Our Lord and Our Lady give us the graces we will need for whatever lies ahead, and may we take to heart the following words of Dom Prosper Guéranger found in *The Liturgical Year* (Feast of St Cyril of Alexandria, February 9):

> When the shepherd becomes a wolf, the first duty of the flock is to
> defend itself.... The true children of Holy Church at such times are
> those who walk by the light of their baptism, not the cowardly souls
> who, under the specious pretext of submission to the powers that be,
> delay their opposition to the enemy in the hope of receiving instruc-
> tions which are neither necessary nor desirable.[26]

---

25   Peter Kwasniewski, *True Obedience in the Church: A Guide to Discernment in Challenging Times* (Manchester, NH: Crisis Publications, 2021), 52–53, citing *ST* I-II, Q. 96, art. 4.
26   Guéranger, *The Liturgical Year*, vol. 4, *Septuagesima*, pp. 379–80.

41

We Oppose to *Traditionis Custodes* Not *"Non Possumus"* but *"Non Licet"*[1]

RÉMI FONTAINE

T HE MOTU PROPRIO *TRADITIONIS CUSTODES* OF JULY 16, 2021 was felt like a blow:

• a slap in the face to Pope Emeritus Benedict XVI, whose letter and spirit of the motu proprio *Summorum Pontificum* of 2007 taught and decreed almost the opposite of this unjust and accusatory text;

• a slap in the face to what could be called the "Ecclesia Dei" people, against whom he immediately and globally addresses a reckless judgment and with whom he breaks his word;

• a humiliation inflicted on the Church itself, "Jesus Christ diffused and communicated" (Bossuet), by the offense thus given to the principle of non-contradiction, which is incompatible with a "hermeneutic of rupture," as well as to the natural and canonical law relative to the Mass.

In this way, one could rightly react by repeating the words of Our Lord before the High Priest, when a servant slapped him: "If I have spoken wrongly, bear witness to what is wrong. If I have spoken well, why do you strike me?"

In this regard, we can reread what Jean Madiran (who died in July 2013) wrote just after Benedict XVI's motu proprio but which is valid a posteriori for Pope Francis's motu proprio: "With benevolence, everything becomes possible and livable, even possible disagreements. With malice, everything is weakened, everything is contaminated, even possible agreements."

Certainly, one might say, there are the two sentences of Benedict XVI in his Letter to the Bishops accompanying his motu proprio (the equivalent of which is not, however, among the obligatory norms laid down therein): "Obviously, in order to live full communion, the priests of communities that adhere to the old usage cannot, on principle, exclude the celebration according to the new books. The total exclusion of the new rite would not be consistent with the recognition of its value and sanctity."

---

1   This chapter was first published in French in three parts at *Le Salon Beige* on November 5, 2021, March 31, 2022, and June 1, 2022. The internal quotations are drawn from the writings of Jean Madiran. An English translation was published at *Rorate Caeli* on July 7, 2022.

Again, Madiran responds, as if in anticipation:

> There are two licit ways to hold to the traditional Mass while excluding
> the other Mass, without it being an exclusion "on principle" [or total].
> First, one can exclude the other Mass in virtue of the proper rule of
> a community or institute. Secondly, it must be understood that to
> exclude the other Mass on principle would be to exclude it as heretical,
> schismatic or blasphemous. Now, the most representative opponents
> of the other Mass [including the Priestly Society of St Pius X, but even
> more so and without exception in the so-called "*Summorum Pontificum*
> movement"] have *not* contested, and have even explicitly recognized,
> its licitness and validity when it is celebrated in accordance with its
> official text. Even in this case, however, its use can be refused, if not
> on principle but for pastoral reasons, for example.

A MISLEADING SYMMETRY

Benedict XVI's motu proprio *Summorum Pontificum* and his Letter to the Bishops did confirm that the traditional Mass had "never been juridically abrogated"
(because it could not be) and that any prohibition had been (or would be) an abuse
of power that did not bind in conscience. Conversely, they did not oblige one to
celebrate the Mass of Paul VI as well, according to a false symmetry, convenient but
misleading. One could adhere to the traditional Mass as others adhere (exclusively)
to the new Mass, without excluding in principle the other form of the Roman
Rite. This is the substance of the motu proprio of Benedict XVI and its "pluralist"
application as an armistice and a liturgical peace to be built over time.

This is analogous to the distinction that the Church makes between a commandment (which is obligatory) and a counsel (which is optional). The evangelical
counsel to turn the other cheek depends on the circumstances (Jesus Himself did
not always follow it!), unlike the commandment not to kill the innocent. Not
to pursue every therapeutic means of extending a person's life is, for example, a
case of advice: a relative no, a matter of prudential choice, unlike the absolute no
to euthanasia, which is a case of doctrine. While one may legitimately interrupt
a treatment considered unreasonable, one must absolutely proscribe euthanasia.

Similarly, because it is not possible to *prohibit the traditional Mass*, there can be
no *obligation to celebrate the new Mass*, especially since the latter, despite its undeni-
able recognition, is subject to significant circumstantial reproaches (according to
Benedict XVI himself and many theologians). Let us also recall the *Brief Critical
Examination of the New Order of Mass*, consigned by Cardinals Ottaviani and Bacci,
which points to the promotion of a different conception of the Mass, moving
from an essentially sacrificial reality to a communal gathering.

The pastoral reasons that some have for bypassing the new Mass (related
to doctrinal reasons) deserve to be listened to, considered, or respected: they
belong to the second option of the maxim attributed to St Augustine: "Unity
in what is necessary, freedom in what is not necessary, charity in all things."

May the hierarchy meditate on this crucial distinction, making its pastoral and disciplinary choices less arbitrary! Perhaps we could return to the wisdom and benevolence of Pope Benedict XVI, an eminent servant of the common good of the Church: there are many paths and dwellings in the House of Tradition, unity not being uniformity.

IN THE LIGHT OF JEAN MADIRAN BUT ALSO OF GUSTAVE THIBON

As Jean Madiran claimed in the past with regard to the falsifications that were being made of Scripture, to the unheard-of prohibition of the old catechism and the inherited rite of Mass, what we are opposing today to the brutality of the motu proprio *Traditionis Custodes* — specifically, to its restrictions, which are ordered to the same unjustified prohibition — is *not*, N.B., a *non possumus* (we cannot) but a *non licet* (it is not permitted)! This is not a matter of sensitivity to the circumstances but of an impossibility intrinsic to (super)natural and canonical law, intrinsic to the organic continuity of the ecclesial tradition:

> A *non possumus* causes a disorder in the Church, an apparent or real disorder; it raises a de facto exception in front of a commandment that is not intrinsically legitimate. This disorder may be a lesser evil when the *non possumus* is well founded. Nevertheless, however well-founded it may be, the extent and inconvenience of the resulting disorder must be taken into consideration. On the contrary, a *non licet*, if it is well founded, is not a factor of disorder, but of order: *it is order itself*, insofar as it needs to be proclaimed, defended, or restored. [2]

Like Antigone facing Creon. Or like Thomas More facing Henry VIII.

Benedict XVI had recognized that the new Mass broke excessively with the traditional Mass, which had "never been abrogated" and could not be. Whatever one thinks of the undoubted validity of this new Mass and its links with the old one, its artificial fabrication and ambiguous institution are too far removed from the legacy of the old one handed down from generation to generation to legitimize an abrogation or even an obrogation of that legacy. One can let a secular custom that has become obsolete die out on its own, but one does not have the right to *forbid* it (St Pius V's provisions preserved all the rites or uses that were at least two hundred years old at the time: Milanese, Mozarabic, Lyonnais, Dominican, Carthusian . . .). Unless one can *demonstrate* that this custom, which was that of the Latin Church, sanctifying its faithful for centuries, was bad, we say: *Non licet!*

No doubt traditions also have their dangers, as Pope Pius V had considered (freeing the Roman Rite from recent overloads judged to be useless), as Pope Paul VI no doubt also imagined he was doing (in reality deconstructing what his predecessor had precisely wanted to protect, purify, and unify in the tradition of the Roman Rite). Gustave Thibon puts it in his own graphic way:

---

2   Madiran, *Itinéraires*, July–August 1969.

> There is the tradition-source and the tradition-freeze, the second gener-
> ally succeeding the first as soon as the original inspiration cools down
> and the letter suffocates the spirit: we then see rites freeze into formal-
> isms, virtue into moralism, art into academicism . . . This inclines us
> to deny the source when all we need to do is to break the ice.[3]

In believing he was breaking the ice, did not the liturgical reform of Paul VI
deviate from, if not deny, the source itself? To the point of "renewing" the letter
in the absence of a manifest adequacy to the spirit that gives life . . . Under the
guise of a return to the sources and of archaeology, has one not "multiplied the
waterworks without taking care lest the source dry up," to use another image of
Thibon? He also likes to recall the warning Chateaubriand already gave to the
giddy innovators of his time: "Let us beware of shaking the pillars of the temple:
the future can be brought down upon itself!" The living tradition consists more
in a *reliance* on the sources than in a "return" to them.

"NON LICET!"

In view of the current fruits of the Vetus Ordo (gradually rediscovered by a
youthful and growing population with multiple vocations) and those of the Novus
Ordo (practiced by an aging population that is dwindling and whose vocations
in many places are drying up), we can at least reflect on the relevance of these
general words of the peasant philosopher on the living tradition: "Only artificial
flowers do not need roots . . ."

The emergence, as a survival reflex, of multiple "experiments" of tradition,
unforeseen but salutary, which did not always allow themselves to be incorporated
into the forms of ritual and parish organization imposed by the liturgical reform,
verified that "what is organic is more important than what is organized" — organized also artificially by experts and clerics, even if they are the best-intentioned
in the world! — according to the words Benedict XVI addressed in December 2009
to Cardinal Cordes about new communities attached to the transmission of the
faith. Regarding these charismatic communities, the pope added what can also
be applied to traditionalists: "Certainly, these movements must be ordered and
brought back into the fold; they must learn to recognize their limits and become
part of the Church's communitarian reality." Nevertheless, in the event of a
major crisis, the perfect society (in the philosophical and theological sense) that
is the Church really needs these imperfect but organic microsocieties, capable
of regenerating it like antibodies in a sick organism. This is what Benedict XVI
understood and wanted.

Even if it was a stopgap measure, the cohabitation of the two forms of the
Roman Rite decreed by his motu proprio *Summorum Pontificum* was certainly the
right political (in the noble sense of the word: in accordance with the common

---

3   Gustav Thibon, *Au secours des évidences* (Paris: Mame, 2022).

good) and theological path: an act of justice and charity capable of reconciling Catholics after decades of gaping wounds and liturgical abuses. Subject to certain pastoral norms, one could and should have the leisure to choose the form of the Latin rite. Leisure: "a state in which it is permitted to do what one wishes" (according to the *Littré*). From the Latin precisely: "*licere*," to have the permission to. It is in this sense that leisure differs from work, which is subject to constraint, whereas in leisure one is free to choose one's activity. This is why the motu proprio of Benedict XVI did not absolutely oblige one to (con)celebrate the Mass of Paul VI (and vice versa).

We can therefore say again with Jean Madiran about "the forbidden Mass"— that of our ancestors but also that of our children—which is again stigmatized without legitimate reason: *non licet!* "We refuse to separate ourselves from the Church, to allow ourselves to be separated from it . . . nothing and no one can replace the apostolic succession and the primacy of the Roman See," nor can anyone else do for them what is specifically their charge, despite their weaknesses or even their crimes.

COMMUNION IN ALL ITS NECESSITY

It is not a challenge to the apostolic succession or the primacy of the Roman See to respectfully oppose Pope Francis's motu proprio of July 16, 2021 with a "*non licet*" ("it is not permitted!"). We are not sinning against the necessity of ecclesial communion, which is treated so badly elsewhere. But it is well known: "The more hierarchical authority becomes 'lax,' as they say, even evanescent, in matters of dogmatic fidelity, the more its militarism increases in practical or subsidiary matters."[4] Now Catholic communion, which is first of all the communion of saints that we profess in the Creed and that the catechism explains to us, is not a union or an obedience that would have no conditions or limits.

Faced with a submission that is brutally and arbitrarily demanded as a secondary and contingent ("clericalist"?) sign of this communion, traditional Catholics simply practice an objection of conscience. In this legitimate objection of sons of the Church, not being members (with some exceptions) of the teaching Church, they can be more or less right, even more or less wrong, but communion and ecclesial unity are not broken:

> Clerics, laymen, ordinary Catholics and even saints have found themselves in discussion, in contestation, in quarrel with their bishop; with the Holy See; with the pope. See, for example, when the Holy See dissolved and suppressed the Jesuit Order, it did not declare them excommunicated; of the Jesuits who, in spite of the Holy See, desired, organized, and finally obtained from the Holy See the reconstitution of the Society of Jesus, no one fulminated against them that they were "not in communion with the Holy See."

4 Madiran, *Itinéraires*, March 1987.

Without even mentioning the case of Joan of Arc, the waverings of the holders of the apostolic succession and of the Roman See in the face of the Protestant Revolt and later the French Revolution also had their unhappy hours cut short by the pathfinders of the Counter-Reformation and the Counter-Revolution ...

Besides, the "trads," as they are called, have no unity as such, with no other commanding authority than the Church's (which is nowadays quite deficient), to which they consent and submit themselves, so to speak, as much as, if not far more than, mainstream and progressive Catholics. With variations among the trads, following different interpretations, and remaining subject to the definitive judgment of the Church (which always eventually comes after the objective malfunctions of its history):

> Since the crisis of the Mass began, they [the trads] have always been deeply divided as to the attitudes to hold and the initiatives to take in regard to the Mass, according to the diversity of particular opinions, sensitivities, arguments, tactics ... The "trads" are not and cannot be a party, an army, or a Church; theirs is a state of mind. And, of course, a behavior. A *professio* and a *devotio*.[5]

THE ROLE OF THE LAITY (FOLLOWING THE EXAMPLE OF THE PILGRIMAGE OF CHRISTENDOM)

If, in history, it is the priests who preach the crusade, it is not they who lead it and undertake it. By their condition, the lay faithful are undoubtedly better able than the clergy, according to this metaphor, to express and ostensibly lead the kind of moral insurrection that this pluralist behavior *in medio Ecclesiae* and even more so *in corde Ecclesiae* represents today. The prudential and religious options of the traditionalist movement — this legitimate objection of conscience, this self-defense of the people of God — can certainly be found in many places without any "parallel hierarchy" or any attempted substitution for ecclesiastical power. The faithful who join the places where the traditional liturgy is celebrated are led there by what Jean-Pierre Maugendre calls the triptych "coherence, exigency, transcendence": they want first of all to be spoken to about God, to be taught the faith, and to be helped to pray with beauty. The rest appears to be accessory.

The history, *devotio*, and *professio* of the Pilgrimage of Christendom [i.e., the Chartres pilgrimage] bear witness to this: "The temporal powers of the Christian laity remain what they are, in fact and in law, whatever the failings, maneuvers, or impostures of various representatives of the hierarchical Church." With their own institutions and temporal authorities, nothing prevents the laity, in order to better fulfill their temporal tasks spiritually — to survive as families in the religious crisis while keeping to the fixed points of the Christian people — from calling upon traditionalist clerics not as leaders but as chaplains or religious

---

5   Madiran, *Itinéraires*, January 1987.

advisors (as the non-reformed scouts, the MJCF,[6] and the non-contracted schools have done, with the missionary spirit and vocations that we know), to assist them spiritually, to distribute the sacraments, to enlighten, instruct, and comfort them spiritually according to a moral authority of advice, of supplementation. This authority cannot, of course, claim to be an authority of religious decision or jurisdiction. Tradition, as the constitutive source of the Church, obliges the traditionalist resistance to respect the structure of the visible Church and to work with it despite its deficiencies.

Jean Madiran spoke of a certain "militarism" [*caporalisme*], where the present pope would say "clericalism" today:

> Religious militarism is perhaps the most unbearable phenomenon of all. It consists at present in regarding any objection as blasphemy, any discussion as disobedience, any disobedience (legitimate or not) as schism. The most necessary distinctions are bulldozed by unintelligence. This does not promote unity. On the contrary. See: it is in pieces.

Regardless of the momentary wielders of power in the Church, the ecclesial Creons, and even after the administrative *Responsa* of Archbishop Roche and the wavering of Pope Francis, we can nevertheless persist and characterize ourselves as did the late founder of the magazine *Itinéraires*: "In communion, yes, but with the Holy See"!

> Traditional Catholics by conviction (and by pleonasm), we are in communion with the faith in the apostolic succession and in the primacy of the Roman See. To this succession, to this primacy, we strive to bring a Christian and not a servile obedience.[7]

---

6   Mouvement de la Jeunesse Catholique de France. For more on the history of this traditional resistance movement, see "Resistance is never futile: An interview with Christian Marquant, founder of Paix Liturgique," *Rorate Caeli*, December 16, 2020.

7   Preface to *Église interdite: Le livre blanc de Port-Marly*, Alain Sanders and Rémi Fontaine (Fontenay-sous-Bois: Éditions de L'Orme Rond, 1987).

42

Finishing Off Traditionalists[1]

ENRICO ROCCAGIACHINI

A S TIME PASSES, WE UNDERSTAND MORE AND MORE clearly how the civil war unleashed by the Church leadership against the "traditionalists" has developed and toward what goals it tends. We properly speak of a civil war because it is really an internal struggle, albeit one that began in terms opposite to the prevailing dynamic of such a phenomenon: it is not a portion of the people that rises up against those in power and seeks to undermine them, but rather those in power who seek to crush a portion of the people. All this is because, in the regime that is to be established at all costs, it has no place: there is a dominant group that has gained power precisely to introduce "irreversible changes," and that portion of the people, by its mere albeit peaceful existence, constitutes an insurmountable impediment to the realization of the revolutionary utopia.

Instead, strictly speaking, we should not speak of "traditionalists," except to simplify for convenience. Not only because, for us, traditionalist and Catholic *tout court* should be synonymous, but also because the part of the people that they want to eliminate is not confined to "classical traditionalists" (those — to be clear — "of the traditional Latin Mass") but, as has been appropriately noted,[2] includes those who believe that the Church cannot change her definitive moral and doctrinal teachings — that these are irreformable. If this were not the case, why, for example, should Opus Dei be targeted, despite all the mimetic efforts it has made in recent years (including a rigorous distancing of itself from the traditional liturgy) in order not to be even remotely perceived as belonging to the "opposition"?

Therein lies a key juncture for understanding what is happening: the "traditionalists" are not persecuted in order to suppress the resistance, the opposition, the possible disobedience that they oppose to the new course (for those who *openly* oppose it are there, but they are not representative of the whole group, and in Rome they know it very well); on the contrary, they are persecuted *even if*, concretely, operationally, they do *not* oppose it, and *even if* they expressly condemn their more belligerent colleagues.

The "traditionalists" are persecuted *for the mere fact of being there*, because by their very existence, however silent and hidden, they show the world the

---

1 First published at *Rorate Caeli* on August 16, 2022.
2 See Eric Sammons, "The Liturgy Wars Have Become Doctrinal Wars," *Crisis Magazine*, August 2, 2022.

impossibility and substantial injustice of the ongoing revolution; they show the fruitfulness of the counterrevolutionary alternative, the vigor of "Church 1.0" and the concrete, factual impossibility of replacing it with "Church 2.0." They stand to the project of irreversible changes, the project of the Catholic catching-up from an alleged two-hundred-year lagging behind on modernity, as the kulaks stood to the violent project of Stalin and the full Sovietization of Russia. Such were not to be "converted," nor were they to be defeated or bent to the will of the revolution: they were simply to be suppressed, eliminated (even physically), because in the new world they just were *not supposed to exist*; because, just by existing, even in perfect silence, in the midst of that new world and its magnificent fates and progressives, they would empirically show its inherent fallacy.

We are thus witnessing yet another version of a historically recurring phenomenon: the search for the Final Solution. The current one, in fact, also exhibits its characteristics.

It began by considering the traditionalists as a freak show, tending to be comical, destined to spontaneously die out. This phase is the one in which they were made to coincide totally with the devotees of the ancient liturgy, and were thought to be old nostalgics already out of touch with reality and now close to dying off, or insignificant and harmless misfits. It was the phase of amused tolerance, of more or less good-natured mockery.

Then, however, the ones in charge realized that things were not exactly like that—that the "infatuation" with Tradition was taking root and spreading. However, while no longer being able to see it as a folkloric phenomenon, traditionalism was still not seen as a real danger but as a kind of accident along the way, a manageable and controllable problem: after all, some traitor will always be there, it was said; it is a nuisance one has to reckon with and somehow live with . . . That was the phase of the "Indian reservation," of apartheid, of containment and ghettoization: "All of you go to the SSPX or some other ghetto that might segregate you from the rest of the faithful—and do not get in the way of the majority's path to its unfailingly bright future. You are not worth worrying about any further; faith in the certain success of the revolution and the new Pentecost is so firm that it does not fear you."

But as time went on, even this thesis collided with the facts. The traditionalists cannot be contained: they are *attractive*, their communities do not allow themselves to be ghettoized and are multiplying, they are full of young and fertile Christian families, they peacefully fit into parishes, and they are even producing priestly and religious vocations at a rate that the mainstream Church can no longer even imagine, let alone compete with; they could really represent the future! At the same time, the revolution itself is beginning to run out of steam, the sun of the future has been slow to rise, and those who are really in danger of dying from old age are precisely . . . the revolutionaries. These cannot and will not allow their new world to be corrupted by the existence of the traitors, for their existence would (as we said above) prove inexorably the new world's fallacy. Therefore, they can no longer be tolerated or segregated; they must be *suppressed* — and it must be done quickly. The Final Solution must be reached soon.

And so, that brings us to the present moment. The first ones in the cross-hairs can only be the liturgical traditionalists, because it is easy to find them and strike them. But then it must include also all the others, the "fanatics" of orthodoxy and of perfect continuity, wherever they are nested and however they are camouflaged — even if they are perfectly aligned with the Novus Ordo in its official documentation.

There is little to add. Except that historical experience would seem to teach that, sooner or later, perhaps decades later (but what are a few decades in the designs of Providence?), the *real* Final Solution annihilates the persecutors, not the persecuted. Not least because they may not necessarily try to defend themselves: the self-defense of the betrayed — think especially of the laity — is still largely to be put into play, and may turn out to be the next chapter in this dramatic and painful saga.

43

Yes, Francis is the Pope— and His Office Binds Him[1]

SEBASTIAN MORELLO

TRADITIONAL CATHOLICS CONDEMNED

Recently, fellow writer for *The European Conservative*, Felix Miller, wrote a piece strongly criticizing traditional Catholics who, in his view, have routinely been overly critical of Pope Francis.[2] In the opening two paragraphs, three times Miller invokes the name of Satan to point his readers to the spirit he thinks is leading trad Catholics in their general attitude to current Church affairs. Then Miller tells us that "contemporary conservative and traditional speech to and about the Church hierarchy crosses the line from proper Christian fraternal correction to scandalous disobedience or even schism." Given, then, that Miller pulls no punches, no doubt he expects the same in any response to his piece. I shall try not to disappoint him.

Miller singles out for denunciation those groups that promote and provide the ancient apostolic form of the Roman Rite, naming Sedevacantists, Lefebvrists (SSPX), and mainstream traditional Catholics like fellow *European Conservative* writer Peter Kwasniewski, whom he names by name. Miller groups these three together as if there were no substantial differences between them, only some fine discrepancies that amount to mere differences of degree rather than of kind. Sedevacantists, however, deny that the Chair of St Peter has any incumbent at all, and thus the man in white for whom the other two groups pray every day is just an imposter. This is not a mere difference of degree. This is a radically different position to those of Lefebvrists and mainstream trad Catholics.

Many mainstream trad Catholics have made enormous sacrifices and received astonishing mistreatment from their own bishops merely for worshiping as did their forebears in the faith, and for protecting their children from the heresy preached or irreverence practiced at the local parish (sometimes necessitating travel over vast distances every Sunday). They've often undergone terrible bullying by the Church's ministers precisely because, rather than deny that there's a pope in Rome like the Sedevacantists or opt to be in a canonically irregular situation like the Lefebvrists, they chose to tough it out in submission to the Church's law and Her hierarchy—undergoing frequent persecution as a

---

1 First published at *The European Conservative* on February 23, 2023.
2 Felix James Miller, "Francis is the Pope," *The European Conservative*, February 18, 2023.

consequence. Miller contributes to the bullying of these faithful Catholics and calls his hounding of them "a spiritual work of mercy."

Miller leaves his readers guessing as to what, exactly, he is referring: what criticisms in particular does he think "cross the line"? Certainly, trad Catholics *have* routinely criticized Pope Francis's "family synods," which promoted homosexuality and divorce, and which saw ideological "LGBT" terminology make its way into official Church documents.[3] They've criticized his public support for Eucharistic sacrilege (in his 2016 letter to the Argentinian bishops). They've criticized his "synodal path," which has officialized dissent and helped to foment a real schism with the Church in Germany. They've criticized his tampering of the *Catechism of the Catholic Church*, so that it now teaches notions condemned as heresy by Pope Innocent III. They have also criticized his arranging of pagan fertility-idol worship in the Vatican gardens, his declaration that God wills a plurality of religions as He wills the distinction of the sexes, his public affirmations of homosexuality, his support for communist regimes, his throw-them-under-the-bus treatment of Chinese Catholics, his critical remarks on the "breeding" habits of large families, his corruption of curial offices, his mishandling of abuse cases (especially when his friends are involved), his invitations to outspoken pro-abortion and population-control fanatics to be curial advisors, and his attempt to wipe the ancient apostolic Roman Rite off the face of the planet—to name but a few on a much longer list of disapprovals about which trad Catholics invariably criticize Pope Francis.

Does Miller think that the faithful ought to just shut up and watch the Church they love, and the faith that is Her gift to the world, be attacked by those who hold Her highest offices? Does Miller believe that Catholics shouldn't criticize such abuses of ecclesiastical power, even though it's their canonical right to voice their concerns (can. 212, sec. 3)?

Traditional Catholics are denounced by Miller for their disobedience—making no distinction between disobedience and resistance—but he does not seem to believe that the Church's pastors are bound by obedience too. The Church's pastors are bound by the requirements of their offices, by the tradition of the Church, by divine law, by positive ecclesiastical law, by the just civil laws of the states in which they reside, and above all by the teaching of Jesus Christ. If pastors disobey, does Miller believe that the faithful may not complain, despite the fact that, as noted, it is their canonical right to do so?

Traditional Catholics in general and Kwasniewski in particular are criticized by Miller for a theory circulating among them. This theory holds that, due to repeated heretical and heterodox teaching—which Pope Francis has been recurrently asked to withdraw by members of the faithful in public letters and

---

3   See Peter Kwasniewski, "'LGBT' appears for the first time in a Vatican document. Catholics should grieve," *LifeSiteNews*, October 4, 2018; Leila Marie Lawler, "Beware Church Use of 'Transgender' Language," *The Catholic Thing*, November 18, 2023.—*Ed.*

statements (some of which I've signed) — Francis's teaching authority may have been "suspended." This is a theory, as Miller notes, that was put forward by St John Henry Newman in his analysis of the Arian heresy. Miller suggests that this theory ought to be rejected on the grounds that Newman argued for it over a decade before he became a Catholic. Newman, however, never retracted the work as a whole or that argument in particular, and he continued to have *The Arians of the Fourth Century* published after his reception into the Catholic Church, as he did much of his work (like every one of his Anglican sermons), all of which he considered orthodox from a Catholic perspective.

It is especially odd that Miller takes aim at trad Catholics for entertaining this Newmanian theory in relation to the current papal situation. Traditional Catholics like Kwasniewski have had recourse to this theory precisely to sustain their continuing recognition of Francis as pope whilst trying to show that the ongoing abuses of papal power during his pontificate may not possess the full authoritative force of his office. To accuse trad Catholics like Kwasniewski of disobedience — *satanic* disobedience, even — whilst attacking their very attempts to maintain fidelity to Pope Francis (despite the chaos he's heaped upon the Church) seems bizarre, to say the least. Miller entitles his essay "Francis is the Pope," and then he denounces trad Catholics for utilizing resources of Church history, theology, and law to support the truth of this claim whilst minimizing its damage at the present time.

THE POWER-AUTHORITY DISTINCTION

Perhaps the most disturbing aspect of Miller's piece is his conception of how ecclesiastical authority works. He doesn't seem to see that the Catholic Church is in a post-authority epoch in any case, at least regarding the healthy function of the ordinary magisterium. He doesn't appear to realize this because he makes no distinction at all between *power* and *authority* — a very common error among nominalists, voluntarists, and legal positivists, but not one I expected from Miller. He seems to think that any resistance to the use of brute power by a pope is a denial of the pope's authority. But the power and legal force of the Holy See rests on its authority, and that authority is derived from the Lord, the only head of the Church — of whom the pope is a mere servant.[4] If the servant acts in disobedience to his Lord, he ought to be resisted, lest the wrath of the Lord be provoked.

For those members of the faithful who have either apostatized or adopted a strongly progressivist conception of the Church and Her Faith, the Church's authority has no meaning. They will deny dogmas of the faith and violate the moral law, irrespective of what the Church teaches. Traditional Catholics, on the other hand, actually take the law very seriously — for them, it has authority over them, regardless of whether it is enforced — which is why Pope Francis

---

4   See chapter 6.

uses the law to attack them. He knows that they think the law is important.

Unlike the trad faithful whom he mistreats, however, for Pope Francis the law seems to mean very little. There are ample examples of this, helpfully presented in volume 2 of Kwasniewski's *The Road from Hyperpapalism to Catholicism.* But even a book of that size does not contain all the many examples this infelicitous papacy has provided. One interesting case that won't be found in that volume is that of Vatican City, over which Pope Francis is temporal lord as well as bishop, mandating that all Vatican employees be vaccinated with a COVID-19 vaccine. The Church's most authoritative statement concerning the morality of receiving vaccinations derived from (or tested on) aborted human babies' cells, however, clearly states that whilst it may be *permissible* in some instances to receive such vaccines, reception of them should never be obligatory. Pope Francis, then, showed flagrant disregard for the Church's moral teaching, for the Church's law, and for the just exercise of temporal coercion – to the point of threatening people with loss of employment if they didn't take experimental medicines of malign origin. Perhaps Miller, though, thinks that Vatican employees should have just shut up and done what they were told, or they would have been "denying the pope's authority."

Pope Francis's behavior has led trad Catholics, rightly in my view, to wonder how papal authority can persist during such scandalous abuses of power and ongoing dissemination of error. As noted, one theory they've suggested is that during such abuses the pope's authority is "suspended." This theory may be incorrect, but it seems preferable to denying that Francis is the pope (like the Sedevacantists) or declaring canonical disunity with him (like the Lefebvrists), but to Miller it's all the same. Thus, he condemns all traditional Catholics in one sweep. And this remarkable lack of charity towards his fellow coreligionists is called by him "a spiritual work of mercy."

THE SSPX, MAINSTREAM TRADITIONAL CATHOLICS, AND THE SAINTS

Miller explicitly moves on to the Lefebvrists. According to Miller, the SSPX are "interested in their own manmade structures of authority" rather than "following Christ's." What manmade structures? The SSPX recognize the apostolic succession, they have bishops, priests, deacons, and laity. They recognize Francis as the pope, and they pray for him every day in the Church's most solemn prayer, the Roman Canon. The full ecclesiastical structure bestowed by Christ is the one they follow. They are, however, in a canonically irregular situation, the meaning of which no one knows, and about which the Vatican has never said more since the lifting of all excommunications by Pope Benedict XVI.

Francis recognizes SSPX bishops and priests, and by his universal authority he has granted them faculties – wherever they are in the world – to hear confessions and (with the local ordinary's consent) witness marriages. Indeed, SSPX clergy seemingly possess more canonical rights than any clergy in the entire Church, straight from the Holy Father. And yet, Miller denounces them in a way that Pope Francis has not, and he declines to show the charity that Pope Francis has expressed towards them. Perhaps it's Miller, in fact, who has a problem with papal authority.

Eventually, Miller confesses that he is without the knowledge or qualifications to really enter this debate, and so he declares that whilst he may not have all the correct arguments, he has the saints on his side. Or at least he thinks he does. In his piece, Miller refers only to one saint in support of his case. He presents to us the example of St Pius of Pietrelcina ("Padre Pio") who, Miller tells us, despite the fact that he was "deeply skeptical of the Second Vatican Council and the liturgical reform that occurred in its wake," offered the new form of the Mass promulgated after the so-called liturgical reforms. This, however, is impossible given that the new order of the liturgy didn't come out until 1969 and Padre Pio died in 1968.

The comparison with Padre Pio is misplaced in any case. The persecutions that he suffered during his lifetime at the hands of both his religious order and the Church's senior clerics were aimed at him personally. Traditional Catholics don't think that they're being *personally* attacked by the Church (except when they're diagnosed with cod psychology by the pope as "rigid" or must endure his criticisms of large families). Rather, they think the tradition and liturgical heritage of the Church has been — and continues to be — repudiated by the postconciliar regime, in an unprecedented spirit of rupture that has only intensified during the most recent papacy. They think that this tradition and liturgical inheritance belongs to all the Church's faithful by right. They think that the wielding of ecclesiastical power to destroy the Church's tradition and liturgical inheritance is an abuse and undermines the authority on which that power rests. In turn, they criticize such abuse of power, which Miller mistakes for a denial of papal authority due to his failure to make some very simple distinctions. Moreover, Padre Pio, as a Franciscan, was under a vow of obedience which he was rightly keen not to break. The lay faithful and secular clergy of the Church are under no such vow, and are free to voice their concerns, which — I repeat — is their canonical right.

Miller then turns to the person of Archbishop Marcel Lefebvre, founder of the SSPX, contrasting him with Padre Pio. Miller claims that whilst the latter was obedient in the face of persecution, Lefebvre simply opted for disobedience. Miller concludes that that's why one is now a canonized saint and the other is not. In fact, Lefebvre obediently cooperated with the Vatican for as long as he could. It's well documented that it was only when the Vatican sent emissaries to investigate the teaching in Lefebvre's seminary in Écône, Switzerland, and criticized the seminary for teaching the historicity of the Lord's resurrection, that he decided to secure his work's future by continuing with the formation and ordination of priests. Much later, when it was clear that the Vatican wouldn't support the continuation of this work after his death, Lefebvre took the step of consecrating bishops. Canon law, in fact, permits the consecration of bishops without papal approval during times of crisis in the Church. The question is, then, was the latter half of the twentieth century a time of crisis? I'm confident that future Church historians, looking at the period of greatest apostasy and dissemination of heresy in the whole history of the Church, will agree that it was indeed a time of crisis. It should be noted too that those familiar with the life of Archbishop Lefebvre, even those who strongly disagree with his decisions, don't doubt the outstanding depth of his personal holiness.

Continuing to group together Sedevacantists, Lefebvrists, and mainstream trad Catholics—a grouping that is convenient for Miller's purposes despite its dishonesty—Miller writes that "there is not a single hagiography of which I am aware that details a saint denying that there is a pope." But of course, Lefebvrists and mainstream traditional Catholics think there *is* a pope, and Miller knows that; he just apparently wants his reader to assume that *all* trad Catholics are basically schismatics. Seemingly, when it comes to dealing with his fellow Catholics, Miller is not going to let truth get in the way of making his argument.

As for the approach taken by mainstream trad Catholics, the saints may very well be more on their side than Miller thinks. Prof. Roberto de Mattei's book *Love for the Papacy and Filial Resistance to the Pope* details a great many examples of saints who disputed papal acts and decrees, which Miller may like to read at his leisure. Missing from Miller's piece is any consideration of the life of St Athanasius, Father and Doctor of the Church, who repeatedly resisted the bishops and the pope—a pope who was content to compromise with the Arian heresy—until Athanasius was eventually excommunicated by Pope Liberius. How might Miller make sense of such abuse of papal power and such saintly resistance to St Peter's successor, given that Miller has already rejected Newman's explanation? I'm most keen to know.

LOVING AN ABUSIVE FATHER

The ancient liturgy of the Church, that great gift of the centuries that traditional Catholics love above anything else in this world, is currently being targeted by those who are meant to be its greatest defenders. The incumbents of the Church's highest offices are working boundless mischief and wickedness in their ideological and pathological desire to repudiate the Church's tradition. They have brought into the Church that very impulse which persecuted Her from without in the form of successive revolutions, and that heaped terrible chaos on Her mission throughout modernity. Such revolutionary mayhem now governs the Church. Despite all this, traditional Catholics seek to make sense of this situation, that they may remain in a canonically regular situation, recognizing Francis as their pope and praying for him as such. For this, Miller implies that they're led by Satan. I can only assume that Miller somehow really does believe that his remarkable lack of charity towards his brethren in Christ is a "work of mercy," for otherwise it would be truly inexcusable.

Finally, Miller accuses trad Catholics of "falling into doubt about the Holy Spirit's protection of His Church." Miller clearly hasn't considered the obvious counterargument to his entire approach: namely, that the Holy Spirit may be protecting the Church precisely by raising up worldwide outcry among the remaining faithful against the current attacks on the Faith and the bimillennial inheritance that this same Holy Spirit inspired.

Traditional Catholics don't deny the pope's authority, as Miller claims, but they *do* deny that the power attached to that authority is arbitrary. They hold that the capricious, scandalous, sacrilegious use of such power undermines the authority to which it appeals. Thus, these faithful sons and daughters of the Church have tried to make sense of how such abuse has occurred and how the faithful are to respond to it. The pope's authority exists to protect and conserve the Church's revealed teaching, Her moral doctrine, and the liturgical and devotional tradition handed down to us. When this authority is exercised in contradiction to revelation, morals, or tradition, not only do the faithful have a right to criticize such abuse, but they may also—as canon law rightly states—have a duty to do so. If a family resists an abusive father, that doesn't mean that its members say they have no father, or refuse to call him father, or cease to strive for his good. It means that the father is failing to do that to which fatherhood has bound him, or he is doing that which fatherhood forbids. A family that resists an abusive father is not inspired by Satan, but by love of the family itself.

44

How to Obey the Church[1]

JOSEPH SHAW

A MONG THE FAMILIAR PHRASES OF THE DEBATE ON the liturgy are ones involving obedience to the Church. "The Church asks us . . . ," "we must obey the Church..." and the like, generally employed by supporters of the liturgical reform. It is not immediately clear what they mean. What are these people saying when they refer to "the Church"?

When theologians want to discern the "teaching of the Church" they may be able to pick out some "extraordinary" act of the magisterium, such as an *ex cathedra* definition by the pope, but very often there isn't one available. This being so, they go to Scripture and Tradition, as containing the Deposit of Faith: they will tell us what the Church teaches. The Fathers and Doctors are witnesses to the Tradition and also draw out its implications. This is the "ordinary" magisterium of the Church, and the ordinary way in which the Church passes on the teaching which has been entrusted to her by Our Lord.

This is how, ordinarily, God has chosen to reveal Himself to us; this is how, ordinarily, the Holy Spirit speaks to the Church: through what has been passed down. When people are moved to overturn established Tradition in favor of a radical new reading of Scripture, perhaps inspired by a private revelation, we can expect to hear some heresy.

This I hope is not controversial, but when it comes to the liturgy a very different attitude often takes hold. Liturgical progressives tell us that the Spirit has called them, or is calling the entire Church, to adopt some liturgical innovation: to take just one example, consider the service of the altar by females (altar girls). This overturns a tradition of only men and boys serving at Mass going back as far as the records go, which is the late fourth century (see canon 44 of the Council of Laodicea).

The unanimity of the liturgical tradition here is impressive, but it is brushed aside for two reasons. One is that it is not a dogmatic but a disciplinary matter; the other is that at a certain point the legal apparatus of the Church permitted us not to follow the tradition (at least, in the reformed version of the liturgy of the Western Church).

These two arguments are besides the point, however, if we accept that the Holy Spirit habitually speaks to us through the Tradition of the Church. If the Spirit tells us about the doctrine God has revealed through Tradition with a

---

1 First published at *OnePeterFive*, June 12, 2023.

capital "T," it seems very strange to say that we should ignore a liturgical tradition, when it tells us about how God wishes us to worship Him. Of course
liturgy is not doctrine; nevertheless there is an obvious parallel with the ordinary
magisterium. God has revealed a certain amount about how we are to worship
in Scripture, and it would be strange if this were not supplemented by the
liturgical writings of the Fathers and Doctors and by the practice of the Church.

The role of liturgical traditions in communicating God's will to us about
how we should worship is supported by the idea that the liturgy is a "theological source," and also directly by the magisterium. We read in Pius XII's 1947
encyclical *Mediator Dei* that the development of the liturgy over the centuries
was guided by Providence: "Just as obviously unwise and mistaken is the zeal
of one who in matters liturgical would go back to the rites and usage of antiquity, discarding the new patterns introduced by disposition of divine Providence
to meet the changes of circumstances and situation." This idea is echoed by
Memoriale Domini, the 1969 Instruction forbidding (with the inevitable exceptions) the reception of Holy Communion in the hand. These two documents
were defending developments in the liturgy against those who wanted to make
use of what they claimed was an older custom. When it comes to an issue in
which there has been *no* development that we can see—when the practice of
the Church has been continuous and unchanging from the earliest records that
exist right up to the 1990s, when priests were permitted to use female servers
for "specific local reasons"[2]—the case is that much stronger. God is surely telling
us, by means of this tradition, that the service of the altar by men and boys is
something He wants. How could that message be set aside?

One alternative approach would be to say this. The liturgy is the creature of
the Church, continually subject to change by legislative *fiat*, and yet it is also
a theological source, and conveys to us God's will: which is to say, what the
liturgy tells us is neither more nor less than what our superiors, those with
authority over the liturgy, want to tell us, and God is speaking through *them*.
(It should be noted that we are not necessarily talking about the pope: until
Trent, bishops and religious orders had extensive authority over their liturgy;
the Eastern Churches have a high degree of autonomy; and so on.)

This is a positivistic conception of the liturgical tradition: the liturgical tradition just is whatever a legislator with the appropriate legal authority tells us it is.
However, it is one thing to accept that various people had or have legal authority
over the liturgy; it is another to suggest that this amounts to a new organ of
the magisterium. The point of saying that the liturgy is a theological source, a
witness to the Tradition alongside, if subordinate to, Scripture and the Fathers, is
that it is the product of organic development, under Divine Providence, and has
in a certain sense the approbation of centuries of use in the Church. If it turns

---

2 *Notitiae* 30 (1994): 333–35.

out to be the product, instead, of the arbitrary whims of particular officeholders, then the idea that it is a theological source becomes impossible to maintain. Those officeholders may have magisterial authority, and if so they can exercise that authority in the normal way. The point of according special significance to the liturgy is that it is a *different* source, not simply another version of the authority held by bishops and popes.

When we talk about what the liturgical tradition, as a theological source, tells us, the reformed liturgies of the 1960s naturally have less weight than liturgical traditions stretching back millennia, not because the latter were established by legislators with greater authority, but because they were used in and approved by the Church over these vast stretches of time. What "the Church" is telling us to do, liturgically, is not a matter of looking at the most recent legislation, but at what Providence has impressed on countless generations of Catholics.

The Church tells us things in a range of ways, and these things may even be in tension with each other. The liturgical tradition, nevertheless, has special authority to tell us how to *worship*: that, surely, is its core competence. If we accept that "the Church" has anything more than mere human regulations to guide Catholic worship, then we must look at the broad and deep tradition: even when this may make for uncomfortable reading.

45

The Significance of
Pope Francis for the Church[1]

JOHN LAMONT

JORGE MARIO BERGOGLIO WAS ELECTED POPE IN 2013, and is now 87. He is in poor health. Most of his pontificate is behind him, and we are in a position to draw some general conclusions about the nature and significance of the man and his tenure of the papal office.

One conclusion that can be drawn is that a dominating goal of Pope Francis's pontificate has been the destruction of the work of his two predecessors. This work must be understood in the context of the Second Vatican Council (1962–1965). During this council and its aftermath, every aspect of Catholic faith and practice was attacked by powerful forces within the Church. These attacks were described by their initiators as being the implementation of that council, and they were largely successful, producing a transformation of the Catholic Church, a deep crisis, and a catastrophic decline that began in the 1960s and continues unabated to the present day. Neither John Paul II nor Benedict XVI opposed these attacks on a broad front and as a whole. Instead, each of them concentrated on preserving and promoting a particular feature of Catholic teaching and tradition, hoping that their favored element of tradition would provide the solution to the crisis in the Church.

John Paul II upheld and defended Catholic teaching on priestly celibacy, the impossibility of ordaining women to the priesthood, marriage, sexual morality, and the existence of moral absolutes. Benedict XVI's initiative was to attempt to free the traditional Latin liturgy of the Church and make it accessible to all Catholics. Neither of these projects reversed the decline of the Church, but both of them had some success. Francis is ideologically committed to the total attack on Catholic faith and practice. He has accordingly made it his aim to defeat the counterattacks of his two predecessors.

Pope Francis's attack on the legacy of John Paul II was a major effort that involved calling a synod of the bishops of the Church. His strategy was to verbally affirm the indissolubility of marriage, but to insist that persons in a valid Catholic marriage who were civilly married to someone else could receive the Eucharist. The Catholic Church has always refused the Eucharist to such persons, on the ground that they were publicly living in an adulterous relationship. John

---

1   First published at the blog of the Society of St Hugh of Cluny on March 21, 2023.

Paul II had firmly upheld this refusal. The strategy was largely successful. Pope Francis understood that his doctrinal opponents were weak and afraid of a direct confrontation with him. A small number of Catholic scholars and ecclesiastics denounced him for attacking the faith, but no cardinals and almost no bishops put up any real opposition to his initiative. This initiative effectively denied the existence of marriage. It did not accept that one can cease to be married to one person and can then marry someone else, as is the case with Protestant and Jewish teaching and the civil law of marriage. Such a concept of dissoluble marriage at least stipulates that one has an exclusive relationship to a spouse when a marriage exists, and certain duties towards that person alone that follow from the relationship; and that this relationship must cease to exist, via divorce, before one can enter into another relationship of that sort with a different person. Pope Francis's position, on the other hand, permits simply walking away from a marriage that continues to exist, and taking up with someone else. This empties the notion of marriage of content.

Pope Francis's attack on the legacy of Benedict XVI has focused on the traditional Latin liturgy. Some historical background is needed to understand this attack. In the twentieth century, two movements concerned with the liturgy arose within the Roman Catholic Church. The first of these saw the traditional liturgy as a neglected treasure that needed to be better known and practiced by Catholics, both lay and clerical. According to this movement, unfortunate historical and intellectual developments had led Catholics to turn away from the liturgy as a source of salvation and sanctification. The influence of the Jesuits, whose approach to the spiritual life centered on individual prayer rather than the liturgy, was considered to be one of these regrettable developments. This thesis was advanced by the Benedictines Dom Lambert Beaudoin and Dom Maurice Festugière in the first half of the twentieth century, and opposed by the Jesuits Jean-Jacques Navatel and Louis Peeters. The Benedictines argued for the priority of the public liturgy of the Church in the spiritual life, whereas the Jesuits argued for the priority of personal prayer.[2] The Italian priest Romano Guardini took the Benedictine side, and his book *The Spirit of the Liturgy* was a formative influence on the young Joseph Ratzinger. The liturgy here was understood to be the traditional Latin liturgy that took its substantive form under Pope Gregory the Great (ca. 540–604). It included not only the ceremonies for the Mass, but the rites of the other sacraments, the Divine Office (the public prayer of the Church said by religious and priests), and the various blessings and other prayers reserved to the clergy. Substantial initiatives of this first liturgical movement were the publication of missals containing the liturgy of the Mass in Latin with a facing-page translation in the vernacular, and an effort to restore sung Masses with Gregorian chant as the normal form of worship.

---

2 On this debate, see Peter Kwasniewski, *Noble Beauty, Transcendent Holiness: Why the Modern Age Needs the Mass of Ages* (Kettering, OH: Angelico Press, 2017), 115–33.

The second movement was concerned not with reviving the Latin liturgy, but with replacing it. The Latin liturgy of the Church was seen as obsolete and inadequate not just in its use of the Latin language, but in its theology, ceremony, music, and architecture. In a sense this movement accepted the Jesuit idea of the primacy of personal prayer, and sought to implement it by changing the liturgy to suit the personal preferences of its adherents. This second movement had the goals of eliminating the use of Latin in Catholic worship, changing the dogmatic content of Catholic liturgy, and replacing traditional Catholic music, art, and architecture with modern forms. These goals were presented as necessary to make Catholic worship accessible and attractive to modern man, and as a means of attracting Protestants to the Church, but this presentation was largely a sales tactic. In fact the members of this movement hated the old Catholic liturgy and the dogmas it embodied, and sought their destruction as an end in itself.

The new Catholic liturgy introduced by Pope Paul VI in 1970 carried out the program of this second movement. This liturgy was not a translation of the old Latin liturgy into vernacular languages, but a new production. Only 13% of the old prayers of the Mass were preserved in a substantially expanded liturgy. The composition of the new ritual was entrusted to mediocrities, whose lack of talent gave a free field of operation to their ideological zeal. References to divine punishment, hell, the devil, dependence on divine grace, salvation of the soul, reliance on the merits and intercessions of the saints, and the sacrificial character of the Mass were purged from prayers and Bible readings. Scriptural texts containing these unwelcome elements were bowdlerized or removed entirely (Psalms 57, 82, and 108, for example, have been excised). The traditional architecture and music of Catholic worship, one of the great cultural treasures of the human race, was rejected—in a process often involving vandalism and destruction—and replaced by modern design and pop music of the most banal and talentless kind.

The importance of this liturgical change has sometimes been acknowledged by sociologists, but is not widely understood. The destruction of Catholic worship was one of the most important and damaging events of the twentieth century. It abolished the religious culture of the Roman Catholic countries of Europe and Central and South America, and of the substantial Roman Catholic minorities in other countries. In Europe, the traditional Catholic culture was not replaced by a different religious culture that could be made to serve as the basis for a society, as happened when Islam replaced Christianity in the Middle East and North Africa. It was replaced by unbelief. In the first five years after the liturgical changes of Paul VI, a large percentage of priests, religious, and lay Catholics walked out of the Church. This decline has continued, slowing down at times but never ceasing. The Catholic Church in Western Europe is facing extinction. The formerly Catholic cultures of Europe, having lost their spiritual and cultural foundation, are threatened with the same fate. Even the secular and anticlerical currents in European society have been mortally wounded by this change. Having lost their Catholic competition, they have no inducement to keep up their own intellectual and cultural standards, and have declined into imbecility.

Cardinal Joseph Ratzinger saw that this change was a disaster, and attacked it as an abuse of papal authority:

> The pope is not an absolute monarch whose will is law; rather, he is the guardian of the authentic Tradition and, thereby, the premier guarantor of obedience. He cannot do as he likes, and he is thereby able to oppose those people who, for their part, want to do whatever comes into their head. His rule is not that of arbitrary power, but that of obedience in faith. That is why, with respect to the Liturgy, he has the task of a gardener, not that of a technician who builds new machines and throws the old ones on the junk-pile.[3]

And:

> What happened after the Council is quite different: instead of a liturgy that is the fruit of a continuous development, a fabricated liturgy has been put in place. They left the living process of growth and becoming and entered into the manufacturing process. They no longer wanted to continue the organic becoming and maturation of a living thing that lives through the centuries, and replaced it—in the manner of technical production—by a fabrication, a banal product of the moment.[4]

After his election to the papacy, Benedict XVI acted on this conviction. He issued a decree, *Summorum Pontificum*, acknowledging the right of priests to celebrate the traditional Latin liturgy, and obliging bishops to provide this liturgy to lay groups who requested it. The decree produced or expanded traditionalist communities all over the world, whose congregations were characterized by large families, low average age, and doctrinal orthodoxy. Traditionalist communities also produced vocations to the priesthood and religious life out of all proportion to their numbers.

This was an extraordinary result. Anyone looking at the preservation of the Latin language in the Catholic Church prior to 1965, when it quickly began to be abandoned, would have seen the civilizational connections of that language as an essential part of the case for using it. Latin was the language of civilization for Western Europe from the establishment of the Roman Empire up until the thirteenth century. The use of Latin in the Roman Catholic Church meant that the Catholic Church preserved that heritage of civilization. Keeping Latin meant not just keeping alive the Catholic theology and worship that was bound up with that heritage, but keeping alive the heritage itself, and extending it beyond Europe to people who would benefit from it.

---

3 Ratzinger, Foreword to Reid, *Organic Development of the Liturgy*, 10–11.
4 Ratzinger, "Preface to the French [1992] Edition of Klaus Gamber."

This was a good argument prior to 1965, but by the time Benedict XVI restored the Latin Mass, it had become obsolete. Cultural links to the Latin civilization of Europe had been largely obliterated. The traditional communities that sprung into being after his restoration were almost entirely composed of Catholics to whom the heritage of Latin literature, culture, and history were unknown. In Europe and North America, the culture, if it can be called that, in which these communities were born was a complete negation of the cultural basis of the Latin Mass. The success of these communities has few parallels in religious history. Africans and Native Americans had adopted the Latin liturgy with enthusiasm when exposed to it by missionaries in the sixteenth to the nineteenth centuries, but this adoption could be seen as benefiting from the prestige and power of the European states from which the missionaries had come. There is now no prestige attached to the Latin Mass, which is still often celebrated in school gyms and the chapels attached to funeral homes. Its growth can only be reasonably explained by a purely religious power inherent in the traditional liturgy.

Pope Francis moved against the Latin Mass in July 2021, after addressing the legacy of John Paul II. This was no doubt partly due to a prudent policy of dealing with one enemy at a time. He issued a decree, *Traditionis Custodes*, which imposed severe restrictions on the celebration of the Latin Mass that were designed to lead to its eventual extinction. Prior to issuing the decree, he sent a questionnaire to all the Roman Catholics bishops of the world inquiring about the use of the Latin Mass in their dioceses. Reliable leaks of the responses to the questionnaire indicate that the majority of the bishops reported favorably on the Latin Mass and the communities attached to it, which would explain why these responses were not made public by the Vatican. In his public letter accompanying the decree, Francis announced that "the responses reveal a situation that preoccupies and saddens me, and persuades me of the need to intervene"; this need not be taken to be a lie, since he would consider a favorable attitude of the bishops towards the Latin Mass to be extremely undesirable. In a typical maneuver, he has used one of his creatures, Cardinal Arthur Roche, to enforce the program of the destruction of the traditional liturgy set forth in *Traditionis Custodes*. Roche, a mediocrity who is nothing without Francis, is to attract the blame and opprobrium for doing his master's will.

There is a sense in which Francis has failed in destroying the legacies of both John Paul II and Benedict XVI, and a sense in which he has succeeded. He has failed in suppressing belief in the religious and moral truths that John Paul II insisted on, and in suppressing the traditional Latin Mass that Benedict XVI restored. He has succeeded in destroying the projects of harmonization that accompanied both those legacies. John Paul II's project was the harmonization of the Second Vatican Council with the Catholic truths he chose to uphold, and Benedict XVI's project was some sort of fusion of the traditional Latin Mass and the Novus Ordo—with the former being dominant—rather than a simple scrapping of the ritual of Paul VI and a return to the old Mass. Benedict XVI included both of these projects of harmonization under the term "hermeneutic of reform" (or "hermeneutic of continuity"), which he opposed to the "hermeneutic of rupture." The latter hermeneutic was the understanding of the Second Vatican Council as a rejection of Catholicism, and the attack on the faith that implemented this understanding. The projects were the personal initiatives of these popes, who did not manage to impose them in a way that would survive after their pontificates. Pope Francis rejects both of them, and thanks to him they are now dead.

Pope Francis has not restricted himself to a reactive policy of destroying the work of his predecessors. He has taken positive steps to advance the program of eradicating the faith. One of these steps is the adoption of a theme from the pontificate of John Paul II. John Paul II made a number of gestures and statements that could be seen as favoring the idea that all religions are paths to salvation. The best known is his interfaith meeting at Assisi in 1986, where Catholics, Buddhists, Hindus, and an assortment of other religious believers all prayed, sacrificed, or performed other rituals together. His kissing the Koran and praying together with Togolese animists are other examples. (Animism is the African ancestor of Haitian Voodoo, and furnished Voodoo with some of its gods; it is largely concerned with detecting and eliminating witches and placating malign spirits.) Implicit in these actions of John Paul II was the idea that all religions are ways to God, with Christianity being simply the best developed of these ways. Pope Francis has explicitly endorsed this idea and participated in a number of activities that embody it. These activities include presence at an idol-worshipping ceremony in the Vatican gardens and the co-signing in Abu Dhabi, with the imam of Al-Azhar University in Cairo, of the syncretistic "Document on Human Fraternity for World Peace and Living Together."

Pope Francis's other positive initiative is a personal one. It is an attack on the legal and institutional structure of the Church. By "institutional structure" is meant the actual personnel that compose the Church leadership, and the agreed practices and traditions outside of canon law itself that determine the way the Church is governed. These include administrative practices and the criteria and practice concerning the selection of men to fill ecclesiastical offices.

Francis does not follow canon law, and he prefers not to use it as an instrument to enforce his will. His policy on marriage and the Eucharist contradicts canon law, but he does not deal with this contradiction by changing the law; he leaves it on the books and ignores its existence. He has consistently shielded sexual abusers from ecclesiastical and civil authorities. Of course the usual practice in the Church is for bishops and religious superiors to protect sexual criminals and conceal their crimes. But the goal of this policy is to prevent these criminals being caught. Once they are caught, the policy is to say that no one knew anything about them. Francis's approach is different. He protects and even promotes such men after they have been caught as well as before. This can be seen in the cases of Fr Julio Grassi, Fr Mauro Inzoli, Fr Marko Rupnik, and Bishop Gustavo Zanchetta. He seems to consider that having been caught for such acts gives a priest a title to respect.

When confronted with a task or a subject matter to be examined and pronounced upon, Francis generally does not make use of the responsible curial office. He uses other advisors, and often makes his bypassing of the responsible office obvious, in order to demonstrate its impotence and establish that his untrammeled will decides everything. He does not show loyalty to his subordinates, official or unofficial, and eventually turns on them after having made use of them. As far as possible he only appoints bishops and cardinals who agree with his agenda, and he has no standards of education or experience that his appointees must meet.

Francis's policy, especially when it comes to appointments that carry real power with them, is to choose individuals who are compromised in some way, either by having committed crimes, or by having covered them up, or both. His approach to American appointments is worthy of note. Francis is a Latin American leftist and as such detests the United States. He detests the American Catholic Church in particular for its support of John Paul II's role in the fall of communism in Eastern Europe. He appears to have made a special effort to appoint leaders of the American church who will cause the most possible discredit.

Francis's approach to governance is a tried and tested one. It has been well described by one of its more talented practitioners:

> If you really want to do something new, the good won't help you with it. They are self-satisfied, lazy, they have their God and their own pig-headedness—you can't do it with them. "Let me have men about me that are fat." An anointed king can say that, but not a leader that has made himself. Let me have men about me that are arrant knaves. The wicked, who have something on their consciences, are obliging, quick to hear threats, because they know how it's done, and for booty. You can offer them things, because they will take them. Because they have no hesitations. You can hang them if they get out of step. Let me have men about me that are utter villains—provided that I have the power, absolute power over life and death. The sole and absolute leader, whom no one can interfere with. What do you know of the possibilities in evil! Why do you write books and make philosophy when you only know about virtue and how to acquire it, whereas the world is fundamentally moved by something quite different?[5]

This policy was known in influential circles before his election to the papacy, and helped his rise to that office. Cardinal McCarrick before his disgrace boasted of how he helped to secure Bergoglio's election. McCarrick had addressed the

---

5   Hermann Göring, quoted in Joachim Fest, *The Face of the Third Reich: Portraits in Nazi Leadership*, trans. Michael Bullock (New York: Ace Books, 1970), 124–25.

General Congregation before the conclave that elected Francis, and urged upon the assembled cardinals the desirability of choosing a Latin American pope. No influential cardinal supports a papal candidate without first informing himself about that candidate and about what the candidate has to offer him. McCarrick knew that Francis was his man and that he was Francis's, because he knew that Francis's method of government relied on men like himself.

What is the significance of Pope Francis? I think the answer to this question is suggested by Johann Chapoutot, the brilliant French scholar of Nazism. In 2018 Chapoutot and Christian Ingrao published a biography of Adolf Hitler that sought to understand Hitler's significance. In a talk presenting the biography, Chapoutot gave this account of their thesis:

> One of the most common explanations for Nazism, without explaining it in relation to one's self, and in the end evacuating it of significance, is to say that Hitler was a madman and that all those Nazis were caught up in a sort of St Vitus's dance, morbid and macabre, that carried away Europe and their era in a whirlwind of suffering and horror. This is an explanation that does not explain. It is far too convenient; one can see how it provides psychological reassurance, but it is not accurate. Hitler poses a problem for us not because he is a madman, but because he is a monster. He is a monster. What is a monster? A monster is an individual that we find difficult to explain today — today, and for let us say perhaps two hundred years. A monster is a thing, a phenomenon, that several centuries ago had a meaning and made sense. Consider the etymology of "monster"; it comes from "monstrare" in Latin, which means to indicate, to show, to give a sign of something, to be a sign of something. And in fact, in a world saturated with the divine, saturated with transcendence, saturated with magic perhaps, the monster, the one who is an extreme departure from normality, who is extreme by his evil acts for example, is the sign of something; a sign of the anger of God, of the divine vengeance that is striking us.[6]

---

6   The original text of Johann Chapoutot's remarks, in full, is as follows (transcribed from www.youtube.com/watch?v=LEQvVDGVWNE): "Hitler est un paravent commode pour nous tous. C'est celui que nous identifions au nazisme, au mal absolu, et qui au fond fait écran et nous empêche de penser un phénomène, le nazisme, dont nous participons nous aussi, puisque ce phénomène est né culturellement et pratiquement et s'est déployé en Allemagne, c'est à dire en Europe, c'est-a-dire en occident. Et jusqu'à preuve du contraire nous sommes aussi des européens et des occidentaux. Mais avoir affiché — voyez la couverture [c-à-d du livre, montré sur un écran derrière les auteurs] — le paravent Hitler, cet écran-là — nous détourne de ce questionnement-là, puisque nous attribuons beau-coup de choses à ce personnage et a son entourage avec une réduction personnelle, personnalisante, psychologique, psychologisante, qui nous empêche encore une fois de penser le phénomène. Et une des explications les plus courantes pour expliquer le nazisme, sans en expliquer vis-à-vis de soi-même, et au fond de l'évacuer, c'est de dire que Hitler était fou et que tous ces gens-la étaient saisis d'une forme de danse de saint-guy sadique, morbide, macabre, qui a emporté l'Europe et cette époque dans un tourbillon de malheur et d'horreur. C'est une explication qui n'en est pas une, elle est beaucoup trop commode, on en voit le, comment le dire, le confort psychologique, celui qu'on en retire, mais elle n'est pas exacte. Hitler de fait nous pose problème, non pas parce qu'il serait fou, mais parce qu'il est un monstre. Il est un monstre. Qu'est que c'est qu'un monstre? Un monstre c'est un individu

Chapoutot and Ingrao's discussion of Hitler has merits and defects that do not concern us here. What does concern us is their explication of the concept of a monster. This concept provides the interpretive key for an understanding of Francis and his papacy. Francis is a monster. He has been described and explained as a Peronist, a modernist heretic, a Jesuit who exhibits the worst failings that characterize members of that order. These descriptions are not wrong, but they do not get to the important truth about him. The extremity of his evil acts identifies him as outside the normal order of things, as a phenomenon that does not belong to the natural or supernatural structure of human life.

What is he a sign of? Francis, in his personality, actions, and beliefs, is a sign of the true nature of the transformation of the Church that occurred during and after the Second Vatican Council. The arrogance, hatred, criminality, and love of destruction that he manifests so clearly were the motive forces for this transformation and its leaders. He is a sign of the failure and the fundamental dishonesty of the projects of "harmonization" undertaken by Popes John Paul II and Benedict XVI. He is also a sign of the corruption of the Catholic priesthood and episcopate. With very few exceptions, Catholic priests and bishops have either supported his destructive acts or kept quiet about them. There have been other manifestations of this corruption. The offence of criminal sexual abuse is widespread among Catholic priests and religious. The persons who are best informed about these offences are other Catholic priests and bishops. The offenders are however absolutely never denounced by their fellow clerics. These offences are kept secret as far as possible by the criminals, but Pope Francis's crimes are public knowledge. The silence of priests and bishops in the face of his crimes reveals their baseness and treachery in an unmistakable way.

When the topic of the sins of priests is raised, one often encounters this quotation from St Anthony Mary Claret:

> When His just indignation reaches its climax, He sends the last and most atrocious of His punishments by allowing unfaithful ministers, stained priests, scandalous shepherds to appear among men. Then it

---

dont on a du mal à rendre raison ou à se rendre raison aujourd'hui — aujourd'hui, disons, depuis peut-être deux cents ans. Un monstre, c'est quelque chose, c'est un phénomène qui il y a quelques siècles était porteur de sens. Voyez l'étymologie du terme monstre; ça vient de monstrare en latin, qui veut dire faire signe vers, envoyer un signe, être un signe de quelque chose. Et de fait, dans un monde saturé du divin, saturé de transcendance, saturé de magie peut-être, le monstre, celui qui est exorbitant à la normalité, celui qui est exorbitant par ses actes maléfiques par exemple, est le signe de quelque chose; de la colère de Dieu, de la vengeance de la divinité qui s'abat sur nous. Le monstre a un sens; il a une signification. Dans un monde désenchanté, désenchanté au sens positif du terme, dont l'enchantement, dont la magie a disparu, eh bien l'aubépine qui fleurit dans l'hiver n'a plus de sens, de la même manière que le monstre n'a plus de sens; d'où notre fascination méduseé devant les grands criminels, devant les tueurs en série, qui font l'objet de séries et d'émissions à répétition, de romans. Nous nous interrogeons sur ces personnages. Eh bien, nous avons voulu prendre le monstre au sens étymologique au pied de la lettre, Christian Ingrao et moi, et nous avons voulu le lire comme un signe. Ce personnage-là est un monstre que nous avons voulu relire comme un signe; sans l'apparat de transcendance, sans l'appareil de transcendance, mais tout simplement en historien."

happens that the abominations of the people are the cause of the bad priests, and the bad priests are the greatest punishment with which God chastises the people.

This quotation is often used to support the fallacious inference that since God sends bad priests to punish a bad people, if priests are bad it is because the people have sinned. The responsibility for a corrupt priesthood is thus handily shifted from the priests to the laity. There is no evidence that this shifting is justified when it comes to Francis and the progressive, "conciliar" cause that he champions. In 1960, the Catholic laity around the world were not notably corrupt, certainly not in comparison to many other historical epochs. Fr Bryan Houghton asserts that the opposite was the case:

This issue was that the new reforms in general and of the liturgy in particular were based on the assumption that the Catholic laity were a set of ignorant fools. They practised out of tribal custom; their veneration of the Cross and the Mass was totem-worship; they were motivated by nothing more than the fear of hell; their piety was superstition and their loyalty, habit. But the most gratuitous insult of all was that most Catholics had a Sunday religion which in no way affected their weekly behaviour. This monstrous falsehood was—and still is—maintained by bishops and priests who, for the most part, have never been adult laymen. Every day the Catholic workman had to put up with the jeers of his colleagues, as the more educated with their sneers. Every night they took their religion to bed with them.... I am not in a position to judge other priests' parishioners. I am, however, in a position to judge what were my own. No words are adequate for me to express my admiration for the conscious faith and piety of my flock, both in Slough and in Bury. This is where the trouble lay. The reforms were based on criticism; I was unwilling to take any action which might make me appear to criticise the wonderful people whom I was ordained to serve. I was perfectly conscious that I learned more about God from them than they were likely to learn from me.[7]

The significance of Pope Francis is that Catholic priests and bishops as a body have betrayed Our Lord and the Catholic faithful, and that they must repent, make atonement for their sins, and work to undo the harm they have done.

---

7   Fr Bryan Houghton, *Unwanted Priest: The Autobiography of a Latin Mass Exile* (Brooklyn, NY: Angelico Press, 2022), 81.

46

Pope Francis: How Much Lower Can We Sink?[1]

HENRY SIRE

WHEN JOSEPH SHAW PROPOSED THIS TALK TO ME in early September [2023], I suggested the title "Pope Francis: how much lower can we sink?", but the fact is that even since then we have been overtaken by events. Over the past eleven years we have all seen Pope Francis's pontificate in a trajectory of accelerating descent into more and more overt betrayal of Catholic doctrine, but I must say I did not foresee the Gadarene rush we have seen just within the last three months. If we want to assess the very grave events that are happening around us, we need to try and understand the man we now have sitting on the throne of Peter. So before I comment on recent developments I would like to add some details to the picture of Pope Francis which I gave in my book *The Dictator Pope*, first published six years ago.

To give you some background on this book, I should explain that I arrived to work in Rome in April 2013, less than a month after the election of Pope Francis, and I lived there for the next four years. I was working for the Order of Malta, an organization which has close links to the Holy See, and I quickly began to hear the reports that were privately coming out of the Vatican. They showed a very different Francis from the genial, liberal figure who was being presented by the world's media. Insiders were saying that, as soon as the publicity cameras were off him, Francis became a different figure: arrogant, dismissive of people, given to foul language, and notorious for furious outbursts of temper which were known even to the Vatican chauffeurs. Over the next couple of years I continued to hear inside information, for example from the late Cardinal Pell about the internal politics involved in the two Synods on the Family in 2014 and 2015. Let us bear in mind that in his first years Pope Francis had barely shown his hand and that people assumed he was the liberal reformer that the Church supposedly needed. Early in 2016 I wrote an article for Angelico Press titled "Pope Francis: Where is the reformer behind the media idol?" I was beginning to think that somebody needed to write a book disclosing the gulf between the public image of Pope Francis and the reality as seen within the Vatican; but at that stage I did not think that I would be the one to write it.

---

1 Text of a talk given to the Latin Mass Society in London on November 24, 2023. First published at *OnePeterFive* on December 11, 2023.

Besides the information gulf I have described, there was another one stemming from the language barrier. There was in fact a great deal of information which had been available for years about Jorge Bergoglio and his career in Argentina, but it simply had not come through to the rest of the world because it had not been translated into English. Since I am half-Spanish, this was another of the factors that pointed to my shouldering the task that was needed. When I decided to start work on the book, the first thing I did was to make a trip to Argentina, in March 2017, to speak to people who could tell me about Bergoglio's past record. This was the information that had been sadly lacking to the cardinals when they elected Bergoglio in 2013. In particular, there was a very revealing book which had been written shortly after the papal election, but which had been quickly stamped on, and had since become almost unavailable. The title was *El Verdadero Francisco (The Real Francis)*, by Omar Bello. The author was a public-relations executive who had known Bergoglio personally over the past eight years, having worked for him in a television channel run by the archdiocese of Buenos Aires. As a professional in the field of public relations, Bello was quick to recognize in Bergoglio a master in self-promotion. He also described a man who was accomplished in the covert exercise of power and the manipulation of people.

For example, Bello tells in his book two stories which were already well known in Buenos Aires. One was the way in which Bergoglio took a dislike to a member of the archiepiscopal staff, Mr Felix Botazzi, and decided to sack him without showing his hand. The aggrieved ex-employee then sought an interview with Bergoglio, who affected ignorance. "I knew nothing about it, my son. What did they sack you for? Who did it?" Mr Botazzi did not get his job back, but the archbishop presented him with a new car, and he went away convinced that Bergoglio was a saint, dominated by a circle of malicious subordinates. The other story that Bello repeats is of a Buenos Aires priest on the diocesan staff who sought psychiatric help, exhausted by the merry dance that he and his colleagues were being led by their archbishop. After listening to his woes, the psychiatrist said to him: "I can't treat you. To solve your problems I would need to treat your archbishop."

These and other revelations were made shortly after Bergoglio had been elected pope, but in fact there had been revealing reports appearing in the Spanish-language media even before that. For example, in 2011 the Spanish journalist Francisco de la Cigoña published an article describing how Bergoglio was building himself a network of power in the South American hierarchies through followers he had planted in various departments in the Vatican. De la Cigoña summed up his report:

> That is how Bergoglio proceeds to generate a network of lies, intrigue, espionage, mistrust and, more effective than anything, fear. Bergoglio is a person who above all knows how to generate fear. However much he may work carefully to impress everyone with the appearance of a plaster saint, austere and mortified, he is a man with a mentality of power.

We should note that this was written well over a year before Bergoglio was elected pope, before anyone had reason to suspect that he might be more widely dangerous.

When I started my book, I set myself the objective of transmitting Spanish-language reporting of this sort to the English-speaking world, but there was another piece of evidence whose non-emergence had not been due to the language barrier. While I was living in Rome, I began to hear from journalists of a document called the "Kolvenbach Report," which several of them had been trying to track down without success. It was the report that Fr Kolvenbach, the General of the Jesuits, had written back in 1991, when it had been proposed to make Fr Bergoglio an auxiliary bishop in Buenos Aires, and it was rumored to be distinctly unfavorable. A copy of the report had been kept in the archive of the Jesuit General Curia in Rome, but it swiftly disappeared as soon as Bergoglio was elected pope. In the course of my research, I discovered that at least one copy of the report existed in private hands, but its owner could not bring himself to share it with me for the purpose of publication. The nearest I was able to get to it was through a priest who had read it before it disappeared from the Jesuit archive, and he gave me the gist of it as follows: Fr Kolvenbach accused Bergoglio of lack of psychological balance, deviousness, disobedience cloaked under a mask of humility, and habitual use of vulgar language. He also pointed out, with a view to his suitability as a bishop, that Bergoglio had shown himself a divisive figure while Provincial of the Jesuits in Argentina. After eleven years of the Francis papacy, we can fairly say that Fr Kolvenbach had got him completely right.

Another key to Bergoglio's mode of acting is the political background of Argentina, which is so alien to the Anglo-Saxon understanding. One of the first things I heard about Bergoglio when I went to Rome was from an Argentinian priest who said: "What you've got to understand about him is that he's a pure politician." At the time, I did not grasp the bearing of this, but one needs to add that Francis's politics are modelled by the great figure in Argentina in the twentieth century, Juan Perón, who was dictator of the country from 1946 to 1955, the years in which Bergoglio was growing up. Perón dazzled a whole generation of Argentinians with his unscrupulous, opportunistic style, and his legacy has continued to dominate the country's political life ever since. Bergoglio was more than a generic disciple of the great man. When he was novice-master of the Argentinian Jesuits in the early seventies, he was actively assisting a party called the Iron Guard who were working, successfully, to bring back Perón from exile for his final months in office as President until his death in 1974. By ordinary standards this was an unusual way for the novice-master of a religious order to spend his spare time, but it illustrates the comment that was made to me by one Argentinian who had been a pupil of the young Bergoglio when he taught at a Jesuit school in the sixties. On the strength of a lifetime's personal knowledge, he described Bergoglio to me as *"un enfermo del poder"* — a man for whom power is a mania, or a sickness.

So, on the basis of reports like these I proceeded to write my book, and I included in it a chapter on Bergoglio's career before his election. In it, my purpose was to provide something of a character study which had been sadly lacking to the cardinals when they elected him pope in 2013. Since publication, however, I have discovered a great deal of new information which shows that in fact things were far, far worse than I imagined.

The first revelation was about the financial malpractice involved in Bergoglio's government of the archdiocese of Buenos Aires. I mentioned earlier the article by Francisco de la Cigoña about the network of power that Cardinal Bergoglio had built up in the Vatican, but we need to add that that network was made possible by the deployment of large sums of money. The background to this was the near-bankruptcy that had been incurred by the Holy See in the eighties and nineties by the criminal activities of its financial managers, Archbishop Paul Marcinkus and his less well known but equally corrupt successor Donato De Bonis. In these conditions, the ability to transfer large sums to the Vatican coffers would give a churchman enormous influence. Cardinal Bergoglio did this through his control of the Catholic University of Argentina, which had a rich endowment of 200 million dollars. Specifically, between 2005 and 2011 some 40 million dollars were transferred from the University of Argentina to the Vatican, in a transaction which was supposed to be a deposit, but which the Vatican Bank promptly proceeded to treat as a donation. Not until a year or two ago has this misappropriation begun to be rectified.

This however is only the tip of the iceberg of huge financial corruption in the archdiocese of Buenos Aires which has been kept secret, although it was known to the Vatican from an early date. In 2009, eleven years into Cardinal Bergoglio's rule as archbishop, Pope Benedict ordered a secret visitation of the archdiocese by a monsignor who was sent there ostensibly as a diplomatic member of the papal nunciature, and he uncovered grave irregularities including money-laundering and Mafia links. To be fair, these malpractices dated from before Bergoglio's appointment as archbishop in 1998, but they remained unreformed owing to Bergoglio's habitual policy of cover-up and protection of the guilty. It is said that the information that the papal investigator gained during his visit has given him a hold over the pope and enabled him to pursue a well-protected Vatican career despite the enmity of powerful figures.

The archdiocese that Cardinal Bergoglio headed was thus steeped in financial wrongdoing. To give you some history of this, I will go back to Bergoglio's first appointment as auxiliary bishop of Buenos Aires in 1991. As I mentioned, he earned this position at the request of the then Archbishop of Buenos Aires, Cardinal Quarracino, but the man who was most influential in pressing for it was Msgr Roberto Toledo, a member of the archiepiscopal staff. Why Msgr Toledo was such an advocate of Bergoglio's I am unable to say, but he emerges as the central figure in the next major scandal to arise in the archdiocese. This relates to a large pension fund of the Argentinian military, which in 1997 was asked to make a loan to the archdiocese of ten million dollars. By that time Cardinal Quarracino was ailing and Bishop Bergoglio had already been appointed his suffragan with right of succession. At the meeting held to finalize the loan, Cardinal Quarracino was too ill to attend, but he was represented by Msgr Toledo. When the time came to sign the contract, Msgr Toledo left the room, ostensibly to obtain Cardinal Quarracino's signature, and he returned presently with a signature which, as later transpired, had in fact been forged by himself. Soon afterwards the military pension fund found itself in difficulties, and it made efforts to recover its loan to the archdiocese of Buenos Aires, whereupon Cardinal Quarracino denied that he had ever signed the contract.

Cardinal Quarracino soon afterwards died, and Bergoglio succeeded him as Archbishop of Buenos Aires. What stands out is his kid-glove handling of Msgr Toledo when the fraud was discovered. He was first sent back to his hometown without any sanctions. Finally, eight years later, in 2005, he was tried for fraud, but no sentence was ever passed. It should be added that Msgr Toledo was well known to be a homosexual and to have a male lover, a gym instructor, who had played a go-between's role in the financial relations I have described. The most macabre detail in this case emerged in 2017, when Msgr Toledo, who had been working for the past eighteen years as a parish priest without any sort of ecclesiastical sanction, was accused of murdering a long-time friend of his and forging his will to obtain an inheritance of millions.

Msgr Toledo is an example of a prelate who was already in place when Bergoglio arrived as auxiliary bishop, but it is equally revealing to look at those whom he promoted once he became archbishop. The first to notice is Juan Carlos Maccarone, whom Bergoglio made an auxiliary bishop in 1999. In 2005 Maccarone was dismissed from the episcopate by Pope Benedict after he was filmed having sexual relations with a homosexual prostitute in the sacristy of his cathedral. Yet Cardinal Bergoglio publicly defended him, asserting that the filming was a set-up to bring the bishop down because of his left-wing political commitment. Another protégé was Joaquín Sucunza, whom Bergoglio consecrated auxiliary bishop in 2000, although he had by then been cited in a divorce case as the lover of a married woman. Bishop Sucunza continued as auxiliary and was even appointed by Pope Francis as temporary administrator of the archdiocese in 2013 after his own elevation to the papacy.

These cases display a pattern of moral cynicism and clerical cronyism which Bergoglio has shown behind the scenes, while he presented the public image of a reformer. The most blatant examples of it relate to his record as a protector of clerical sex abusers. One case is that of the Buenos Aires priest Rubén Pardo, who was reported for sexually abusing a fifteen-year-old boy. The mother of the boy had great difficulty in getting the archdiocese to admit the case; she complained that Cardinal Bergoglio was protecting the guilty priest, that he gave him lodging in a diocesan residence, and that when she tried to speak to the Cardinal at the archiepiscopal residence he had her ejected by the security staff. The priest was finally convicted by the civil courts and shortly afterwards died of AIDS, and a Buenos Aires court obliged the Catholic Church to pay the family compensation for what they had suffered. The mother's opinion of Bergoglio's claim to be cracking down on such crimes was: "Bergoglio's commitment is just talk."

Another well-known case was that of Father Julio Grassi, who had been running children's homes which he used to exploit young boys' ambitions to escape from poverty through the medium of professional football. In 2009 Fr Grassi was convicted of sexually abusing a teenage boy, but while the case was in progress the Argentinian bishops' conference, headed by Cardinal Bergoglio, went to great expense to commission a document of 2,600 pages to assert his innocence. The report was condemned by the Argentinian court as a gross attempt to interfere with justice and to prejudice the judicial hearing. Meanwhile, Fr Grassi himself testified that throughout the hearings he had had the personal support of Cardinal Bergoglio himself. As we know, there are many bishops in the world whose careers have been ended by allegations less serious than this, yet Bergoglio has managed to ride them out untouched. Moreover, as pope he has shown in many instances that he has no scruples in protecting clerical sexual offenders, regardless of the supposed zero-tolerance policy he professes to enforce.

I think it is worth offering a general or generic explanation of this strange laxity, which at bottom is rooted in the macho sexual culture of Latin America. That is nowhere more evident than in Argentina, where it has been traditionally said that a "poof" is defined as a man who only sleeps with his own wife. This culture contaminates the clergy themselves. Very often among these Latin Americans, and indeed among the Italians and others, there is an inclination to treat the less tolerant view of sexual wrongdoing as a manifestation of Anglo-Saxon puritanism. With this attitude, the sexual corruption that has been rampant in the Church and in the Vatican has little hope of being reformed, and in fact has grown far worse under the present pope.

The facts I have just mentioned have been published in various articles, or in some cases discovered by me, in the last five or six years, and my comment on them is as follows: when I wrote *The Dictator Pope* the state of my information led me to give a picture of Bergoglio as a man with certain defects of character which ought to have been known to the cardinals when they elected him in 2013; but the reality is far worse. What we find existed in 2013 was a situation of horrific clerical corruption in the Argentinian Church, and we see Bergoglio sitting squarely in the center of it. Now, I am not accusing him of being himself financially or sexually corrupt like the clerics he protected. I hark back to the journalist de la Cigoña's description of him as "working carefully to impress everyone with the appearance of a plaster saint." One has to admit that Bergoglio has always been personally austere, indeed ostentatiously so, but he has combined this with a policy of surrounding himself with morally weak and corrupt persons, precisely so that he could control them and build up his own power through them, and this policy he has continued throughout his pontificate.

We need to look at the situation that existed at the Conclave of 2013, after the surprise abdication of Pope Benedict XVI. It was generally recognized that the Church was facing a crisis, and Cardinal Bergoglio was explicitly elected to make reforms particularly in three areas: firstly the world-wide scandal of clerical sexual abuse which had gravely undermined the Church's moral authority; secondly the morass of the Vatican finances; and thirdly the moral and political corruption within the Roman Curia, of which Benedict XVI had received crushing evidence in a report presented in December 2012. In all three of these areas Pope Francis's pontificate, far from delivering reform, has made things infinitely worse. In case after case, we have seen clerical sex offenders protected with an impudence that eclipses anything in the past. In the area of the Vatican finances, it looked at first as if Pope Francis was espousing genuine reform. He appointed Cardinal Pell with wide powers to reform the finances of the various Vatican departments, but within two years it became clear that this was an empty promise. The audit of the Vatican departments that Pell had launched was cancelled, and it was cancelled by two of the men whom Francis himself had put in power: Cardinal Parolin, as Secretary of State, and Cardinal Becciu, his Deputy at the time. Cardinal Becciu, after four years of increasing power, lost the favor of Pope Francis in 2020, was effectively stripped of his cardinalate, and is at present on trial for financial crimes.[2] Back in 2017, Parolin and Becciu between them ordered a stoppage of Cardinal Pell's financial reform, in a series of incidents which illustrate the regime of lawless dictatorship which now prevails in the Vatican. One of them was the treatment of the layman Libero Milone, who had been appointed General Auditor of the Vatican two years earlier to carry out the financial reform. In 2017 he was sacked in circumstances suggestive of a fascist state, with the Vatican police breaking into his offices and confiscating his computers, while he was given an ultimatum there and then to resign or be arrested. As part of the explanation for this treatment Cardinal Becciu complained that Mr Milone had been spying on his superiors, in other words that he was doing the job he had been appointed to do.

The most notorious aspect of this clamp-down was the way Cardinal Pell was got rid of. In 2017 he had to return to Australia to face historic charges of sexual abuse, for which he was sentenced to prison, until his conviction was quashed on appeal three years later. By that time, it was too late for him to resume his post at the Vatican. There is every reason to believe that the Australian prosecution

---

2   The trial of Cardinal Becciu ended on December 16, 2023 with a conviction for embezzlement and a prison sentence of over five years. — *Ed.*

was instigated and assisted by figures in the Vatican as a means of stopping his reform, and Cardinal Becciu has been specifically named as the agent of this policy.

When we turn to the reform of the Curia as a whole, the experience of the past eleven years has been just as disastrous as the financial story. And the reason is that Pope Francis's interest is not in reforming the Curia but in controlling it. As I mentioned before, he has always exercised his control by appointing morally weak and compromised characters to office, and they become his unconditional tools. Thus, in the first half of his pontificate we saw the few individuals of real integrity in the Curia removed one by one — Burke, Sarah, Müller, Pell — and an unparalleled collection of clerical villains took their place. For example, the Administration of the Patrimony of the Holy See, which controlled the Vatican's money, remained under the presidency of Cardinal Calcagno, an Italian clerical crook of the old school, in spite of the fact that he was under investigation for real-estate dealings in his previous diocese which harmed the diocese's finances; he was also a known protector of clerical sex offenders. He remained in his powerful office and had the privilege of dining every night with Pope Francis until he retired on age grounds in 2018.

An even more scandalous appointment for different reasons was that of the South American Archbishop Edgar Peña Parra, who stepped into the shoes of Cardinal Becciu as Deputy to the Secretary of State in 2018. Peña is a man who, as a student, was dismissed from his first seminary as morally suspect, and he is said to have made his career under the cover of a circle of homosexual clergy who protected and advanced him. It has been alleged that he fled his native Venezuela and took refuge in Rome after a serious incident which incurred the intervention of the Venezuelan police. This background has been no obstacle to Peña's becoming the second most powerful man in the Secretariat of State, the position that he still holds. He is just one example of the circle of unsavory Latin Americans who have been promoted to the top of the Church under the present pope. And so it goes on, with one scandalous appointment after another that plunge the moral reform of the Curia ever further into the realm of impossibility.

Yet the world's media, which so savagely attacked Benedict XVI at every opportunity, have remained silent in the face of scandals which would have destroyed any other papacy. The reason is simple: Pope Francis gives them exactly what they want. They are looking for a pope who will weaken the Church and bend it to their own secularizing agenda, and that is exactly what Pope Francis is giving them. This therefore is the key to the question: what exactly is Francis about in his pontificate? From the first, the gallery to which he has been playing has been the secular media, together with the woke intellectual and political establishment, and for their sake he espouses every fashionable secular cause, to the detriment of actual Catholic teaching. His words and actions have been calculated exclusively to win the approval of the world, and he has succeeded entirely. So entirely that he can afford to ignore any other constituency, and to get away with a clerical

cronyism and corruption for which the media would have savaged him if it had
come from a conservative pope.

A corollary of this is his drive against tradition. Pope Francis realizes perfectly well that the only real obstacle to his revolution comes from traditionalists in the Catholic Church, the only element with any backbone prepared to
recognize that the emperor has no clothes. Hence the campaign he has waged
throughout his pontificate against so-called "rigid" and "backward" Catholics,
whom he derides at every opportunity. He repeated this theme just a few weeks
ago, when he said what a scandal it was that young priests should be going to
ecclesiastical tailors to order soutanes and traditional vestments. We all know
what the real scandals in the modern Church are, but the only ones that bother
Pope Francis are those of priests following tradition. Hence also his promotion
of Cardinal Roche to be Prefect of Divine Worship in place of Cardinal Sarah,
and the motu proprio *Traditionis Custodes* to undo the work of Benedict XVI.
(By the way, it has been pointed out that a possible translation of *Traditionis
Custodes* is "the jailers of tradition," which is certainly the job that Cardinal Roche
and Pope Francis would like to be doing.) Like Pope Francis, Cardinal Roche is
also fond of lecturing traditional Catholics on how out-of-date they are. It has
been remarked that the Catholic Church is the only institution in which men
in their seventies and eighties are continually telling people in their twenties
and thirties that they need to get with it. It suits Pope Francis to pretend that
Catholic traditionalism is a matter of priests liking to wear cassocks and to use
incense in church, but he knows very well that it is a matter of doctrine, of the
Deposit of Faith, of the perennial philosophy of the Church, of the treasures of
spirituality; and that is why it is an unbreakable obstacle to a pope who tries
to lead the Church into the paths of modern secularism.

Before I close, I ought to comment on the situation in which we find ourselves now. As I said at the beginning, the events of the past three months have
taken by surprise even those who had no illusions about the present regime. The
downward spiral has accelerated to an extent that I for one did not foresee. What
we have seen in the past three months is the scandals of Pope Francis's papacy
in their most concentrated form. I will begin with the scandal of clerical sexual
abuse and cover-up, of which the most blatant example has been very much in
the news. This was the case, which I am sure you have all heard of, of the Jesuit
Fr Rupnik, who has been accused of sexual abuse of the most horrendous kind
inflicted on religious sisters of whom he was supposed to be the spiritual director.
The abuse included appalling sacrilegious elements which I will not go into, and
it had been going on for decades, yet the Jesuits failed to do anything about it.
Earlier this year they decided belatedly they had better be without Fr Rupnik
and expelled him from the Society, but the protection of him continued on the
Vatican's part. Fr Rupnik had been found guilty of the serious canonical crime
of absolving one of his sexual partners in the confessional, and had incurred

the automatic penalty of excommunication, but the excommunication had been lifted within a month. Not only that, but at precisely that time Fr Rupnik was invited to preach a retreat within the Vatican itself. Attempts to bring this priest to ecclesiastical trial were impeded by the fact that his offences fell under the statute of limitations; this can be lifted in appropriate cases, but Pope Francis failed to do so. He publicly denied involvement in the case, but Christopher Altieri has written: "senior churchmen close to Francis have strongly suggested that Francis had pretty much everything to do with the management of it." Fr Rupnik is in fact typical of the immoral clerical cronies whom Pope Francis has been consistently protecting throughout his pontificate and before it.

By the middle of this year the Rupnik cover-up was reaching its peak. There were figures, such as the fellow Jesuit Cardinal Ladaria, the Prefect of the Doctrine of the Faith, who wanted Fr Rupnik to be fully punished; that is said to have been the reason for Ladaria's being notoriously disinvited to the recent Synod on Synodality. Vatican forces were even trying to get Fr Rupnik's earlier excommunication quashed as irregular. Finally, a public outcry was provoked, firstly when a report by the Vatican's own Commission for the Protection of Minors criticized the laxity being shown, and secondly when it was revealed that Fr Rupnik, in spite of his expulsion from the Jesuits and the accusations still hanging over him, had been newly incardinated in the diocese of Koper. In late October the Vatican finally issued an announcement that defects in the handling of Fr Rupnik's case had been brought to the pope's notice and he'd decided to waive the statute of limitations so as to allow him to stand trial. On this, Altieri has commented: "Implausibly timed and preposterously explained, this announcement only gives further confirmation that Responsibility, Accountability, Transparency are transparently cynical bromides. The act of raw power shows that rule of law in the Church is a farce."

What are the other papal acts we have been assailed with in the last weeks? We have had the Apostolic Exhortation *Laudate Deum*, on the so-called climate crisis, in which (as somebody has remarked) Pope Francis has gone full Greta Thunberg. The exhortation declares, "It is no longer possible to disbelieve the primarily human cause of climate change." So many other articles of Christian belief have been shaken, but let us be glad that Pope Francis still upholds one dogma of unquestionable faith. Then there have been the further moral scandals we have seen — the fact that, for example, Cardinal Ricard of France has been allowed to keep his cardinalate in spite of having admitted molesting a fourteen-year-old girl years ago, or that Pope Francis has yet again, in the case of Bishop Gisana of Sicily, defended a bishop accused of protecting sexual abusers and has denigrated his accusers.

All this is shocking, but what we need to look at is an event of graver consequence for the Church. This is the overtly schismatical course of the German Synodal Way, which has proceeded with no serious attempt by Pope Francis to check it or rebuke it. On November 3, the Bishop of Speyer announced that he was authorizing the blessing of homosexual couples, and compiling a list of priests in his diocese willing to perform them. Again, complete silence from Rome.[3] Just a few days later came the announcement that Bishop Strickland of Tyler has been dismissed for failing to toe the Modernist line. Here we see demonstrated with perfect symmetry the pattern of Pope Francis's pontificate: the heretic is protected and the faithful Catholic bishop is dismissed. Cardinal Müller has publicly called Bishop Strickland's dismissal an abuse of the divine right of the papacy. An Italian journalist has been prompted to describe this papacy as "The pontificate of purges," and to contrast Francis's practice with his professed slogan of Mercy. Peter Kwasniewski has commented:

> Years ago Henry Sire called Pope Francis "the dictator pope." Time and again this evaluation has been vindicated, and never more so than when the pope deposes a bishop without due process, against canon law and for no imaginable grave wrongdoing. He has combined the "I am the Tradition" mentality of Pius IX with the motto of Juan Perón: "To the friend, everything. To the enemy, not even justice."

Serious as all this is, we need to pay more attention to the recently closed Synod on Synodality, because it is the means by which Pope Francis is attempting to institutionalize his revolution. The first comment to make is that all these synods, including the two previous ones on the Family, have been managed so as to enable a clique of Modernists to advance their program under the pretense of consultative process. To quote an Italian observer:

> The development of the various Synods of this pontificate, starting with the one on the family, and finishing in resounding fashion with the latest, shows that the rules of the discussions and deliberations, prepared before that with the selection of the participants themselves, have been changed repeatedly so as to silence the obvious rejection on the part of the ecclesial majority of the single line of thought which its proponents were attempting to impose on it, and to prevent the emergence within the Synod of a line that did not agree with the one predetermined from the top.

Nevertheless, when the final report emerged from the Synod we all received a surprise; it proved to be unexpectedly inconclusive. Many of us were puzzled by this for a moment, but we got the explanation from a news revelation that appeared shortly afterwards. This was the disclosure of a plan to change the rules

---

3 On December 18, 2023, Cardinal Fernández released a Declaration of the Dicastery for the Doctrine of the Faith entitled *Fiducia Supplicans*, which laid out a pseudo-theology of blessings and, with torturous reasoning and far-fetched distinctions, officially approved the worldwide blessing of same-sex couples. The Declaration provoked a firestorm of criticism, with many bishops and priests refusing to implement it, and prominent theologians writing against its compatibility with the Catholic religion. — *Ed.*

for the papal conclaves so as to introduce the participation of lay people, including women. What this showed us was that the point of the preceding Synod had not been the document to emerge from it, but the process itself. It was designed to soften up the Church for a revolution in the papal election. Thus, we had had bishops making declarations like: "It will be impossible from now on to hold a Synod without lay participation." If that was so, people would also be demanding a papal election under similar conditions.

This news story disclosed that conversations had been in progress for months between the pope and Cardinal Ghirlanda, to change the conclave rules. Cardinal Ghirlanda, by the way, besides being a Jesuit, is the propounder of an extreme theological view of papal power which makes him the ideal agent to entrench the regime of papal dictatorship. As soon as the story broke, there was a prompt denial from the Vatican, accompanied by furious efforts within the various dicasteries to find out who had been responsible for the leak. The lesson this showed was that the Vatican found it had lost control of the narrative, as they say nowadays, and had been embarrassed by a revelation which pre-empted its plans. I think there can be little doubt that the reform, so called, will go ahead, but I presume that the premature revelation has upset Pope Francis's schedule.

However, not all the papal news is made by Rome itself. One very significant development has come from Argentina, in the shape of last Sunday's presidential election and the coming to power of Javier Milei. In the first place, this was directly contrary to the policy of the Church, which, apparently on orders from Rome, had been canvassing openly against Milei and urging voters to vote against him. More particularly, Milei is a declared enemy of Pope Francis and has publicly insulted him, while his Vice-President, Victoria Villarruel, is a traditionalist Catholic. *La Croix* has commented on the result: "Frankly, if a group of church affairs junkies were to sit down in a bar and try to sketch a ticket on a cocktail napkin that would amount to a rejection *tout court* of a sitting pope's agenda, it's doubtful they could have come up with anything more vivid than what actually happened." A more stringent commentary has come from an Argentinian political expert, Professor Rubén Peretó Rivas, who stated in a recent interview that Milei's victory

> represents a rebuff to Bergoglio, and confirms what everybody knows: the Argentinians do not like Pope Francis and don't want him. For years now, when news about Bergoglio has appeared in newspapers and portals, the administrators find themselves obliged to close readers' comments, which are for the most part contemptuous and harsh. Many people may have thought that the rejection of Bergoglio was widespread only among those who read and keep informed. It has now been shown that it's present in all social strata, even among the poor. For that very reason, Bergoglio will never come to Argentina, because his journey would be a failure. It is certain that the majority

of the lower clergy, especially the younger priests, are sick of Bergoglio and don't want anything to do with him: a rejection which embraces everything that the pope does and advocates.

That is the view from Argentina, which the rest of the world might be advised to take heed of, as the cardinal electors would have been in 2013.

Thus, it seems that in this area too Pope Francis's plans have come unstuck, and we shouldn't underestimate the consequences of it for a pope who's so naked a politician as Francis. So, to sum up, what can we expect for the immediate future? I hesitate to make any predictions, but what the events of the past few weeks have shown us is that Pope Francis is an old man in a hurry. He's desperate to institutionalize his revolution before he dies, and he'll stop at nothing to achieve that. So the answer to the question "how much lower can we sink?" is that there's probably no limit to it, and we can expect to be scandalized by worse and worse enormities. However, Pope Francis needs to bear in mind that he's not in control of everything. Besides presidential elections in Argentina, closer to home there's one very traditional law that he has no power to repeal, and that's the law of human mortality. The final reality is that Pope Francis will not be here for ever, but that Christ has told us, "Behold I am with you always, even to the consummation of the world."

47

Pope Francis as Public Heretic[1]

JOHN LAMONT

P OPE FRANCIS HAS RECENTLY PUBLISHED ANSWERS TO
two sets of *dubia* submitted to him by members of the College of Cardinals:
one set submitted by Cardinals Brandmüller, Burke, Sandoval, Sarah, and
Zen on July 10, 2023, and the other set submitted by Cardinal Dominik Duka
on July 13, 2023. Pope Francis responded to the *dubia* of the five cardinals on
July 11 and made this response public on October 2. On September 25, 2023, the
Dicastery for the Doctrine of the Faith responded to *dubia* proposed by Cardinal
Dominik Duka; the response was endorsed by the pope. On November 1, 2023,
Pope Francis issued, motu proprio, the apostolic letter *Ad Theologiam Promovendam*
to accompany revised statutes for the Pontifical Academy of Theology. His answers
to these *dubia* and his apostolic letter openly and unmistakably contradict the
Catholic faith (see Annexe II, p. 432 for the texts in question).

Concerns have already been expressed about contradictions between the statements of Pope Francis and the Catholic faith.[2] A number of Catholic scholars
made their concerns about the apostolic exhortation *Amoris Laetitia* known to
the College of Cardinals and the Patriarchs of the Catholic Church, in a document that listed the propositions advanced by Pope Francis that appeared to be
contrary to Catholic teaching, and that assigned theological censures to these
propositions.[3] A group of Catholic scholars addressed a filial correction to Pope
Francis on account of his propagation of heresies by the apostolic exhortation
Amoris Laetitia and by other words, deeds, and omissions.[4] The filial correction
met with no response from Pope Francis, and he did not clarify or withdraw
any of the words or actions which it identified as heretical. In consequence, a
number of Catholic scholars issued an open letter to the bishops of the Catholic
Church, stating that Pope Francis had committed the canonical delict of heresy.[5]
A further appeal to the cardinals of the Catholic Church denounced Pope Francis's
statements on the death penalty as contrary to the teachings of the Scriptures and
to the magisterium of the Church.[6]

---

1 First published at *Rorate Caeli* on November 24, 2023.
2 The documents mentioned in this paragraph, with the lists of their signatories, are collected
in Lamont and Pierantoni, *Defending the Faith*.
3 "Theological Censures of *Amoris Laetitia*," in *Defending the Faith*, 49–73.
4 "*Correctio filialis de haeresibus propagatis*," in *Defending the Faith*, 75–123.
5 "Open Letter to the Bishops of the Catholic Church," in *Defending the Faith*, 125–59.
6 "An Appeal to the Cardinals of the Catholic Church," in *Defending the Faith*, 161–65, first
published in *First Things*.

Pope Francis's answers to the *dubia* of the cardinals surpass his earlier statements in the clarity of their rejection of the Catholic faith. In consequence, they place his tenure of the papal office in doubt.

The following statement contains four parts: I. heresies asserted by Pope Francis; II. heresy as a personal sin and as a public crime; III. Pope Francis's pertinacity in maintaining heresy; IV. consequences of Pope Francis's heresy.

I. HERESIES ASSERTED BY POPE FRANCIS

(1) By stating that "both the texts of the Scripture and the testimonies of Tradition require interpretation in order to distinguish their perennial substance from cultural conditioning" (Response to first Dubium, f.), Pope Francis contradicts the following infallibly taught doctrines of the Catholic Church.

> Since human beings are totally dependent on God as their Creator and Lord, and created reason is completely subject to uncreated truth, we are obliged to yield to God the revealer full submission of intellect and will by faith. This faith, which is the beginning of human salvation, the Catholic Church professes to be a supernatural virtue, by means of which, with the grace of God inspiring and assisting us, we believe to be true what He has revealed, not because we perceive its intrinsic truth by the natural light of reason, but because of the authority of God himself, who makes the revelation and can neither deceive nor be deceived.[7]

> For the doctrine of the faith which God has revealed is put forward not as some philosophical discovery capable of being perfected by human intelligence, but as a divine deposit committed to the spouse of Christ to be faithfully protected and infallibly promulgated. Hence, too, that meaning of the sacred dogmas is ever to be maintained which has once been declared by Holy Mother Church, and there must never be any abandonment of this sense under the pretext or in the name of a more profound understanding. May understanding, knowledge, and wisdom increase as ages and centuries roll along, and greatly and vigorously flourish, in each and all, in the individual and in the whole Church: but this only in its own proper kind, that is to say, in the same doctrine, the same sense, and the same understanding.[8]

> If anyone says that it is possible that at some time, with the progress of knowledge, a sense should be assigned to the dogmas propounded by the Church which is different from that which the Church has understood and does understand: let him be anathema.[9]

Pope Francis's distinction between the "perennial substance" of the testimonies of Tradition and the "cultural conditioning" of these testimonies asserts that *only a part of the content of these testimonies* must always be accepted by Catholics. This

---

7   First Vatican Council, *Dei Filius*, ch. 3.
8   First Vatican Council, *Dei Filius*, ch. 4.
9   First Vatican Council, *Dei Filius*, ch. 4, can. 3.

part is their so-called "perennial substance." The rest of the content of all of the testimonies of tradition is produced by the cultural conditions of their time. This element is not part of their perennial substance, and hence does not need to be accepted by all Catholics at all times.

This position might be acceptable if applied solely to some non-infallible expressions of Tradition, but Pope Francis does not apply it only to these non-infallible expressions; he applies it to all expressions of Tradition whatsoever, which includes infallible teachings. Moreover, the first dubium to which he is responding *specifically asks about Divine Revelation* to which the obedience of faith is due. This includes *only* expressions of Tradition that are infallibly taught. Pope Francis's response should be understood as referring entirely or at least primarily to the expressions of Tradition that are referred to in the dubium to which he is responding. The response therefore applies to expressions of Tradition that infallibly teach divinely revealed dogmas.

The bare statement that not all of the content of any testimony of tradition needs to be accepted in its entirety is heretical. Pope Francis does not limit himself to this bare statement; he asserts that some elements of the culturally conditioned content of the testimonies of tradition may or must be rejected as deficient. But the teaching of *Dei Filius* cited above asserts that the entire meaning of the dogmatic teaching of the Church must be accepted by all Catholics at all times in the sense that the teachings had when they were first made. It does not deny that dogmatic utterances are expressed in the cultural and conceptual forms of their time. It asserts that the utterances that these cultural and conceptual forms were used to produce give an entirely true description of what is, and do not and could not contain any false or dispensable elements.

Purely human assertions can contain erroneous elements because of the influence of the cultural and conceptual forms of their time. This is not true of God. The statements made by the Scriptures and by Sacred Tradition are uttered both by God and by human beings. The fact that these statements are made by the free action of human will and human intellect does not make them any the less fully and directly divine statements. Since God is all-knowing and all-powerful, He can ensure that any statements that He makes in human language, using human instruments, are entirely free of error of any kind. Since He is perfectly good and truthful, He will ensure that His statements are free of any error. These are the reasons given by the First Vatican Council for holding that Catholic dogma cannot be mistaken, cannot change, and must be believed by Catholics. Pope Francis's claim that all of the testimonies of tradition may contain erroneous elements because of the influence of the cultural and conceptual forms of their time thus implies that none of these testimonies are divinely revealed.

In paragraph (g) of his reply to the first dubium, Pope Francis states:

> In this regard, I would like to recall what St Thomas Aquinas affirmed: "The more one descends to matters of detail, the more frequently we encounter defects" (*Summa Theologiae* I/II q. 94, art. 4).

Since the dubium refers to Divine Revelation and the question of whether or
not this revelation is immutable, the natural sense of this statement should
be understood as applying this affirmation of St Thomas Aquinas to Divine
Revelation. In this sense, the statement asserts that Divine Revelation contains
defects, and that the more one descends into the details of Divine Revelation
the more defects are to be found in it. This expresses and expands on the heresy
plainly stated in paragraph (f). The citation from St Thomas Aquinas does not
support this heresy, because St Thomas is referring to practical, contingent matters that are the subject matter of the practical reason ("contingentia, in quibus
sunt operationes humanae"), not to Divine Revelation or to speculative truths in
general. However, the words of this citation by Pope Francis, taken in isolation
independently of their original meaning when used by St Thomas, are heretical
as applied to Divine Revelation, the subject of the first dubium.

The contradiction between Pope Francis's statement and this teaching of the
First Vatican Council is apparent from the explication of this teaching given in
other magisterial statements.

> For the Church of Christ, watchful guardian that she is, and defender of
> the dogmas deposited with her, never changes anything, never dimin-
> ishes anything, never adds anything to them; but with all diligence she
> treats the ancient documents faithfully and wisely; if they really are
> of ancient origin and if the faith of the Fathers has transmitted them,
> she strives to investigate and explain them in such a way that the
> ancient dogmas of heavenly doctrine will be made evident and clear,
> but will retain their full, integral, and proper nature, and will grown
> only within their own genus—that is, within the same dogma, in the
> same sense and the same meaning.[10]

> Every truth, if it is authentic, presents itself as universal and absolute,
> even if it is not the whole truth. If something is true, then it must be
> true for all people and at all times.[11]

> The word of God is not addressed to any one people or to any one
> period of history. Similarly, dogmatic statements, while reflecting at
> times the culture of the period in which they were defined, formulate
> an unchanging and ultimate truth.[12]

> The truth about God is not abolished or reduced because it is spoken
> in human language; rather, it is unique, full, and complete, because
> he who speaks and acts is the Incarnate Son of God.[13]

Pope Francis might reject the teaching of Vatican I and of these magisterial

---

10   Pius IX, Bull *Ineffabilis Deus*.
11   John Paul II, *Fides et Ratio*, 27.
12   John Paul II, *Fides et Ratio*, 95.
13   Congregation for the Doctrine of the Faith, *Declaration* Dominus Iesus *on the Unicity and
Salvific Universality of Jesus Christ and the Church*, 6.

pronouncements as products of cultural conditioning, and therefore as not binding on Catholics. But such a move would simply reveal the depth of the rejection of faith involved in the modernist heresy that he is espousing. Since every part of every magisterial pronouncement is influenced by the cultural conditions in which it was produced, this approach permits the modernist to reject any part of the teaching of the Church that he chooses, while still claiming to be Catholic. It is a strategy that has been used by modernist theologians to reject various parts of Catholic teaching on faith and morals.

Pope Francis does not specify if all the testimonies of Tradition require interpretation in order to distinguish their perennial substance from cultural conditioning, or if only some of them do. Either one of these positions is heretical.

If all the testimonies of Tradition require interpretation in order to distinguish their perennial substance from cultural conditioning, then the perennial substance of magisterial teaching can never be set forth by the magisterium of the Church. This is because every magisterial teaching exists in some cultural context or other. A magisterial teaching that attempts to identify the perennial substance in a previous teaching will thus itself be a compound of perennial substance and cultural conditioning, which must be distinguished in order to know what part of it must be accepted; and so on *ad infinitum*. We will never get to a magisterial teaching whose content can simply be accepted as it stands.

Pope Francis does not seem to hold that all the testimonies of Tradition require interpretation in order to distinguish their perennial substance from cultural conditioning, because he expects his own statements to be accepted as they stand. This position makes him the supreme and sole arbiter of Revelation, since he can reject any part of Scriptural and magisterial teaching as culturally conditioned while requiring that his own position on the contents of the faith be accepted in its entirety.

(2) In stating that the texts of Scripture require interpretation in order to distinguish their perennial substance from cultural conditioning, and claiming that three Scriptural texts (offered as examples of presumably many more) cannot be accepted as true in their original meaning, Pope Francis contradicts the following infallibly taught doctrine of the Catholic Church:

> Now this supernatural revelation, according to the belief of the universal Church, as declared by the sacred council of Trent, is contained in written books and unwritten traditions, which were received by the apostles from the lips of Christ himself, or came to the apostles by the dictation of the Holy Spirit, and were passed on as it were from hand to hand until they reached us. The complete books of the Old and the New Testament with all their parts, as they are listed in the decree of the said council and as they are found in the old Latin Vulgate edition, are to be received as sacred and canonical. These books the Church holds to be sacred and canonical not because she

subsequently approved them by her authority after they had been composed by unaided human skill, nor simply because they contain revelation without error, but because, being written under the inspiration of the Holy Spirit, they have God as their author, and were as such committed to the Church.[14]

If anyone does not receive as sacred and canonical the complete books of Sacred Scripture with all their parts, as the holy council of Trent listed them, or denies that they were divinely inspired: let him be anathema.[15]

Pope Francis does not give what he understands to be the meaning of the Scriptural passages that he asserts to be false. He is not distinguishing between different possible understandings of these passages, and maintaining that some particular interpretation of these passages is not what God in fact meant to express by them, and should be rejected as false; he is claiming that *the passages themselves* are false. Denying that some Scriptural passage is true is heretical in itself, since the Catholic faith holds that every assertion of Scripture is a divinely revealed truth.

Pope Francis uses this claim about these Scriptural passages to argue for the general claim that some or all of the Scriptures must be rejected as false in their original meaning. This general claim is heretical, since it contradicts Catholic dogma on the divine inspiration and consequent complete truth of the Scriptures. The different methods of interpreting the Scriptures, the varying interpretations of Scriptural texts, and the original meaning of the Scriptural passages that he mentions are immaterial when it comes to the heretical character of this general claim. It is however easy to show the falsity of Pope Francis's claim that the Scriptural passages he mentions are unacceptable in their original meaning (see Annexe I below).

Pope Francis's general claim about the Scriptures is a far graver heresy than his more circumscribed heresy of denying the truth of several Scriptural passages. As well as denying the Catholic teaching that Scriptural passages must be true because they are divinely revealed, it asserts that any part of a Scriptural passage can be judged to be false on the grounds of the cultural conditioning of that passage. But every biblical text, like every other text, is culturally conditioned in its entirety. Biblical texts are expressed in human languages, which are cultural forms, and they are of necessity formulated using the concepts and assumptions of their human authors. Pope Francis's position lets us reject any part of a biblical text on the grounds that it is culturally conditioned, if we come to disagree with something that the people of the culture that produced it assumed or held to be true. It is a heresy that permits any Scriptural assertion to be dispensed with at will.

---

14   First Vatican Council, *Dei Filius*, ch. 2.
15   Chapter 2, canon 4.

The teaching that divine inspiration extends to every part of the Scriptures and that this inspiration rules out any error is asserted in the following pronouncements, which repeat and explain the teaching of the First Vatican Council on this subject:

> For all the books which the Church receives as sacred and canonical, are written wholly and entirely, with all their parts, at the dictation of the Holy Ghost; and so far is it from being possible that any error can coexist with inspiration, that inspiration not only is essentially incompatible with error, but excludes and rejects it as absolutely and necessarily as it is impossible that God Himself, the supreme Truth, can utter that which is not true. This is the ancient and unchanging faith of the Church, solemnly defined in the Councils of Florence and of Trent, and finally confirmed and more expressly formulated by the Council of the Vatican. These are the words of the last: "The Books of the Old and New Testament, whole and entire, with all their parts, as enumerated in the decree of the same Council (Trent) and in the ancient Latin Vulgate, are to be received as sacred and canonical. And the Church holds them as sacred and canonical, not because, having been composed by human industry, they were afterwards approved by her authority; nor only because they contain revelation without error; but because, having been written under the inspiration of the Holy Ghost, they have God for their author." Hence, because the Holy Ghost employed men as His instruments, we cannot therefore say that it was these inspired instruments who, perchance, have fallen into error, and not the primary author. For, by supernatural power, He so moved and impelled them to write—He was so present to them—that the things which He ordered, and those only, they, first, rightly understood, then willed faithfully to write down, and finally expressed in apt words and with infallible truth. Otherwise, it could not be said that He was the Author of the entire Scripture.[16]

> It is absolutely wrong and forbidden "either to narrow inspiration to certain passages of Holy Scripture, or to admit that the sacred writer has erred," since divine inspiration "not only is essentially incompatible with error but excludes and rejects it as absolutely and necessarily as it is impossible that God Himself, the supreme Truth, can utter that which is not true. This is the ancient and constant faith of the Church." This teaching, which Our Predecessor Leo XIII set forth with such solemnity, We also proclaim with Our authority.[17]

> For Holy Mother Church, relying on the belief of the Apostles (see Jn 20:31; 2 Tim 3:16; 2 Pet 1:19-20, 3:15-16), holds that the books of both the Old and New Testaments in their entirety, with all their parts, are sacred and canonical because, written under the inspiration of the Holy Spirit, they have God as their author and have been handed on

---

16 Leo XIII, *Providentissimus Deus*, 20.
17 Pius XII, *Divino Afflante Spiritu*, 3-4.

as such to the Church herself. In composing the sacred books, God chose men and while employed by Him they made use of their powers and abilities, so that with Him acting in them and through them, they, as true authors, consigned to writing all those things and only those things which He wanted.

Therefore, since everything asserted by the inspired authors or sacred writers must be held to be asserted by the Holy Spirit, it follows that the books of Scripture must be acknowledged as teaching the truth, which God wanted to be recorded by means of sacred writings for the sake of our salvation, solidly, faithfully and without error.[18] Therefore "all Scripture is divinely inspired and has its use for teaching the truth and refuting error, for reformation of manners and discipline in right living, so that the man who belongs to God may be efficient and equipped for good work of every kind" (2 Tim. 3:16–17, Greek text). [The encyclicals *Providentissimus Deus* and *Divino Afflante Spiritu* as cited above are referenced in the footnotes to this passage from *Dei Verbum*, in order to explain the doctrine that is being asserted.][19]

(3) In his apostolic letter *Ad Theologiam Promovendam*, Pope Francis asserts:
• theology must develop using an inductive method, which starts from the different contexts and concrete situations in which peoples are inserted, and allows itself to be seriously challenged by reality;
• the knowledge of people's common sense is a "locus theologicus" that must be privileged first of all by theology;
• theology must enter into the culture, worldview, and religious tradition of a people, and develop into a culture of dialogue and encounter between different traditions and different knowledge, between different Christian denominations and different religions.

These statements contradict the following teaching of the Catholic Faith.

Since human beings are totally dependent on God as their Creator and Lord, and created reason is completely subject to uncreated truth, we are obliged to yield to God the revealer full submission of intellect and will by faith. This faith, which is the beginning of human salvation, the Catholic Church professes to be a supernatural virtue, by means of which, with the grace of God inspiring and assisting us, we believe to be true what He has revealed, not because we perceive its intrinsic truth by the natural light of reason, but because of the authority of God himself, who makes the revelation and can neither deceive nor be deceived.[20]

---

18   This famous sentence is rendered correctly here from the Latin; as Fr Thomas Crean demonstrates, the standard translation of this sentence is grammatically incorrect and theologically misleading. See *"Letters from that City . . .": A Guide to Holy Scripture for Students of Theology* (Lincoln, NE: Os Justi Press, 2022), 25–27.
19   Second Vatican Council, *Dei Verbum*, 11–12.
20   First Vatican Council, Dogmatic Constitution *Dei Filius*, ch. 3.

If anyone says that divine faith is not to be distinguished from natural knowledge about God and moral matters, and consequently that for divine faith it is not required that revealed truth should be believed because of the authority of God who reveals it: let him be anathema.[21]

Even though faith is above reason, there can never be any real disagreement between faith and reason, since it is the same God who reveals the mysteries and infuses faith, and who has endowed the human mind with the light of reason. God cannot deny himself, nor can truth ever be in opposition to truth. The appearance of this kind of specious contradiction is chiefly due to the fact that either the dogmas of faith are not understood and explained in accordance with the mind of the Church, or unsound views are mistaken for the conclusions of reason. Therefore we define that every assertion contrary to the truth of enlightened faith is totally false (see Lateran V, session 8). Furthermore the Church which, together with its apostolic office of teaching, has received the charge of preserving the deposit of faith, has by divine appointment the right and duty of condemning what wrongly passes for knowledge, lest anyone be led astray by philosophy and empty deceit (see Col 2:8). Hence all faithful Christians are forbidden to defend as the legitimate conclusions of science those opinions which are known to be contrary to the doctrine of faith, particularly if they have been condemned by the Church; and furthermore they are absolutely bound to hold them to be errors which wear the deceptive appearance of truth. Not only can faith and reason never be at odds with one another but they mutually support each other, for on the one hand right reason established the foundations of the faith and, illuminated by its light, develops the science of divine things; on the other hand, faith delivers reason from errors and protects it and furnishes it with knowledge of many kinds.

Hence, so far is the Church from hindering the development of human arts and studies, that in fact she assists and promotes them in many ways. For she is neither ignorant nor contemptuous of the advantages which derive from this source for human life, rather she acknowledges that those things flow from God, the Lord of sciences, and, if they are properly used, lead to God by the help of his grace. Nor does the Church forbid these studies to employ, each within its own area, its own proper principles and method: but while she admits this just freedom, she takes particular care that they do not become infected with errors by conflicting with divine teaching, or, by going beyond their proper limits, intrude upon what belongs to faith and engender confusion. For the doctrine of the faith which God has revealed is put forward not as some philosophical discovery capable of being perfected by human intelligence, but as a divine deposit committed to the spouse of Christ to be faithfully protected and infallibly promulgated.[22]

---

21   Ibid., canon 2.
22   Ibid., chapter 4.

If anyone says that human studies are to be treated with such a degree
of liberty that their assertions may be maintained as true even when
they are opposed to Divine Revelation, and that they may not be
forbidden by the Church: let him be anathema.[23]

Catholic theology takes God as its object, and it takes the study of divinely revealed
truths contained in Scripture and Sacred Tradition as its method. Its knowledge
of these truths is based on an act of the theological virtue of faith, which assents
to the truths divinely communicated by God in Scripture and Sacred Tradition
"because of the authority of God himself, who makes the revelation and can neither
deceive nor be deceived." The goal of theology is to understand these divinely
revealed truths more deeply, discern the connections between them, and discover
the conclusions that logically follow from them.

If theology starts from the different contexts and concrete situations in which
peoples are inserted, then these contexts and concrete situations are where Divine
Revelation is to be found. But this is incompatible with the definition of Divine
Revelation given above. The contexts and situations in which peoples are inserted
do not have the authority of God himself, who makes the revelation and can
neither deceive nor be deceived, and they cannot be believed on the grounds
of God's authority, or provide material for beliefs that are accepted because of
the authority of God who reveals it. They are not divine communications that
demand the assent of faith. They provide natural knowledge that is not Divine
Revelation and cannot be identified with it. The same applies to the knowledge
of people's common sense. This is a natural form of knowledge that is not Divine
Revelation. It is not a "locus theologicus," that is, it is not a fundamental principle
or source of theological science. Human common sense is subject to instruction
and correction by Divine Revelation and has no authority over it.

Nor can Divine Revelation be known through induction. Belief in Divine
Revelation does not involve inductive inference. It is directly based on the authority of God who cannot deceive or be deceived. Belief on this basis involves a
deductive inference from properties that God possesses necessarily. It confers
absolute certainty — as the Church teaches — which inductive inference cannot do.
The absolute certainty of divine knowledge, and the absolute trustworthiness of
Divine Revelation, are the reasons why the Church anathematizes the claim that
human studies can be treated with such a degree of liberty that their assertions
may be maintained as true even when they are opposed to Divine Revelation. The
apostolic letter *Ad Theologiam Promovendam* thus goes farther than the denial of
individual divinely revealed truths. It proposes a theological message that denies
the existence of Divine Revelation as the Catholic Church understands it.

Ad Theologiam Promovendam describes the task of theology as reading and interpreting the Gospel, as penetrating and communicating the truths of faith and

---

23   Ibid., canon 2.

transmitting the teaching of Jesus in today's languages, and as the proclamation of the salvific event of God-*agape* communicated in Jesus Christ. This presents the object of theology as the Christian revelation, and the task of theology as being the understanding and communication of this revelation. This description of the object and task of theology is in accordance with Catholic teaching, as far as the ordinary meaning of its words go. But these words do not make explicit mention of divinely revealed truths or of the theological virtue of faith. And as noted above, the theological method prescribed in *Ad Theologiam Promovendam* indicates that the apostolic letter does not understand the truths of faith and the teaching of Jesus as being divinely revealed in the sense of Catholic teaching. It excludes the possibility of these truths and these teachings being divinely revealed in this sense.

The apostolic letter in fact proposes a common understanding of theology and Divine Revelation; it is the understanding that is held by progressive theologians who deny that Divine Revelation is propositional in nature—they deny the existence of truths that are communicated by God, and reject the conception of faith as consisting in or including belief in such truths on the grounds that God has literally asserted them. Pope Francis is correct in asserting that Catholic theology is called to a turning point, a paradigm shift, and a cultural revolution by *Ad Theologiam Promovendam*: the apostolic letter requires the rejection of the Catholic conceptions of Divine Revelation, faith, and theology. The term "cultural revolution" is an apt one. This term refers to the movement launched by Mao in China in 1966. The method proposed by *Ad Theologiam Promovendam* aims at complete destruction of Catholic tradition and belief, just as Mao's Cultural Revolution aimed at complete destruction of Chinese tradition.

(4) In the apostolic exhortation *Amoris Laetitia*, in his letter to the pastoral region of Buenos Aires on September 5, 2016, and in the response to the *dubia* of Cardinal Duka, Pope Francis states that the Church can and must abandon her perennial discipline of refusing the Eucharist to the divorced who live *more uxorio* with a person who is not their spouse, and of refusing absolution to such persons unless they express contrition for their state of life and a firm purpose of amendment with regard to it. Pope Francis thereby contradicts the following divinely revealed teaching:

> *Exodus 20:14.* You shall not commit adultery.

> *Matthew 19:3-12.* And Pharisees came up to him and tested him by asking, "Is it lawful to divorce one's wife for any cause?" He answered, "Have you not read that he who made them from the beginning made them male and female, and said, 'For this reason a man shall leave his father and mother and be joined to his wife, and the two shall become one flesh'? So they are no longer two but one flesh. What therefore God has joined together, let not man put asunder." They said to him, "Why then did Moses command one to give a certificate of divorce, and

to put her away?" He said to them, "For your hardness of heart Moses allowed you to divorce your wives, but from the beginning it was not so. And I say to you: whoever divorces his wife, except for unchastity, and marries another, commits adultery." The disciples said to him, "If such is the case of a man with his wife, it is not expedient to marry." But he said to them, "Not all men can receive this saying, but only those to whom it is given. For there are eunuchs who have been so from birth, and there are eunuchs who have been made eunuchs by men, and there are eunuchs who have made themselves eunuchs for the sake of the kingdom of heaven. He who is able to receive this, let him receive it."

Mark 10:2-12. And Pharisees came up and in order to test him asked, "Is it lawful for a man to divorce his wife?" He answered them, "What did Moses command you?" They said, "Moses allowed a man to write a certificate of divorce, and to put her away." But Jesus said to them, "For your hardness of heart he wrote you this commandment. But from the beginning of creation, 'God made them male and female.' 'For this reason a man shall leave his father and mother and be joined to his wife, and the two shall become one flesh.' So they are no longer two but one flesh. What therefore God has joined together, let not man put asunder." And in the house the disciples asked him again about this matter. And he said to them, "Whoever divorces his wife and marries another, commits adultery against her; and if she divorces her husband and marries another, she commits adultery."

Luke 16:18. Every one who divorces his wife and marries another commits adultery, and he who marries a woman divorced from her husband commits adultery.

1 Corinthians 6:9-10. Do you not know that the unrighteous will not inherit the kingdom of God? Do not be deceived; neither the immoral, nor idolaters, nor adulterers, nor sexual perverts, nor thieves, nor the greedy, nor drunkards, nor revilers, nor robbers will inherit the kingdom of God.

1 Corinthians 7:10-11. To the married I give charge, not I but the Lord, that the wife should not separate from her husband (but if she does, let her remain single or else be reconciled to her husband) — and that the husband should not divorce his wife.

1 Corinthians 11:27-30. Whoever, therefore, eats the bread or drinks the cup of the Lord in an unworthy manner will be guilty of profaning the body and blood of the Lord. Let a man examine himself, and so eat of the bread and drink of the cup. For any one who eats and drinks without discerning the body eats and drinks judgment upon himself. That is why many of you are weak and ill, and some have died.

He also contradicts the apostolic exhortation *Familiaris Consortio* of Pope John Paul II issued in 1981. *Familiaris Consortio* states:

> 84. Daily experience unfortunately shows that people who have obtained a divorce usually intend to enter into a new union, obviously not with a Catholic religious ceremony. Since this is an evil that, like the others, is affecting more and more Catholics as well, the problem must be faced with resolution and without delay. The Synod Fathers studied it expressly. The Church, which was set up to lead to salvation all people and especially the baptized, cannot abandon to their own devices those who have been previously bound by sacramental marriage and who have attempted a second marriage. The Church will therefore make untiring efforts to put at their disposal her means of salvation.
>
> Pastors must know that, for the sake of truth, they are obliged to exercise careful discernment of situations. There is in fact a difference between those who have sincerely tried to save their first marriage and have been unjustly abandoned, and those who through their own grave fault have destroyed a canonically valid marriage. Finally, there are those who have entered into a second union for the sake of the children's upbringing, and who are sometimes subjectively certain in conscience that their previous and irreparably destroyed marriage had never been valid.
>
> Together with the Synod, I earnestly call upon pastors and the whole community of the faithful to help the divorced, and with solicitous care to make sure that they do not consider themselves as separated from the Church, for as baptized persons they can, and indeed must, share in her life. They should be encouraged to listen to the word of God, to attend the Sacrifice of the Mass, to persevere in prayer, to contribute to works of charity and to community efforts in favor of justice, to bring up their children in the Christian faith, to cultivate the spirit and practice of penance and thus implore, day by day, God's grace. Let the Church pray for them, encourage them and show herself a merciful mother, and thus sustain them in faith and hope.
>
> However, the Church reaffirms her practice, which is based upon Sacred Scripture, of not admitting to Eucharistic Communion divorced persons who have remarried. They are unable to be admitted thereto from the fact that their state and condition of life objectively contradict that union of love between Christ and the Church which is signified and effected by the Eucharist. Besides this, there is another special pastoral reason: if these people were admitted to the Eucharist, the faithful would be led into error and confusion regarding the Church's teaching about the indissolubility of marriage.
>
> Reconciliation in the sacrament of Penance, which would open the way to the Eucharist, can only be granted to those who, repenting of having broken the sign of the Covenant and of fidelity to Christ, are sincerely ready to undertake a way of life that is no longer in contradiction

to the indissolubility of marriage. This means, in practice, that when, for serious reasons, such as for example the children's upbringing, a man and a woman cannot satisfy the obligation to separate, they "take on themselves the duty to live in complete continence, that is, by abstinence from the acts proper to married couples" [John Paul II, Homily at the Close of the Sixth Synod of Bishops, 7 (October 25, 1980)].

Similarly, the respect due to the sacrament of Matrimony, to the couples themselves and their families, and also to the community of the faithful, forbids any pastor, for whatever reason or pretext even of a pastoral nature, to perform ceremonies of any kind for divorced people who remarry. Such ceremonies would give the impression of the celebration of a new sacramentally valid marriage, and would thus lead people into error concerning the indissolubility of a validly contracted marriage.

By acting in this way, the Church professes her own fidelity to Christ and to His truth. At the same time she shows motherly concern for these children of hers, especially those who, through no fault of their own, have been abandoned by their legitimate partner. With firm confidence she believes that those who have rejected the Lord's command and are still living in this state will be able to obtain from God the grace of conversion and salvation, provided that they have persevered in prayer, penance and charity.

Familiaris Consortio clearly states what *Amoris Laetitia* denies: the divorced and remarried who do not undertake to live as brother and sister cannot be granted absolution, and cannot be admitted to Eucharistic communion. This is not the full extent of the contradiction between the two documents. *Familiaris Consortio* explicitly considers those "hard cases" that *Amoris Laetitia* raises, such as persons who are subjectively convinced that their previous marriages were not valid, those who have been unjustly abandoned by their spouses, and those who enter into or remain in civil partnerships for the sake of their children's upbringing. It teaches that these "hard cases" *cannot* be a basis for changing the Church's discipline concerning absolution and reception of the Eucharist. It agrees with *Amoris Laetitia* in saying that the Church cannot abandon to their own devices those Catholics who have entered into second unions. However, its understanding of what it means for the Church to not abandon these people is the *opposite* of the one proposed by *Amoris Laetitia*. *Familiaris Consortio* describes the pastoral help of the Church in these cases as having the object of enabling such persons to cease their adulterous and bigamous relations. *Amoris Laetitia* does not propose this as the object of their pastoral care; instead it proposes that in some cases they should be assisted to live their adulterous and bigamous relations in a good way.

Amoris Laetitia recognizes "limitations that mitigate responsibility and culpability" for the situations of the civilly divorced and remarried living *more uxorio* with one another, and that in consequence permit them to be absolved and to receive the Eucharist. But the character of these limitations is not plainly specified. There are two possible ways in which such a specification could be made. The limitations in question could be understood as circumstances that make the actions and lives of such persons objectively good, and hence not in need of forgiveness. This is certainly what is suggested by the text of *Amoris Laetitia*. However, these limitations could instead be understood as circumstances that do not make the actions and lives of such persons objectively good, but do make them subjectively guiltless for their cohabitation and sexual relationship. It is therefore necessary to determine what Scripture and Tradition teach on both these possibilities.

The above Scriptural passages express an absolute prohibition upon adulterers receiving the Eucharist. They state that those guilty of grave sins may not receive the Eucharist, that adultery is a grave sin, and that those who divorce their spouse and marry someone else commit adultery. The Scriptural texts are much clearer on this subject than they are on many doctrines that have been solemnly defined as divinely revealed. The question is therefore whether the Eucharist can be received by persons who are objectively acting in an evil way by their cohabitation and sexual relationship, but whose responsibility for this evil action is for some reason reduced or nonexistent.

The possibility of such persons receiving the Eucharist can be excluded in two ways. The first way is through a divine commandment addressed to the civilly divorced and remarried that absolutely forbids them to receive the Eucharist. The second way is through a divine commandment addressed to priests and bishops absolutely forbidding them to dispense the Eucharist to persons who are civilly divorced and remarried.

It is certainly true that Catholics are forbidden to choose to receive the Eucharist when they are in a state of mortal sin. But it does not follow from this that it is the defiled state of the soul in mortal sin that furnishes the sole reason for the prohibition on grave sinners receiving the Eucharist, so that the absence of this defiled state of soul removes the basis for this prohibition. The Scriptural passages that express this prohibition do not qualify it by saying that those who commit grave sins with full knowledge and consent of the will must not choose to receive the Eucharist. What the Scriptural texts say is that committing grave sin is a bar to reception of the Eucharist. It is not hard to see why this commandment is not qualified by adding that the grave sin in question is one that is done with full knowledge and consent of the will. The Eucharist is the holiest thing in the universe, and nothing evil can be permitted to approach it. In the hypothetical case of a person blamelessly living in an adulterous relationship, the evil of mortal sin in the person's soul is lacking, but the objectively evil act, with its violation of the order of justice and its evil consequences, remains. Reception of the Eucharist by a person committing this evil would be a profanation of the sacrament, and hence is contrary to divine law. As the *Dictionnaire de théologie catholique* states, receiving communion in a state of merely material sin is in itself a very grave sacrilege, because objectively speaking it involves a profanation of the body and blood of Jesus Christ.[24]

This requires that the civilly divorced and remarried be forbidden by the Church to attempt to receive the Eucharist, regardless of their degree of responsibility for their state. Are priests also required to refuse the Eucharist to such persons? The profanation of the sacrament involved in reception of the Eucharist even by someone in a merely material state of grave sin is one reason why this is required. Such reception could not benefit the persons receiving the Eucharist in any way, because the benefit that is sought in receiving the Eucharist is grace and union with Christ. This benefit will not be granted by a communion that profanes the Eucharist, even if the persons receiving it are guiltless of the profanation that occurs. Scandal given to other Catholics by such reception is another compelling reason for refusing it.

There is also a divine command that forbids giving the Eucharist to public grave sinners. Such a command is to be found in a number of places in the Scriptures. There are several Scriptural texts that command the expulsion of public grave sinners from the Christian community. We may take it that such expulsion includes refusal of the Eucharist. 1 Corinthians 5:1–6 refers to the expulsion of a man for an irregular marriage (to his father's wife). The chapter then generalizes this measure in verses 10 to 11, commanding the expulsion of a number of categories of public sinners, and concludes "Put away the evil one from among yourselves" (v. 13). 1 Timothy 1:20 refers to another such expulsion. 2 Thessalonians 3:6 states "And we charge you, brethren, in the name of our Lord Jesus Christ, that you withdraw yourselves from every brother walking disorderly, and not according to the tradition which they have received of us." These passages together constitute a clear Scriptural command to refuse the Eucharist to public sinners. This includes public adulterers such as the civilly divorced and remarried. Some obvious reasons can be suggested for this command; respect for the meaning and function of the Eucharist as the bond of union in Christ, the avoidance of the desecration of the Eucharist by a sacrilegious communion, and the prevention of the spiritual harm caused to those who make sacrilegious communions. To them may be added the grounds that *Familiaris Consortio* provides for the specific prohibition on giving the Eucharist to the civilly divorced and remarried.

There is a general moral issue at stake as well. The assumption behind the position of Pope Francis is that it is not reasonable to assert that there is situation where complete sexual continence can be demanded of Catholics. The teaching that Christians must accept that there are circumstances where complete sexual continence is required of them, and that they cannot refuse such continence under those circumstances if they wish to be saved, is plainly asserted in the Scriptures.

---

24   "La communion, faite en état de faute matérielle, est par elle-même un très grave sacrilège, puisque, objectivement parlant, il y a profanation du corps et du sang de Jésus-Christ": *DTC* III, "Communion eucharistique," col. 505.

It is essential to all Christian teaching on sexual activity. By rejecting it, Pope Francis makes a clean sweep of Christian sexual morality.

Pope Francis's position on the reception of the Eucharist is thus heretical on a number of counts. It should be noted that this position implements the heretical positions put forward in his response to the *dubia* of the five cardinals and in the apostolic letter *Ad Theologiam Promovendam*. The teaching of the Scriptures on this subject could not be clearer. Pope Francis flatly contradicts these Scriptural teachings, without troubling to offer any justifications or explanations for doing so. His theological method and his positions on Scripture and Tradition enable him to do this.

II. HERESY AS A PERSONAL SIN AND AS A PUBLIC CRIME

In order to clarify the nature of Pope Francis's heretical statements and the response that is due to them, it is necessary to elucidate the nature of heresy.

A heretic is a baptized person who accepts the divine authority of Christ as revealer of truths, but knowingly denies or actively believes to be doubtful one or more of the truths that Christ has revealed.[25] The truth in question must be one that has been proposed by the Church as divinely revealed and as demanding the assent of divine and catholic faith, and it must be known to be so proposed by the person who denies it. Heresy is not of course denial of a proposition that one believes to be divinely revealed; it is denial of a proposition that one knows to be proposed by the Catholic Church for belief as divinely revealed. If a Christian denies a divinely revealed truth that he does not know to be proposed by the Church as divinely revealed, he is not thereby a heretic, but only in error. The knowledge that the proposition being denied by the heretic is proposed by the Church as divinely revealed and as requiring the assent of faith is termed pertinacity. Pertinacity does not demand a long and obstinate rejection of the revealed truth, or a repeated rejection of monitions on the part of Church authority. As soon as the revealed truth that is denied is known to be authoritatively taught by the Church as divinely revealed, the denial of the truth is pertinacious and the sin of heresy is committed.

The theological virtue of faith requires that we both believe inwardly the truths of Divine Revelation and confess them outwardly to be true.[26] The personal sin of heresy can be committed purely by inward disbelief, with no outward denial of the truth that is rejected. In such a case, there are no public, legal consequences of heresy in the Church. The sin is between the heretic and God, and it is only subject to the judgment of the Church if it is mentioned in the sacrament of confession.

Public heresy involves outward rejection of a divinely revealed truth by a baptized person, and outward pertinacity in this rejection. Pertinacity is made public when the heretic makes it clear by some exterior manifestation that he

---

25 See St Thomas, *ST* II-II, Q. 11, art. 1.
26 Rom 10:9; St Thomas, *ST* I-II, QQ. 1-3.

knows that the proposition he is publicly denying is authoritatively taught by the Church as divinely revealed. Inner disbelief in the teaching is presumed if outward denial and pertinacity exist. Public heresy is a crime that by its nature separates the heretic from the Church. This is the teaching of the Scriptures.[27] Pius XII asserts this in *Mystici Corporis* 23: "Not every sin, however grave it may be, is such as of its own nature to sever a man from the Body of the Church, as does schism or heresy or apostasy." The Church has accordingly always punished heresy by excommunication. Such excommunication is a recognition of the separation caused by heresy, not simply a penalty whose existence is due to its imposition by ecclesiastical law.

The Church has employed various criteria to determine pertinacity in heresy. She has not required that in every instance, an individual must be warned to reject heresy one or more times before being found guilty of heresy. Cardinal de Lugo points this out:

> Neither is it always demanded in the external forum that there be a warning and a reprimand as described above for somebody to be punished as heretical and pertinacious, and such a requirement is by no means always admitted in practice by the Holy Office. For if it could be established in some other way, given that the doctrine is well known, given the kind of person involved, and given the other circumstances, that the accused could not have been unaware that his thesis was opposed to the Church, he would be considered as a heretic from this fact . . . The reason for this is clear: the exterior warning can serve only to ensure that someone who has erred understands the opposition which exists between his error and the teaching of the Church. If he knew the subject through books and conciliar definitions much better than he could know it by the declarations of someone admonishing him then there would be no reason to insist on a further warning for him to become pertinacious against the Church.[28]

Such warnings are mentioned in the Epistle to Titus, which requires that a person who rejects admonition one or two times be avoided (Tit 3:10-11). However, the epistle does not require that a person be admonished one or more times before avoiding him. These warnings are in some circumstances issued or required to be issued by ecclesiastical superiors out of pastoral solicitude for the person being warned, and as an effective way of verifying pertinacity in heresy. In the past, rejection of such warnings and perseverance in heresy after receiving them has been considered by the Church to be the crime of obdurate heresy, a crime that was considered to be graver than the crime of simple heresy and that had more severe penalties attached to it. What is universally required of evidence

---

27   See Mt 18:17; Mk 16:16; Gal 1:9; 2 Jn 10; 1 Tm 1:18-20; Gal 5:19-21; Jude 1; Tit 3:10-11; Heb 3:7-17; 2 Pet 2; Rev 22:18-19.

28   Cardinal Juan de Lugo, *Disputationes scholasticae et morales; de virtute fidei divina* (Lyon, 1546), disp. 20, sect. 5, nos. 157-58, p. 769.

of pertinacity for heresy is that it be public evidence that suffices to establish pertinacity beyond a reasonable doubt.

There is moral unanimity among canonists and theologians that a pope who is a public heretic can and must lose the papal office.[29] As Suárez states:

> It would be extremely harmful to the Church to have such a pastor and not be able to defend herself from such a grave danger; furthermore it would go against the dignity of the Church to oblige her to remain subject to a heretic Pontiff without being able to expel him from herself; for such as are the prince and the priest, so the people are accustomed to be.[30]

This unanimity also extends to the position that the pope cannot be deposed by the Church for heresy. Deposition is the act of a superior, and the pope has no superior on earth. The deposition of a pope for heresy cannot be the implementation of canon law on heresy. The pope is not subject to canon law as such, and in any case this law describes the actions to be taken by superiors judging inferiors. The juridical procedures prescribed by canon law for dealing with heretics therefore do not apply to the case of a heretical pope, except to the extent that they are independently required by natural justice and divine law. The divine law on heresy indicated in the Scriptures governs the situation of a heretical pope. There is disagreement among theologians about what action if any the Church must take to bring about the deposition of a heretical pope; no definite account of how a heretical pope must fall from office can be proposed as certainly correct.[31]

III. POPE FRANCIS'S PERTINACITY IN MAINTAINING HERESY

Pope Francis's pertinacity in maintaining the heresies is established by the following public facts.

(a) Expertise in Catholic theology counts as evidence of pertinacity when a Catholic publicly denies a divinely revealed truth. Pope Francis possesses this expertise. He completed the theological studies necessary for ordination, obtained a licentiate in philosophy and a licentiate in theology, and became a university professor in theology at the Facultades de Filosofía y Teología de San Miguel, a Jesuit university and seminary in Argentina. He subsequently became the Rector of these faculties.

---

29   See, e.g., Thomas de Vio Cajetan, *De comparatione auctoritatis papae et concilii cum Apologia eiusdem tractatus* (Rome: Angelicum, 1936); Melchior Cano, *De locis theologicis*, Bk. 6, ch. 8; Bañez, *In IIaIIae*, q. 1, a. 10; John of St Thomas, *Cursus theologici II-II, De auctoritate Summi Pontificis*, d. 8, ad 3, De depositione papae; Suárez, *De fide*, disp. 10; Bellarmine, *De Romano Pontifice*, Bk. 2; Billuart, *Cursus theologiae*, Pt. II-II; St Alphonsus Liguori, *Vindiciae pro suprema Pontificis potestate adversus Iustinum Febronium*; Charles Journet, *L'Église du Verbe incarné*, vol. 1: *L'hiérarchie apostolique* (Saint-Maurice: Éditions Saint-Augustin, 1998), 980–83.

30   Suárez, *Tractatus de fide divina*, disp. 10, sec. 6, §7, in *R. P. Francisci Suárez opera omnia* (Paris: Vivès, 1857), vol. 12, p. 317.

31   See chapters 9, 10, and 11.

(b) Pope Francis is the pope. Knowledge of the Catholic faith may be presumed in the pope. If this were not the case, it would be irrational to consider papal teaching of the Catholic faith as having authority and as being worthy of belief.

(c) Pope Francis has made many statements whose natural meaning is heretical, and has never withdrawn them or explained them in an orthodox sense even when asked to do so. These statements are documented in the Filial Correction, the Open Letter to the Bishops of the Catholic Church, and the Appeal to the Cardinals of the Catholic Church. This is evidence for his rejection of the duty to believe and profess the Catholic faith.

(d) Cardinals Brandmüller, Burke, Sandoval, Sarah, and Zen have the right and duty to advise the pope, in virtue of their membership of the Sacred College. The *dubia* they submitted to Pope Francis are official utterances made as part of the exercise of this right and duty. When they asked in their first dubium if "Divine Revelation is binding forever, immutable and therefore not to be contradicted, according to the dictum of the Second Vatican Council," they clearly indicated to Pope Francis that the Church teaches that Divine Revelation is immutable. The form of a dubium does not imply that the question being asked is in any way open to doubt; the question in a dubium can be asked in order to state established doctrine and obtain a restatement of it. The *dubia* of the cardinals were submitted to obtain such a restatement. They were a reminder and an assertion of Catholic teaching.

In response to being advised by the proper persons of the content of Catholic doctrine in this first dubium, Pope Francis clearly denied this doctrine. When given the opportunity to withdraw or correct this denial by the reformulated *dubia*, he refused to do so, and instead ordered that his original denial of the faith be made known to the entire Church through official publication by the Vatican.

(e) The apostolic letter *Ad Theologiam Promovendam* is an official document formally promulgated by the Holy See. Such documents are the result of careful preparation. They involve consultation with Vatican officials with expertise in theology, and are reviewed and discussed by the pope before being made public. It repeats the heresies found in the *dubia* of the five cardinals, which Pope Francis had responded to prior to issuing the apostolic letter. The content of the apostolic letter therefore represents and conveys Pope Francis's considered opinion. The whole message of the letter, not just some parts of it, is heretical; it is in fact a program for heresy.

The actions of the five cardinals and the response of Pope Francis mean that he has been officially advised of the doctrine of the Church, and that he has knowingly, publicly, and repeatedly denied that doctrine. This establishes beyond a reasonable doubt that he has repudiated the Catholic faith and is guilty of the public crime of heresy. There are no remotely credible grounds for denying this. Pope Francis is a public and notorious heretic through notoriety of fact.

IV. CONSEQUENCES OF POPE FRANCIS'S HERESY

The public crime of heresy committed by the pope is the worst form that this crime can take. This is because the pope has a greater responsibility to preserve and uphold the faith than anyone else, and because open heresy on the part of the pope causes more damage to the Church than heresy committed by any other person. The gravity of Pope Francis's crime means that Catholics should follow the directions of the Scriptures on the subject of heresy. They should recognize that Pope Francis has separated himself from the Church through his heresy and they should shun him as a heretic.

The following conclusions can also be drawn from the facts of the situation as described above;

• Because of the disagreements between theologians over the conditions required for a heretical pope to fall from office, it is not certain that Pope Francis has lost the papal office as a result of his heresy.

• It is defensible to assert that Pope Francis has lost the papal office because of his heresy.

• It is defensible to assert that Pope Francis can no longer exercise jurisdiction because of his status as a heretic. It seems repugnant to accept that a public heretic can exercise supreme jurisdiction over the Church.

• The faithful are not obliged to obey the commands or believe the assertions of Pope Francis, unless these commands and assertions can be known independently to be good and true. It would be imprudent of them to do so, however, because of his demonstrated heresy and hostility to the faith.

• The bishops and cardinals of the Church have a duty to act immediately to remove Pope Francis from the papacy, supposing that he still retains the office. In order to avoid doubt on the matter, they should take the steps that all the principal theologians who have treated of the question of a heretical pope would accept as sufficient for removal of such a pope from office. It is not likely that the bishops will carry out this duty; that does not affect the fact that the duty exists.

• Because of the difficulties involved in removing Pope Francis from office, and the scandal and damage to the Church that would result from it, the best solution would be for Pope Francis to resign the papacy. He should be insistently urged to do so by the cardinals and bishops.

I do not myself think that Pope Francis has ceased to be pope because of his heresy. I am not convinced by St Robert Bellarmine's claim that a pope automatically loses the papal office as a result of heresy. However, this position is indeed a serious one that is held by many theologians and canonists. Since Pope Francis's heresy is not in doubt, the position that he is no longer pope is also a serious one that cannot be dismissed.

The idea that the papal office is vacant as a result of its former occupant publicly embracing heresy is sometimes treated by Catholics as too horrifying to contemplate, and therefore as being impossible. It is not clear though why this possibility is more horrifying than the possibility of a heretical pope systematically using the papal office to attack the faith and the Church, which is what Pope Francis is now doing. There is no good reason in any case to suppose that disaster cannot happen to the Church. The priority is not to argue about the nature of the current disaster, but to do something about it. What needs to happen is for Pope Francis to cease to be pope, and for him to be replaced by a believing pope who can set to work to correct the damage he has done.

ANNEXE I

ELUCIDATION OF BIBLICAL AND MAGISTERIAL
TEXTS REJECTED BY POPE FRANCIS AS FALSE

> *Exodus 21:20-21.* When a man strikes his slave, male or female, with a rod and the slave dies under his hand, he shall be punished. But if the slave survives a day or two, he is not to be punished; for the slave is his money.

The punishment referred to in verse 21 is the punishment for murder, as appears from verse 20; so the meaning of the text is that the master will not be given the punishment for murder if his slave survives a day or two after being struck by his master. This is a standard legal principle in many legal codes — an injured person must die within a certain period of time after an injury for the person responsible for the injuries to be charged with murder. The text does not say that there are no consequences at all for a master who injures his slave. This is not the case, as appears from later verses of that chapter (vv. 26–27):

> When a man strikes the eye of his slave, male or female, and destroys it, he shall let the slave go free for the eye's sake. If he knocks out the tooth of his slave, male or female, he shall let the slave go free for the tooth's sake.

The Mosaic law differed from other legal codes of antiquity in giving rights to slaves, rather than conferring on masters the absolute right of life and death over the slave. The text of Exodus 21:20–21 is an indication of this.

～⌒～

> *1 Timothy 2:11-15.* Let a woman learn in silence with all submissiveness. I permit no woman to teach or to have authority over men; she is to keep silent. For Adam was formed first, then Eve; and Adam was not deceived, but the woman was deceived and became a transgressor. Yet woman will be saved through bearing children, if she continues in faith and love and holiness, with modesty.

The teaching in this verse refers to teaching the faith. This appears from the context of the epistle, which is addressed to Timothy, the leader of a local Christian church, and discusses the problem of false doctrines and false teachings in the Church. The prohibition of women teaching and having authority over men is thus a prohibition on women functioning as authoritative teachers, i.e., as priests. The assertion that women may not be ordained as priests is a magisterial teaching that all Catholics must accept. The New Testament does not rule out all prophesying by women, as the text of 1 Corinthians 11:5 cited below indicates. The text does not assert that women must bear children in order to be saved, as is apparent from other New Testament texts that recommend celibacy for the sake of the kingdom of God. The meaning of the statement that women will be saved through childbearing is not transparent. It is meant to be a contrast to Genesis 3:16, where Eve is told by God that she shall bear children in sorrow as a punishment for her sin. There is probably also a Marian reference in the text. There is no identifiable meaning of the text that is objectionable.

> *1 Corinthians 11:3-12.* But I want you to understand that the head of every man is Christ, the head of a woman is her husband, and the head of Christ is God. Any man who prays or prophesies with his head covered dishonors his head, but any woman who prays or prophesies with her head unveiled dishonors her head—it is the same as if her head were shaven. For if a woman will not veil herself, then she should cut off her hair; but if it is disgraceful for a woman to be shorn or shaven, let her wear a veil. For a man ought not to cover his head, since he is the image and glory of God; but woman is the glory of man. (For man was not made from woman, but woman from man. Neither was man created for woman, but woman for man.) That is why a woman ought to have a veil on her head, because of the angels.

The assertion that the husband is the head of the wife is made in other New Testament passages (Eph 5, Col 2). It is a part of Christian teaching that is directly connected by the New Testament to the mystery of Christ. It must not be understood as conferring a tyrannical authority on the husband, but it must be believed by Catholics in its proper sense. The assertion that the man is in the image and glory of God does not imply that women are not also made in the image of God (cf. Gen 1:27, "So God created man in his own image, in the image of God he created him; male and female he created them"). St Paul's apostolic authority gave him the right to command men to bare their heads during worship and to command women to cover their heads during worship. There is no reason for objecting to this disciplinary regulation. The reference to angels in verse 10 is obscure, but there are no grounds for objecting to it.

Bull Dum Diversas *of Pope Nicholas V.* The bull of Pope Nicholas V to which Pope Francis refers is not a magisterial teaching that requires assent, but a legal enactment that did not have the authority to require Catholics to agree to the truth or justice of its content.

ANNEXE II

TEXTS CONTAINING POPE FRANCIS'S
DENIALS OF CATHOLIC DOGMA

The texts that contain Pope Francis's denials of Catholic dogma are provided here in a more complete form for reference, together with other material that gives context for them.

POPE FRANCIS'S ANSWER TO THE *DUBIA* OF CARDINALS BRANDMÜLLER, BURKE, SANDOVAL, SARAH, AND ZEN

On July 10, 2023, Cardinals Brandmüller, Burke, Sandoval, Sarah, and Zen submitted a number of *dubia* to Pope Francis and to the prefect of the Dicastery for the Doctrine of the Faith. The first of these *dubia* was the following:

> 1. *Dubium about the claim that we should reinterpret Divine Revelation according to the cultural and anthropological changes in vogue.*
>
> After the statements of some bishops, which have been neither corrected nor retracted, it is asked whether in the Church Divine Revelation should be reinterpreted according to the cultural changes of our time and according to the new anthropological vision that these changes promote; or whether Divine Revelation is binding forever, immutable and therefore not to be contradicted, according to the dictum of the Second Vatican Council, that to God who reveals is due "the obedience of faith" (*Dei Verbum* 5); that what is revealed for the salvation of all must remain "in their entirety, throughout the ages" and alive, and be "transmitted to all generations" (7); and that the progress of understanding does not imply any change in the truth of things and words, because faith has been "handed on . . . once and for all" (8), and the Magisterium is not superior to the Word of God, but teaches only what has been handed on (10).

Pope Francis responded to these *dubia* in a letter of July 11, 2023 that was signed with his own hand. His response to the first dubium was as follows:

> (a) The answer depends on the meaning you give to the word "reinterpret." If it is understood as "interpret better," the expression is valid. In this sense, the Second Vatican Council affirmed that it is necessary that with the work of exegetes — and I would add of theologians — "the judgment of the Church may mature" (Second Vatican Council, Dogmatic Constitution *Dei Verbum*, 12).
>
> (b) Therefore, while it is true that the Divine Revelation is immutable and always binding, the Church must be humble and recognize that she never exhausts its unfathomable richness and needs to grow in her understanding.
>
> (c) Consequently, she also matures in her understanding of what she has herself affirmed in her Magisterium.

(d) Cultural changes and new challenges in history do not modify Revelation but can stimulate us to express certain aspects of its overflowing richness better, which always offers more.

(e) It is inevitable that this can lead to a better expression of some past statements of the Magisterium, and indeed, this has been the case throughout history.

(f) On the one hand, it is true that the Magisterium is not superior to the Word of God, but it is also true that both the texts of the Scripture and the testimonies of Tradition require interpretation in order to distinguish their perennial substance from cultural conditioning. This is evident, for example, in biblical texts (such as Exodus 21:20–21) and in some magisterial interventions that tolerated slavery (cf. Pope Nicholas V, Bull *Dum Diversas*, 1452). This is not a minor issue given its intimate connection with the perennial truth of the inalienable dignity of the human person. These texts need interpretation. The same applies to certain considerations in the New Testament regarding women (1 Corinthians 11:3–10; 1 Timothy 2:11–14) and other texts of Scripture and testimonies of Tradition that cannot be materially repeated today.

(g) It is important to emphasize that what cannot change is what has been revealed "for the salvation of all" (Second Vatican Council, Dogmatic Constitution *Dei Verbum*, 7). Therefore, the Church must constantly discern between what is essential for salvation and what is secondary or less directly connected with this goal. In this regard, I would like to recall what St Thomas Aquinas affirmed: "The more one descends to matters of detail, the more frequently we encounter defects" (*Summa Theologiae* I/II q. 94, art. 4).

(h) Finally, a single formulation of a truth can never be adequately understood if it is presented in isolation, detached from the rich and harmonious context of the entire Revelation. The "hierarchy of truths" also implies placing each of them in proper connection with the central truths and with the entirety of the Church's teaching. This can ultimately lead to different ways of presenting the same doctrine, even though "for those who long for a monolithic body of doctrine guarded by all and leaving no room for nuance, this might appear as undesirable and leading to confusion. But in fact such variety serves to bring out and develop different facets of the inexhaustible riches of the Gospel" (*Evangelii Gaudium*, no. 40). Every theological current has its risks, but also its opportunities.[32]

The cardinals reformulated their *dubia* and resubmitted them to Pope Francis on August 21, 2023. The first dubium was reformulated as follows:

> We therefore re-propose our questions to You, so that they can be answered with a simple "yes" or "no."

---

32 *Vatican News* translation at www.vaticannews.va/en/pope/news/2023-10/pope-francis-responds-to-dubia-of-five-cardinals.html.

Your Holiness insists that the Church can deepen its understanding
of the deposit of faith. This is indeed what *Dei Verbum* 8 teaches and
belongs to Catholic doctrine. Your response, however, does not capture
our concern. Many Christians, including pastors and theologians, argue
today that the cultural and anthropological changes of our time should
push the Church to teach the opposite of what it has always taught. This
concerns essential, not secondary, questions for our salvation, like the
confession of faith, subjective conditions for access to the sacraments,
and observance of the moral law. So we want to rephrase our *dubium*:
is it possible for the Church today to teach doctrines contrary to those
she has previously taught in matters of faith and morals, whether by
the pope *ex cathedra*, or in the definitions of an ecumenical council,
or in the ordinary universal magisterium of the bishops dispersed
throughout the world (cf. *Lumen Gentium* 25)?

This resubmission gave Pope Francis an opportunity to withdraw or correct
the statements he made in his response. Pope Francis did not respond to these
reformulated *dubia*. Instead, he made public his response to the original *dubia*.
This response was placed on the Vatican website on October 2, 2023. Cardinal Victor Manuel Fernández, the prefect of the Dicastery for the Doctrine
of the Faith, publicly reprimanded the cardinals for submitting reformulated
dubia rather than publishing Pope Francis's original response after receiving
it: "Instead of publishing those answers, they now make public new questions,
as if the pope were their slave for errands."[33] These steps indicate that Pope
Francis is firmly committed to the contents of his response to the *dubia*, and
chooses to make them public.

POPE FRANCIS'S ANSWER TO THE *DUBIA* OF CARDINAL DUKA

On September 25, 2023, the Dicastery for the Doctrine of the Faith responded
to *dubia* proposed by Cardinal Dominik Duka on July 13, 2023 regarding the
administration of the Eucharist to divorced couples living in a new union.

These *dubia* were prompted by debate over the meaning of a number of passages
in the apostolic exhortation *Amoris Laetitia*. The relevant passages are the following:

AL 298: The divorced who have entered a new union, for example,
can find themselves in a variety of situations, which should not be
pigeonholed or fit into overly rigid classifications leaving no room for a
suitable personal and pastoral discernment. One thing is a second union
consolidated over time, with new children, proven fidelity, generous
self-giving, Christian commitment, a consciousness of its irregularity
and of the great difficulty of going back without feeling in conscience
that one would fall into new sins. The Church acknowledges situations
"where, for serious reasons, such as the children's upbringing, a man

---

33   *Catholic News Agency* article, October 2, 2023, at www.catholicnewsagency.com/news/255540/
vatican-releases-pope-francis-responses-to-pre-synod-dubia-criticizes-cardinals.

and woman cannot satisfy the obligation to separate. [Footnote 329: In such situations, many people, knowing and accepting the possibility of living "as brothers and sisters" which the Church offers them, point out that if certain expressions of intimacy are lacking, "it often happens that faithfulness is endangered and the good of the children suffers."] There are also the cases of those who made every effort to save their first marriage and were unjustly abandoned, or of "those who have entered into a second union for the sake of the children's upbringing, and are sometimes subjectively certain in conscience that their previous and irreparably broken marriage had never been valid." Another thing is a new union arising from a recent divorce, with all the suffering and confusion which this entails for children and entire families, or the case of someone who has consistently failed in his obligations to the family. It must remain clear that this is not the ideal which the Gospel proposes for marriage and the family. The Synod Fathers stated that the discernment of pastors must always take place "by adequately distinguishing," with an approach which "carefully discerns situations." We know that no "easy recipes" exist.

AL 299: I am in agreement with the many Synod Fathers who observed that "the baptized who are divorced and civilly remarried need to be more fully integrated into Christian communities in the variety of ways possible, while avoiding any occasion of scandal. The logic of integration is the key to their pastoral care, a care which would allow them not only to realize that they belong to the Church as the body of Christ, but also to know that they can have a joyful and fruitful experience in it. They are baptized; they are brothers and sisters; the Holy Spirit pours into their hearts gifts and talents for the good of all. . . . Such persons need to feel not as excommunicated members of the Church, but instead as living members, able to live and grow in the Church and experience her as a mother who welcomes them always, who takes care of them with affection and encourages them along the path of life and the Gospel."

AL 300: Since "the degree of responsibility is not equal in all cases," the consequences or effects of a rule need not necessarily always be the same. [Footnote 336: This is also the case with regard to sacramental discipline, since discernment can recognize that in a particular situation no grave fault exists.]

AL 301: It is [sic] can no longer simply be said that all those in any "irregular" situation are living in a state of mortal sin and are deprived of sanctifying grace. More is involved here than mere ignorance of the rule. A subject may know full well the rule, yet have great difficulty in understanding "its inherent values, or be in a concrete situation which does not allow him or her to act differently and decide otherwise without further sin."

AL 303: Conscience can do more than recognize that a given situation does not correspond objectively to the overall demands of the Gospel. It can also recognize with sincerity and honesty what for now is the most generous response which can be given to God, and come to see with a certain moral security that it is what God himself is asking amid the concrete complexity of one's limits, while yet not fully the objective ideal.

AL 304: I earnestly ask that we always recall a teaching of Saint Thomas Aquinas and learn to incorporate it in our pastoral discernment: "Although there is necessity in the general principles, the more we descend to matters of detail, the more frequently we encounter defects . . . In matters of action, truth or practical rectitude is not the same for all, as to matters of detail, but only as to the general principles; and where there is the same rectitude in matters of detail, it is not equally known to all . . . The principle will be found to fail, according as we descend further into detail." It is true that general rules set forth a good which can never be disregarded or neglected, but in their formulation they cannot provide absolutely for all particular situations.

AL 305: Because of forms of conditioning and mitigating factors, it is possible that in an objective situation of sin—which may not be subjectively culpable, or fully such—a person can be living in God's grace, can love and can also grow in the life of grace and charity, while receiving the Church's help to this end. [Footnote 351: In certain cases, this can include the help of the sacraments. Hence, "I want to remind priests that the confessional must not be a torture chamber, but rather an encounter with the Lord's mercy." I would also point out that the Eucharist "is not a prize for the perfect, but a powerful medicine and nourishment for the weak."]

AL 308: I understand those who prefer a more rigorous pastoral care which leaves no room for confusion. But I sincerely believe that Jesus wants a Church attentive to the goodness which the Holy Spirit sows in the midst of human weakness, a Mother who, while clearly expressing her objective teaching, "always does what good she can, even if in the process, her shoes get soiled by the mud of the street."

These passages had already been the subject of *dubia* proposed to Pope Francis by Cardinals Burke, Brandmüller, Caffarra, and Meisner in 2016:

1. It is asked whether, following the affirmations of *Amoris Laetitia* (nn. 300–305), it has now become possible to grant absolution in the Sacrament of Penance and thus to admit to Holy Communion a person who, while bound by a valid marital bond, lives together with a different person *more uxorio* (in a marital way) without fulfilling the conditions provided for by *Familiaris Consortio* n. 84 and subsequently reaffirmed by *Reconciliatio et Paenitentia* n. 34 and *Sacramentum Caritatis*

n. 29. Can the expression "in certain cases" found in note 351 (n. 305) of the exhortation *Amoris Laetitia* be applied to divorced persons who are in a new union and who continue to live *more uxorio*?

2. After the publication of the Post-synodal Apostolic Exhortation *Amoris Laetitia* (cf. n. 304), does one still need to regard as valid the teaching of St John Paul II's Encyclical *Veritatis Splendor* n. 79, based on Sacred Scripture and on the Tradition of the Church, on the existence of absolute moral norms that prohibit intrinsically evil acts and that are binding without exceptions?

3. After *Amoris Laetitia* (n. 301) is it still possible to affirm that a person who habitually lives in contradiction to a commandment of God's law, as for instance the one that prohibits adultery (cf. Mt 19:3–9), finds him or herself in an objective situation of grave habitual sin (cf. Pontifical Council for Legislative Texts, Declaration, June 24, 2000)?

4. After the affirmations of *Amoris Laetitia* (n. 302) on "circumstances which mitigate moral responsibility," does one still need to regard as valid the teaching of St John Paul II's Encyclical *Veritatis Splendor* n. 81, based on Sacred Scripture and on the Tradition of the Church, according to which "circumstances or intentions can never transform an act intrinsically evil by virtue of its object into an act 'subjectively' good or defensible as a choice"?

5. After *Amoris Laetitia* (n. 303) does one still need to regard as valid the teaching of St John Paul II's encyclical *Veritatis Splendor* n. 56, based on Sacred Scripture and on the Tradition of the Church, that excludes a creative interpretation of the role of conscience and that emphasizes that conscience can never be authorized to legitimate exceptions to absolute moral norms that prohibit intrinsically evil acts by virtue of their object?

No response to these *dubia* was officially given by Pope Francis or any organ of the Roman Curia. Their content was however addressed in the response given by the Dicastery for the Doctrine of the Faith to the *dubia* proposed by Cardinal Duka. This response was officially endorsed by Pope Francis. It stated:

2. Can Pope Francis's response to the question from the pastoral section of the diocese of Buenos Aires, given that the text was published in the *Acta Apostolicae Sedis*, be considered an affirmation of the ordinary magisterium of the Church?

As indicated in the rescript accompanying the two documents in the *Acta Apostolicae Sedis*, these are published "velut magisterium authenticum," that is, as authentic magisterium (teaching).

3. Is it a decision of the ordinary magisterium of the Church based on the document *Amoris Laetitia*?

As the Holy Father recalls in his letters to the delegate of the pastoral region of Buenos Aires, *Amoris Laetitia* was the result of the work and prayer of the whole Church, with the mediation of two synods and the pope. This document is based on the magisterium of previous popes, who already recognized the possibility for divorced people in new unions to access the Eucharist, as long as they assume "the duty to live in complete continence, that is, by abstinence from the acts proper to married couples," as it was proposed by John Paul II, or "commit (themselves) to living their relationship . . . as friends," as proposed by Benedict XVI. Francis maintains the proposal of full continence for the divorced and remarried in a new union, but admits that there may be difficulties in practicing it and therefore allows in certain cases, after adequate discernment, the administration of the sacrament of reconciliation even when they fail to be faithful to the continence proposed by the Church.

9. Wouldn't it be appropriate for the entire issue to be explained better in the text of your competent dicastery?

Based on the words of the Holy Father in the letter of response to the delegate of the Buenos Aires pastoral region, in which it was stated that there are no other interpretations, it seems that the issue is sufficiently explained in the aforementioned document.

Pope Francis's letter to the pastoral region of Buenos Aires was a response to a statement issued by the bishops of the Buenos Aires region on September 5, 2016, on the application of the post-synodal apostolic exhortation *Amoris Laetitia*. The statement gave the following directions for the application of *Amoris Laetitia* (the number references are to that document's paragraphs):

6) In other, more complex cases, and when a declaration of nullity has not been obtained, the above mentioned option may not, in fact, be feasible. Nonetheless, a path of discernment is still possible. If it comes to be recognized that, in a specific case, there are limitations that mitigate responsibility and culpability (cf. 301–302), especially when a person believes they would incur a subsequent wrong by harming the children of the new union, *Amoris Laetitia* offers the possibility of access to the sacraments of Reconciliation and Eucharist (cf. footnotes 336 and 351). These sacraments, in turn, dispose the person to continue maturing and growing with the power of grace . . . .

9) It may be right for eventual access to sacraments to take place privately, especially where situations of conflict might arise. But at the same time, we have to accompany our communities in their growing understanding and welcome, without this implying creating confusion about the teaching of the Church on the indissoluble marriage. The community is an instrument of mercy, which is "unmerited, unconditional and gratuitous" (297).

10) Discernment is not closed, because it "is dynamic; it must remain ever open to new stages of growth and to new decisions which can enable the ideal to be more fully realized" (303), according to the "law of gradualness" (295) and with confidence in the help of grace.

Pope Francis wrote an official letter dated the same day to Bishop Sergio Alfredo Fenoy of San Miguel, a delegate of the Argentinian bishops' Buenos Aires region, stating that the bishops of the Buenos Aires region had given the only possible interpretation of *Amoris Laetitia*:

> Beloved brother,
> I received the document from the Buenos Aires Pastoral Region, "Basic Criteria for the Application of Chapter Eight of *Amoris Laetitia*." Thank you very much for sending it to me. I thank you for the work they have done on this: a true example of accompaniment for the priests . . . and we all know how necessary is this closeness of the bishop with his clergy and the clergy with the bishop. The neighbor "closest" to the bishop is the priest, and the commandment to love one's neighbor as one's self begins for us, the bishops, precisely with our priests. The document is very good and completely explains the meaning of chapter VIII of *Amoris Laetitia*. There are no other interpretations.

This letter to the bishops of Buenos Aires was then published in the *Acta Apostolicae Sedis* of October 2016, with a note saying that Pope Francis had ordered its publication together with that of the Buenos Aires statement as an act of the authentic magisterium. This note does not assert that the statements of *Amoris Laetitia* or of the Buenos Aires bishops themselves constitute part of the authentic magisterium; it states with magisterial authority that the Buenos Aires bishops' understanding of what Pope Francis meant to say in *Amoris Laetitia* is correct.

POPE FRANCIS'S APOSTOLIC LETTER *AD THEOLOGIAM PROMOVENDAM*

In the apostolic letter *Ad Theologiam Promovendam*, Pope Francis describes the nature, tasks and method of theology. The entire letter is important, but the following passages are particularly worthy of consideration:

> 4. Theological reflection is therefore called to a turning point, to a paradigm shift, to a "courageous cultural revolution" (Encyclical Letter *Laudato Si'* 114) that commits it, first and foremost, to be a fundamentally contextual theology, capable of reading and interpreting the Gospel in the conditions in which men and women daily live, in different geographical, social and cultural environments, and having as its archetype the Incarnation of the eternal Logos, its entering into the culture, worldview, and religious tradition of a people. From here, theology cannot but develop into a culture of dialogue and encounter between different traditions and different knowledge, between different Christian denominations and different religions, openly confronting everyone, believers and non-believers alike. . . .

> 5. This relational dimension connotes and defines, from the epistemic point of view, the status of theology, which is urged not to close itself in self-referentiality, which leads to isolation and insignificance, but to

grasp itself as embedded in a web of relationships, first and foremost
with other disciplines and other knowledge. This is the approach of
transdisciplinarity, that is, interdisciplinarity in a strong sense, as distinct from multidisciplinarity, understood as interdisciplinarity in a
weak sense. The latter certainly promotes a better understanding of the
object of study by considering it from multiple points of view, which
nevertheless remain complementary and separate. Instead, transdisciplinarity should be thought of "as the placement and fermentation
of all knowledge within the space of Light and Life offered by the
Wisdom that emanates from God's Revelation" (Apostolic Constitution
Veritatis Gaudium, Proem., 4c). Hence the arduous task for theology
to be able to make use of new categories elaborated by other knowl-
edges, in order to penetrate and communicate the truths of faith and
transmit the teaching of Jesus in today's languages, with originality
and critical awareness.

8. It is a matter of the pastoral "stamp" that theology as a whole,
and not only in one of its particular spheres, must assume: without
opposing theory and practice, theological reflection is urged to develop
using an inductive method, which starts from the different contexts
and concrete situations in which peoples are inserted, allowing itself
to be seriously challenged by reality, in order to become discernment
of the "signs of the times" in the proclamation of the salvific event
of God-*agape*, communicated in Jesus Christ. Therefore, it is necessary that the knowledge of people's common sense, which is in fact
a "locus theologicus" in which so many images of God dwell, often
not corresponding to the Christian face of God, only and always love,
be privileged first of all.

48

The Culture of Totalitarian Ultramontanism[1]

STUART CHESSMAN

B Y NOW, THE INCREASINGLY ERRATIC AND DESPOTIC acts and pronouncements of Pope Francis and his entourage are attracting greater and greater attention among Catholics. Even such stalwarts of the progressive Catholic establishment as Robert Mickens and Massimo Faggioli, and media outlets such as *katholisch.de* and *La Croix*, are now acknowledging these issues.[2] At the same time, there is a perception that we are in the last stages or the "endgame" of the Bergoglian papacy. It's appropriate to revisit a topic we had addressed a year and a half ago—in its broadest sense, the constitution and culture of the Roman Catholic Church. This consists of two elements. First, ultramontanism: the centralized power, teaching authority, and jurisdiction of the pope. Second, Vatican II's call to openness (really deference) to the world and renewal (really, revolution) within the Church.

In recent attempts to come to grips with the phenomenon of Francis, critical commentators turn to terms such as Peronism or dictatorship. These concepts are inadequate: they represent an unacknowledged attempt to divorce the phenomenon of Francis from the culture of the Church as a whole, reducing it to a personal quirk of the current incumbent of the See of Saint Peter. Francis did not elect himself pope. He rose to power based on support centered in Western Europe. Furthermore, these comparisons are politically inaccurate. In no way, for example, is Francis a figure like Mussolini, the early Hitler, or, of course, Juan Perón: a charismatic mob leader rising to power on the strength of a popular movement. The Francis phenomenon is totally different.

Similarly, it is misleading to focus on Francis's "Argentinian" culture. Undeniably, the personal heritage of each pope directly influences his style of government: Paul VI was an Italian curial functionary; John Paul II shared the thespian gifts of his countrymen; and Pope Benedict always remained a German academic bureaucrat. But these native influences hardly offer a complete interpretive key to their reigns.

Let us review the main features of Catholic institutional culture today to better understand this affair. I hope the reader accepts these critical remarks as

---

1   First published at the blog of The Society of St Hugh of Cluny, December 15, 2023.
2   E.g., Roland Juchem, "Papst Franziskus: Die Unruhe im Auge des Sturms," *katholisch.de*, December 12, 2023.

earlier generations regarded Antonio Rosmini's *On the Five Wounds of the Church* or even the much more forceful diatribes of the medieval writers on the defects of the clergy.

Centralized and unlimited papal authority. The Church is centralized in all respects. Pope Francis makes decisions without consulting anyone beyond his close associates and without giving notice. He directly intervenes at any level from the College of Cardinals to the ordinary parish. He has assumed the direct leadership of numerous functions, like the Diocese of Rome and the Dicastery for Evangelization. The rule of Francis is detached from any institutions within the Church. All Vatican functions have been remade into mouthpieces for Francis. Even the College of Cardinals no longer serves any real advisory role for Francis, but functions only as a means for rewarding friends and stacking the vote at the next conclave. Recently the pope has made the claim that his temporal power as head of the Vatican city-state is of divine origin — a claim last asserted before Vatican I.

"Formless despotism."[3] The culture of the Church of Francis is lawless and amorphous. Only the will of Francis counts. Francis expresses his will in forms ranging from offhand remarks to an endless series of interviews with the media to formal legislative decrees. He endorses decisions made by the Vatican offices reporting to him, and then disregards or rejects them himself. In areas like foreign policy or media relations, the pope works not only through the official Vatican institutions having responsibility for these matters but also on the side through his trusted associates. Under Francis, tradition, canon law, custom, and even the words of the Scriptures themselves have only relative value. Francis generally does not repudiate these authorities, but simply disregards them or renders them irrelevant. Legal procedures are either rendered meaningless or become totally chaotic (like the current Vatican trials of the perpetrators of failed financial investments). Most recently, in the area of theology, Francis has even formalized these characteristics (*Ad Theologiam Promovendam*).[4]

Bureaucracy. The bishops, priests, and lay employees of the Church have been assimilated into one bureaucracy. The Church had been reduced to this bureaucracy well before Francis, but the status of each member of the bureaucracy now potentially depends on his personal relationship with Francis, not on any official position or title. Loyalty to Francis is the defining criterion of a good cleric or even of a good Catholic. Bishops — there have been several very recent examples — are installed or removed in a completely arbitrary manner without any explanation or legal procedure.[5] Moreover, a whole population of bishops exists who serve only at the discretion of the pope: some have handed in their resignation and are waiting a papal decision on it; many others have surpassed the official age limits.

---

3   A concept of Oswald Spengler's.
4   See chapters 46 and 47.
5   See John Lamont, "On the Papal Deposition of Bishops," *Rorate Caeli*, December 18, 2023; Kwasniewski, *Bound by Truth*, 178–99.

A papal cult of personality. A clique of sycophants and a vast publicity apparatus praise the pope's every act and word. Francis is described as a reformer, a champion of the poor, a humble man, even as an existential philosopher. An already endless list of books by Francis or those lauding Francis continues to grow: Francis is now working on his autobiography. And the books are joined by cartoons, films, videos, and television programs. Francis is the center of gigantic Catholic events like World Youth Day. This campaign is not confined to the Vatican or to the official Catholic media. The pope's portrait is found in most churches—sometimes, as in St. Patrick's Cathedral, New York, provided with a fake halo. In many parish bulletins we encounter the face of Francis or a weekly message from Francis; his thought is constantly cited in Catholic academia and local diocesan events. Indeed, the Vatican media have expressed the wish that Francis and his message should be brought into the private home of every Catholic.

A climate of fear. Especially among those in the clerical ranks, a climate of fear has taken hold. In Rome and at the Vatican, courtiers dread attracting the attention of Francis or his watchdogs either because their opposition to him would be discovered or, paradoxically, they might attract his favorable attention. For the favor of Francis tends to be fleeting! But the climate of fear is not limited to the pope's immediate entourage. The entire Church is ever more strongly divided into friends and enemies of Francis. The latter are mocked, disciplined, and excluded from Church life. In the traditionalist world, for example, institutions, individuals, and parishes do not want reports written or photographs published lest they attract the notice of the local nuncio or the Vatican itself. Catholic traditionalists who have seen their Masses abolished or transferred to gymnasiums can testify to the reach of Francis and his agents.

Systemic dishonesty. Dishonesty dominates the discourse of the Catholic Church in all areas and at all levels. We saw this in the papal manipulation of synods in preparation of *Amoris Laetitia* and in the management of the (never disclosed) survey supposedly supporting *Traditionis Custodes*. We see this today in the manipulated synodal discussions up to and including the ongoing "Synod on Synodality" where the real objectives remain disguised and the main problems facing the Catholic Church are studiously avoided. The pope himself sets a personal example, routinely saying one thing and doing another—such as in his financial reform initiatives, his policies against clerical sexual abuse, his war on "clericalism," his advocacy of "synodal" governance—the list is endless. Once again, the culture of dishonesty is by no means limited to the highest levels of leadership in the Church; throughout the world, the official Catholic media are its leading practitioners and purveyors. In any given diocese anyone can verify this by comparing the public record of closed or merged school and parishes, declining ordinations, dissolving and declining religious orders, and never-ending financial and sexual scandals with the optimistic narrative to be found in the local Catholic media.

Ideology. This entire system, however, is not the mere underpinning of a personal dictatorship but serves an ideology—that of Vatican II, reduced to a few basic beliefs. This ideology's principles are clear, however crudely Francis expresses them: Vatican II and the accompanying liturgical changes are the will of the Holy Spirit, so those who oppose or even question them are opposing God. One cannot go back but must go forward. All are welcome in the Church "as they are." Indeed, Aldo Maria Valli and Aurelio Porfiri have written an entire book on the now-dominant platitudes of the pope and the Catholic Church:

• Dialogue	• Fragility
• Listening	• Mercy
• Pastoral	• Ecumenism
• Accompaniment	• Discernment
• Synodality	• Diversity
• Bridges	• Peripheries

Often this doublespeak has a meaning totally different from its normal sense in the language.[6]

Remoteness from reality. The Church leadership inhabits a world distant from the lives of ordinary lay Catholics (and of much of the lower clergy as well), as we see with the current "Synod on Synodality," where the papacy, episcopacy, and Church bureaucracy seem to lack any contact with historical, political, or sociological reality. This isolation is evident in recent news reports of the views of cardinals allegedly "papabile" in the next conclave. Moreover, a pervasive lack of accountability applies within the Church. Only where the mainstream secular media become involved—such as in issues involving sexual abuse—do the higher clergy face any consequences for their bad judgment or even criminality.

The regime I have described above is no mere autocracy or dictatorship. It is a genuine form of *totalitarianism*, a culture which informs the entire body of the Church. The most obvious comparison in the recent past was the Soviet Union. The constant repetition of meaningless official clichés, the systemic dishonesty, and a certain element of fear are indeed reminiscent of the last decades of the life of the Soviet Union and its satellites.

Even though that specific regime has disappeared, a more recent secular role model has emerged: the United States, Western Europe, and their dependencies in their current "woke" phase. Here, in the last fifteen years or so, a unity among news media, government, think tanks, universities, businesses, scientific-medical institutions, and even internal security forces has consolidated its power under the banner of the woke ideology. The Roman Catholic Church of the last decades has been assimilating more and more closely to the secular world around it. Indeed, in many respects the Roman Catholic Church resembles the subordinate educational

---

6   Aldo Maria Valli and Aurelio Porfiri, *Decadenza: Le parole d'ordine della Chiesa postconciliare* (Hong Kong: Chorabooks, 2020).

institutions of the secular establishment, like universities and school districts. Here too we find the same mix of exploding bureaucracy, restricted speech and thought, ideological conformity, fear, and, similar to the Catholic Church, an ongoing and increasing failure to achieve the stated purposes of the institution. (Such secular educational "fiefdoms" typically lack, however, a "pope" — an omnipotent leader exercising centralized charismatic rule.)

THE SOURCES

What are the origins of the current system? We have previously treated the ultramontane doctrines of Vatican I, relentlessly expanded over subsequent decades.[7] But equally important is Vatican II. For it was Vatican II that introduced into the Church a fierce ideological element. For the first time, the Church bureaucracy — up to the 1960s, overwhelmingly the clergy and religious — was inspired to repudiate Catholic tradition in liturgy, theology, and morality in favor of, in the best case, a somewhat uncertain core of Catholicism. Vatican II gave the ultramontane system a purpose and direction beyond that of merely defending the institution against adversaries and maintaining tight clerical control.

The best evidence of the importance of both Councils is the role of the Jesuit order. Jesuits were of decisive importance in the birth of ultramontanism in the years leading up to 1870 (e.g., the editors of *Civiltà Cattolica*; Joseph Kleutgen, SJ). The Jesuit order, of course, also advanced the most aggressive interpretations of Vatican II from the very beginning of that council. Pope Francis is a product of this order. Today, he relies on the Society of Jesus and publicly favors it and its institutions. He has appointed many of his confreres to leading positions in the Church. In turn, Jesuits play a key role as advocates of the agenda of Francis.

Yet two other influences within the Church need to be considered. First, the transformation of the Church into a bureaucracy after 1870 would have far-reaching effects on the faith. The attitude of a bureaucrat, especially a government bureaucrat, is decisively different from that of an apostle. As the church approximated more and more to a secular bureaucracy, its leaders (consciously or not, as the case may be) adopted attitudes and limitations resembling those of functionaries in the various governmental, academic, and economic bureaucracies of the modern age. Indeed, the basic division in the Church is no longer between clergy and laity, but between the Church bureaucracy (including, bishops, clergy, religious, and lay employees, both men and women) — and everyone else. This bureaucracy has supported the progressive agenda with remarkable unanimity since the 1960s. It is currently spearheading the "Synodal Path" in Germany (where it is strongest and best financed) and, more generally, the "Synod on Synodality" throughout the Catholic world.

---

7   See especially chapters 19 and 37.

Second, the novel Catholic institution of the "movement" emerged, starting even before the Second World War. Despite their bewildering diversity in membership requirements, organization, and objectives (compare two early examples: Opus Dei and the Catholic Worker!), the movements all rested on similar foundations: irrational loyalty and absolute obedience to a "visionary" founder, a degree of separation from mainstream Catholic life, formulas for addressing alleged economic and spiritual failures of the Church, and, usually, a blurring of the traditional roles of clergy and laity. Often the movement would establish a direct relationship with the Vatican.

What had been a fringe phenomenon before Vatican II subsequently acquired a growing influence over the Church, especially under Pope John Paul II. The number of movements grew even though their absolute membership remained small. They departed from, or even challenged, the ordinary Catholic life of the clergy and laity, yet reinforced both the centralized absolute papacy and Vatican II (e.g., devotion and obedience to a charismatic leader having absolute authority, an emotional and irrational culture, and, often, arbitrary liturgical and devotional practices). Pope Francis generally has not shared Pope John Paul II's enthusiasm for the movements — except for certain communities aligned with his objectives, like Sant'Egidio or, at least until recently, the Neocatechumenal Way. But the pope's leadership style with its accompanying cult of personality is very much like that of a movement founder.

THE LIMITS OF TOTALITARIAN ULTRAMONTANISM

We have labeled the current culture of the Catholic Church as totalitarian. Yet the limits to ecclesiastical totalitarianism are great indeed. These divergences from the secular model mean that the Roman Catholic Church is totalitarian only in an analogous, or qualified, sense. It is a "soft totalitarianism."

Above all, Pope Francis depends on the goodwill of the secular world and its media. This is the key to his entire regime. It was a series of conflicts with the media that motivated forces within the Church to work for Pope Benedict's departure and his replacement with someone more accommodating to the world. Now, in the person of Pope Francis, the media obtained a pope who has worked to implement within the Church their vision of the world. And the media have here succeeded beyond their wildest dreams. For Francis has in large part transformed the Catholic Church from an obstacle or even an adversary to the secular agenda, to an active cooperator with the Western establishment. At each stage of his papacy, Francis has enjoyed the support of the media, either by their adulation of "the reformer, the humble man, the visionary" — or by their studied suppression of adverse news. Let's not forget that the overwhelming majority of the laity — and of the clergy as well — derive their knowledge of Church affairs from the mainstream secular media. The media's (both secular and Catholic) attitude has been described for us with remarkable frankness by

John Allen. He had written previously of the role of the media in building up "progressive" heroes (referring specifically to Cardinal McCarrick) and, more recently, has pointed out that many journalists today see Francis "as a moral hero, a champion of the underdog."[8]

Now this relationship has not been necessarily untroubled—at times, Francis has strayed from the party line. Witness his initial reluctance to condemn Russia in the Ukrainian crisis, or to express unqualified support for Israel, or his clumsy attempt to rehabilitate Fr Marko Rupnik, SJ. In these cases, Francis and the Vatican either capitulated or "clarified" their language quickly after the media called them on the carpet.

Francis's dependence on the clerical bureaucracy is equally strong. By 2023, of course, the "clerical" bureaucracy in chanceries, schools, and universities consists mainly of lay employees. They tend to be imbued with the revolutionary spirit of the 1960s. Their loyalty is thus not primarily to Francis personally, but to the progressive values they share with him. Francis has been very careful to avoid a confrontation with these forces—his handling of the German synodal path is evidence of that. At times he has felt the need to restrain them. But the Germans are by no means willing to defer to Francis and "go slow" with their agenda. This is particularly so because the warnings of the pope and various Vatican functionaries are obviously only tactical in nature.

There is also the resistance of those bishops who are not at all active participants in the Francis regime. This is not because of any deep ideological convictions, but because they dread being forced into confrontations with organizations, such as those of the traditionalists, or more generally with their own laity. It's clear that, because of this silent resistance, the major policy initiatives of Francis, such as divorce, LGBT acceptance in the Church, and the war on traditionalism, have only been imperfectly transformed into action. Going beyond the mere dragging of feet, there has undoubtedly been a more active, behind-the-scenes opposition to Francis's policies.

Finally, outside of this entire clerical, bureaucratic structure is the realm of the laity—those of the laity *not* in the employ of the Church, that is. Theologically speaking, of course, they form part of the Church, indeed, overwhelmingly the largest part. In most places the majority has ceased practicing the faith; those that remain are largely silent. The laity provides continuing financial support for the Church—paying taxes in Germany, making donations in the United States. They serve as extras at Church functions and events (like World Youth Days or Eucharistic conferences). Yet they have no role in the governance of the Church. They may see their parishes and schools summarily closed or merged without warning. In the case of the traditionalists, they will even be banished from churches and publicly denounced by the pope and the bishops. Archbishop

---

8 John L. Allen, "Pope Francis and the Sharron Angle Strategy of Media Relations," *Crux*, November 5, 2023.

Wilton Gregory of Washington, for example, recently denied to the laity the capacity of coming to any informed opinion about the liturgy.[9] Incoming Archbishop Coyne of Hartford, Connecticut, placed the blame for the decline of Catholic life in the Archdiocese squarely on the laity.[10]

To summarize, many bishops, an even greater percentage of the lower clergy, and a percentage of the laity greater still, while by no stretch of the imagination active opponents of the Bergoglian regime, are also not actively advancing it. Francis thus by no means has obtained that total freedom from any control, including that of his own party and ideology, that was achieved by Stalin or Hitler. This reflects the declining influence of the papacy. Pope Francis may assert the boldest ultramontane claims, but in fact he can no longer draw on the absolute obedience and indeed the willingness to go beyond the letter of the law that characterized the implementation of the "spirit of Vatican II" by Paul VI the 1960s.

FURTHER REFLECTIONS

Throughout the last ten years the level of practice and knowledge of the faith among the laity, the number of vocations, and the number of Catholic institutions (schools, parishes, etc.) have dramatically declined. The Catholic laity is a "resource" that steadily diminishes each year. In that regard, the submission of the Church to the COVID restrictions was utterly disastrous in accelerating this decline in the active presence of the lay faithful in the Church. The Church establishment regards these facts with indifference. If we consider that the main objectives of the currently-ruling Catholic establishment are the retention of power over the Church and conformity to the world's ideology of progress and change, this is understandable—whether anything remains in the Church other than the rulers themselves is irrelevant to them.

But this, viewed in purely secular terms, is the Achilles' heel of the institutional Church. The entire continued existence of the Catholic Church depends on the freely-chosen faith of the laity. Without it, there are no more congregations, no more vocations—and no more money. Nowhere in the Catholic Church, not even in Poland, can major secular benefits be obtained by practicing the Catholic faith. There are no significant positions or benefices available to those seeking a professional career in the Church. Thus, the steady diminution in the practice of the faith among the laity inevitably will lead to a crisis of the institution.

What of the conservatives? Bergoglio's war ultimately is directed not just against liturgical traditionalists but against the entirety of Catholic tradition in

---

9   For a discussion, see my article "Cardinal Gregory Explains," blog of The Society of St. Hugh of Cluny, December 10, 2023.

10   Daniel Payne, "Connecticut archbishop calls for female deacons, moving Vatican out of Rome," *Catholic News Agency*, November 22, 2023.

liturgy, theology, philosophy, and morality.[11] The only exception is what can be tolerated as folklore, like certain Marian cults. In the past, the conservative Catholics were the most vocal defenders of papal authority; now they find themselves with a pope who is not only *not* a leader, but a real adversary. Generally speaking, with the exception of some noisy apologists of low mental wattage, these forces tend to fall silent on the subject of the papacy.

Some conservative institutions, such as the Institute for Human Ecology at Catholic University or its counterpart at Notre Dame, the Center for Ethics and Culture, continue to talk of "the intellectual heritage of Catholicism" and how it can save the world. According to them, Catholicism has given rise to ideas and insights that, if implemented, would make possible a healthier secular society. The same can be said for the integralist movement (which is otherwise viewed as an adversary by most of the conservatives). But the best evidence of Catholicism is not what was written or preached in the past about distributism, subsidiarity, or justice. It is not past philosophical reflection on the relationship of Church and State. It is the actual practice of Catholicism at *this* moment, the culture of the Catholic Church that is lived every day. And the governing culture of the Catholic Church today—which I have sought to outline above—in no way can serve as a model for the secular world.

Let's remember that it was under the medieval papacy that the whole concept of the rule of law was resurrected in the West; that universities were established; that natural science experienced its beginnings. In the Middle Ages, parliamentary or representative government and the nation-state had their origins. The current state of the Catholic Church forms a terrible contrast with those prior ages.

Catholics in the United States, when confronted with dire problems, always ask what can be done. Examining the perfection of the ultramontane system, an impartial observer's frank reaction would be: *nothing*. A Catholic should not be so pessimistic. But he should be prepared to admit the need to revise the definitions of papal power to clarify that it must always be exercised within the tradition of the Church. This would return the papacy to its role as the defender of the tradition and doctrine of the Catholic faith, not as their creator. That would also allow authentic dialogue with the Orthodox, the form of ecumenism that really makes sense. The Orthodox have retained elements of tradition—such as their liturgy and art, and the priority accorded contemplative spirituality—which should be of critical importance to a recovery of the Western Church.

Is this possible? Indeed it is—but only with the aid of some event or situation that would shake up the current regime of the Catholic Church and redirect the

---

11   See Fr Serafino Lanzetta's *"Super Hanc Petram": The Pope and the Church at a Dramatic Moment in History* for a pithy account of the concrete ways in which Francis is undermining each of these areas of Catholicism.

attentions of the clergy from worldly goals to the defense and propagation of the Faith. Before that occurs, prayer and the dedication to the totality of Catholic tradition—in liturgy, theology, and morality—are required of each individual Catholic. At the time of Vatican II, did not various thinkers speculate about an apocalyptic collapse of the institutional Church that would lead to the rebirth of some kind of smaller, purer institution?[12] Can it be that this will in fact occur—but in a way that those progressives could not have imagined? For are not the "purer" forces, alive and active in the Church today, the traditionalists and the conservatives?

---

12   See, e.g., "'Is it really a Phoenix?' Ida Görres and the Collapse of German Catholicism, Part II," blog of The Society of St. Hugh of Cluny, March 30, 2020.

49

The Pontiff's New Clothes[1]

CHARLES A. COULOMBE

Accipe tiaram tribus coronis ornatam, et scias te esse patrem principum et regum, rectorem orbis in terra, vicarium Salvatoris nostri Jesu Christi, cui est honor et gloria in saecula saeculorum.

(Receive the tiara adorned with three crowns and know that you are the father of princes and kings, the ruler of the world, the vicar of our Savior Jesus Christ on earth, to whom be all honor and glory, world without end.)
— Prayer at the traditional Papal Coronation

IN THE PAST FEW WEEKS, THE WORLD HAS BEEN "treated" (if that is the right word) to the spectacle of the Holy Father ordering the deposition of a bishop in an extracanonical manner and ordering the stripping of a cardinal of his stipend and flat in Rome because he is an "enemy."[2] In a pontificate that has seemed to many to be powered more by personal prejudices and the settling of scores than by a concern for the salvation of souls, coupled with the Supreme Pontiff's hardline defense of associates of questionable morals, this sort of pettiness and legal irregularity has been compared unfavorably with such papal low points as the pornocracy of the tenth century.

Without wanting to enter into that particular argument at the moment, this author will contend that the Church's current leadership dilemma owes its origin to a development that, although symptomatic of a greater problem, was positively hailed when it first appeared in the 1960s: the transformation of the papal monarchy into a republic. The irony is that the Ultramontanism originally advanced to defend that papal monarchy became itself the chief means by which this development was imposed.

The major difference between the Christian monarchy of yore and the liberal republic of the present may be found in the difference between two key elements of governance: authority and power. The former is the right to say what ought to happen; the latter is the ability to make it so.[3] My doctor has the authority to prescribe medicine, but only I have the power to actually take it. In the Christian ideal — as described by the writings and examples of the Church Fathers, the

---

1 First published at *The European Conservative* website on December 30, 2023.
2 Referring to Bishop Strickland and Cardinal Burke. — *Ed.*
3 For a different account of this distinction, see chapter 6. — *Ed.*

Ecumenical Councils, and countless sovereigns, popes, and theologians—the union of the Davidic Kingship inherited by Christ and the *Communio* of the Church He established at the Last Supper meant that, henceforth, Christian monarchy would be a participation in His Kingship. Legitimacy and authority would be bestowed by Him through the Church upon the various sovereigns: popes crowning emperors; emperors convoking ecumenical councils; emperors and kings serving in set liturgical roles at papal Masses and acting as canons of Roman basilicas (and at select churches in their own countries); the role of the pope as sovereign of the Papal States—indeed, the whole panoply of Church and State that arose as a result (regularly attacked since the beginning of the Age of Revolution as corrupting to both) was extremely fruitful to both, despite disputes of the sort that are inevitable in human relations. Not least was this true in terms of the production of saints in every stratum of society, from kings to peasants. Later, when Europe expanded overseas, millions of souls were brought salvation by the united efforts of Church and State.

The role of authority as wielded by the heads of Church and State was indispensable in guiding empowered clergy and laity to use their offices for the end to which God had committed both power and authority to men: the common good. In earlier times, there was no confusion about the definition of the common good; for the Church, it meant the salvation of individual souls; for the State, it meant assisting the Church in this area by ensuring sufficient security and well-being so that people would be able to worry about their souls rather than their safety and sustenance.

Authority being concentrated and power diffused, a good leader was like an orchestra conductor; bad leaders produced, as a rule, not tyranny but anarchy. It was a maxim of both moral theology and historical experience that either authority or power exercised for the mere benefit of the wielder would inevitably come to a bad end. Human law was a noble thing, but only if it was in accord with justice—that is, God's law.

After the rise of liberal republics in the late eighteenth century (and earlier in the Three Kingdoms of the British Isles), this entire schema was altered. Rather than being in the hands of God via the Church, authority was held to reside in the "people," whose will would be explained to them and wielded on their behalf by the nascent political class. These worthies, in turn, would be the satellites of the leading (and contending) economic and social interests in the State. From this reality emerged the party system. Whether in a constitutional monarchy (where the sovereign, despite having his hands effectively tied behind his back, nevertheless served as a focus of popular loyalty above political faction) or in a complete republic (where all offices, including the highest, were available to the most effective politico), power became increasingly divorced from authority as authority became increasingly obscured and enfeebled. As a result, power became ever more sought for its own sake, and the whole notion of the "common good" was submerged beneath the ever more shrill demands of party loyalty. Moreover, what remained of the common good became ever more secular in nature. It simply became the ability of supporters of the dominant party to do whatever they wished — preferably at the expense of their opponents.

As regards the Church and the Papacy, and as witnessed by the Gelasian canon and the Codes of Theodosius and Justinian, pope and emperor — theoretically, at least — worked as partners in the ultimate rank of governance, under Christ Himself, of the *Res publica Christiana*. This system was always subject to stresses and strains, but even so great a Ghibelline as Dante recognized the spiritual superiority of the pope, and even such a deep-dyed Guelph as Innocent III accepted the necessity of the role of the emperor. So it was that the two were both monarchies, albeit of different sorts.

Despite the disruption of this system by the Protestant Revolt, the overthrow of monarchies, and the end of both the Byzantine Empire by the Turks and the Holy Roman Empire by Napoleon, the monarchical aspect of the Holy See survived. Even the loss of the Papal States did not affect it immediately in that sense because, at the same time, the pope became, as it were, the immediate Father of a body of faithful who were persecuted or harassed in very many countries around the globe. But in what sense was that monarchy comparable to the ones we know around the globe even to-day?

Symbolism is an important factor in any monarchy; for the Holy See, there was none so omnipresent as the papal tiara — the triple crown. Descending from the regular bishop's miter, it acquired the first crown when the popes became temporal rulers. The second made its appearance in the thirteenth century to show the superiority of the papal crown to mere earthly crowns. At the beginning of the fourteenth century, the third made its appearance. Unlike so many imperial and royal crowns, there was no single specimen of this diadem; twenty-two such tiaras survive to-day. From the Middle Ages on, the triple crown was the principal heraldic symbol of the Holy See and could be found anywhere in the papal dominions in Italy and the South of France.

The tiara was bestowed upon successive popes at a coronation rite, with the words that opened this article. Impressive as they were, however, this placing of the tiara and assurance of the wearer's power was immediately followed by a Capuchin friar burning a brand before the new pope, then extinguishing it with the words, "Thus passes the glory of this world" — of which the fledgling pontiff had just been assured he was spiritual ruler. Indeed, as with last year's coronation rite of Charles III, everything about the ceremony was intended to exalt the office above its recipient, and to remind the recipient of his solemn duty to use his office wisely.

Indeed, for centuries, the papal court was as rigorously hedged about with ceremony as any in Europe. As with his secular monarchical children, the pope was expected to subordinate his personal preferences to an endless round of rituals, which were intended to force him to subject himself to the awe-full role God had laid upon him. In addition to the clerics with whom each pope ran the Church, there were laymen who helped him administer and defend the Papal States. There was the Roman nobility, who saw him as their feudal lord, and the soldiers who served in his army, as well as the lay members of his court. Even after the loss of the Papal States ended the adventures of the Papal Zouaves, who had come from all over the Catholic world to fight for Bl. Pius IX, there were still quite a few laity to be found at the papal court. Those Roman nobility who gave up all hope of social, political, or financial betterment in order to remain loyal to the popes — the so-called "Black" nobility — would later be rewarded with Vatican citizenship after the 1929 Lateran Treaty. In the meantime, and after, they filled the ranks of the Noble Guard and the hereditary positions at the papal court. There were various kinds of lay staff, including the Swiss Guards and the papal chamberlains, in their Renaissance garb.

The late nineteenth and early twentieth centuries saw some truly colorful characters serve in the ranks of the latter body: the Norwegian convert Baron Wilhelm Wedel-Jarlsberg; his fellow countryman and convert, Christopher de Paus; Charles Owen O'Conor, heir to the High Kings of Ireland; Old Oxonian and Newman Society founder Hartwell de la Garde Grissell; and the American diplomat and friend of Empress Zita, Francis Augustus MacNutt. There was also the papal nobility — created by popes in recent times — as opposed to the ancient Roman aristocracy. Even Americans received the honor, such as Duke Nicholas Frederic Brady, Countess Estelle Doheny, and Count John Crimmins.

The fall of the monarchies resulting from the two World Wars and various revolutions caused this aspect of the Holy See to look antiquated to churchmen who had converted to the cult of progress. Bound up with this was a sort of unconscious political Manichaeism, about which this author has written else-where.[4] In turn, the pontificate of Paul VI and the aftermath of Vatican II saw a desire to "update" every aspect of Catholic life. In an atmosphere where the Mass itself — the very heart of the Catholic Faith — was up for alteration according to the playful attitudes of self-described experts, it could not be supposed that the lay element of the papal court and its hallowed disciplines could or would be spared. The loyal Black nobility lost its Vatican citizenship, and most lay offices — including the Noble Guards, the Palatine Guards of Honor, and most hereditary positions — were abolished. The chamberlains, *sediari pontifici*, *bussolanti*, and other such groups were stripped of their costumes and transformed into the white-tied gentlemen of His Holiness.

Even as the liturgical life of the Church would become a matter of clerical whim, so too would the ceremonial life of the Holy See become more clericalized. But it also became ever more of a sort of clerical republic. Although Catholic

---

4   See my article "Vatican II and the Political Manichees," *Crisis Magazine*, June 26, 2023.

monarchs are circumscribed by tradition and law, republican leaders seldom are, preferring to enact whatever pops into their heads regardless of precedent or even true utility. John Paul I, when made Patriarch of Venice, did away with the traditional entrance by gondola and likewise replaced the papal coronation with a presidential-style inauguration, which has been the case ever since. Pope Benedict eliminated the tiara from his personal heraldry while retaining it in general, but he abandoned the age-old title of "Patriarch of the West" — a move that predictably annoyed the Eastern Orthodox, the five oldest patriarchates of which predicate their relationship with the pope upon this position. That said, he did restore several papal articles of clothing, understanding that it was and is the office of the papacy that the faithful really need, rather than the elevation of the office-holder's own personality.

So it is that we find ourselves in the current pontificate, which — its critics assert — has become an entirely authority-free zone, where power is exercised in a petty and arbitrary manner reminiscent of a banana republic. Pope Francis's jettisoning of the title of "Vicar of Christ" is seen by such critics as the pontiff's refusal to play second fiddle to anyone, no matter how exalted. He is seen as having the same relationship with the salvation of souls as most recent American presidents have had with their country's constitution. No matter how harsh such judgements may be, it is up to the current leadership in the Holy See to deprive them of any grain of truth they may have. If the Vicar of Christ is anything, he is not the representative of some kind of supernatural president but rather of the King of Kings. For to forget is to invite disaster, such as those that have occasioned the unfortunate times when ecclesiastical and political figures alike have forgotten the awesome responsibility of the Supreme Pontiff.

50

If It Depended on Genius, This Office Would Be Madness

MARTIN MOSEBACH & THOMAS STERNBERG

In 2019, Herder Korrespondenz published the following "polemical discourse." [1] *Lucas Wiegelmann is the interviewer. Thomas Sternberg is a politician and a quintessential member of the establishment of the German Catholic Church: he is president of the (lay) Central Committee of German Catholics, which is at the forefront of the current "Synodal Path" agitation. I assume our readers know who Martin Mosebach is. — Ed.*

T O BE "THE VICAR OF CHRIST"? FUNDAMENTALLY THE inconceivable is expected from the successors of Peter. The president of the Central Committee of German Catholics, Thomas Sternberg, and the author Martin Mosebach discuss whether God has wanted the way Francis has handled things so far and how the papacy will develop.

LUCAS WIEGELMANN: Mr. Mosebach, Professor Sternberg—when you meet the pope how do you conduct yourself?

MARTIN MOSEBACH: I bend the left knee and kiss his ring. Then I wait for the pope to address me. The only pope whom I have met so far was Benedict XVI. For me it was surprising: he mentioned my address on receiving the Büchner prize, had obviously read it, and quoted from it. Like a true monarch, he was prepared for my visit.

THOMAS STERNBERG: I have had the opportunity several times to speak with Pope Francis. I shook his hand and greeted him in our first meeting. I tried to explain to him quickly, in Italian, what organization I represented, what I did there, etc. But this didn't particularly interest him. That evening an authority on the curia explained that for this pope, there's a rule of thumb. The more ties and titles a visitor displays, the more uninteresting the pope finds him. So, in the next encounter with him, I just said in German: "Thanks for *Amoris Laetitia*." Then he beamed at me in a friendly and happy way.

WIEGELMANN: Among the peculiarities of the papal office is that the first man to occupy it never could have heard anything about it—I'm referring to the Apostle Peter, and also to many of his legendary first successors. The papacy arose only gradually, in the course of centuries. Did God want this office, or could things have taken a totally different path?

---

1   "Käme es auf Genie an, wäre dies Amt ein Irrsinn," *Herder Korrespondenz Spezial* 1/2019. Published here with permission of *Herder Korrespondenz*.

MOSEBACH: But of course, Peter had heard about it—from Our Lord Himself! "And I will give unto thee the keys of the kingdom of heaven, and whatsoever thou shalt bind on earth shall be bound in heaven, and whatsoever thou shalt loose on earth shall be loosed in heaven" (Mt 16:19). By the way, these words allude to the Old Testament. There, using an almost identical formulation, a man called Eliakim is appointed the treasurer of the king. "And the key of the house of David will I lay upon his shoulder: so, he shall open, and none shall shut: and he shall shut and none shall open" (Is 22:22). The entrusting [of the Church] to Peter thus stands in the spirit of Jewish tradition. As a Catholic, I have an untroubled relationship to tradition. In the present day we have an instinctive distrust of every kind of tradition. But for me, a tradition is valid until it is refuted beyond any doubt. In the early Church, who the bishop of Rome was might be fiercely contested, but not the special status of Peter's successor. Eastern Orthodoxy, hostile to Rome, also acknowledges the primacy of honor of the successors of Peter based on Matthew 16. I don't know any historical argument that permits excluding the special empowerment of Peter.

WIEGELMANN: You're saying that Peter was the first pope?

MOSEBACH: Of course!

STERNBERG: Excuse me, but I can't agree. That's simply nonsense! The office of pope developed in the course of time. There were bishops relatively early in the Church. A certain theological precedence crystalized around those bishops who had dioceses in the government centers. These were the later patriarchs, in Alexandria, Antioch, Jerusalem, Constantinople, and Rome. Within this group, Rome achieved only bit by bit a preeminent position. On the one hand, on its own initiative, the papacy made corresponding claims, arguing that the graves of the princes of the Apostles were in Rome. On the other hand, its preeminence arose out of a praxis: the bishops of the West appealed ever more frequently to the bishop of Rome to settle their disputes. In this way the pope's authority grew by influence from without. He acquired the function of a preserver of unity. The legitimating expressions from the Bible only came to be applied later. Being a historian, I am too critical to be able to say that Jesus Christ wanted the office of the pope.

WIEGELMANN: Why then does the papacy have for you a religious authority?

STERNBERG: At least 1,500 years have elapsed between the establishment of the papacy and the current office-holder. You cannot simply ignore this lengthy period of time. Accordingly, the current pope naturally has a leading function and is also for me the head of the Roman Catholic Church. We owe it to the papacy that this Church could, on the whole, preserve its unity over the centuries despite all the difficulties. You can assess how important this mission is by what happened when the papacy failed as the guarantor of unity, such as occurred in the Great Schism or at the time of the Reformation. If Adrian VI (1522–1523) had had the chance to serve for longer, and had he not been so quickly marginalized by the curia as the "stranger from Utrecht," he might have succeeded in assimilating and integrating the reforming impulses of Martin Luther and thus avoiding schism. Today, once more, we most urgently need the papacy as the guarantor and servant of unity.

WIEGELMANN: Do you have a favorite pope in history?

STERNBERG: I especially admire Paul VI—the greatest reforming pope of recent history.

MOSEBACH: The most terrible pope of recent history.

STERNBERG: On the occasion of his very first public appearance he sent a signal: he sold his tiara to an American museum and donated the proceeds to the poor. That was a gesture that was part of a great tradition and ultimately adopts a demand made by the Doctor of the Church Ambrose: charity has priority over church property. Afterwards, Paul VI always wore a miter and thus placed himself in the ranks of the bishops. He viewed himself as the bishop of Rome, as the first among the bishops. All the other papal titles and official attributes were less important to him. It was also fitting that he radically pruned the court ceremonies of the Vatican. You see a gigantic difference if you compare his processions with those of his predecessor, John XXIII. The Noble Guards were abolished; the diverse ranks and special offices, the ostrich feather fans—all that was eliminated.

MOSEBACH: Paul VI did what a pope has no right to do. With his reform of the Mass, he destroyed the organically developed Catholic liturgy and left us an "order for church services"[2] that obscures the Eucharistic mystery. Paul VI abused papal authority. You yourself have said that up to the Middle Ages, the papacy was characterized by deciding controversies. Therein lies the pope's area of authority—not in the unleashing of religious and political forces. It's a passive authority. The office of *Vicarius Christi* would place completely insuperable demands on anyone who would understand it as an active office. This office can be exercised only in a passive manner. It's an office that Mr. Everyman has to be able to assume. Peter, not Paul, became the first pope. If genius and charisma were essential, this office would be madness. By the way, the old pomp, which Paul VI abolished, accomplished exactly this—it covered up the person of the pope. When the pope entered, one didn't see the little old man anymore because he was hidden under a mass of brocade. Then, in the twentieth century this cult of the solitary man in white developed under the influence of the news media—the *Pastor Angelicus* shining out over the crowds. The pope as charismatic leader, however, contradicts Catholic tradition. The pope isn't free; he is subject not only to the Gospel but to the entirety of tradition. Only within this can he act, and in the end, that means he cannot *act* at all. And, indeed, he absolutely shouldn't!

WIEGELMANN: In the course of history popes have, however, said and done completely different, even contradictory things. To name just one example, for a long time the successors of Peter thought that the Sun circled the

---

2   *Gottesdienstordnung*: the German word here refers to the regulations or agenda governing worship services of the German (Lutheran) church.

Earth—now they have a different opinion. How imaginary is the supposed continuity of the Magisterium?

MOSEBACH: Here we really have to make distinctions. Are we talking about essentials, or some kind of accident limited to a specific time? The astounding thing in the history of the Church is not the flux of time but rather the clear continuity in the essentials.

STERNBERG: Continuity is an extremely important category for the Church and especially for the pope. It always has been so. Nevertheless, major distinctions exist. For me it is a sign of the activity of the Holy Spirit in history that at certain times popes appear who react to their surroundings and give specific, new answers to the questions of their age. That means that the papacy precisely does not remain "always the same." It always has to guard against becoming antiquated.

WIEGELMANN: The curia administers the Magisterium. There, fine specialists sit at their desks, process files, compile dossiers, and finally a stamp is given—or not given—to a religious procedure. Can you really get a handle on something as supernatural as Christianity with files and binders?

STERNBERG: I find this question beside the point. Naturally, the Church is a theological entity. But at the same time the Church is also an entity that can be sociologically described. As such, the Church is subject to totally normal human processes and events. In considering the eternally repeated question as to how the Church should be best organized, we should first treat with caution the argument that this or that doesn't work because it doesn't fit into the [prevailing] ecclesiology. For theology and the order of the organization are different spheres. In the Vatican it's also a question of organizing an administration. And this administration isn't optimally ordered, and still isn't. One of my predecessors as president of the Central Committee of Catholics, Hans Meier, had already pointed this out again and again. He asked why in the curia something like a cabinet principle does not exist: that all the prefects of the dicasteries regularly sit down with the pope at one table. No, they only ever have their individual audiences. So nobody should be surprised that many things start to diverge.

MOSEBACH: That a religion takes the form of an existing state that had previously persecuted it with all its might is one of the most remarkable processes in the history of the world. There has never been anything like it anywhere else; it cannot be compared with the theocratic states of the Orient. The Catholic Church absorbed the Roman imperial state . . .

STERNBERG: . . . and surprisingly, separated itself once again from the state!

MOSEBACH: Correct. It's also unique in history that the Church survived the collapse of the Roman state and could create a totally new amalgam with the barbarian kingdoms. Protestantism views this as a perversion of religion. On the contrary, I, as a Catholic, say that this process obviously was providential. Christ became a man in the "fullness of time." He became man both in the universal Roman Empire and at the same time in the most national of nations, the Jewish people, uniting these two poles, like the divine and the human, bearing in Himself the national and the universal. If the religion He started was to survive, it had to do so in the Roman empire – it had to become Roman. This may contradict exceedingly a fundamentalist understanding of the Gospel. Yet not only the Gospel, but also the *fact* of the Incarnation in the Jewish, Greek, and Roman culture belongs to Revelation. Long duration, by the way, is also an argument. The Roman Church model has proved itself extraordinarily durable. And everything that the Church had to drag around as a filthy burden by reason of becoming a state – that prevented her from becoming presumptuous.

WIEGELMANN: What does it mean to you when the Holy Father does or says something that goes against the grain? How do you deal with it? The pope is the pope.

STERNBERG: The times in which one held a statement to be true because an official appointed by authority said it are largely over. Authority today is primarily based on the assignment of authority: I have to grant somebody authority first. Once I have done that, I personally receive his statements very exactly. A simple structure of obedience doesn't work in the Catholic Church anymore – nor, for that matter, outside of it. I'm ready to admit that a whole host of problems arises on account of this. The real problem, however, is that many a priest and many a bishop has not yet noticed this change.

MOSEBACH: It's clear: the entitlement to infallibility exists only when the pope speaks in submission to tradition. When he doesn't do that, then he quite simply is not binding [on us]. He possesses his authority by being a mere submissive mouthpiece of the Infinite that existed before him.

STERNBERG: With this formulation, you open the door to resistance against the pope. The judgment whether something is in accord with tradition or not depends very much on the historical convictions, knowledge, and perceptions of the individual.

MOSEBACH: You are probably thinking of Cardinal Lehmann, who once reinterpreted the papal directive to withdraw from "pregnancy conflict counseling" as a papal directive to remain in it.[3] He supported this with the infamous words: "I've learned how to handle texts." Especially Jesuits are very much engaged in handling tradition in this way. I almost have the feeling that only in our days has Pascal's cruel caricature of the Jesuits in *Lettres à un Provincial* been truly and completely vindicated. In that book Pascal wrote this beautiful sentence about the Jesuits: "*Ecce patres, qui tollunt peccata mundi.*"[4] One would think he is talking

---

3   This refers to the engagement of the Catholic Church in Germany in centers which advised women seeking an abortion. Once a consultation had taken place, such centers issued a certificate that was a legal requirement to obtain an abortion. In this way it appeared that the Church was in some sense consenting to the abortions. Starting in 1999, the Vatican intervened to prohibit the practice, against massive resistance from the German hierarchy. – *Ed.*

4   "Behold the [Reverend] Fathers, who take away the sins of the world." Pascal is saying that Jesuit casuistry explains away sins or gives them a pass. – *Ed.*

about Francis. But these maneuvers, these cunning ideological reinterpretations, collapse after a certain amount of time. What endures is the gigantic block of tradition by means of which a believer can take the measure of something. First of all, a glance at the Gospels suffices. The Gospels are radical. Every line of the Gospels denounces the cunning that would make Christianity acceptable. But everyone can also take the measure of a thing using, for example, a Gothic cathedral. Stand before Notre Dame de Paris and ask if this or that encyclical, this or that papal address stands comparison to this building. And if not, it's certainly not the fault of the cathedral.

WIEGELMANN: Then you agree: when the pope says something, both of you first reflect how seriously it should be taken. The pope is the pope only as long as Catholics treat him as such.

STERNBERG: We have to distinguish here two areas. What we have just said is valid at the level of the individual person, the individual believer. But there is a second level, namely, the question of how I deal with a papal pronouncement as a member of the Church or, in my case, as a leader of an ecclesiastical organization. On this level, within the institution, statements and directives of the pope have a dignity and meaning that can't be simply subject to the judgment of individual taste.

WIEGELMANN: In his encyclical *Evangelii Gaudium* Pope Francis himself said, regarding papal writings: I know very well that today documents don't raise the same interest as in other times and are quickly forgotten. When a new encyclical comes, what do you do with it?

MOSEBACH: [*addressing Sternberg*] You're still in office — you have to read it!

WIEGELMANN: Or first let it be digested for you by a subordinate?

STERNBERG: No, no, I read these myself! I am so very happy that we have a pope now who, for example, on the topic of marriage, family, and partnership — of all things — issues a text that has the surprising title *Amoris Laetitia*, the joy of love. In it are such lovely passages on love in old age, preparation for marriage, and similar topics. I actually gave it to my daughter for marriage preparation and said: just read this text of the pope. Twenty years ago, I could not have imagined even dreaming that this would be possible. Now, I'm not of the opinion that every Catholic must read every papal encyclical. But when I look at the encyclicals of the recent past — of John Paul II, of Benedict XVI, and also of Paul VI — I can always say that I recommend them very much as reading. There are very insightful things to be found there.

MOSEBACH: It would be bad if there weren't! Nevertheless, my curiosity in this regard is limited as a matter of principle. I remember the splendid statement Robert Spaemann put at the beginning of one of his books (I'm citing it from memory): "If in this book there should be anything new, it would disturb me, because then it would be wrong." Now I find it very strange that in *Amoris Laetitia*, next to passages that are acceptable — I would readily grant that to you — we find a gigantic, disputed issue like communion for divorced and remarried people mentioned in a footnote! And that this question is then not *decided* [but simply broached] — although we have already stated that the office of the pope consists above all in the resolution of disputes. Well, if that kind of thing continues, it won't be rewarding anymore for a Catholic to read encyclicals, because the pope will refuse to exercise his office. His private views are unimportant.

WIEGELMANN: Francis wants it to be the case, after all, that in the future Rome doesn't have to decide everything. In *Evangelii Gaudium* he writes: "I don't believe that one has to expect from the papal magisterium a final or complete answer to all questions which concern the Church and the world."

MOSEBACH: Pope Francis here is trying in a rather unclear way to address a mistaken development. The First Vatican Council in *Pastor Aeternus* confirmed, in the midst of a political crisis, the infallibility of the pope in questions of faith and morals. It thereby launched, in part through dramatic formulations, an exaltation of the papal office that couldn't bear comparison with Catholic tradition. Post-conciliar papalist theology in particular has inflated the papal office to a height that is incompatible with tradition. This omnipotent papacy, which seems to have copied the absolutist fantasies of Joseph de Maistre, has revealed its full danger really only now, when suddenly everything is supposed to depend on this one very special personality, Bergoglio. Perhaps Catholics should be thankful for this situation, because it renders more urgent the correction of such exaggerations. Leading the papacy back to its old constraints would be fortunate for the Church. The Pope as supreme judge, who decides controversies in submission to tradition — that suffices.

STERNBERG: In the past there was always a level of authority situated between Rome and the local churches. There were provincial synods, provincial councils (the records from those in Gaul and in North Africa have come down to us best), metropolitan bishops. These layers have disappeared. Vatican II proceeded on the assumption that each local church relates solely to its bishop and that there is nothing between these local churches and the pope. That is unhistorical and also inappropriate. The Church was for a long time a Roman church because originally she covered the Roman region, that is, Western Europe from the eighth century onwards. Today, as a world Church, she occupies totally different territories. Thus, one has to ask whether a European bishops' conference, an Asiatic or an African bishops' conference, should be conceded greater "continental" individuality. More and more topics on different continents must be decided differently. God knows, the question of unity naturally will not thereby become easier.

WIEGELMANN: How much of the "sacrality" of the papacy is left since Benedict XVI abdicated?

STERNBERG: I believe that since Benedict XVI the aura of the papacy has not diminished at all. Rather, the papacy has once again obtained a totally new coloration with Francis, the first Argentinian and Latin American on the papal throne. A pope who does many things totally differently, beginning with the point-blank assertion in *Evangelii Gaudium* that religion is not something to muddle through sullenly but involves joy. I really very much admire Francis's opening to the perception of other people. The way he deals with handicapped people; the way he lifts them out of the wheelchair, how he walks first to them and then afterwards to the officials. Those are more than details — it's an approach to life. Francis teaches me: the handicapped, the sick, the weak, the non-intellectual, the ignored person is especially important for me as a Christian.

MOSEBACH: But you must certainly know, Mr Sternberg, that that's part of the ritual of modern dictators: kissing children, comforting the sick, visiting field hospitals, and so forth. Since publicity has existed, since we have had propaganda, rulers have displayed themselves in this manner. When there were still ostrich feather fans at the papal court, that was an old-fashioned practice, almost touching in its antiquity. The strong men of the modern age — a Hitler or a Stalin — have used far different stylistic means to exhibit themselves in the best light. It's the same with the current pope. A football stadium, where tens of thousands zero in on a solitary white form in the middle — that's a far more totalitarian language than the ponderous, old-fashioned court etiquette of the past! Then there's the utilization of the sick in their wheelchairs: lined up in a row, they are now used to demonstrate our charity and mercy towards them. A shiver runs through me whenever the reigning Holy Father speaks of the "tenderness of God." I'd just like to roll up and die! The tenderness of God — that, in the face of the hard language of Scripture! It's a criminal trivialization, a deception, to deprive the faithful of the *Rex tremendae majestatis* of the regrettably abolished *Dies irae.* I would also like to take the liberty of drawing attention to the close connection between kitsch and heterodoxy...

STERNBERG: I really have to object strongly here because I have experienced it differently. Once I was at a general audience in St. Peter's Square. Next to me was a Latin American family with a small girl who was obviously disabled. When the pope came by, he took the girl into his arms. And when he noticed that she was blind, he took her hands and let her feel his face. There were no cameras there, it wasn't a show.

WIEGELMANN: Pope Francis also says at every appearance that one should pray for him.

STERNBERG: I will leave aside the question of my personal prayer life. Otherwise, praying for the pope is part of every celebration of the Eucharist.

MOSEBACH: I pray every day for the priests and monks. He is of course one of them.

⟨ BIBLIOGRAPHY ⟩

MAGISTERIAL OR ECCLESIASTICAL DOCUMENTS

Acta Synodalia Sacrosancti Concilii Oecumenici Vaticani Secundi. Rome: Typis Polyglottis
 Vaticanis, 1970–99.

Benedict XV. Encyclical Letter *Ad Beatissimi Apostolorum*, November 1, 1914.

Benedict XVI. *Farewell Address to the Cardinals*, February 28, 2013.

——. Homily, Mass of Possession of the Chair of the Bishop of Rome, May 7, 2005.

——. *Last General Audience*, February 27, 2013.

——. Letter to Andrea Tornielli, February 18, 2014, published in *La Stampa*, February 27, 2014.

Boniface VIII. Bull *Unam Sanctam*, November 18, 1302.

Bullarum Sanctorum Romanorum Pontificum a Gregorio XIII ad Sixtum V. Edited by Francisco
 Gaude. Turin: Seb. Franco et Henrico, 1868.

Code of Canon Law: Latin-English Translation. Washington, DC: Canon Law Society of
 America, 1998.

Congregation for the Doctrine of the Faith. Declaration *"Dominus Iesus" on the Unicity and
 Salvific Universality of Jesus Christ and the Church*, August 6, 2000.

——. "Il Primato del Successore di Pietro nel Mistero della Chiesa." *Documenti (1966–2013)*.
 Città del Vaticano: Libreria Editrice Vaticana, 2017.

——. Instruction *Donum Veritatis*, May 4, 1990.

——. Letter to Archbishop José H. Gomez, from Luis Ladaria, SJ, on Catholics in public
 office who support legislation allowing abortion, euthanasia, or other moral evils.
 https://wherepeteris.com/wp-content/uploads/2022/07/Ladaria-Letter-to-Gomez.pdf.

Constance, Council of. Thirty-ninth session, October 9, 1417. Ratified by Pope Martin V.

Corpus Iuris Canonici. Edited by Emil Friedberg. Leipzig: Tauchnitz, 1879.

Davis, Raymond, trans. *The Eighth-Century Popes (Liber Pontificalis)*. Liverpool: Liverpool
 University Press, 1992.

Denzinger, Heinrich. *Compendium of Creeds, Definitions, and Declarations on Matters of Faith and
 Morals*. 43rd edition. Edited by Peter Hünermann with Helmut Hoping; English edition
 edited by Robert Fastiggi and Anne Englund Nash. San Francisco: Ignatius Press, 2012.

Denzinger-Schönmetzer. *Enchiridion*. Freiburg: Herder, 1965.

Francis. Apostolic Constitution *Veritatis Gaudium*, January 29, 2018.

——. Apostolic Exhortation *Evangelii Gaudium*, November 24, 2013.

——. Apostolic Exhortation *Gaudete et Exsultate*, April 9, 2018.

——. Apostolic Exhortation *Querida Amazonia*, February 2, 2020.

——. Apostolic Letter *Ad Theologiam Promovendam*, November 1, 2023.

——. Encyclical Letter *Fratelli Tutti*, October 4, 2020.

——. Encyclical Letter *Laudato Si'*, June 18, 2015.

——. "New Revision of Number 2267 of the *Catechism of the Catholic Church* on the Death Penalty—Rescriptum 'Ex Audientia Ss.mi,'" August 2, 2018. www.vatican.va/roman_curia/
 congregations/cfaith/ladaria-ferrer/documents/rc_con_cfaith_doc_20180801_catechis-
 mo-penadimorte_en.html.

——. "Pope Francis clarifies two points of 'Traditionis custodes,'" *Vatican News*, February
 21, 2023.

——. "Pope Francis Speaks with Mexican Television," *America*, March 13, 2015.

——. Post-Synodal Apostolic Exhortation *Amoris Laetitia*, March 19, 2016.

———. "Saluto del Santo Padre Francesco ai Padri Sinodali, 6 ottobre 2014." *La famiglia è il futuro. Tutti i documenti del Sinodo straordinario 2014*. Edited by Antonio Spadaro. Milano: Àncora Editrice, 2014. English translation: "Pope Francis's invitation to the Synod Fathers at the opening of the General Congregation: With honesty and humility." *L'Osservatore Romano*, October 10, 2014.

Foerster, Hans, ed. *Liber Diurnus Romanorum Pontificum*. Bern: Francke Verlag, 1958.

Gasser, Vincent. *The Gift of Infallibility: The Official* Relatio *on Infallibility of Bishop Vincent Gasser at Vatican Council I*. 2nd edition. Translated with commentary by James J. O'Connor. San Francisco: Ignatius Press, 2008.

Gelasius. Letter *Famuli Vestrae Pietatis* to Emperor Anastasius I Dicorus. AD 494.

Gregory VII (attr.). *Dictatus Papae*. English translation: Ernest F. Henderson, *Select Historical Documents of the Middle Ages* (London: George Bell and Sons, 1910).

———. Letter to Hermann of Metz, March 15, 1081. *Registrum*, Bk. 8, Letter 21. In *The Correspondence of Pope Gregory VII*, translated with an introduction by Ephraim Emerton. New York: W.W. Norton & Company, 1969.

———. *Propriae auctoritates apostolicae sedis*. The text may be found in Hubert Mordek, "Proprie auctoritates apostolice sedis. Ein zweiter Dictatus Papae Gregors VII?" *Deutsches Archiv für Erforschung des Mittelalters* 28 (1972): 105–32.

Gregory XIII. Bull *Sancta Mater Ecclesia*. 1584.

Gregory XVI. Letter *Quo Graviora*. October 4, 1833.

Innocent III. Sermon III for the Consecration of the Pontiff. *PL* 217.

John Paul II. Address to the Bishops from the United States of America [of New York] on Their *Ad Limina* Visit, October 15, 1988.

———. Apostolic Letter *Ad Tuendam Fidem*, May 18, 1998.

———. Encyclical Letter *Ut Unum Sint*, May 25, 1995.

———. Post-Synodal Apostolic Exhortation *Familiaris Consortio*, November 22, 1981.

———. Encyclical Letter *Fides et Ratio*, September 14, 1998.

———. General Audience, March 24, 1993.

———. Apostolic Constitution *Universi Dominici Gregis*, February 22, 1996.

Leo XIII. Apostolic Letter *Notre Consolation*, May 3, 1892.

———. Decree *Quemadmodum*, December 17, 1890.

———. Letter *Epistola Tua*, June 17, 1885. https://novusordowatch.org/leo13-epistola-tua/.

———. Letter *Testem Benevolentiae*, January 22, 1899.

———. Encyclical Letter *Aeterni Patris*,

———. Encyclical Letter *Au Milieu des Sollicitudes*, February 16, 1892.

———. Encyclical Letter *Providentissimus Deus*, November 18, 1893.

Levada, William. "Theological Reflections on Catholics in Political Life and the Reception of Holy Communion," June 13, 2004.

Mansi, Giovanni Domenico. *Sacrorum conciliorum nova et amplissima collectio, in qua praeter ea quae P. Labbeus et G. Cossartius et novissime N. Coleti in lucem edidere, ea omnia insuper suis in locis optime disposita exhibentur quae J. D. Mansi evulgavit*. Ed. Novissima ab eodem Patre Mansi curata accedunt etiam notae, et dissertationes quam-plurimae, etc. Florence and Venice: 1759–1798. Tomes 36–53, *Sacrorum conciliorum nova et amplissima collectio continuata*, edited by J.B. Martin and L. Petit. Paris: H. Welter, 1901–1927.

Nicholas V. Bull *Dum Diversas*, June 18, 1452.

Paul VI. Apostolic Constitution *Romano Pontifice Eligendo*, October 1, 1975.

Pius IV. Bull *Iniunctum Nobis*, with Tridentine Profession of Faith. November 13, 1565.

Pius VI. Bull *Auctorem Fidei*. August 28, 1794.

Pius IX. Apostolic Constitution *Reversurus*, July 12, 1867.

——. Apostolic Letter *Mirabilis Illa Constantia*, March 4, 1875.

——. Bull *Ineffabilis Deus*, December 8, 1854.

——. Encyclical Letter *Quanta Cura*, with the *Syllabus of Errors*, December 8, 1864.

——. Profession of Faith, January 6, 1870.

Pius XII. Encyclical Letter *Divino Afflante Spiritu*, September 30, 1943.

——. Encyclical Letter *Mediator Dei*, November 20, 1947.

——. Encyclical Letter *Mystici Corporis*, June 29, 1943.

Supreme Sacred Congregation of the Holy Office. Instruction *Crimen Sollicitationis*, June 9, 1922. Reissued by the same office, with an appendix, on March 16, 1962.

Tanner, Norman J. *Decrees of the Ecumenical Councils*. Volume 2: *Trent to Vatican II*. Washington, DC: Georgetown University Press, 1990.

United States Conference of Catholic Bishops. *National Synthesis of the People of God in the United States of America for the Diocesan Phase of the 2021-2023 Synod*, www.usccb.org/resources/US%20National%20Synthesis%202021-2023%20Synod.pdf.

Vatican Council I. Dogmatic Constitution *Dei Filius*, April 24, 1870.

——. Dogmatic Constitution *Pastor Aeternus*, July 18, 1870.

Vatican Council II. Declaration on Religious Freedom *Dignitatis Humanae*, December 7, 1965.

——. Decree Concerning the Pastoral Office of Bishops in the Church *Christus Dominus*, October 28, 1965.

——. Dogmatic Constitution on the Church *Lumen Gentium*, November 21, 1964.

——. Dogmatic Constitution on Divine Revelation *Dei Verbum*, November 18, 1965.

OTHER WORKS CITED

Abbo, John A. and Jerome D. Hannan. *The Sacred Canons: A Concise Presentation of the Current Disciplinary Norms of the Church*. St Louis, MO: B. Herder Book Co., 1952.

Adler, Alfred. *The Individual Psychology of Alfred Adler: A Systematic Presentation in Selections from His Writings*. New York, Basic Books, 1956.

Allen, John L. "Pope Francis and the Sharron Angle Strategy of Media Relations." *Crux*, November 5, 2023.

Alphonsus Maria de Liguori. *Dogmatic Works*, volume 8. Turin, 1848.

Anonymous. "Taming the *Action* — II. The Decree," *Rorate Caeli*, January 21, 2012, https://rorate-caeli.blogspot.com/2012/01/taming-action-ii-decree.html.

Aron-Beller, Katherine. *Jews on Trial: The Papal Inquisition in Modena 1598-1638*. Manchester, UK: Manchester University Press, 2011.

Athanasius of Alexandria. *Four Letters to Serapion of Thmuis*. In William A. Jurgens, ed., *The Faith of the Early Fathers*. Collegeville: The Liturgical Press, 1970.

Aubert, Roger. "The Backwardness of Religious Studies and the Controversy about the 'German Theologians.'" In *History of the Church*, vol. 8: *The Church in the Age of Liberalism*, eds. Roger Aubert, Johannes Beckmann, Patrick J. Cornish, Rudolf Lill, 228-47. New York: Crossroad Publishing Co., 1981.

——. "Ultramontane Progress and Final Gallican Resistance." In *History of the Church*, vol. 8: *The Church in the Age of Liberalism*, eds. Roger Aubert, Johannes Beckmann, Patrick J. Cornish, Rudolf Lill, 304-7. New York: Crossroad Publishing Co., 1981.

Bachofen, Charles Augustine. *A Commentary on the New Code of Canon Law*. Volume 8. St Louis, MO: Herder, 1918.

Basil of Caesarea. *On the Holy Spirit*. www.newadvent.org/fathers/3203.htm.

Bauers, Walter, and Frederick William Danker. *A Greek Lexicon of the New Testament and Other Early Christian Literature.* Chicago and London: University of Chicago Press, 2000.

Baunard, Louis. *Histoire du cardinal Pie: Évêque de Poitiers.* Poitiers: H. Oudin, 1886.

Bellarmine, Robert. *De Controversiis,* volume 2. Paris: Vivès, 1873.

——. *De Romano Pontifice.* Ingolstadt, 1599.

——. *On the Most Holy Sacrifice of the Mass.* Translated by Ryan Grant. Post Falls, ID: Mediatrix Press, 2020.

Benson, Robert L. *The Gelasian Doctrine: Uses and Transformations.* Paris: Presses Universitaires de France, 1982.

Bernardi, Peter J. "Louis Cardinal Billot, SJ (1846–1931): Thomist, Anti-Modernist, Integralist." *Journal of Jesuit Studies,* 8.4 (2021): 585–616; https://doi.org/10.1163/22141332-08040004.

Berthelot du Chesnay, C. and J. M. Gres-Gayer. "Gallicanism." In *New Catholic Encyclopedia,* 2nd ed., vol. 6. Detroit: Gale, 2003.

Billot, Louis. *De Ecclesia Christi.* Prato: Giachetti, 1909.

——. *Tractatus de Ecclesia Christi.* Rome: Aedes Universitatis Gregorianae, 1927.

Blanchard, Shaun. *The Synod of Pistoia and Vatican II: Jansenism and the Struggle for Catholic Reform.* Oxford: Oxford University Press, 2020.

Blennerhassett, Sir Rowland. "The Hohenlohe Memoirs." *The Eclectic Magazine,* vol. 148. University of Iowa, 1907.

Bogle, James. "Is the Pope Really the 'Head of the Catholic Church?'" *Inside the Vatican,* no date given. https://insidethevatican.com/magazine/is-the-pope-really-the-head-of-the-catholic-church/.

Bonneterre, Didier. *The Liturgical Movement.* Kansas City, MO: Angelus Press, 2002.

Brugger, E. Christian. "Capital Punishment Is Intrinsically Wrong: A Reply to Feser and Bessette." *Public Discourse,* October 22, 2017

——. *Capital Punishment and Roman Catholic Moral Tradition.* Notre Dame, IN: University of Notre Dame Press, 2014.

——. "Catholic Tradition, St. John Paul II, and the Death Penalty." *Public Discourse,* October 23, 2017.

Butler, Cuthbert. *The Vatican Council (1869–1870): Based on Bishop Ullathorne's Letters.* Edited by Christopher Butler. Westminster, MD: The Newman Press, 1962.

Campbell, Phillip. "Gregory the Great and the Reform of Penance." *Unam Sanctam Catholicam,* November 21, 2021, www.unamsanctamcatholicam.com/gregory-the-great-and-the-reform-of-penance.

——. *"Propriae auctoritates apostolicae sedis." Unam Sanctam Catholicam,* April 15, 2012, http://unamsanctamcatholicam.blogspot.com/2021/04/propriae-auctoritates-apostolicae-sedis.html.

Campo, Cristina. "Introduzione a Simone Weil, Attesa di Dio" (1966). In idem, *Sotto falso nome.* Milan: Adelphi Edizione, 1998.

Cano, Melchior. *De Locis Theologicis.* In *Opera,* edited by Hyacinthe Serry. Padua, 1734.

Cantor, Norman F. *Church, Kingship, and Lay Investiture in England,* 1089–1135. Princeton, NJ: Princeton University Press, 1958.

——. *Medieval History,* 2nd ed. Toronto: MacMillan Co., 1971.

Chadwick, Owen. *The Secularization of the European Mind in the Nineteenth Century.* Cambridge: Cambridge University Press, 1975.

Chapman, John. *The Condemnation of Pope Honorius.* London: Catholic Truth Society, 1907.

——. *Studies on the Early Papacy.* Port Washington and London: Kennikat Press, 1928.

Chessman, Stuart. "Cardinal Gregory Explains." Society of St. Hugh of Cluny blog, December 10, 2023.

——. "The 'Dazzling Catholic Intellectual Tradition' — The Institute for Human Ecology at Catholic University." Society of St Hugh of Cluny blog, September 26, 2022.

——. "'Is it really a Phoenix?' Ida Görres and the Collapse of German Catholicism, Part II." Society of St. Hugh of Cluny blog, March 30, 2020.

Cocchi, Guido. *Commentarium in Codicem Iuris Canonici.* Turin: Marietti, 1930.

Congar, Yves. *Diario del Concilio: 1960-1966,* in 2 vols. Cinisello Balsamo: San Paolo, 2005.

——. *My Journal of the Council.* Translated by Mary John Ronayne and Mary Cecily Boulding. Adelaide: ATF Press, 2012.

Coppen, Luke. "Rome silent on German diocese's appointment of lay 'vicar general representative.'" *The Pillar,* October 14, 2022.

Coriden, James, Thomas Green, and Donald Heintschel, eds. *The Code of Canon Law: A Text and Commentary.* London: Geoffrey Chapman, 1985.

Corrêa de Oliveira, Plinio. "A perfeita alegria," *Folha de S. Paulo,* July 12, 1970, www.pliniocorreadeoliveira.info/1970_236_CAT_A_perfeita_alegria.htm.

——. "Luther, Absolutely Not!" December 27, 1983, www.tfp.org/luther-absolutely-not/.

——. "Luther Thinks He Is Divine." January 10, 1984, www.tfp.org/luther-thought-he-was-divine/.

——. "O direito de saber." *Folha de S. Paulo,* January 25, 1970, www.pliniocorreadeoliveira.info/FSP_700125_direito_de_saber.htm.

——. *Revolution and Counter-Revolution.* 3rd edition. Spring Grove, PA: The American Society for the Defense of Tradition, Family, and Property, 1993.

——. "Saint of the Day." January 10, 1976. Portuguese original at www.pliniocorreadeoliveira.info/Mult_760116_Vaticano_vida_quotidiana.htm; translation by José Ureta.

——. "The Vatican Policy of Détente with Communist Governments — Should the TFPs Stand Down? Or Should They Resist?," September 1, 1974, www.tfp.org/vatican-policy-detente-communist-governments-tfps-stand-resist/.

Costigan, Richard. *Rohrbacher and the Ecclesiology of Ultramontanism.* Rome: Gregorian University, 1980.

Coulombe, Charles. *Blessed Charles of Austria: A Holy Emperor and His Legacy.* Gastonia, NC: TAN Books, 2020.

Crean, Thomas. *"Letters from that City . . .": A Guide to Holy Scripture for Students of Theology.* Lincoln, NE: Os Justi Press, 2022.

Cuchet, Guillaume. *Comment notre monde a cessé d'être chrétien: Anatomie d'un effondrement.* Paris: Seuil, 2018.

Cummings McLean, Dorothy. "No evidence Pope Benedict said 'the Pope is one; it is Francis.'" *LifeSiteNews,* July 4, 2019.

Daniel-Rops, Henri. *A Fight for God 1870-1939.* Volume 1. Translated by John Warrington. Garden City: Image Books/Doubleday, 1967.

Dante. *Paradiso.* Longfellow translation. Public domain.

Davies, Michael. *Pope John's Council.* Chawleigh, Chulmleigh: Augustine Publishing Company, 1977.

Davis, Michael Warren. "Politics of Reason and Beauty." *The American Conservative,* September 29, 2022.

de Broglie, Albert. *Questions de religion et d'histoire.* Paris: Michel Lévy Frères, 1860.

Dee, Dacian, OFM. *The Manifestation of Conscience.* Washington, DC: Catholic University of America Press, 1960.

de Lugo, Juan. *Disputationes scholasticae et morales; de virtute fidei divina.* Lyon, 1546.

del Val, Merry. *The Truth about Papal Claims.* Boonville, NY: Preserving Christian Publications, 2012.

de Maistre, Joseph. *Considérations sur la France.* In *Œuvres,* edited by Pierre Glaudes. Paris: Robert Laffont, 2007.

——. *Du Pape.* Lyon-Paris: H. Pélagaud, 1878.

——. "Lettre à une dame russe sur la nature et les effets du schisme et sur l'unité catholique." In *Lettres et opuscules inédits,* vol. 2. Paris: A. Vaton, 1863.

de Mattei, Roberto. *Apologia della Tradizione.* Turin: Lindau, 2011. English edition: *Apologia for Tradition. A Defense of Tradition Grounded in the Historical Context of the Faith.* Translated by Michael J. Miller. Kansas City, MO: Angelus Press, 2019.

——. *Il crociato del secolo XX. Plinio Corrêa de Oliveira.* Casale Monferrato: Piemme, 1996. English edition: *The Crusader of the Twentieth Century: Plinio Corrêa de Oliveira.* Leominster: Gracewing, 1998.

——. *Love for the Papacy and Filial Resistance to the Pope in the History of Church.* Brooklyn, NY: Angelico Press, 2019.

——. "Modernismo e antimodernismo nell'epoca di Pio X." In *Don Orione negli anni del modernismo,* ed. Michele Busi, Roberto de Mattei, Antonio Lanza, Flavio Peloso. Milan: Jaca Book, 2002.

——. "The 'Ninth Crusade' of the Papal Zouaves." *The Remnant* online, April 1, 2020.

——. *Le ralliement de Léon XIII – L'échec d'un projet pastoral.* Paris: Éditions du Cerf, 2016.

——. *The Second Vatican Council: An Unwritten Story.* Translated by Michael J. Miller et al. Fitzwilliam, NH: Loreto Publications, 2012.

Dischner, Margit. *Humbert von Silva Canida: Werk und Wirkung des lothringischen Reformmönches.* Munich: Ars Una, 1996.

Döllinger, Ignaz von. *Declarations and Letters on the Vatican Decrees, 1869–1887.* Edinburgh: T&T Clark, 1891.

——. *The Pope and the Council.* London, Oxford, and Cambridge: Rivington's, 1869.

Dounot, Cyrille, Nicolas Warembourg, and Boris Bernabé, eds. *La déposition du pape hérétique: Lieux théologiques, modelès canoniques, enjeux constitutionnels.* Sceaux: Mare & Martin, 2019.

Douthat, Ross. "How Catholics became Prisoners of Vatican II." *The New York Times,* October 12, 2022. Also in Kwasniewski, ed., *Sixty Years After,* 63–67.

Doyle, Thomas. "The 1922 Instruction and the 1962 Instruction 'Crimen Sollicitationis,' Promulgated by the Vatican." October 3, 2008. www.awrsipe.com/doyle/2008/2008 -10-03-Commentary-on-1922-and-1962-documents.pdf.

Dreher, Rod. "Uncle Ted's 'Special Boy.'" *The American Conservative,* July 25, 2018.

Dublanchy, Edmond. "Église" (1911) and "Infaillibilité du pape" (1923). *Dictionnaire de théologie catholique.* Paris: Letouzey et Ané, 1907–51.

Dulles, Avery Cardinal. "Authority in the Church." In *Civilizing Authority: Church, State, Society,* ed. Patrick McKinley Brennan. Lanham, MD: Lexington Books, 2007.

Ellicott, Charles. *A Bible Commentary for English Readers.* Volume 1. London: Cassell, n.d.

Fastiggi, Robert. "Capital Punishment and Magisterial Authority." Published in four parts at *Where Peter Is,* August 14–17, 2023.

——. "Capital Punishment and the Papal Magisterium: A Response to Dr. Edward Feser." *Catholic World Report,* October 24, 2017

——. "Is There Really a Definitive Teaching of the Church on Capital Punishment?" *Catholic World Report,* November 10, 2017.

Ferrara, Christopher. *False Friends of Fatima*. Pound Ridge, NY: Good Counsel Publications, 2012.

Feser, Edward. "A Hart that pumps bile," December 21, 2017, edwardfeser.blogspot.com.

——. "Aquinas on St. Paul's correction of St. Peter," August 15, 2022, edwardfeser.blogspot.com.

——. "Bellarmine on capital punishment," March 23, 2018, edwardfeser.blogspot.com.

——. "Benedict XVI, Cardinal Pell, and criticism of Pope Francis," January 14, 2023, edwardfeser.blogspot.com.

——, with Joseph M. Bessette. *By Man Shall His Blood Be Shed: A Catholic Defense of Capital Punishment*. San Francisco: Ignatius Press, 2017.

——. "Can Pope Honorius be defended?," October 6, 2022, edwardfeser.blogspot.com.

——. "Capital Punishment and the Infallibility of the Ordinary Magisterium." *Catholic World Report*, January 20, 2018.

——. "Catholic Theologians Must Set an Example of Intellectual Honesty: A Reply to Prof. Robert Fastiggi." *Catholic World Report*, October 30, 2017.

——. "The Church Cannot Teach That Capital Punishment is Inherently Wrong: A Reply to John Finnis." *Public Discourse*, September 13, 2018

——. "The Church permits criticism of popes under certain circumstances," May 20, 2018, edwardfeser.blogspot.com.

——. "The error and condemnation of Pope Honorius," October 4, 2022, edwardfeser.blogspot.com.

——. "Fastiggi on the revision to the Catechism (Updated)," September 20, 2019, edwardfeser.blogspot.com.

——. "Hart, hell, and heresy," July 22, 2020, edwardfeser.blogspot.com.

——. "Hot Air vs. Capital Punishment: A Reply to Paul Griffiths and David Bentley Hart." *Catholic World Report*, November 28, 2017.

——. "Prof. Fastiggi's pretzel logic," January 25, 2018, edwardfeser.blogspot.com.

——. "St. John Paul II Did Not Change Catholic Teaching on Capital Punishment: A Reply to E. Christian Brugger." *Public Discourse*, November 20, 2017.

——. "Traditional Catholic Doctrine on Capital Punishment is Irreversible: A Reply to E. Christian Brugger." *Public Discourse*, November 19, 2017.

——. "Unnatural Lawyering: John Finnis's Brief against Traditional Catholic Teaching on Capital Punishment." *Catholic World Report*, January 4, 2019.

——. "Yes, Traditional Church Teaching on Capital Punishment Is Definitive." *Catholic World Report*, November 21, 2017.

Fest, Joachim. *The Face of the Third Reich: Portraits in Nazi Leadership*. Translated by Michael Bullock. New York: Ace Books, 1970.

Fiedrowicz, Michael. *The Traditional Mass: History, Form, and Theology of the Classical Roman Rite*. Translated by Rose Pfeifer. Brooklyn: Angelico Press, 2020.

Figueiredo, Anthony J. *The Magisterium-Theology Relationship: Contemporary Theological Conceptions in the Light of Universal Church Teaching Since 1835 and the Pronouncements of the Bishops of the United States*. Rome: Editrice Pontificia Università Gregoriana, 2001.

Fimister, Alan. *The Iron Sceptre of the Son of Man: Romanitas as a Note of the Church*. Lincoln, NE: Os Justi Press, 2023.

Finnis, John. "The Church Could Teach That Capital Punishment Is Inherently Wrong," *Public Discourse*, August 23, 2018.

——. "Intentional Killing Is Always Wrong: The Development Initiated by Pius XII, Made by John Paul II, and Repeated by Francis." *Public Discourse*, August 22, 2018.

Flanders, Timothy S. *City of God vs. City of Man: The Battles of the Church from Antiquity to the Present*. N.p.: Our Lady of Victory Press, 2021.

——. "Pornocracy and the Coming Reign of Antichrist," *OnePeterFive*, December 23, 2021.

——. "The Post-Vatican II Decline of Theology." *OnePeterFive*, June 13, 2022.

——. "The Pre-Vatican II Decline of Theology." *OnePeterFive*, June 7, 2022.

——. "The Third Pornocracy: What We Are Living Through." *OnePeterFive*, December 16, 2021.

——. "Unite the Clans to Rebuild Christendom!" *OnePeterFive*, August 31, 2021.

Fonbaustier, Laurent. *La déposition du pape hérétique: Une origine du constitutionnalisme?* Paris: Mare & Martin, 2016.

Fortesque, Adrian. *The Mass: A Study of the Roman Liturgy*. Fitzwilliam, NH: Loreto Publications, 2003.

Fromm, Erich. *Beyond the Chains of Illusion: My Encounter with Marx and Freud*. London: Abacus, 1980.

Geraghty, Chris. Interview on Australian Broadcasting Corporation radio, July 6, 2003; transcript at www.abc.net.au/radionational/programs/spiritofthings/priest-factory/3534652.

Gherardini, Brunero. *Quod et tradidi vobis: La Tradizione, vita e giovinezza della chiesa*. Frigento: Casa Mariana, 2010.

Gill, James F., SJ. "A Jesuit's Account of Conscience." *Studies in the Spirituality of Jesuits*, IX/5 (November 1977).

Granfield, Patrick. *The Limits of the Papacy: Authority and Autonomy in the Church*. New York: Crossroad, 1987.

Gratian. *Decretum Magistri Gratiani*. Leipzig: Tauchnitz, 1879.

Greaney, Michael D. "New Things." Foreword to Thomas P. Neill, *They Lived the Faith: Great Lay Leaders of Modern Times*. Post Falls, ID: Mediatrix Press, 2020; originally published 1951.

Gregory the Great. *Moralia in Iob*. PL 76.

Guéranger, Prosper. *The Liturgical Year*. Translated by Laurence Shepherd. Great Falls, MT: St. Bonaventure Publications, 2000.

Hall, Kennedy. "The Pope that Broke the Camel's Back." *OnePeterFive*, August 12, 2021.

Hart, David Bentley. "Christians and the Death Penalty." *Commonweal*, November 16, 2017.

——. "Further Reflections on Capital Punishment (and on Edward Feser)." *Church Life Journal*, December 19, 2017.

——. "Good God? A Response." *Theopolis*, October 7, 2019.

Hartmann, Christoph. "Wie der Papst die Feier der vorkonziliaren Messe einschränken könnte." *Katholisch.de*, July 14, 2021.

Hefele, Charles. *A History of the Christian Councils*. Translated by William Clark. Edinburgh: T. & T. Clarke, 1872.

Hitchens, Dan. "Leading theologian: change canon law to correct papal errors." *Catholic Herald*, August 18, 2017, www.catholicherald.co.uk/leading-theologian-change-canon-law-to-correct-papal-errors/.

Hollingsworth, Mary. *Conclave 1559: Ippolito d'Este and the Papal Election of 1559*. London: Head of Zeus, 2021.

Houghton, Bryan. *Judith's Marriage*. Brooklyn, NY: Angelico Press, 2020; originally published 1987.

——. *Unwanted Priest: The Autobiography of a Latin Mass Exile*. Brooklyn, NY: Angelico Press, 2022.

Howard, Thomas Albert. *The Pope and the Professor: Pius IX, Ignaz von Döllinger, and the Quandary of the Modern Age*. Oxford: Oxford University Press, 2017.

Iggers, George. "Historicism: The History and Meaning of the Term." *Journal of the History of Ideas*, vol. 56, no. 1 (1995).

Ignatius of Loyola. *Constitutions of the Society of Jesus*. In George E. Ganss, SJ, *The Constitutions of the Society of Jesus*. St Louis: The Institute of Jesuit Sources, 1970.

——. Letter 3304 to the members of the Society in Portugal (the "Letter on Obedience"), March 26, 1553. In *Letters of St Ignatius of Loyola*. Translated by William J. Young, SJ. Chicago: Loyola University Press, 1959.

Inés San Martin. "Pope removes Puerto Rican bishop from office after he refused to resign." *Crux*, March 9, 2022.

Isidore, *Sententiae*. PL 83.

Jestin, Laurent. "The End of Conciliation Efforts." *Rorate Caeli*, January 10, 2022.

Journet, Charles. *The Church of the Word Incarnate*. Volume 1: *The Apostolic Hierarchy*. London: Sheed & Ward, 1955.

——. *L'Église du Verbe incarné*. Volume 1: *L'hiérarchie apostolique*. Saint-Maurice: Éditions Saint-Augustin, 1998.

Joy, John P. *Disputed Questions on Papal Infallibility*. Lincoln, NE: Os Justi Press, 2022.

Jugie, Martin. "Constantinople, IVème Concile de." *Dictionnaire de théologie catholique*. Paris: Letouzey et Ané, 1907–51.

——. *Joseph de Maistre et l'Eglise greco-russe*. Paris: Maison de la Bonne Presse, 1923.

Kallio, Albert. "Collegialità nel Vaticano II: una nuova dottrina?" *Chiesa e post concilio*, June 26, 2018, https://chiesaepostconcilio.blogspot.com/2018/06/collegialita-nel-vaticano-ii-una-nuova.html.

Kasper, Walter. "Gott in der Geschichte." In *Gott heute: 15 Beiträge zur Gottesfrage*, ed. Norbert Kutschki. Mainz: Matthias-Grünewald-Verlag, 1967.

Ker, Ian. *John Henry Newman: A Biography*. Oxford: Clarendon Press, 1988.

Knibbs, Eric. "Ebo of Reims, Pseudo-Isidore and the Date of the False Decretals." *Speculum* (2017): 144–83.

Kwasniewski, Peter A. *Bound by Truth: Authority, Obedience, Tradition, and the Common Good* (Brooklyn, NY: Angelico Press, 2023).

——. "Games People Play with the Holy Spirit." In *Illusions of Reform: Responses to Cavadini, Healy, and Weinandy in Defense of the Traditional Mass and the Faithful Who Attend It*, ed. Peter A. Kwasniewski, 134–50. Lincoln, NE: Os Justi Press, 2023.

——. "It's Time to Imitate Our Forefathers: Never Give Up!" *OnePeterFive*, July 28, 2021.

——. "'LGBT' appears for the first time in a Vatican document. Catholics should grieve." *LifeSiteNews*, October 4, 2018.

——. *Noble Beauty, Transcendent Holiness: Why the Modern Age Needs the Mass of Ages*. Kettering, OH: Angelico Press, 2017.

——. *The Once and Future Roman Rite: Returning to the Traditional Latin Liturgy after Seventy Years of Exile*. Gastonia: TAN Books, 2022.

——. *The Road from Hyperpapalism to Catholicism: Rethinking the Papacy in a Time of Ecclesial Disintegration*. Two volumes. Waterloo, ON: Arouca Press, 2022.

——, ed. *Sixty Years After: Catholic Writers Assess the Legacy of Vatican II*. Brooklyn, NY: Angelico Press, 2022.

——. *True Obedience in the Church: A Guide to Discernment in Challenging Times*. Manchester, NH: Crisis Publications, 2021.

Lamont, John R.T., and Claudio Pierantoni, eds. *Defending the Faith Against Present Heresies: Letters and Statements Addressed to Pope Francis, the Cardinals, and the Bishops with a Collection of Related Articles and Interviews*. Waterloo, ON: Arouca Press, n.d. [2021].

Lamont, John R.T. "Conscience, Freedom, Rights: Idols of the Enlightenment Religion." *The Thomist* 73/2 (2009): 169–239.

——. "In Defence of Michel Villey." In *Truth and Faith in Ethics*, ed. Hayden Ramsay. St Andrews Studies in Philosophy and Public Life. Exeter: Imprint Academic, 2011.

——. "On the Papal Deposition of Bishops." *Rorate Caeli*, December 18, 2023.

——. "Tyranny and Sexual Abuse in the Church: A Jesuit Tragedy." *Catholic Family News*, October 27, 2018.

Lanzetta, Serafino M. *"Super Hanc Petram": The Pope and the Church at a Dramatic Moment in History*. Lincoln, NE: Os Justi Press, 2023.

Lavaud, B. "L'obéissance religieuse d'après la correspondance de saint Ignace de Loyola." *La vie spirituelle* (October 1929).

Lawler, Leila Marie. "Beware Church Use of 'Transgender' Language." *The Catholic Thing*, November 18, 2023.

Lecanuet, Édouard. *L'Église et le Second Empire (1850–1870)*. Volume 3: *Montalembert*. 4th ed. Paris: Ancienne Librairie Poussièlgue, 1912.

Le Goff, Jacques. *Medieval Civilization*. Translated by Julia Barrow. Oxford: Blackwell Publishers, 1999

Löffler, Klemens. "Pope Leo X." *The Catholic Encyclopedia*. New York: Robert Appleton Company, 1910. www.newadvent.org/cathen/09162a.htm.

MacDougall, H.A., ed. *Lord Acton on Papal Power*. London: Sheed and Ward, 1973.

Magister, Sandro. "If the Conclave Wants a Second Francis, Here Is the Name and the Program." *Settimo Cielo*, February 10, 2022.

Manning, Henry Edward. *The Vatican Council and its Definitions*. London: Longmans, 1870.

Marquant, Christian. "Resistance is never futile: An interview with Christian Marquant, founder of Paix Liturgique." *Rorate Caeli*, December 16, 2020.

McGrath-Merkle, Clare. "Fallen Failsafes and a Revolutionary Modern Priesthood." *The Regensburg Forum*, August 23, 2020, https://regensburgforum.com/2020/08/23/fallen-failsafes-and-a-revolutionary-modern-priesthood/.

McShea, Bronwen. "Bishops Unbound: The History Behind Today's Crisis of Church Leadership." *First Things*, January 2019, www.firstthings.com/article/2019/01/bishops-unbound.

——. *La Duchesse: The Life of Marie de Vignerot – Cardinal Richelieu's Forgotten Heiress Who Shaped the Fate of France*. New York: Pegasus Books, 2023.

——. "When Rome Policed Art." *First Things*, August 2021, www.firstthings.com/article/2021/08/when-rome-policed-art.

Megivern, James J. *The Death Penalty: An Historical and Theological Survey*. Mahwah, NJ: Paulist Press, 1997.

Meloni, Julia. "The Weapon of the St. Gallen Mafia Is Synodality." *OnePeterFive*, September 20, 2021.

Meyendorff, John. *Imperial Unity and Christian Division: The Church 450–680*. Yonkers, NY: St Vladimir's Seminary Press, 2011.

Miceli, Vincent P. "Detroit: A Call to Revolution in the Church." Item 4544 at Catholic Culture.org; originally published in *Homiletic & Pastoral Review*, March 1977.

Michelson, Emily. *Catholic Spectacle and Rome's Jews: Early Modern Conversion and Resistance*. Princeton, NJ: Princeton University Press, 2022.

——. "Conversionary Preaching and the Jews in Early Modern Rome." *Past and Present* 235 (2017): 68–104.

Miller, Felix James. "Francis is the Pope." *The European Conservative*, February 18, 2023.

Miller, J. Michael. *The Shepherd and the Rock: Origins, Development, and Mission of the Papacy.* Huntington, IN: Our Sunday Visitor, 1995.

Molano, Eduardo. "Potestad del Romano Pontifice." *Diccionario General de Derecho Canónico,* vol. VI. Cizur Menor (Navarra): Editorial Aranzadi, SA, 2012.

Monumenta Germaniae Historica. Epistolarum Karolini Aevi. Volume 4. Berlin: Weidmann, 1895.

Mosebach, Martin. *Der Ultramontane: Alle Wege führen nach Rom.* Augsburg: Sankt Ulrich Verlag, 2012. English edition: *Subversive Catholicism: Papacy, Liturgy, Church.* Translated by Sebastian Condon and Graham Harrison. Brooklyn, NY: Angelico Press, 2019.

Moynihan, James. *Papal Immunity and Liability in the Writings of the Medieval Canonists.* Rome: Gregorian University Press, 1961.

Müller, Gerhard Ludwig. "By What Authority: On the Teaching Office of the Pope." *First Things,* January 16, 2018.

——. "Statement on the Limits of Papal Authority." Translated by Susan Johnson. In *Roman Encounters: The Unity of the Faith and the Holy See's Responsibility for the Universal Church.* Irondale, AL: EWTN Publishing, 2019.

Müller, Wolfgang. *Huguccio: The Life, Works, and Thought of a Twelfth-Century Jurist.* Washington, DC: Catholic University of America Press, 1994.

Murphy, Yvonne, et al. *Report by Commission of Investigation into Catholic Archdiocese of Dublin,* November 29, 2009. www.gov.ie/en/publication/13804-report-by-commission-of-investigation-into-catholic-archdiocese-of-dublin/.

Murr, Charles Theodore. *The Godmother: Madre Pascalina, A Feminine Tour de Force.* Self-published, 2017.

Murray, Placid, ed. *Newman the Oratorian.* Dublin: Gill and Macmillan, 1969.

Newman, John Henry. *Letter Addressed to the Duke of Norfolk.* London: Longmans, 1900.

——. *Letters and Diaries of John Henry Newman,* vol. 24: *A Grammar of Assent: January 1868 to December 1869.* Edited by Charles Stephen Dessain and Thomas Gornall, SJ. Oxford: Clarendon Press, 1978.

——. *Letters and Diaries of John Henry Newman,* vol. 25. Edited by Charles Stephen Dessain and Thomas Gornall, SJ. Oxford: Clarendon Press, 1973.

Nichols, Aidan. *The Latin Clerk: The Life, Work, and Travels of Adrian Fortescue.* Cambridge: The Lutterworth Press, 2011.

——. "Thomism and the Nouvelle Théologie." *The Thomist* 64 (2000): 1–19.

Oakley, Francis. "Authoritative and Ignored: The Overlooked Council of Constance." *Commonweal,* October 11, 2014.

O'Connell, Marvin. "Ultramontanism and Dupanloup: The Compromise of 1865." *Church History,* vol. 53, no. 2 (June 1984): 201–5.

O'Malley, John. *Vatican I: The Making of the Ultramontane Church.* Cambridge, MA: Belknap Press of Harvard University Press, 2018.

Ottaviani, Alfredo, Antonio Bacci, and a group of Roman theologians. *Brief Critical Study of the New Order of Mass* ("Ottaviani Intervention"). Kansas City, MO: Angelus Press, 2015. The text may be found online at https://lms.org.uk/ottaviani-intervention.

Parente, Pietro. "Supr. S. Congr. S. Officii Decretum 4 febr. 1942 — Annotationes." *Periodica de Re Morali, Canonica, Liturgica* 31 (February 1942). Originally published as "Nuove tendenze teologiche." *L'Osservatore Romano,* February 9–10, 1942.

Pattenden, Miles. *Pius IV and the Fall of the Carafa.* Oxford: Oxford University Press, 2013.

Payne, Daniel. "Connecticut archbishop calls for female deacons, moving Vatican out of Rome." *Catholic News Agency,* November 22, 2023.

Pelikan, Jaroslav. *The Christian Tradition: A History of the Development of Doctrine.* Volume 1: *The Emergence of the Catholic Tradition (100–600).* Chicago: University of Chicago Press, 1971.

——. *The Riddle of Roman Catholicism.* New York: Abingdon Press, 1959.

Pennington, Kenneth and Wolfgang Müller. "The Decretists: The Italian School." In *The History of Medieval Canon Law in the Classical Period*, ed. Pennington and Müller, 121–73. Washington, DC: Catholic University of America Press, 2008.

Pentin, Edward. "Archbishop Scicluna: We Are Following the Pope's Directives." *National Catholic Register*, January 30, 2017.

Pepino, John. "Anatomist of the Catholic Collapse in France and Beyond." *Catholic World Report*, September 13, 2022.

Pereiro, James. "'Am I my brother's keeper?' Cardinal Manning and the Jewish People." *Bulletin of the John Rylands Library* 97 (2021): 195–208.

Perrone, Giovanni. *Il protestantesimo e la regola di fede.* 3 volumes. Rome: Civiltà Cattolica, 1953.

Peters, Edward. "A canonical primer on popes and heresy." *In the Light of the Law*, December 16, 2016, https://canonlawblog.wordpress.com/2016/12/16/a-canonical-primer-on-popes-and-heresy.

Picciotti-Bayer, Andrea. "Counterfeit Catholicism, Left and Right." *The Wall Street Journal*, September 23, 2022.

Pie, Louis-Édouard-François-Desiré. *Lettre pastorale*, July 14, 1866. In *Oeuvres de Monseigneur l'évêque de Poitiers*, 5th edition. Poitiers: Librairie Henri Oudin, 1876.

——. *Oeuvres de Monseigneur l'évêque de Poitiers.* 9th edition. Poitiers: Librairie-Éditeur H. Oudin, 1887.

Pinckaers, Servais. *The Sources of Christian Ethics.* Translated by Mary Thomas Noble. Washington, DC: Catholic University of America Press, 1995.

Pink, Thomas. "John Finnis's alternative history of Trent," www.academia.edu/37861294/John_Finniss_Alternative_History_of_Trent.

——. "Vatican II and Crisis in the Theology of Baptism." In *Integralism and the Common Good: Selected Essays from* The Josias, vol. 2: *The Two Powers*, ed. Edmund Waldstein, OCist, 290–334. Brooklyn, NY: Angelico Press, 2022.

Poinsot, John. *Cursus Theologicus, IIa IIae, qq. 1–7.* Paris: Vivès, 1885.

Popenoe, David. *Families without Fathers.* New ed. New Brunswick: Transaction Publishers, 2009.

Porfiri, Aurelio, and Aldo Maria Valli. *Uprooted: Dialogues on the Liquid Church.* Hong Kong: ChoraBooks, 2019.

Pound, Ezra. *Guide to Kulchur.* New York: New Directions, 1970; originally published in 1938.

Quinn, John R. "The Claims of the Primacy and the Costly Call to Unity" (June 29, 1996). Item 5301 at CatholicCulture.org.

Quinones, Ricardo. *The Changes of Cain: Violence and the Lost Brother in Cain and Abel Literature.* Princeton, NJ: Princeton University Press, 1991.

Rabban, R. "Chaldean Catholic Church (Eastern Catholic)." *New Catholic Encyclopedia* (2003), vol. 3, p. 369. Cited from Encyclopedia.com.

Rao, John C. "Louis Veuillot and Catholic 'Intransigence.'" In idem, *Catholic Christendom versus Revolutionary Disorder*, 26–53. Waterloo, ON: Arouca Press, 2023.

Ratzinger, Joseph. "Best Quotes on the Liturgy by Joseph Ratzinger/Benedict XVI." *New Liturgical Movement*, January 2, 2023.

——. "Translation of Ratzinger's Preface to the French [1992] Edition of Klaus Gamber" [referring to Msgr Gamber's book *The Reform of the Roman Liturgy: Its Problems and Background*]. *New Liturgical Movement*, February 8, 2023.

——. "Worthiness to Receive Holy Communion: General Principles," www.ewtn.com/catholicism/library/worthiness-to-receive-holy-communion-general-principles-2153.

Reid, Alcuin. Introduction to Adrian Fortescue's *The Early Papacy*. San Francisco: Ignatius Press, 2008.

——. *The Organic Development of the Liturgy*. 2nd edition. San Francisco: Ignatius Press, 2005.

Richards, Jeffrey. *The Popes and the Papacy in the Early Middle Ages, 476-752*. London & Boston: Routledge & Kegan Paul, 1979.

Rifan, Fernando. *Tradition und lebendiges Lehramt*. Bad Schmiedeberg: Renovamen Verlag, 2022.

Ripperger, Chad. "Operative Points of View." *Christian Order*, March 2001, https://christianorder.com/features/feature_2001-03.html.

——. "Ten Problems in the Traditional Catholic Movement." Transcript of lecture: www.tumblarhouse.com/blogs/news/problems-in-the-traditional-catholic-movement.

Roche, Georges. *Pie XII devant l'Histoire*. Paris: Editions Robert Laffont, 1972.

Rodriguez, Alphonsus (Alonso). *Practice of Perfection and Christian Virtues*. Translated by Joseph Rickaby. London: Manresa Press, 1929.

Salza, John, and Robert Siscoe. *True or False Pope*. Winona: STAS Editions, 2015.

Sammons, Eric. "The Liturgy Wars Have Become Doctrinal Wars." *Crisis Magazine*, August 2, 2022.

——. "Rethinking the Papacy." *Crisis Point Live* (video), September 28, 2021.

Sanders, Alain and Rémi Fontaine. *Église interdite: Le livre blanc de Port-Marly*. Fontenay-sous-Bois: Éditions de L'Orme Rond, 1987.

Scalfari, Eugenio. "Francesco, papa profeta che incontra la modernità." *la Repubblica*, July 1, 2015, www.repubblica.it/cultura/2015/07/01/news/francesco_papa_profeta_che_incontra_la_modernita_-118048516/.

Scarisbrick, J.J. *Henry VIII*. Los Angeles: University of California Press, 1970.

Schatz, Klaus. *Papal Primacy: From Its Origins to the Present*. Collegeville, MN: Liturgical Press, 1996.

Schoenig, Steven. *Bonds of Wool: The Pallium and Papal Power in the Middle Ages*. Washington, DC: Catholic University of America Press, 2016.

Schmaus, Michael. *Dogmatica cattolica*. Casale Monferrato: Marietti, 1963.

Schmidberger, Franz. "Kasper's New Pastoral Approach to Marriage." March 25, 2014, https://sspx.org/en/news-events/news/kaspers-new-pastoral-approach-marriage-3886.

Seewald, Peter. *Benedict XVI: A Life*. Volume 1: *Youth in Nazi Germany to the Second Vatican Council 1927-1965*. Translated by Dinah Livingstone. London: Bloomsbury, 2020.

Shaw, Joseph. "Can the Church forget doctrine?" *LMS Chairman*, June 12, 2018.

Silveira, Arnaldo Xavier da. *Can a Pope Be a Heretic? The Theological Hypothesis of a Heretical Pope*. Portugal: Caminhos Romanos, 2018.

Solimeo, Luiz Sérgio. "Against Traditionalist Neo-Gallicanism." *OnePeterFive*, August 25, 2022.

——. "One Cannot Destroy the Papacy to Save the Church: True Ultramontanism and the Right to Resist." *The American Society for the Defense of Tradition, Family, and Property*, January 16, 2020.

Spadaro, Antonio. "A Big Heart Open to God: An Interview with Pope Francis." *America*, September 30, 2013, www.americamagazine.org/faith/2013/09/30/big-heart-open-god-interview-pope-francis.

Steiger, J. "Causes majeures." *Dictionnaire de théologie catholique*. Paris: Letouzey et Ané,

1907–51.

Suárez, Francisco. *Defensio Fidei Catholicae.* In *Opera omnia*, vol. 24. Paris: Vivès, 1859.

——. *De Fide* and *De Caritate.* In *Opera omnia*, vol. 12, edited by Charles Berton. Paris: Vivès, 1858.

Tanquerey, Adolphe. *Précis de théologie ascétique et mystique*, 7th ed. Paris: Desclée et Cie, 1923. English edition: *The Spiritual Life: A Treatise on Ascetical and Mystical Theology.* 2nd rev. ed. Translated by Herman Branderis. Tournai: Desclée & Co., 1930.

Tapsell, Kieran. "Canon Law and Child Sexual Abuse through the Ages." *Journal of the Australian Catholic Historical Society* 36 (2015): 113–36; posted by the author at www. academia.edu/65995747/Canon_Law_and_Child_Sexual_Abuse_through_the_Ages.

"The Teaching of the Catholic Faith on the Reception of the Holy Eucharist." *Rorate Caeli*, September 17, 2022.

Thibon, Gustav. *Au secours des évidences.* Paris: Mame, 2022.

Thomas Aquinas, St. *Summa theologiae.* Translated by Fathers of the English Dominican Province. Second and revised edition, 1920. Online edition by Kevin Knight, 2017.

Thomas de Vio (Cajetan). *De comparatione auctoritatis papae et concilii.* In *Opuscula omnia.* Lyons, 1525.

——. *De comparatione auctoritatis papae et concilii cum Apologia eiusdem tractatus.* Rome: Angelicum, 1936.

Tierney, Brian. *Foundations of the Conciliar Theory: The Contribution of the Medieval Canonists from Gratian to the Great Schism.* Leiden: Brill, 1998.

——. *Origins of Papal Infallibility, 1150-1350: A Study on the Concepts of Infallibility, Sovereignty, and Tradition in the Middle Ages.* Leiden: Brill, 1972.

Torquemada, Juan de. *Summa de Ecclesia.* Salamanca, 1560.

Trochu, François. *The Curé d'Ars: St Jean-Marie-Baptiste Vianney.* Charlotte: TAN Books, 2007.

Ureta, José A. "The Faithful Are Fully Entitled to Defend Themselves Against Liturgical Aggression — Even When It Comes from the Pope." *The American Society for the Defense of Tradition, Family, and Property*, July 25, 2021.

——. *Pope Francis's "Paradigm Shift": Continuity or Rupture in the Mission of the Church?* Translated by José Aloisio Schelini. Spring Grove, PA: The American Society for the Defense of Tradition, Family, and Property, 2018.

Vacandard, Elphège. "Déposition et Dégradation des clercs, VI. Déposition des Papes." *Dictionnaire de théologie catholique.* Paris: Letouzey et Ané, 1907–51.

Valli, Aldo Maria, and Aurelio Porfiri. *Decadenza: Le parole d'ordine della Chiesa postconciliare.* Hong Kong: Chorabooks, 2020.

Van Hove, Brian. "Blood-Drenched Altars." *Faith and Reason* (Summer 1994). Reprinted at *EWTN*, www.ewtn.com/catholicism/library/blooddrenched-altars-4082.

Vian, Giovanni. "Il modernismo durante il pontificato di Benedetto XV, tra riabilitaziioni e condanne." https://iris.unive.it/retrieve/handle/10278/3691556/113213/Il%20modernismo%20durante%20il%20pontificato%20di%20Benedetto%20XV%20-%20testo %20atti%20Bologna.pdf.

Villey, Michel. *Le droit et les droits de l'homme.* Paris: PUF, 1983; 3rd ed., 1998.

——. *La formation de la pensée juridique moderne.* Paris: Éditions Montchrestien, 1968; repr. Paris: Presses Universitaires de France, 2003.

——. *Questions de saint Thomas sur le droit et la politique, ou, Le bon usage des dialogues.* Paris: PUF, 1987.

——. *Seize essais de philosophie du droit, dont un sur la crise universitaire.* Paris: Dalloz, 1969.

Ware, Timothy (Kallistos). *The Orthodox Church.* London: Penguin, 1993.

Watt, J. A. "The Use of the Term 'Plenitudo Potestatis' by Hostiensis." In *Proceedings of the Second International Congress of Medieval Canon Law*, Boston College, August 12–16, 1963, ed. Stephen Ryan and Joseph Kuttner, 161–87. Città del Vaticano: S. Congregatio de Seminariis et Studiorum Universitatibus, 1965.

Weigel, George. "What Vatican II Accomplished." *The Wall Street Journal*, September 30, 2022; also in Kwasniewski, *Sixty Years After*, 154–60.

Weil, Simone. *Waiting for God*. Translated by Emma Craufurd. New York: Capricorn Books, 1959.

Wernz, Francisco and Peter Vidal. *Ius Canonicum ad Codicis Normam Exactum*. Rome: Gregorian University, 1937.

Whalen, Brett Edward. *Dominion of God: Christendom and Apocalypse in the Middle Ages*. Cambridge, MA: Harvard University Press, 2009.

Wolf von Glanvell, Victor, ed. *Die Kanonessamlung des Kardinals Deusdedit*. Paderborn: Ferdinand Schöningh, 1905.

Zagorin, Perez. "Lord Acton's Ordeal: The Historian and Moral Judgment." *The Virginia Quarterly Review*, vol. 74, no. 1 (Winter 1998).

⟨ ABOUT THE CONTRIBUTORS ⟩

RAYMOND LEO BURKE attended seminary in La Crosse, Wisconsin, Washington, DC, and Rome, where he was ordained a priest by Pope Paul VI in 1975. Ordained a bishop in 1995 by Pope John Paul II, he served for almost nine years as Bishop of La Crosse, where he founded the Shrine of Our Lady of Guadalupe, and over four years as Archbishop of St. Louis. He was named a cardinal in 2010 by Pope Benedict XVI. Cardinal Burke has written and spoken widely on Roman Catholic canon law, the Holy Eucharist, devotion to the Sacred Heart of Jesus, devotion to Our Lady of Guadalupe, and the sanctity of human life. He is a member of the Supreme Tribunal of the Apostolic Signatura.

PHILLIP CAMPBELL holds a BA in European History from Ave Maria University and a certificate in Secondary Education from Madonna University. He is the author of the popular "Story of Civilization" series by TAN Books, as well as *Heroes and Heretics of the Reformation* and *Power from on High*. Campbell is also the founder of Cruachan Hill Press, which specializes in works of Catholic history and spirituality. He is the creator of the blog and website *Unam Sanctam Catholicam*.

STUART CHESSMAN has been a financial executive with several large multinational corporations. Since 2007 he has been a leader of the Society of St. Hugh of Cluny, which is dedicated to the preservation and spread of the Traditional Latin Mass. He is the author of *Faith of Our Fathers: A Brief History of Catholic Traditionalism in the United States, from "Triumph" to "Traditionis Custodes"* (Angelico Press, 2022).

CHARLES A. COULOMBE is a contributing editor at *Crisis* and the magazine's European correspondent. He previously served as a columnist for the *Catholic Herald* of London and a film critic for the *National Catholic Register*. A celebrated historian, his books include *Puritan's Empire* and *Star-Spangled Crown*. He resides in Vienna, Austria and Los Angeles, California.

ROBERTO DE MATTEI graduated from the University of Rome with a degree in Contemporary History; he was a student and assistant of philosopher Augusto del Noce, and considers himself a disciple of Professor Plinio Corrêa de Oliveira. After further studies he became titular chair of Modern History in the Faculty of Letters at the University of Cassino (1985–2009), then Associate Professor in the European University of Rome (since 2005). He directs the magazine *Radici Cristiane* and the *Corrispondenza Romana* News Agency. He is the author of numerous books that have been translated into multiple languages, including a major biography of *Saint Pius V* (Sophia Institute Press, 2021); *Love for the Papacy and Filial Resistance to the Pope in the History of the Church* (Angelico Press, 2019); and *The Second Vatican Council: An Unwritten Story* (Loreto Publications, 2012).

EDWARD FESER is Professor of Philosophy at Pasadena City College in Pasadena, California. He holds a BA in philosophy and religious studies from the California State University at Fullerton, an MA in religion from the Claremont Graduate School, and a PhD in philosophy from the University of California at Santa Barbara. The author of numerous philosophical works on epistemology, metaphysics, and natural theology, he has also published extensively on politics and culture from a traditional Catholic perspective.

TIMOTHY S. FLANDERS is the editor-in-chief of *OnePeterFive*. He is the author of *City of God vs. City of Man: The Battles of the Church from Antiquity to the Present* and *Introduction to the Holy Bible for Traditional Catholics*. His writings have appeared at *OnePeterFive*, *Crisis*, and *Catholic Family News*. In 2019, he founded The Meaning of Catholic, a lay apostolate dedicated to uniting Catholics against the enemies of Holy Church. He holds a degree in classical languages from Grand Valley State University and has done graduate work with the Catholic University of Ukraine.

RÉMI FONTAINE obtained a master's in philosophy at the Sorbonne and studied at the Université libre des sciences de l'homme. With a team from the Fédération catholique des étudiants de France (FCEF), he founded the academic journal *Disputatio*. He went on to teach philosophy in a number of schools, as well as at the Institut universitaire Saint-Pie-X (IUSPX) in Paris. Mr Fontaine enjoys the honor of having been one of the instigators and first organizers of the Chartres Pilgrimage launched in 1983.

MATT GASPERS is the Managing Editor of *Catholic Family News* and an author whose work has been published by *OnePeterFive*, *LifeSiteNews*, and *The Fatima Crusader*.

JEREMY HOLMES is Academic Dean and Associate Professor of Theology at Wyoming Catholic College. He earned a BA in Liberal Arts at Thomas Aquinas College, an STB in Theology at the International Theological Institute, Gaming, Austria, and a PhD in Biblical Studies at Marquette University. His book *Cur Deus Verba: Why the Word Became Words* (Ignatius Press, 2021) unfolds a systematic theology of Scripture.

JOHN P. JOY is the Dean of Faculty at St Ambrose Academy in Madison, Wisconsin. He earned his undergraduate degree in theology from Ave Maria College, his master's and licentiate in theology from the International Theological Institute in Austria, and his doctorate in dogmatic theology from the University of Fribourg in Switzerland. Prior to his current position he was Director of Evangelization and Catechesis for the Diocese of Madison, as well as Senior Theologian to the Bishop. He has published *Disputed Questions on Papal Infallibility* (Os Justi Press, 2022) and *On the Ordinary and Extraordinary Magisterium from Joseph Kleutgen to the Second Vatican Council* (Arouca Press, 2023).

Robert W. Keim is a professional writer, editor, and educator who has worked in Catholic and secular publishing since 2010. He studied applied science, history, and Spanish as an undergraduate, earned a Master of Arts in literature and linguistics, and is currently pursuing a PhD in English literature and literary theory. A secular brother of the Oratory of St. Philip Neri in London, Robert lives physically in the southeastern United States and spiritually in Cangues d'Onís, Spain.

Peter A. Kwasniewski holds a BA in Liberal Arts from Thomas Aquinas College and an MA and PhD in Philosophy from the Catholic University of America, with a specialization in the thought of St. Thomas Aquinas. After teaching at the International Theological Institute in Austria, he helped establish Wyoming Catholic College in 2006, where he taught theology, philosophy, music, and art history and directed the choir and schola until 2018. Today, he is a full-time writer, publisher, and speaker whose work has been translated into over twenty languages; he runs a popular Substack called *Tradition & Sanity*. He is also a composer whose sacred choral music has been performed around the world.

John Lamont is a Canadian Catholic philosopher and theologian. He studied philosophy and theology at the Dominican College in Ottawa and at Oxford University, and has taught philosophy and theology in Catholic universities and seminaries. He is the author of *Divine Faith* (Ashgate, 2004) and the co-editor of *Defending the Faith Against Present Heresies* (Arouca Press, 2021), and has published a number of academic papers.

Sebastian Morello holds a BA in philosophy from the Open University and MA and PhD degrees in philosophy from the University of Buckingham; his postgraduate supervisor was Sir Roger Scruton. A lecturer, public speaker, and writer, and Senior Editor of *The European Conservative*, he is the author of *The World as God's Icon* (Angelico, 2020), which explores the Neoplatonic themes in the thought of Thomas Aquinas, and *Conservatism and Grace* (Routledge, 2023), a work of political philosophy.

Martin Mosebach was born in Frankfurt am Main in 1951. His literary work includes novels, short stories, and dramatic works; in 2007 he was honored with Germany's highest literary award, the Georg Büchner Prize. He has also published non-fiction as a traditionalist Catholic, of which *The Heresy of Formlessness* is best known.

Clemens Victor Oldendorf is the pen-name of a traditionalist writer from central Europe who specializes in the history of liturgical books, rubrics, customs, and legislation.

Thomas Pink is a professor of philosophy at King's College, London. He is the author of *Free Will: A Very Short Introduction* and *The Ethics of Action*, and has edited a collection of Francisco Suárez's moral and political writings. He is currently editing *The Questions Concerning Liberty, Necessity and Chance* for the Clarendon edition of the works of Thomas Hobbes.

ENRICO ROCCAGIACHINI is the pen name of an Italian author who publishes at the blog *Messainlatino*.

ERIC SAMMONS, a convert to the Faith, holds a Master's in Theology from Franciscan University of Steubenville and serves as Executive Director of Crisis Publications and Editor-in-Chief of *Crisis Magazine*. A contributor to numerous websites, including *OnePeterFive, Catholic Answers, AntiWar.com, The Federalist, CatholicVote*, and *Bitcoin.com*, he has published several books, including *Deadly Indifference* about the impact religious indifference has had on the Church over the past five decades; *The Old Evangelization: How to Spread the Faith Like Jesus Did*; *Holiness for Everyone: The Practical Spirituality of St. Josemaría Escrivá*; and a sacramental preparation textbook on the Sacrament of Confirmation.

ATHANASIUS SCHNEIDER is the Auxiliary Bishop of Astana, Kazakhstan, and a member of the Canons Regular of the Holy Cross of Coimbra. He is the author of several books, including *Dominus Est*, on reverence for the Holy Eucharist; *Christus Vincit: Christ's Triumph Over the Darkness of the Age* (in conversation with Diane Montagna); *The Springtime That Never Came* (in conversaton with Paweł Lisicki); and *Credo: Compendium of the Catholic Faith*, a fully traditional Catholic catechism.

JOSEPH SHAW has a Doctorate in Philosophy from Oxford University, where he also gained a first degree in Politics and Philosophy and a graduate Diploma in Theology. He is the editor of *The Case for Liturgical Restoration* (Angelico Press), and the author of *The Liturgy, the Family, and the Crisis of Modernity* (Os Justi Press). He is the Chairman of the Latin Mass Society of England and Wales and President of Una Voce International. He was a member of the Philosophy Faculty at Oxford University for eighteen years and is now an independent scholar and freelance writer. He lives outside Oxford with his wife and nine children.

HENRY SIRE, historian, is author of six books on Catholic history and biography, including one on the famous English Jesuit Father Martin D'Arcy. His best-known work, *The Dictator Pope*, is the fruit of Sire's four-year residence in Rome from 2013 to 2017. During that time he became personally acquainted with many figures in the Vatican, including cardinals and curial officials, together with journalists specializing in Vatican affairs.

THOMAS STERNBERG, Dr. phil, Dr. theol., was born in 1952. He is President of the Central Committee of German Catholics. From 1988 to 2016, he was Director of the Franz-Hitze-Haus Catholic Academy in Münster, and from 2005 to 2017 he was a member of the North Rhine-Westphalia state parliament for the CDU.

DARRICK TAYLOR earned his PhD in History from the University of Kansas. He lives in Central Florida and teaches at Santa Fe College in Gainesville, FL. He also produces a podcast, *Controversies in Church History*, dealing with controversial episodes in the history of the Catholic Church.

JOSÉ ANTONIO URETA is co-founder of Fundación Roma (Chile) and advisor of its pro-life and pro-family project Acción Familia; a senior researcher at Société Française pour la Défense de la Tradition, Famille et Propriété (Paris); and author of *Pope Francis's Paradigm Shift: Continuity or Rupture in the Mission of the Church?* (2018).

Printed in Great Britain
by Amazon

37910806R00288